FINDING
OUR
FATHERS

FINDING OUR FATHERS

A Guidebook to Jewish Genealogy

Dan Rottenberg

RANDOM HOUSE  NEW YORK

All rights reserved under International and Pan-American Copyright Conventions.
Published in the United States by Random House, Inc., New York,
and simultaneously in Canada by Random House of Canada Limited, Toronto.

Library of Congress Cataloging in Publication Data

Rottenberg, Dan.
Finding our fathers.

Bibliography: p.
1. Jews—Genealogy. I. Title.
CS3010.R57   929'.1'028   76–53493
ISBN 0–394–40675–3

*Grateful acknowledgment is made to the following for permission to reprint
previously published material:*

Doubleday & Company, Inc.: The list of archives in the section on Poland comes
from *American Origins* by L. G. Pine. Copyright © 1960 by L. G. Pine.

Keter Publishing House, Ltd. (Jerusalem): Chart on p. 56–57, "Dynasty of David,"
from *Encyclopaedia Judaica.* Copyright © 1975 by Keter Publishing House, Ltd.

KTAV Publishing House, Inc.: Coats of arms on p. iv of the photo insert from
The Universal Jewish Encyclopedia, Copyright 1948, Vol. 3, p. 227.

Macmillan Publishing Co., Inc.: The map on p. 119 is Map No. 67 from *Jewish
History Atlas* by Martin Gilbert. Copyright © 1969 by Martin Gilbert.

Manufactured in the United States of America

2 4 6 8 9 7 5 3

FIRST EDITION

Designed by Carole Lowenstein

*For Barbara,
Lisa and Julie*

We are the children of many sires, and every drop of blood in us in its turn betrays its ancestor.

—EMERSON

You may say you have been oppressed and persecuted—that has been your power! You have been hammered into very fine steel, and that is why you have never been broken.

—LLOYD GEORGE, 1925

Preface

THE IDEA for this book first occurred to me one day during the early 1970s when I was leafing through a copy of Leslie G. Pine's *Genealogist's Encyclopedia.* For years I had been tracing my family tree as a hobby, but I had always done so without help from others, primarily because no help seemed to be available. Even though ancestor hunting has become a major American pastime, and even though dozens of books have been published to advise people how to go about it, very few of the publications were of any use to me because my background was exclusively Jewish. All the references to church and parish registers, to Revolutionary War pension records and to European coats of arms were meaningless to someone whose ancestors never belonged to a church or parish, came to America long after the Revolution and knew nothing about coats of arms except to run for their lives when they saw one coming.

Even Pine's book, which offered a rare attempt to deal with problems faced by Jews in tracing their ancestors, devoted only nineteen pages to the subject, and fifteen of those pages were consumed by an article on registration of Jewish birth, death and marriage records in Germany. As I studied every word of Pine's for something I could use, I found myself wishing someone would write a guidebook for Jewish genealogists. I thought about that some more and wondered, Why shouldn't *I* write it?

There was, in fact, a good reason why I shouldn't. Ideally, a book on Jewish genealogy should be written by a scholar or a professional genealogist or an expert on Judaica, and I am none of these. I am simply a journalist who happens to be Jewish and who enjoys tracing his ancestors in his spare time. I had no real desire to write a book on Jewish genealogy because I cared only about my own family and I did not change my mind until I realized, as my research took me further and further back in time, that all Jews are, in fact, members of my family.

I originally set out to compile a book that would offer everything that is known on the subject of Jewish genealogy. I should have listened to the Talmud, which tells us: "It is not upon thee to finish the work; neither art thou free to desist from it." This book is certainly not the last word on Jewish genealogy; it's more like the *first* word on the subject, and I hope others will follow the Talmud's advice and take up where I have left off.

While I have included information of use to Jews of all backgrounds and types, the sheer volume of the available material has led me to gear the book primarily toward American Jews of European ancestry, and especially East European ancestry. The reasons should be obvious: nearly half the world's Jews today are American, and 85 percent of the world's Jews have their roots in Europe, especially Eastern Europe. Moreover, it is in Eastern Europe that the greatest persecutions of Jews took place, along with the sloppiest record keeping, and so the problem of tracing ancestors there is greatest. If your ancestors came from medieval Spain or Italy, you may very well find a published history of your family in some Jewish book or encyclopedia; if they were in the United States before 1840, you will probably find your ancestors neatly grouped in one of the charts in Rabbi Malcolm Stern's *Americans of Jewish Descent.* The Americans of East European Jewish descent, so many in number, have no such handy aid, and it is on them that I have focused most of my efforts.

D. R.

Philadelphia
October 1976

Acknowledgments

JUST AS an individual human being is a product of many ancestors, so a book by a single author is actually the work of many hands. A great number of people contributed their time, labor, expertise, moral support and even lodging toward my labors. Some of them are capable of writing superb books of their own on this subject, and I am deeply grateful for their unselfishness in sharing their knowledge with me.

I'm especially grateful to my research assistant, Robert Strauss, who worked alongside me in compiling the list of 8,000 names that comprises the bulk of this book. Among other things, this task involved combing through every line of the *Jewish Encyclopedia,* the *Universal Jewish Encyclopedia* and the *Encyclopaedia Judaica* for genealogical references. Strauss has since become a newspaper reporter, but after this project he could probably qualify for the rabbinate.

My particular thanks also to Steven Siegel of New York, a researcher for Jewish organizations who carefully led me through the intricacies of public and Jewish institutions and also reviewed three of my chapters. Other chapters were reviewed by Dr. Rela Monson and Rabbi Ivan Caine, both of Philadelphia, to whom I am greatly indebted. My thanks also to Dr. Monson for loaning me her set of the *Jewish Encyclopedia.*

This book was undertaken with the advice and encouragement of Rabbi Malcolm Stern, the dean of American Jewish genealogists, and Charles Bernstein, a Chicago lawyer and part-time ancestor hunter. The value of their encouragement cannot be overestimated because others actively tried to dissuade me from the project—some because they sincerely felt I had set myself an impossible task, others because they wished they had thought of the idea themselves.

Librarians, archivists and scholars at virtually every institution I visited went out of their way to help. My thanks, then, to Tim Beard and Frank Bradley at the New York Public Library's genealogy room; to Sybil Milton and Steve Lowenstein at the Leo Baeck Institute; to Daniel Cohen, Hadassah Assouline, Simon Schwarzfuchs and Shlomo Avayou at the Central Archives for the History of the Jewish People in Jerusalem; to Frannie Zelcer at the American Jewish Archives; to Nathan Kaganoff and Bernard Wax at the American Jewish Historical Society; to Marek Web at the YIVO Institute; to Berl Kagan and Adina Feldstern at the Jewish Theological Seminary; to Elkan Buchalter at Gratz College; to Yehuda Komlosh at Dropsie University; to Ludovit Sturc of the Society for the History of Czechoslovak Jews; to Moses Rischin of the Western Jewish History Center; and to Lindsay Nauen of the Philadelphia Jewish Archives.

In addition, I'm indebted to Society Hill Synagogue and Beth Zion Synagogue, both in Philadelphia, for giving me the use of their libraries, and to the staff of the religion department at the Free Library of Philadelphia for allowing me to work up to the closing minute on countless nights.

This book was also made possible by my ability to travel considerable distances on a shoestring budget, thanks to the hospitality of friends and relatives in several cities: Lenore and Herman Rottenberg in New York, Judith and Hillel Shuval in Jerusalem, Margaret Ann and Peter Rothman in Boston, and Claire and Ronald Gordon in Cincinnati. I'm also indebted to Mrs. Gordon and to Diane Rubin and Nancy Rigg of Philadelphia for their research help.

Thanks are due my editor, Charlotte Mayerson of Random House, for the personal interest she took in this project above and beyond her considerable professional skills. And to my agent, Julie Fallowfield, for her perceptiveness in matching me with such an editor. I should also like to thank Carole Lowenstein, who designed the book, and Barbara Willson, who copyedited it.

Finally, I suppose it's appropriate in a book of this sort—and *only* in a book of this sort—to thank my ancestors for whatever skills they passed on to me.

Contents

Preface   ix

Acknowledgments   xi

I. Our Links with the Past   *3*

II. Starting Out   *15*

The basic steps: (1) Arm yourself with the proper materials. (2) Make up a chart and fill in as much as you can. (3) Locate your relatives, close and distant. (4) Write, telephone or visit your relatives for information. (5) Visit the graves of your ancestors and relatives for more clues. (6) Fit your clues together and see where they take you.

III. Public Records in the United States   *26*

Birth, death and marriage records—Federal census records—Ships' passenger lists—Naturalization records—Newspaper obituaries—City directories—Probate records

IV. A Quick Course in Judaica   *40*

The Diaspora—Sephardim and Ashkenazim—Jewish population— The Khazar Connection—Hebrew dates—Marriage ages— Consanguinity—Family size—Prefixes on names—Naming of children—Adoption of family names—Sources of Jewish family names

V. Tradition, History and the Bible   *54*

CONTENTS

VI. Jewish Sources in America 66

*Libraries—Mormon Genealogical Society—American Jewish Archives
—American Jewish Historical Society—YIVO Institute for Jewish
Research—Leo Baeck Institute—Jewish Theological Seminary—
Yeshiva University—Dropsie University—Philadelphia Jewish Archives
Center—Western Jewish History Center—Early American Jewry—
Society for the History of Czechoslovak Jews—World Federation of
Hungarian Jews—Landsmanshaften—United HIAS Services—
Tracing missing relatives—Jewish historical societies—Sources in
Canada*

VII. Back across the Ocean . . . 86

*Foreign boundaries—Jewish libraries and guidebooks—Algeria and
Morocco—Argentina—Australia—Austria—Belgium—Brazil—Britain
—Bulgaria—The Caribbean—Czechoslovakia—Denmark—France—
Germany—Greece—Hungary—Iraq—Italy—Latvia—Lithuania—
Netherlands—Poland—Portugal—Rumania—South Africa—Soviet
Union—Spain—Switzerland—Turkey—Yugoslavia*

VIII. . . . back to Israel 127

*The best research sources in Israel: the Central Archives for the
History of the Jewish People—Jewish National and University
Library—Diaspora Research Institute—Archives of the Sephardi
Community—Ghetto Fighters' House—Yad Vashem*

A Source Guide to Jewish Family Genealogies

Introduction 141
Abbreviations 147
Alphabetical List of Family Names 149

Bibliography

Jewish Family Histories 376
Genealogy and General Reference 390
Jewish Reference Books 392
International Judaica 394

FINDING
OUR
FATHERS

I

Our Links with the Past

MY GREAT-GREAT-GRANDFATHER MOSES was a poor Jewish baker struggling to support a wife and five daughters in the Russian town of Suwalk. In 1882 his third daughter, my great-grandmother Dora, was married through an arranged match to a young man she barely knew; the following year, at the age of nineteen, she was a mother. A few months later her husband left for America to avoid the harsh military service that the czar was then imposing on Jewish males. At twenty, Dora said goodbye to her parents for the last time, and clutching her baby—my grandfather—in her arms, made her way alone across the Atlantic to join her husband in New York. Thirteen years later her husband died, leaving Dora, at thirty-three, a widow with five children to support. In fifteen years she had undergone the metamorphosis of a lifetime. Yet the life she had known was typical of her generation.

When Dora herself died fifty years later, in 1947, I was not yet five years old. I had visited her apartment in the Bronx several times with my parents, and I can recall the faded furniture in her living room, the street scene from her window, and an iron gate in her hallway on which I liked to swing. But I remember very little of the woman herself; just a vague awareness that some-one was quietly watching me as I hung on that gate. I am told by my elders that Dora was a tall, stately woman of great courage. All I remember is a little old lady.

How do you bridge the gap between that little old lady in the Bronx and the innocent young bride in Suwalk? And how do you pass on the thread of these experiences to a four-year-old who is more interested in swinging on the gate or looking out the window? How did we get where we are, and what does that tell us about ourselves?

Today, at last, there is time for most of us to ponder these questions. The Cossacks and the Nazis are no longer at the door; the Spanish Inquisition is over; the Crusaders have vanished; Pharoah is dead. Jews whose families have been in North America for two generations or more have both the freedom and the self-confidence to assert their backgrounds. And in the relative security of twentieth-century America we find not merely Jews but Italians, Poles, Irish, Latins, Greeks and blacks aggressively taking up genealogy, the hobby of tracing family trees—in addition, of course, to the white Anglo-Saxon Protestants, who have been doing it all along. And all to one end: to discover who we are.

Genealogy is simply history on a personal scale. The anarchist's bomb that killed Czar Alexander II in St. Petersburg in 1881 led to the Russian pogroms and the anti-Semitic May laws of 1882, which in turn caused thousands of Jews to flee Russia and come to the United States. The failure of the German revolution of 1848—which sought, among other things, to grant equal rights to Jews—was the catalyst for the migration of many liberal German Jews to America. It is remarkable that thousands of unrelated experiences involving unrelated people stretching back over thousands of years can be forged into the personality of a single individual. Yet that is the case for every one of us.

The urge to discover one's roots is probably as old as civilization itself. It distresses us to think that our existence may eventually be all but forgotten, reduced to a yellowed picture stashed at the bottom of someone's closet. So we dig into the history of our ancestors in the hope that someday our descendants will do the same for us.

I first got into the subject at my grandmother's funeral in 1958, when I found myself copying names and dates from relatives' tombstones. Over the following years, as I visited or wrote to relatives, many asked for a chance to study my research at their leisure. Finally, in 1969, I assembled my findings into a book, which I sent to some two hundred relatives around the world. They responded with so much additional information that the book soon became obsolete and I set out to produce a revised edition, which will no doubt generate still more additions and thus keep the cycle going endlessly.

This process of discovering new relatives produced wonderful opportunities to meet and bring together people who share common ancestors with me. My research turned up such distant relatives as Alan Pakula, the movie director; Alan and Marilyn Bergman, the Academy Award-winning songwriters; Don

Rickles, the comedian; Hope Lange, the actress; Helen Sobel, probably the greatest woman bridge player of all time; John Roberts, who financed the Woodstock rock festival in 1968; Don Taussig, a former outfielder for the San Francisco Giants, St. Louis Cardinals and Houston Astros; Kenneth Reiner, the inventor of Lady Ellen hair clips; David Milsten, the author of the official Oklahoma Will Rogers memorial poem; Samuel Ungerleider, who was Warren Harding's stockbroker; Emma Tamarin, a colonel in the Soviet army during World War II; and Polly Cleveland Roberts, who is a direct descendant of Presidents John Adams and John Quincy Adams and a grand-niece of Grover Cleveland. Cleveland, of course, was President of the United States when many of my ancestors arrived as immigrants, so this discovery is especially delicious.

Perhaps my greatest satisfaction came as the result of sending out my family history book to my far-flung relatives, most of whom I had never met. After receiving copies of the book, two families living next door to each other on Long Island discovered that they were distantly related; their children, who had been playmates for years, ran through the streets shouting, "We're cousins! We're cousins!"

But beneath the fun of stalking one's ancestors and relatives is the humbling —and inspiring—realization that each of us is merely a link in a chain. We may someday be forgotten, but the contribution we made to the chain, however slight, will always be there, and as long as the chain exists, a piece of us will exist, too.

Jews, of course, possess more of this sort of perspective than most people. For thousands of years our ancestors have been wandering over Europe, Asia and Africa, watching civilizations rise and fall—the just and compassionate as well as the cruel and barbaric—and this experience has left an indelible message. It is that all nations die sooner or later; even cities, towns and neighborhoods come and go. Ultimately, only families provide an unending link between the past and the future.

Yet to most Jews this awareness is subconscious rather than conscious, and general rather than specific. We know a great deal about the history of the Jews, yet remarkably little about the lives of individual Jews who may have been our ancestors. Until recently, genealogy in the United States has been primarily the preserve of Anglo-Saxon Protestants, and with good reason: WASPs stay pretty much in the same part of the world from one century to the next, they keep neat and well-preserved records, their ancestors spoke the same language they do, and they have ancestral homelands that aren't behind the Iron Curtain. Most Jews, on the other hand—chased from country to country, their records obliterated, their synagogues and cemeteries destroyed —have assumed that it's simply impossible to trace their ancestries back more than a few generations, and so they haven't even tried.

It *is* difficult, but it's not impossible. If Jews face special obstacles in tracing their family histories, they also enjoy special advantages. The most intriguing of these is the fact that there is only a finite number of Jews in the world—there were never more than 17 million at any one time, and there are only 14 million today—and by and large Jews have tended to intermarry within Judaism. Thus most Jews are related to one another somewhere in the past, however distant.

In my case, for example, I was able to trace my grandmother's family back only to her grandfather, Charles Margulies, who was born in Galicia about 1840. However, by poking about in the original *Jewish Encyclopedia*, published in 1901, I discovered strong evidence that this Margulies was descended from a family of Galician rabbis named Margolioth that traces its tree back to the fifteenth century. Using that clue, I questioned my older Margulies relatives until I found one who did indeed recall being told as a child that the family was descended from rabbis. The rabbinic Margolioth family is in turn intermarried with families like Heilprin, Landau and Schor, so by looking up the histories of these families I have been able to further extend my own.

In theory, if we put together the genealogies of everyone in the world, they would all fit together like parts of an enormous jigsaw puzzle. Mathematically, if we figure twenty-five years to a generation, each of us had more than a million ancestors walking the earth in the fifteenth century, and more than a billion in the thirteenth century. Obviously no one really had a billion ancestors in the thirteenth century: many of those billion names would turn out to be the same people popping up on your tree dozens of times. Nevertheless, each of us did have thousands of ancestors a few centuries back. And the further back you go in your research, the more likely you are to find other contemporaries who share the same ancestors with you.

The ultimate dream of most genealogists is that someday all existing genealogies can be cross-indexed and computerized so that your family history can be linked up with the histories of any other families that are related to you, thus making your own task much easier. This is a far-fetched and, in fact, impossible task if we are talking about cross-indexing the entire population of the world. But it is not an impossible dream if we limit ourselves solely to Jews. As recently as 1700, according to one estimate, the world Jewish population was only one million. Other estimates place the figure higher, but certainly it was no more than two million. Presumably almost all of the Jews living today were descended from those one to two million Jews. That means that it should not be all that difficult to link up your family tree with the tree of some related family that can trace itself back to 1700 or earlier. Especially in the computer age, it may well be possible to gather and cross-index enough material about Jewish family histories so that each of us can find missing interlocking pieces in our own histories.

To be sure, few Jews in medieval times kept family records. But one section of the Jewish community—the rabbis—considered the keeping of such records a solemn duty. Long before the introduction of the Ph.D. thesis, the Jews had their own equivalent exercise in the responsa and commentaries written by rabbinical students. The introductory section of such a scholarly work usually contained genealogical information about the author. Many of these Hebrew works have been published and can be found in major libraries in books or on microfilm; still others were never published but survive in archives in manuscript form. And the laws of probability and mathematics being what they are, there's a good chance that most modern Jews are somehow descended from some of those medieval rabbis. The problem is to figure out how. The cross-referenced alphabetical list at the end of this book is a first step in that direction, and the information I have gathered on Jewish archives and libraries is another step.

Despite the upheaval and destruction of European Jewry, there are some advantages for American Jews tracing their family trees. While many records of European Jewish communities have vanished, the ones that have been preserved—and there are a great many, as we will see—can be found in a few centralized locations, basically in the United States and in Israel. An American gentile whose family emigrated from Eastern Europe would have to spend months or years searching behind the Iron Curtain to find the sort of records American Jews can find at places like the Leo Baeck Institute or the YIVO Institute in New York or the American Jewish Archives in Cincinnati.

There is an obstacle for English-speaking Jews in that much Jewish historical material is in Hebrew or in European languages (as recently as 1900, 81 percent of the world's Jews lived in Europe). On the other hand, the dominant language of the world's Jews today is English: fully 50 percent of all Jews live in English-speaking lands, and more of the world's Jewish knowledge is being produced in English or translated into English than ever before. It is no accident, for example, that the greatest compendium of Jewish knowledge ever printed—the 16-volume *Encyclopaedia Judaica,* published in Israel in 1971— is written not in Hebrew, but in English.

There are, of course, other fundamental differences between Jewish and gentile genealogy. Let me put it this way: several years ago while I was working in the Newberry Library in Chicago, I found a genealogy of the McCormicks, who are best known for two major enterprises, the Chicago *Tribune* and International Harvester Company. One of the charts traced the family's lineage back to medieval English kings, and one line went back as far as Charlemagne. Next to many of the names was a small cross, and when I looked at the bottom of the page to see what it meant, I read: "Denotes Crusader." It was all I could do to keep from bursting out laughing, despite the library's prohibition against unseemly noise. In *my* upbringing, you see, the Crusaders had always been regarded as religious fanatics who swept through Europe in a senseless orgy of burning, looting and killing. To my way of thinking, one might just as proudly have constructed a family tree with symbols labeled

"Denotes Nazi" or "Denotes rapist." But one man's meat is another man's poison.

If Jews can't point to ancestors who were Crusaders, most Jews can find at least one line on which they can trace some ancestors in the Bible. Disraeli, denounced once for his Jewish background by an anti-Semite in Parliament, responded with an ancestral put-down of his own: "When the ancestors of the right honorable gentlemen were savages living in caves, my ancestors were priests praying in the temple of the Most High."

That sort of reminder may be necessary to maintain your sense of personal pride in an age when the greatest status symbol seems to be an ancestor who came over on the *Mayflower* or fought in the American Revolution. But snob appeal and ancestral one-upmanship are frivolous reasons for anyone to trace his genealogy. For Jews, there is a more solid justification in the teachings of Judaism itself.

Nearly two thousand years ago, the sages of the Mishnah considered the question of why God had created just one Adam and Eve instead of several men and women at the same time. They concluded that God was motivated by a desire to demonstrate the brotherhood of all people. Thus the Judaeo-Christian tradition teaches that everyone, no matter what his culture or religion, no matter if he be a king or a beggar, is descended from one root; ultimately, no one may say, "My ancestor was greater than yours." Most people are unable to feel this sense of universality, but many Jews can indeed trace their lineage back to Adam, with a little help from the Bible and some inductive leaps of faith.

Consider the lineage I constructed after discovering in some old Hebrew books that the Margulies branch of my family claimed to be descended from Rashi, the famous Talmudic commentator of eleventh-century France. Rashi is supposed to have been descended in the thirty-third generation from Johanan ha-Sandalar, who lived in second-century Egypt. Johanan was a great-grandson of Rabbi Gamaliel the Elder, who was in turn the grandson of Hillel the Great, the sage who lived in Jerusalem during the time of King Herod and Jesus. And Hillel, you may recall, is the scholar who was once asked by a scornful heathen to explain Judaism while standing on one foot. Hillel replied, "What is hateful to thee, do not unto thy fellow man. This is the whole law; the rest is mere commentary."

There is something comforting about finding those words at the roots of one's family tree, for that is really what genealogy is all about. It teaches us that we are all brothers and sisters, and that whatever harm we do to one another, we do to ourselves.

But my ancestral search did not end with Hillel. Tradition holds that Hillel was a direct descendant of King David. And from there, with a little research into the Good Book, it's an easy jump back to Adam himself. I've never been one to believe in the literal interpretation of the Bible, but there are powerful inducements to do so when you discover that you may be descended from King David, not to mention Adam, Noah, Abraham, Isaac, Jacob and Judah.

Perhaps the best argument for tracing your family tree, though, is simply that it's fun. Genealogy involves assembling seemingly unrelated tidbits until they all fit together into one big picture. And it's an endless puzzle, because births, deaths and marriages keep occurring. Once you've dipped into genealogy, you're likely to be hooked for life.

I know what you're thinking: "My family has been in the United States for only three generations [or two, or four]. My ancestors came from towns whose Jewish communities and Jewish records were destroyed in World War II. My parents or grandparents don't like to talk about the old country, or remember too little about it from their own antecedents."

Do not be discouraged! My own East European Jewish ancestors settled in the United States between 1875 and 1900, yet I have traced all the branches of my tree back at least to about 1800, and I fully expect to go back a great deal further in what I hope is the long life ahead of me. My wife's family came here from Russia and Lithuania early in the twentieth century, yet I've traced her ancestry back to about 1820, and in one line have found a connection with the Khazar kingdom in the Crimea, which dates back to the eighth century.

There is much more information floating around about your family and mine than you would expect. A great deal of it is in obscure and unlikely places. As we will discuss later, the Mormon Church in Salt Lake City, Utah, for example, has what may well be the most complete set of genealogical records in the world—including Jewish records. Mormons study their genealogies—and, by extension, everybody's genealogies—in order to identify their ancestors and gain salvation for them.

That may sound like silly superstition. And yet . . . each time I have uncovered the name of one of my long-forgotten ancestors I have been filled with the mystical feeling that I was indeed rescuing that ancestor—not from hellfire, perhaps, but from oblivion. They did walk this earth, our ancestors, once upon a time, and they are still out there, somewhere. There is much they can teach us even now, if we can find them. So let us begin.

No family has ever been traced in an unbroken line from Adam down to the present day, but the following four charts make a noble effort to do so. The Bible traces the descent from Adam down to King David (Chart A), Jewish tradition traces the descent from King David through Hillel the Great to Rashi (Chart B), and numerous descendants of Rashi have been identified (Chart C), including the Luria family, which traces itself in an unbroken line from the fourteenth century through the twentieth (Chart D). A fifth chart (E) shows some intermarriages of prominent rabbinic families of the Middle Ages. Chart B, which covers the 2,000 years from David to Rashi, is taken from Ma'alot Ha-Yu-hasin, *by Ephraim Zalman Margolioth of Galicia (1762–1828), himself a descendant of Rashi. This chart was apparently concocted in seventeenth-century Italy, and Judaica scholars agree with surprising unanimity that it is total nonsense, but I pass it on here for curiosity's sake. Chart C, which shows Rashi and his descendants, is considered historically sound. As you can see, no one can trace his ancestry back to Rashi in an unbroken line. But the Treves, Luria and Zarfati families come close. As you can also see, there are many descendants of Rashi unaccounted for. Anna and Bellette, daughters of Dolce and Eleazar of Worms (right center on Chart C), were killed by Crusaders, but other branches presumably continued, and it's interesting to speculate as to who those descendants might be. You, maybe?*

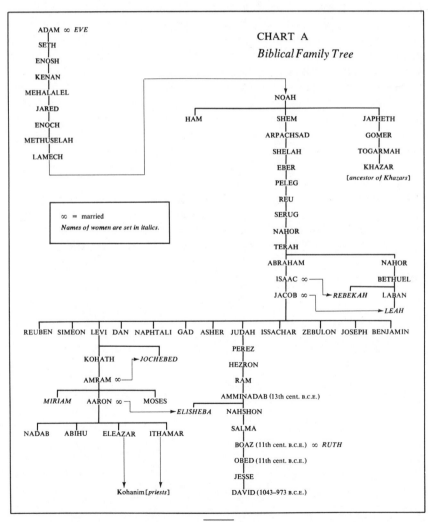

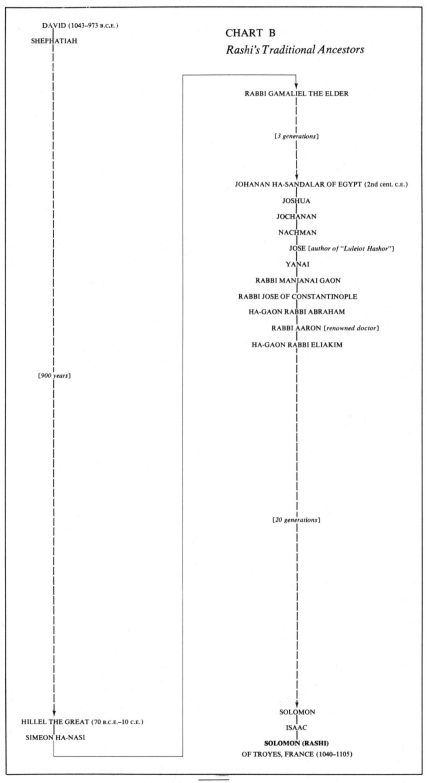

DAVID (1043–973 B.C.E.)

SHEPHATIAH

CHART B

Rashi's Traditional Ancestors

RABBI GAMALIEL THE ELDER

[*3 generations*]

JOHANAN HA-SANDALAR OF EGYPT (2nd cent. C.E.)

JOSHUA

JOCHANAN

NACHMAN

JOSE [*author of "Luleiot Hashor"*]

YANAI

RABBI MANJANAI GAON

RABBI JOSE OF CONSTANTINOPLE

HA-GAON RABBI ABRAHAM

RABBI AARON [*renowned doctor*]

HA-GAON RABBI ELIAKIM

[*900 years*]

[*20 generations*]

HILLEL THE GREAT (70 B.C.E.–10 C.E.)

SIMEON HA-NASI

SOLOMON

ISAAC

SOLOMON (RASHI)
OF TROYES, FRANCE (1040–1105)

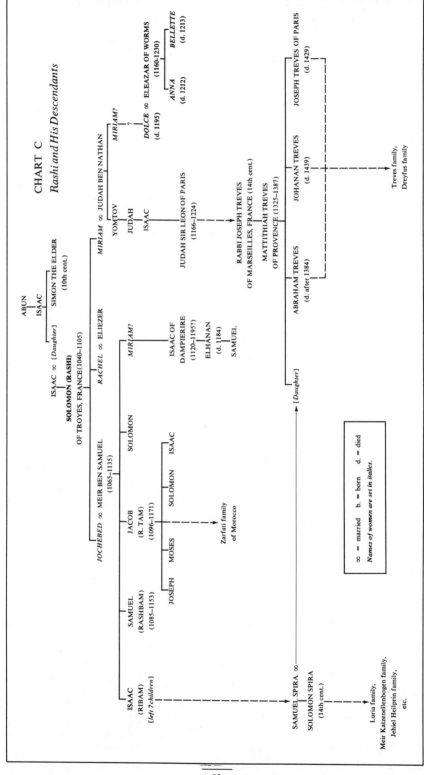

CHART C
Rashi and His Descendants

ABUN
ISAAC
SIMON THE ELDER (10th cent.)

ISAAC ∞ [Daughter]

SOLOMON (RASHI)
OF TROYES, FRANCE (1040–1105)

RACHEL ∞ ELIEZER   MIRIAM ∞ JUDAH BEN NATHAN

JOCHEBED ∞ MEIR BEN SAMUEL (1065–1135)

MIRIAM?   MIRIAM?

YOMTOV
JUDAH
ISAAC

ISAAC (RIBAM) [left 7 children]

SAMUEL (RASHBAM) (1085–1153)

SOLOMON

JACOB (R. TAM) (1096–1171)

JOSEPH   MOSES   SOLOMON   ISAAC

Zarfati family of Morocco

ISAAC OF DAMPIERRE (1120–1195?)

ELHANAN (d. 1184)

SAMUEL

DOLCE ∞ ELEAZAR OF WORMS (1160–1230)

ANNA (d. 1212)   BELLETTE (d. 1213)

JUDAH SIR LEON OF PARIS (1166–1224)

RABBI JOSEPH TREVES OF MARSEILLES, FRANCE (14th cent.)

MATTITHIAH TREVES OF PROVENCE (1325–1387)

[Daughter]

ABRAHAM TREVES (d. after 1384)

JOHANAN TREVES (d. 1439)

JOSEPH TREVES OF PARIS (d. 1429)

Treves family,
Dreyfus family

SAMUEL SPIRA ∞

SOLOMON SPIRA (14th cent.)

Luria family,
Meir Katzenellenbogen family,
Jehiel Heilprin family,
etc.

∞ = married   b. = born   d. = died
Names of women are set in italics.

12

CHART D

The Luria Family
—An Unbroken Line almost back to Rashi

∞ = married   b. = born   d. = died

Names of women are set in italics.

SOLOMON SPIRA (14th cent.) [*descendant of Rashi*]

MIRIAM ∞ SAMSON LURIA (14th cent.)

JEHIEL LURIA

NATHANIEL LURIA

AHARON LURIA (d. 1456)

JEHIEL LURIA (d. 1470)

ABRAHAM LURIA

JEHIEL LURIA

SOLOMON LURIA (1510–1573) (b. Lublin, d. Brest-Litovsk)

MIRIAM ∞ ELIEZER ISSERLES

MOSES ISSERLES (17th cent.)

JEKUTHIEL SALMAN   [*Daughter*] ∞ MOSES MENKES
ISSERLES   ABRAHAM SOLOMON

JOCHANAN LURIA OF ALSACE (late 15th, early 16th cent.)

AHARON LURIA OF ELSASS

SCHLOMO LURIA

JOSHUA MOSES LURIA (d. 1591 at Worms)

AHARON LURIA (d. 1613 at Frankfurt)

ZE'EV WOLF LURIA

ABRAHAM LURIA

JEHIEL LURIA

ZE'EV WOLF LURIA

ABRAHAM LURIA

AARON LURIA

MOSES LURIA

JACOB LURIA

YAKOV LURIA

ASHER LURIA

ZE'EV WOLF LURIA

BARUCH BENDET LURIA

ABRAHAM LURIA

PINHAS SELIG LURIA

ISAAC EISIK LURIA

DAVID LURIA OF MOGILEV

JACOB AARON LURIA (d. 1783 in Mogilev)

ISRAEL ISSER LURIA OF MOGILEV

AARON LURIA (d. 1835 in Pinsk)

DAVID LURIA OF PINSK (1828–1883)

ALEX LOURIE OF VIENNA (b. Pinsk) (1861–?)

LEOPOLD LOURIE OF VIENNA (b. Pinsk) (1850–?)

ISIDOR LOURIE OF LIBAU (1851–1920)

SAMUEL LOURIE (1850–1888) (b. Pinsk, d. Wiesbaden)

SAMUEL LURIA (b. 1826, Pinsk)

YEHUDA IDEL LURIA OF BYCHOW

JACOB AARON LURIA OF MINSK

DAVID LURIA OF MINSK

DAVID LURIA OF BYCHOW (1798–1855)

MOSES LURIA (d. Wiesbaden) (1824–1906)

RACHEL ∞ MOSES CHAIM ELIASBERG OF BERLIN

ZEVI HIRSCH LURIA OF BYCHOW

BELE ∞ IDEL LURIE OF WIESBADEN

SELDE ∞ ELIAS ELIASBERG OF PINSK

AARON LOURIE OF PINSK (1841–1910)

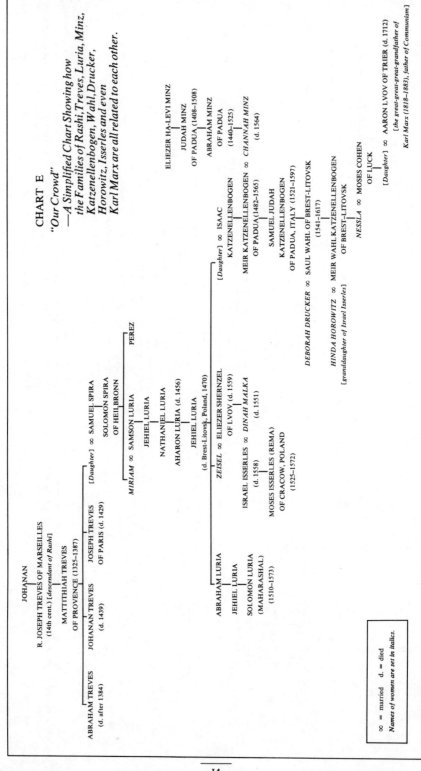

CHART E

"Our Crowd"

—*A Simplified Chart Showing how the Families of Rashi, Treves, Luria, Minz, Katzenellenbogen, Wahl, Drucker, Horowitz, Isserles and even Karl Marx are all related to each other.*

JOHANAN

R. JOSEPH TREVES OF MARSEILLES (14th cent.) [*descendant of Rashi*]

MATTITHIAH TREVES OF PROVENCE (1325–1387)

JOHANAN TREVES (d. 1439)

JOSEPH TREVES OF PARIS (d. 1429)

ABRAHAM TREVES (d. after 1384)

[*Daughter*] ∞ SAMUEL SPIRA

SOLOMON SPIRA OF HEILBRONN

MIRIAM ∞ SAMSON LURIA

PEREZ

JEHIEL LURIA

NATHANIEL LURIA

AHARON LURIA (d. 1456)

JEHIEL LURIA (d. Brest-Litovsk, Poland, 1470)

ELIEZER HA-LEVI MINZ

JUDAH MINZ OF PADUA (1408–1508)

ABRAHAM MINZ OF PADUA (1440–1525)

CHANNAH MINZ (d. 1564)

ABRAHAM LURIA

JEHIEL LURIA

SOLOMON LURIA (MAHARASHAL) (1510–1573)

ZEISEL ∞ ELIEZER SHERNZEL OF LVOV (d. 1559)

ISRAEL ISSERLES ∞ *DINAH MALKA* (d. 1558) (d. 1551)

MOSES ISSERLES (REMA) OF CRACOW, POLAND (1525–1572)

[*Daughter*] ∞ ISAAC KATZENELLENBOGEN

MEIR KATZENELLENBOGEN ∞ *CHANNAH MINZ* OF PADUA (1482–1565)

SAMUEL JUDAH KATZENELLENBOGEN OF PADUA, ITALY (1521–1597)

DEBORAH DRUCKER ∞ SAUL WAHL OF BREST-LITOVSK (1541–1617)

HINDA HOROWITZ ∞ MEIR WAHL KATZENELLENBOGEN OF BREST-LITOVSK [*granddaughter of Israel Isserles*]

NESSLA ∞ MOSES COHEN OF LUCK

[*Daughter*] ∞ AARON LVOV OF TRIER (d. 1712) [*the great-great-great-grandfather of Karl Marx (1818–1883), father of Communism*]

∞ = married   d. = died
Names of women are set in italics.

14

II

Starting Out

IT'S BEEN SAID that no matter how often you read *War and Peace* or see *Citizen Kane,* you'll never be able to relive the thrill of that first time. So it is with discovering your ancestors. Speaking as someone who has been ancestor hunting for fifteen years, I envy you for the adventure you are about to undertake. The excitement of sitting down with a family chart and discovering how many names you can fill in, just off the top of your head—that's an experience the veteran genealogist will never again know.

It is not, however, an easy task. As Ethel Williams put it in her book, *Know Your Ancestors,* all you need to trace your family tree is the attributes of "a full-time detective, a thorough historian, an inveterate snoop, a confirmed diplomat, a keen observer, a hardened skeptic, an apt biographer, a qualified linguist, a part-time lawyer, a studious sociologist and, above all, an accurate reporter." She might have added that you'll also need a degree of inner strength, since genealogy is a very lonely hobby: nobody is likely to be interested in your particular family other than you and your relatives.

And while the aim of this book is to help you overcome the special obstacles faced by Jews in finding their forefathers, it is conceivable that even *with* this book you may find yourself up against a stone wall from the very start—if you have no living relatives or written records, for example. Except for extreme cases, if you follow this book closely you should certainly learn more about your family than you know now.

1. Arm yourself with the proper materials

Begin with the following:

• A *three-ring binder* and some *three-hole paper* to go with it. On these sheets you will create your charts and keep biographical details about your ancestors and their brothers and sisters.

• *Manila file folders.* Label one for each branch of your family. If these folders get too bulky, you can break them down into even smaller branches—say, one for each of your sixteen great-great-grandparents. Use these folders to keep correspondence and miscellaneous material you collect about each branch of the family. As your files grow, you may want to replace the folders with boxes.

• *A good notebook.* The best kind, I've found, are the spiral-type notebooks with 240 pages, subdivided into five sections. This format is ideal for a genealogist because you can devote one section to each of your grandparents' families, with one section left over for miscellany. This way, as you interview people you'll have all your notes in one book—a great convenience when you are traveling to a distant city to see relatives from two or three different branches. If you are just beginning, such an arrangement may seem overly complicated, but please take my word for it: before you know it, you'll be so inundated with notes that you'll be glad you had the foresight to organize them beforehand.

That's really all you need, aside from the star of the show: yourself. This entire project, never forget, involves discovering how hundreds or even thousands of ancestors combined their genes and chromosomes to make you the unique person you are. So begin with yourself and work backward.

2. Make up charts and fill in as much as you can

To prepare a genealogy, you must construct two types of charts; each feeds on the other. The first is a *direct-ancestry chart,* showing yourself, your parents, your grandparents, your great-grandparents and so on, as far back as you can go. The second is a series of *descendants' charts,* one for each branch of your family. These charts should start with your most ancient ancestor in each branch and should show his children, grandchildren, great-grandchildren, etc.

In other words, a direct-ancestry chart begins with the present and works backward in time, and everyone mentioned on the chart is a direct ancestor of yours. A descendants' chart begins in the past and works forward to the present, and everyone mentioned on it will be some kind of relative of yours —a cousin, sibling, aunt, uncle, parent, grandparent, etc. Forms for these charts can be purchased at genealogical societies, genealogy departments of

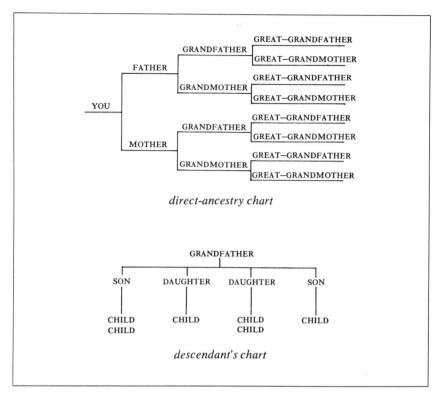

GREAT—GRANDFATHER

GRANDFATHER

GREAT—GRANDMOTHER

FATHER

GREAT—GRANDFATHER

GRANDMOTHER

GREAT—GRANDMOTHER

YOU

GREAT—GRANDFATHER

GRANDFATHER

GREAT—GRANDMOTHER

MOTHER

GREAT—GRANDFATHER

GRANDMOTHER

GREAT—GRANDMOTHER

direct-ancestry chart

GRANDFATHER

SON   DAUGHTER   DAUGHTER   SON

CHILD   CHILD   CHILD   CHILD
CHILD   CHILD

descendant's chart

libraries and at some bookstores, but it's easy enough to make the charts yourself, with a ruler and pencil.

Every genealogist seems to have a different method for compiling his data, ranging from the very complicated—complete with codes and symbols—to the simple. I've always opted for simplicity and tried to avoid codes of any sort. A person's name, the years of his birth and death, and his native country or city should be enough to identify him on your charts; additional information about him can be provided on supplemental sheets, where he can be identified by his name and dates.

As you fill in your direct-ancestry chart, you'll soon notice gaps where you are unable to write in the appropriate names. Don't worry about them. This is where the fun begins.

3. Locate your relatives, close and distant

To learn more about your ancestors than you know yourself, your first, best source of information is your pool of living relatives. Your older relatives may not remember dates and ages off the tops of their heads, but they will probably be very good indeed on names, places and circumstances that could confirm or refute the information you will find in documents.

Most people have some memory of their grandparents, and just about everyone remembers his or her parents. And you have many more relatives than you may think.

For example, if you are thirty-five, both of your parents may be living. Even if only one of your four grandparents is still living, brothers or sisters of those who are dead may still survive. Thus you may be able to call or write to check your findings with members of the immediate families of at least some of your grandparents. In my own case, no fewer than fifty-four first cousins of my grandparents are living at this writing; each of those fifty-four cousins had grandparents who were ancestors of mine, so anything these cousins can remember about their grandparents will be useful to my own genealogy. And many more cousins of my grandparents have widows or widowers still living. (In addition, I have found six living cousins of my *great*-grandparents.)

Your powers of deduction are valuable in sniffing out relatives who might be two or three generations in your past. Persistence helps, too. Among your sixteen great-great-grandparents, for example, the first may have been born in 1830 and the last in 1860. Thus there is a wide spread in age between members of the same generation, which explains why it's possible for someone from your grandparents' generation, say, to be older than someone from your great-grandparents'.

One day while pondering the chart of descendants of my youngest great-great-grandmother (born in 1853), I noticed that she had had a younger brother, named Isaac Kirschbaum, who was born in 1861 and died in Brooklyn. Based on his birth date, I reasoned that it was entirely possible that Isaac Kirschbaum had children who were still living—even though they would be first cousins of my great-grandparents. My close relatives in that branch of the family recalled that Isaac had five children, but no one seemed to know what became of them. For a year or two I made inquiries as to the whereabouts of Isaac Kirschbaum's children, without success. Finally I took an extreme step: I looked in the Brooklyn phone book and found twelve Kirschbaums listed there. I wrote letters to all twelve. Sure enough, two of them turned out to be children of Isaac Kirschbaum. I had a memorable "reunion" with one of them; from her I learned, among other things, the town that the Kirschbaum branch of my family had come from (Jaroslav, in Galicia) and that her grandfather, who was my great-great-great-grandfather, was a teamster.

On a similar occasion I was searching for an eighty-five-year old relative on Long Island named Joe Sobel. Again, no one seemed to know his exact address. Again, I looked in the Nassau County phone book and sent letters to all six Joe Sobels I found there. The correct one contacted me and shortly after arranged a small party where I met not only him but sixteen of his and my relatives. Postal rates being what they are lately, I do not recommend such mass mailings as a routine matter. As a last resort, though, they are excellent, and not all that expensive, if you consider that the time you spend hunting for distant relatives is worth something.

I have found that old relatives are usually eager to talk about the past and will welcome your interest. As for their memories—they may be fuzzy about what they did last week, but they're often remarkably clear about events of sixty or seventy years ago.

Some people find it difficult to interview older men and women, but it's easy when you consider the alternative. You can spend years searching fruitlessly through books and records for the answer to a question that one living human being could supply in seconds. Your older relatives, whatever their recall, have valuable memories inside their heads which they will take to their grave unless you get to them first.

I ran that kind of race against time in the mid-1960s when I learned that a first cousin of my great-grandmother, a man then in his nineties, was living in Rockaway Beach, New York. I was then living in Chicago, and each time I visited my parents in New York, I telephoned his home in the hope that I could come to see him. Each time, his daughters told me that his mind was not lucid at that particular moment and a visit would be futile. This went on for several years until the summer of 1970, when his daughters said they thought he was in condition to see me. By then he was 101 years old. To my delight he recounted many stories and relationships which jibed with facts I had gathered from other sources and opened doors to new research; when I left, his daughters told me he hadn't been that lucid in years. Six months later the man died—content, I like to think, in the knowledge that he had discharged his obligation to future generations.

4. Write, telephone or visit your relatives for information— preferably the oldest first

When you've located relatives who might be able to help you fill in the missing spaces on your charts, get in touch with them. Ask specific questions. For example, "Do you know the names of Grandpa's children? When were they born? Whom did they marry? Did they have any children? Where did they live? When did they come to this country?" These questions are best asked in a personal interview, conducted in a comfortable place where your relative can look at your charts while the two of you are talking. The answers you get may be vague guesses or simply wrong, but your living relatives (and their spouses) are generally your best starting point in your hunt for useful clues.

Genealogists have traditionally frowned on oral interviews as reliable sources of information, preferring concrete evidence such as official records, family Bibles, personal letters or tombstones. As you'll see in chapter 3, you will make much use of birth, death and marriage certificates, wills, and immigration and naturalization papers. And it is true that for determining specific dates, written or engraved records are best. But they are hardly infallible, especially concerning Jews.

Many Jewish immigrants from Europe never knew their birthdays or anniversaries, and so official papers dealing with these matters might simply reflect educated guesses, and in some cases wild guesses.

Often people deliberately lied about their ages in official papers, perhaps to make them appear old enough to be legally married, perhaps out of vanity. There was almost no sense of rapport or understanding between turn-of-the-century Jewish immigrants and the officials who filled out birth, death and marriage certificates. The Jews had always been suspicious of government bureaucrats in Europe, and that suspicion persisted in America. The American bureaucrats, for their part, couldn't understand the nuances of Jewish names and usually didn't care; just about every American Jewish family has a story similar to that of a family who upon their arrival from Russia in 1883 were asked their name by an immigration official. "Mayakovsky," they replied, whereupon the officer dutifully wrote down "Greenstein," thus changing the family name permanently for no reason other than that it was noisy in Castle Garden and he couldn't understand them.

If in the course of your research you find no discrepancies at all among what people tell you and what you find in official records and on gravestones, you will be a rare bird indeed. The main thing to keep in mind as you go about asking questions is that you should never place all of your trust in any single source of information. (Come to think of it, this is sensible advice for *any* situation, genealogical or not.) Official records and tombstones have the advantage of permanence: whatever is written down or inscribed does not change with the passage of time, as people's memories often do. But ultimately, facts derived from official documents, tombstones and personal interviews all originate with human beings and are subject to human fallibility. Your best bet is to double-check and triple-check your information with as many sources as possible. Your own powers of deduction are every bit as important in genealogical research as the hard information you'll find in official records. And it is in personal interviews that the powers of deduction come into play.

I personally don't use a tape recorder during these interviews because I find transcribing all those tapes to be too time-consuming. But it's actually a good idea to use *both* tape recorder and notes when interviewing relatives—the former because ancient recollections have a way of tumbling out in disorganized fashion, faster than you can write them down; the latter because you (and the person you are interviewing) have to be able to see what subjects you have covered while the interview is in progress. Family relationships can get very confusing in conversation; it's of enormous help if you can point to names and dates on a chart as you talk.

5. *Visit the graves of your ancestors and relatives for more clues*

While you're talking to relatives, you can be checking cemeteries, old letters, diaries, family Bibles and photo albums for corroborating evidence. It's been my experience that tombstones are usually more reliable than official papers, if only because people tend to give more thought to something as permanent (and expensive) as a tombstone.

This is not to say that tombstones are entirely reliable either. I have found too many gravestones with ages rounded off to the nearest five years—"75 years old," "65 years old," etc.—not to suspect that a lot of these are simply educated guesses made by relatives who were certainly not trained genealogists. From your own research you may well be able to make a much more educated guess than the people responsible for either your relative's tombstone or his death certificate.

Nevertheless, the Hebrew inscription on the stone usually tells not only the name of the deceased, but also the name of the father of the deceased. And if the deceased belonged to the priestly tribe *(Kohanim)* or to the Levites, the gravestone will tell you that, too, and provide you with a personal link back to the Bible. It's a good idea to copy the entire gravestone inscription, both the Hebrew and English, or better still, take a photo of it. You never can tell what nuggets will be contained in a seemingly innocuous word or two.

The easiest way to find the appropriate cemeteries for your ancestors is to question your relatives; usually there is some relative who can tell you which cemetery to go to. If no relative can help you, you can take the circuitous route of searching for your ancestor's death certificate (see chapter 3); the certificate will tell you the name of the cemetery. Or if your family belonged to a certain synagogue, you may be able to find the cemetery through the congregation, since many synagogues used specific cemeteries.

If you do find the cemetery and are especially lucky, you may find your ancestors are buried in a family plot with other relatives. Needless to add, the relatives' gravestones contain valuable information, and you should copy everything you find on these stones. (On the other hand, don't assume that everyone buried on a family plot is a relative; I know of families who have buried their cook and their bookkeeper on the family plot, cheek by jowl with bona-fide relations.)

When you visit a cemetery, always stop first at the cemetery office to learn the location of the grave. Get directions that are as specific as possible, because cemeteries are easy places to get lost in. Most cemeteries can provide you with a map which will show you how to locate the grave you seek. If there is no map, ask the clerk to draw one for you. It's important to have a map even if you know the section, row and grave number—there may not be any number when you get to the section, row or grave.

It is best to wear old clothes and heavy shoes or boots to a cemetery. The ground may be soft on the day you visit, or you may have to push your way through brush and weeds if the grave you seek is in a neglected section. Some gravestones sink into the ground with the passage of time, and in those cases you may have to get down on your knees and clear dirt and moss away with your fingers in order to read the bottom lettering. If you want to photograph a gravestone, bring chalk to trace over the lettering so that it will show up clearly in your picture.

Some old headstones are difficult to read because the markings have all but faded away. In these cases it may help to come back at another hour of the day; an inscription may be more legible depending on how the sun strikes it. Copy the stone exactly as it is written, including all punctuation. If parts of the inscription are illegible, say so in your notes. A gravestone copied incorrectly can throw you off your trail and into hopeless confusion.

As you will discover, ancestor hunting basically involves dealing with two types of people: relatives, who are likely to feel some bond with you, and bureaucrats, who are likely to see you as a pain in the neck. With the former you must be patient and loving; with the latter, you must be persistent and pointed. Some of the most difficult bureaucrats, unfortunately, are those who work in cemetery offices, perhaps because cemeteries have their customers right where they want them—in the ground, where they are unlikely to be moved if the service isn't suitable. Once, at a large New York cemetery office, I overheard a little old woman begging a clerk to tend to some problem regarding a grave there. The clerk gave the woman no satisfaction, nor even the slightest bit of sympathy. "But . . . this is a dear relative of mine," the little old woman whimpered uncomprehendingly.

"Lady," the clerk replied matter-of-factly, "to you it's a dear relative, to us it's only a grave."

Some cemetery clerks seem to have forgotten that the purpose of their work is to perpetuate respect for and memory of the past. However, many are genuinely interested in helping you track down records. If you have a name and date, it should be no problem for them to tell you where a grave is located, and their files may yield other information as well. If, on the other hand, you want to pore over a cemetery's annual burial books, it is best not to go on a Sunday—the one really busy day at Jewish cemeteries, which are closed on Saturdays. Or if you must go on a Sunday, go during the winter, when few other visitors are there. Do *not* go on Mother's or Father's Day, the busiest time for cemeteries, or around the time of the High Holy Days. Any weekday is usually sufficiently slow for most clerks to be happy to help you.

6. Fit your clues together and see where they take you

No bit of information from any of your research is too minor to be ignored. Your grandmother's story about an uncle who lived in a neighboring town in the Ukraine might provide you with future clues about that branch of your family. Consider, for example, the arcane route I took to locate the grave and name of a sister of my great-grandmother.

Over the years, in the course of wandering through the Hungarian Cemetery in Brooklyn, New York, I had found the graves of a number of my relatives (as well as the tomb of the magician Harry Houdini). I had also found graves of people whose names were familiar but who didn't seem to be related to me. One of these was a Bernat Klein who died in 1903 and was buried next to his wife, Lydia, who died in 1920. My great-great-grandfather's name was Morris David Klein, but of course Klein is a very common name. Nevertheless, I copied their names and dates into my notebook and promptly forgot about them.

Meanwhile, I was assembling information about the children of that great-great-grandfather, Morris David Klein. All of my relatives agreed that Morris had four children—a son and three daughters—and that all four were buried in the Hungarian Cemetery. In time I found the grave of the son, William, who was supposed to be the oldest, and of two of his sisters, including my great-grandmother Julia Klein (who married a Klein and thus kept her family name). But the relatives all insisted there had been another sister, named Rifka, who had died around 1918 or 1920 and had been a widow for many years at the time of her death. Strangely, none of the relatives could remember Rifka's married name, and without that I could not find her grave.

Fortunately, I was able to find the grave of her daughter, Fanny Gelbman, at the Hungarian Cemetery, and with the information it provided, obtain a copy of Fanny's death certificate. The certificate, I reasoned, would give me the names of Fanny's parents and thus tell me Rifka's married name.

But things rarely come that easily in genealogy. Fanny Gelbman's death certificate listed her father as "Bernat Klein," and under "maiden name of mother" it said "Rebus Schwartz." As I've said earlier, death certificates are often full of mistakes, and this seemed to be such a case. "Rebus" was perhaps a passable variation of "Rifka," but I already knew that Rifka's maiden name was Klein, not Schwartz. I seemed to have hit a dead end.

Finally, one Sunday night I spread out all my notes and death certificates in front of me, then tried to clear my mind and reason anew the mysterious matter of the sister named Rifka. It was indeed odd, I told myself, that my older Klein relatives could remember Rifka quite vividly, but not one of them could remember her married name. Usually it's the other way around: when a woman is long-departed, people remember her only by her married name.

And then there was the strange business of the death certificate. Perhaps, I conjectured, the reason nobody remembered Rifka Klein's married name was that her *married* name was actually Klein. Perhaps Rifka was not a sister at all to the Kleins, but a sister-in-law whose husband had died so long before that relatives fifty years later recalled her as a full-blooded sister. Or there was another possibility: Rifka was indeed a sister to the Kleins, but she had married someone *else* named Klein, and thus she had never had any name but Klein.

Idly I began thumbing through my notebooks, reviewing my old jottings in the light of my new logic. And that's when the note about the graves of Bernat Klein and Lydia Klein, copied down and forgotten years before, jumped out at me. This Lydia Klein died in 1920, or around the time that Rifka Klein was supposed to have died. Lydia was seventy-five years old at death, an age which would have been about right for Rifka. What's more, Lydia's husband's name was Bernat, and the death certificate of Fanny Gelbman said that *Rifka*'s husband was Bernat. Finally, Lydia's husband Bernat had died in 1903, or seventeen years before his wife Lydia died, and my Klein relatives had always told me that Rifka had been a widow for many years. On the basis of all this, it seemed highly likely to me that the Lydia Klein in this grave and the Rifka Klein for whom I was searching were one and the same person.

On my next trip to New York I hurried out to the Hungarian Cemetery to check the graves of Bernat and Lydia Klein firsthand. The English notations on the graves yielded nothing new—I had copied them down years before—but the Hebrew inscriptions, which I had ignored originally, confirmed my hunch. "Rifka bat Moshe David"—Rifka, daughter of Morris David—read the Hebrew words on Lydia Klein's grave, and I was home free; the mystery was solved. Rifka—whose Anglicized name was apparently Lydia—was indeed the daughter of my great-great-grandfather Morris David Klein, and she had married Bernat Klein, which explained why no one had ever known her by any name but "Klein." (The notation of "Schwartz" on Rifka's daughter's death certificate had simply been a mistake.)

All right, you are probably telling yourself, after years of hunting and hunching down many a blind alleyway, I finally found the grave of Rifka Klein. So what? After all, Rifka was not a direct ancestor of mine: she was merely a sister of my great-grandmother. Was it so important to find her grave?

As a matter of fact, it was. In the jigsaw-puzzle world of genealogy, even the most seemingly obscure fact can be important, and finding Rifka's grave was a major element in confirming my discovery of the grave of Rifka's mother, my great-great-grandmother Lena Klein, the widow of Morris David Klein, and that led to my discovery of the names of *her* parents—my great-great-great-grandparents—thus adding one more generation to my family tree. The process of finding ancestors is not unlike that of squeezing blood from a stone.

The search for the Rifka Klein of my family provides one other general lesson. In many cases, the Hebrew names by which people were familiarly known have been given fancy Anglicizations for official purposes in the United States, and the Anglicized version frequently bears little or no resemblance to the Hebrew. Rifka Klein's gravestone, for example, called her "Lydia," although I never heard any relative refer to her by that name. The Hebrew name Chaya has been rendered as Cornelia or Charlotte or Anne. Moses, depending on the vogue then current, has been transformed into Morris or Martin or Moe.

III

Public Records in the United States

THERE ARE JOYS and pitfalls to be found in sifting through official records. They may or may not be accurate, and they can be hit-or-miss affairs (in my own case, I was able to find the births of my great-aunts and great-uncles listed in a microfilm index, but I was unable to find any listing for my grandmother herself, even though she was born in New York about 1885). Nevertheless, official records are usually accessible to the public, and if used wisely in conjunction with your interviews of relatives, other sources of information and your own analytical powers, they can open many a new door out of many a formerly blind alley.

A wide variety of public records in the United States can provide useful pieces in your family puzzle: death certificates, birth certificates, marriage records, census records, wills and administrations, ships' passenger lists, immigration and naturalization records, newspaper obituaries, and back issues of city directories—all may be of value to you.

Some records are more readily available than others, and some are more reliable than others. There is nothing more frustrating than finding contradictory information in official documents, especially for twentieth-century Americans, who are so precise about dates and spellings of names. Our ancestors were not. Indeed, some of them could not read or write. Others, as we have said, deliberately altered information on official forms.

What is most frustrating, I think, is that death certificates, census forms, ships' passenger lists and the like *look* so exact that it's hard to believe they are wrong. Yet in fact little or no effort was made, at the time these documents were filled out, to verify their accuracy.

The key thing to remember in sifting through public records is that the closer in time a document is to the event it is recording, the more likely it is to be accurate. A turn-of-the-century American birth certificate may be off by a few days, weeks or even months, but never more than that. On the other hand, if your grandmother's death certificate in 1958 lists her age as eighty, that is hardly reason to assume that she was born precisely in 1878.

Similarly, every death certificate is supposed to list the name of the father and the maiden name of the mother of the deceased. It is this feature that makes a death certificate such a valuable source for genealogists: if these names are accurate, you will then have another generation to add to your family tree. But if a woman died in 1958 at the age of eighty or so, there may not have been anyone around when her death certificate was filled out who remembered the names of her parents. On the other hand, if the woman was *married* in the United States, the names of her parents on her marriage certificate would be more likely to be accurate; after all, she probably filled that out herself. And if she was *born* in the United States, the names of her parents listed on her birth certificate will be more accurate still, since they were probably provided by her parents themselves.

On to specifics:

BIRTH, DEATH AND MARRIAGE RECORDS

Because these records almost always list the names of the subject's parents, they are the most obvious tool for adding new generations of ancestors to your family tree. If any of your ancestors—or any of your ancestors' brothers or sisters—died in the United States, you can with a bit of searching obtain a death certificate.

To be sure, a death certificate is usually filled out not only in haste, but at the worst possible time for rational thinking. In the typical turn-of-the-century tableau, the death certificate is completed by the physician or the undertaker, who naturally knows little about the biographical or family details of the deceased. And the spouse and children of the deceased, who might be able to provide these details, are beside themselves with grief at the moment. So all too often the doctor or undertaker turns to some cousin sitting in the corner of the room, who may or may not know specific details about the life of the departed. Or the doctor or undertaker simply fills in the biographical details himself as best he can, leaving blank spaces where he's completely at a loss.

Information on these certificates varies from state to state and from year to year, but a death certificate will usually provide the following information:

- Date and hour of death
- Cause of death
- Place of death
- Home address of the deceased
- Age of the deceased, and possibly his birth date
- Birthplace of the deceased
- Name of father and maiden name of mother of the deceased
- Birthplace of father and mother of the deceased
- Number of years the deceased was in the United States
- Marital status of the deceased
- If married, name of spouse
- Name of the attending funeral home
- Name of cemetery where the deceased was buried
- In some cases, the name of a relative who furnished information for the death certificate

If you know the date of your relative's death and the city in which he died, it should not be too difficult to obtain a photocopy of the original death certificate. Fees for these copies range from 50 cents in Puerto Rico to $3 in Alaska ($4 for a marriage certificate in New York City), and it's a good idea to send for the certificates as soon as possible, since the fees always seem to be going up.

If your relative died in a major city, for the sake of precision it's a good idea to try to learn the index number of the death certificate before you send away for it. For example, in New York you can find it by looking in the city's annual indexes of death certificates, which go back to August 1888, in the Local History and Genealogy Division of the New York Public Library. Indexes for marriages and births are also available there.

In some states all birth, death and marriage records are kept in a single place at the state capitol; in others, the records are kept in the county where the event occurred. For precise information, send for copies of the following federal government booklets:

> *Where to Write for Birth and Death Records*
> (DHEW Pub. No. HRA 75–1142)
>
> *Where to Write for Marriage Records*
> (DHEW Pub. No. HSM 72–1144)
>
> *Where to Write for Divorce Records*
> (DHEW Pub. No. HSM 73–1145)

Each of these booklets costs 35 cents and can be obtained by writing to the Superintendent of Documents, U.S. Government Printing Office, Washington, D.C. 20402. If you live in a city with a U.S. Government Printing Office bookstore, you'll usually find these booklets there. Look first in your local phone book for such an office. Specific state-by-state information can also be found in the book *How to Trace Your Family Tree,* by the American Genealogical Research Institute staff ($1.95).

Some cities have a prepared form which you should fill out when requesting a birth, death or marriage certificate. In these cases, ask for a copy of the form before you send in any money. (Or ask for several: you never can tell when you may need another. I've photocopied a pile of forms to save me the trouble of requesting a new one each time I need it.)

When you send for a copy of a certificate, be sure to provide as much information as possible about the person whose record is being requested: his full name; the month, day, year and place of birth, death or marriage; his sex and race; and his parents' names, if you know them. You should also mention your relationship to the person, and the reason you need the copy of the certificate ("genealogical research" is sufficient). In addition to the check covering the fee, it's always a good idea to enclose a stamped, self-addressed envelope.

FEDERAL CENSUS RECORDS

The federal census, an attempt to enumerate the entire population of the United States, has been compiled every ten years since 1790. The reliability of its information has varied from one decade to the next, but if you can find your relatives in the census, you're likely to pick up some new tidbits about them. The 1880 census, for example, listed the name, age, sex and color of each person in a household; the relationship of each person to the head of the family; the birthplace of each person and the marital status of each person. The censuses for 1850, 1860 and 1870 also listed weddings within the past year, value of real estate and personal property owned, and the profession of each person over fifteen years of age. The 1790–1840 censuses give only the names of the head of the household; other family members are tallied unknown by age and sex.

Bear in mind that all censuses are subject to human frailties. The census taker interviewing the head of a household in 1900 asks for the birth dates of all the children in the house—since the form provided spaces for such dates. But the father doesn't know the exact birth dates of his children; he knows only their ages. The census taker, meanwhile, is in a hurry. "OK," he tells the father. "You say your daughter is two years old, and she was born in the spring? We'll put down April 1898." The father nods and the census taker is on his way. Seventy-five years later, some descendant peering at this form on a microfilm reader at the National Archives sees this notation and accepts it as holy writ, which it is not. It is, however, useful as a means of double-checking other information you have gathered.

Let's suppose that the baby girl we've been talking about in our 1900 census scenario is today your grandmother. For as long as you can remember, your grandmother has been telling everyone that she was born in 1901. Obviously, the mere fact that she is listed at all in the 1900 census is solid evidence that she was born before then and that she has been fibbing about her age all these years. Perhaps she wasn't born exactly in April 1898, but she was probably born within a year of that date, one way or the other.

Similarly, suppose you know that your great-grandfather died in New York in 1909. You obtain a copy of his death certificate, which tells you, among other things, that he had been in the United States for thirty years when he died. This is by no means proof that he arrived in America in 1879; the "30 years" notation may simply be a rough estimate made by someone who hardly knew your great-grandfather. To narrow down the date, you can look him up in the 1880 census; if you find him, you'll know he was in the United States before 1880. If the 1880 census shows him to have had a five-year-old child born in Austria and a three-year-old child born in New York, you can surmise that he probably came to the United States sometime between 1875 and 1877. By finding the birth certificate of that three-year-old child born in New York, you can narrow down even more precisely the range of possible dates of arrival. If you can find your great-grandfather's name on the passenger list of a ship arriving in the United States, you can of course pin down the date exactly. Census material from 1790 through 1880 is widely available in local, state, college and historical society libraries throughout the country. The same material is also available, of course, at the National Archives in Washington. The census records for 1890, unfortunately, will never be available: all but a handful of them were destroyed in a fire in Washington in 1921. From 1900 on, the census is supposed to be confidential, but in fact the 1900 census has been microfilmed and can be studied at the National Archives and at National Archives branches, provided you sign a form declaring that your interest is in bona-fide historical, legal or genealogical research.

Finding a name in the census is no easy task because it is compiled geographically, not alphabetically by name, if the person lives in a city or town. For the censuses prior to 1880, you must first learn the street address of the relative you seek. You can probably find this by checking through old copies of the local city directory (more on this in a moment). If the city is a large one, once you have the address you must consult old maps of the city to learn what ward the house was located in, since censuses were conducted by wards. (Such maps are available at the National Archives, the Library of Congress and major local public libraries.) Once you know this, *then* you can look through the actual census roll and find your relative.

It's an involved process, but not as bad as it may sound. Most major municipal libraries have city directories on microfilm dating back to the early nineteenth century; they have map rooms where you can locate the necessary ward numbers; and they have the census rolls for their area on microfilm, so everything you need to make a census search may well be there under one roof.

If that still sounds too complicated, the National Archives offers blessed relief for anyone searching through the 1880 or 1900 censuses. During the Depression, the Work Projects Administration (WPA) compiled an alphabetical card index for both of these censuses. The 1880 index lists every household with children aged ten or less (apparently this index was used to verify the age of people who claimed to be sixty-five when Social Security was introduced in 1935). The 1900 index lists all families, couples and individuals living alone. In other words, for the 1880 census you can find most names (and all names in 1900) simply by looking them up in the alphabetized microfilm indexes for your particular state.

To be sure, the indexed 1880 and 1900 census rolls aren't in strictly alphabetical order, but are arranged according to an ingenious system known as Soundex, which orders names not according to their spelling, but according to their phonetic sound (on the valid theory that many names on census forms were misspelled). Do not, repeat not, let this scare you away: once you get accustomed to it, Soundex is fun, easy to use and certainly more convenient than the crusty old alphabet. And don't worry about figuring out the Soundex code for the particular names you need. The National Archives or any other library that uses Soundex will have a simple guide you can use.

If you can't visit the National Archives, one of its branches or a public library that has census records, the National Archives will do what it can to help you by mail. Ask the National Archives for GSA Form 7029, "Order for Copies—Census Records," to make your requests. When you do, be as specific as possible and include as much pertinent information as possible. The mailing address:

> National Archives and Records Service
> NNC
> Washington, D.C. 20408

The National Archives also handles mail requests for copies of 1900 census returns, but these must be applied for on a different federal form, GSA Form 7163, "1900 Census Application."

Information about more recent censuses—that is, from 1900 through the present—can be obtained for a fee by writing to the U.S. Department of Commerce, Bureau of the Census, Pittsburg, Kansas 66762, if you are a bona-fide relative or historical researcher. Ask for Form BC–600. Again, be specific.

If the task isn't too time-consuming, the National Archives staff will search its records for you at no charge. They will also supply you with photocopies of their records for a moderate fee per page. (Don't send money when you apply; you'll be billed after the search, and only if they find something.) If the task *is* too time-consuming, you'll have to do the job yourself. In any case, sooner or later it's a good idea to visit the National Archives in person. No surrogate can sniff out your family's records as well as you can.

The National Archives Building is at Eighth Street and Pennsylvania Avenue NW, Washington, D.C. 20408. Branch offices of the National Archives (formally known as Federal Archives and Records Centers), often contain census and other records for their particular regions. There are eleven branches, as follows:

- 380 Trapelo Road, Waltham, Mass. 02154
- Military Ocean Terminal, Building 22, Bayonne, N.J. 07002
- 5000 Wissahickon Avenue, Philadelphia, Pa. 19144
- 1557 St. Joseph Avenue, East Point, Ga. 30044
- 7358 S. Pulaski Road, Chicago, Ill. 60629
- 2306 E. Bannister Road, Kansas City, Mo. 64131
- 4900 Hemphill Street, Fort Worth, Tex. 76115
- Building 48, Denver Federal Center, Denver, Colo. 80225
- 1000 Commodore Drive, San Bruno, Calif. 94066
- 24000 Avila Road, Laguna Niguel, Calif. 92677
- 6125 Sand Point Way, Seattle, Wash. 98115

For more information on records inside and outside the National Archives, send for the following two leaflets:

- *Genealogical Records in the National Archives*
(Natl. Archives general information leaflet no. 5)
- *Genealogical Sources Outside the National Archives*
(Natl. Archives general information leaflet no. 6)

Both are available free of charge from the Publication Sales Branch (NATS), National Archives (GSA), Washington, D.C. 20408. (Don't worry about what those initials mean; just include them in the address.) You can also get, on request from the same address, a complete packet of National Archives leaflets plus sample copies of order forms. You may also be able to get copies of these leaflets at your local U.S. Government Printing Office bookstore. For $1.65 you can get even more detailed information in the following book:

- *Guide to Genealogical Sources in the National Archives,* by Meredith Colket Jr. and Frank E. Bridgers. 145 pp. (Natl. Archives publication no. 64–8)

This can be obtained at most U.S. Government bookstores or by writing to the Superintendent of Documents, U.S. Government Printing Office, Washington, D.C. 20402.

SHIPS' PASSENGER LISTS

The passenger list of virtually every ship that ever arrived at an American port on the Atlantic or the Gulf of Mexico since 1820 can be found at the National Archives, and many can be found at Archives branches or public libraries. (Most of the West Coast lists have been destroyed in fires, but fortunately for us, not many Jews arrived in the United States on the West Coast.) If you know the name of the ship your ancestor was on and the date of arrival, it's an easy matter to find the appropriate microfilm roll at the National Archives. The early lists are very inconsistent and sometimes difficult to read (nobody used ball-point pens in those days), but at the very least they should contain the age, occupation and former residence of the person in question. Some lists provide a good deal more, such as the name of a relative in the United States whom the newly arrived immigrant intended to join. Such a tidbit is of course tremendously valuable to a genealogist. Some turn-of-the-century passenger lists also mention the immigrant's final destination in the United States, who paid his passage, whether he could read and write, and even whether or not he was a polygamist.

If you don't know your ancestor's exact date of arrival and the name of the ship, there is still hope. For one thing, you may find his date of arrival in his naturalization records (more on that below). If you know the approximate date of arrival, or the name of the ship, or the port of embarkation, or the port of arrival, or any combination of these, you can consult the *Morton Allan Directory of European Passenger Steamship Arrivals,* available at the National Archives and major libraries. It lists ship-by-ship dates of arrival in New York, 1890–1930, and in Baltimore, Boston and Philadelphia, 1904–1926. For example, a friend's grandfather recalls that he arrived in New York as a small boy in the early years of the century aboard the S.S. *Bremen;* he thinks his family came in September. By consulting the Allan directory, my friend found the exact dates of September arrivals of the *Bremen* in New York in the early twentieth century. Now he can consult the passenger lists for these particular crossings by the ship. Combing through these long lists is still like searching for a needle in a haystack—as witness the fact that he hasn't yet found his grandfather's family on any of the lists—but the use of the Allan directory does reduce the size of the haystack considerably. Other similar directories cover earlier periods.

If you are especially lucky, your ancestors arrived during a period and at a port whose passenger lists have been indexed. If this is the case, it's just a matter of looking up the name on the indexed microfilm rolls (although names aren't always spelled right or alphabetized correctly, due to illegible handwriting). Indexes are available for the following ports and periods:

- Baltimore, 1820–1897
- Boston, 1848–1891, 1902–1906
- New Orleans, 1853–1899
- New York, 1820–1846; June 16, 1897–June 30, 1902
- Philadelphia, 1800–1906
- Some other, minor ports, 1890–1924

Indexes have also been compiled for more recent periods, but to protect the privacy of immigrants still living, there is a fifty-year restriction on these records by the Immigration and Naturalization Service. Thus indexes which include periods within the past fifty years are not accessible to the public. However, if a particular reel of microfilm has no data more recent than fifty years ago, you can examine it at the National Archives. And if you write to the National Archives, the staff will look up names for you on the more recent restricted indexes. These later indexes cover the following ports and periods:

- Baltimore, 1898–1952
- Boston, 1906–1920
- New Orleans, 1899–1952
- New York, July 1, 1902–1943
- Philadelphia, 1907–1948

Requests for searches should be made on GSA Form 7111, "Order for Copies —Passenger Lists." If you want the Archives staff to consult an index, provide at least the name of the immigrant, the port of entry and the supposed year of arrival. If you want the Archives staff to search specific passenger lists— that is, those not covered by an index—you should also state the name of the vessel and the exact date of arrival. There is no charge for such a search, only for the copies of the lists.

Whether indexed or not, the following passenger lists are available on microfilm—more than 11,000 rolls of them—at the National Archives:

- Baltimore, 1820–1909
- Boston, 1820–1874; 1883–1943
- New Orleans, 1820–1945
- New York, 1820–1942
- Philadelphia, 1800–1945
- Other, minor ports, 1820–1873; 1893–1945

To some extent, these passenger lists are available in the city where the ships arrived, along with some nonfederal lists not available elsewhere. The Local History and Genealogy Division of the New York Public Library, for example, has indexed passenger lists of ships arriving in New York, 1820–1846. The city of Baltimore maintains an alphabetically indexed list of aliens who arrived there from 1833 to 1866 (write to Department of Legislative Reference, City Hall, Baltimore, Md. 21202). Massachusetts has lists of aliens who arrived there from 1848 through 1891 (Archives Division, Office of the Secretary of the Commonwealth, State House, Boston, Mass. 02133). Indexes to the Boston lists are also in the Boston Public Library (Copley Square, Boston, Mass. 02117), the Genealogical Society of the Church of Latter-day Saints (50 E. North Temple Street, Salt Lake City, Utah 84150), as well as in the National Archives.

NATURALIZATION RECORDS

Naturalization—that is, citizenship—procedures were standardized by the federal government as of September 26, 1906. If you have an ancestor who was naturalized after that date, the record is on file at the Immigration and Naturalization Service, Washington, D.C. 20536. Ask for Form G-641, which explains how to get information from the Service. These records provide the names of the new citizen's spouse and children, and the date and place of his arrival in the United States—information that can help you pinpoint the ship on which he arrived. Inquiries about citizenship granted after September 26, 1906, should be sent to the Immigration and Naturalization Service on a form that you can obtain from any of the Service's district offices. If there is no district office in your city, your local post office can give you the address of the nearest one.

If your ancestor was naturalized *before* September 26, 1906, you may have a harder time finding his citizenship records, and the information contained in them may be less valuable. Before 1906, naturalization proceedings could be held in any court—federal, state or local. Thus the records will most likely be found in the court where the naturalization took place. The clerk of the court should have these records; the problem is finding the right court.

This problem is completely avoided, though, if you are looking for a naturalization in New York City, Maine, Massachusetts, New Hampshire or Rhode Island. During the 1930s the WPA compiled cumulative Soundex indexes of naturalization records for these areas, so it's simply a matter of consulting the appropriate name in the index. The naturalization index for all courts in what are now the five boroughs of New York City—covering 1790 through 1906—is in the Federal Records Center at Bayonne, N.J. (Military Ocean Terminal, Building 22). Records for Maine, Massachusetts, New Hampshire and Rhode Island cover 1787 through 1906 and are available at the National Archives in Washington. The National Archives staff will search these indexes for you at no charge if you provide the full name of the new citizen and the approximate date of his or her naturalization. (Requests for New York City should be directed to the Federal Records Center in Bayonne.)

Once you've located these citizenship papers, though, it's a hit-or-miss matter as to what information you'll find, since there were no standardized citizenship forms prior to 1906. Often the only information contained in pre-1906 naturalizations is the new citizen's country of origin. But you never can tell what other information might be there.

There are, incidentally, three types of naturalization papers: the "declaration of intention," often filed soon after an immigrant arrived; the "final petition," filed after the required length of stay in America (five years throughout most of our history); and the "certificate of naturalization." Often the declaration of intention contains more information than the other papers. For more details on these papers, see *Locating Your Immigrant Ancestor,* by James and Lila Neagles.

One last note: the Federal Records Center in Bayonne, N.J., where naturalization and other federal records for New York City are kept, is so out of the way that few people use it in person, and the staff seems to be so lonesome that should you pay a visit there, they will probably be overjoyed to see you and help you. That makes it something of a rarity among federal institutions!

NEWSPAPER OBITUARIES

Most public libraries in major cities have back issues of local newspapers (and usually the *New York Times* as well) on microfilm. Even if your ancestors weren't sufficiently prominent to merit a news story when they died, their family may have inserted a paid obituary notice in the local paper. If there is (or was) a Yiddish newspaper in your city, it carried many obituaries, too. By checking back issues of such papers for these obituary notices, you can often find a great deal of vital information—names of descendants, the funeral home and the cemetery, for example. An obit notice usually lists the survivors of the deceased, thus giving you a clue as to whether the deceased outlived his or her spouse, siblings, children, and so on.

At the very least, obits are a quick and cheap way to double-check what you have learned elsewhere. Let us suppose you are looking for the death certificate of your great-grandfather, George Schwartz, who died in New York City in 1925. At the New York Public Library's Local History and Genealogy Division you would look up your great-grandfather's name in the 1925 index to New York City deaths. Suppose you find three George Schwartzes who died in New York that year, and you don't know which one is your ancestor. You could send away for all three death certificates—at $2.50 each—and hope that one of the three is the one you're looking for. But it's much easier and more reliable to step into the library's microfilm room just next door, order the *New York Times* rolls for a day or two after the three dates you have found, and look up the obituaries for George Schwartz on each of those three dates. (Don't overlook microfilms of defunct newspapers as a possible source, too.) If one of them lists survivors whose names are familiar to you as relatives, you can be sure you have the right person. *Then* you can send away for his death certificate, and it will cost you only $2.50 instead of $7.50.

The same process is useful in confirming gravestones. If, for example, you discover a grave that you *think* belonged to a relative, you can confirm his relationship by checking the obituary page of your local paper for the day after the date on the gravestone. If the obituary notice refers to brothers or sisters or children of the deceased, and if you recognize the names as relatives of yours, you will know that the grave in question indeed belongs to a relative.

Today most American Jews receive an obituary notice in their local daily newspaper. That was not always the case, of course, especially in the heyday of Jewish immigration when many Jews didn't speak English. In searching English-language newspapers for obituaries of my own relatives, I have found notices for virtually all of them from 1923 onward, but none for any relatives who died before 1923. The cutoff date for your family may be somewhat earlier or later, but it seems that sometime in the 1920s most Jewish funeral directors began routinely placing obit notices in the major local English paper. Before that time you may have little luck finding your relatives on the obit page of the *New York Times,* the Chicago *Tribune* or the Philadelphia *Bulletin.* On the other hand, you may very well find their obituaries in the back issues of the local Jewish paper, such as New York's *Jewish Daily Forward* (45 East 33rd Street, New York, N.Y. 10016). The *Forward,* of course, is in Yiddish.

If your relative lived in New York and/or was a prominent person, the *New York Times Obituary Index* may help you locate the date of his death without even scouring cemeteries or death-certificate indexes. The *Times Obituary Index,* available at major public libraries, is a cumulative index of obituary articles in the *Times* from 1858 through 1966. It's haphazard for the years before World War I, but complete since then. If a news article about your relative's death—even one or two paragraphs—appeared in the *Times* before 1966, his or her name should be listed in the index. This book does not, however, index the actual obit notices—the paid advertisements inserted by relatives, friends and organizations. So the fact that a death isn't listed in the *Times Obituary Index* doesn't necessarily mean you won't be able to find that death in a back issue of the *Times.*

The American Antiquarian Society in Worcester, Mass., has compiled an extensive unpublished index of newspaper obituaries since 1800; it will furnish you references from this index on request. Some libraries carry a typescript of *Index to the Obituary Notices in the Boston Transcript (1875–1930).* The California State Library in Sacramento has valuable indexes to obituaries of even minor people in the news in California.

For more detailed information as to where to find back issues of newspapers, consult:

- *American Newspapers, 1821–1936: A Union List Available in the United States and Canada,* by Winifred Herould
- *Newspapers on Microfilm*

CITY DIRECTORIES

Before telephones were commonplace, most people relied on city directories to tell them who lived where. And, indeed, directories are still published for most cities (although not New York). In the nineteenth century these directories generally listed only the head of the household, his occupation and his address. Old editions of these directories can be found (on microfilm, if not the originals) in most municipal libraries and historical societies. Both the Library of Congress and the National Archives in Washington have a huge collection of old city directories. A checklist of these directories in the Library of Congress was published by Philip M. Smith in the July 1936 issue of *American Genealogist* (Vol. 13, pp. 46–53), and was revised in the July 1951 issue (Vol. 27, p. 142).

These directories can be helpful in pinpointing your ancestor's arrival or date of death. Obviously, if you find him listed in the directory, you can be reasonably certain that he was alive and in the United States at the time the directory was published. The first year you find his name listed will give you some clue as to the date of his arrival in that particular city; the last year will provide some clue as to when he died. It helps in identifying your ancestor, of course, if you know his occupation or his address. Don't be surprised, incidentally, to find one person constantly changing his address from year to year. Families, especially immigrant families, moved quite often around the turn of the century. In those days, when rents were very low and families had few bulky possessions, it was usually easier to move into a freshly painted apartment every year or two than to paint the old place while you were living in it.

Bear in mind that city directories, like today's telephone directories, were compiled by private companies which had no legal means of extracting information from people. We've already seen that inaccuracies are all too frequent even in official documents like death certificates and census records; city directories, then, should be taken with even more than the usual dose of salt. In any given year's directory, many names were no doubt missing. The reliability of city directories depends largely on the particular companies that compiled them. The old New York City directories, I have found, are more reliable than the directories for Brooklyn (Brooklyn was a separate city until 1898). As for insights into the reliability of other directories, consult the librarian at your local library, historical society or genealogical society.

PROBATE RECORDS

The last will and testament of an individual is a valuable genealogical source because people usually will their property to their relatives, and thus a will should be able to help you ascertain the names of additional relatives and perhaps even determine whether the person who wrote the will is indeed your relative.

Let's suppose, for example, that you've come across the grave of someone you think is an ancestor of yours. You note his date of death, age and any other pertinent information from the gravestone (and *anything* is likely to be pertinent—the Hebrew inscription may tell you his father's name; "My beloved husband" that his wife outlived him; "Our dear father" that he left children, and so on). From the cemetery records you learn where he died. You then proceed to obtain this person's death certificate, which tells you the names of the parents of the deceased. This is all well and good, but you still haven't established that the deceased is actually an ancestor of yours. You may be able to do this by looking for his obituary notice in a back issue of the local newspaper. But if there is no such obit notice, a last will and testament is your best alternative.

All wills are open to public inspection once they are filed after a person's death (this enables all potential heirs to see to their own satisfaction that they are getting what is coming to them). Probate laws vary from state to state, but usually you can find wills in your local courthouse, usually in the surrogate's court; ask for the "Index to Administrations and Estates." To be sure, many people never get around to making a will; even today, about a third of all Americans die without one. If someone dies without a will and has property that must be disposed of, the court will appoint an administrator, and the record of this administration can also be found in the same index; it is not, however, likely to yield as much information as a will.

Despite the value of a will in tracing your family tree, I'm devoting little space to the subject here because it's my impression that few immigrant Jews around the turn of the century left wills. I have yet to find a single will left by any relative of mine prior to 1920. Even in the case of one of my great-great-uncles, who owned a chain of variety stores, there was only a single sheet noting that an administrator had been appointed for his estate, without further elaboration. For relatives who died more recently, wills probably are available, but since the children and grandchildren of these relatives may still be living, you probably don't need a will to answer any questions you may have.

On the other hand, since wills and administrations are always indexed (usually year by year), it doesn't take much time or trouble to look them up.

IV

A Quick Course
in Judaica

UP TO THIS POINT we've dealt with information you can extract from your living relatives, from gravestones of dead relatives, and from public records in the United States. The fact that you are Jewish has made very little difference in your research so far: most of the methods I've discussed apply equally well to gentiles and Jews alike.

We are now ready, however, to plunge deeper into the past, and this excursion will inevitably take us into that dark, strange, confusing and very exciting land known as the Diaspora. Just as a tourist is likely to be left behind on a safari if he shows up wearing a fedora and loafers instead of pith helmet and swamp boots, so you are likely to get lost in the Diaspora if you're unprepared. This chapter represents an attempt to assemble the various bits and pieces of Judaica that you may stumble over as you search further for your ancestors. Some of the pieces may seem obvious and elementary, others arcane and obscure, but all are relevant and valuable. I've made no attempt to offer a historical overview of Jewish civilization; this you can find in many other books. The following is presented simply as a chance to catch your breath as well as your perspective. Rest assured that you will need both from here on in.

THE DIASPORA

This is the Greek word for "dispersion," first used in a Jewish connection to refer to the Jews who were exiled after the Babylonian conquest of Palestine in 586 Before Common Era. That scattering has continued for such a long time that today the word has almost an exclusively Jewish connotation, especially when spelled with a capital *D*. Even today, for many purposes it is common to divide the world's Jewish population into two groups: those in Israel, and those in the Diaspora. A flexible word, used both as a noun and as an adjective, it applies both to Jews living outside of Israel and to the specific places where Diaspora Jews live. Since those places have changed from one century to the next, the connotation of the word has changed, too: in the nineteenth century it usually meant "Europe"; in the twentieth century it usually means "America." As the Americans might say, the Diaspora isn't so much a state as a state of mind.

SEPHARDIM AND ASHKENAZIM

The world's Jews are usually divided into two broad ethnic classifications: Sephardic Jews and Ashkenazic Jews. The Sephardim (also known as Spanish-Portuguese Jews) came to Northern and Eastern Europe from Palestine through North Africa, Spain and Portugal. The so-called Oriental Jews, those from North Africa and the Middle East, share many characteristics with the Sephardim and are usually grouped with them. The Ashkenazim—at least a great number of them—came by way of Babylonia and Mesopotamia through southern Russia and wound up in medieval times in Germany, Poland and elsewhere in Europe, and are sometimes referred to as German-Polish Jews.

There are sharp differences between the two groups, above and beyond their physical differences (Sephardim tend to have darker complexions). They speak different dialects of Hebrew: the Sephardim use the pronunciation of ancient Judea, while the Ashkenazim are considered to have brought with them the language spoken in Galilee and/or Babylonia. (Sephardic Hebrew, though strange-sounding to many American Jews, is the official dialect of the State of Israel today.) The Sephardim, at least those from Spain and Portugal, have an aristocratic tradition that stems from seven hundred years of Moslem rule in Spain, when Jews were among the upper classes and many intermarried with the nobility; Ashkenazim were restricted to the bottom of society throughout their history until the last century. Traditions in marriage, naming of children and many other matters differ between the two groups (more on these differences below). The Ashkenazim, for example, mark their graves with vertical standing stones; the Sephardim, with stones that lie horizontally on the earth.

Most of the Sephardic Jews who left Spain and Portugal during the Inquisition went to Holland or England; Sephardim were also the first Jews to settle in America, in 1654. But some Sephardim did emigrate from Spain to Germany and Poland, where they intermarried with Ashkenazim. Of all the Jews in the world today, only about one million are thought to be pure Sephardic; the rest are Ashkenazic.

JEWISH POPULATION

The science of counting heads has long been an uncertain one, and most demographers maintain that any attempts to arrive at precise population figures for any group prior to 1800 are little more than exercises in fantasy. Even today, any estimates of the number of Jews in the world must be rough guesses, because most countries, like the United States, do not enumerate citizens according to religion, and in any case, there is no single accepted way to define who is a Jew.

Nevertheless, Jews have all along made at least serious attempts to count their numbers, beginning with the census enumerations in the Bible. The estimates of various demographers suggest that the world Jewish population has had its ups and downs over the millennia, and that its greatest growth occurred during the relatively peaceful nineteenth century.

There are today believed to be some 14.2 million Jews in the world, of whom about 5.8 million are in the United States, 2.6 million in the Soviet Union, and 2.6 million in Israel. Other countries with more than 100,000 Jews, in order of Jewish population, are France, Argentina, Britain, Canada, Brazil, South Africa and Rumania. This is not the largest the Jewish population has ever been—it peaked at 16.7 million just before World War II—but it is considerably greater than figures from any previous century. Statistics from earlier ages suggest that the Jews of today are descended from a relatively small group of Jews of the past.

The Census of King David (about 1000 B.C.E.) is said to have recorded 1.3 million males over the age of twenty, which would imply a population of over 5 million. This seems rather high, especially considering that the entire population of the world at the time of Jesus was only about 250 million, but I pass it on because in this case, as in so many others, the estimates of the Bible are the only ones we have. After the Babylonian conquest of 586 B.C.E. and the exile of the Jews to Babylonia, the number of exiles who returned to Israel from Babylonia in 522 B.C.E. is given at 42,360. Tacitus, the Roman historian, declared that Jerusalem at its second destruction in 70 Common Era had 600,000 inhabitants; the historian Josephus maintained that the city's population was more like 1.1 million, of whom 97,000 were sold as slaves. These 97,000 slaves were probably the ancestors of most European Jews.

Although today we tend to think of population as something that inevitably increases with the passage of time, this has been the case only since about 1800 —for the world population as well as for the Jews. Until then, Jews did a great deal of moving around but precious little increasing, because often their numbers were decimated by persecutions and plagues. Martin Gilbert's *Jewish History Atlas* says that in 300 C.E. there were 3 million Jews, of whom 1 million were already in Central and Western Europe. But by the end of the twelfth century, according to the *Encyclopaedia Judaica*, the world Jewish population was only 1 million or at the most 2 million, the majority of whom still lived in Moslem countries. This situation began changing shortly afterward as Jews began moving to Western lands. In 1300, according to the *Encyclopaedia Judaica,* there were 450,000 Jews living in Europe; by 1490 the number was up to 600,000.

Yet by 1700, according to the *Jewish Encyclopedia,* the world Jewish population was still only about 1 million, and while this estimate may be low, it is probably not low by much. But in the nineteenth century, while the population of Europe was doubling, the world Jewish population quadrupled.

The demographer A. Ruppin has estimated that there were 2.5 million Jews in the world in 1800. By 1825, according to Jacob Lestchinsky, the number was about 3.25 million, of whom 85 percent were in Europe. Subsequent estimates provide the following comparisons:

YEAR	WORLD JEWISH POPULATION
300	3 million
1200	1 million
1700	1 million
1800	2.5 million
1825	3.25 million
1840	4.5 million
1880	7.7 million
1900	10.7 million
1925	14.9 million
1939	16.7 million
1946	10.8 million
1962	13.0 million
1975	14.2 million

The composition of this group has changed radically, of course. Throughout the nineteenth century more than 80 percent of the world's Jews lived in Europe; the proportion was as high as 88.3 percent in 1880, just before the first wave of emigration to the New World. Today, as we have mentioned, more than 50 percent of the world's Jews live in North and South America, and less than 30 percent live in Europe (including those in the Soviet Union). Jews in Africa (mostly in Morocco and Algeria, and more recently, South Africa) accounted for only 4.4 percent of the world's Jews in 1840, and since then their proportion has dwindled to about 1.4 percent today, as most have migrated to Israel.

The greatest single source of Jews since the Middle Ages, by far, has been Poland. In 1939 the Jewish population of Poland was 3.25 million. The Jewish population of the Soviet Union then was about 2.8 million—but virtually all Soviet Jews then (and now) lived in areas that had once been part of Poland. Thus on the eve of World War II, nearly 40 percent of the world's Jews lived in Poland itself or in formerly Polish territories, and at least another 20 percent were descendants of Polish Jews who had emigrated to America. Medieval Jews lived in Poland and Lithuania because they were among the last countries to be Christianized. Poland was still a pagan country until the end of the tenth century, and Lithuania did not accept Christianity until about 1400. Pagan kings, having no religion of their own to promote, were much more tolerant of Jews than Christian kings, who believed that their salvation depended on the elimination of heretics. While the land of Israel may be the ancient ancestral homeland of the Jewish people, Poland is the more immediate ancestral homeland of most of today's world Jewish population.

THE KHAZAR CONNECTION

One of the most bizarre episodes in Jewish history concerns the Khazars, a nomadic Turkic people who appeared in Transcaucasia in the second century C.E. and later settled in southern Russia between the Volga and Don rivers. About the year 700 they conquered the Crimea and established a huge empire that ruled or exacted tribute from perhaps a dozen other lands.

The Khazars were a pagan, warlike people, but in 740 the king of the Khazars astonished the world by embracing Judaism, and most of the upper classes of the kingdom followed his example. The Khazar kingdom thus became the only nation in the history of the world, aside from Israel, whose state religion was Judaism.

According to legend, the king of the Khazars settled on Judaism after listening to presentations from leaders of the Christians, the Jews and the Moslems. When questioned, both the Christian and Moslem spokesmen acknowledged that they traced their religious roots to Judaism, and thus the king decided to make his kingdom Jewish. If this story is true, it probably represents the only time a state religion was ever chosen on solely rational grounds. The more likely reason the king chose Judaism is that he wanted to avoid the Christian-Moslem wars then raging, and Judaism offered a convenient way to retire to the sidelines gracefully.

In any case, the Khazar kingdom existed as a Jewish state for more than two hundred years, although it apparently practiced tolerance toward all religions. As such it became a haven for some Jewish refugees from other parts of the Diaspora. Even after the Khazar empire was largely destroyed by the Russians in 969, the Khazars retained their independent, albeit smaller, kingdom and their Judaism well into the thirteenth century.

What ultimately happened to the descendants of the Khazar Jews? Most Jewish historians contend that they were absorbed into other East European populations and that all but a handful lost their Jewish identity. Some scholars maintain, though, that most of today's East European Jews, and perhaps even most of the world's Jewish population, are descendants of the Khazars.

Arthur Koestler, in *The Thirteenth Tribe,* makes a tantalizing case for this viewpoint. He notes that after the breakup of the Khazar kingdom, settlements of Khazars were mentioned in the Crimea, the Ukraine, Hungary, Poland and Lithuania—"all areas," he says, "where the greatest concentrations of Jews were at the dawn of the modern age." The common belief is that the Jews of Eastern Europe migrated there from France, Germany and Italy, but Koestler notes that the number of Jews in Poland and Lithuania in the seventeenth century has been estimated at 500,000, whereas only a fraction of that number lived in France, Germany and Italy during the preceding centuries. The Khazar kingdom, on the other hand, had a population of about 500,000—just about the same number of Jews who later turned up in Eastern Europe. How else, Koestler asks, can we explain the sudden appearance of such a huge number of Jews in Eastern Europe?

The issue can't be settled definitively, because population estimates are extremely frivolous tools. Historians who theorize about the Khazars and their descendants must do so by piling conjecture upon conjecture. The Khazar kingdom may have been a Jewish state with a population of 500,000, but as Koestler himself notes, the great mass of the Khazars remained heathens and worshipped idols; others were Christians and Moslems, so Jews probably represented only the ruling classes—a small minority of the total Khazar population.

Even among the Khazar Jews, not all had come into Judaism via the Khazar conversion. Some were of Palestinian Jewish descent who had been in the Crimea long before the Khazars conquered the area. Others, as we have said, had fled to the Khazar Jewish kingdom to escape persecution elsewhere.

In any case, *some* East European Jews, and perhaps a great many, are descended from the Khazars. Figuring out whether you are or aren't of Khazar ancestry may be impossible, but some families seem to have clues. For example, a branch of my wife's family named Tamarin, from Russia, maintains that the family came into Judaism via the Khazar conversion and that the family took its name from Tamara, queen of Georgia in the thirteenth century.

HEBREW DATES

The Hebrew calendar was probably designed by the patriarch Hillel II in the fourth century C.E. He calculated the age of the world by computing literal ages of Biblical characters and other chronological references in the Scriptures and came up with a calendar that begins 3,760 years before the Christian calendar.

Thus, to translate Hebrew dates to Christian-era dates, subtract 3,760 from the Hebrew date. To translate Christian to Hebrew, add 3,760. The Christian year 1977, for example, is the Hebrew year 5737. Since the Hebrew year begins in the preceding September or October, the dates listed for the months of Tishri, Heshvan, Kislev and sometimes Tebet must be read in the Christian calendar as applying to the preceding year. In other words, for those months, subtract 3,761 from the Hebrew year to arrive at the Christian year. (The terms B.C.E. and C.E. are the Jewish variations of B.C. and A.D., respectively. B.C.E. stands for "before Common Era," C.E. for "Common Era." They are simply the form Jews use for referring to dates in the Christian calendar without using the name of Christ.)

The *Universal Jewish Encyclopedia* has a perpetual Hebrew-Christian calendar covering the Christian years 1800 to 2000. The *Encyclopaedia Judaica* has a perpetual calendar covering 1900 to 2000. These enable you to translate precise Hebrew dates into precise Christian dates. The *Jewish Encyclopedia* provides a formula for converting any precise Hebrew date into a precise Christian date; see its article on Calendars.

MARRIAGE AGES

Into the nineteenth century and even up to 1900, Jews in Eastern Europe tended to marry quite early, certainly earlier than the average couples in Central and Western Europe. According to the *Encyclopaedia Judaica,* marriages of boys aged between fifteen and eighteen with girls from fourteen to sixteen years old were quite common, although not the rule.

In the Middle Ages, early marriages were a protective device at a time when Jewish girls were often carried off by landlords or other gentiles seeking to harass Jewish families. Later, early marriages were encouraged so that young scholars would not be distracted by thoughts of sex while studying their books. In *Life Is With People,* a description of East European *shtetl* culture, Mark Zborowski and Elizabeth Herzog note: "The more talented the student, the more effort is made to have him marry young, even at 14 or 15." The late teens were the more usual marriage age in the *shtetl,* the authors add.

An eighteenth-century Polish census mentions a Jewish wife aged eight. Even in the West, the burgomaster of Amsterdam in 1712 had to prohibit the marriage of a Jewish couple under the age of twelve. As late as 1891 a Russian landowner who employed Jews remarked to an English visitor that the Jews "have no vice, unless early, improvident and fruitful marriages can be deemed a vice."

Some of the youthful marriages in Eastern Europe were of course arranged matches in which the bride and groom did not actually live together until a few years after the wedding ceremony.

CONSANGUINITY

In the past, Jews have married their near relatives more often than the rest of the world has done. A study in England in 1875, for example, indicated that 7.5 percent of all English Jewish marriages were among first cousins—a proportion that was about three times as great as that among gentiles.

Marriages of first cousins and even of uncles to nieces are common among Jews and quite legal according to Jewish law. Indeed, the complex limitations placed on prospective marriage partners of *Kohanim* could be interpreted to restrict their choice to those nearly related to them. In other cases, first-cousin or uncle-niece marriages were necessitated in small towns where there simply weren't any other Jews of marriageable ages. The proportion of such marriages has generally been much greater among Sephardic Jews than among Ashkenazic.

FAMILY SIZE

East European Jews, and many West European Jews as well, tended to have larger families than gentiles, for two reasons. For one thing, the words in the very first chapter of Genesis, "Be fruitful, and multiply, and replenish the earth," were interpreted by most rabbis not so much as a blessing as the first commandment of the Bible. Thus the Jews shunned any form of birth control.

Second, the infant mortality rate among Jews was sharply lower than that of European gentiles. This was due largely to the favorable hygienic conditions that resulted from the Jews' ritual food controls and religious bathing requirements. The greater accessibility to medical help, even in crowded East European ghettoes, and the extreme rarity of illegitimate births among Jews were other factors. (While the Jews may have had a relatively low infant mortality rate through the Middle Ages, they had a high *persecution* mortality rate that prevented their total numbers from increasing.)

NAMES—PREFIXES

Ben, as in "Moshe ben Mordecai," means "son of" in Hebrew. So does *bar.* On gravestones the word will often appear as בּ׳ר , an abbreviation for *ben reb,* that is, "son of the worthy," followed by the father's name.

Bat means "daughter of."

Ibn or *aben* means "son of" in Arabic. This prefix is common among Sephardic Jews. Although the Hebrew *ben* usually is a literal reference to a person's father, the prefix *ibn* is often compounded with a permanent family name, perhaps taken from the founder of the family. Thus the Ibn Ezra family, for example, claims to trace its origin to Ezra the Scribe.

NAMING OF CHILDREN

Contrary to popular belief, there are no rules in Jewish law regarding names that can or cannot be given to children, but there are any number of traditions. In Jewish folklore it was commonly believed that a person's soul was bound up with his name. From this belief it followed that a person's soul would be deprived of its rest after death if his name was bestowed during his lifetime on one of his descendants. Thus arose the Jewish practice, still widely followed today, of naming a child after an ancestor *only* after the ancestor has died.

This practice, however, is not followed by Sephardic Jews. They traditionally name the oldest grandson for his paternal grandfather, the oldest granddaughter for her paternal grandmother, whether the grandparents are alive or dead. Succeeding children are named for the maternal grandparents, then for uncles and aunts. This pattern isn't strictly followed by all Sephardim, of course, but knowledge of it can be a help in tracing ancestors.

Whatever their differences, both Ashkenazim and Sephardim seem to believe in naming children after ancestors. It's a curious tradition because there is no trace of the custom in the Bible. Almost every name in the Bible is an original: in two thousand years of Biblical history you will find no repetition of names like Adam, Eve, Noah, Abraham, Isaac, Jacob, Moses, David or Solomon.

The custom of naming children after departed relatives apparently began during the age of the Maccabees (second century B.C.E.). By the first century C.E. it was fairly well established, but it was not until some eight hundred years later that Jews began to give their children Biblical names (Abraham, Isaac, Rachel, Sarah, etc.).

In Christian lands, Jews very early began giving their children Christian names, and the practice became so widespread after the twelfth century that the rabbis required every Jewish boy to be given a purely Jewish name. Thus began the custom of giving *two* names—a religious name used in synagogue, and a non-Jewish name used for secular affairs—that persists even today.

While this "double-name" system may be confusing, it can be a help in tracing your family's origins, for the non-Jewish names chosen for children tended to conform to local Christian practice. As European Jews moved from country to country, they would continue to name children after ancestors but would alter those names to suit their new homelands. Thus a name like Shprinzel is actually a Polish variation of the Italian Esperanza. A European name like Yente comes, believe it or not, from the Spanish Juanita. This suggests that Yente the Matchmaker in *Fiddler on the Roof,* for all her Russian *shtetl* ambiance, probably had a Sephardic ancestor somewhere in her distant past.

The practice of modifying names continues in America, of course. When American Jews name a child today, very often all that remains in the secular name is the ancestor's first initial. (The Hebrew name, of course, continues to be given.) Thus the Hebrew name Abraham becomes Arthur or Alan, Broucha becomes Barbara, and Rezel becomes Rhoda or Roberta.

For more information on Jewish first names, see the articles on "Names" in the *Jewish Encyclopedia, Universal Jewish Encyclopedia* and *Encyclopaedia Judaica;* also "Jewish First Names Through the Ages," by Benzion Kaganoff in *Commentary* (November 1955).

ADOPTION OF FAMILY NAMES

Until the nineteenth century the question of whether to take on a family name was left to the individual Jew. Some Jews had already had family names for centuries: in Spain, Portugal and Italy, especially, family names were common among Jews as early as the fourteenth century. Many of these names were adopted from the town the family came from and are thus the easiest to trace.

The great bulk of the Jews in Germany and Eastern Europe, unfortunately for us, still followed the tradition of using merely the personal name and the father's name—Zevi ben Moshe, and so on. Zevi's son would then be known as, say, Avraham ben Zevi. Thus there would be no common name by which the three generations could be identified. Although this is a major obstacle for Jewish genealogists, many Jews at the time preferred this disorderly arrangement because it helped them avoid tax collectors, army recruiters and other government nuisances. There are, however, some East European families that did maintain family names, and if you can trace a connection to one of these families, your research may very well lead you back all the way to the age of Christopher Columbus.

Emperor Joseph II of Austria, who issued the Edict of Toleration for the Jews in 1781, was the first to require Jews to take family names—in Galicia, in 1785. Two years later the requirement was extended to all the Austrian provinces except Hungary. Jews were given names based on the size of the registration fee they could afford. The most expensive were names derived from flowers and gems, like Rosenthal or Goldstein; for a smaller amount, you could get a name like Stahl (steel) or Eisen (iron); and if you had no money at all, you would be saddled with a nonsensical name like Ochsenschwanz (ox tail), Temperaturwechsel (temperature change), Wanzenknicker (bug squasher) or Galgenstrick (dirty trick).

In 1808 Napoleon required all the Jews of his empire to take family names, but his decree forbade Jews to take names based on localities or to adopt names of famous families. (This condition is of some interest to me because my family name is Rottenberg and my earliest known Rottenberg ancestor was born, as far as I know, in the town of Rotenburg-on-the-Fulda in Hesse-Nassau (now Germany) about 1805. I had always assumed that the family had taken its name somehow from the town, but Napoleon's edict makes that seem unlikely. It does, however, open up another exciting possibility—that my family may be related to a family that took the name Rothenberg because it is descended from Rabbi Meir of Rothenburg-on-the-Tauber, who lived in Bavaria in the thirteenth century.)

On the other hand, in some parts of Europe, especially southern Germany, Jews were forced to change their names if they were of Biblical origin. Under the Baden law of January 13, 1809, for example, Levites who customarily were named Levi were forced to choose new family names, most of which were derived from place names.

The kingdom of Prussia emancipated the Jews in 1812, on the condition that Jews adopt family names. This requirement was extended to the province of Posen in 1833 and to other parts of the Prussian empire in 1845. Check your historical atlas to see which areas were covered. (Also see the section on national boundaries in chapter 7.)

In Russia the statutes of 1804 and 1835 allowed Jews to alter their family names but did not require them to adopt them. It wasn't until 1844, when Russian Jews were first compelled to enter their names in the public register, that they were obliged to assume family names. In Poland a decree requiring family names was issued in 1821, but it wasn't strictly enforced until the Russian regulations were enacted in 1844. Thus some Jews have had family names for less than 150 years.

Five generations of a German family are grouped around their progenitor (front, center) in this intriguing study made about 1890. Notice that the relatives did not all pose together; the picture is a composite of several group photos.

A ketubah *(marriage certificate) from Amsterdam, dated 1718. The border, which may have been a standard form, is dated 1693.*

This Hebrew marriage certificate, printed in New York in 1915, provides such information as the date and the parents of the bride and groom. Actually, the marriage recorded above took place in Russia in 1903; the bride and groom, Joseph and Celia Biderman, lost their original and so had this copy made when they arrived in the United States. Note that in the fourth line they have crossed out "Bemedinat Amerika" ("in the state of America") and have substituted the name of their Russian town, Zvenigorodka.

Jüdische Familien-Forschung

The twelve tribes of Israel adorned the nameplate of Jüdische Familien-Forschung, *a Jewish genealogy quarterly published in Germany from 1924 to 1938.*

Some Jewish coats of arms.

Rothschild (England)

Pirbright (Austria)

Elkan von Elkansberg
(Austria)

Bassevi von Trenenfeld
(Austria)

Teixeira (Holland)

Halevi (Spain)

Medieval Hebrew gravestone in Mainz, Germany.

A Levite's grave in Leipzig, Germany, indicating a direct descendant of Levi, son of the Biblical Jacob. The jug symbolizes the Levite duty of washing the feet of the priests. From this emblem (Kanne in German), some Levite families took the surname Kann.

A kohen's *grave (right) in Boedigheim/Baden, Germany, indicating a direct descendant of Aaron, brother of Moses. The hands on the stone are outstretched, in the manner of the* kohanim *(priests) when they bless the congregation.*

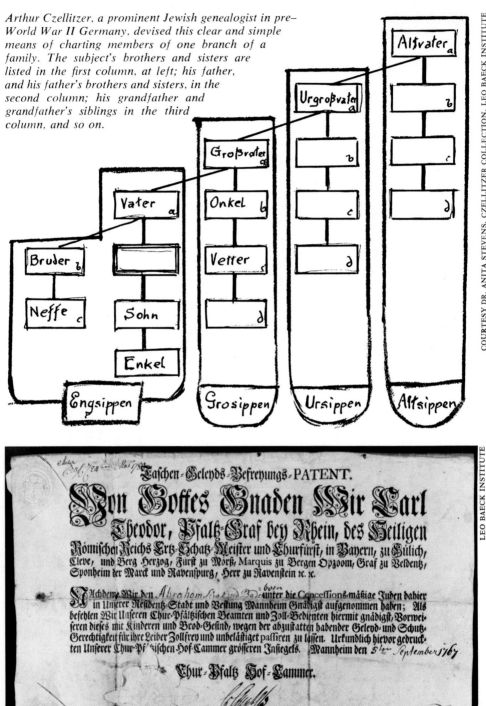

Arthur Czellitzer, a prominent Jewish genealogist in pre–World War II Germany, devised this clear and simple means of charting members of one branch of a family. The subject's brothers and sisters are listed in the first column, at left; his father, and his father's brothers and sisters, in the second column; his grandfather and grandfather's siblings in the third column, and so on.

Altvater *a*

Urgroßvater *a*

b

Großvater *a*

b

c

Vater *a*

Onkel *b*

c

d

Bruder *b*

Vetter *c*

Neffe *c*

Sohn

d

Enkel

Engsippen

Grosippen

Ursippen

Altsippen

Taschen-Geleyds-Befreyungs-PATENT.

Von Gottes Gnaden Wir Carl

Theodor, Pfaltz-Graf bey Rhein, des Heiligen

Römischen Reichs Ertz-Schatz-Meister und Churfürst, in Bayern, zu Gülich, Cleve, und Berg Herzog, Fürst zu Mörß, Marquis zu Bergen Opzoom, Graf zu Veldentz, Sponheim der Marck und Ravensburg, Herr zu Ravenstein rc. rc.

Nachdem Wir den *Abraham Siek und Bade* unter die Concessions-mäßige Juden dabier in Unserer Residentz-Stadt und Vestung Mannheim Gnädigst aufgenommen haben; Als befehlen Wir Unseren Chur-Pfältzischen Beamten und Zoll-Bedienten hiermit gnädigst, Vorweiseren dieses mit Kindern und Brod-Gesind, wegen der abzustatten habender Geleyd- und Schutz-Gerechtigkeit für ihre Leiber Zollfrey und unbelästiget passiren zu lassen. Urkundlich hievor gedruckten Unserer Chur-Pf lischen Hof-Cammer grösseren Insiegels. Mannheim den *5ten September 1767*

Chur-Pfaltz Hof-Cammer.

This Schutzbriefe, *issued in eighteenth-century Hannover, is typical of the internal passports issued to German Jews to permit them to travel within a German state. The Leo Baeck Institute in New York has a large collection of these papers, which provide basic information about the bearer. All date from before 1830.*

In Nazi Germany, Jews were required to prove their German ancestry by producing an Ahnenpass, *on which their ancestors were identified after certification by the appropriate community officials. This* Ahnenpass *shows six generations of the family of Herman Vierfelder.*

French birth certificate, issued for a Fanny Loewenstein in 1912, indicates her father and the maiden name of her mother.

Turn-of-the-century Rumanian passport of a Hersch Goldstein, filled out in both Rumanian and French. On this page alone, a genealogist can find such valuable information as the names of the bearer's children, their ages, and what they looked like.

A last will and testament often provides valuable clues about relatives. In the past a Hebrew will was often an elaborate affair, as the above opening page will attest. It was written in 1724 by Moses Laemmle Rheingarum.

SOURCES OF JEWISH FAMILY NAMES

Jewish family names (surnames) spring from a limited number of sources, and if you can trace yours back to its origin, you may be able to learn something about your ancestors—where they came from, perhaps, or what they did for a living. The original family name tends to become corrupted and eroded over the generations as a family moves from place to place—who would suspect that Falk could become Wallach and then Block, or that Dreyfus is really Treves? But if you study names carefully, useful insights may emerge. A few general observations:

Patronymics. The earliest form of Jewish surname was some conjunction of the father's given name, which was especially common among Sephardic and Oriental Jews. Thus Moses ben Maimon took the surname Maimonides. The Ibn Dana family became Abendana. A name like Belish might be traced back to the common Sephardic surname Benelisha, a conjunction of the Hebrew words for "son of Elisha."

Among Ashkenazic families, patronymics are also popular, but where a Sephardic patronymic often begins with a prefix like Ben or Aben, Ashkenazim more often apply suffixes on the end of the original name. Thus the son of someone named Abraham might have taken the surname Abramowitz, Abramson, Abrahamowski or the shortened Abrahams or Abrams. The German ending *-witz*, Slavic *-vitch* or *-icz* or *-wicz*, and Rumanian *-vici* all mean "son of." (On the other hand, the German ending *-er* and the Slavic *-ski* denote place of origin: Krakauer means "from Cracow," Poznanski means "from Poznan," the modern name for Posen.)

Local place names. These may be the greatest source of surnames among modern Jews. Names like Hollander, Deutsch and Pollak refer to nationalities. Sephardic Jews often took their surnames from the towns in which they lived, as in Almanzi, Carvajal, Castro, Leon, Navarro, Robles, Toledano (Spanish) and Almeida, Carvallo, Miranda and Pieba (Portuguese). The same is true among many Italian families.

Among Ashkenazic Jews, a family often adopted the name of its hometown as a surname after it had moved elsewhere. The Katzenellenbogen family, a line of rabbis widely dispersed throughout Eastern Europe, originated in the German town of Katzenellenbogen but didn't take that name until the family moved to Padua, Italy, in the fifteenth century. Similar logic accounts for such German surnames as Hess (from Hessen), Preuss (Prussian), Bayer (Bavarian), Schlesinger (Silesian), Schwab (Swabian), Frank and Frankel (Franconian), Posner (from Posen, now Poznan), Berlinger or Berlinsky (from Berlin), Halpern or Heilprin (from Heilbrunn), Dreyfus (from Treves), Spira or Shapiro (from Speyer), Sulzberger (from Sulzberg), Fould (from Fulda), Oppenheimer (from Oppenheim), and countless others.

Vocational names. These are probably the second greatest source of surnames among Ashkenazim, although they are much less common among Sephardim. Most of them arose from the descriptions attached to the names of Jews in official registers. Most obviously, the names "Cohen" and "Levy" refer to the ancient priestly functions performed by the *Kohanim* and the Levites, and names like Rabinowitz or Cantor suggest a rabbi or cantor somewhere in the family. Some names are strictly secular and follow the local language: Kaufman (merchant), Spielmann (player), Schneider (tailor), Schuster and Sandler (cobbler), Wechsler (moneychanger), Drucker (printer), Goldschmidt (goldsmith), Metzger (butcher). Others are more distinctively Jewish. Chait and Keith are derived from the Hebrew *hayyat,* for tailor. Schechter comes from the Hebrew *shochet,* for "butcher." Singer and Chazan refer to singers of Israel; Rokeach is derived from the Hebrew for "spice merchant."

Family symbols. Especially in southern and western Germany, families often adopted names from the distinctive escutcheons on their homes. A family of Levites might have a jug carved on their door, since the Levites are traditionally supposed to pour water over the hands of the priests before the priests bless the congregation. From this symbol the family might become known as Kann —from German *Kanne* for "jug." Similar explanations account for names like Rothschild (red shield), Kahn (boat), Nussbaum (nut tree), Schwarzschild (black shield) and Flesch from *Flasche* for "flask."

Animal names. Some Ashkenazic Jews chose family names by identifying their given names with characters in the Bible who had symbolic connections with animals. For example, the Biblical Judah was symbolized by a lion, and so a man named Judah might call himself Judah Lowe, "Judah the Lion" (*Löwe* in German). This name has subsequently taken on such forms as Loeb, Lyon, Leibowitz, Lowensohn, Lefkowitz. Benjamin is symbolized in the Bible by a wolf, and the name Wolf has since become Wolk, Walk, Wolfberg, Lupo (Rumanian), López (Spanish), Siff (from the Hebrew *ze'eb*) and many other variations. Naphtali is associated with a stag—*Hirsch*—from which has come Hertz, Hartwig, Harris, Cerf, Herzl and Jellinek. *Bär* (bear) produces Berman and Berish. *Ochs* (ox) corresponds to Schorr, Byk, Wahl, Wohl and Volov in various languages. Other Jewish animal names include Fuchs (fox), Adler (eagle), Fink (finch), Hahn (cock) and Falk (falcon).

Names describing characteristics. Some family names refer to features of the people who received them: Gross (large), Klein (small), Alt (old), Neu (new), Schwarz (black), Weiss (white), Schoen or Jaffa (German *schön* and Hebrew for "beautiful"), *süss* (Sussmann, Susskind) and *gut* (Guttmann, Gutkind).

Surnames from feminine names and words. Sometimes a Jewish family name was derived from the name of a mother or wife. Usually in these cases, an *s* or *-es* was added to the end of the woman's name; such an ending on a name is a tip-off that the name was taken from a woman. Thus Samuel Edels, the seventeenth-century Polish rabbi, took his name from his wealthy mother-in-law, Edel, whose generosity enabled him to open a yeshiva. (The name Edels later became Atlas.) A name like Perles or Perls is probably derived from the female Perle. Eventually, of course, the ending may have changed as the name took on new forms. Other examples of feminine names and words similarly used are Bella or Beile (Beilis, Beilin), *Freude* (Freudenberg, Freudenthal), Miriam (Mirkin), Hannah (Hahnemann, Hensel), *Rose* (Rosenmann, Rosen), Chaya (Chajes, Chaikin) and *Liebe* (Liebmann, Lipmann).

Names from acronyms. Some names have arisen from abbreviations formed out of the initials of a man's name and that of his father. Thus we have Brill (Ben Rabbi Yehudah Lowe), Bry (Ben Rabbi Israel), Schach (descendants of Shabbetai Cohen), Bruck or Brockmann (Ben Rabbi Akiba) and Badt (Ben David). Other names were sometimes taken from initials of official titles. Katz is short for *Kohen tzeddek* (priest of righteousness); Segal and its variations substitute for *segan leviyyah* (assistant of the Leviteship.)

For more information on surnames, consult the articles on Names in the *Jewish Encyclopedia, Universal Jewish Encyclopedia* and *Encyclopaedia Judaica.* Also helpful are the article "Jewish Surnames Through the Ages," by Benzion Kaganoff in *Commentary* (September 1956), p. 249; an article on Jewish names by Edgar Samuel in *Genealogist's Magazine* (1961); and "Notes on Transformation of Place Names by European Jews," by Max Markreich, in *Jewish Social Studies* (October 1961), p. 265.

V

Tradition, History and the Bible

MANY TRADITIONS about ancestral descent, Jewish and otherwise, have been handed down over centuries and even millennia. Because they have survived for so long, they are often accepted as truth. It's fun to consider these traditions, and impossible to say flat out that they are false, but at the very least they are highly suspect. If you examine any such tradition closely, you will find that the people maintaining it had some particular ax to grind.

A number of medieval rabbinic families, for example, claimed descent from Rashi, the famous Talmudic commentator of eleventh-century France. Certainly it is possible that some of them *were* descended from Rashi, but I have yet to find a family that can trace its ancestry back to him in an unbroken line (the Treves family comes closest: it goes back to Rabbi Joseph Treves of Marseilles in the fourteenth century, supposedly a descendant of Judah Sir Leon of Paris [1166–1224], a great-great-great-grandson of Rashi. See chart on page 11). The likely reason rabbis claimed descent from Rashi, though, is that Rashi was simply a very good person to be descended from if you wanted to get ahead in the rabbinical world.

Similarly, in the nineteenth century many Hungarian Jews claimed to be descended from the Khazars. Again, perhaps their claim was valid, but this claim also happens to have been very convenient in an age when Hungarian nationalism was strong and suspicion of outsiders widespread. The Khazar tradition enabled Hungarian Jews to maintain that they did not come originally from Israel at all, but were Magyars just like the rest of the Hungarian population. On the other hand, it is worth noting that the traditional view—that most Jews descend from German and French Jews who moved eastward during the persecutions of the fourteenth and fifteenth centuries—also has political implications: if it could be shown that a major part of the world's Jews were descended from the Khazars, and not from the ancient Israelites, this might seem to some people to undercut the Jews' claim to Israel as their rightful homeland.

Or consider the Sephardic Jews in Spain during the early Inquisition. Many of these Jews constructed elaborate genealogies purporting to show that their families had been in Spain before the time of Jesus. Again, perhaps they were: it is not unlikely that there were some Jews in Spain before the Christian era. But there was a specific purpose to these genealogies: if the Spanish Jews could prove to have been in Spain continuously since pre-Christian times, they would have a very good alibi in case some Inquisitor accused them or their ancestors of crucifying Christ. (While this logic may have seemed unassailable to the Sephardim, it apparently didn't do them much good during the Inquisition.)

And just about every great religious leader worth his salt is claimed by tradition to have descended from King David. Again, there is good reason: the Old Testament said that the Messiah would be a descendant of David, and thus anyone claiming to be the Messiah must find David somewhere in his family tree. The New Testament goes to some pains to demonstrate that Jesus was descended from David—on both sides of his family. Some Britons maintain Queen Victoria was a descendant of David. Hillel the Great (first century B.C.E.) is supposed to have been a descendant of David, and tradition claims that Rashi was descended from Hillel, which means Rashi had Davidic blood too. Actually, King David died about 970 B.C.E. and his descendants can historically be traced in an unbroken line to the fourth century B.C.E., but no further. (See chart on page 56.) Traditions about the House of David were probably a great comfort to an oppressed people during the Middle Ages—and that is probably the main reason these traditions were devised.

After the death of King Solomon, about 930 B.C.E., the empire built by his father, David, and enlarged by Solomon began to crumble. Vassal states like Moab, Edom, Ammon and Zobah revolted against Solomon's son Rehoboam, and the country itself was broken up into two small kingdoms, Israel in the north and Judah in the south. In 722 B.C.E. the Kingdom of Israel was conquered by the Assyrians, and its inhabitants were carried off into captivity and never heard from again. It is assumed that in time these "lost tribes" were absorbed into the populations of other countries, but the identity of their

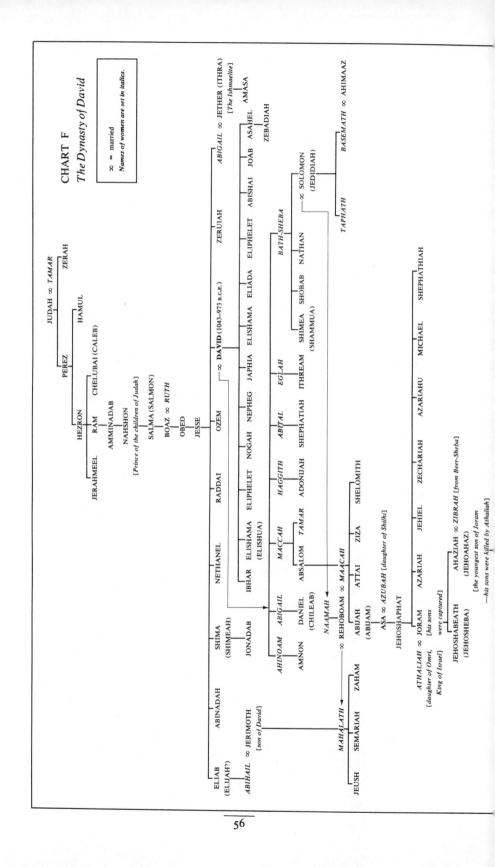

CHART F
The Dynasty of David

∞ = married
Names of women are set in italics.

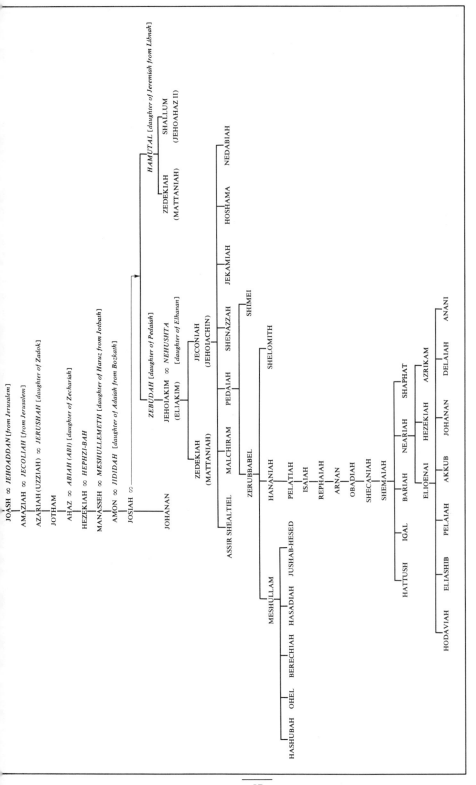

JOASH ∞ JEHOADDAN [from Jerusalem]

AMAZIAH ∞ JECOLIAH [from Jerusalem]

AZARIAH (UZZIAH) ∞ JERUSHAH [daughter of Zadok]

JOTHAM

AHAZ ∞ ABIAH (ABI) [daughter of Zechariah]

HEZEKIAH ∞ HEPHZI-BAH

MANASSEH ∞ MESHULLEMETH [daughter of Haruz from Jotbath]

AMON ∞ JIDIDAH [daughter of Adaiah from Bozkath]

JOSIAH ∞

ZEBUDAH [daughter of Pedaiah]

HAMUTAL [daughter of Jeremiah from Libnah]

SHALLUM
(JEHOAHAZ II)

ZEDEKIAH
(MATTANIAH)

NEDABIAH

HOSHAMA

JEKAMIAH

SHIMEI

SHENAZZAH

SHELOMITH

PEDAIAH

JECONIAH
(JEHOIACHIN)

NEHUSHTA
[daughter of Elnanan]

JEHOIAKIM ∞
(ELIAKIM)

ZEDEKIAH
(MATTANIAH)

MALCHIRAM

ZERUBBABEL

JOHANAN

ASSIR SHEALTIEL

HANANIAH

PELATIAH

ISAIAH

REPHAIAH

ARNAN

OBADIAH

SHECANIAH

SHEMAIAH

SHAPHAT

NEARIAH

AZRIKAM

HEZEKIAH

ANANI

DELAIAH

JOHANAN

AKKUB

ELIOENAI

BARIAH

IGAL

HATTUSH

MESHULLAM

HASHUBAH OHEL BERECHIAH HASADIAH JUSHAB-HESED

PELAIAH

ELIASHIB

HODAVIAH

57

descendants has been a matter of speculation and whimsy among scholars, writers and screwballs even until today. (At one time or another the Yemenis, Ethiopians, American Indians, Peruvian Indians, Mexican Indians, the Berbers of North Africa, the Ibos of Nigeria, the Khazars, the Persians, the Afghans, the Ganges Indians and even the Shindai Tribe of Japan have claimed descent from the lost tribes of Israel.)

Despite the defeat of Israel, Israelite independence survived in the neighboring Kingdom of Judah, whose capital was Jerusalem and whose population consisted of two Hebrew tribes—Judah and Benjamin—plus the *Kohanim* (priests), the Levites (temple servants), and members of the former tribe of Simeon, which had been absorbed into the tribe of Judah. In 586 B.C.E. this kingdom, too, was conquered by the Babylonians, and its Hebrew population was exiled to Babylon. Some of these exiles returned to Palestine fifty years later, after Babylonia had been conquered by Cyrus of Persia; the rest stayed in Babylonia or ventured out into the broad reaches of the Persian empire, thus becoming the vanguard of the Diaspora. It is from these two groups, exiled from the land of Judah by the Babylonians in 586 B.C.E., that most modern Jews are believed to descend.

The primary source of the above information is the Bible. And there is plenty more where that came from. Anyone who has even casually leafed through the Jewish Scriptures and the New Testament is aware that the Bible is a genealogist's playground. Whole sections comprise long lists of "begats"; there are ten genealogies in the Book of Genesis alone, and genealogy occupies a great deal of Numbers and First Chronicles.

But can we believe the Bible? How reliable is it as a historical document? Are parts of it more valid than others? If so, which parts? Beyond that, even if we know that certain accounts and family lists in the Bible refer to real historical people and real relationships, how do we connect them to our own particular families? Are today's Jews in fact blood descendants of the ancient tribes that lived in Israel and Judah, or is that simply wishful thinking?

Any layman who ventures opinions on these issues runs the risk of being burned at the stake. So I will simply pass on the insights of others more learned —and braver—than I.

As to the historical accuracy of the Bible, the evidence uncovered by archaeologists and historians suggests that much of the Old Testament was simply a clerical record of the people of Israel, and that such people and their relationships did literally exist—although the literalness is less likely the further back you go. There seems no doubt that King David was a real king. The various estimates of the dates of his birth and death are all remarkably close —within fifteen years or so. One scholar has pinpointed David's dates down to exact years: born in 1043 B.C.E., became king in 1013, died in 973. Moses and his brother Aaron, the first *Kohen,* were probably real people, too, who led the Hebrews out of Egypt perhaps in the thirteenth century B.C.E.

Some historians even believe that Abraham, Patriarch of the Hebrews, was a real person; his lifetime has been fixed as early as the twenty-first century B.C.E. and as late as the sixteenth century B.C.E. by various scholars. But back beyond the generation of Aaron and Moses there is greater disagreement among historians as to whether Biblical names represent (a) literal persons, (b) groups of people, or (c) fictitious characters. It is well established that there were some twelve tribes in ancient Israel and Judah, each with a specific portion of land. But there is less agreement as to whether the members of those tribes were literal descendants of the twelve sons of Jacob, as the Bible suggests, or whether those twelve sons really existed at all, or whether Jacob existed at all.

Nevertheless, it has been demonstrated by anthropologists that complex historical material can be passed on orally for hundreds of years with remarkable accuracy, so it may well be that the relationships mentioned in the Old Testament are historically valid further back than we might guess—especially since genealogy was once taken just as seriously by Hebrews, Israelites and Jews as it is today by Mormons. This was so because personal status in ancient Hebrew society was determined by one's ancestry.

Until the destruction of the First Temple in 586 B.C.E., possession of a family or clan genealogical list was a personal asset, although generally not a necessity. Those who belonged to the *Kohanim*—the highest social group, composed of the male descendants of Aaron and their families—had little trouble proving their membership because the tribes lived a relatively settled existence. But the destruction of the Temple and the exile from the land of Israel made it more difficult, and more necessary, for priests and others to record their lineage so as to regain their rightful privileges when they returned to Jerusalem. The ensuing problems led the scholars of the Talmud, centuries later, to devote volumes to sorting out the genealogical confusion of the Temple destruction, the exile, and the return to Israel over the next century and a half.

(Incidentally, the Talmud is a prime source of genealogical data in its own right. The rabbis of the Talmud, who flourished between 200 B.C.E. and 450 C.E., invariably included with their commentaries information about their own families as well as many others. The last volume of the Soncino translation contains an index which includes all references to scholars and rabbis mentioned in the Talmud. This could be a tool with which to construct a massive interlocking Talmudic family tree of Palestinian and Babylonian sages, much like the trees some people have constructed for the Bible. I pass over this possibility quickly, though, because there do not seem to be any modern Jews who can trace their families back to the Talmudic era.)

During the Second Temple period (522 B.C.E. to 70 C.E.), genealogy played an increasingly important role in Jewish life. A general genealogical list of *Kohanim* was maintained in the Temple compound; even *Kohanim* living in the Diaspora supplied the necessary information to the Temple record keepers.

The Mishnah lists ten social groups that returned from Babylonia with Ezra about 430 B.C.E. Among these categories there were complex rules regarding who could marry whom, for the groups constituted a distinct social pecking order, as follows, starting at the top:

(1) *Kohanim* (priests)—male descendants of Aaron, who was a brother of Moses and a descendant of Levi.
(2) Levites—other male descendants of Levi, who served as assistants to the *Kohanim.*
(3) Israelites—all other Jews of unblemished heritage (that is, descendants of Jacob who had not intermarried with non-Jews).
(4) *Halalim*—offspring of some forbidden marriages entered into by priests.
(5) *Gerim*—converts to Judaism.
(6) *Harurim*—freed slaves.
(7) *Mamzerim*—bastards.
(8) *Netinim*—descendants of the Gibbeonites, who were circumcised at the time of Joshua (1200 B.C.E.?) and were not regarded as full Jews because their conversion was effected by trickery.
(9) *Shetukim*—persons unable to identify their father.
(10) Persons unable to identify either their father or their mother.

Not included in this list were gentiles and slaves, who had no legal status at all in Jewish law at the time, since Jewish law applied only to Jews. It is also interesting to note that this social order applies only to Jews who returned to Israel from the Babylonian exile. As late as the third century C.E. the Jews still in Babylonia continued to claim that their lineage was superior to that of the Palestinian Jews, on the theory that the only Jews who had returned to Israel with Ezra were those of lower social groups who didn't like being treated as second-class citizens in Babylonia.

Actual genealogical data in the Jewish Scriptures include the following:

• The pedigree of Moses, listing the "heads of their fathers' houses" of the sons of Reuben, of Simeon, and finally of Levi. Levi's three sons were Gershon, Kohath and Merari. Out of Kohath came Amram, from whom came Miriam, Aaron and Moses. The pedigree continues this chain of descent, through Aaron's sons Eleazar and Phinehas. (Exodus 6:14–25.)
• Genealogy of the Aaronites (Num. 3:1–5).
• Genealogy of the Levites (Num. 3:17–39).
• Families of the Levites (Num. 26:57–61), with details about the births of Aaron, Moses and Miriam and the names and fate of Aaron's sons.
• A list with genealogical notes of priests who took "strange wives," and of Levites and Israelites (Ezra 10:18 and following).
• Genealogies of some of the descendants of Judah and Benjamin (Nehemiah 11:4 and following).

- Lists of priests and Levites (Neh. 12:1–26).
- Genealogy of the sons of Israel (I Chronicles 2:1–33) down to Jerahmeel, continued (a) in the part-Egyptian line of Sheshan through his daughter's marriage to Jarha the Egyptian (I Chron. 2:34–41), and (b) in the family of Caleb coming down to David (I Chron. 2:42–55).
- David's pedigree (Ruth, 4:18–22).
- Descendants of David (II Samuel 3:3–5; 5:14–16; I Chron. 3:1–9; also 14:4–7), of Solomon, of Jehoiakim, of the sons of Jeconiah, of Pedaiah, of Zerubbabel and of Hananiah (I Chron. 3:10–21).
- Genealogy of Judah and Simeon (I Chron., 4).
- Genealogy of the Levites, according to families (I Chron., 6).

Even when all this nit-picking over birth and blood was going on, though, Jewish law still considered ability to be more important than birth. Some religious leaders were of noble descent, but others had no genealogical records at all, and some were even descended from proselytes. And the Mishnah notes: "A learned bastard takes precedence over an uneducated High Priest."

After the destruction of the Second Temple by the Romans in 70 C.E., when the *Kohanim* lost their function, they cherished their purity of descent even more, for it was the last vestige of their exalted status. In Israel and Babylonia, their preoccupation with genealogical purity continued until the sixth century to such a degree that a *kohen* who wished to ensure the continued purity of his family would marry only his sister's daughter.

Today the notion of status by birth has all but disappeared from Judaism, except in Hasidism, in which descent from the *zaddik* (righteous man) of the community is endowed with special significance because the *zaddik* is believed to be close to God and able to transmit some of his sanctity to his descendants. Most medieval and modern rabbis have stressed the concept of a person creating his own good name. (Some rabbis today have even come so far as to stress the concept of a person creating *her* own good name.) But some circles still follow the concept of *yichus* (lineage), emphasizing one's family background, especially in the choice of a marriage partner.

There is also in Judaism the interesting doctrine of *zekhut avot* (merit of the fathers), which teaches that people benefit from the righteous acts of their ancestors. A corollary concept holds that the righteousness of the living person favorably affects the fate of his dead ancestors. Thus the bridge between us and our dead ancestors, according to Jewish tradition, is our mutual virtue.

If the Jews of Biblical times and later were such sticklers about genealogy, it is likely that the long family lists in the Bible were passed on not as casual matters, but as sacred obligations. Certainly these lists were not included in the Bible for their entertainment value—anything but—or to enhance any particular story. The accuracy of the Biblical scribes in the mundane business of recording generations is all the more credible when you consider that even some of the more fantastic episodes in the Bible have been shown to have had some historical basis, such as the crossing of the Red Sea (at low tide?) or the great flood (which may have been a glacier).

But even if there was such a person as Abraham, could he really have lived 175 years? In the first ten generations of the Bible, from Adam to Noah, each of the men is supposed to have lived anywhere from 600 to 969 years, except for Enoch, who was cut down in the prime of life at age 365. I, for one, don't believe it. But as in the story of the crossing of the Red Sea, even the account of the first ten generations might hold some historical truth if interpreted broadly. For example, perhaps Adam, Seth, Enoch, Methuselah, Noah and the rest were not names of individuals, but of families or dynasties.

Since Biblical families were constantly intermarrying, many Bible genealogies appear there two or three times. If you are combing through the Bible with some single-minded purpose, such as tracing specific relationships, you will be struck by the overwhelming consistency from one account to the next. To be sure, there are *some* contradictions. For example, in Genesis 10:23, Uz is listed as the son of Aram, but in Genesis 22:20–21 Uz is a son of Nahor and an uncle of Aram. In I Chron. 2:9, Ram is a son of Hezron and brother of Jerahmeel, yet in the same chapter, verse 27, Ram is the eldest son of Jerahmeel.

But such slip-ups are so rare that it is possible, using only the Bible as a source, to fit virtually all of the Bible's characters together into one gigantic family tree. Indeed, such a chart, on a two-foot-by-three-foot wall poster containing some 1,100 names, has been compiled by Dr. Mary Lou Farris, an Oklahoma City Sunday school teacher. (It is available for $5 from Good Things Company, P.O. Box 60706, Oklahoma City, Okla. 73106.)

The Farris chart purports to show, among other things, the descent from Adam and Eve through David all the way down to Jesus. Two of the Gospels, Matthew and Luke, include genealogies tracing Jesus directly back to David, but most scholars say there is no historical validity to this ancestry; indeed, the genealogies of Matthew and Luke contradict each other.

This is not to say that Jesus could not have been a descendant of David. Perhaps he was. But the genealogies put forth in Luke and Matthew merely reflect the belief among the followers of Jesus that he was the Messiah—and if he was the Messiah, it followed that he must, by definition, be descended from David, for Jewish Scriptures and tradition maintained that the Messiah would come from the House of David.

The genealogy of the House of David has been singled out for special attention in the Bible and has endured through the ages as a symbol of hope for the future redemption of the Jews. Thus numerous luminaries (Hillel, Rashi, even Queen Victoria) have been alleged to be descendants of David. Actually, as we have mentioned, documentation of the House of David ends about 400 B.C.E., although some scholars would stretch this to the middle of the third century B.C.E. (See chart on page 56.) There is no information concerning the House of David between the fourth century B.C.E. and the second century C.E. In the fifth century C.E. a work called *Seder Olam Zuta* tried to connect the exilarchs (the heads of the Jewish community in Babylonia until the eleventh century C.E.) to the House of David, and this work was in turn used as the basis for others who later claimed descent from David. Its historical value, though, is extremely dubious.

In short, the Bible seems historically reliable for perhaps a thousand-year stretch from, say, the thirteenth century through the fourth century B.C.E. No purist would venture back beyond that point. And yet . . . the information is there, it's fun to fool around with, and if you keep in mind that you are dealing with highly speculative material, my inclination is to shrug your shoulders and include it.

But all of this begs the crucial question: these Biblical characters may well have been directly related to each other, but were any of them direct ancestors of ours? Almost all historians agree that the answer is "yes" (although some anthropologists have expressed doubts). While no Jewish family can be traced in an unbroken line back to Biblical times, the movement of Jewish groups and communities can be traced continuously from the fall of the Kingdom of Judah in 586 B.C.E. to the present. Some made their way over the centuries through Persia, Turkey and the Crimea and finally into Europe, where they became today's Ashkenazim. Others moved across North Africa and into Spain, where they became today's Sephardim. The same process occurred, albeit later, among the exiles who returned to Palestine in the fifth century B.C.E. The descendants of these people constituted the Jews who were in Jerusalem at the time the Second Temple was destroyed by the Romans in 70 C.E. Again, the Jews who survived that slaughter—97,000, according to Josephus—largely made their way to Europe either via Persia or North Africa.

Thus, of the 14 million Jews in the world today, all of them fit into at least one of five groups:

• The greatest number, probably, are descendants of the tribes of Judah, Benjamin and Simeon. When Jews of the Second Temple period spoke of themselves as *"Kohanim,* Levites and Israelites," the latter term referred to these three tribes, and it still does. Before the Second Temple period, of course, it referred to twelve tribes, but nine of them have disappeared and are presumably no longer Jewish. The Israelites who survived in the Kingdom of Judah to build the Second Temple were from the tribes of Judah, Benjamin and Simeon (which was absorbed by the tribe of Judah). It is impossible to determine now which of these tribes is yours (no doubt most of us had ancestors in all three tribes). In any case, descendants of all three tribes can rightfully claim direct descent from Jacob, the father of Judah, Simeon and Benjamin.

Incidentally, Biblical reference books always fudge when discussing the number of tribes in ancient Israel. The number 12 had special tribal significance in the Bible and the ancient Near East (twelve tribes, twelve disciples, etc.), so the popular notion holds that there were twelve tribes—one for each son of Jacob—and that after the fall of the northern kingdom of Israel there were ten lost tribes. But actually, even from the evidence in the Bible itself there were thirteen "groups." One of Jacob's twelve sons, Joseph, was the forefather of two tribes, Manasseh and Ephraim, named for his sons. The remaining eleven sons of Jacob founded one group each, including Levi, whose group had no land and thus was not really a tribe. As for what happened to those thirteen groups, we can account for four of them: Simeon was merged into the tribe of Judah, and Judah, Benjamin and most of the Levites lived in the southern kingdom of Judah and thus preserved their identity as Jews. By my count, that means there were only nine lost tribes: Reuben, Manasseh, Gad, Asher, Naphtali, Issachar, Zebulon, Dan and Ephraim.

• The *Kohanim* (priests). Aaron, brother of Moses, of the tribe of Levi, was the first of the *Kohanim,* and he passed the title on to his two surviving sons. I have yet to come across any book or article that explicitly says all *Kohanim* are direct descendants of Aaron, but certainly the title, as well as some ceremonial duties and customs, have been passed down from father to son even to today. Many *Kohanim* have taken the surname "Cohen" or some variation (Kogan, Kagan, Cohn, etc.) or Katz (for *Kohen Tzedek*—legitimate priest). But the name alone, however, is insufficient proof of priestly descent, and on the contrary, many *Kohanim* have names that sound totally different. If you find an ancestor referred to as "Ha-Kohen" in writings or on his gravestone, that is a good indication that he belongs to the *Kohanim.* Another is the sign of the priestly benediction—two outspread hands touching, the fingers grouped in pairs—on a tombstone. And if your relatives can remember an ancestor who was called to the altar to recite the *Kohen*'s prayer on the High Holy Days, there is probably no doubt that you are a genuine *Kohen.*

The *Kohanim* are descended from both the family of Levi, through Aaron, and from the family of Judah through Aaron's wife, Elisheba.

• The Levites. The descendants of Levi, unlike the families of Jacob's other sons, were designated to render service in the temple. Thus, the Levites owned no land, but were assigned the revenues of certain cities and lands of the other tribes. One branch of the Levites, descended from Aaron, became the priests, or *Kohanim,* mentioned above; the rest became known as Levites. They functioned as gatekeepers and caretakers of the sanctuary, and as judges, teachers, scribes, temple musicians and assistants to the *Kohanim.* Like the *Kohanim,* the Levites have passed the title down from father to son to the present day; if you find an ancestor referred to on his grave or elsewhere as "Ha-Levi," you can claim Levi, son of Jacob, as your direct ancestor.

• Descendants of the Khazars. As mentioned in chapter 4, some Jews, and perhaps a great many, are descended from the Khazars, who were converted to Judaism in the eighth century C.E. and thus have no Biblical lineage to speak of. It is hard to tell, of course, whether you have Khazar blood. Some of the Karaite Jews of the Crimea and modern Israel are probably Khazar descendants. If a branch of your family was *Kohanim* or Levites, or if a branch has no roots whatever in Eastern Europe, you can be sure that that branch is *not* of Khazar ancestry.

If you *do* have Khazar ancestors, of course, they are not descended from the Twelve Tribes of Israel. But that's no reason to toss out your Bible. An Arab historian in the ninth century traced the Khazars back to the Biblical character Khazar, seventh son of Togarmah. Togarmah, considered the ancestor of all Turkish tribes, was a grandson of Japhet, the third son of Noah. And Noah, of course, was the great-great-great-great-great-great-great-great-grandfather of Abraham, patriarch of the Palestinian Jews.

• Descendants of other converts to Judaism, past or present.

In any case, if you figure four generations to a century, there have been more than 150 generations of Jews since Abraham. That's an extraordinary amount of marrying and breeding. In earlier times, when conscious attempts were made to maintain purity of bloodlines, the breakdown I have just provided might have meant something. But today it is likely that almost every Jew is partly descended from Judah, partly from Benjamin, partly from Levi if not Aaron, partly from the Khazars, and partly, no doubt, from gentiles. This means that at the very least, each of us can claim direct descent from Jacob, who was father of Judah, Benjamin and Levi. And from Jacob we can go backward to his father Isaac, to his father Abraham, to his father Terah and all the way back through another eighteen generations to Adam.

There is no need to conclude your research here, of course: in genealogy every doorway opened into the past merely leads to another doorway. For further investigation, consult Darwin's *Origin of Species.*

VI

Jewish Sources in America

BACK TO your research—by this point it may seem that you have stretched the limits of your resources in America. You have tracked down all of your known relatives on this continent, and you have communicated with them. You have located all the appropriate birth, marriage and death certificates, ships' passenger lists and census records. You have sloshed through the mud and brambles of every conceivable cemetery. You may now think there is nothing more for you to do at home, that if you wish to trace your tree further back, you will have to do it in Europe or Israel.

Think again. Swarms of records relating to Jews, Jewish families, Jewish congregations and Jewish communities in America and overseas can be found in libraries and research institutions in the United States and Canada. These records may provide you with details about your relatives, but even if they don't, there is a wealth of books and manuscripts available about Jews in specific countries and towns that can give you valuable background insights and will help you evaluate and reconstruct the information you gather about your family.

Because of the uncertain nature of the Jewish past, there is no central clearing house for Jewish records, but many records have found their way to the United States. Chance often plays a great part in determining which records will survive and which ones will be lost forever.

Consider what happened to the records of the Holy Inquisition in Mexico in the nineteenth century. Transcripts of inquisitional trials in medieval Mexico, Spain and Portugal are of great value to Jewish genealogists because the courts carefully studied the background of each defendant to determine whether he was or was not a true Christian. In 1882, when the government of Mexico was cleaning out its storage space, most of the records of the Mexican Inquisition were sold to a junk dealer for their value as waste paper. Somehow, thirty-three volumes of these records fell into the hands of one David Fergusson of Seattle, who recognized their value and forwarded them to Charles Lea of Philadelphia, a leading historian of the Inquisition. Still another volume of the same lot was discovered by chance in the rubbish of an antiquary's shop in Washington by—of all people—the president of the American Jewish Historical Society; it provided enough material of interest to fill an entire issue of the society's publication in 1899.

The following agencies and institutions may help you advance your research a good deal without requiring you to cross the ocean.

LIBRARIES AND ARCHIVES

Many major public libraries and many large universities in the United States have substantial Judaica collections which often contain obscure Jewish family histories or books and articles on specific Jewish communities. It is important to keep in mind the difference between a library and an archive. A library houses published books, and thus most major Judaica libraries will largely duplicate each other's holdings. An archive, on the other hand, holds unpublished manuscripts, documents, papers and all sorts of miscellaneous odds and ends (one archive even has old dental appointment cards in one of its collections). Thus the holdings of each archive are likely to be unique (although, to be sure, microfilm is reducing that uniqueness). In short, it is probably not necessary to travel across the country to a major Jewish library if there is a major Jewish collection near you; on the other hand, each of the Jewish archives in the United States and Canada may be worth a special trip.

Obviously, the larger the library, the more likely it is to have detailed books on obscure Jewish families and Jewish communities. On the other hand, in relatively small and disorganized libraries I have sometimes come across rare books that I couldn't find elsewhere. Still, the big libraries are your best starting point.

Based on estimates from the *American Jewish Yearbook* and other sources, the largest Judaica libraries in the United States are as follows:

	Judaica volumes
YIVO Institute, New York	300,000
Klau Library, Hebrew Union College, Cincinnati	250,000
Jewish Theological Seminary, New York	200,000
Harvard University, Cambridge, Mass.	150,000
Library of Congress, Washington, D.C.	150,000
Jewish Division, New York Public Library	135,000
Yeshiva University, New York	100,000
University of California at Los Angeles	90,000
Hebrew Union College—Jewish Institute of Religion, New York	90,000
Brandeis University, Waltham, Mass.	78,000
University of Judaism, Los Angeles	60,000
American Jewish Historical Society, Waltham, Mass.	54,000
Dropsie University, Philadelphia	50,000
Columbia University, New York	50,000
Yale University, New Haven, Conn.	50,000
Leo Baeck Institute Library, New York	50,000
Zionist Archives and Library, New York	50,000
Frances Henry Library, Hebrew Union College, Los Angeles	45,000
University of California, Berkeley	40,000
Blaustein Library, American Jewish Committee, New York	40,000

Other Judaica collections of 15,000 or more volumes can be found at Gratz College, Philadelphia; Spertus College of Judaica, Chicago; Baltimore Hebrew College; Herzliah-Jewish Teachers Seminary, New York; Hebrew College, Brookline, Mass.; University of Wisconsin, Madison; University of Texas, Austin; and Ohio State University, Columbus.

Probably the most popular of these libraries is the Jewish Division of the New York Public Library, because of its location and public accessibility. My favorite is the Klau Library at Hebrew Union College in Cincinnati, which offers an extensive collection, a well-organized card catalogue, a modern building, and perhaps most important, open stacks through which you can browse.

If you plan to photocopy anything in libraries, here is one more tip: college libraries (the Klau in Cincinnati, for example) seem to offer the least expensive photocopying machines. The most expensive is the New York Public Library, which charges 30 cents a page at this writing.

Synagogues are another source of good Jewish libraries. Most synagogue libraries are geared toward Hebrew schools and do not provide the sort of obscure books likely to turn up details about your particular family. However, at least three large congregational libraries are exceptions to this rule: Temple Emanu-El Library in New York, Tifereth Israel (The Temple) Library in Cleveland, and Wilshire Boulevard Temple Library in Los Angeles.

Public genealogical libraries are relatively few. Most libraries scrupulously avoid the subject altogether, because family history books probably have less general interest than any other type of book found in a library. And because genealogy is often a matter of finding a single name in a book and linking it to a name in another book, and so on, genealogists go through books much more quickly than other library users. At a genealogy library like the New-berry in Chicago, it's not unusual for a single researcher to call for fifty books in the course of a day, thus monopolizing the time of the staff.

What genealogical libraries and societies do exist, I have found, have relatively little information helpful to Jews. Perhaps the best resource in such a place will be the librarians themselves, who can give you advice on your particular problems. Of genealogy sections open to the public, the best are:

• The Mormon Genealogical Society in Salt Lake City (more on this in a moment).
• The Local History and Genealogy Division of the New York Public Library. It has some 40,000 family histories, indexes to New York City births, deaths and marriages, and histories of towns and cities in the United States, Britain and Ireland.
• The Genealogy Room of the Library of Congress, Washington, D.C.
• Boston Public Library, Copley Square, Boston
• The New England Historic Genealogical Society Library, Boston
• The Newberry Library, Chicago
• The Los Angeles Public Library
• The Virginia State Library, Richmond
• The Indiana State Library, Indianapolis
• The Pennsylvania State Library, Harrisburg

MORMON GENEALOGICAL SOCIETY

The Genealogical Society of Utah
50 E. North Temple Street
Salt Lake City, Utah 84150

Painful though it may be to admit, the best records for Jewish ancestor hunters are not to be found in Jewish institutions, but in the Mormons' genealogical library in Salt Lake City. No other religious institution is as ancestor-conscious as the Mormons, nor does any other institution approach the dollar figures that the Mormons devote to genealogy: $10 million a year to maintain their archives of six million family group sheets, 36 million index cards, 90 million feet of microfilm, and 250 microfilm machines, a network of branch genealogical libraries around the United States, and six massive storage vaults, blasted out of the insides of Granite Mountain and protected by six-hundred-foot-thick granite ceilings, nine-ton metal doors, iron gates and closed-circuit television systems.

Genealogy is a very serious business to the Mormons because their religion holds that people born before the faith was founded in 1830 cannot enter heaven unless they are baptized posthumously. Thus, as we have seen, Mormons study their genealogies to identify their relatives and to ensure that their ancestors will attain salvation. And since a twentieth-century Mormon can never be sure who his ancestors were, Mormons are zealous about everyone's genealogy—including those of Jews. U.S. census reports, baptismal records from England, marriage licenses and millions of other documents have all been stored and recorded on a computerized family index, so that simply by pushing a button you can be referred instantly to any families related to families with your name. This won't do you much good if your name is "Smith" or "Cohen" —you'll simply be referred to thousands of families, most of them not related to you—but it could be helpful if you have a relatively rare name, like, say, Sobel or Kirschbaum.

If you can't travel to Salt Lake City, you can use the collections by working through any of the society's dozens of branch libraries scattered throughout the United States and other countries. Consult your telephone book under "Church of Jesus Christ of Latter-day Saints"; if there is no specific listing for a genealogical library, call the church number and you can learn where the nearest branch library is. Most of these branches are small rooms offering only a few microfilm readers and a bare minimum of reference books; however, they serve as clearing houses from which you can borrow virtually anything from the Main Library in Salt Lake City, whether you are a Mormon or not. At the branch you will find microfilmed indexes of the Genealogical Society's card catalogue; from these, you can order actual microfilm reels from Salt Lake City. Once these arrive, you can study them on the microfilm readers at the branch library for several weeks or longer, if you wish. The only fee charged for this service is the cost of mailing—usually 75 cents per reel, plus renewal fees if you use the reels for more than two weeks.

Of course, the microfilmed indexes of the Genealogical Society's card catalogue are probably a year or two out of date. Since cards are being added to the catalogue every day, your best bet, if it's at all possible, is to go to Salt Lake City in person. Another alternative is to correspond with the society's staff; the library has specialists in virtually every European country who can help you with your particular problem; they can also refer you to a number of books and pamphlets that deal with genealogical research in specific countries. Simply write to "Specialist: [Your country]" at the Genealogical Society Library. In 1976 the society added a specialist in Jewish genealogy, Dr. Jeffrey Kahn. Unlike most bureaucrats, the Mormon specialists will serve you with efficiency, interest and even pleasure. To them, this is not merely a job: it's a matter of salvation.

Because the Mormons don't represent any government or any political viewpoint, they have in some cases gained access to records in Communist countries that have turned a cold shoulder to other researchers, including Israeli archivists. The Mormons, and only the Mormons, have been allowed to microfilm all of the existing communal birth, death and marriage records from Hungary for the period before vital statistics were centralized in 1895. Some of these records go back to the late eighteenth century, and since they were kept according to religious denomination, the Jewish records are isolated from the others. There are more than 250 microfilm reels of Hungarian Jewish community records alone—including those of former Hungarian communities that are today in Czechoslovakia, Rumania and Yugoslavia. (The Hungarian Jewish community records are identified as "Israelita Hitkozseg" or "Israelitische," *not* "Jewish.") These communities are indexed according to present-day county; the county in which your ancestors' town was located can be found by consulting *Ritters Geographisch-Statistiches Lexikon* in the map department of most public libraries (see the section on foreign boundaries in chapter 7). If your ancestors were nineteenth-century Hungarian Jews, you should have a surprisingly easy time locating their birth, death and marriage records once you find the appropriate microfilm roll.

Similarly, the Mormons, and only the Mormons, have been permitted to microfilm old vital statistics in Poland. Again, these go back to the eighteenth century and earlier—and again, they include Jewish records. At this writing, the microfilming of Polish records is still in progress. However, just randomly browsing through the Mormons' Poland index, I have already found such entries as an inventory of lists of Jewish births, marriages and deaths in East Prussia from 1812 to 1850, and a register of births, marriages and deaths of the Jewish congregation of Osterode district, from 1865 to 1936. (Both of these districts were German then; now they belong to Poland).

It is likely that the Polish records are incomplete, since some of them were lost or destroyed during the two world wars. On the other hand, the records of Czechoslovakia and Yugoslavia are believed to be quite complete, and the Genealogical Society hopes to microfilm those (and also the records of Rumania) when its Poland project is finished. (Also see the sections on Poland, Czechoslovakia, etc., in chapter 7.)

Another valuable resource at the Genealogical Society library is an indexed microfilm set of the complete records of all emigrations out of Hamburg, Germany, from 1850 to 1934. (Many East European Jews, not only Germans, sailed from Hamburg.) These records contain a good deal of information about the emigrant, where he came from and where he was going. The Genealogical Society has indexes for these emigration lists on a year-by-year basis (although the names are grouped only by the first letter of the last name, not in strict alphabetical order).

For more information on the facilities in Salt Lake City, consult *A Handy Guide to the Genealogical Library and Church Historical Department,* by Ronald Cunningham and Evan Evans.

AMERICAN JEWISH ARCHIVES

3101 Clifton Avenue
Cincinnati, Ohio 45220

The American Jewish Archives (AJA) seeks to preserve any documents illuminating the history of Jews in the Western hemisphere, especially the United States, but also including Canada, Mexico, the West Indies and South America. Since its founding in 1947 by Dr. Jacob Rader Marcus (still its director), the Archives has developed a reputation as a place that will accept and preserve virtually anything Jewish that is given to it. Today its catalogue numbers well over 500,000 cards, a great many of them testifying to AJA's generous cross-referencing policy. The Archives stands on the Hebrew Union College campus in a building that was originally the home of the college library; the present Hebrew Union College library is just two doors away from AJA—and since that library is probably the best Judaica library in the United States, a trip to Cincinnati is well worth the trouble for any serious Jewish researcher.

The Archives contains, among other things, documents, letters, memoirs, organizational records and hundreds of family trees. Many of these are merely scraps of paper which obscure people have sent in and AJA has meticulously preserved, so you never can tell—your own relatives may be in there. Records and publications of more than a thousand congregations are listed on a city-by-city basis; look for these in AJA's card catalogue under "synagogue activities" in the section for your city. (Most of these synagogues tend to be reform congregations because Hebrew Union College is a reform seminary, but AJA is interested in all congregations and does have some orthodox and conservative synagogue records, too.)

In addition to the card catalogue, the Archives also has unique indexes—by cities, topics and individuals—of some nineteenth-century Jewish-American publications. *The Occident,* for example, was published from 1843 to 1869 by Isaac Leeser of Philadelphia; he had agents across the country who provided him with all sorts of details, from new congregations to obituaries to complete lists of subscribers to his newspaper. Other indexes cover *Die Deborah,* published (in German) by Isaac Mayer Wise from 1855 to 1900; the *Israels Herald* (1849–1850); and the *Sinai* (1856–1863). These indexes are not available anywhere else (although AJA will loan them to other libraries). The same is true for its "Deutsch index," a remarkable catalogue of American and European Jewish periodicals from 1850 to 1920, indexed according to topic, city and individual by the late Gotthard Deutsch, a Hebrew Union College history professor. (The Deutsch index is in two sections: American listings are in the

American Jewish Archives; European listings are next door at the Hebrew Union College library.)

Also extremely helpful is the American Jewish Periodical Center next door in the Klau Library, which has microfilmed every Jewish periodical published in the United States between 1823 and 1925, and many more since then. These are not only in English but also in German, Hebrew, Yiddish, Polish, Ladino, Serbo-Croatian and Hungarian. If you can't visit Cincinnati, these materials are available on loan to other libraries. (See *Jewish Newspapers and Periodicals on Microfilm Available at the American Jewish Periodical Center.*).

AJA contains almost no books, only manuscripts. Its card index to its holdings has been reproduced in a 4-volume catalogue available at most major libraries, but the catalogue covers only holdings as of June 30, 1971. (Reports of some subsequent additions can be found in the semiannual publication *American Jewish Archives.*)

Because Cincinnati is off the beaten path for most American Jews, AJA is a relatively quiet place, and the staff is both competent and anxious to help anyone who travels there. They often handle mail requests from people seeking information about their ancestors. Such requests should provide as much detail as possible. In return, the staff will provide a very brief reply advising what is available on the particular subject; AJA will also provide photocopies for a small fee.

AMERICAN JEWISH HISTORICAL SOCIETY

2 Thornton Road
Waltham, Mass. 02154

The library and archives of the American Jewish Historical Society (AJHS) contain about four million items relating to all areas of American Jewish history, including such fields as family histories, family papers, community histories, and immigration and synagogue records, all of which may be useful in your search for family clues. The society's home on the Brandeis University campus is bright, modern, spacious, comfortable, efficient and—because of its location—little used. AJHS moved its quarters to Brandeis from New York in the 1960s because of the high cost of real estate in New York and because of its desire to be affiliated with a university. The location does have its advantages: when you come to do research at AJHS, there are no distractions, as there would be, say, in downtown New York or Chicago. And the society is conveniently close to the Brandeis Library, which has one of the largest Judaica collections in the United States.

The society's archives and library holdings are integrated into a single card catalogue, which means you have to look up family names, towns and subjects only once. The archives' collections include several hundred genealogies and family histories, and hundreds of synagogue histories and journals, virtually all of them American. AJHS also has records of numerous organizations, lodges, hospitals, immigrant aid societies, orphanages, community councils, college fraternities, etc. Its *Publications* and *Quarterly* have contained useful articles over the years; among other things, the *Quarterly* lists all new Jewish family history books received by the society.

The librarian says the staff frequently receives mail requests for information about ancestors and does not mind looking things up for people. One hour is the maximum they will spend on a research request. Beyond that, people must come themselves. The best way to trace an ancestor at the society is to provide the name of an institution with which the ancestor was affiliated—a synagogue, say, or a charitable organization—since the society has multitudes of records of such groups.

YIVO INSTITUTE FOR JEWISH RESEARCH

1048 Fifth Avenue
New York, N.Y. 10028

Unlike the American Jewish Historical Society and the American Jewish Archives, YIVO is primarily concerned with European Jewry, and particularly East European Jewry, and it is by far the best source in the United States for material on East European Jews and Jewish communities. Its library is said to contain about 300,000 volumes—which would make it the largest Judaica library in the country—and its archives contain at least ten million items, filling nearly a mile of shelf space. It has valuable records of East European Jewish communities, thousands of case files on immigrants to the United States (especially after 1920), family histories and genealogies, and *yizkor* (memorial) books written by survivors of East European communities in memory of their neighbors who perished in the Holocaust. There is only one slight problem at YIVO: finding anything you are looking for.

Part of YIVO's organizational problem stems from the fact that unlike American-oriented libraries and archives, its library catalogues are separated into four different language-alphabet sections: Roman (English, French, German, etc.), Yiddish, Hebrew, and Cyrillic (Russian, Ukrainian, etc.). But most of the problem is due to the fact that YIVO fulfills every popular stereotype of a disorganized East European archives-library. In the library, books are catalogued not by categories, as in the Library of Congress system, but in order of acquisition. This means that a book's catalogue number has no relation to its subject, so a book which is accidentally misshelved may be lost for eternity. There is a subject index, of sorts, in the library, but the archives are catalogued by the collections with which they originally arrived at YIVO, not by subject, so to find material on a particular subject, place or name, you may have to comb through dozens of collections. In addition, a great deal of archival material is piled up in nooks and crannies throughout YIVO's huge old mansion at 86th Street and Fifth Avenue and few people know where much of it is.

But if YIVO's system hasn't caught up with its holdings, at least some members of the staff do seem to know where almost everything is, and you will find their help indispensable. "Genealogists will have a hard time here," the YIVO archivist acknowledges, "because they must check through many collections. We cannot conduct any genealogical research for anyone." At this writing, YIVO hopes to have a complete inventory of its archives published by 1978, but until then, chaos reigns for the uninitiated visitor.

Nevertheless, there are some areas in which YIVO may be helpful to ancestor hunters with relatively little trouble. A few possibilities:

• YIVO has complete records of the Hebrew Immigrant Aid Society (HIAS), covering every immigrant assisted by HIAS from the 1920s onward. It also has incidental immigration items from the 1890s through the 1920s.
• More than a thousand autobiographies written by East European Jews or U.S. immigrants from Eastern Europe, 1882–1955.
• Collections of testimonies of Holocaust survivors.
• YIVO serves as a clearing house for information about *landsmanshaften* — organizations formed by groups of Jews in America who came from particular towns in Eastern Europe. YIVO has a card file listing more than eighty of these societies in New York and providing names, addresses and phone numbers of officers. Members of these societies can of course be helpful in remembering details about your relatives from their particular towns.
• YIVO has some four hundred *yizkor* books. Many of these books are in Yiddish, and they are not always complete, but usually they attempt to list all of the Holocaust victims from a particular town, and often they contain a history of the town's Jewish community as well. Most of YIVO's *yizkor* books memorialize towns in Poland, but there are also books for communities in Bulgaria, Russia (46), Germany (4), Hungary (15), Yugoslavia, Greece, Latvia (7), Lithuania (40), Czechoslovakia (7) and Rumania (12).
• Records of numerous European *kehillot* and other communal organizations, including Vilna, Ostrow (Poznan, or Posen, area), Briesen (Danzig area), Minsk, Kiev and many other Russian and Polish communities, as well as about a hundred Jewish communities in Lithuania during the autonomy period of 1919–1923.

LEO BAECK INSTITUTE

129 East 73rd Street
New York, N.Y. 10021

The library and archives of the Leo Baeck Institute are devoted to preserving any and all records of the German-speaking Jewish culture which was destroyed in the Holocaust. Its emphasis is thus on the Jews of Germany, but its materials also cover other German-language areas, such as Austria and parts of Poland and Czechoslovakia. It also has a small amount of material on Russian Jews who moved to Germany.

The institute, founded in 1955, is housed in a town house built at the turn of the century by a prominent New York Jewish family. Considering the extent of the institute's holdings, the quarters are cramped, but it's a pleasant place to work because the staff is more efficient than most, and usually the staff outnumbers the visiting researchers.

Most of the books and materials at the Baeck Institute are in German, while others are in English. Relatively few are in Hebrew or Yiddish. The library contains 50,000 volumes, including broad collections of community and family histories. A printed catalogue of part of the library's holdings was published in 1970, edited by Max Krautzberger *(Lèo Baeck Institute Bibliothek und Archiv, Katalog,* Band I). If you live outside New York, you might look up this catalogue at your local library for its references to the institute's holdings on Jewish communities in Germany, unpublished memoirs, newspapers and other periodicals. Of course, the institute has added many books since that catalogue was published, and in any case, the catalogue doesn't cover the whole library.

The institute's archive holds thousands of private and institutional papers, including hundreds of family trees, business documents, community histories, and a unique collection of 550 unpublished memoirs written by German Jews from 1790 to 1945.

The archive's holdings also include fifteen microfilms pertaining to 446 destroyed synagogues in the states of Bavaria, Hesse and Bremen. And in 1976 the institute acquired the complete collection of the late Rudolf Simonis, a German Jewish genealogist who fled to Sweden during the Holocaust. His collection includes literally hundreds of family trees, genealogical notes and family histories of German and Swedish Jewish families, all alphabetized and in impeccable order.

In any case, the staff members of the Baeck Institute are sufficiently knowledgeable about German-Jewish affairs so that if you can't find what you need there, they should be able to direct you to other sources helpful to you elsewhere—assuming, of course, that the family you are tracing is of German ancestry.

JEWISH THEOLOGICAL SEMINARY (LIBRARY)

3080 Broadway
New York, N.Y. 10027

Although the seminary library is regarded by many as the pre-eminent Jewish library in North America, it has two drawbacks. First, its archive suffers from a lack of space; thus it takes a long time for the staff to process all the papers it receives. Second, the library has never quite recovered from a disastrous fire in 1966 that destroyed thousands of books and manuscripts, many of them rare copies that couldn't be replaced elsewhere. The losses from that fire haven't yet been inventoried, so it's still possible to find a card in the library's catalogue, only to discover that the corresponding book no longer exists.

The library does have an extensive collection of books and manuscripts about Jewish communities in Europe. Look in the card catalogue under "Jews in . . .," followed by the appropriate country or town.

In addition to its 200,000 books, the seminary library has an archive providing material on Jewish life in France, Spain, Italy, Morocco, Central Europe, North Africa and the United States. The manuscripts include a number of *pinkasim* (record books) of European Jewish communities in the sixteenth through nineteenth centuries, containing minutes of meetings, lists of officers, tax assessments, fines and numerous other entries reflecting the life of the local community.

Another valuable resource at the seminary library is *Sefer Hapremumerantin (Hebrew Subscription Lists)*, by Berl Kagan, a member of the library staff. In nineteenth-century Europe it was common for Hebrew books to be financed through "subscriptions" from Jews in the particular town where the book appeared; a list of these subscribers would then appear in the book. *Hebrew Subscription Lists* is a guide to such lists that still exist for 8,767 communities in Europe and North Africa. These lists cover the eighteenth, nineteenth and twentieth centuries and contain more than 350,000 names, some of which, perhaps, could be your ancestors. The actual lists are not in Kagan's book—it merely enumerates them—but most are available at the seminary library or elsewhere in New York City. The book is in Hebrew, but it does contain an English-language introduction and an index to towns, which is also in English.

YESHIVA UNIVERSITY LIBRARY

Mendel Gottesman Library
of Judaica and Hebraica and Archives
Amsterdam Avenue and 185th Street
New York, N.Y. 10033

Yeshiva is the pre-eminent Orthodox rabbinical seminary in the United States. Its library has more than 100,000 volumes. Between the library and the archives there are a great many books, periodicals, documents and manuscripts dealing with Jewish life in pre–World War II Europe as well as early American Jewish communities. Yeshiva also has a large collection of records of Orthodox congregations in the United States. Since most East European Jews were Orthodox, at least when they first arrived in the United States, you might be able to find some of your immigrant ancestors in these records and thus get a better idea of when they arrived or where they lived.

DROPSIE UNIVERSITY

Broad and York streets
Philadelphia, Pa. 19132

Dropsie's library and archives are similar to the YIVO Institute in New York, though on a smaller scale, in the sense that it has many remarkable and rare manuscripts, documents and books, but because its cataloguing is weak, you may have a hard time finding them. Until a few years ago, Dropsie's 50,000 books were catalogued only by author and title, not by subject, and the library has only recently begun to catalogue its books according to the Library of Congress decimal system.

Nevertheless, I have found several rare old family histories at Dropsie that I couldn't get elsewhere. For years, for example, I searched for *Ma'alot Ha-Yuhasin,* a Hebrew history of the Margulies and Landau families of Galicia written in the 1820s and published in Cracow in 1900. I could not find it in any New York library, but at Dropsie this book—the original, not a microfilm copy—was standing innocuously out on the public reference shelves.

"Are you aware," I said to the librarian, "that this is an extremely rare book that I've spent years searching for?"

He laughed and said, "We have a lot of books like that here. Nobody knows the extent of what we have, not even we."

Dropsie also has an archive whose items include the Abraham Katsh microfilm collection of rare Hebraica manuscripts from the USSR, Poland and

Hungary, and the Isaac Leeser Collection, containing 30,000 letters and documents dealing with American Jewry from colonial times through the mid-nineteenth-century emigrations from Germany.

PHILADELPHIA JEWISH ARCHIVES CENTER

625 Walnut Street
Philadelphia, Pa. 19106

The Philadelphia Jewish Archives Center, established in 1972, is the only Jewish archive which deals exclusively with the records of one city. Its goal is to collect and organize all records, papers, manuscripts, pictures and other material relating to the Philadelphia Jewish community. It has no money for acquisitions and relies entirely on donations, so its holdings thus far are small. It does, however, have a few collections that may be of interest to Philadelphia-area ancestor hunters.

• Hebrew Immigrant Aid Society records, 1884–1921. These record books list virtually all Jewish immigrants arriving in Philadelphia and include such information as name, age, country of origin, occupation and final destination.
• Records of the Neighborhood Center Day Nursery and Nursery School, 1904–1952, including correspondence, minutes, records, reports, statistics and case files, which contain family data, names of relatives, etc.
• Orphans' records of the Association for Jewish Children, 1855–1974.
• Records of various Philadelphia-area synagogues.

The Archives Center publishes a newsletter twice a year, which lists new additions. It is available at no charge by writing to the center.

WESTERN JEWISH HISTORY CENTER

Judah L. Magnes Memorial Museum
2911 Russell Street
Berkeley, Calif. 94705

The center was established in 1967 as a division of the Judah Magnes Museum. It is rapidly building a unique archive of Western Jewish Americana, including family histories and memoirs of Jewish families in the western United States. The center's director, Moses Rischin, has written a brochure, *Family History Guide,* especially oriented toward Jews preparing family histories in the western states. It is available from the center for $1.

EARLY AMERICAN JEWRY

The figure of Rabbi Malcolm H. Stern looms sufficiently large over the American Jewish genealogical scene to merit his inclusion in this chapter as an institution in himself. For more than twenty years Rabbi Stern has been keeping track of the genealogies of America's oldest Jewish families, and he has become so proficient that he now serves as a virtual one-man clearing house on the subject. His 1960 book, *Americans of Jewish Descent,* is a compendium of charts of descendants of Jews in the United States before 1840; its index alone contains 26,000 entries. The publication of that book generated a flood of mail to Rabbi Stern containing additions and corrections, and at this writing he is preparing a revised and greatly expanded edition of his book, which will include early Jewish families in Canada as well as the United States.

Stern is so widely known for his genealogical work that it sometimes comes as a surprise to people to learn that genealogy is merely a sideline which he sandwiches in when the isn't doing his real job as director of placement for the Central Conference of American Rabbis. In any case, if your family was in North America before 1840, your task in tracing your ancestors is considerably simplified by Stern's interest in the subject. For more information, consult Rabbi Stern's book or contact him personally at the Central Conference of American Rabbis, 790 Madison Avenue, New York, N.Y. 10021.

One caveat. Stern picked 1840 as his cutoff date for a good reason: it was just before the first great wave of Jewish immigrants arrived from Germany. In 1840 there were only some 40,000 Jews in the United States, and their descendants are a tiny fraction of today's American Jewish population.

A JEWISH GENEALOGY NEWSLETTER

As this book went to press we were advised of the launching of *Toledot: The Journal of Jewish Genealogy,* a bimonthly newsletter intended to serve as an ongoing clearing house for information about Jewish family trees. Editors are Steven Siegel and Arthur Kurzweil, and Rabbi Malcolm Stern is a contributing editor. Address: P.O. Box 126, Flushing, N.Y. 11367.

SOCIETY FOR THE HISTORY OF CZECHOSLOVAK JEWS

25 Mayhew Avenue
Larchmont, N.Y. 10538

This group, successor to a similar organization in Czechoslovakia before World War II, is dedicated to researching any information pertaining to Czechoslovak Jewry. Its primary, although not exclusive, concern is Czech Jewry between the two world wars. The nucleus of the group is some thrity to forty serious researchers of Czechoslovak Jewish descent who have compiled a 2-volume series, *The Jews of Czechoslovakia,* covering mid-nineteenth century to 1938. At this writing they are working on a third volume, to cover 1938 to 1948. Much of the research they have done is original. Some members of the society have done genealogical research in Czechoslovakia and can offer advice as to how to proceed there. Contact Ludovit Sturc, president.

WORLD FEDERATION OF HUNGARIAN JEWS

136 East 39th Street
New York, N.Y. 10016

Like the Society for the History of Czechoslovak Jews, this group devotes most of its time to publishing research works on the Jews of Hungary. Its 3-volume series, *Hungarian Jewish Studies,* is filled with useful information for Hungarian ancestor seekers, including an article on Hungarian Jewish migrations and a list of Jewish communities.

LANDSMANSHAFTEN

When Jews emigrated to the United States from Europe they often banded together in their new surroundings with their old neighbors from Europe to form what is known as *landsmanshaften* societies. Usually these societies were social clubs, but sometimes they constituted congregations. In many cases these societies have put together histories of their old Jewish communities and memorials to the Holocaust victims of those communities. While many of these organizations are defunct, some still exist. Members of the society from your family's particular town may be able to give you some clues in your research.

Unfortunately, in most American cities there is no directory of these societies; they are known largely by word of mouth in particular neighborhoods where most of their members live; nor can you find them listed in the telephone book because they generally operate out of the home of an officer. In New

York, however, the YIVO Institute for Jewish Research (1048 Fifth Avenue) acts as a clearing house for information on *landsmanshaften*. It has a card catalogue listing some eighty such societies in the New York area, together with names, addresses and phone numbers of officers.

UNITED HIAS SERVICES

200 Park Avenue South
New York, N.Y. 10003

United HIAS Services was founded in 1892 as the Hebrew Immigrant Aid Society and has long been the most important Jewish migration agency, with offices throughout the world. Its New York office has microfilm records of every immigrant met by HIAS workers since 1911. Each name is listed in a master file, which will refer you to an individual case file that should yield considerable detail as to the immigrant, his family, where he came from and where he was going. These records are restricted, but if you write to HIAS and explain your relationship and provide the name and approximate date of your relative's arrival, HIAS will reply with information. (Also see the section in this chapter on YIVO Institute, which has some records of predecessor agencies.)

United HIAS Services also operates an international missing persons bureau. See below.

TRACING MISSING RELATIVES

If you don't know where your relatives are, a number of Jewish agencies have facilities to help you find them. Five examples:

1) United HIAS Service, mentioned above (200 Park Avenue South, New York, N.Y. 10003), operates an international missing persons bureau through its Search and Location Department. During the course of a year, HIAS Search and Location handles between two and three thousand requests from Jews throughout the world to locate friends and relatives, sometimes involving separations of up to half a century. Although the multilingual staff often works with mere shreds of information, it locates about two thirds of the missing relatives it seeks, working through the HIAS network of international contacts established in more than a hundred years of rescue and resettlement work.

If a missing relative is believed to be in the United States, HIAS first checks its own central files, which include records of every refugee aided by HIAS in the United States since 1911. HIAS also checks with Jewish family service agencies and runs notices in Yiddish and Anglo-Jewish papers across the country, and in the German-language *Aufbau*.

If an American is seeking relatives in the Soviet Union, the information is sent to the HIAS office in Geneva. From there it is transmitted to the International Red Cross, which carries out the search in Russia. In sixty other countries, the Search and Location Department works with HIAS offices and cooperating agencies. The department also handles requests from people who want to find out what happened to relatives who were presumably murdered during World War II.

Needless to add, some of the department's searches fare better than others. In one recent case a young Jewish dancer, recently arrived from the Soviet Union, asked Search and Location to find his uncle. He knew only four facts about the man: his name, birth date (1903), birthplace ("somewhere in the Ukraine") and last known residence (Omaha, Nebraska). With the help of the Jewish federation in Omaha, HIAS found the dancer's relatives in the Midwest.

Less successful has been the case of an elderly man who asked HIAS to find his wife and two sons. He has not seen them since they got out of a railroad car at Bergen-Belsen in 1940; the men were sent to one line and the women and children to another. At this writing, HIAS has been searching for more than a year for some clue as to what happened to his family.

HIAS charges no fee for any of its search and location services, although it does accept donations.

2) Yad Vashem, the Holocaust Memorial in Israel (Har Hazikaron, P.O. Box 84, Jerusalem), provides a service that registers Holocaust victims who were either killed during World War II or are thought to be living somewhere in the world. It has lists of people who came from Europe to Israel after the war, and in some cases addresses.

3) The International Tracing Service in Arolsen, West Germany, specializes in tracing Holocaust survivors. It is the best of such tracing organizations, and has millions of names on file. Most of its records are also available at Yad Vashem in Israel.

4) The Jewish Agency has a section that traces missing relatives in Israel. Its address: Missing Relatives Department, P.O. Box 92, Jerusalem.

5) Americans and Canadians Aliyah (53A Hayarkon Street, Tel Aviv, Israel) also traces missing relatives in Israel.

JEWISH HISTORICAL SOCIETIES

There are sixteen regional Jewish historical societies in the United States. Those that emphasize local communities often have detailed local records or can provide specific advice on local Jewish sources. Their addresses:

Jewish Historical Society of
Southern California
6505 Wilshire Boulevard
Los Angeles, Calif. 90048

Jewish Historical Society of
New Haven
1156 Chapel Street
New Haven, Conn. 06511

Jewish Historical Society of
Greater Hartford
335 Bloomfield Avenue
West Hartford, Conn. 06117

Jewish Historical Society of
Delaware
204 Hitching Post Drive
Wilmington, Del. 19803

Jewish Historical Association of
Southern Florida
4200 Biscayne Boulevard
Miami, Fla. 33137

Jewish Historical Society of
Indiana
215 E. Berry Street
Fort Wayne, Ind. 46892

Jewish Historical Society of
Annapolis
24 Romar Street
Annapolis, Md. 21403

Jewish Historical Society of
Maryland
5800 Park Heights Avenue
Baltimore, Md. 21215

Jewish Historical Society of
Michigan
163 Madison Avenue
Detroit, Mich. 48226

Jewish Historical Society of
Trenton
999 Lower Ferry Road
Box 7249
Trenton, N.J. 08628

Jewish Historical Society of
New York
8 West 70th Street
New York, N.Y. 10023

Columbus Jewish History Project
Ohio Historical Society
I-71 & 17th Avenue
Columbus, Ohio 43211

Oregon Jewish Historical Society
c/o Oregon Jewish Oral History
and Archives Project
6651 S.W. Capitol Highway
Portland, Oregon 97219

Rhode Island Jewish Historical
Association
130 Sessions Street
Providence, R. I. 02906

Jewish Historical Society of
Greater Washington
4501 Connecticut Avenue N.W.
Apt. 807
Washington, D.C. 20005

Southern Jewish Historical Society
c/o Congregation Beth Ahadah
1111 W. Franklin Street
Richmond, Va. 23220

Jewish Archives Project
University of Washington Libraries
Manuscripts Collection
Seattle, Wash. 98195

Wisconsin Jewish Archives
State Historical Society of
Wisconsin
816 State Street
Madison, Wis. 53706

SOURCES IN CANADA

Montreal's Jewish community was developed in the late 1760s. Today there are nearly a dozen Jewish historical organizations, libraries and archives in Canada that may be helpful to you in your search. All birth and death registers in Montreal are held both by individual synagogues and by the Archives of the City of Montreal. Other possible sources:

• The Canadian Jewish Congress Archives has numerous records of synagogues and organizations, including records of the Jewish Colonisation Association (from the 1890s to World War I), which contain information about immigrants. The Archives has two branches, one covering Montreal, at 1590 MacGregor Avenue, Montreal, Que.; the other covering Central Canada, at 150 Beverly Street, Toronto, Ont., home of the Jewish Historical Society of Canada.
• *Americans of Jewish Descent,* the huge genealogy compendium by Malcolm Stern, will in its revised edition contain family-tree charts for Jewish families that settled in Canada before 1840.
• The Jewish Immigrant Aid Society has records of immigrants. Address: 5151 Cote St. Catherine Road, Montreal, Que.
• The Jewish Public Library of Montreal, located in the same building as the Jewish Immigrant Aid Society, has little in the way of genealogical data, but has a great deal of general books and manuscripts about Jews and Jewish communities in Canada.
• Toronto Jewish Historical Society, 19 Rostrevor Road, Toronto, Ont.
• Ottawa Jewish Historical Society, 151 Chapel Street, Ottawa, Ont.
• Jewish Historical Society of British Columbia, 2867 Grainville Street, Vancouver, B. C.
• Jewish Historical Society, Archives and Museum of Western Canada, Suite 403, 322 Donald Street, Winnipeg, Manitoba.
• Bronfman House, 1590 MacGregor Avenue, Montreal, Que.
• Reverend Jacob Raphael Cohen (1738–1811) kept a small record of births, deaths and marriages in Montreal during the early years of the Jewish community there. He later held pulpits in New York and Philadelphia, and his records from Montreal can now be found at Congregation Mikveh Israel, 6th and Walnut streets, Philadelphia, Pa. 19106. (They were also published in the *American Jewish Historical Quarterly,* Vol. 59 (September 1969).
• Copies of birth, death and marriage certificates can be obtained from the Registrar of Vital Statistics at the Department of Health in the respective capital in each of the provinces.
• *Tracing Your Ancestors in Canada* is a guide booklet that contains addresses of the ten provincial record offices in Canada, a bibliography of printed material on genealogy in Canada, information about census returns, vital statistics, land records, wills, notorial records, military and immigration papers and their availability.

VII

Back across the Ocean . . .

SOONER OR LATER, your search for your ancestors should take you on a personal trip to the lands they came from. It can be a frustrating experience and one that depends to some extent on good luck. But if you persist, it can be an exhilarating adventure, and you can learn many things that you would not find out any other way.

If you reach the point at which relatives and records in the United States are no longer sufficient, you must see what is available across the Atlantic. For most North American Jews this means corresponding with archives or vital-statistics bureaus in their country of origin in Europe. But in some cases, especially in countries where records are poor or inaccessible, you might be wiser to start hunting first in Israel (see chapter 8) or even in individual family histories (see the alphabetical list of names at the end of the book) before wading in among the cobwebs of European archives. In this chapter I've provided a rundown on sources of family records, especially Jewish family records, in each country, and how to go about writing for them if you can't go there in person. More details are provided in the Bibliography.

FOREIGN BOUNDARIES

When dealing with foreign countries, keep in mind that national boundaries have changed constantly over the centuries, especially in Europe. My grandfather, for example, considers himself a Hungarian, yet his birthplace is today in Czechoslovakia. Another of my ancestral towns, Zbarazh, was in Poland during the Middle Ages, was part of Austria when my great-grandfather was born there, and is today part of the Soviet Union. The town hasn't moved; only the boundaries have. The entire area known as the Russian Pale of Settlement was part of Poland until it was annexed by Russia between 1772 and 1815. Indeed, in the Middle Ages, Poland was the largest country in Europe, but from 1795 to 1918 it vanished from the map altogether. Germany, too, was not really Germany until Bismarck unified a collection of miscellaneous kingdoms and duchies in 1870.

All of this is important to remember because if official records are available, they are likely to be kept in the country where the town is located *now*. Hungary, for example, has centralized records for all births, deaths and marriages since 1895, but these records apparently cover only areas that are part of Hungary today.

Specific boundary problems will be discussed at greater length elsewhere in this chapter. In any case, a good historical atlas would be a help in discovering what government your ancestors were living under at what particular time. The *Atlas of European History,* by Edward Whiting Fox, is available in paperback. Also useful in a number of ways is Martin Gilbert's *Jewish History Atlas,* which contains 112 maps tracing Jewish history and migrations from Biblical times to the present.

As national boundaries have changed, names of towns have changed, too. What was once Pressburg is now Bratislava; what was once Lemberg is now Lwow (also known as Lvov); what was once the Hungarian Nagy Becskerek is now the Yugoslav Zrenjanin. Thus, if your ancestors left Europe before the maps over there were redrawn by World War I, you may have a hard time locating your ancestral towns today.

You should be able to solve this problem, though, by making use of the map room in any major public library or the Map Division in the Library of Congress in Washington. Not only should you be able to find exceptionally detailed maps of European countries, past and present, but you can also make use of old gazetteers and atlases which can help you locate towns according to the names by which your ancestors knew them.

Especially valuable is *Ritters Geographisch-Statistiches Lexikon.* This German gazetteer is an alphabetical listing of every town in the world at the turn of the century, in some cases down to communities as small as ten people.

Simply look up the name of the town as it's been given to you by your ancestors, and you are likely to find it listed along with its country, state, district, county, population and other details, such as whether it had a post office. For larger towns and districts, *Ritters* sometimes breaks down the population according to Protestants, Catholics and Jews. The one thing *Ritters* doesn't provide is the precise longitude and latitude of the towns it lists. Nevertheless, *Ritters* gives you enough other clues (county, district, etc.) so that by scouring an old, detailed map of the region—ask for one at your local library map room—you may be able to find the town you're looking for.

Don't be shy, incidentally, about asking for help in a library map room. Most of these places, I've found, are underutilized by the public, and the librarians are only too happy to expose you to the rare treasures in their map departments. I spent several years, for example, searching for a map which located my grandfather's tiny village in Czechoslovakia. Even when I went to Czechoslovakia, and even when I visited the village itself, I could not find such a map. But in the Map Division of the New York Public Library I found a military map of Hungary made in 1880 which was drawn to such a large scale that not only did it include my grandfather's village, it actually had a mark for every *house* in the village.

Also helpful in library map departments is another German book, *Stielers Hand Atlas,* published in several editions between about 1890 and 1920. Its listings aren't as minute as *Ritters,* but it has detailed maps of Europe together with an index. (*Ritters* is merely a gazetteer; it has no maps at all.)

If you know the *present* name and country of your ancestral village, the easiest way to locate it is in the country-by-country gazetteers published by the U.S. Board on Geographic Names. These books, too, should be available in your library's map room, and they are even more detailed than *Ritters Lexikon.* They provide longitude and latitude of all geographic locations, bar none, within a country's current borders—towns, counties, districts, lakes, hills, rivers, forests, islands, you name it. The series covers 128 countries, including all the countries of Europe except present-day Poland and Czechoslovakia. Of course, if you don't know the present name of your ancestral town, these books won't do you much good.

If you *do* know the town's present name but not its country, look for it in the *London Times World Index-Gazetteer.* This is not as detailed as *Ritters Lexikon*—nothing is—but it lists many small towns and provides longitude and latitude for each, which will enable you to find the towns on maps.

JEWISH LIBRARIES AND GUIDEBOOKS

A trip to Europe is valuable not only for finding your ancestral town but because Europe still offers some of the best Jewish libraries in the world. Especially notable are the British Museum and the Bodleian Library in London, Cambridge University Library, the W. H. Low Library of Hebraica in Trinity College, on the Cambridge campus, and Oxford University Library, all in England. Other outstanding libraries are mentioned throughout this chapter. For a complete rundown, consult the *Guide to Jewish Libraries of the World,* by Josef Fraenkel, or the *European Library Directory,* by Richard C. Lewanski.

Another source worth checking is the "Tentative List of Jewish Cultural Treasures in Axis-Occupied Countries" that appeared in the January 1946 issue of *Jewish Social Studies* (Vol. VIII, No. 1). This 103-page supplement listed Jewish libraries, museums, archives and other resources in countries that had been occupied during World War II by Germany and Italy, and it breaks down these resources according to countries and towns. It does not provide any information as to the state of these resources in 1946, and many of the cultural treasures listed in the supplement have since been moved to Jerusalem, New York or elsewhere. But at the very least, the supplement might provide some leads as to what kinds of information exist from your ancestral town.

Jewish people who are living in Europe may be just as important in your search as archives or libraries. By locating a Jewish institution of any sort in your ancestral town—synagogue, Jewish center, Jewish museum, kosher restaurant, etc.—you may be able to find someone who knows of your family. To find such Jewish institutions, check the following books:

- *Jewish Travel Guide,* published annually by the *Jewish Chronicle* (London).
- *The Selective Guide for the Jewish Traveler,* by Warren Freedman.
- *The Traveler's Guide to Jewish Landmarks of Europe,* by Bernard Postal and Samuel H. Abramson.

Also, before you go, be sure to read the articles on your particular country and town in the *Encyclopaedia Judaica* (Jerusalem, 1971). It is filled with articles on Jewish communities throughout Europe, and in many cases describes their status today.

The following four books are especially good for details on genealogical research in foreign countries:

- *American Origins,* by Leslie G. Pine.
- *The Genealogist's Encyclopedia,* by Leslie G. Pine.
- *A Guide to Foreign Genealogical Research,* by Maralyn Wellauer.

• *Genealogical Research: Methods and Sources,* by Milton Rubincam and Jean Stephenson.

On to business:

ALGERIA AND MOROCCO

Jews have been in these two lands at least since the first century C.E. Some North African Jews are descended from Spanish and Portuguese Jews who fled to Morocco and Algeria from the Inquisition after 1492. These Jews are relatively easy to trace because they had family names in Spain, and once in Africa, continued to keep communal records separate from those of the Jews who had been in these countries all along.

These Jews from Spain, like the Spanish Jews who settled in the Ottoman Empire, were known as Ladino Jews. (See the section on Turkey, below, for more background.) As in Turkey, rabbis were very meticulous about the spelling of names and sometimes compiled lists of precise spellings of family names. Some such lists of names from Morocco are on microfilm at the Central Archives for the History of the Jewish People in Jerusalem (see chapter 8). That archive is probably the best place to start before you journey to North Africa.

As mentioned before, many Jewish families had no family names until the twentieth century, and very few were aware of their family histories. But especially in Morocco, it was customary to refer to a man not merely by his father's name but by his grandfather's as well: e.g., Avraham, son of Hayyim, son of Avraham. Thus, if you can find the name of your ancestor, you may find two additional generations as well.

Because record hunting in Algeria and Morocco is a dubious prospect, sources in Israel and the alphabetical listing of names in the back of the book are your best starting points. Other aids:

• *Directory of Archives, Libraries and Schools of Librarianship in Africa,* by E. W. Dadzie and J. Y. Strickland (Paris: UNESCO, 1965).
• *The Scloma Directory of Libraries and Special Collections on Africa,* by Robert Collison (Hamden, Conn.: Archon Books, 1967).
• *The Jews of North Africa,* by Nahum Slouschz.
• *A World Passed By: Scenes and Memories of Jewish Civilization in Europe and North Africa,* by Marvin Lowenthal (New York: Harper's 1933).
• *Reflexions sur l'onomastique judeo-nord-afrique,* by D. Corcos.

ARGENTINA

The first Jews arrived with the early Spanish settlers in the sixteenth century, but the bulk of Argentina's Jews came from Eastern Europe between 1890 and 1920; others came after World War II. Today Argentina's Jewish community comprises 500,000 people, fifth largest in the world, and a figure that represents two thirds of all Jews in Latin America. The Jewish population of Buenos Aires alone is some 360,000.

Birth and marriage certificates can be obtained from the Registro Civil (Civil Registry Office) of the municipality or rural district in which the birth or marriage occurred.

AUSTRALIA

Jews did not arrive in Australia until about 1817, and the greatest number of them have come from Europe since the 1930s. There are today some 70,000 Jews in Australia, of whom more than 60,000 live in Melbourne and Sydney.

Civil registration of births, deaths and marriages has been kept in all states at least as far back as 1856; some go all the way back to the first fleet in 1788. You should apply by mail or in person to the Registrar General of the state concerned. If you fill out an application and pay the fee in advance, the Registrar General's office will search its records for you if you don't know the exact date.

The Great Synagogue in Sydney has material dating back to 1828, including an alphabetically indexed register of births, marriages and deaths. Synagogues in other towns also have records, although Sydney's is by far the oldest.

The best source of information on Australia is an article by Anthony Joseph, "On Tracing Australian Jewish Genealogy," in *Genealogist's Magazine.* Other sources:

• The Australian Jewish Historical Society. Its headquarters at the Falk House in Sydney contains many genealogies.
• The Society of Australian Genealogists, History House, 8 Young Street, Sydney, New South Wales, Australia. It also has branch offices in every Australian state.
• *Guide to Genealogical Sources of Australia and New Zealand,* by Niel Hansen (Melbourne, 1961).

AUSTRIA

The nation today known as Austria is a mere shadow of its former self. If your ancestors were from Austria, they may very well have come from lands that are now part of Czechoslovakia, Poland, the Soviet Union or Germany. Austria has known its present boundaries only since the Austro-Hungarian Empire was broken up in 1918. To determine which present-day nation you want, visit the map room of your local public library, or consult a historical atlas.

Until 1938, the registration of births, deaths and marriages was handled by the various religious denominations. While this means the Austrian government has no vital records prior to 1938, it is an advantage of sorts because Jewish vital records are separate and thus easier to sift through. A great number of Austrian Jewish communal histories, registers, documents, etc., can be found at the Leo Baeck Institute in New York (see chapter 6) and at the Central Archives for the History of the Jewish People in Jerusalem. For birth, death or marriage records in Austria itself, write to:

> Israelitische Kultusgemeinde
> Bauernfeldgasse 4
> A-1190 Vienna

Another address I've been given for the same information is:

> Jewish Record Center
> Schottenring 25
> Vienna 1

Other handwritten sources related to Jewish families can be found at the Vienna Town Hall:

> Wiener Stadtarchiv [or Wiener Stadtbibliothek]
> Rathaus
> A-1010 Vienna

Other possible sources:

• The Institute for Jewish History at the University of Vienna is relatively new and doesn't have much in the way of original sources. Its staff can give you useful advice as to where to turn, though. The address:

> Institut für Judaistik der Universität Vienna
> Ferstelgasse 6/12
> A-1090 Vienna

• Latter-day Saints research paper C-16, "Major Genealogical Record Sources in Austria"; paper C-18, "The Austro-Hungarian Empire Boundary Changes and Their Effect Upon Genealogical Research." (See section on Mormons in chapter 6.)

• The Israelitisch-Theologische Lehranstalt in Vienna has an outstanding Jewish library.
• A genealogical society in Vienna is Heraldisch-Genealogische Gesellschaft "Adler," Haarhof 41, A-1010 Vienna.
• General information in Vienna can be obtained at the U.S. Information Center, Kärntnerstrasse 38, A-1010 Vienna.
• The Central Archives for the History of the Jewish People in Jerusalem has microfilmed Jewish material from the Central State Archives in Vienna (fifteenth–nineteenth centuries). The Central Archives also provides an inventory of Jewish community archives and schools in Burgenland; these data were confiscated in 1938 and are now at the state archives in Eisenstadt. These cover Deutschkreuz (1747–1938), Eisenstadt (1703–1938), Frauenkirchen (1840–1938), Gattendorf (1801–1906), Gussing (1753–1904), Kittsee (1758–1938), Kobersdorf (1804–1931), Lackenbach (1819–1912), Mattersburg (1708–1926), Rechnitz (1687–1938) and Stadtschlaining (1780–1926).
• *Archiv für jüdische Familienforschung* was the publication of a society devoted to Austrian Jewish genealogy. A similar publication by a similar society is *Jüdisches Archiv—Zeitschrift für jüdisches Museal und Buchwesen, Volkskunde und Familienforschung.*
• The Austrian National Library has a good Jewish collection. Its address: Österreichische Nationalbibliothek, Josefplatz, A-1014 Vienna.

BELGIUM

As a sovereign state, Belgium dates only from 1831; prior to that its territory was part of Holland or France. What Belgian records do exist were in some cases removed to France and even to Austria during World Wars I and II. The address of the national archives is:

> Archives Générales du Royaume
> 78 Galerie Ravensteen
> Brussels

There are also state archives in Antwerp, Arlon, Bruges, Hasselt, Liège, Mons, Namur, Ghent and Flanders. Each state archive holds civil-act books recording births, marriages and deaths.

For recent birth, marriage and death records, write to:

> Officier de l'Etat Civil [Officer of Vital Statistics]
> [Name of your town], Belgium

Some Belgian mayors have been helpful to inquiring genealogists. They may be able to tell you where to turn. Write to:

> La Mairie [Town Hall]
> [Name of your town], Belgium

The Belgian state archives contain no Jewish communal records of births, deaths and marriages. The best possible sources of Jewish records are the major Jewish congregations:

Communauté Israelite de Bruxelles
2 rue Joseph Dupont
B-1000 Brussels

Communauté Israel Orthodoxe
67a rue Clinique
B-1070 Brussels

Communauté Israelite Sephardite
47 rue Pavillon
B-1030 Brussels

Israelitische Gemeente van
 Antwerpen
Terlistraat 35
B-2000 Antwerp

Israelitische Orthodoxe Gemeente
 van Antwerpen
Jacob Jacobstraat 22
B-2000 Antwerp

Other sources:

• "L'Organisation du culte israelite en Belgique," by Theodore Baudin, in *Res Publica,* Vol. 1 (1963).
• *Directory of Belgian Research Libraries and Documentation Services* (Brussels, 1967).
• *Les Archives Générales du Royaume,* by M. Van Haegendoren, an inventory of the national archives collection in Brussels.
• Two genealogical societies: (1) Antwerpsche Kring voor Familiekunde, 25 Moonsstraat, Antwerp; (2) Service de Centralisation des Études Généalogiques et Démographiques de Belgique, 26 rue aux Laines, Brussels.

BRAZIL

Large numbers of Marranos—forced converts who observed their Jewish faith in secret—arrived in Brazil from Portugal early in the sixteenth century, but only when the Dutch conquered Pernambuco in 1630 were they finally able to observe Judaism openly. When the Portuguese recaptured Dutch Brazil in 1654, the few Jews there fled the country and came to Nieuw Amsterdam (now New York). There was no Jewish community in Brazil again until the nineteenth century, and the bulk of it came from Europe between 1924, when the United States began restricting immigration, and 1934, when Brazil began restricting immigration. Today the Jewish population of Brazil is about 135,-000, second in Latin America behind Argentina.

For birth, death or marriage records, write to the Registro Civil (Civil Registry Office) of the district or city where the event took place.

BRITAIN

Jews were recorded among the population of England when William the Conqueror arrived in 1066, and William himself brought some French Jews from Rouen. But whatever Jewish families were there then presumably disappeared from England after the Jews were expelled in 1290. There were some 200 Jews in England in the sixteenth century, but they fled after the execution of one of their leading members. Jews did not return in any sizable number until the mid-seventeenth century. First to arrive were Sephardim, who came from France and Portugal, sometimes by way of Holland; in 1680 there were some 2,000 Sephardic Jews in London. The first Ashkenazic Jews arrived from Poland, Germany, Central Europe, Alsace and Holland in the late seventeenth century. By 1738 there were supposedly 6,000 Jews living in England, and presumably most of those 6,000 have descendants today, probably in England or in America. Many of them, however, were absorbed by intermarriage into the general population.

Whatever the case, if your ancestors were English, you should have a reasonably good chance of finding them. For one thing, complete birth, death and marriage registrations for all England are on file and may be inspected by anyone at Somerset House, London W.C. 2. If you can't get there in person, you can apply for a copy of a certificate by mail. There is a small fee, but all inquiries are answered promptly.

For another thing, while the English are generally reserved and understated about most things, they go positively haywire over the subject of genealogy, and English Jews are no exception. Any number of books and articles have been written on the subject of Jewish genealogy in Great Britain. A few possible starting points:

• The British Museum has one of the best Jewish collections in the world— not just for Britain, but for all countries. It has records of Jewish business and taxation from the pre–1290 period, but no synagogue registers have survived from that era. Excellent British collections can also be found at Oxford and Cambridge universities. Also at Cambridge is the W. H. Low Library of Hebraica in Trinity College.

• The Jewish Historical Society of England, 33 Seymour Place, London W. 1, has a great deal of material, including a collection of Anglo-Jewish genealogies bequeathed by the late Sir Thomas Colyer-Fergusson. The society's *Transactions* (1893 onward) and its *Miscellanies* (1925 onward) contain birth and death records and other genealogical data, and the volumes from 1893 through 1945 have been cumulatively indexed.

• The Anglo-Jewish Historical Exhibition of 1887 in London produced two notable sources for Anglo-Jewish genealogists. The first is the catalogue of the exhibition itself, by Lucien Wolf and Dr. Joseph Jacobs. It lists 2,600 exhibits, including a mass of biographical data and family documents. Note especially exhibit No. 762, a collection of fifty-eight Jewish family-tree charts. The second is *Bibliotheca Anglo-Judaica,* a bibliographical guide to Anglo-Jewish History, also by Lucien Wolf. It covers the period from 1657 to 1886 and includes a small section (pp. 120–122) devoted to biographies, followed by an abridged biographical dictionary with references on some 230 Anglo-Jewish figures.

• *Bevis Marks Records.* Bevis Marks Synagogue was the original post-Cromwellian Sephardic congregation of London; this book contains, among other things, marriage registers from 1687 through 1837. Birth and burial records can be seen at the synagogue itself (London, E.C.3).

• *Archives of the United Synagogue,* by Cecil Roth. The United Synagogue served the Ashkenazic Jews of London; this book catalogues many valuable genealogical records. The records themselves can be seen at the offices of the United Synagogue at Woburn House, London W.1.

• *Burke's General Armoury of 1884* contains over sixty entries of Jewish families. Other entries can be found in subsequent editions.

• There are about seven inactive Jewish cemeteries in London, some dating back to the early eighteenth century. Most are supervised by the Jewish Board of Deputies, London. The *Jewish Year Book* lists Jewish cemeteries under the heading "London—Ecclesiastical Administration." Burial registers are usually kept at the grounds if there is a resident caretaker; otherwise, they are at the appropriate synagogue.

• Outside London, there are perhaps a dozen congregations formed before 1830: Brighton (1823), Dublin (seventeenth century), Edinburgh (1816), Exeter (1775), Hull (1826), Liverpool (1790), Manchester (about 1780), Nottingham (1823), Plymouth (1767), Portsmouth (1747), Sheffield (1790) and Swansea (about 1780). These should be consulted for records in their respective areas.

• The first London city directory of 1677 (reissued in 1878 by Chatto & Windus) contains names and addresses of at least fifty Jewish merchants, although only two appear to be Ashkenazic. Jewish names can also be found in late-eighteenth-century London and provincial directories, as well as subsequent directories.

• The first purely Jewish directory to appear was *The Jewish Directory for 1874,* by A.I. Myers (London). Then came *The Jewish Calendar, Manual and Diary,* by Rachel Myers (London, 1888–1899), and then *The Commercial Directory of the Jews of the United Kingdom,* by G.E. Harfield (London, 1893). The *Jewish Chronicle* began publishing its *Jewish Year Book* in 1896; among other things, it contains a large "Communal Directory" each year. *Service for the Two First Nights of Passover,* by A. Alexander (London, 1770) has 145 names and addresses, while *Fast Day Services,* Vol. VI, by D. Levi (London, 1793), provides over two hundred names and addresses of English and American Jews.

• *Anglo-Jewish Notabilities,* by the Jewish Historical Society of England, is a concise biographical dictionary and catalogue of Anglo-Jewish coats of arms.

• An alphabetical index of all wills of Jews, compiled by Arthur Arnold, is available at Somerset House, London W.C.2.

• Perhaps the best overview can be obtained from "Sources of Anglo-Jewish Genealogy," by Wilfred Samuel, in *Genealogist's Magazine* (December 1932); his information was updated by his son, Edgar Samuel, in "Jewish Ancestors and Where to Find Them" in the same magazine (December 1953).

• Other English libraries with major Jewish collections include the Wiener Library in London, Jews College in London, the Mocatta Library at University College, London, and the Bodleian Library in London.

• *The Western Synagogue Through Two Centuries,* by Arthur Barnett, has some details on Ashkenazic settlements in London.

• "Old Anglo-Jewish Families," by Lucien Wolf, in *Essays in Jewish History.*

• *A List of Jews and Their Households in London, Extracted from the Census List of 1695,* by Arthur P. Arnold.

• "Jewish Obituaries in the *Gentleman's Magazine*" (1731–1868), by Albert Montefiore Hyamson, in *Miscellanies of the Jewish Historical Society of England.*

• *Sources for Roman Catholic and Jewish Genealogy and Family History,* by D. J. Steel and Edgar R. Samuel, contains numerous specific source references for Jewish data in Britain.

BULGARIA

Records of Jews in Bulgaria have been found from as early as the year 811 C.E. Some were Sephardim who later came from Spain and Portugal during the Inquisition. There were 30,000 Jews in Bulgaria in 1900. (Bulgaria was long part of the Ottoman Empire. See the section on Turkey, below).

Civil registration of births, deaths and marriages began in 1893. Write to the District People's Council in the place the event occurred. Older documents are with the Ministry of Justice in Sofia, but it is not known whether these include any Jewish records. Religious groups began keeping registers in 1860; again, it's not clear whether this applies to Jews as well.

Wills are kept by the local notary public, or if made privately, with the notary of the People's Court in the appropriate district.

This vague information is the best I can provide about a country that has not thus far been open in its dealings with the rest of the world. Perhaps you can learn more through a personal visit.

One last suggestion:—*Spravochnik na Bibliotekitev Bolgariya*, by Snezhina Tosheva (Sofia, 1963), is a directory to libraries in Bulgaria. Needless to add, it's in Bulgarian.

THE CARIBBEAN

The first Jews arrived in this area from Spain and Portugal in the seventeenth and eighteenth centuries; some came from Holland, although generally they, too, were of Spanish origin. Many of these families have since migrated to the United States and Canada.

Barbados, the West Indies—Birth and marriage certificates are obtainable from the Registrar of Barbados. Marriage certificates can also be obtained from the head of the appropriate Jewish community, if one still exists.

Jamaica—Birth and marriage certificates may be obtained from the Registrar General, Spanish Town, Jamaica.

Netherlands Antilles—Birth and marriage certificates may be obtained from the Civil Registrar's Office of the island of the birth or marriage.

The following books may be of use to you:

• *Jewish Memorial Inscriptions in Barbados*, by E. M. Shilstone, lists inscriptions on tombstones and makes some cross-references to public documents.
• *Precious Stones of the Jews of Curaçao: Curaçaoan Jewry, 1656–1957*, by I. S. Emmanuel. Contains biographies, genealogies and tombstone inscriptions.
• *History of the Jews of Jamaica*, by J. A. T. Andrade. This book is full of names, tombstone inscriptions, documents, etc.
• *History of the Jews in the Netherlands Antilles*, by S. M. Emmanuel.
• *A Guide to Jewish History in the Caribbean*, by Malcolm Stern and Bernard Postal.

CZECHOSLOVAKIA

This country was created in 1918 out of the former regions of Bohemia, Moravia, Slovakia and parts of Silesia. From 1867 to 1918 it was part of the Austro-Hungarian Empire; since 1947 it has been Communist.

An Austrian law of 1726 provided for the registration of heads of Jewish families, and for more than a hundred years, restricted the number of Jewish families to 8,600 families in Bohemia, 5,400 in Moravia and also a limited number in Silesia. To keep the number of Jewish families constant, only one son from each registered Jewish family was permitted to marry (families which had no sons were regarded as extinct), and even that son could not marry until his father had died. The law wasn't repealed until the Jews were emancipated in 1849.

The advantage of this law for us is that it is one of the earliest known cases of a government attempt to register Jews; the disadvantage is that it forced Jews into secrecy and subterfuge and thus makes it even more difficult to trace families. Many Jews reacted to these "Familianten" laws by marrying secretly according to Jewish ritual, or by marrying in other countries, such as Slovakia, which was not then a part of Austria.

Nevertheless, Czechoslovakia is the only Communist country that has a formal procedure for handling requests from genealogists. American researchers from the Society for the History of Czechoslovak Jews say that it is possible to obtain individual documentation of the birth, marriage and death data from old Jewish records (Matriky-Matriken) that survived the Nazi Holocaust. Records in Prague apply to Jews in Bohemia and Moravia; in Bratislava, to Jews in Slovakia.

Individual requests for genealogical records should be addressed to the Consular Division of the Embassy of the Czechoslovak Socialist Republic, 3900 Linnean Avenue N.W., Washington, D.C. 20008. The embassy will then forward your request to the Administration of the Archives of the Ministry of the Interior in Prague. The embassy will also send you a brochure entitled *Information on Securing Family History from Czechoslovakia.*

The Czech archivists can't trace Holocaust victims, but they do have Jewish records going back to the nineteenth century, and some registration data from the fifteenth and sixteenth centuries. There is a fee of $5.50 per hour for searching out your records, and an advance deposit of $30 is required. Americans who have used the service say the fee for a search usually comes to $50 or $60, and that the results have been well worth the cost. One other caveat: the report you receive will be in the Czech or Slovak language only.

The Society for the History of Czechoslovak Jews is itself a good source if you need more specific advice. Its address is 23 Mayhew Avenue, Larchmont, N.Y. 10538. For background on Czechoslovakia, consult the society's two-volume series, *The Jews of Czechoslovakia.* Among other things, Vol. II has a valuable chapter on Jewish cemeteries in Slovakia.

The Central Archives for the History of the Jewish People in Jerusalem (see chapter 8) has microfilmed Jewish material from the Archives of the Ministry of the Interior in Prague. This material covers 1591 through 1745 but isn't specifically genealogical.

Civil registration of births, deaths and marriages did not start in Czechoslovakia until 1918, and even then it was not compulsory except for people who did not belong to any church. Since 1950 all registration has been taken over by the state, and you can obtain copies of birth, marriage and death certificates since 1950 by applying to the Consular Division of the Czech Embassy in Washington (3900 Linnean Avenue NW) or the Ministry of Foreign Affairs in Prague.

Although the registers for 1918–1950 are unlikely to yield much of value to Jews, you can peruse them at town halls, where they are kept. (In the case of villages, one register may cover several places in one book.) A list of the existing registry offices is available. All information regarding civil registration, but not actual copies of the records, can be obtained from two main archives: for Bohemia and Moravia, write to Archivni Sprava, Trida Obrancumiru 133, Prague 6. For Slovakia, write to Slovenska Archivni Sprava, Vajanskeho, Nabrezi 8, Bratislava.

There are state-operated Jewish archives in both Prague and Bratislava; you can learn more about these at the two addresses above.

Regional archives, for whatever they're worth, are located in:

> Ceske Budejovice-Trebon
> Ostrava-Kinstat
> Jihlava-Telc
> Karlovy-Vary-Kasterec nad Ohri

You can also get general information from Cedok, the Czechoslovak Travel Bureau, in virtually every town of 10,000 or more population in Czechoslovakia, and in the United States at:

> Cedok
> 10 East 40th Street
> New York, N.Y. 10016

Ask Cedok for its brochure on *Jewish Monuments in Czechoslovakia.*

There was a genealogical society in Czechoslovakia prior to 1947, but it was one of the first casualties of the Communist regime. In recent years, though, the state publishing house has been producing some useful books for genealogists.

• *Ceskoslovensky Vojensky Atlas* (Prague, 1965) is an excellent state-published world atlas with maps of Czechoslovakia so detailed that barely a hamlet is missing. It can be found in the map rooms of most major American public libraries.

• *Die Deutschen in der Tschechoslowakei,* 1933–1947, ed. by Vacloc Kral (Prague, 1964), lists place-name changes from German to Czech on pages 641–643. This is a good way to find towns which were once part of Austria-Hungary but have since changed names.

• *O Ceskych Prymenich,* by Josef Benes (Prague, 1962), contains information about Czech surnames.

Another book that might be helpful is

• *In Search of Freedom: A History of American Jews From Czechoslovakia,* by Guido Kisch.

Of seven synagogues still standing in Prague, only two serve congregations; the rest have been converted by the government into Jewish museums. They are fascinating to visit, but somewhat disturbing too, for they give the impression that they are memorials to an extinct civilization. There is not much of genealogical use in these museums, but you never can tell. Also worth looking at—but again a long shot in terms of genealogical value—is the old Jewish cemetery. It was used until 1787 and contains 12,000 graves, many piled on top of one another because of the limited burial space that Jews were permitted.

DENMARK

Jews have been in Denmark since about 1600; there were about 4,000 Jews there in 1893. Civil registration of births, deaths and marriages began in Denmark in the 1850s. Registrations since then are kept in the Public Record office, of which there are four: (1) in Copenhagen, which includes Zeeland, Lolland-Falster, Bornholm and the former Danish colonies; (2) in Aabenraa, which covers South Jutland; (3) in Viborg, which covers North Jutland; and (4) in Odense, which covers Funen.

Records of Jewish interest can be found in the state archives (Rigsarkivet), covering 1619–1849. The address is:

> Rigsarkivet
> Rigsdagsgården 9
> 1218 Copenhagen

An inventory of available Jewish records there and at the German Chancery in Copenhagen can be obtained from the Central Archives for the History of the Jewish People in Jerusalem (see chapter 8). The Central Archives in Jerusalem also has inventories for material on the Jewish communities of Copenhagen, Aalborg, Aarhus, Assens, Faaborg, Fredericia, Horsens, Nakskov, Randers, Slagelse and Viborg, 1720–1956.

In the United States, the Genealogical Society of the Mormon Church has microfilmed Danish census records for 1787 through 1911. Its research papers, Series D, nos. 5 through 10, provide specific information about genealogical records in Denmark.

Other possible helpful sources:

• The Royal Library in Copenhagen includes the Bibliotheca Judaica Simonseniana, a large Jewish collection. Look particularly for the works of the Danish Rabbi Josef Fischer (1871–1949), who wrote extensively on the genealogies of Danish Jewish families. Separate from its Jewish collection, the library also has a large genealogy collection, although few books in it are Jewish. Its address:

Det Kongelige Bibliothek
Christians Brygge 8
1219 Copenhagen

• *The Genealogical Guidebook and Atlas of Denmark,* by Frank Smith and Finn A. Thomsen. This is an excellent general guidebook describing Danish census returns, church records, probate records, military levying rolls, Danish words and their meanings, and 64 pages of large-scale maps with an index of 12,000 communities.
• Danish Embassy, 3200 Whitehaven Street N.W., Washington, D.C. 20008.
• *History of the Danish Jews,* by Benjamin Balsler.

FRANCE

Jews were in France in the first century C.E. During the twelfth, thirteenth, and fourteenth centuries there were several expulsions of Jews, the last in 1394. During some of this time, at least, Jews remained in the south of France, in the Perpignan and Avignon regions. After 1492 some of the Jewish population of France were Sephardim fleeing from Spain. In 1799 French Jews were emancipated, and in 1900 there were about 100,000 Jews in France, of whom 60,000 were in Paris. Today the French Jewish population is about 550,000, of whom some 300,000 are North African Jews who came in the 1960s after Algeria and Morocco became independent of France.

Civil registration began in France in 1791, and Jews were required to take family names in 1808. By French law, municipalities can keep their records as long as they want; that is, they don't have to turn the records over to the *département* (county) or the national government in Paris. Still, 99 percent of French registration records, including communal lists of Jews in Paris and Alsace, survive today. As one of my French friends observes, "We French keep our records very faithfully. The problem is finding them."

Fortunately for Jews, many of the French registers have been microfilmed by the Central Archives for the History of the Jewish People in Jerusalem (see chapter 8), which also has registers for scattered French Jewish communities going back to Metz in 1711. It also has a list of Alsatian Jews, by family and town, printed in 1784 (the number of Jews in Alsace was restricted by law); lists of Jews, probably mostly Sephardic, in Bordeaux and Bayonne before the Revolution; Hebrew books from eighteenth-century Avignon and the Papal States in southern France. Jews who had professions in 1808 needed a permit; the Jerusalem Archives has some of these on microfilm too. But to find individual French Jewish records before 1720, you must be very dedicated indeed.

The Jerusalem archives has microfilmed Jewish material at the following French public sources:

- Avignon, Departmental Archives of Vaucluse (15th–18th centuries); Museum Calvet (17th–18th centuries).
- Bayonne, Municipal Archives (18th century).
- Bordeaux, Departmental Archives of Gironde (18th century).
- Carpentras, Municipal Archives and Library (16th–18th centuries).
- Chambery, Departmental Archives of Savoie (13th–14th centuries).
- Colmar, Departmental Archives of Haut-Rhin (16th–18th centuries); Municipal Archives (17th–18th centuries).
- Dijon, Departmental Archives of Côte d'Or (14th century).
- Grenoble, Departmental Archives of Isère (14th–15th centuries).
- Marseilles, Chamber of Commerce (18th century).
- Metz, Departmental Archives of Moselle (16th–18th centuries); Municipal Archives (18th century).
- Paris, National Archives (12th–18th centuries); National Library (13th–19th centuries); Arsenal Library (18th century).
- Strasbourg, Departmental Archives of Bas-Rhin (16th–18th centuries); Municipal Archives (16th–18th centuries); National and University Library (17th–18th centuries).
- Troyes, Departmental Archives of Aube (13th–14th centuries).

The Central Archives in Jerusalem also has inventories of Jewish material at other archives and museums in Avignon, Bayonne, Carpentras, Chambery, Colmar, Marseilles, Metz, Orange, Paris and Strasbourg.

If you are in France and would prefer to visit the departmental archives offices personally, a complete list of these offices and their addresses is available in Leslie G. Pine's *Genealogist's Encyclopedia.* The National Archives' address is:

> Archives Nationales de France
> 60 rue des Francs-Bourgeois
> Paris 3

The National Archives in Paris is considered very good for registrations of births, deaths and marriages from 1800 on.

For records of births, deaths or marriages since 1791, write to La Mairie (Town Hall) of the place where the event occurred. Some large cities have a number of districts, each having a mayor.

There are no functioning Jewish cemeteries in France today, since municipal governments have a monopoly on burials (except in Alsace-Lorraine, where cemeteries are still privately operated). However, some municipal cemeteries may have sections for Jews. And most of the old Jewish cemeteries in France still exist; some French Jews have found graves in these cemeteries dating back to the fifteenth century. One of the great problems with Ashkenazic cemeteries, though, is that the standing tombstones have sunk over the years and are today buried under the ground, presumably next to the corpses they represent.

Other useful sources (the French consulate in New York, tel.: 212/535–0100, can supply addresses for the first three):

- The Bibliothèque de l'Alliance Israelite Universelle in Paris is a substantial Jewish library; there is also a good library at the École Rabbinique de France in Paris.
- The Centre de Documentation Juive Contemporaine in Paris also has a large Jewish library and can provide information on tracing more recent relatives.
- The Bibliothèque Nationale in Paris has an extensive Jewish collection.
- The Strasbourg University library also has a large Judaica and Hebraica department.
- *Guide des Recherches Généalogiques aux Archives,* by Jacques De Tupigny (Paris, 1956), is a genealogical inventory of the French National Archives.
- "Major Genealogical Record Sources in France," Latter-day Saints research paper, Series G, no. 1, 1973. (See section on Mormons in chapter 6.)
- YIVO Institute in New York has an extensive set of records from World War II dealing with the disposition of French Jews and Jewish refugees in France, 1941–1943. (See section on YIVO in chapter 6.)
- *Les Noms des israelites en France: Histoire et dictionnaire,* by P. Levy.
- *Franco-Judaica: A Bibliography, 1500–1788.*
- *Analytical Franco-Jewish Gazetteer, 1939–1945,* with an introduction to some problems in writing the history of Jews in France during World War II, by Zosa Szajkowski.

GERMANY

From the peculiar viewpoint of a modern Jewish genealogist, it might seem that the Germans of the past have spent virtually all their time in two pursuits: (1) exterminating Jews, and (2) keeping meticulous records of all the Jews they exterminated. There is, in fact, a wealth of Jewish birth, death and marriage data available today from countless German communities back to the eighteenth century and beyond, notwithstanding the fact that there is only a handful of Jews living in Germany today.

Before you set foot in Germany, pay a visit to the Leo Baeck Institute in New York (see chapter 6). Also, the Central Archives for the History of the Jewish People in Jerusalem (see chapter 8) is largely run by German Jews, and its most complete genealogical data come from Germany.

Another prelude to a visit to Germany should be the reading of an article entitled "Registration of Births, Deaths and Marriages in European Jewish Communities, in Palestine and in Israel," by Mrs. R. Blumenthal, Mrs. C. Fraenkel, Dr. J. Raba and P. A. Alsberg. The article first appeared in *Archivum,* Vol. 9 (Paris, 1959), and a reprint can be obtained from the Central Archives in Jerusalem (again, see chapter 8); the article is also largely reprinted in the section on Jewry in Leslie Pine's *Genealogist's Encyclopedia.* It outlines procedures for eighteenth- and nineteenth-century registration of births, deaths and marriages in Jewish communities in the seventeen kingdoms, duchies, protectorates and free cities that united into Germany in 1870. To find which of these areas your ancestors came from, check the map room of your nearby public library or consult a good historical atlas.

Civil registration has been compulsory in Germany since 1876; records since then are kept in the civil-registry office of the place of the birth, death or marriage. I have no information about vital records in East Germany, but in the Federal Republic of Germany, write to:

Standesamt [Civil Registry Office]
[Name of your town], Germany

The Germans have also kept emigration records, and as we have seen, for $3 the staff of the state archives in Hamburg will search through passenger lists of ships departing from the Hamburg-Kiel area. (Passenger lists for the port of Bremerhaven were destroyed in World War II.) Write to:

Staatsarchiv
Rathaus Markt I
2000 Hamburg, Federal Republic of Germany

These same records are also available on microfilm, at the Genealogical Society Library in Salt Lake City, Utah (for 1850 through 1934, indexed) and at the Manuscript Division of the Library of Congress in Washington (for 1850 through 1873), both discussed in chapter 6. This Staatsarchiv also has detailed records of old and recent Jewish congregations.

If all this isn't enough, in recent years there has been a new wave of studies and exhibits about German Jewish communities of the past. Much of this valuable work is being done by non-Jews, perhaps as a form of guilt therapy. Just about every city in Germany has Jewish records in its archives or local library, and Jews who write to these archives and libraries invariably seem to get a prompt and warm response. Histories of individual German Jewish communities have been appearing in Germany recently at the rate of about thirty new books a year. Most of these, though, can be found without going to Germany: check with the Leo Baeck Institute in New York. Some of them delve into the sort of minute detail that will delight genealogists: a book on the Jews of Hamburg now in the works, for example, will include inscriptions from Jewish gravestones beginning in 1712.

The Institute for the History of German Jews does not have specific genealogical material, but it is engaged in gathering records and producing Jewish community histories, and its staff might be able to point you in a worthwhile direction. Its address:

Institut für die Geschichte der deutschen Juden
Rothenbaumchaussée 7
2 Hamburg 13, Federal Republic of Germany

Germany is also one of the few countries where there has been organized interest in the past in specifically Jewish genealogy. A society for German-Jewish genealogy flourished before World War II; its quarterly publication, *Jüdische Familienforschung,* was published from 1924 through 1938 and contains numerous family and community histories, mostly German but some from other countries. The back issues can be found at most Jewish libraries, along with a cumulative index that covers the first thirty-eight issues (there were fifty issues altogether). The names in that index have been integrated into the alphabetical listing at the end of this book.

Other sources:

• *Mein Stammbaum: Eine genealogische Anleitung für deutsche Juden,* by Arthur Czellitzer, tells how to trace Jewish ancestors in Germany. It's written in German, of course, and dates from before the war, so some of the sources it cites may no longer be available.
• *Die Familiennamen der Juden in Deutschland,* by G. Kessler.
• *Grosse jüdische National-Biographie.*
• "Namen der Juden, 1837," by Leopold Zunz, in *Gesammelte Schriften,* Vol. II (1876), pp. 1–82.
• The state libraries in Berlin, Munich and Hamburg have extensive Jewish collections; so do the municipal libraries of Frankfurt and Leipzig (East Germany).
• *The Atlantic Bridge to Germany,* by Charles M. Hall, is filled with large-scale maps and indexes of the tiniest communities; it's a good aid to locating the town your ancestors came from.
• *Encyclopedia of German-American Genealogical Research* has a chapter on German Jews.
• "German-Jewish Names in America," by Rudolf Glanz, in *Jewish Social Studies* (July 1961), pp. 143–167.
• The *Yearbook* of the Leo Baeck Institute has articles which may be of some use to researchers.
• The Mormons' Genealogical Society library in Salt Lake City has microfilmed birth, death and marriage records in East Prussia (1812–1950) and Osterode (1865–1936), which were German at the time but are now part of Poland. (See chapter 6 for details.)
• A new comprehensive handbook to archives in all German-language areas (West Germany, East Germany, Austria, Switzerland, some of Czechoslovakia) includes mention of Jewish archives. Title: *Archive im deutschsprachigen Raum, Minerva Handbücher.* It is available at the Leo Baeck Institute in New York.

GREECE

Jews here date to pre-Christian times. The Jewish population was 9,000 in 1903, of whom most were Ladino Jews—that is, of Sephardic descent—whose ancestors had fled from the Inquisition in Spain and Portugal. For much of the past six hundred years Greece was part of the Ottoman Empire; see the section on Turkey, below, for a greater description of Jewish records under Ottoman rule. Suffice it to say here that they are haphazard at best.

Since 1912, religious groups have been required to register births, deaths and marriages in Greece. In some areas these statistics were registered as early as 1856. The names of all Greek citizens are maintained in local archives, a system that was begun in 1933 but was not practiced efficiently until 1954.

HUNGARY

The fact that your ancestors considered themselves Hungarians does not necessarily mean they came from the area known today as Hungary. Modern Hungary is only a small part of the pre–World War I Hungary, which embraced some areas of what are now Czechoslovakia, Yugoslavia, Rumania and the Soviet Union.

Nevertheless, if you *do* have roots within the boundaries of modern Hungary, you are luckier than most East European Jews, for the records here are better and more accessible than in neighboring countries. Civil registration of births, marriages and deaths in Hungary began on October 1, 1895, and those records are kept in the National Center of Archives. (The records held by the Archives apply only to areas within Hungary's present borders, even though many other areas were part of Hungary from 1895 until 1918.) Relatives may apply for registration records to the Archives at this address:

> Leveltarak Orszagos Kozpontja
> Uri Utca 54–56
> Budapest I

Besides this center, there are twenty-two provincial archives where more information may be available. A directory of archives offices and libraries in Hungary can be found in an article on "Hungary's Libraries," by Aurelien Hencz, in *Library Journal,* Vol. 81 (1956). Also useful is the two-volume *Hungarian Library Directory,* published in Budapest in 1965. The Hungarian National Library in Budapest has a sizable Jewish collection.

If your ancestors were in Hungary *before* October 1, 1895, their birth, death and marriage records may be even *more* accessible, believe it or not. Shortly after World War I, the Hungarian government gathered the pre-1895 records as they had been kept by all religious denominations—Catholic, Protestant and, yes, Jewish. These include not only present-day Hungary, but areas that were Hungarian before 1918, and some of these records go as far back as the late eighteenth century. These records have since been microfilmed by those genealogical zealots, the Mormons, and are available at the Genealogical

Society library in Salt Lake City or at any of its branch libraries around the country. The Jewish records are conveniently separate from the rest—there are 250 reels for Hungarian Jews alone—and they are also conveniently broken down by present-day counties and towns, and also by present countries. (The tiniest towns, however, are often included in the registrations of larger nearby communities.)

Other valuable guidance in the United States can be obtained from the World Federation of Hungarian Jews (136 East 39th Street, New York, N.Y. 10016). Among other things, it has published a 3-volume work entitled *Hungarian Jewish Studies.* One article in Vol. I, "Family Tree of Hungarian Jewry," discusses Hungarian Jewish migrations; another in the same volume, "Hungarian Jewry: Settlement and Demography, 1735 to 1910," contains a list of Jewish communities in Hungary, but it is not complete.

Some Hungarian Jewish material is also available at the Diaspora Research Institute of Tel Aviv University in Israel. (See chapter 8 for details.)

Also possibly helpful is the *Magyar Zsido Lexikon* (Hungarian Jewish encyclopedia), by Peter Ujvari, which has articles on Hungarian Jewish communities and individuals.

IRAQ

Jews have been in Iraq continuously almost since the Babylonian exile of 586 B.C.E. Even today there is a small Jewish community there, probably numbering not more than 5,000.

Birth certificates for persons born prior to 1921 can be obtained from heads of religious communities (including rabbis) or from local dignitaries (mukhtars). Official public records, based on public records and issued by municipal offices or by the Census Department, are available only for persons born after 1921.

For background, see *A History of the Jews in Baghdad,* by D. S. Sassoon.

ITALY

Some Italian Jewish families claim to be descendants of Jews who lived in Italy in the first century C.E., and since Jewish family names came into use here early in the Middle Ages, many Italian families can be traced back seven or eight hundred years. This is helpful to East European Jews, too, since the great number of Italian Jews moved on to Poland in the latter part of the Middle Ages.

Because of this background, Italy was until the nineteenth century the leading source of Jewish libraries and still contains many important book and manuscript collections. The Hebrew department of the library in Parma has over 2,000 old manuscripts. Other extensive Judaica collections can be found in the Vatican Library, the Biblioteca Casanatense, Biblioteca Angelica, Biblioteca Nazionale, Biblioteca Vittorio Emmanuele, and Biblioteca della Pia Casa dei Neofiti, all in Rome; the Biblioteca Mediceo-Laurentiana in Florence; the University Library of Bologna; the Royal Library at Modena; the Biblioteca Marciana in Venice; and the Ambrosiana in Milan.

On the other hand, Italy itself has been a unified nation only since 1870, and while the civil records since then are well preserved, records before that date are haphazard. For information about birth, death or marriages in Rome, write to:

> Istituto Centrale di Statistica
> Via Cesare Balbo 16
> Rome

For civil records from other communities, write to:

> Ufficio di Stato Civil [Office of Vital Statistics]
> [Name of your town], Italy

A great deal of Jewish material exists in the national archives and in the thirteen state archives and various municipal archives. Much of this has been microfilmed and/or inventoried by the Central Archives for the History of the Jewish People in Jerusalem, and is available there (see chapter 7). Microfilmed Jewish material at the Central Archives in Jerusalem includes:

- Como, State Archives (16th century).
- Cremona, State Archives; Municipal Archives (16th–17th centuries).
- Ferrara, Municipal Archives (1507–1831).
- Milan, State Archives (15th–19th centuries).
- Modena, State Archives (15th–18th centuries).
- Parma, State Archives (1451–1750).
- Pavia, State Archives (16th–18th centuries).
- Rovigo, Accademia dei Concordi (17th century).
- Trieste, Municipal Library (18th century).
- Venice, State Archives (14th–18th centuries); Museum Correr (16th–18th centuries).

This material is, of course, available at the various Italian archives themselves, in addition to being on microfilm in Jerusalem. The Central Archives there has also made up inventories of other materials still in Italy on the Jewish community of Rome (1566–1852) and of Jewish materials in state archives and other archives at Acqui, Alexandria, Bergamo, Crema, Cremona, Florence, Guastalla, Milan, Modena, Novara, Padua, Palermo, Perugia, Siena, Turin, Venice, Verona and Vicenza.

The national archives are located at:

Archivio Centrale della Stato
Corso Rinnascimento 40
Rome

Other helpful sources:

• "The State Public Libraries of Italy," by Anne Martinelli, in *Library Quarterly,* Vol. 25 (1955), pp. 163–170.
• "Major Genealogical Record Sources in Italy," Latter-day Saints research paper, Series G, no. 2.
• "Stemmi di famiglie ebraice italiane" (Family Trees of Italian Jews), by Cecil Roth, in *Scritti in memoria di Leone Carpi.*
• Back issues of *Corriere Israelitico,* an Italian monthly founded in 1863 and devoted to Jewish history and literature.
• Italian genealogical societies include Genealogico Italiano (Castelli 19, Florence) and the Istituto Italiano di Cultura (686 Park Avenue, New York, N.Y. 10021).
• Italian Embassy, 1601 Fuller Avenue, Washington, D.C. 20009.
• Some Italian Jewish material is available at the Diaspora Research Institute, Tel Aviv University, Israel. (See chapter 8.)

LATVIA

Jews have been in Riga, the capital of Latvia, at least since 1560; in the 1897 census there were 30,700 Jews in the city. In Courtland (Kurland), a region of western Latvia, there were 8,000 Jews counted in 1800, and 49,000 in 1897. Except for the period between the two world wars, Latvia through most of its history has been incorporated into other countries. Today it is a Soviet Socialist Republic. For more information, see the section on the Soviet Union.

LITHUANIA

Jews have been in Lithuania since the eighth century, and in the eighteenth century their population numbered 250,000. For virtually all of the past six hundred years, Lithuania has been under the rule of some other country. It was once a grand duchy, but in 1385 it was united with Poland. When Poland was dismembered, the section that had been Lithuania came under the aegis of Russia in 1796. In 1918 Lithuania finally became an independent country, but this arrangement lasted only twenty-two years: Lithuania was overrun by the Nazis in 1940, was annexed by the Soviet Union in 1944 and is now a Soviet Socialist Republic.

Even during its brief independence, Lithuania maintained the practice of having heads of religious denominations keep registers of births, deaths and marriages. These registers and many older registers have been sent to the Central Archives in Kaunas, Lithuania, but it is not clear how accessible they are to the public. Wills were probated in local courts of justices of the peace prior to 1933, and after that in the district courts, where wills were part of the public record and accessible to any interested party in the archives of the particular court. There was no central depository of these documents. Leslie Pine, in *American Origins,* speculates that the probating of wills in Lithuania is today done by notaries public.

The best source of information about Lithuanian Jews may well be the YIVO Institute in New York, which has extensive records of the Vilna Jewish community as well as about a hundred other Jewish communities in the period 1919 to 1923, some of which include vital statistics. (See chapter 6, and also the sections on Poland and the Soviet Union in this chapter.)

THE NETHERLANDS (HOLLAND)

Jews have been in the Netherlands at least since the early fourteenth century, when groups arrived there after having been expelled from France and England. In 1536, Spanish and Portuguese Jewish refugees from the Inquisition were permitted to settle there, and Dutch cities, especially Amsterdam, became centers of Sephardic Jewry. Throughout most of its history Holland has been a haven for Jews fleeing oppression in other countries, and thus it attracted Ashkenazic Jews as well. Even during the Nazi occupation of Holland, Dutch gentiles were notable in their efforts to shelter and hide Jewish families. The country had 105,000 Jews in 1900.

Civil registration of births, deaths and marriages began with Napoleon's conquest of the Netherlands (which then included present-day Belgium) in 1811 and was continued after his defeat. Recent birth, death and marriage records can be obtained from the Civil Registry Office of the burgomaster of the community. For the more distant past, write to the state archive. Its address:

> Algemeen Ryksarchief
> 7 Bleijenburg
> The Hague

The state archive has records of the central government and those of the province of Zuid-Holland. There are ten other provincial archives in Holland, located in Assen, Leeuwarden, Arnheim, Groningen, Maastricht, s'Hertogenbosch, Haarlem, Middelburg, Utrecht and Zwolle. The state archive can direct you to the proper provincial archive for your search. Among other things, the provincial archives have wills prior to about 1925 (more recent wills are in the Central Testamenten Register, The Hague).

Since about 1850, each Dutch municipality has maintained a register which provides details about people living there. Inquire at the appropriate town hall.

The Central Archives for the History of the Jewish People in Jerusalem has extensive material on the Jews of Amsterdam, and some material on other communities. These include records of the Portuguese community (17th–19th centuries), records of the Ashkenazic community (1698–1815), and marriage contracts and deeds for 1786–1787, 1845–1848 and 1879–1880. The Central Archives also has register books for Oldenzaal (1801–1803 and 1822–1904), and a circumcision book for Roermond and vicinity (1888–1926).

Other sources:

• Prominent Jewish libraries can be found at the Sephardi, Ashkenazi and Ez Hayyim seminaries in Amsterdam, in the Amsterdam University Library, and in the Academy Library of Leyden.
• *Libraries in the Netherlands* (Amsterdam, 1961).
• Latter-day Saints research paper C-3, "Major Genealogical Record Sources in the Netherlands." Papers C-5 through C-14 deal with specific provinces. (See section on Mormons in chapter 6.)
• *Searching for Your Ancestors in the Netherlands.*
• *Dutch Emigration to North America, 1624–1860,* by B. H. Wabeke (New York: The Netherlands Information Bureau, 1944).
• The Netherlands Embassy, 4200 Linnean Avenue N.W., Washington, D.C. 20008.

POLAND

Poland, as we have discussed, was once the largest country in Europe, embracing not only the present Polish borders but also Galicia, Lithuania, White Russia and the Ukraine—the greatest sources of European Jewish origin. Its hereditary monarchy ended in 1572 and was followed for more than two hundred years by a system of elective monarchy. According to legend, Saul Wahl, a Jew of the Katzenellenbogen family, served as an interim "king" of Poland in the late sixteenth century for a few days while a new king was being elected. Whether that story is true or not, it is known that Wahl was close to Polish leadership circles and that Jews enjoyed prominent positions and considerable freedom during the elective monarchy.

Beginning in 1772 the country was carved up and apportioned between Germany, Austria and Russia, and by 1795, Poland had disappeared from the map altogether, not to reappear until 1918.

Civil registration in Poland began about 1870. If a birth occurred within the limits of Warsaw, write to:

> Urzad Stanu Cywilnego [Vital Statistics
>   Office for Central Warsaw]
> Warszawa-Strodmiecie

or

> Urzad Stanu Cywilnego [Vital Statistics
>   Office for Praga]
> Warszawa-Praga

If a birth occurred in one of the larger towns or cities outside the Warsaw district, write to:

> Urzad Stanu Cywilnego [Vital Statistics Office]
> [Name of your town], Poland

If a birth occurred in a village or area where there is no Vital Statistics Office, write to:

> Urzad Stanu Cywilnego Gminnej Rady Narodowej [Communal
>   Vital Statistics Office]
> [Name of your town], Poland

The U.S. embassy in Warsaw (c/o Department of State, Washington, D.C. 20521) will help you obtain a copy of recent birth, marriage or death records if you can supply the full name of the people involved, and the date and place of the event.

There are no genealogical societies in Poland, but for a fee you can get help with your research by engaging an attorney-at-law. The appropriate government bureau to contact is:

> Zespol Adwokacki nr 40
> ul. Hibnera 13
> Warsaw

Probably the best source of information within Poland is the Jewish Historical Institute in Warsaw, which was set up after World War II to help Polish Jews look for family records, and thus is attuned to genealogical research. It is mainly geared toward survivors of World War II but does have some earlier records.

Unfortunately, in recent years, as relations have frozen between Israel and the Communist bloc, the condition of the Jewish Historical Institute has become increasingly tenuous. The scholars who originally supervised it are gone, replaced by retired Polish army officers. These ex-officers are at least Jewish—they were purged from the army after Israel's Middle East victory in 1967—but not as knowledgeable as might be hoped. The institute also has a substantial library of Polish Judaica. If you plan to go there, my suggestion is you go soon, because it may not be around much longer. The address:

Zydowski Instytut Historyczny
Al. Gen. Swierczewskiego 79
Warsaw

Miscellaneous vital statistics, some going back to the thirteenth century, can also be found in the national archives in Warsaw and in twenty-five regional archives. The central addresses:

Old records (pre-1918):

Archiwum Glowne Akt Dawnych
Dluga 7
Warsaw

Modern records (post-1918):

Archiwum Akt Nowych
Dluga 7
Warsaw

Before you get involved with these archives in Poland, check the Mormon Genealogical Society or its branches (see chapter 6). Also, the following run-down—for which I am indebted to Leslie Pine's *American Origins*—will give you some idea of what is available at the Polish local archives, some of which cover regions that were part of Germany until 1945.

• Bialystok—Wojewodzkie Archiwum Panstwowe w Bialystoku, Kilinskiego 16. Has public records to 1945 and after 1945.
• Bydgoszcz (German: Bromberg)—Wojewodzkie Archiwum Panstwowe w Bydgoszczy, Dworcowa 65. Public records, archives of educational institutions and political bodies, private collections, maps.
• Torun (Thorn)—Oddzial Terenowy w Toruniu, Ratusz. Archives of Torun, 1252–1945. Archives of the Prussian lands from old Polish era, archives of various institutions and organizations (guilds, churches, etc.), modern documents.
• Gdansk (Danzig)—Wojewodzkie Archiwum Panstwowe w Gdansku, Waly Piastowskie 5. Danzig municipal archives, Elblag (Elbing) municipal archives, cessions of the Prussian states, archives of Danzig for 1919–1939, documents from 1939 to 1945, and from 1945 onward.
• Katowice (Kattowitz)—Wojewodzkie Archiwum Panstwowe w Katowicach, Jagiellonska 25. Public records, industrial records, private archives, modern (post-1945) records.
• Cieszyn (Teschen)—Oddzial Terenowy w Cieszynie, Regera 6. Local records from 1388 to beginning of the 20th century.
• Czestochowa—Oddzial Terenowy w Czestochowie, Narutowicza 16. Records of the Czestochowa municipality guild and industrial, local, legal documents, etc.

- Gliwice (Gleiwitz)—Oddzial Terenowy w Gliwicach, Zygmunta Starego 6. Local records.
- Pszczyna—Oddzial Terenowy w Pszczynie, Zamek. Local records.
- Kielce—Wojewodzkie Archiwum Panstwowe w Kielcach, Rewolucju Pazdziernikowej 17. Public records to 1918, and from 1918, records of denominational, social, cultural bodies, private archives.
- Radom—Oddzial Terenowy w Radomiu, Zeromskiego 53. Local records (1789–1918). Documents from 1918 to present.
- Krakow (Cracow)—Archiwum Panstwowe M. Krakowa i Wojewodztwa Krakowskiego, Sienna 16. Public records to 1795 and from 19th and 20th centuries. Records of denominational, educational and socio-cultural bodies. Guild and trade records, private archives, cartographical collections.
- Lublin—Wojewodzkie Archiwum Panstwowe w Lublinie, Narutowicza 10. Old Polish records. Documents of Poland and Russian administration of 19th century. Documents relating to peasant affairs and to the land reform of 1864. Records from 1918 to 1939. Municipal archives and guild records. Private archives. School records for 19th and 20th centuries.
- Lodz—Archiwum Panstwowe M. Lodzi i Wojewodztwa Lodzkiego, Pl. Wolnosci 1. Public records to 1918, and from 1918 to 1945. Postwar documents, municipal records of Lodz from 1794 to 1949. Industrial documents from 1834 to 1945. Records of banking and financial houses, private archives. Cartographical, iconographical and local-press collections.
- Piotrkow—Oddzial Terenowy w Piotrkowie, Torunska 4. Local records.
- Olsztyn (Allenstein)—Wojewodzkie Archiwum Panstwowe w Olsztynie, Zamek. Public records to 1945. Legal records and land registers from 18th to 20th century. Private archives, public records, 1945 onward.
- Opole (Oppeln)—Wojewodzkie Archiwum Panstwowe w Opolu, Zamkowa 2. Public records from 19th and early 20th centuries. Municipal documents, including parchments from 13th century. Records of social institutions and organizations. Public records from postwar period.
- Brzeg (Brieg)—Oddzial Terenowy w Brzegu, Chrobrego 17. Local records.
- Poznan (Posen)—Archiwum Panstwowe M. Poznania i Wojewodztwa Poznanskiego, 23 Lutego 41/43. Documents from 1215 to 1813. Legal records, 1390–1794. General administrative records, municipal and guild records, 1405–1939. Economic records, 1850–1954. Records of institutions and organizations (educational, legal, ecclesiastical), private archives. Cartographical collections, modern public records.
- Rzeszow—Oddzial Terenowy w Rzeszowie, Rynek 6. Public records, municipal, private and denominational records. Industrial documents.
- Szczecin (Stettin)—Wojewodzkie Archiwum Panstwowe w Szczecinie, Sw. Wojciecha 13. Feudal records. Documents of Prussian administration. Municipal records from 15th to 20th century. Private archives. Postwar public records.

- Warszawa (Warsaw)—Archiwum Panstwowe M. St. Warszawy i Woje-
wodztwa Warszawskiego, Nowowiejska 12. Municipal and *voivod* (county)
records from 19th century. Postwar public records. Cartographical collections.
Library of local history.
- Plozk (Plock)—Oddzial Terenowy w Plocku, Tumska 2. Local records.
- Wroclaw (Breslau)—Archiwum Panstwowe M. Wroclawia i Wojewodztwa
Wroclawskiego, Pomorska 2. Public records to 1943. Records of socio-cultural,
denominational, etc., institutions. Private archives, cartographical collection.
Public records from 1945.
- Jelenia Gora (Hirschberg)—Oddzial Terenowy w Jeleniej Gorze, Podwale
27. Local records (municipal, guild, economic, factory, legal, ecclesiastical).

Much of the material of Jewish interest from these archives at Bialystok,
Kielce, Cracow, Lubin, Lodz, Poznan and Warsaw have been microfilmed by
the Central Archives in Jerusalem (see chapter 8) and are available there. The
Central Archives in Jerusalem also has material from the Ossolineum Library
at Wroclaw (1346–1936), the National Library in Warsaw (1467–1900), the
University Library in Warsaw (1550–1661), the Jagellonic Library (1533–1846)
and the National Museum in Cracow (1539–1794), and the Lopocinsky Library
in Lublin (1521–1780).

Other sources of possible help:

- *Libraries in Poland,* by A. and K. Remerowa (Warsaw, 1961).
- "Some Sources for Polish Genealogy," by B. Klec-Plewski, in *Genealogist's
Magazine,* Vol. XVI (December 1969), pp. 150–159.
- Embassy of the Polish People's Republic, 2640 16th Street N.W., Washing-
ton, D.C. 20009.
- *The Jews of Poland, 1100–1800,* by Bernard Weinryb.
- *History of the Jews in Russia and Poland,* by Simon Dubnow.

PORTUGAL

The first trace of Jews in Portugal is in the twelfth century. Eventually Jews
went to Portugal after they were expelled from Spain, but soon the Inquisition
spread to Portugal, too. In 1903 only 500 Jews were living in the entire country.

The Spanish and Portuguese Jews who moved on to other countries during
the Inquisition are probably the best-documented group in Jewish history.
Consult the sections in this chapter dealing with their countries of settlement
after leaving Portugal; also check the alphabetical list of names in this book.

For birth, death and marriage records from Portugal, Madeira, the Azores
and Cape Verde Islands, write to:

Conservatoria de Registro Civil [Office of the Civil Registrar]
[Name of your town], Portugal [or Madeira, the Azores, etc.]

Also see *The Sephardi Heritage,* ed. by Richard Barnett.

RUMANIA

Rumanian religious denominations were first required to keep birth, death and marriage registers in 1831, although many of them had been doing so voluntarily earlier. Jewish communities apparently were required to begin keeping such lists about 1850, although such registers were not required in Transylvania (then part of Hungary) until 1895. It's hard to say how much material there is of Jewish value in Rumania today, but it can't do any harm to apply for a birth, death or marriage record from the following address:

> Oficiul Starii Civile Statul Popular [Office of
> Vital Statistics of the People's Council]
> [Name of your town], Rumania.

Birth, death and marriage records are kept in these local vital-statistics offices for seventy-five years, then they are transferred to the state archives, whose address is:

> Archivelor Statului
> B-Dul Gheorghe Gheorghui
> Dej nr. 29
> Bucharest

Other sources of possible help:

• *Libraries in the Rumanian People's Republic* (Bucharest, 1961).
• *Dictionar Onomastic Rominesc,* by N. A. Constantinescu (Bucharest, 1963). Provides information about Rumanian surnames. In Rumanian.
• The Diaspora Research Institute of Tel Aviv University in Israel has some Rumanian material. (See chapter 8.)

SOUTH AFRICA

Jews have been in South Africa since the mid-nineteenth century; they numbered 47,000 in 1905 and there are about 115,000 today. Many South African Jewish immigrants came from Eastern Europe.

For records of births, deaths and marriages, write to:

Secretary of the Interior
Private Bag XII4
Pretoria

Other possible sources:

- *Precis of the Archives of the Cape of Good Hope* (Capetown).
- South African Embassy, 3051 Massachusetts Avenue N.W., Washington, D.C. 20008.
- *Directory of South African Libraries* (Pretoria, 1965). Part I (Scientific and Research) lists archives offices.
- *South African Surnames,* by Eric Rosenthal (Capetown, 1965).
- *South African Jewry,* ed. by Leon Feldberg. The major portion of this volume consists of "Who's Who in South African Jewry."

SOVIET UNION (RUSSIA)

Prior to the first partition of Poland in 1772, the Russian government made explicit attempts to ban Jews from living there. Then Poland was carved up by Russia, Germany and Austria, and into Russian hands came the areas we today know as Poland, Lithuania, White Russia, the Ukraine and some of Galicia. Almost overnight, hundreds of thousands of Jews were added to the Russian population.

By laws of 1795 and 1835, the Russian government limited its new Jews to the newly annexed areas, since known as the Pale of Settlement. This area was made up of the governments of Vitebsk, Mogilev, Chernigov, Poltava, Ekaterinoslav, Taurida, Kherson, Kiev, Minsk, Podolia, Bessarabia, Volhynia, Vilna, Kovno, Suwalki, Grodno, Lublin, Syedlitz, Lomza, Plock, Warsaw, Kalisz, Piotrkow and Kielce, the last ten of which are now part of Poland. In 1882 more than 1.5 million Russian Jews who had managed to live outside the Pale were forced into it, so that by 1885 there were 4 million Jews living in the Pale.

Since the 1917 Revolution, births, deaths and marriages have been registered with great care in local offices of the USSR Ministry of Internal Affairs. To obtain a copy of a document in the Soviet Union, write to:

Consular Section
American Embassy, Moscow
c/o Department of State
Washington, D.C. 20521

Ask for a "data sheet" which requests "data which the Soviet Ministry of Foreign Affairs requires to process requests for official extracts of records." After you have received and completed this form, return it to the American Embassy, Moscow, at the address above. The Soviet fee of 1.50 rubles ($2.25)

THE PALE 1835–1917

0   200
Miles

St.Petersburg

1891. 2,000 Jews deported, many of them in chains

1865. Open to Jews

Moscow

1891. 20,000 Jews expelled

Baltic Sea

KOVNO

VITEBSK

GERMANY

SUWALKI

VILNA

PLOCK

LOMZA

WARSAW

GRODNO

MINSK

MOGILEV

KALISZ

SYEDLITZ

PIOTRKOW

RADOM

LUBLIN

KIELCE

VOLHYNIA

CHERNIGOV

Brody

Kiev

KIEV

POLTAVA

AUSTRIA–HUNGARY

PODOLIA

EKATERINOSLAV

BESSARABIA

KHERSON

Nikolaev

RUMANIA

TAURIDA

Principal town from which in 1880 began the exodus of over 2 million Jews from the Pale to the United States, Britain, Europe, South America, and Palestine.

Sebastopol   Yalta

Black Sea

In 1882, 500,000 Jews living in rural areas of the Pale were forced to leave their homes and live in towns or townlets (shtetls) in the Pale. 250,000 Jews living along the western frontier of Russia were also moved into the Pale. 700,000 Jews living east of the Pale were driven into the Pale by 1891.

The Pale of Settlement. Russian Jews confined to this area by laws of 1795 and 1835. By 1885 there were over 4 million Jews living in the Pale.

⊙ Towns within the Pale barred to Jews without special residence permits.

for each document must accompany the completed form, either in a U.S. postal money order, certified check or cashier's check, payable to *American Embassy, Moscow.* The fee will not be refunded even if your request is not fulfilled, according to the Consular Section.

It typically takes from six months to a year before the embassy receives a response to a request to Soviet authorities for a public document. In many cases the document is reported to be unavailable because of the destruction of public records in World War II. A friend of mine who sent away for his father's birth record received a reply in barely two months; however, the reply was: "The Soviet authorities have informed us that no birth record could be found in the archives."

Prior to 1918, Russia had no government bureaus to register births, deaths and marriages. If pre-1918 records do exist, the Communist government there has been reluctant to share them with the rest of the world. It is known that in czarist Russia, Jewish communities kept their own circumcision books, marriage and divorce registrations, records of burials, cemetery lists and so on, and that these were physically kept on the premises of the synagogue or in the home of the rabbi or some other leader of the community. But few of these records seem to have survived.

Nevertheless, the Central Archives for the History of the Jewish People in Jerusalem (see chapter 8) is persisting in its efforts to locate and/or microfilm Jewish records in the Soviet Union. It is also possible that the czarist government did indeed keep some sort of records of Jews; obviously, for example, it had to know the birth dates of Jewish males to be able to conscript them into the army. Indeed, we've all heard stories of Russian Jews who delayed registering their children's birth so as to postpone their future induction into the czar's army.

But all efforts to find such records thus far have been stonewalled. When asked, Soviet officials have told the Jerusalem representatives that the records don't exist. When the Israelis have pointed out that the Soviet Union's own publications indicate the existence of some records, they have been told the files were in disarray and in no condition to be microfilmed. Leslie Pine, in *American Origins,* remarks that he spent eight or nine years writing to the Soviet government for pre-Bolshevik *gentile* information, and never received anything more than a brief acknowledgment. And so it goes.

The bright side of this situation is that the problem largely has to do with the Soviet government's attitude toward the rest of the world, and this attitude could conceivably change in time. When it does, perhaps the records we are all seeking will still be there.

In the meantime, try grasping at these straws:

• *Libraries and Bibliographic Centers in the Soviet Union,* by Paul L. Horecky (Bloomington: Indiana University Press, 1959).

- Extensive Jewish collections can be found at the Asiatic Museum, Leningrad; the Saltykov-Shehedrin Library, Leningrad; the Lenin Library, Moscow; and the Oriental Institute of the Academy of Sciences Library, Moscow.
- USSR Intourist, 45 East 49th Street, New York, N.Y. 10017, and other cities.
- Some information about Bessarabia can be found at the Diaspora Research Institute of Tel Aviv University, Israel (see chapter 8).
- See *History of the Jews in Russia and Poland,* by Simon Dubnow.
- *The Russian Jew Under Tsars and Soviets,* by Salo Baron (1964).
- *The Jewish Community in Russia, 1772–1844,* by Isaac Levitats.
- *World of Our Fathers,* by Irving Howe.
- *Archives and Manuscript Repositories in the USSR,* by Patricia Kennedy Grimsted.
- A "Survey of Manuscript and other Archival Materials in the U.S.A. Pertaining to Russia and the USSR" is being conducted at this writing by the Kennan Institute for Advanced Russian Studies, Woodrow Wilson International Center for Scholars, Smithsonian Institution Building, Washington, D.C. 20560.

SPAIN

Prior to the Inquisition in the fifteenth century, Spain accounted for the largest single group of Jews in Europe—a group which has been celebrated for its culture and position, especially during the seven hundred years of Moslem rule in Spain. Countless books have been written about the Jewish experience in Spain, but with the expulsion in 1492 and the 342-year-long Spanish Inquisition, Jews disappeared from the country, never to return.

If your ancestors lived in Spain at one time, undoubtedly they went somewhere else first before coming to America—perhaps the Netherlands, England, the West Indies, South America, North Africa, Palestine or even Germany and Eastern Europe. Consult the sections on those countries in this chapter, or look up your family name in the alphabetical list at the end of this book. Many Spanish Jewish families have long histories, and you may find yours mentioned there.

If by some wild chance you have had an ancestor living in Spain in the last century or two—and it's highly unlikely—you can send for birth, death or marriage records to the Juzado Municipal (Municipal Court) of the appropriate district.

The actual records of trials in the Spanish Inquisition, incidentally, contain detailed genealogical information about those on trial. Microfilms are available at the Central Archives for the History of the Jewish People in Jerusalem (see chapter 8), and at many other libraries.

Other possible sources:

- *American Archivist,* Vol. 37 (October 1974), p. 605, has a discussion of Spanish archives.
- *A History of the Jews in Christian Spain,* by Y.F. Baer.
- *Noble Families Among Sephardic Jews,* by J. da Costa.
- *The Jews of Moslem Spain,* by Eliyahu Ashtor.
- *Sources of Spanish-Jewish History,* by Joseph Jacobs.

SWEDEN

Jews have been in Sweden since the seventeenth century; the Jewish population there was 4,000 in 1905. Swedish record keeping is highly efficient and its genealogical resources are well organized, even down to the publication of a 13-page booklet entitled *Tracing Your Swedish Ancestry,* published by the Royal Ministry for Foreign Affairs. Religious denominations have been required by law to keep birth, death and marriage records for nearly three hundred years. For records, write to Pastorsämbetet (Parish Registrar) at the place of birth, death or marriage. Also check the national archive:

> Riksarkivet
> Arkivgatan 3
> Stockholm

The Stockholm municipal archive holds census and real-estate records. Its address:

> Kammararkivet
> Stockholm 2

There is also a municipal archive in Malmö.

Before going to Sweden to look for your ancestors, you should look for them at the Leo Baeck Institute in New York (see chapter 6). The Baeck Institute is concerned primarily with German Jewry, but, as we have discussed, it recently obtained the collection of the late Rudolf Simonis, with hundreds of genealogies of German and Swedish Jewish families, all of them in impeccable order and condition. Ask specifically to see the "Simonis Collection"; its family listings haven't been integrated into the institute's card catalogue (although they have been integrated into the family-name list in this book!).

Other sources in Sweden:

- Mosaiska Församlingens Bibliotek in Stockholm is a leading Jewish library.
- A genealogical society is located in Riddarhuset in Stockholm.
- *Libraries and Archives in Sweden,* by Gösta Ottervik, trans. into English by R. Cox (Stockholm, 1964).

• Latter-day Saints research paper D-3: "Major Genealogical Record Sources in Sweden" (see section on Mormons in chapter 5).
• Royal Swedish Embassy, Suite 1200 Watergate, 600 New Hampshire Avenue N.W., Washington, D.C. 20037.

SWITZERLAND

Jews have been in what is now Switzerland since as early as 1213. In 1291, three independent cantons—Uri, Schwyz and Unterwalden—formed an alliance against the Hapsburgs which was the predecessor of modern Switzerland. As a political state, Switzerland formally began in 1848. There were 10,000 Jews in Switzerland in 1900.

The Swiss civil registration system records extensive details about each person. Before 1848, registration of births, deaths and marriages was up to each canton, so some started before others. From 1848 to 1876 registration was handled by religious denominations; after 1876 by civil authorities. Consult the Registrar's Office in the appropriate canton.

The Episcopal Archives in Basel has some material of Jewish concern; this has been microfilmed by the Central Archives for the History of the Jewish People in Jerusalem and can be seen there (more easily, too, since you won't have to weed through non-Jewish records). For details on the Jerusalem archives, see chapter 8.

The Jewish community library in Zurich may be useful.

Also see the article on "Swiss Archives," by Ulrich Helfenstein, in *American Archivist,* Vol. 37 (October 1974), pp. 565–571.

TURKEY

The area that is today Turkey, Greece, Bulgaria and lower Yugoslavia was part of the Ottoman Empire from the fourteenth century until the empire collapsed in 1922. Jews were in this region before the time of Christ; the Jewish population of Turkey in 1906 was 211,000. Jewish records from Ottoman times are difficult to come by; your best bet is the Central Archives for the History of the Jewish People in Jerusalem. I pass on here what I have learned about Jewish record keeping in the Ottoman lands from the staff of the Archives in Jerusalem.

The Jews of central and eastern Turkey are of Kurdic stock; they speak Aramaic and Targum, and some families have lived there continuously for more than two thousand years. But the greatest number of "Ottoman" Jews were in western Turkey and the Balkan countries. They are known as Ladinos because they speak a Spanish dialect of Hebrew, stemming from the fact that their ancestors were Sephardim who came to the Balkan area from Spain and Portugal during the Inquisition. Even before them, though, Jews had come to the Balkans from Italy and Sicily in the ninth, tenth and eleventh centuries. There are also in the Balkans more recent Ashkenazic Jewish arrivals from Hungary, Bavaria and, during the nineteenth- and twentieth-century pogroms, from Russia.

Usually the Jews from Spain and Portugal tried to stay together when they arrived in the Balkans, and often they would name their synagogue after their old town in Spain—a fact which might be of some help in ancestor hunting. Because of social pressures, people usually stayed in one congregation all their lives. However, if there was a quarrel among two factions within a synagogue, one group of families might quit and join the other synagogue in town. Thus some Sephardim did join Ashkenazic congregations, and vice versa, and over centuries their families might well take on all the characteristics of their new congregation.

Turks were not required to have family names until 1927, after the establishment of modern Turkey, but many Jews had family names well before that. The Spanish Jews, of course, had family names which they brought from Spain. Some other Turkish Jews can trace their family names back to about 1840.

Records *were* kept by the Jewish communities. The Central Archives in Jerusalem is presently microfilming some records of Greek Jewish communities, and it has some remnants of other records as well. They vary in character and are widely dispersed. Not the least of the problems with Turkish records is that for centuries all Turkish houses were built of wood, and whole cities were periodically destroyed by fires. If you still want to persist, though, here are some other clues that may help you make use of what you find:

• In Ottoman lands, the Jewish community was responsible to the government for collecting taxes, and it kept records of these collections, listing the head of each family.

• In Turkey, a newborn boy's circumcision was recorded in the Jewish community records.

• Marriage records were also preserved. Even more important than the record of the wedding was the engagement contract. Among Spanish-Portuguese Jews and Ashkenazim, this contract would specify the dowry the woman would pay to the man. Jews in central and eastern Turkey, on the other hand, followed the Arab custom whereby the groom "buys" his wife. In any case, Turkish rabbis were surprisingly fussy about the spelling of names in marriage contracts and other documents. Some of them even compiled lists of precise spellings of family names, a few of which have survived and are at the Central Archives in Jerusalem.

• Even if you can't pinpoint your ancestors, your name may help you discover your ancestral town. Most Turkish Jewish names can be traced to specific cities, because only the traders and the very rich moved about from town to town. Specialists in Turkish Jewry at the Central Archives in Jerusalem may be able to help you.

• Synagogues also kept records of "selling of *mitzvot*" (blessings).

• Sometimes the mere knowledge of first names can help trace your ancestors. Most Turkish Jews followed the Sephardic tradition that the first son is named for his paternal grandfather, the second son for the maternal grandfather, and so on. Of course, this tradition wasn't always followed strictly.

• For individual family names, consult the alphabetical list at the end of the book.

• For background, read *Jewish Life in Turkey in the 16th Century,* by Morris Goodblatt. It gives a good picture of diverse Jewish groups in Salonika.

• A discussion of Sephardic families in Salonika and the origins of their names can be found in "Usos y Costumbres de los Sefardies de Salonica," by M. Molho, in *Biblioteca Habraicoespanola.*

YUGOSLAVIA

Yugoslavia was created in 1918 out of the regions of Serbia, Croatia, Slovenia, Bosnia-Herzegovina, Macedonia and Montenegro. The centers of Jewish population, in the north of what is now Yugoslavia, were under Hungarian rule before 1918. If your ancestors were born in that area before October 1895, you may be able to find records of their birth, death or marriage in the Hungarian microfilm rolls held by the Mormon Genealogical Society in the United States. (See section on Hungary in this chapter.)

Civil registration of vital statistics began in Yugoslavia only in 1946 (1895 in the territory of Voivodina); before then they were kept by churches and, presumably, synagogues. For records since 1946, write to:

Maticar [Registrar]
Mesni Narodni Odhor [Village People's Committee]

or

Gradski Narodni Odhor [Municipal People's Committee]
[Name of your town], Yugoslavia

In the larger cities, you must write to the People's Committee of the appropriate ward *(rejon).* Good luck.

The American consul in Zagreb suggests that the hiring of an attorney is the best way to begin searching for genealogical information in Yugoslavia. All legal practice in Yugoslavia is private, but the U.S. consulate in Zagreb will supply you with a list of attorneys who provide genealogical research services. The consulate doesn't assume any responsibility for the ability or integrity of the names it sends you, though.

The Central Archives for the History of the Jewish People in Jerusalem (see chapter 8) has an inventory of material at the Jewish Museum in Belgrade (1749–1952), and of Jewish-related material at the Municipal Archives at Zemun (registers, 1751–1834) and at the Macedonian State Archives in Skopje (registers, 1621–1692).

Two last possibilities:

• *Yugoslav Libraries,* by M. Rojnic, translated into English by M. Partridge (Zagreb, 1954).
• *A Guide to Yugoslav Libraries and Archives,* compiled by Slobodan Jovanovic and Mtako Rojnic (Columbus, Ohio: American Association for the Advancement of Slavic Studies, 1975).

VIII

...back to Israel

MOST DIASPORA JEWS visit Israel to discover their roots in a general sense. But it is also an extremely good place to discover your specific roots. There are now twenty major archives and about fifteen minor ones in Israel dealing with Judaica all over the world. Somewhere amid this mass of documents, which now consume more than twenty-eight miles of shelf space, may be some clues about your own particular family. Many of these archives—the various Israeli municipal archives, the Israeli State Archives, the Military Archives and the Labour Movement Archives, for example—are of little or no interest to genealogists whose families come from other countries. Others may have some use, depending on your background; if your ancestors were active Zionists, you might find something on them in the Central Zionist Archives.

I have concentrated here on the particular archives, libraries and agencies that should be especially useful in researching family roots in other countries. Each of these institutions provides a great deal of material or service that can't be found elsewhere, and the volume of records stored in Israeli archives is likely to grow with the passage of time.

Since the resources and degree of organization vary from one place to another, it is important to prepare yourself properly and to allow yourself ample time at any library or archives you plan to visit—especially if you don't speak Hebrew. I've tried to provide such preparation in the descriptions below, but of course there is a certain amount you must discover for yourself. A research visit to one or two of these places during a vacation in Israel is not merely a good way to get some research done, it is also a simple but appropriate way to relate yourself to the country you are visiting. Indeed, that's really the only way to go about researching your ancestors in Israel: my impression is that there isn't yet that much family material available exclusively in Israel to justify making a trip there solely for the purpose of genealogical research. But you can judge for yourself as you read on.

CENTRAL ARCHIVES FOR
THE HISTORY OF THE JEWISH PEOPLE

Sprinzak Building
Hebrew University (Givat Ram Campus)
P.O. Box 1149
Jerusalem

The Central Archives, founded in 1939, probably possesses the single most extensive collection of documents, registers and records concerning Jewish history in the Diaspora from the twelfth century to the present. Its primary function is the gathering and transferring to Jerusalem of the archives of Jewish communities, organizations, institutions and private personalities of the Diaspora and to classify and arrange them for historical research. Its collections include source material from Western, Central and Eastern Europe, North Africa, North and South America and East Asia. At last count, the Central Archives had assembled and microfilmed more than 3 million documents consisting of some 1,400 archives (or parts of archives) of communities and institutions consuming some 1,500 meters of shelf space.

Many of these archives are records of Jewish communities themselves. In other cases, the staff of the Central Archives has gone to governmental, provincial and municipal archives in different countries and has microfilmed records concerning Jews. These include birth, death and marriage registers, *mohel* (circumcision) books, gravestone registrations, and so on. The Central Archives also has nearly 200 lists, inventories and calendars describing records of Jewish interest in archives in other countries. It has collections of photographs, press clippings, reports and leaflets. And it has a collection of Jewish genealogies and family histories.

Of special interest to genealogists at the Central Archives will be the following:

- The family histories.
- Town-by-town registration of Jewish births, deaths and marriages in Germany, most from about 1800, although some go back much earlier. Generally these continue until 1876, when the government took over the registration function. Fragmentary registration records also exist for Jewish communities in other countries.
- Family records.
- Genealogical notes, listed by families.
- The collection of Paul Diamant, an Austrian Jewish genealogist. It has some 300 genealogies and notes filling about twenty boxes on Jewish families in what is now Germany, Austria, Poland, Hungary and Czechoslovakia. Many of these notes, however, are extremely fragmentary.
- The genealogical collection of the Jewish Cultural Reconstruction in Darmstadt, Germany, which contains some three dozen genealogies, many in outstanding condition.

Each of the categories mentioned above is indexed separately at the Central Archives, so you must ask to see the card catalogue on each. A family history in the Diamant collection, for example, will not be indexed in the general file of family histories.

The Diaspora Jew who has read this far will no doubt envision a huge Israeli equivalent of the Library of Congress, fully computerized and tended by dozens of researchers and librarians fluent in many languages, all waiting eagerly to serve the novice visitor. Indeed, after Leslie G. Pine mentioned the Central Archives in his 1969 book, *The Genealogist's Encyclopedia,* the Central Archives was swamped with letters from people who assumed that it could tell them the maiden name of their great-grandmother Sadie, even if the only thing they knew about Sadie was that her husband was a butcher in Budapest sometime in the nineteenth century.

Such people are bound to be disappointed. The Central Archives may very well be the greatest single repository of information about Jews and their communities in the Diaspora; in time it may indeed be a mecca for Jewish scholars and lay people—what the Library of Congress is to Americans, and the Mormon Genealogical Society is to genealogists. Right now, though, the Central Archives falls well short of its goal, partly because the state of Jewish records in the Diaspora has always been so inconsistent, and partly because the survival needs of the State of Israel are such that support of the Central Archives is a relatively low priority. Nevertheless, the Central Archives and its limited staff can be of tremendous help—if you come properly prepared.

First, keep in mind that hardly anyone in Israel has heard of the Central Archives. Its primary tasks so far have been the gathering and classifying of Jewish records from other countries rather than making these records available to the general public. Its clientele until now has consisted of a small circle of serious scholars, government officials, wartime-reparations claims examiners from Germany, and other insiders. As it is currently constituted, the Central Archives is only marginally equipped to deal with the general public, and so it keeps a low profile. Even on the Givat Ram campus of the Hebrew University you will have a hard time finding it unless you ask people to direct you to the Sprinzak Building. Here, the Central Archives carries on its work safely out of public view in the basement, a cold, austere, dungeonlike place where the sun rarely shines. It's a good idea to take a heavy sweater with you regardless of the summer heat outside. In the winter, what with Israel's fuel shortage, two sweaters would not be excessive. (You will find the staff of the Archives similarly attired.)

Second, the space available to the public is severely limited. The small reading room seats only four people comfortably, and it has only one microfilm reader, which you would do well to reserve in advance. Moreover, two days a week the microfilm reader is reserved for the use of the Archives staff. Do not, however, let these limitations scare you away. Despite the lack of space, I've never had an occasion on which I was unable to get a seat in the reading room; it simply isn't used that much. And the use of the microfilm reader is not crucial to most genealogical research, since the great portion of family histories and communal records are available in their original copies. (Indeed, if you are a researcher accustomed to handling nothing but Xerox and microfilm copies of records, it is somewhat startling, and exciting, to fill out a request form at the Central Archives, and after perhaps a fifteen-minute wait, to be matter-of-factly handed a folder containing the original moth-eaten records of a synagogue in seventeenth-century Germany.)

Third, the staff is limited. Just about everyone at the Central Archives speaks English as well as several other languages, and there is always a librarian available to help you find what you need. But the staff members don't have the time to do your research for you. They *may* be able to give you insights into where to turn for your particular problem, if you catch them on the right day: the Central Archives has specialists who deal in specific regions (Western Europe, Eastern Europe, North Africa, etc.), but most are there only two or three days a week.

Fourth, hardly any of the documentary material is in English. Jewish communal records are either in Hebrew or Yiddish or in the national tongue in which the community was located. To make matters worse, many of the old German municipal records at the Central Archives are written in Gothic script. Even some of the index cards in the Archives' own catalogue are handwritten and hard to decipher.

But again, the linguistic barrier is not *that* formidable, if you are properly prepared. I personally have had a great deal of luck at the Central Archives, even though my ability to read Hebrew is only good enough to recognize names of families or towns. As for official records or genealogies in foreign languages that use the Roman alphabet—German, say, or French, Italian, Hungarian, Polish, Spanish, Czech—it is easy enough to recognize names and dates and figure out what's going on if you know a few key words: *geboren* means "born" and *gestorben* means "died" in German, for example. Translation dictionaries from most languages into English are available in pocket sizes for only a few dollars.

The biggest problem at the Central Archives, however, is the fact that its greatest abundance of records comes from Germany, Austria, France and Italy and not from Eastern Europe, where most Jewish families come from. The Central Archives records on German Jewish communities, for example, are marvels of thoroughness, some of them going back to the eighteenth century and earlier, because German Jewish communities were required by law to keep their own records. These were confiscated and destroyed by the Nazis during the 1930s, but the photocopies made by the Nazis survive—in tiny booklets that can be read with a magnifying glass the librarian will provide for you. Ironically, we can also thank the Nazis for methodically recording not only vital information about all Jews then living in Germany but also such minutiae as the inscriptions on all Jewish tombstones in many German cities. The records for countries like Poland and Russia, on the other hand, are haphazard and few, and much of what does exist from Eastern Europe deals with the period after World War I. Of the pre–World War I Polish records, in addition, most are only from parts of Poland that were under German control from 1772 to 1918. During that time, of course, most Polish Jews lived in areas controlled by czarist Russia.

The situation won't necessarily always remain this way, although it could. The staff of the Central Archives is persisting in its efforts to find and microfilm records pertaining to Jewry in East European countries. But the problems are twofold. First, as we've seen already, record keeping in East European countries wasn't that good to begin with. Second, most Communist countries, thus far, have been reluctant to cooperate with outside researchers, especially Israelis.

Perhaps the best that can be said is that the Central Archives is as good a single repository as now exists for documents on the history of Diaspora Jewry; that if and when more documents on East European Jewry are made available, they are likely to turn up at the Central Archives; and that at the very least, if such documents are available elsewhere, staff members of the Archives are likely to know their whereabouts.

If you are to find anything of personal value at the Central Archives, you will almost certainly have to go to Israel in person and be willing to spend some time in research—a day or two at least, and possibly a few weeks. If you're unable to go to Israel, the staff will do what it can for you by mail—but only if you send precise information. If, for example, you know the date and place where an ancestor was born, the staff members will see whether they have a birth register for that particular community. If they do, they will look up your ancestor for you and let you know what they find. But to get this kind of service you must be willing to provide precise data. The staff doesn't have the time to comb through birth, death or marriage registers for a ten-year period or for a vague geographical region. If you want to do that, you must go to Jerusalem and do it yourself—and, indeed, you may very well find something.

Upon request, the Central Archives will send you a copy of its guidebook, published as an edition of the *Central Archives Newsletter* in 1973. This contains a brief description of the Archives as well as a listing of archives of Jewish communities, institutions and organizations in its possession. These are grouped by country and city, following the national boundaries of 1919. Each listing mentions the time period covered as well as the amount of space the material takes up on the Central Archives shelves, so you can get a rough idea of how much information is available. The guidebook also lists the Central Archives holdings dealing with international organizations and private archives and collections. And the guidebook contains two appendices, one listing non-Jewish archives in which material concerning Jews was microfilmed (usually state or municipal archives in Europe), the other listing archives in other countries for which the Central Archives has prepared inventories. These two appendices might be useful to you if you can't make it to Israel but would like to do some research in Europe.

The guidebook does not, however, list genealogies or communal birth, death and marriage registers on file at the Central Archives, the most valuable resources for ancestor hunters. The genealogies can be discovered simply by consulting the list of the family names at the end of this book. And the staff will tell you, by mail, whether it has birth, death or marriage records for particular communities.

Another possibly useful publication offered by the Central Archives on request is an 18-page paper, in English, entitled *Registration of Births, Deaths and Marriages in European Jewish Communities, in Palestine and in Israel.* This is a collective research work by Archives staff members that appeared in 1959 in *Archivum,* a publication of the Conseil International des Archives (Paris; Presses Universitaires de France). It has also been included virtually verbatim in Leslie Pine's *Genealogist's Encyclopedia* and, indeed, comprises almost everything Pine has to say on the subject of Jewish genealogy.

This report contains a brief introduction discussing, in general terms, the ways in which European Jewish communities kept internal records prior to the Napoleonic era. Most of the report, though, is a survey of specific kinds of records kept by German Jewish communities from 1808, when Napoleon first required Jewish communities to keep vital records and turn at least one copy over to the state, until 1876, when all such record keeping became the function of the government. The authors of the survey chose Germany as their example because of the abundance of material at their disposal; they had planned to write similar surveys on Jewish records in other countries, but they have not yet done so. The survey does give exact data about the ways in which Jews were registered in each of the various German kingdoms and dukedoms—

Baden, Bayern (Bavaria), Braunschweig (Brunswick), Frankfurt-am-Main, Hamburg, Hannover, Hessen, Hohenzollern-Hechingen, Holstein, Lübeck, Mecklenburg-Schwerin, Oldenburg, Preussen (Prussia), Sachsen (Saxony)-Weimar-Eisenach, Schleswig (Sleswig), Westfalen (Westphalia) and Württemberg. Thus by extension it provides some idea of what actual registers are available at the Central Archives itself. But if you are interested in other countries it is of relatively little use. And even Jews with German ancestors will find the survey no substitute for a trip to the Central Archives in person. I speak on this point from personal experience.

JEWISH NATIONAL AND UNIVERSITY LIBRARY

Hebrew University (Givat Ram Campus)
Jerusalem

The library grew from a small private collection in 1892 to the present modern building housing about 2 million books and 16,500 periodicals. It is just across the Givat Ram campus from the Central Archives for the History of the Jewish People. When you are finished with your research at the Central Archives at its 2 P.M. closing time—assuming you are not already bleary-eyed —you can walk over to the library and continue working there for another eight hours.

The archives of the library has a number of *pinchassim* (registers) of births, deaths and other listings for scattered communities in Algeria, Austria, Czechoslovakia, France, Germany, Greece, Hungary, Italy, Latvia, Morocco, Poland, Lithuania, Rumania, Turkey, the Soviet Union and Yemen. Many of the registers for Poland, Lithuania and Russia go back to the eighteenth century or even beyond. They are, of course, far from comprehensive, but they do cover seventeen communities in the Soviet Union and twenty-nine in Poland and Lithuania—and these are areas in which the Central Archives is notably weak. A town-by-town list is included in the *Guide to the Archives in Israel* (Jerusalem: Israel Archives Association, 1973).

DIASPORA RESEARCH INSTITUTE

Tel Aviv University

The institute has collections of original material shedding light on the Jews of Bessarabia, Hungary, Rumania and the Bilu movement. It also has copies of documents deposited by researchers after their studies have been completed. At this writing, the Bilu collection deals mainly with the history of Jewish communities in Italy.

ARCHIVES OF THE SEPHARDI COMMUNITY

Hahavazelet Street 12a
Jerusalem

This contains documents of Eastern (i.e., Greek, Turkish, North African, etc.) Jews in Palestine beginning with the Ottoman conquest of Palestine in the sixteenth century. Most of the older records are Muslim court documents, such as contracts for the purchase or lease of land. Also included are official decrees on the status of the Jewish community, appointments, taxation, repairs of synagogues, etc. The archives contain many volumes of letters sent to Jewish communities throughout the world, records of contributions and charitable works, and detailed accounts of the yearly income and expenses of the community. The most recent section, covering the first half of the twentieth century, is classified according to subjects, such as "Sephardi local and international organizations," "Sephardi synagogues," "Oriental and other communities in Jerusalem," "Rabbinic matters," etc.

GHETTO FIGHTERS HOUSE

Kibbutz Lohamei Haghetaot
Akko Post Office

The Ghetto Fighters' House is best known for its museum of the Warsaw Ghetto Uprising, but it also contains 20,000 volumes and thousands of documents, manuscripts, photographs and eyewitness accounts dealing with the Holocaust and particularly the Warsaw Ghetto Uprising. The accounts of what happened to survivors after the war might be of some use to genealogists.

YAD VASHEM

Har Hazikaron
P.O. Box 84
Jerusalem

Most tourists know of Yad Vashem as the museum which provides a gruesome (yet remarkably tasteful) perpetual reminder of the horrors of the Nazi period, 1933–1945. Yet this well-known museum is adjoined on either side by two lesser-known buildings that may contain useful information for ancestor hunters, especially those from Eastern Europe. To the left of the museum is the Hall of Names, where Yad Vashem is assembling personal information on each of the six million Jewish victims of the Holocaust. To the right is the Yad

Vashem Archives building, the primary repository for books and archives dealing with the Holocaust period.

Although Yad Vashem's scope is much narrower than that of the Central Archives for the History of the Jewish People, it has two important advantages. First, because it stands along a well-worn tourist path, it is much better equipped to deal with the general public. The reading room of its library is moderately large, bright and—by golly—above ground. Second, its resources tend to be strongest in the very area where the Central Archives is weakest —that of Eastern Europe, where most of the Holocaust persecution of Jews took place.

To be sure, most of this material deals with the Holocaust period, and if your grandparents came to America from Poland in 1890, this may not be of much help to you. But don't rule it out. There is a great deal of historical material at Yad Vashem, and many of the accounts of Jewish communities destroyed by the Nazis extend back to the nineteenth century and even earlier. If you know the town from which your ancestors came, it is worth at least a visit to the Yad Vashem Archives to see what is available.

The idea of the Yad Vashem Archives was conceived in the European ghettoes and concentration camps during World War II. After the war, some survivors who emigrated to Israel brought with them records, documents and memorabilia from their old communities, to be placed in the yet-to-be-established center. In the same postwar period, Jewish historical commissions were established in Germany and countries formerly occupied by the Nazis to collect documents and take testimonies from Jewish aid and rescue societies and Displaced Persons organizations. Material from these commissions in Munich, Poland, Bratislava, Budapest, Vienna and Linz formed another nucleus for the Yad Vashem Archives, which was formally created in 1953.

Since then Yad Vashem has photocopied entire collections from foreign countries and has also generated its own collection of interviews with Holocaust survivors. By now Yad Vashem has over 25 million pages of documents in its archives. The material includes, among other things, records of concentration camps, German occupation authorities, the Gestapo and Jewish rescue agencies; diaries of German officials; transcripts and exhibits from the Nuremberg trials; press clippings from the period; miscellaneous collections for each country; and some 15,000 photographs.

The archives are organized in five departments: (1) archives of institutions and legal records; (2) collections from documentation centers, private papers, testimonies and single documents; (3) exhibits; (4) testimonies department (Holocaust survivors—in Tel Aviv); (5) the reference department.

The reference department is especially useful because its catalogue covers Holocaust material available not only at Yad Vashem, but elsewhere in Israel and also in other countries.

Probably most valuable of all for genealogists is Yad Vashem's collection of *yizkor* (memory) books from East European communities. When survivors from a particular town got together after the war in Israel or New York or wherever they had relocated, they often formed a *landsmanshaft* and published a *yizkor* book to commemorate their late community and the names of their dead neighbors. Yad Vashem has collected such books for some six hundred European towns. Many of these books can also be found elsewhere, of course—most notably the YIVO Institute in New York (see chapter 6), but if you are in Jerusalem it can't do you any harm to stop at Yad Vashem to see whether there are any books dealing with your relatives' communities. Most of these books make some attempt to provide a comprehensive list of Holocaust victims from each particular town, so at the very least you can find names and possibly dates.

Sometimes just a browse through one of these books may yield an unexpected helpful clue. For example, a branch of my mother's family from the vicinity of Miskolc, Hungary, came to the United States in 1875, long before the Holocaust. Recently I was told that this family was related to a family named Spielberger, or some variation of that name. The name seemed odd to me, nor was I sure how to spell it. But at Yad Vashem I found a *yizkor* book for the Miskolc area and there, in one of the long columns of Holocaust victims, I found three people named Spilberger. Not my relatives, perhaps, but at least it gave me something to go on, for I now know that the name did exist in the Miskolc neighborhood.

Here is a partial list of local Jewish histories—*yizkor* books—in the library at Yad Vashem. Although very few are in English, many have introductory sections in English which might give you at least a name and address you could contact for more information on that community.

In English or German:

Alsenz	Braunschweig	Fulda
Altona	(Brunswick)	Giessen
Andernach	Buchau	Gdansk (Danzig)
Antwerp	Butzbach	Gmünd
Baden	Chemnitz	Göttingen
Baden-Württemberg	(Karl-Marx-Stadt)	Hagen
Bamberg	Cologne (Köln)	Hamburg
Bensheim	Constance (Konstanz)	Hannover
Berlin	Danzig (Gdansk)	Heilbronn
Bergeb-Enkheim	Dés (Dej)	Hessen
Beuel (Vilich)	Dresden	Hohenzollern
Bielefeld	Einbeck	Iserlohn
Bitolj (Monastir)	Eisenstadt	Kalisch (Kalisz)
Böhmen (Bohemia)	Eitorf	Karl-Marx-Stadt
Bonn	Essen	(Chemnitz)
Bonyhád	Fehérgyarmat	Kitzingen
Brandenburg	Frankfurt	Klagenfurt
Bratislava (Pressburg)	Freiburg	Köln (Cologne)

Konstanz (Constance)
Lackenbach
Landau
Leeuwarden
Lettland (Latvia)
Mähren (Moravia)
Mainz
Mannheim
Memmingen
Mergentheim
Moisling/Lübeck
Monastir (Bitolj)
Moravia (Mähren)
Munich (München)
Münster
Neupest (Ujpest)
Nordhorn
Nuremberg (Nürnberg)
  (1146–1945)
Nyíregyháza
Oberhausen
Offenburg
Oldenburg
Osnabrück
Pápa
Pressburg (Bratislava)
Radom
Rheinland-Pfalz
Ruppichteroth
Saarbrücken
Saarland
Salonika
Salzburg
Schaumburg-Lippe
Schlesien (Silesia)
Senica
Siegerland
Silesia (Schlesien)
Solingen
Stettin (Szczecin)
Stuttgart
Sulzburg
Talheim
Tübingen
Ujpest (Neupest)
Ulm
Vas
Vienna (Wien)
Viersen
Vilich (Beuel)
Wandsbek

Weinheim
Westfalen (Westphalia)
Wien (Vienna)
Wiesbaden
Württemberg
Zborow
Zholkva (Zolkiev)
Zundorf
Zwickau

In Hebrew or Yiddish:
Beliza
Belz
Bereczany
Bershad
Bessarabia
Bialystok
Brest-Litovsk
Brisk
Brody
Bulgaria
Byelorussia
Chelm
Chisinau (Kishinev)
Cracow (Krakow)
Danzig (Gdynia)
Debrecen
Dembitz
Dubno
Dubromil
Dukla
Falstein
Frankfurt-am-Main
Fünfkirchen (Pécs)
Galicia
Galina
Gardinas (Grodno)
Gdynia (Danzig)
Glogau (Glogow)
Golob
Grodno (Gardinas)
Horodenka
Jampol
Jaworow (Yavorov)
Kalisch (Kalisz)
Kamenets Podolski
Kaunas (Kovno)
Kishinev (Chisinau)
Kobrin (Kobryn)
Kovel (Kowel)

Kovno (Kaunas)
Krakow (Cracow)
Kremnitz (Kremnica;
  Körmöczbanya)
Lemberg (Lwow; Lvov)
Lettland (Latvia)
Levartov
Lodz
Lublin
Lubomil
Lusk
Lwow (Lemberg; Lvov)
Minsk
Miskolc
Munkács (Mukachevo;
  Mukacevo)
Nemerov
Neustadt
Pécs (Fünfkirchen)
Pinsk
Plonsk
Plozk (Plock)
Polnoi
Radom
Radziwilov
Rohatyn
Rovno (Rowne; Rowno)
Slutsk
Sokolov
Sokolow Podlaski
Stanislav (Stanislau;
  Stanislawow)
Stropkov
Suwalki (Suvalki;
  Suvalkai)
Tarnograd
Tarnopol (Ternopol)
Tarnów
Tiktin
Tours
Troky
Venice
Vilna (Wilna)
Vitebsk
Vladimir Volynsk
  (Wlodzimierz)
Volkovysk (Wolkowysk)
Warsaw (Warszawa)
Yavorov (Jaworow)
Zevartkov
Zwihil

If you cannot go to Israel in person, you can obtain by mail from Yad Vashem a copy of any document, photograph or microfilm in its possession, provided you pay all related expenses. Selections of documents appear in two publications, *From the Yad Vashem Archives* and *Yad Vashem Studies* (both in English and Hebrew), which can be found in most Jewish libraries. An 8-page survey of the holdings of the Yad Vashem Archives can be found in *Guide to the Archives in Israel* (Jerusalem: Israel Archives Association, 1973).

Before we leave Yad Vashem, don't forget the Hall of Names, on the other side of the museum, where records of the six million Holocaust victims are kept. The hall serves as a reminder that the victims were not mere statistics, but live human beings. Nevertheless, the sheer volume of the project is overwhelming: allowing one 8 1/2" by 11" sheet for each victim, the pile of sheets stretches the length of two football fields—and, of course, many Holocaust victims are still unaccounted for. The sheets provide as much information as is known about the victim's name, date of birth and death, family, home address, and place and circumstances of death. Some sheets are in Hebrew, some in other languages, and you can't browse through them: you must give specific names to the attendant, and he will fetch them for you. If the name you are looking for is missing, you might want to fill out a sheet for that particular person yourself. (Of course, you don't have to go to Yad Vashem to do this: simply write to Yad Vashem and ask for a "page of testimony" for registration of a relative or friend who died in the Holocaust.)

If you *do* find sheets for relatives, they may contain new information that will give you further clues for your research. For example, the sheet may be filled out by a distant relative whom you didn't know you had.

Even if your immediate family left Europe long before the rise of Hitler, it is likely that you had some relatives who perished in the Holocaust. After all, three of every eight Jews then walking the earth were killed. If you can go back four or five generations on your family tree, and if you can then go forward and list all the descendants of your great-grandparents or great-great-grandparents, you will probably find some distant cousins who never left Europe and were instead swept away in World War II. If you know of similar names in your own family, you should look them up at Yad Vashem's memorial hall. Even if the sheets you find tell you nothing new, it is a powerful and meaningful sensation to hold a piece of paper testifying that someone of your blood could, in the twentieth century, be stamped out like an ant by a government's decree.

Alas, even at Yad Vashem, of all places, bureaucrats occasionally have to be reminded of their functions. On my last trip there, I was the only visitor at the Hall of Names, and the attendant was sitting at his desk, apparently with nothing to do. So I filled out a form requesting sheets for twelve relatives who had been killed by the Nazis.

"*Twelve names!*" the attendant howled. "I don't have time to look for twelve names!"

I fixed him with what I like to think was a conscience-penetrating stare. "I'm terribly sorry," I said, "to have inconvenienced you by having had so many relatives who perished in the Holocaust." The message got through, and I got all twelve sheets. But of course, I suppose that is the lesson of Yad Vashem, and of the State of Israel: if you want something—be it your life, your survival as a state, or a simple piece of paper—you must assert yourself.

A Source Guide
to Jewish Family
Genealogies

Introduction

THE GREATEST DISCOVERY of my genealogical adventures occurred in 1970 after I received a phone call one night from my friend Chuck Bernstein, a Chicago lawyer. Like me, Chuck is a Jewish genealogy fanatic, but he is also blessed with a photographic memory, which means that he had memorized not only the entire genealogy of his own family but of mine as well.

"Take a look in the *Jewish Encyclopedia,*" Chuck told me on this particular night. "There's an article about a Saul Margolioth who was a rabbi in Zbarazh in the eighteenth century. Maybe he's related to you." With his phenomenal memory, Chuck had recalled that I had ancestors named Margulies who had lived in the town of Zbarazh, Galicia.

At the time, I had not even heard of the *Jewish Encyclopedia.* It had never occurred to me to look for my ancestors in an encyclopedia because it never occurred to me that any of them might have been famous. Nor had it occurred to me that a name like Margulies might have been derived from another name, like Margolioth, although today that seems so obvious that I am appalled at my previous lack of imagination.

A few days later I followed Chuck's advice and went to the public library to look through the 12-volume *Jewish Encyclopedia.* There I found not only an article on Rabbi Saul Margolioth of Zbarazh but articles on countless other Margolioths from Galicia, including two who, like Saul Margolioth, had lived in Zbarazh during the eighteenth and early nineteenth centuries. In addition, the encyclopedia provided a family tree tracing most of these Margolioths all the way back to the sixteenth century. Finally, the encyclopedia suggested that this Margolioth family is the ancestor of most Galician Jews with names like Margulies, Margolis, Margolin, and so on—a fact I have subsequently verified through other sources. Through all my years of genealogical research, my wildest fantasy had been that someday I would discover a document that would open the door to the Middle Ages and trace my own family back hundreds of years. Now my wildest fantasy had been fulfilled.

That experience with the *Jewish Encyclopedia* taught me that there is more than one way to search for your ancestors. The most obvious and most popular method is to work through your relatives and go as far back in time as you can. The less obvious and far less direct method is to trace everybody else's family trees on the theory that other people's ancestors may turn out to be your ancestors too. This is the approach being taken by the Mormon Genealogical Society, which would like to assemble family trees for the entire population of the world, undoubtedly an impossible task. Jews, on the other hand, represent only one half of one percent of the world's population. This means that the family tree of the world's Jews can be painted on a relatively small canvas; if enough of that canvas is filled, perhaps we can see the whole picture. If a sufficient number of Jews exchanged family information with one another in some centralized form, might we not be able to fill in enough of the missing pieces of our past to enable us to discover more of our own ancestors?

Inspired by my experience with the *Jewish Encyclopedia,* I have attempted to take the first step toward such an information exchange by compiling the alphabetical list of some 8,000 Jewish family names which follows. It summarizes whatever genealogical and biographical information I have found about each family name after combing through every line of the *Jewish Encyclopedia,* the *Universal Jewish Encyclopedia,* and the *Encyclopaedia Judaica,* after looking through hundreds of published and unpublished books of Jewish family histories, and after studying the genealogy holdings of some half-dozen major Jewish archival institutions in the United States and Israel.

Ideally, you should be able to look up your family name in this guide and find information about the derivation of the name, some description of families which have carried the name and where they came from, references to family trees, records and histories, and cross-references to families which I have found to be related to families with your name. You can then look up the entries for these related families, which will perhaps provide helpful information for tracing your own family.

Please note that the key word in the preceding paragraph is "ideally." Do not expect to look up your family name in this guide and find, right there, a history of your own particular family. You *might* be that lucky, but the likelihood is small. Many Jewish family names are so common—Cohen, Levy, Goldstein, for example—that the name alone is inadequate for determining family relationships. However, some other Jewish family names *do* share common origins: among Central and East European Jews, names like Margulies, Rappaport, Weill, Halpern, Falk, Shapiro, Wallach, Schorr, Jaffe, Horowitz, Ginsberg and Auerbach are examples, and there are many more. But in many cases I have found nothing at all for particular family names, or just the merest sliver of information. Small though the Jewish population may be compared to the rest of the world, it is still a staggering task to assemble all of the world's Jewish genealogies, which perhaps explains why no list of this sort has ever before been attempted. To my knowledge, the only previous guide dealing with this subject was the 21-page manuscript *Bibliographia Genealogica Judaica,* a list of about a thousand Jewish family histories, genealogies and community histories compiled in 1942 by the late Hermann M. Z. Meyer, to whom I am greatly indebted for some of my information. But only twenty-two copies of Meyer's bibliography were produced, and they barely scratched the surface of the subject.

The following guide delves a bit deeper, but still, the true depths of Jewish genealogy remain to be plumbed. Before you start flipping through the pages to look up the entries for your various related families, it is important that you read the following instructions and caveats so you will know precisely what this guide can do for you and precisely what it cannot. The list was intended only as a supplement to this book and is no substitute for the basic research and interviews you must do on your own. You may strike gold by looking in this guide; on the other hand, it is possible that it will be of no use to you at all.

In the first place, this guide is organized according to family names (also called surnames), and prior to 1800 the great preponderance of Jews had no surnames at all. Many who *did* have surnames changed them from one generation to the next.

Second, in order to keep the list manageable (and to preserve my own sanity), I have limited my attention almost entirely to references to family relationships *prior* to 1900 and *outside* the United States. Thus, if you cannot trace your family back to 1900, this guide won't be of much use to you, nor will it provide much help in tracing ancestral relationships within the United States. My assumption is that most of us *can* trace our families at least back to 1900 and that you can find your American ancestors on your own, using the suggestions in chapters 2, 3, and 6.

The further back you have traced your family tree, the more useful this guide is likely to be to you. If you know the names of your grandparents, for example, you will have four family names to look up in the guide. If you know all of your great-grandparents, you will have eight names; if you know your great-great-grandparents, sixteen names, and so on. The more ancestral names you know, the greater is the likelihood that you can find an entry that might bear directly on your own family. It is also important that you look for the family name in its earliest known form. If your family was named "Goldstein" by an immigration officer at Ellis Island, it will do you little good to look up "Goldstein" in this list; you must find out what the family's name was in the old country and look under that entry.

Keep in mind also that Jewish family names were often modified or changed as Jews moved from one country to another. (I have therefore not used any umlauts in the listings.) In addition, the same name may have been spelled several different ways and in several different alphabets. A name like Horowitz, for example, is synonymous with Horovitz, Horwitz, Hurwitz, Urwicz and many other forms; in Russia it became Gorwitz, Gurwicz and Gurewicz. Wherever possible, I have grouped together and cross-referenced names that have a common root; in other cases I have cross-referenced names that *may* have a common root. But I've doubtless missed many such combinations, so it's a good idea to play detective yourself by running your finger quickly down the pages in search of names that may be similar to your own. Just as Margulies is a modern adaptation of Margolioth, so your name might be a shortening, refinement or Anglicization of a more ancient name.

Remember, too, that some letters are often used interchangeably when Jewish family names are written in the English alphabet. The letter *A* is sometimes interchangeable with *E,* for example (as in Adelson and Edelson). Some other interchangeable uses:

> *B* and *V* (as in Abigdor and Avigdor).
> *Y* and silent *J* (as in Yaroslav and Jaroslav).
> *F* and *P* (as in Saffer and Sapir).
> *V* and *W* (as in Volovsky and Wolowsky).
> *F* and *V* (as in Fogel and Vogel).
> Hard *C* and *K* (as in Cohen and Kohen)
> *Ch* and *Sh* (as in Elyachar and Elyashar)
> *S* and soft *C* and *Z* (as in Sinberg, Cinberg and Zinberg)

In some cases a name may have been kept intact from one country to another except for a change of a single letter to make the name sound more comfortable in its new surroundings. A name like Zitomer, for example, might become Gitomer in the United States, and Zavin might be changed to Gavin. In searching for names, in short, do not constrict yourself to the exact present spellings of the particular names you seek. Use your imagination. Your ancestors certainly used theirs.

Other points to keep in mind before you plunge into the guide:

• The guide is intended merely to provide a taste of what resources are available regarding each Jewish family name. In some cases where hardly any information is available, I have included everything that I could find about a particular family. In the case of more prominent names, the Rothschilds, for example, I have merely provided a sampling of the voluminous material available.

• All names have been listed in strict alphabetical order, whether they are two words or one. Thus a name like Villa-Real is alphabetized as Villareal.

• Most surnames evolved informally rather than formally. In the Middle Ages men often had two given names, as in Judah Lowe, Dov Baer, Menahem Mandel, Naphtali Hirsch or Benjamin Wolf, and it's impossible to pinpoint when Lowe, Baer, Mandel, Hirsch and Wolf began to be spoken of as family names rather than given names. Similarly, a man with no family name might be referred to as Schechter ("the butcher") or Ashkenazi ("from Germany"), and his descendants two or three generations later may have taken those appellations as surnames. In deciding at what point a given name or an appellation becomes a surname, I have followed the judgment of the three major Jewish encyclopedias: if they have used a name as a surname, so have I. (Incidentally, if your ancestors had *first* names that are also family names —such as Hirsch or Wolf—it wouldn't hurt to look up those names, too, in this list. It's a long shot, but there may be a connection.)

• At the close of each entry I've included cross-references (in small capital letters) to related family names, usually in a sentence beginning "Related to . . ." Most of these collateral references have been gleaned from the three Jewish encyclopedias; some have been taken from actual family trees and other sources. But these collateral names are not necessarily related to the families mentioned in the entry, unless I've specifically indicated that they are. For example, consider the following fictitious entry:

> SMITH—JE has article on 18th-cent. German horse thief John Smith, grandson of Fred JONES (1682–1763). Related to SCHWARTZ, COHEN and BERNSTEIN.

This means, obviously, that John Smith is related to Fred Jones, and if you are related to this particular John Smith you should look him up in JE (the *Jewish Encyclopedia*) and also look up the entry in this list for JONES to learn more about your family. But it does *not* mean that the Schwartz, Cohen and Bernstein families are related to this John Smith—only that they are related to *someone* named Smith. By consulting the cross-reference, you may learn which Smith is their relative.

• If a listing says "JE has biographies" (referring to the *Jewish Encyclopedia*); that does not mean that the same biographies can't also be found in UJ *(Universal Jewish Encyclopedia)* or EJ *(Encyclopaedia Judaica);* it only means that UJ and EJ don't have any biographies other than the ones found in the *Jewish Encyclopedia.* Obviously, the information in these biographies varies from one encyclopedia to another, so for the best results, consult all three encyclopedias. I've placed the greatest emphasis in this list on JE because it is more concerned with genealogy than the two later encyclopedias.

• Many of the entries in this guide contain references to family history books. Most of these books have been published in limited editions, and many of them are not in English. Additional information about these books, and where to find them, is provided in the Bibliography.

• When I refer to a family as "beginning in" or "dating from" or "originating in" a particular country or century, obviously I am referring to the family's earliest known existence. Technically, families don't "begin," unless we are speaking of the family of Adam.

• In some cases I have indicated whether a family name is Ashkenazic or Sephardic. If I haven't, you can figure it out easily enough yourself. Families originating in Spain, Portugal, North Africa, the Middle East and the Orient are almost always Sephardic. All others are Ashkenazic.

• You'll find some names in the guide that clearly are not Jewish. These are gentiles who married Jews, or Jews who took Christian names after forsaking Judaism.

• Although this is a guide to Jewish family names, I have also included entries on six notable figures from Jewish history who do not have family names: King David (1043 B.C.E.–973 B.C.E.), Hillel the Great (70 B.C.E.–10 C.E.), Rashi (1040–1105), the Maharal of Prague (1525–1609), the Baal Shemtob (1700–1760) and the Gaon of Vilna (1720–1797). They are included because their lives are touchstones for numerous other Jewish families that claim them as ancestors or relatives.

• Finally, if you search through this guide and find nothing at all about your family or family name, do not despair: there is still a chance that some information exists somewhere. For one thing, new books, records, histories and family trees are being acquired by libraries and archives every day. Second, my assistant and I are only human, and we no doubt missed some names and some resources here and there. While we did personally check through a large number of family history books, cross-referencing the family names we found, in most cases we simply used whatever information was provided about a book on its card catalogue. In some archives, the family histories and genealogies were organized haphazardly, and we simply copied down the names of as many as we could find without making a serious attempt to be comprehensive. Thus your family name may well be mentioned in a Jewish library, archive or book somewhere, even if it isn't mentioned in this guide.

(At press time I learned of the publication of *The Unbroken Chain*, by Neil Rosenstein (Shengold), an extraordinarily valuable 700-page book which not only translates many East European rabbinic genealogies into English, but also traces many of those families down to the present day. Fully indexed.)

Abbreviations

AJA—American Jewish Archives. For more details, see chapter 6.

AJF—*Archiv für jüdische Familien-Forschung* (a publication put out in Vienna, 1912–1916), dedicated to Jewish family histories, primarily Austrian. In German; available at major Jewish libraries.

BJGL—*Blätter für jüdische Geschichte und Literatur,* by L. Löwenstein, Vols. I–V (Mainz, 1899–1904).

CAJ—Material from the "genealogy" or "family" file at the Central Archives for the History of the Jewish People in Jerusalem. For more details, see chapter 8.

CAJD—Material in the file on the *Jewish Cultural Reconstruction in Darmstadt,* available at the Central Archives for the History of the Jewish People in Jerusalem. For more details, see chapter 8.

CB—*Catalogus librorum hebraeorum in Bibliotheca Bodleiana,* by M. Steinschneider, 3 vols. (Berlin, 1931).

EJ—*Encyclopaedia Judaica,* 16 vols. (New York and Jerusalem, 1971). Available at all major public and Jewish libraries.

JA—*Jüdisches Archiv* (published by Leopold Moses in Vienna, 1927–1929).

JE—*Jewish Encyclopedia,* 12 vols. (New York, 1901–1906). Available at all major public and Jewish libraries.

FFJ—*Jüdische Familien-Forschung.*

JHSE—Jewish Historical Society of England (see section on England in chapter 7).

JJLG—*Jahrbuch für jüdische Literatur und Gesellschaft.*

JQR—*Jewish Quarterly Review.*

KB—M. Kayserling's *Bibliotheca Espanola-Portugueza-Judaica* (Strasbourg, 1890).

KS—M. Kayserling's *Sephardim. Romanische Poesien der Juden in Spanien* (Leipzig, 1859).

LBI—Archives of the Leo Baeck Institute, 129 East 73rd Street, New York, N.Y. 10021. The presence of records here indicates that the family is probably of Germanic background. For more details, see chapter 6.

LBIS—Rudolf Simonis collection at the Leo Baeck Institute, 129 East 73 Street, New York, N.Y. 10021. For more details, see chapter 6.

MGWJ—*Monatsschrift für Geschichte und Wissenschaft des Judentums.*

PD—Paul Diamant collection at the Central Archives for the History of the Jewish People in Jerusalem. Diamant was a Jewish genealogist; his work covers Germany plus some of what is now Poland, Hungary and Czechoslovakia, but many of the family records in his collection are extremely fragmentary. See chapter 8.

REJ—*Revue des Études Juives* (Paris).

UJE—*Universal Jewish Encyclopedia,* 10 vols. (New York, 1939–1948). Available at all major public and Jewish libraries.

VR—*Geschichte der Juden in Rom,* by H. Vogelstein and P. Rieger (Berlin, 1895–1896).

ZGJD—*Zeitschrift für die Geschichte der Juden in Deutschland.*

ZGJT—*Zeitschrift für die Geschichte der Juden in Tschechoslowakei.*

ZS—*Gesammelte Schriften,* by Leopold Zunz.

ZL—*Literaturgeschichte,* by Leopold Zunz.

Zunz GL—*Geschichte und Literatur,* by Leopold Zunz.

Alphabetical List of Family Names

AARON (also Aarons, Aaronsohn, etc.)—
LBIS has tree for an Aaron family from
Mecklenburg. AJA has Aarons family
tree beginning Holland, 18th cent. JE, UJ
and EJ have biographies from Rumania,
U.S.A., England and Palestine, including
Jonas Aaron, first known Jewish resident
of Philadelphia (1703), and English boxer
Barney Aaron (1800–1850). Related to
JAFFE, L'ARRONGE, ABRAHAM.

AARONS—See AARON.

AARONSOHN—See AARON.

ABARBANEL—See ABRAVENEL.

ABBADY—UJ has article on Isaac Abbady
(b. 1898), descendant of a Sephardic family.

ABBAS (also Abbasi)—Sephardic name.
EJ has articles on Turkish poet Moses Abbas (1601–1671), who came from a Spanish
family, and Spanish translator Jacob Abbasi (13th cent.).

ABBASI—See ABBAS.

ABDALA—JE article on "Coat of Arms"
includes a description of the Abdala arms.

ABEATAR—See ATTAR.

ABEDROTH—See ABT.

ABEL (also Abele, Abeles, Abelman,
Abelmann, Abelson)—Name found in
Moravia as early as 17th cent., elsewhere
in Eastern Europe later. AJA has family
tree beginning in Prussia, 1837; LBIS
also has tree. PD has records of Abeles
family. JE, UJ and EJ have several biographies, including Judah ben Isaac
Abelson, a merchant at Sherwenty,
Lithuania, late 18th cent. Related to
HERZL, JAFFE.

ABELE—See ABEL.

ABELES—See ABEL.

ABELMAN—See ABEL.

149

ABELMANN—See ABEL.

ABELSON—See ABEL.

ABEN—Related to YULY.

ABENAES—EJ has article on Portuguese Marrano Solomon Abenaes (1520–1603), whose name was originally MENDES.

ABENAFIA—Sephardic name. EJ has article on Spanish Rabbi Joseph Abenafia (d. 1408).

ABENALAZAR—See ELEAZAR.

ABENARDUT—See ARDUT.

ABENATAR—See ATTAR.

ABENDANA (also Ibn Dana, Abendanan) —Name of a number of Sephardic families living in London, 1900. The name is traced to the Marrano Francisco Nunez PEREYRA, who fled Spain to Amsterdam in early 17th cent. and took the name David Abendana. JE lists his descendants. Histories of the family can be found in *Transactions of the Jewish Historical Society of England,* Vol. 8, p. 98, and Vol. 10, p. 221. JE article on "Coat of Arms" has two Abendana family crests. The Moroccan rabbinic family of Abendanan is traced to 13th cent.; see EJ. Related families include NUNES, OSORIO, BELMONTE, NAHMIOS, MENDES and de BRITO.

ABENDANAN—See ABENDANA.

ABENEFEIA—See ABULAFIA.

ABENGALEL—See BENGALEL.

ABENMENASSE—Family of courtiers in Spain that dates from 13th cent. Related to ABINNAXIM. See EJ. Also see IBN MENASHEH.

ABEN SCHOSCHAN—Sephardic name. See Zunz GL, p. 436, for family history.

ABENSOUR (also Abensur)—Sephardic family that originated in Spain; after 1492 there were branches in Morocco, Italy, Amsterdam and Hamburg. The Hamburg branch descended also from the MILLAO family. See EJ. Related also to MILAN.

ABENSUR—See ABENSOUR.

ABENVIVES (also Vives)—Spanish family that dates to 13th cent. See EJ, which also has an article on Juan Vives, Spanish humanist (1492–1546).

ABERL—Related to JAFFE.

ABIATAR—See ATTAR.

ABIATHAR—See ATTAR.

ABIGDOR (also Avigdor, d'Avigdor)— Name that first appeared in the Middle Ages with the French physician Abraham Abigdor (b. 1350 in France); see JE. In Eastern Europe the name was subsequently changed to VIGDOR, VIGDER, VIGDORTSHIK or VIGDOROWITZ; see UJ. EJ has a family tree of the prominent 19th-cent. English family of d'Avigdor, which was related to LYON, GOLDSMID, JACOBS. Other d'Avigdors and Avigdors were in Constantinople and Nice, France, in 19th cent. Other relatives include APTOWITZER, FLETCHER, NATHAN, LANDAU, GOLDSCHMIDT, CLAPCOTT and EPSTEIN. See also FIGDOR.

ABI-HASIRA—Family of Moroccan origin that was living in Syria in 16th cent.; some descendants were in Israel in 1970. See EJ.

ABINNAXIM—Related to ABENMENASSE.

ABIOB—EJ has article on Turkish Rabbi Aaron Abiob (1535–1605).

ABITBOL—Moroccan family. EJ has two biographies from 18th and 19th cent.

ABI ZIMRA—EJ has article on Algerian poet Isaac Abi Zimra (16th cent.).

ABOAB (also Aboaf, Abof, Abohab, Abohaf)—Ancient and widely distributed Spanish family, noted for its many scholars. JE has family biographies beginning in 1263, tracing descendants in Holland, Italy, Turkey, Africa and U.S.A. EJ has a family-tree chart. JE article on "Coat of Arms" has the family crest. Also see *Die Familie Aboab.* Relatives include BELILHOS, TEIXEIRA, FRANCO, GOMEZ, DINIS, HENRIQUES, FONSECA, CURIEL, FALEIRO, LEVI, DIAS and VITORIA.

ABOLAFIA—See ABULAFIA.

ABOLAYS—See ALAISH.

ABRABALIA—See ALBALIA.

ABRABANEL—See ABRAVENEL.

ABRAHAM (also Abrahams, Abrahamson, Abrahamsohn, Abrahamsen)—Ashkenazic name. JE article on Bazarjik, Rumelia, mentions a Samuel Abraham who died there in 1644. JE also refers to Levi Abraham, a Hannoverian Jew who came to Antwerp in 1769. JE, UJ, EJ have many biographies. AJA has family tree beginning 18th cent.; CAJ has family tree beginning 1804; LBI has family tree; LBIS has Abrahamson family tree. Also see *Abraham Elias af Haus-esterhousmere* for a history of the Abrahamsen family. Related families include MONTEFIORE, WARBURG, EPSTEIN, JOHNSON, JAFFE, BRAHAM, AARONSOHN, COHEN, DAVID, KATZ, NONES, YATES, SAMUEL, NATHAN and BRAHM. Also see ABRAMS, BRAHAM.

ABRAHAMS—See ABRAHAM.

ABRAHAMSEN—See ABRAHAM.

ABRAHAMSOHN—See ABRAHAM.

ABRAHAMSON—See ABRAHAM.

ABRAHAO—Sephardic name. UJ has article on Portuguese agent Coje Abrahao, who lived in Gao, India (16th cent.).

ABRAMOWITSCH—See ABRAMOWITZ.

ABRAMOWITZ (also Abramowitsch)— Russian name. UJ has four biographies from 19th cent.

ABRAMS (also Abramsky, Abramson)— Ashkenazic name. UJ has two biographies, also an article on Abraham Abramson of Germany (1754–1811), the son of Jacob ABRAHAM. AJA has Abramson family trees from Poland, related to GRAETKE, SOLOMON and RUBIN. EJ has other biographies.

ABRAMSKY—See ABRAMS.

ABRAMSON—See ABRAMS.

ABRASS—UJ has article on Russian cantor Joshua Abrass (1820–1884).

ABRAVANEL (also Abarbanel, Abrabanel) —One of the oldest and most distinguished Spanish families. The German scholar Herman Reckendorf maintained that the Abravenels were direct descendants of King David, through Zerubbabel, Hillel and certain Jewish kings in Arabia. JE and EJ have family-tree charts and biographies; also see JE article on Herman Reckendorf and on "Coat of Arms," which includes the Abravenel crest, as well as those of the families Abarbanel de Sousa and Abarbanel de Veiga. LBIS has Abrabanel family tree. Also see KB, p. 6. Related to LINDO.

ABSABAN—EJ has article on Palestinian scholar Solomon Absaban (d. 1592).

ABT (also Abterode, Abedroth, Aptrod) —Ashkenazic name derived from the town of Abterode in Hesse. EJ has article

on German Rabbi David Abterode (d. 1728); UJ has a biography from U.S.A., 19th cent.

ABTERODE—See ABT.

ABTSHUK—UJ has article on Russian writer Avraham Abtshuk (b. 1897).

ABUAB—See ABOAB.

ABUDARAM—See ABUDARHAM.

ABUDARAN—See ABUDARHAM.

ABUDARHAM (also Abudaram, Abudaran, Abudarhan, Abudarhen)—Spanish family that dates from 13th cent.; see EJ.

ABUDARHAN—See ABUDARHAM.

ABUDARHEN—See ABUDARHAM.

ABUDIENTE (also Obediente)—Sephardic family of Marranos, traced back to Lisbon in late 16th cent. Members of the family moved to Amsterdam in 17th cent., then to Hamburg and London. Some called themselves Gideon-Abudiente, but in England most changed their name to GIDEON. See JE and KB.

ABUKARA—EJ has article on Tunisian Rabbi Abraham Abukara (d. 1879).

ABULAFIA (also Abenefeia, Afia, Abolafia, Bolaffi, Bolaffey, Bolaffio)— Widely scattered family of Spanish origin, traced back to 12th cent. The name means "father of medicine." Related branches can be found in Italy (Bolaffi) and England (Bolaffey). JE and EJ have family-tree charts. EJ also has an article on Aaron Afia, Sephardic physician living at Salonika in 16th cent. Also see Zunz GL. Relatives include MELDOLA, FORMIGGINI, BERAB, ALGAZI.

ABULKER—Algerian family, originally from Spain; after expulsion in 1492, went to Italy. EJ has biographies dating back to 15th cent.

ABZARDIEL—EJ has article on Spanish Rabbi Moses Abzardiel (d. 1354).

ACAN (also Azan)—EJ has article on Spanish poet Moses Acan (14th cent.). Another variation of the name is HAZZAN.

ACERRAF—See ANKAVA.

ACHRON—EJ has article on composer Joseph Achron (b. 1886 in Russia).

ACHSELRAD (also Axelrod)—Ashkenazic name. JE has article on Benedict Achselrad, a Levite who lived in Lemberg, Galicia (17th cent.). UJ has article on Pavel Axelrod (b. 1848 in Russia). Also see EJ article on *Abraham* ben Alexander (13th cent.).

ACKERMAN (also Akerman)—Ashkenazic name, sometimes meaning "farmer" in Hebrew, sometimes referring to the town of Akkerman in Bessarabia, southwest of Odessa. JE has article on Austrian poet Rachel Akerman (1522–1544).

ACKORD—EJ has article on Russian physician Elias Ackord (d. 1811).

ACOSTA—See COSTA.

ACSADY—UJ has article on Hungarian historian Ignac Acsady (1845–1906). Related to SZENDE.

ADADI—EJ has article on cabalist Abraham Adadi (1801–1874), born in Tripoli. See also RACCAH.

ADALBERG—See ADELBERG.

ADAM (also Adams)—UJ has article on French sculptor Antony Adam-Salomon (1818–1881), U.S. columnist Franklin P. Adams (b. 1881). Also see EJ article on Fanny Arnstein. Related to SALOMON.

ADAM-SALOMON—See ADAM.

ADAMS—See ADAM.

ADANI—Family name in Yemen and Aden, 15th cent. to present. EJ has five biographies.

ADARBI—UJ has article on Rabbi Isaac Adarbi of Salonika (d. 1583).

ADELBERG (also Adalberg)—Ashkenazic name; UJ has biographies from Lithuania and Poland, 19th cent.

ADELKIND—EJ has article on Italian printer Israel Adelkind (16th cent.).

ADENI—EJ has article on Palestinian scholar Solomon Adeni (1567–1625).

ADERCA—EJ has article on Rumanian novelist Felix Aderca (1891–1962).

ADERSHLEGER—UJ has article on writer Moses Adershleger (b. 1881 in Galicia).

ADHAN—See DAHAN.

ADIBE—UJ has article on Jacob Adibe, who left Portugal in 1496 and settled in Morocco.

ADJIMAN—Family in Constantinople, originally from Spain. See EJ.

ADLER—Family of *Kohanim* originally from Frankfurt-am-Main, Germany, 18th cent. The name is derived from the eagle on the signboard over the family's house. Tradition traces the family to Simon, author of *Yalkut Shimeoni.* The family is probably related to the WORMS and ROTHSCHILD families of Frankfurt; later, in England, the Adlers merged with the SCHIFF family, prominent rabbis. JE, EJ and LBI have family-tree charts. A second Adler family originated in Worms, 18th cent.; see EJ. JE also mentions a Rabbi Nathan Adler, cabalist from Boskowitz, Moravia, who died 1783. See also *The Family of Max and Sophie Adler.* Related families include HALBAN, SPEYER, SULZBERGER, LEVITZKI, MANDL, FRAENKEL, LEHFELD, EICHHOLZ, LICHTENSTEIN, STERNHELL, CARLEBACH, GOLDMARK, WAHL, SHEUERMAN, KAHN and KRAUS.

ADLERBLUM—UJ has article on author Nina Adlerblum (b. 1891 in Jerusalem).

ADMON—EJ has article on Israeli composer Yedidyah Admon, (b. 1897 in Russia); his name was originally GOROCHOV.

degli ADOLESCENTOLI—One of four or five noble families which, according to legend, were transported by Titus from Jerusalem to Rome after the destruction of the Second Temple in 70 C.E. The name means "the youths," after the captive youths brought to Rome. The family can be traced in Italy back to 14th cent.; see JE. Relatives include NAGARI, dei FANCIULLI, dels INFANZ and dels FILS.

ADOLPHUS—Ashkenazic name. UJ mentions an English attorney John Adolphus (1768–1845) of German origin; also a Hetty Adolphus who married Jacob HAYS of New York (18th cent.). AJA has family tree beginning Germany, 18th cent. EJ has additional biographies.

ADRET—EJ has biographies from Spain, 13th cent., and Smyrna, 18th cent.

ADUMIM—Related to EBORENSIS.

AELION—See AYLLON.

AFANASIEVA—Related to EHRENFEST.

AFENDOPOLO (also Efendopolo)—UJ has article on scholar Caleb Afendopolo

(1464–1524), brother-in-law of Elijah BASHYAZI.

AFFACHINER—CAJ has family records.

AFIA—See ABULAFIA.

AFTALION—EJ has article on economist Albert Aftalion (born 1874 in Bulgaria).

AGA—EJ has article on Crimean Karaite leader Benjamin Aga (d. 1824).

AGAI—UJ has article on Hungarian physician Adolf Agai (1836–1916), son of Joseph ROSENZWEIG.

AGHMATI—EJ has article on North African Talmudist Zechariah Aghmati (12th–13th cent.).

AGLOBLIN—CAJ has family records.

AGMON—EJ has article on Israeli dramatist Nathan Agmon (b. 1896 in Russia); originally BISTRITSKI.

AGNON—UJ has article on novelist Samuel Agnon (b. 1888 in Galicia); originally CZACZKES. See also MARX.

AGRON (also Agronsky)—EJ has article on Jerusalem Mayor Gershon Agron (b. 1894 in Russia); originally Agronsky.

AGUADO—UJ has article on banker Alexander Aguado (1784–1842).

AGUILAR—Sephardic name taken from a district in the province of Valencia, Spain, where Jews can be traced back to 1290; see JE. JE article on "Coat of Arms" includes the family crest. Diego d'AGUILAR (1699–1759), was born PEREIRA; see EJ. Related to COSTA, MELDOLA, CASTRO, SAMUDA.

AGURSKY—EJ has article on Russian Communist Samuel Agursky (b. 1884).

AHARONI (also Aharonovitch, Aharonowitz)—Name derived from the Hebrew *aharon*, "the last." UJ and EJ have biographies from Russia and Lithuania, 19th cent. Also see EJ article on Zalman Aranne.

AHARONOVITCH—See AHARONI.

AHARONOWITZ—See AHARONI.

AHIMAAZ BEN PALTIEL—This is not the name of a family, but of the Italian liturgical poet (1017–1060). He is included here because he compiled a family chronicle going back seven generations before him; see family-tree chart in EJ.

AHRON—CAJ has family tree from Germany.

AHRONHEIM—LBIS has family notes.

AHRWEILER—Ashkenazic family name taken from the Prussian town of the same name, northwest of Coblenz (or Koblenz), where Jews lived as early as 1248. In 17th cent. the family name appeared in Frankfurt, Worms and Prague. See JE.

AIKHENVALD—EJ has article on Russian essayist Yuli Aikhenvald (b. 1872).

AISENSTADT—See EISENSTADT.

AIZMAN—EJ has article on Russian writer David Aizman (1869–1922).

AKAVYA—EJ has article on writer Avraham Akavya (b. 1882 in Poland); originally YAKOBOVITS.

AKERMAN—See ACKERMAN.

AKLAR—EJ has article on Persian Rabbi Mordecai Aklar (1856–1936).

AKNIN—EJ has article on Spanish philosopher Joseph Aknin (1150–1220).

AKRA—UJ has article on 16th-cent. Italian Talmudist Abraham Akra.

AKRISH—UJ has article on Spanish scholar Isaac Akrish (1489–1578).

ALAISH (usually Abu Alaish; also Abolays, Bolaix, Belais, Balaiss)—Spanish family traced back to Barcelona, 1391. See JE, which also has an article on Rabbi Abraham Belais (b. 1773 in Tunis, d. 1853 in London). JE article on "Coat of Arms" has the Abolays family crest. Related to de SOLA.

ALAMAN (also Alami)—Many-branched family in the Ottoman Empire, descended from Joseph ben Solomon of Ofen (Buda), early 16th cent. In 1900 he had about 450 descendants living in Constantinople, Adrianople, Brusa, Damascus, Gallipoli, Cairo, and several cities in Bulgaria; their names include ASHKENAZI and DEUTSCH. See JE. Also, EJ has biographies of the Alami family from Palestine, 12th cent., and Spain, 14th–15th cent.

ALAMI—See ALAMAN.

ALASHKAR—Spanish family name derived from the Arabic word for "red." JE traces it to mid-14th cent., and mentions another branch of the family that lived in Egypt from late 15th cent.

ALATINI—See ALATRINI.

ALATINO—See ALATRINI.

ALATRI—See ALATRINI.

ALATRINI (also Alatini, Alatino, Alatri, degli Alatrini, Alatrino, Alterini)—Distinguished Italian family from the town of Alatri; JE traces it to Fermo in 1295, and provides a family-tree chart. The Alatino family, which is probably related, is known to have been in Italy from 16th cent.; see JE. Also see VR. Related to POMIS.

degli ALATRINI—See ALATRINI.

ALATRINO—See ALATRINI.

ALATZAR—See ELEAZAR.

AL-AVANI—EJ has article on Persian poet Isaac Al-Avani (13th cent.).

ALBA—EJ has article on Italian Rabbi Jacob di Alba (16th–17th cent.).

ALBALA—See ALBALIA.

ALBALAG—UJ has article on 13th-cent. philosopher Isaac Albalag.

ALBALAH—See ALBALIA.

ALBALI—See ALBALIA.

ALBALIA (also Abrabalia, Albala, Albalah, Albali)—One of the more ancient Jewish families of Spain, traced to 11th-cent. Cordova and supposed to be descended from a noble family of Judea at the time of the Emperor Titus, 70 C.E. See JE. According to UJ, Isaac Albalia (1035–1094) was an ancestor of Abraham ibn DAUD. EJ has article on Zionist David Albala (b. 1886 in Yugoslavia). Related to BARUCH.

ALBARADANI—EJ has article on Baghdad poet Joseph Albaradani (10th cent.).

AL-BARGELONI—Sephardic name meaning "of Barcelona." EJ has article on 11th-cent. Spanish Talmudist Isaac Al-Bargeloni.

ALBASIR—UJ has article on 11th-cent. Babylonian philosopher Joseph Albasir.

ALBAZ—EJ has article on 16th-cent. Moroccan cabalist Moses Albaz.

ALBECK—UJ has two biographies from Poland, 19th cent.

ALBELDA—Family name taken from a town in Castile, Spain, where Jews can be traced back to the 11th cent. Moses Albelda of Turkey, 16th-cent. Bible commentator, is descended from this family. See JE.

ALBERT—Ashkenazic name usually derived from Albertin in northern France.

ALBO (also Albu)—Philosopher Joseph Albo (1380–1445) was an ancestor of industrialist George Albu (b. 1857 in Germany, d. 1935 in South Africa). See UJ. LBI has family tree.

ALBORN—Related to FRIEDENWALD.

ALBOTINI (also Albutaini)—EJ has article on Portuguese scholar Judah Albotini (d. 1519).

von ALBRECTSBURG—Related to ARNSTEIN.

ALBU—See ALBO.

ALBUTAINI—See ALBOTINI.

ALCALAY—See ALKALAI.

ALCAN—See ALKAN.

ALCASTIEL—EJ has article on Spanish cabalist Joseph Alcastiel, (15th cent.).

ALCHATEV—See Zunz GL.

ALCONIERE—EJ has article on Hungarian painter Theodore Alconiere (1797–1865), originally COHN.

ALCONSTANTINI—Family of Jewish courtiers in 13th-cent. Aragon, probably originally from North Africa. See EJ.

ALCORSONO—EJ has article on 14th-cent. Moroccan scholar Judah Alcorsono.

ALDABI—EJ has article on philosopher Meir Aldabi (1310–1360).

ALDROPHE—UJ has article on French architect Alfred Aldrophe (1834–1895).

ALDUBI—EJ has article on 14th-cent. Spanish Talmudist Abraham Aldubi.

ALEGRE—EJ has article on Rabbi Abraham Alegre of Constantinople (1560–1652), father-in-law of Levi TEGLIO.

ALEMAN—EJ has article on Spanish novelist Mateo Aleman (1547–1615). See also ALAMAN.

ALETRINI—See ALATRINI.

ALETRINO—See ALATRINI.

ALEX—See ALEXANDER.

ALEXANDER (also Alex, Alexandrow)—English family of printers and translators, traced back to the 18th cent.; see JE. JE also has biographies of various other Alexanders in Hungary, Germany, Poland, Palestine, England and Australia, 18th and 19th cent. LBI and ABA have family trees; LBIS has family notes. Also see *The Family History of Nicholas Paul Alexander* and *Notes on the Alexander Family of South Carolina and Georgia and Connections.* Relatives include LINDO, GOMEZ, ERNST, SCHNEIDER, SCHNEERSOHN.

ALEXANDROW—See ALEXANDER.

ALFAKAR—Sephardic name meaning "potter." One of the oldest Jewish Spanish families, traced back to 12th cent. See UJ.

ALFALAS—EJ has article on 16th-cent. Moroccan preacher Moses Alfalas.

ALFANDARI—Family of Eastern rabbis prominent in Smyrna, Constantinople and Jerusalem in 17th and 18th cent.; descendants were known in Constantinople and Beirut in 1900. The name may be taken from a Spanish locality, possibly Alhambra. The family claims descent from Bezalel of the tribe of Judah. See JE, which has a family-tree chart; also EJ.

ALFAQUEIN—See ALFAQUIN.

ALFAQUI—See ALFAQUIN.

ALFAQUIN (also Alfaquein, Alfaqui, Alfuqui)—Surname given in Spain generally to the physician of the king, and also to his secretary and interpreter. The name can be traced back to 12th cent. See JE.

ALFARABI—UJ has article on Arabian philosopher Abu Alfarabi (870–950).

ALFASI—Family of Tunisian rabbis originating in Fez, Morocco, 18th cent.; see EJ. UJ has article on Talmudist Isaac Alfasi (1013–1103), who died in Spain.

ALFES—UJ has article on writer Ben-Zion Alfes (b. 1851 in Vilna). Another variation of the name is Alfas.

ALFUAL—Family of Spanish Jews traced back to 11th cent.; see JE.

ALFUQUI—See ALFAQUIN.

ALGAZI—Rabbinical family found in the eastern Mediterranean, 17th through 19th cent. See UJ and EJ. Related to SE-GOVIA, YA'ISH, HAZZAN, ABULAFIA, CATTAUI.

ALGRANATI—Sephardic name taken from Granada, Spain, where the family originated. See JE.

ALGUADES (also Alguadez)—EJ has article on Spanish physician Meir Alguades (d. 1410).

ALHADIB—Sephardic family traced back to 14th-cent. Spain and Italy. See JE.

AL-HAKAM—Baghdad family traced back to 18th cent. See EJ.

AL-HARIZI—EJ has article on poet Judah Al-Harizi (1170–1235), born in Spain.

ALHAYK—EJ has article on Tunisian Rabbi Uzziel Alhayk (1740–1820).

ALKABETZ (also Alkabez, Alkabiz)—Near Eastern family; EJ has family tree. UJ has article on poet Solomon Alkabetz (d. 1580 in Palestine). Also see JE article on *Moses* ha-Levi Alkabiz. Relatives include CORDOVERO, COHEN.

ALKABEZ—See ALKABETZ.

ALKABIZ—See ALKABETZ.

ALKALAI (also Alcalay)—Sephardic name of an Italian family originally from Kalai, near Madrid, Spain; hence the name. UJ has two biographies from 19th cent., also an article on the Yugoslav Rabbi Isaac Alcalay (b. 1881 in Bulgaria).

ALKAN (also Alcan)—French family; see JE and EJ. French pianist Charles Alkan (1813–1888) was originally MORHANGE.

ALLEMANO—EJ has article on Italian philosopher Johanan Allemano (1435–1504), who was of French ancestry. Possibly related families are ALAMAN and ALEMAN.

ALLEN—AJA has family tree beginning in England, 1762. UJ has two biographies. Related to HACKENBURG.

ALMAGIA—EJ has article on Italian geographer Roberto Almagia (b. 1884).

ALMALI—See ALMOLI.

ALMAN—UJ has article on composer Samuel Alman (b. 1878 in Russia).

ALMANSI—See ALMANZI.

ALMANZI (also Almansi)—Italian family traced back to 1700. The name is supposed to be derived from Almansa in Murcia,

Spain. JE has a family-tree chart. See also "The Family Almanzi," in *Jewish Quarterly Review,* Vol. IV, p. 500.

ALMEIDA—See ALMEYDA.

ALMEYDA (also Almeida)—Sephardic family. *Jewish Quarterly Review,* Vol. XVI, p. 702, has a family tree. Related to BELMONTE, CARABAJAL, NUNES.

ALMOG—EJ has article on Israeli leader Yehuda Almog (b. 1896 in Lithuania); originally KOPELIOWITZ.

ALMOLI (also Almali, Almuli)—Spanish name derived from the Arabic *almu'alli,* "the one who raises up." Can be traced back to 13th cent. See JE.

ALMOSNINO—Distinguished family originally from Aragon, Spain. The name is derived from Arabic and denotes "an orator." The family, which can be traced to 16th cent., later moved to England. EJ has family-tree chart. Also see JE and *La Famille Almosnino.* Related to COCUMBRIEL, SIMHAH.

ALMUL—CAJ has family records.

ALMULI—See ALMOLI.

ALNAQUA (also Alnequa, Alnakar, Aluncawi, Ankoa)—Important family of Spanish Jews that can be traced back to 12th cent. JE has family tree. Also see Zunz GL. Relatives include ANKAVA.

ALNEQUA—See ALNAQUA.

ALOE—UJ has article on U.S. civic leader Louis Aloe (1867–1929).

ALONSO—UJ has article on Mexican Hernando Alonso (d. 1528).

ALOOF—Related to LINDO.

ALPERN—See HEILPRIN.

ALPERSON—UJ has article on writer Mordecai Alperson (b. 1867 in Russia).

ALPINER—AJA has family tree. Related to FELSENTHAL.

ALPRON—See HEILPRIN.

AL-RAGIL—See ARRAGEL.

ALROY—See AROLLIA.

ALSBERG—UJ has two biographies from U.S.A., 19th and 20th cent.

ALSCHULER—See ALTSCHUL.

ALSHECH (also Alshekh, Alsheikh)—UJ has article on Rabbi Moses Alshech (1508–1600). EJ has article on Yemenite Rabbi Shalom Alsheikh (b. 1859).

ALSHEIKH—See ALSHECH.

ALSHEKH—See ALSHECH.

ALTAR—Family of Bohemian rabbis, 18th cent. See JE.

ALTARAS—Family of Italian rabbis traced back to 16th cent. The name may be related to the Spanish Karaite Sidi ibn al-Taras. See JE.

ALTENKUNSTADT—JE has article on rabbi of this name at Verbo, Hungary, first half of 19th cent.; he was also known as Jacob KOPPEL.

ALTER—Ashkenazic name meaning "old." EJ has article on Polish bund leader Victor Alter (b. 1890). Also see UJ article on *Geren* Rebbe.

ALTERINI—See ALATRINI.

ALTFELD—UJ has article on U.S. legislator Emanuel Altfeld (b. 1889).

ALTHEIMER—UJ has article on U.S. banker Benjamin Altheimer (b. 1850 in Germany).

ALTMAN (also Altmann)—UJ has five biographies from Russia and U.S.A.

ALTMANN—See ALTMAN.

d'ALTON—Related to SCHADOW.

ALTSCHUELER—See ALTSCHUL.

ALTSCHUL (also Altschuler, Altschueler, Alschuler)—Name borne by Ashkenazic Jews in many countries, all of whom seem to have had a common origin in Prague, Bohemia, 14th cent. The name is derived from Alt Shul, the "old synagogue," which still stands; the first Altschuls were prominent patrons of this synagogue. The family came to Prague from Provence about 1302. From 16th cent. on, it was prominent in Russia, Poland, Lithuania and Italy; in the 19th cent. it spread to Hungary, Germany, Russia, England and U.S.A. JE has three family trees and many biographies. AJA has Altschuler family tree beginning 1791. LBI has Altschueler family tree. Also see *The Altschuler Family Tree.* Related to PERLES, CHAJES; also ASH, which is sometimes an abbreviation for "Alt Shul."

ALTSCHULER—See ALTSCHUL.

ALUNCAWI—See ALNAQUA.

ALVARES—See ALVAREZ.

ALVAREZ (also Alvares)—Spanish-Portuguese family containing many scholars and martyrs. It can be traced back to 16th cent.; by 1900 there were branches in Holland, France and U.S.A. See JE, which also has the Alvarez family crest in its article on "Coat of Arms." Also see *The Alvares Correa Families of Curaçao and Brazil.* Related to de SOLA, MONTEFIORE, ZACUTO.

ALZEY—See BELMONT.

AMARI—UJ has article on Italian historian Michele Amori (1806–1889).

AMARILLO—Family of Sephardic rabbis prominent in Salonika, 18th cent. See UJ and EJ.

AMBACH—Ashkenazic name. AJA has family tree beginning in Bavaria, 1807. Related to BURGUNDER, GUNDERSHEIMER, GUTMANN, ROSENBAUM, SCHUBART and ULLMANN.

AMBRON—Italian family traced to 16th cent. in VR, No. II. EJ has article on Italian scholar Shabbetai Ambron (17th–18th cent.), who was of Spanish ancestry.

AMBROSIUS—UJ has article on Moses Ambrosius, who arrived in New York with the first Jews in 1654.

AMDUR—Ashkenazic name that probably comes from the Russian town of Amdur (also known as Indura) in the government of Grodno.

AMELANDER—EJ and UJ have articles on Dutch publisher Menahem Amelander (b. 1765), brother-in-law of Eliezer ROEDELSHEIM.

AMERICAN—UJ has article on U.S. civic leader Sadie American (b. 1862).

AMES—Sephardic family of Marranos that settled in London, 1521. See EJ. Related to LOPEZ.

AMIEL—EJ has article on Rabbi Moshe Amiel (b. 1883 in Russia).

AMIGO—Spanish family prominent in Temesvar, Hungary. EJ has biographies beginning in 17th cent.

AMMAR—Sephardic family in North Africa, traced to Moses Ammar in 14th

cent. See *Geschichte der Juden in Spanien und Portugal.*

AMRAM—JE has several biographies.

AMSHEWITZ—EJ has article on British artist John Amshewitz (b. 1882).

AMSTERDAM—Name presumably taken from the city in Holland, a haven for both Sephardic and Ashkenazic Jews. EJ has article on labor leader Abraham Amsterdam (b. 1871 in Russia). Related to CARO.

AMZALAK—UJ has two biographies, from 19th-cent. Palestine and 19th–20th-cent. Portugal. Also see EJ.

ANAKLET—For a family history, see JFF, No. 23.

ANASCHEHON (also Anaschichun)—Spanish family which settled in Palestine and Turkey after 1492. See EJ. Related to ASHKENAZI.

ANATHAN—Related to TELLER.

ANATOLI—UJ has article on Jacob Anatoli of France (1194–1258), son-in-law of Samuel ibn TIBBON.

ANAU—See ANAW.

ANAW (also Anau)—Italian family that can be traced back to Rome, 10th cent.; it's supposedly one of the four prominent Judean families deported by Titus to Rome upon the destruction of Jerusalem in 70 C.E. JE has family-tree charts and sixty-four biographies; EJ also has a tree chart, under Anau. Also see CB, p. 2767, and VR, Vol. I, p. 456, Vol. II, p. 262, as well as JE article on *Solomon* ben Moses ben Jekuthiel, husband of Paola Anaw (13th cent.). Relatives include degli MANSI, PIATELLI, PIETOSI, UMANI, BETHEL, de SYNAGOGA, CASADIO, BOZECCO, BOZECCI, BETHELIDES, POMIS, PISA, SAN MINIATO, TIVOLI and OLMO.

ANCELL—Ashkenazic name, possibly a variation of ANSCHEL.

ANCHEL—See ANSCHEL.

ANCONA—Italian name. JE has article on 15th-cent. copyist Jacob ben Elia d'Ancona. Related to FINZI.

ANDRADA (also Andrade)—French and Portuguese name; JE has biographies from 17th and 18th cent., also the Andrade family crest in its article on "Coat of Arms."

ANDRADE—See ANDRADA.

ANDREWS—AJA has family tree beginning 1753. See also SALOMON, NONES.

ANDREYEV—UJ has article on Russian writer Leonid Andreyev (b. 1871).

ANDRIESSE—For a family history, see "Het Geslacht Andriesse," in *Gens Vostra*.

ANGEL (also Angeli, Angell)—Turkish Jewish name dating back to 16th cent. JE has biographies from Damascus, Constantinople and London, 19th cent.; EJ has biographies from Turkey and Bulgaria, 16th and 17th cent. CAJ has records of the Angeli family.

ANGELI—See ANGEL.

ANGELL—See ANGEL.

ANGERTHAL—LBI has family tree.

ANHAUCH—LBI has family tree.

ANIN—Related to SCHATZ.

ANISIMOV—UJ has article on Russian author Ilia Anisimov (b. 1862). See also NISSIM-OGLU.

ANKAVA (also Ankawa)—Sephardic North African family descended from AL-NAQUA. See JE and EJ. UJ has article on Moroccan Rabbi Raphael Ankava (1848–1935), who married the daughter of Rabbi Issachar ACERRAF.

ANKERBERG—PD has family records. Related to EPSTEIN.

ANKOA—See ALNAQUA.

ANSCHEL (also Anchel, Anschelm, Ansell, Anselm, Anshel)—Ashkenazic name derived from the first name "Anshel," first applied to 15th-cent. Rabbi Anshel ha-Levi of Cologne, who was known as Anschelm or Anselm. Also found in Cracow, Poland, early 16th cent., and Germany, late 19th cent.; see JE and EJ. Also see *The Descendants of Herz Anschel of Bonn*. Related to BIRNBAUM.

ANSCHELM—See ANSCHEL.

ANSELL—See ANSCHEL.

ANSELM—See ANSCHEL.

ANSHEL—See ANSCHEL.

ANSORGE—UJ has article on U.S. lawyer Martin Ansorge (b. 1882).

ANSPACH—Ashkenazic name of French Jews in 19th cent., probably taken from the Bavarian town of Ansbach, or Aspach. See JE. Related to ROTHSCHILD.

ANTEBI—See ANTIBI.

ANTIBI (also Antebi)—Family of rabbis in Egypt and Palestine since 18th cent. The name is derived from Ain Tab, a town in southern Turkey. See EJ, which also has an article on Albert Antebi (b. 1869), descended from a Damascus rabbinical family that may be related. Also see BERAK-HAH.

ANTIN—UJ has two biographies from Russia, 19th and 20th cent. Related to GRABAU.

ANTOINE—JE has article on French theologian Nicholas Antoine (1602–1632), who converted to Judaism and was burned at the stake in Geneva.

ANTOKOLSKI—CAJ has family records. UJ has article on sculptor Mark Antokolski (b. 1842 in Vilna, d. 1902 in Germany).

ANTON—18th-cent. author Carl Anton was born Moses Gershon COHEN at Mitau, Courland (or Kurland), Russia, and claimed descent from Hayyim Vital CALABRESE. He later converted to Christianity. See JE.

ANTONIO—Portuguese family living in Lisbon, first half of 16th cent. See JE. Also see ANTUNYES.

ANTUNYES—Marrano family from Portugal which settled in Brazil in 1557. Branches have also been traced in 17th cent. in Amsterdam, Surinam and the British West Indies; see EJ. Also see ANTONIO.

APOLANT—UJ has two biographies from Germany, 19th and 20th cent.

APOTHEKER (also Aptheker)—Polish name derived from the word for "apothecary." First known to have been used by an Abraham Isaac Apotheker (second half of 16th cent.), of Vladimir, Volhynia, Russia. See JE.

APPEL—Ashkenazic name meaning "apple." LBI has family tree. EJ has article on Lithuanian Zionist Judah Leib Appel (b. 1857).

APPELZWEIG—CAJ has family tree from Hungary.

APT (also Apta)—LBI has family tree. EJ has article on Polish Rabbi Meir Apta (1760–1831). The name may be a variation of ABT.

APTA—See APT.

APTHEKER—See APOTHEKER.

APTOWITZER—UJ and EJ have articles on Galician scholar Viktor Aptowitzer (b. 1871), also known as AVIGDOR.

APTROD—See ABT.

ARA—Related to GUETTA.

ARAMA—UJ has article on Talmudist Isaac Arama (1420–1494).

ARANYI (also Aranyo)—Related to AUFRECHT, BELMONTE, VAMBERY.

ARBIB—UJ and EJ have articles on Italian deputy Eduardo Arbib (1840–1906), who was descended from Isaac ben ARROYO of 16th-cent. Salonika.

ARCHIVOLTI—UJ and EJ have articles on poet Samuel Archivolti (1515–1611), also known as Samuel JACOB.

ARDIT (also Arditi, Ardot, Ardut)—Sephardic family traced to 15th-cent. Aragon (Spain) which emigrated to Turkey, where descendants were living in 1900. It is probably related to a family of physicians named Ardut in 14th-cent. Aragon, and it may also be connected with Ardotial Shem-tov ben Isaac, an early-14th-cent. Spanish poet. See JE and EJ.

ARDITI—See ARDIT.

ARDOT—See ARDIT.

ARDUT—See ARDIT.

ARENDT—EJ has article on Otto Arendt (1854–1936), German economist who married into the MORGENSTERN family. Name may be related to ARNDT.

ARENSDORFF—LBIS has some family notes.

AREZZO—Related to FINZI.

ARHA—EJ has article on Eliezer Arha, Israeli cabalist (d. 1652).

ARIA (also Arias)—Sephardic family name; see JE. EJ has article on Marrano author Joseph Arias of Brussels and Amsterdam (17th cent.).

ARIAS—See ARIA.

ARIPUL—EJ has article on scholar Samuel Aripul (1540–1586).

ARKES (also Arkin)—Ashkenazic name. UJ has article on pathologist Aaron Arkin (b. 1888 in Latvia). See also DEICHES.

ARKIN—See ARKES.

ARLOSOROFF (also Arlozoroff)—CAJ has some Arlozoroff family records. UJ has article on Zionist Victor Arlosoroff (b. 1899).

ARLOZOROFF—See ARLOSOROFF.

ARMIN—UJ has article on painter Emil Armin (b. in 1883 in Rumania).

ARMSTRONG-JONES—Related to MESSEL.

ARNDT—UJ and EJ have biographies from Germany, 19th and 20th cent. Name may be related to ARENDT. See also KISCH.

ARNHEIM—German name dating from 18th cent.; may have been taken from the Dutch city southeast of Amsterdam. See JE and EJ.

ARNHOLD—See ARNOLD.

ARNOLD (also Arnhold)—Ashkenazic name, usually German. AJA has family tree beginning 18th cent.; LBI also has an Arnhold family tree. UJ has two biographies. See also SELIGMAN.

ARNSTEIN (also Arnsteiner, Aronstein, Arnsztajn)—Ashkenazic name taken from the town of Arnstein in Bavaria; another variation of the derivation is ORENSTEIN. Arnstein was a prominent Austrian name in 18th cent., primarily through Fanny von Arnstein of Vienna, daughter of Daniel ITZIG of Berlin; Fanny's daughter married PEREIRA. EJ, LBI and CAJ have family trees; JE article on "Coat of Arms" contains the family crest. Other family histories are in JFF, No. 11 and No. 25, and in *Die Familie Arnstein*. Relatives include WERTHEIMER, STRELITZ, MENDELSSOHN, NYMWEGEN, von HERZ, KAUDERS, WULFF, ADAM, MACHADO, von ALBRECHTSBURG, JEANETTE, LANDAUER, GOMPERZ and MEYERSON.

ARNSTEINER—See ARNSTEIN.

ARNSWALDE—Related to PHILLIPSON.

ARNSZTAJN—See ARNSTEIN.

ARNTHAL—Ashkenazic name. LBI has a family tree.

AROLLIA (also Alroy, Aroyo, Ben Aroloyo, Arroyo)—EJ has entries on two separate 16th-cent. authors in Salonika, one named Arroyo who was an ancestor of the Italian ARBIB family, the other an ancestor of Aroyo, Alroy and Ben Aroloyo. UJ has an article on the false messiah David Alroy (11th–12th cent.).

ARON—French and German name traced to court medalist Philip Aron of Mecklenburg (1750s); see EJ and JE. LBI has a family tree; AJA has a tree of an Aron family of Louisiana. See also FRANCK.

ARONHOLD—UJ has article on German mathematician Siegfried Aronhold (1819–1884). Name may be related to ARNHOLD.

ARONIUS—UJ has article on German historian Julius Aronius (1861–1893).

ARONOWITSCH—Related to RABINOVICH.

ARONS (also Aronsohn, Aronssohn, Aronson)—Ashkenazic name originating in Germany. UJ has biographies from Germany and Russia, 19th cent. AJA has a family tree for Aronson. Other variations are ARON and L'ARRONGE. Related to HACOHEN in Russia.

ARONSOHN, ARONSON—See ARONS.

ARONSTAM—UJ has article on U.S. physician Noah Aronstam (b. 1872 in Latvia).

ARONSTEIN—See ARNSTEIN.

AROYO—See AROLLIA.

ARPA—Italian family of musicians in Mantua; the name is derived from "harp." See EJ article on Abramo Arpa (1542–1577), also known as Abraham LEVI.

ARRAGEL (also Al-Ragil)—Sephardic name. UJ has article on 15th-cent. Spanish Rabbi Moses Arragel.

ARROYO—See AROLLIA.

ARTOM—Family name derived from Asti in Piedmont, probably related to families of the same name in France, 19th cent.; see EJ. UJ has biographies from England and Italy.

ARUNDI—EJ has article on 14th-cent. Italian philosopher Isaac Arundi.

ARUSI—EJ has article on Yemenite folk-poet Abraham Arusi (b. 1878).

ARYE—See "Chronicle of the Family Arye of Samokov, Bulgaria," in Jews in Bulgaria.

ASAEL—EJ has article on Salonika Rabbi Hayyim Asael (1650–1707).

ASCARELLI—UJ has article on Italian poetess Deborah Ascarelli (16th–17th cent.).

ASCH (also Ash)—Ashkenazic family name which is an abbreviation of either "Alt Shul," "Amsterdam" or "Eisenstadt." Families with the name came respectively from Prague, Amsterdam or Eisenstadt, and in some cases are related to families named ALTSCHUL and EISENSTADT. There was a German Rabbi Abraham Asch in Posen (late 18th cent.); see JE. LBI has a family tree beginning 1495. Also see Zur Familiengeschichte Asch. See also BERLIN and DEUTSCH. Another variation is ASCHER.

ASCHAFFENBURG—EJ has article on German criminologist Gustav Aschaffenburg (b. 1866).

ASCHER (also Asher, Ascherson, Aschinsky)—German and Polish name that dates to 17th cent. and is probably a variation of ASCH. LBI has family tree beginning 1801; PD has some family records. JE and UJ have several biographies. See also JAFFE, de SOLA.

ASCHERSON—See ASCHER.

ASCHINSKY—See ASCHER.

ASCHKENASI—See ASHKENAZI.

ASCHROTT—See SAMSON.

ASCOLI—Italian name dating back at least to 15th cent.; see JE. Related to BERR, FINZI.

ASEN—UJ has article on translator Abraham Asen, (b. 1886 in Russia).

ASH—See ASCH.

ASHENHEIM—Scottish family that settled in Jamaica, 18th cent.; see EJ.

ASHER—See ASCHER.

ASHERIDES—Sephardic family of Toledo, Spain. See Zunz GL, p. 421, also JJLG, Vol. 12, p. 237, Vol. 13, p. 142, for a family history from 1267 to 1391.

ASHKENASI—See ASHKENAZI.

ASHKENAZ—See ASHKENAZI.

ASHKENAZI (also Aschkenasi, Ashkenasi, Ashkenaz, Ashkinasi, Askanazy, Askenazy, Asknazi, Asknazy, Eskenazy, etc.)—A Hebrew name meaning "Germany," from where most of its holders originated. The name can be traced as far back as 10th cent.; in most cases it refers to origin in southern and western Germany. People with this name are *not* related to the Biblical people known as Ashkenazi who subsequently settled in western Armenia. Zebi Hirsch Ashkenazi, rabbi of Altona (1660–1718), was the father of Jacob EMDEN, who married NEUMARK. Also see JE article on *Aryeh Loeb ben Saul* (also called Levi Saul Loewenstam), who married the eldest daughter of Zebi Hirsch Ashkenazi. JE and UJ have numerous biographies; also see EJ article on *Adel,* daughter of the Baal Shemtob, who married Jehiel Ashkenazi. An Aschkenasi family tree can be found in JFF, No. 21. Related families include LEVINSON, JAFFE, RAGOLER, ALAMAN, JABEZ, KATZENELLENBOGEN, EDELS, TEMERIS, AZRIEL, TREVES, YERUSHALMI, LAMBERT, STADTHAGEN, KROCHMAL, SPIRA, MIRELS, LORBEERBAUM, GUNZENHAUSER, ULIF, BEKEMOHARAR, ANASCHEHON and WEIDNER.

ASHKINASI—See ASHKENAZI.

ASHLEY—Related to CASSEL.

ASHRIKI—EJ has article on Moroccan adviser Mordecai Ashriki (18th cent.).

ASKANAZY—See ASHKENAZI.

ASKENAZY—See ASHKENAZI.

ASKNAZI—See ASHKENAZI.

ASKNAZY—See ASHKENAZI.

ASKOWITH—UJ has article on educator Dora Askowith (b. 1884 in Lithuania).

ASRO—UJ has article on actor Alexander Asro (b. 1892 in Vilna).

ASSAF (also Osofsky)—UJ has two biographies from Russia, 19th and 20th cent.

ASSER—Dutch name dating back to Moses Asser (18th cent.). May be related to variations of ASCHER, although this isn't necessarily so. JE article on "Coat of Arms" has the Asser family crest, and JE also has several biographies. Related to LEVIN, VARNHAGEN. Also see ASSUR.

ASSING—UJ has article on German writer Ludmila Assing (1827–1880), niece of Varnhagen von ENSE.

ASSUMPCAO—Sephardic name. EJ has article on Diogo da Assumpcao, Marrano martyr (1579–1603).

ASSUR—LBIS has family notes. Also see ASSER.

ASTERLITZ—Related to FLESCH.

ASTRUC—French family that dates back to 13th cent.; the name means "born under a lucky star." JE has an extensive family-tree chart beginning in 17th cent. Related to BONSENYOR.

ASYL—LBI has family tree beginning 1740.

ASZOD—EJ has article on Judah Aszod, Hungarian rabbi (1794–1866).

ATAR—See ATTAR.

ATATORA—Related to MONTEFIORE.

ATHIA—See ATHIAS.

ATHIAS (also Athia, Atias)—Spanish family distinguished by numerous scholars. Some members were in Italy and Palestine in 16th cent.; another branch went to Hamburg, Amsterdam and London. JE has many biographies. Related to CARABAJAL, BELMONTE.

ATIAS—See ATHIAS.

ATLAS—Ashkenazic name derived from EDELS. JE and UJ have biographies from 19th cent.

Ibn ATTAR (also Atar, Abenatar, Abiatar, Benatar, etc.)—Sephardic name that means "apothecary" or "spice dealer" in Arabic. The family name dates to 14th cent. Members were widespread in North Africa at one time; in 1900, descendants with various forms of the name were living in Amsterdam, Italy and Palestine. See family history in KS; JE also has twenty-two biographies. Related to AVILA, MELO, BELMONTE, MELDOLA.

ATTIA—EJ has article on Shem Tov Attia, Salonikan rabbi (1530–1601).

AUB—German name. JE has four biographies, beginning 1805. Related to KOHLER, SULZBERGER.

AUER—German name. See *The Auer Family Tree.* UJ has article on Hungarian violinist Leopold Auer (1845–1930).

AUERBACH (also Auerbacher, Awerbach, Awerbuch, Orbach, Urbach)—Family of scholars descended from Moses Auerbach, court Jew to the Bishop of Regensburg, Germany, 1497. One of his daughters is the reputed ancestress of Rabbi Moses ISSERLES. The family name is taken from the town of Auerbach. Another branch of the family settled in Vienna; JE has a family tree of this branch. EJ also has a family tree. CAJ has family trees from Germany, 1740–1954; LBI has trees beginning 1600 and 1745. LBIS has notes of the family of Meshullam Salman Auerbach of Vienna. AJA also has a family tree. *Reshimoth Aboth,* by Markus Seckbach, shows the family's relationship with other rabbinic families. Also see *The Auerbach Family: The Descendants of Abraham Auerbach.* Relatives include FISCHHOF, ROFE, SINZHEIM, MARGOLIOTH, KATZENELLENBOGEN, LANDESMANN, MALBIM, LOB, LINZ, LURIA, LIPSCHITZ, WAHL, LOWENTHAL, CLASSEN, ANSCHEL, OPPENHEIM, SUSSMANN, JACOB, BINGEN, GREENHUT and KAULLA.

AUERBACHER—See AUERBACH.

AUERNHEIMER—EJ has article on Austrian author Raoul Auernheimer (b. 1876).

AUFRECHT—German name; Hungarian variation is ARANYI.

AUGUSTI—JE has two biographies, 17th- and 18th-cent. Germany.

AULBREGUE—See VALABREGUE.

AUSCHER—CAJ has family tree.

AUSLANDER (also Auslaender)—UJ has two biographies from Russia and U.S.A.

AUSPITZ—Austrian family dating back to 18th cent.; the name is derived from the Moravian town of Hustopece. LBI has family tree beginning 1663. JE has biographies from Austria and Hungary. A family history can be found in *Fünfzig Jahre eines Wiener Hauses.* Related to SHAYE, GOMPERZ, LIEBEN, LIEBER.

AUSTERLITZ—Family name first found in Prague in 1670 among Jews who emigrated from the Austrian town of the same name. The name was also current at that time in Austria and Hungary. JE has five biographies. Related to TAUSK.

AUTOR—CAJ has family records.

AVENEL—French name. JE has several biographies.

AVERNAS-LE-GRAS—The family crest can be found in JE article on "Coat of Arms."

AVICEBRON—Related to GABIROL.

AVIGDOR—See ABIGDOR.

d'AVIGDOR—See ABIGDOR.

AVILA—Moroccan family of prominent rabbis, 17th and 18th cent. A Spanish branch of the family that converted to Catholicism can be traced back to 15th cent. JE has three biographies. Related to ATTAR.

AWANI—JE has biography of Bagdad poet Ishak Ibn Al-Awani.

AWERBACH—See AUERBACH.

AWERBUCH—See AUERBACH.

AXELROD—See ACHSELRAD.

AXENFELD—JE and UJ have biographies, 18th and 19th cent.

AYAS—See AYASH.

AYASH (also Ayas, Ayyash)—Algerian rabbinical family of 17th and 18th cent.; see EJ. JE has article on Leon Ayas, a French army interpreter in the 1846 Algerian campaign.

AYDAN—EJ has article on Tunisian Rabbi David Aydan (1873–1954).

AYLION—See AYLLON.

AYLLON (also Aelion, Aylion, Hillion)—Solomon ben Jacob Ayllon, head of the Sephardic congregations of Amsterdam and London (17th cent.), was born in the Orient, also lived in Salonika. See JE.

AYRTON—English inventor Hertha Ayrton (1854–1923) was the daughter of Levi MARKS; her husband was the father-in-law of Israel ZANGWILL. See UJ.

AYYAS—JE has article on North African commentator Judah Ayyas (b. 1690), who died in Jerusalem. Possibly related to AYASH.

AYYASH—See AYASH.

AZAN—See ACAN.

AZANKOT—JE has article on Moroccan teacher Saadia ben Levi Azankot (early 17th cent.), who lived in Holland.

AZARIA (also Azariah)—JE has biographies from Perpignan, France, 1400, and Furth, Germany, 18th cent. Related to ROSSI.

AZBAN—JE has article on Rabbi Mordecai ben Isaac Azban of Leghorn, Italy (b. 17th cent. in Africa, d. 1740 in Jerusalem).

AZEFF—UJ has article on Russian engineer Evno Azeff (1869–1918).

AZEVEDO—Sephardic family prominent in Amsterdam since 16th cent. The same branch has been in London since 1761, a different branch in Portugal since 1673. JE article on "Coat of Arms" has two family crests. JE and UJ have biographies. Related to MESQUITA and FERME.

AZKARI (also Azikri)—UJ has article on Palestinian Rabbi Eleazar Azkari (16th cent.).

AZIKRI—See AZKARI.

AZRIEL—Ezra ben Menahem ben Solomon Azriel, founder of the speculative cabala, was born at Gerona in 1160; see JE. Families of that name also come from Vilna and Frankfurt-am-Main. JE article on Bazarjik, Rumelia, mentions an Isaac Azriel who died there in 1709.

AZUBI—See AZUBIB.

AZUBIB (also Azubi, Azuby)—Algerian rabbinical family traced back to 17th cent.; see JE. EJ has article on U.S. Rabbi Abraham Azuby (1738–1805). See also MELDOLA.

AZUBY—See AZUBIB.

AZULAI (also Azulay)—Sephardic family descended from Spanish exiles who settled in Fez, Morocco, after the expulsion from Spain in 1492. The family later spread to Italy, England and Palestine. EJ has a chart of the Castilian branch of the family. JE has twelve biographies. Related to DAVID, ISAACI, ZEBI, LEONINI, FRIEDLAENDER, HERSCHELL, PARDO, YIZHAKI and NAVON.

AZULAY—See AZULAI.

BAAL SHEMTOB—EJ has a genealogy of Israel, the Baal Shemtob (1700–1760), founder of Hasidism. Relatives and descendants include HORODEZKY, KUTTOWER, ASHKENAZI, HEILPRIN, LOANS.

BAAR (also Baars)—JE and EJ have biographies from U.S.A. and Holland, 19th and 20th cent.

BAARS—See BAAR.

BAB—UJ has article on critic Julius Bab (b. 1880 in Berlin).

BABAD—Family of Polish rabbis dating from 17th cent., founded by Isaac of Cracow, son of Issachar BERISH. See EJ.

BABEL—UJ has article on Russian author Isaac Babel (b. 1894).

BABENBERG—See BAMBERG.

BABICZ—For a family history, see Babicz Family of Warsaw.

BABITZKY—CAJ has family records.

BABLI—Related to JEHUDAH.

BABOVICH—JE has article on Simha Babovich, head of the Crimean Karaites in early 19th cent.; his children were placed in the care of Abraham FIRKOVICH, who might be related.

BACH—Ashkenazic family name found in Germany, Bohemia and Hungary, 18th and 19th cent. LBI has family trees beginning 1540, 1726 and 1730; AJA has a family tree beginning 1854. JE has several biographies. Related to JAFFE.

BACHARACH (also Bachrach, Bachrich, Bacher, Backer, etc.)—Ashkenazic name indicating origin in Bacharach on the Rhine, in a region that then belonged to Prussia. The name first appears with Samuel Bacharach in 1175, although its accuracy is dubious. The next mention is of Ephraim Gumprecht Bacharach in 16th cent. Three major families bear the name; JE has a chart of one of these. CAJ has a family tree from Germany. Family histories can also be found in ZS; MGWJ, Vol. 43; and in R. Jair Chaim Bacharach. Da'at Kedoshim, by Israel Eisenstadt, shows the family's relation to other prominent families. Bachrach family histories can be found in Zeitschrift für der Geschichte der Juden in Tschechoslowakei. LBI has a Bacher family tree beginning 1799. Relatives include GANS, LOW, LOB, OPPENHEIM, BOHM, BAZALEL, BRILIN, HA-KOHEN, PHOEBUS, NEROL, DUBNOW, JAFFE, EISENSTADT.

BACHE—UJ has two biographies from U.S.A., 19th cent.

BACHER—See BACHARACH.

BACHI—JE has article on 18th cent. French-Italian painter Raphael Bachi.

BACHMAN (also Bachmann)—AJA has Bachmann tree in Germany; LBI has Bachmann tree beginning 1790. UJ has two biographies, 19th cent. Related to KRAUS.

BACHRACH—See BACHARACH.

BACHRICH—See BACHARACH.

BACK—EJ has article on Czech Rabbi Samuel Back (1841–1899). The name is perhaps related to BACH. Also see FRUMKIN.

BACKER—See BACHARACH.

BACRI—Algerian family traced to the 1740s. See EJ. Related to BUSNACH.

BADER—Ashkenazic name. CAJ has family records. UJ has article on Polish author Gershom Bader (b. 1868 in Cracow).

BADHAV—Isaac Badhav (1859–1947), Jerusalem rabbi, was grandson of Isaac COVO; see EJ.

BADIHI—EJ has article on Yemenite author Yahya Badihi (1810–1887).

BADRIAN—LBIS has some family notes.

BADSCHI—See BAGI.

BADT (also Barth)—Ashkenazic name that is an acronym for "ben David." UJ has three biographies from Germany and U.S.A., 19th cent. JE has a Barth biography, Germany, 19th cent. Badt family histories can be found in JFF, Nos. 14 and 21. Also see "The Barths of Missouri," in Jewish Digest (October 1971).

BAECK—UJ has biographies from 17th, 19th and 20th cent. LBI has a family tree beginning 1785. JE has an article on German Rabbi Samuel Baeck (b. 1834 in Moravia), whose family previously came from Hungary.

BAENA—Sephardic name traced to the Spanish poet Francisco de Baena (14th–15th cent.). However, his son took the name of MONTORO. The name de Baena turns up again in the 19th cent. See JE.

BAER (also Beer, Behr, Bar, Berish, Baerke, Baeril, etc.)—Ashkenazic name that was originally gentile but was borrowed by German Jews because *Bär* ("bear") was the equivalent of what the patriarch Jacob called his children. Baeril, Baerush and Baerke are Polish and Russian variations; Hebraic versions are DOB and IS-SACHAR. Another variation is BERMAN. LBI has family trees beginning 1600 and 1785; AJA has a tree beginning 1787. CAJ has some family records. LBI also has a Bar family tree beginning 1650. JE has biographies from Germany and Hungary, 17th cent., and Russia, Prussia and Poland, 18th cent. Also see *The Behr Tree (1683–1949)*. JE has an article on Lithuanian poet Issachar Behr (b. 1746), related to Israel ZAMOSC. Also see EJ article on *Abraham* Hayyim (1750–1816). Relatives include BESHT, CARMOLY, FRIEDENWALD and BABAD. Also see BEER.

BAERIL—See BAER.

BAERKE—See BAER.

BAERMANN—See BERMANN.

BAERUSH—See BAER.

BAERWALD—German name. LBI has family tree beginning 1770; LBIS has some family notes. JE has one biography from Germany, 19th cent. For a family history, see *Geschichte des Hauses Baerwald*.

BAEYER—See BAYER.

BAEZ—Related to CACERES.

BAGDADLI—Related to GABBAI.

BAGI—Prominent Karaite family living in Constantinople from 15th cent. The name is also written BADSCHI, PEGI and POKI. See JE.

BAGINSKY—German family of many physicians living in Ratibor, Prussia, in 1840s; see JE.

BAGNOL—Related to GERSON.

BAGRATIDEN—See family histories in JFF, Nos. 32 and 34.

BAHIEL—JE has article on Ben Moses Bahiel, 13th-cent. Spanish physician.

BAHLUL—Family of rabbis in Meknes, Morocco, 17th cent; see JE.

BAHTAWI—JE has article on Abu Joseph Bahtawi, 9th-cent. Karaite scholar.

BAHUR—Related to LEVITA.

BAHYA—Spanish family dating from 11th cent.; see JE.

BAIERSDORF (also Baiersdorfer, Bayersdorfer)—German name. Samson Baiersdorf (d. 1712), court Jew of Brandenburg-Bayreuth, was the son of Judah SELKE and was related to the HAMELN and GLUCKEL families. See JE and EJ. See also KOHLER and SULZBERGER.

BAIERSDORFER—See BAIERSDORF.

BAIZ—UJ has article on Central American diplomat Jacob Baiz (1843–1899).

BAK—Family of Italian and Czech printers descended from Gerson Bak, who lived in early 16th cent. A branch of the family can be traced in Russia back to 18th cent. See JE and EJ; also CB, p. 2845. Related to STEINITZ and ROKACH.

BAKER—UJ has three biographies from U.S.A.

BAKI—German and Italian family, mostly from Casale, Italy, traced back to 1582. See JE.

BAKISCH—UJ has article on 19th-cent. Bulgarian banker Manasseh Bakisch.

BAKONYI—JE has article on 19th-cent. Hungarian deputy Samuel Bakonyi.

BAKRI—Prominent Algerian family that dates from 1750. See JE and UJ.

BAKST—Russian family from St. Petersburg, first noted in early 19th cent.; see JE. UJ has an article on painter Leon Bakst (1868–1924), who was born ROSENBERG.

BALABAN (also Balabanoff, Balabanov)—CAJ has some family records. UJ has biographies from Russia, Galicia and U.S.A., 19th cent.

BALABANOFF—See BALABAN.

BALABANOV—See BALABAN.

BALAISS—See ALAISH.

BALASSA (also Balazs)—JE and EJ have articles on 19th-cent. Hungarians.

BALAZS—See BALASSA.

BALBO—EJ has article on Cretan Rabbi Michael Cohen Balbo (1411–1484).

BALI—Karaite family living in Cairo from 15th cent.; see JE.

BALIDEH—EJ has article on 15th-cent. Yemenite scholar Moses Balideh.

BALINE—See BERLIN.

BALINT—UJ has article on Hungarian architect Zoltan Balint (b. 1871).

BALL—A family history can be found in Jüdisches Leben einst und jetzt,.

BALLA (also Ballagi)—UJ has two biographies from 19th-cent. Hungary. Related to BLOCH.

BALLAGI—See BALLA.

BALLIN—Names of Danish and British families that are apparently unrelated to one another. CAJ has a family tree and records. AJA has a family tree. JFF, No. 5, has a family history. Also see Die Familie Ballin. The Danish branch is related to TRIER and MELCHIOR.

BALLY—Rumanian family from Wallachia since late 17th cent.; see JE.

BALMES—UJ has article on 15th-cent. Italian physician Abraham de Balmes.

BALOG—Related to KOHN.

BALTHAZAR—Related to CASTRO.

BAMBERG—See BAMBERGER.

BAMBERGER (also Bamberg)—Ashkenazic name derived from the German city of Bamberg, found in Germany, France, Hungary and elsewhere in 19th cent. Some variations are VAMBERY and DOB. LBI has a family tree beginning 1565. LBIS has notes of Bamberger families from Berlin and Duisburg. CAJ has a family tree covering 1692 to 1933. Also see The Descendants of Rabbi Seligmann Bar Bamberger, the "Wurzburger Rav" (1807–1878). A German family of Bamberg is descended from Samuel of Bamberg (13th cent.), also known as Samuel of Babenberg. See also BELMONT, NEUMANN, BISCHOFFSHEIM, FULD, WORMSER, LANDSBERG, STERN, FRIEDENWALD, COHN, LOEWE and ETTLINGER.

BAMBUS—UJ has article on German author Willi Bampus (1863–1904).

BAMPI—JE has article on 19th-cent. Russian scholar Issachar Dob Baer Bampi of Minsk.

BAN—JE has article on 19th-cent. Austrian writer Moritz Ban.

BANETH (also Benet, Panet, Paneth, Ben-edict, Benedicks, Benedictus, Benedite, Bendit, etc.)—German and Hungarian family name traced back to Poland in 1716. CAJ has a family tree. LBI has a Bendit family tree beginning 1746. CAJ has records of the Benet family; Talmudist Mordecai Benet (b. 1753 in Hungary, d. 1829 in Carlsbad) was born Marcus Benedict, and his son died 1857 in Moravia. LBIS has notes of a Benedicks family. JE, UJ and EJ have numerous biographies. Relatives include STOSSEL, BENNETT and FRANZOS.

BANDES—UJ has article on editor Louis Bandes (b. 1866 in Vilna).

BANDMANN—JE has article on U.S. actor Daniel Bandmann (b. 1840 in Germany).

BANDOFF—JE has article on English boxer Ben Bandoff (d. 1865).

BANFI—UJ has article on Hungarian historian Zsigmond Banfi (1857–1894).

BANK—Russian family from Tulchin, 19th cent.; see JE. Related to LEVINSON and LESSING.

BANOCZI—JE and UJ have articles on Hungarian scholar Joseph Banoczi (1849–1926).

BANTH—Related to MUNKACSY.

BAPTISTA—See BATTISTA.

BAPUGEE—JE has article on Haskel Bapugee (d. 1878), one of the Beni-Israelites of Bombay.

BAR—See BAER.

BARACH—Austrian literary family from Neu-Rausnitz, Moravia, 19th cent.; see JE. LBIS has some family notes. Related to MAERZROTH.

BARAFFAEL (also Baruffall)—JE has article on 18th-cent. Italian communal worker Isaac Baraffael.

BARAN—See BARON.

BAR ANINA (also Hanina, Chanina, Chanin)—Palestinian family name dating from 4th cent.; see JE. UJ has article on U.S. architect Irwin Chanin (b. 1891).

BARANOWICZ—EJ has article on Vilna Hebraist David Baranowicz (1859–1915). Also see BARON.

BARANYI—UJ has article on Hungarian physician Robert Baranyi (1876–1936).

BARASCH (also Barash)—Ashkenazic name common in Galicia, taken from the Hebrew acronym for "ben rabbi Schmuel." CAJ has family records. JE and UJ have biographies from 19th cent.

BARASH—See BARASCH.

BARASSA—JE has article on Spanish physician Diego Barassa, a Marrano who lived in Amsterdam, 1640; born Diego de BARROS.

BARATZ—JE has article on Russian lawyer Herman Baratz (b. 1835 in Dubno).

BARAZANI—EJ has article on Kurdish poet Asenath Barazani (1590–1670).

BARBASH—EJ has article on Russian banker Samuel Barbash (1850–1921).

BARBAVEIRA—See JE article on Miles of Marseilles (b. 1294), a physician who took the surname Barbaveira.

BARBER—JE has article on German authoress Ida Barber (b. 1842).

BARBY—Ashkenazic name taken from Barby, a small city near Halberstadt, Prussia. JE has article on Rabbi Meir ben Saul Barby (b. 1725 in Barby, d. 1789 in Pressburg).

BAR COCHBA (also Bar Cochbah, Bar Kokba)—Family name perhaps indicating descent from the leader of the 2nd-cent. rebellion against Rome. See JE.

BAR COCHBAH—See BAR COCHBA.

BARD—UJ has article on Argentine deputy Leopoldo Bard (b. 1888).

BARDACH—Name found in Galicia, Lithuania and Russia, 18th–19th cent. JE has three biographies. Related to MOSES.

BARDAKI—EJ has article on Polish-Israeli Rabbi Isaiah Bardaki (1790–1862).

BARER—UJ has article on pianist Simon Barer (b. 1896 in Russia).

BARGAS—EJ has article on 18th-cent. Marrano author Abraham Bargas, of Spain, France and Italy.

BARIT—JE has article on Russian Talmudist Jacob Barit (1797–1883).

BARKANY—JE has article on Austrian actress Marie Barkany (b. 1862), one of six daughters of a merchant in Kaschau.

BARKI—JE has article on 17th-cent. Salonikan writer Isaac ben Elijah Barki.

BAR KOKBA—See BAR COCHBA.

BARLIN—EJ has article on early 19th-cent. English painter Frederick Barlin.

BARMANN—See BERMAN.

BARNATO—UJ has article on English speculator Barnett Barnato (1852–1897), son of Isaac ISAACS.

BARNAY—UJ has article on German actor Ludwig Barnay (1842–1924), born in Hungary.

BARNERT—UJ has article on U.S. civic leader Nathan Barnert (1838–1927), born in Germany. He was a brother-in-law of Benjamin PHILLIPS of London.

BARNETT (also Barnet)—English name. Jacob Barnett was a Hebrew instructor at Oxford c. 1613; see JE. John Barnett (1802–1890) was the son of Bernhard BEER; see UJ. Related to COHEN, POLOCK, WAHL.

BARNOWSKY—UJ has article on German actor Victor Barnowsky (b. 1875).

BARNSTON—UJ has article on English Rabbi Henry Barnston (b. 1868).

BAROFF—UJ has article on labor leader Abraham Baroff (1870–1932), born in Russia.

BARON (also Baran, Barron)—Ashkenazic name which is sometimes a Hebrew acronym for "ben Rabbi Nachman," the ancestor from whom the name is taken. JE and UJ have biographies from France, Russia, Hungary and U.S.A., 19th and 20th cent. Related to LOITMAN.

BARONDESS—UJ has article on labor leader Joseph Barondess (1867–1928), born in Russia.

BARRASSA—See BARASSA.

BARRIOS—JE has article on Spanish poet Daniel Levi de Barrios (1625–1701), died in Amsterdam.

BARROCAS—JE has article on Mordecai Barrocas, a Marrano in Holland c. 1605. Tamar Barrocas, a relative, was burned at the stake in Lisbon in 1603.

BARRON—See BARON.

BARROS—See BARASSA. Also see EJ article on Arturo Barros Basto (b. 1887), leader of the Marrano revival in Portugal.

BARROW—Related to MONTEFIORE and LOUSADA.

BARRUCHIUS—JE has article on Spanish poet Valentinus Barruchius (12th cent.).

BARSIMON—See BARSIMSON.

BARSIMSON (also Barsimon, Barstinsen, Bersimson)—JE has article on Jacob Barsimson, early Dutch settler in New York, 1654.

BARSTINSEN—See BARSIMSON.

BARTH—See BADT.

BARTHOLDY—German and Italian name. Jacob Salomon Bartholdy (b. 1779 in Berlin, d. 1825 in Rome), uncle of Felix MENDELSSOHN-Bartholdy, was of a prosperous family. See JE. Related to ITZIG.

BARTOLUCCI—UJ has article on Italian Hebraist Giulio Bartolucci (1613–1687).

BARUCH (also Baruchowitz)—Hebrew name meaning "blessed," found in both Sephardic and Ashkenazic families. Baruch ben Moses Ibn Baruch, a 16th-cent. Italian philosopher, belonged to an old noble Spanish family named Baruch; this family may be related to the ALBALIA family. It's also the name of a prominent Polish mechanic in early 18th cent., and the name also appears in France, Germany and Austria; see JE. CAJ has a family tree from the Netherlands; AJA has a tree for the family of U.S. financier Bernard Baruch. See also BORNE and BERENDSEN.

BARUCHOWITZ—See BARUCH.

BARUFFALL—See BARAFFAEL.

BARZILAI—UJ has two biographies from 19th-cent. Italy.

BAS—CAJ has family tree from the Netherlands.

BASAN—Portuguese family in Amsterdam and Hamburg, 18th cent.; see JE.

BASAU—Related to VAN OVEN.

BASCH (also Bash, Brasch, Baschko, Baschwitz)—Ashkenazic name derived from ben Shimeon; in other cases, it's an abbreviation of the town of Bochstein or Borgkunstadt. PD has family records. JE and UJ have biographies from 19th-cent. Germany, Hungary, Austria, France. Polish Rabbi Zebi Baschko (1740–1807), who died in Germany, was related to Ezekiel LANDAU. JE has a tree chart for Baschwitz, a family of German printers from 18th cent.

BASCHKO—See BASCH.

BASCHWITZ—See BASCH.

BASEVI (also Basewi)—Italian and English name. JE has several biographies. George Basevi's sister Maria married Isaac DISRAELI and was the mother of British Prime Minister Benjamin Disraeli. Related to CERVETTO. See also BASSEVI.

BASEWI—See BASEVI.

BASHIRI—EJ has article on Yemenite scribe Yahya Bashiri (17th cent.).

BASHYAZI—Karaite family traced back to Adrianople, 1420; see JE, UJ, EJ. Related to AFENDOPOLO and POKI.

BASILEA (also Basila, Bassola, Basola, Basla)—Family originally from Basel, Switzerland (whence the name), but found in northern Italy and Palestine, 15th–18th cent.; see UJ. EJ has article on Italian Rabbi Moses Basola (1480–1560).

BASIR—EJ has article on 11th-cent. Karaite author Joseph Basir.

BASLA—See BASILEA.

BASLANSKI—See BOSLANSKI.

BASOLA—See BASILEA.

BASS (also Bassista)—JE has article on Polish bibliographer Shabbetai ben Joseph Bass (1641–1718). A Hebrew variation of the name is MESHORER.

BASSAN—See BASSANI.

BASSANI (also Bassan, Bassano)—A name probably of Hebrew origin, although some Jewish families took their names from the Italian city of Bassano, near Florence. JE has biographies from Italy and Constantinople, beginning with the Italian Rabbi Hezekiah Mordecai ben Samuel Bassani (late 16th and early 17th cent.). EJ says 18th-cent. Spanish proofreader Abraham Bassan was the first to shorten the name from Bassani. Also see UJ article on *Benjamin* ben Eliezer. Related to NAVARRE, COEN.

BASSANO—See BASSANI.

BASSERMAN—Related to SAMSON.

BASSEVI—Abraham Bassevi was head of the congregation in Prague (16th cent.); his son, financier Jacob Bassevi von Treuenberg (1580–1634), married the daughter of Ebert GERONIM; see JE and UJ. JFF, Nos. 1 and 15, have family histories. LBI has a family tree beginning 1545. PD has family records. JE article on "Coat of Arms" has the family crest. Relatives include BAT-SHEBA and MAY. See also BASEVI.

BASSISTA—See BASS.

BASSOLA—See BASILEA.

BAS-TIMOV—EJ has article on 17th-cent. Ukrainian author Sarah Bas-Timov.

BASURTO—JE has article on 17th-cent. Marrano poet Diego Enriquez Basurto, born in Spain, the son of Antonio Enriquez GOMEZ; he subsequently lived in Rouen and Holland.

BASY—UJ has article on impresario Alexander Basy (1883–1937), born in Russia.

BAT-SHEBA—Family of 16th- and 17th-cent. printers. The name originates from the feminine Bath-sheba. The first known member is Mattathia Bat-Sheba (d. 1600 at Salonika). The family's descendants include the BASSEVI family of Prague.

BATHYRA (also Betera, Beterah)—Family whose name is probably taken from the city of Bathyra, Syria. The name is mentioned in the Talmud and the Midrash. Two Bathyra brothers were heads of the Sanhedrin under King Herod I in Roman Palestine; see JE.

BATOR—JE has article on Hungarian composer Szidor Bator (b. 1860), also known as BREISACH.

BATTISTA (also Baptista)—JE has article on Giovanni Battista (b. 1588), a baptized Jew who was professor of Hebrew and librarian of the Vatican; his original name was ISAAC. An Egyptian branch of the family was related in 16th cent. to LEVITA.

BATURSKY—UJ has article on Russian socialist Boris Batursky (1879–1920).

BAUER—Ashkenazic name, usually from Germany. CAJ has family tree from Germany. PD has family records. JE has three biographies from Hungary and Austria, 19th cent. See also UJ article on Bauer-Landauer. Related to LEHMANN, GERSHOM and SCHWAB.

BAUERSDORF—PD has family records.

BAUKSER—Related to JAFFE.

BAUM—Ashkenazic name that means "tree" in German. UJ has biographies from 19th-cent. Germany and Austria. CAJ has family records. Also see *We Remember: Saga of the Baum-Webster Family Tree, 1842–1964*. Related to WEBSTER and LERT.

BAUMAN—Related to GOLDMAN.

BAUMGARTEN—JE has biographies from 19th-cent. Austria and Hungary. PD has family records.

BAUMHORN—UJ has article on Hungarian architect Lipot Baumhorn (b. 1860).

BAVLI—EJ has article on 16th-cent. Italian Rabbi Menaham Bavli. UJ has article on Lithuanian poet Hillel Bavli (b. 1893).

BAYER (also Baeyer)—German name meaning "from Bavaria"—Bayern in German. LBI has family tree beginning 1783. EJ has article on German chemist Adolf von Baeyer (1835–1917), whose father married into the HITZIG, or ITZIG, family.

BAYERSDORFER—See BAIERSDORF.

BAYERTHAL—LBI has a family tree beginning 1730.

BAYLINSON—UJ has article on U.S. painter Abraham Baylinson (b. 1882 in Russia). The name may be a variation of BEILIS.

BAYLIS—See BEILIS.

BAZALEEL—See BEZALEL.

BAZALEL—See BEZALEL.

BAZE—JE has article on Abraham de Baze of Orange, Burgundy (early 16th cent.).

BEAR—American variation of BAER. UJ has two biographies from 19th-cent. U.S.A.

BEARSTED—UJ has article on British oil magnate Viscount Bearsted (1853–1927), born Marcus SAMUEL.

BEBRI (also Berbi)—Moses ben Judah Bebri, ambassador from Sultan Mohammed IV to King Charles XI of Sweden, died 1673 in Amsterdam; his son Judah Berbi returned to Constantinople; see JE. JE article on "Coat of Arms" has the family crest.

BECHER—See BECK.

BECHHOLD—UJ has article on German chemist Heinrich Bechhold (1868–1937).

BECHMANN—LBI has family tree beginning 1666.

BECK (also Becker, Becher, Bekker, etc.) —Ashkenazic name. Wolf Becher was a German physician (b. 1682 in Posen, Prussia). Jacob ben Enoch Beck was *dayyan* and *shochet* at Leipnik, Moravia (late 18th–early 19th cent.). JE and UJ have several biographies from 19th-cent. Galicia, Hungary, Rumania, Austria, Germany and U.S.A. Other variations of the name are BAECK and BARUCH. Also see MADARASSY-BECK.

BECKER—See BECK.

BEDARESI—See BEDERSI.

BEDARRIDE—See BEDERSI.

BEDDINGTON—English name. JE has three biographies from 19th cent. Related to LEVERSON, MONTEFIORE and SELIGMAN.

BEDERSI (also Bedaresi, Bedarride)— French name meaning "native of Beziers," first used by 13th-cent. Provençal poet Abraham ben Isaac Bedersi; see JE. UJ has two biographies from 13th-cent. France, also French lawyer Isaie Bedarride (1799–1869). Related to KALIFA.

BEDJARANO—Family from Bejar, Spain. Turkish Rabbi Hayim Bedjarano was born 1846. See UJ.

BEER—Ashkenazic name; a variation of BAER. JE has seventeen biographies from 15th-cent. Italy, 18th-cent. Germany and 19th-cent. Austria, Moravia, France and England. 19th-cent. German banker Jacob Herz Beer married Amalie WOLF, a great-granddaughter of Lipmann Wolf TAUSSIG, or TAUSK. Jacob and Amalie had four sons, including the composer Giacomo MEYERBEER. German author Bernhard Beer was descended from the BONDI family, which came to Dresden in mid-18th cent. 19th-cent. English journalist Rachel Beer was a daughter of SASSOON. CAJD has a tree of a German Beer family related to LOEW. LBI has family trees beginning 1767 and 1823. For family histories, see JFF, No. 14; also the autobiography of Austrian educator Peter (Perez) Beer (1758–1838) and *Urkundliches von Michael Beer und über seine Familie*. Relatives include BING (Beer-Bing), BISCHOFFSHEIM, SELIGMAN, BARNETT and LIEBMANN. Also see BEER-HOFMANN.

BEERBOHM—UJ has article on caricaturist Max Beerbohm (b. 1872 in London).

BEER-HOFMANN—LBI has family tree beginning 1713. EJ has article on Austrian poet Richard Beer-Hofmann (1866–1945). See also BEER, HOFMANN.

BEERMAN—See BERMAN.

BEETH—JE has article on Austrian singer Lola Beeth (b. 1862 in Cracow).

BEGHI—Karaite scholarly family dating from 15th cent.; see EJ.

BEGIN—French name. JE has biographies from late 18th and early 19th cent.

BEHAIM—Related to ZACUTO.

BEHAK—JE has article on writer Judah Behak (1820–1900), born in Vilna.

BEHAR—Possibly a variation of BAER, BEER or BEHR. JE has biographies from 19th-cent. Baghdad, Salonika and Palestine.

BEHR—See BAER.

BEHREND (also Behrends, Behrens, Behrendt, Berend, Berendson, Berendt, Berenson, etc.)—Ashkenazic name first adopted by Leffmann Behrends (1630–1714), financial agent in Hannover whose father was Issachar BARMANN (d. 1675), son of the Talmudic scholar Isaac COHEN of Borkum. Leffmann's first wife, Jente, was the daughter of Joseph HAMELN, president of the Hannover congregation; they had four sons and a daughter who married David OPPENHEIM, chief rabbi of Prague. Leffmann Behrends' second wife was a daughter of Judah Selkele DILMANN. See JE, which has several biographies from 19th-cent. Germany and England. AJA has family tree beginning 17th cent. LBI has Behrens tree beginning 1570, also a Berend family tree. LBIS has some notes on the Behrens and Behrendt families. A family history can be found in *Geschichte der Familien Valentin, etc.* Related to VALENTIN, LOE, MANHEIMER, BELMONT, HAMMERSCHLAG, HEINE, ROSENBERG, GOLDNER, GOLDSCHMID, YOUNG, EDELSTEIN, FRIEDENWALD, ROTHSCHILD, WERTHEIMER, MANNHEIMER, CORINTH and HERTZ.

BEHRENDS—See BEHREND.

BEHRENS—See BEHREND.

BEHRENDT—See BEHREND.

BEHRMAN (Behrmann)—See BERMAN.

BEILIN (also Beilinson, Beilis, Baylis, etc.) —Ashkenazic name derived from the female name Beila. JE and UJ have biographies from Russia and England, 19th cent. Related to CONS. A possible variation is BELIN, BELLIN or BELLIS.

BEILINSON—See BEILIN.

BEILIS—See BEILIN.

BEIM—JE has article on Karaite *hazzan* Solomon ben Abraham Beim (b. 1820 in Odessa).

BEIN—UJ has article on novelist Albert Bein (b. 1902 in Russia).

BEINOS—Related to WAHL.

BEISER—JE has article on Austrian physician Moses Beiser of Lemberg (1807–1880).

BEIT—CAJ has family tree. JE has article on South African financier Alfred Beit (1853–1906), son of a well-known Hamburg family.

BEJA—EJ has article on Bulgarian preacher Isaac Beja (1570–1628).

BEJERANO—EJ has article on Bulgarian Rabbi Bekhor Bejerano (1850–1931).

BEKACHE—EJ has article on Indian-Iraqi printer Shalom Bekache (1848–1927).

BEKE—UJ has two biographies from 19th-cent. Hungary.

BEKEMOHARAR—Family of rabbis in Adrianople, 17th to 19th cent., descended from Menahem ASHKENAZI (1666–1733), who signed his name "Bkmohrr"; see EJ.

BEKHOR SHOR—See SCHOR.

BEKKER—See BECK.

BELAIS—See ALAISH.

BELASCO (also Velasco)—JE has three biographies from 18th- and 19th-cent. England. Related to JAMES and GEST. Also see UJ.

BELENKI—UJ has article on Russian Communist leader Hirsh Belenki (b. 1885).

BELFORTE—EJ has article on Solomon Belforte, 19th-cent. printer in Leghorn, Italy.

BELIAS (also Beliash)—JE has article on Samuel Belias, envoy from Morocco (early 17th cent.).

BELID (also Belitus)—Name of a prominent Jew in 13th-cent. Toulouse, France; see JE.

BELILHOS (also Bellilos, Belilla)—Daniel Belilhos of Amsterdam (17th cent.) was the son-in-law of Isaac de Fonseca ABOAB (d. 1693). David Belilla lived near Cochin, southern India (16th cent.). See JE.

BELILLA—See BELILHOS.

BELIN—JE has two biographies from 15th-cent. Germany. A possible variation is BEILIN.

BELINFANTE—Sephardic family that traces its ancestry back to Joseph Cohen Belinfante, a fugitive from Portugal to Turkey in 1526. Some of his descendants were in Amsterdam in 18th cent. JE has a family-tree chart and biographies. Elijah Hezekiah Belinfante (b. 1699) married Rachel da COSTA of London.

BELINSON—See BEILIN.

BELISARIO—English authoress Miriam Mendes Belisario (b. 1820) was a granddaughter of Isaac MENDES Belisario. See JE.

BELISHA (also Bellis, Hore-Belisha)—Moroccan family of merchants dating from 18th cent.; see JE. The name is a Sephardic contraction of ben Elisha, "son of Elisha." British official Leslie Hore-Belisha was born Belisha and added the name of his stepfather, HORE; see UJ.

BELKIN—See BELKIND.

BELKIND (also Belkin)—Russian teacher Israel Belkind (b. 1861 near Minsk) was the son of Rabbi Meir Belkind; see JE. EJ has family tree. Related to HANKIN, FEINBERG, FREIMAN.

BELKOVSKY—JE has article on Russian economist Gregoire Belkovsky (b. 1865 in Odessa).

BELLELI—JE has article on 19th-cent. Greek writer Lazarus Belleli.

BELLERSTEIN—LBIS has some family notes.

BELLILOS—See BELILHOS.

BELLIS—See BELISHA.

BELLISON—UJ has article on clarinetist Simon Bellison, (b. 1884 in Russia). See also BELISHA.

BELMONTE (also Belmonte, Belmont-Alzey)—Belmonte is a Portuguese-Dutch Marrano family traced back to Don Iago y SAMPAYO, to whom in 1519 King Manuel of Portugal gave the city of Belmonte, allowing Iago to take its name. A later branch is the Belmont family of Alzey in Rhein-Hessen. It is descended from Isaac SIMON, who at the end of 18th cent. took the family name Belmont. His father, Ephraim Simon (d. 1742), was the son of Joseph JESSEL (d. 1738), son of Simhah ben Ephraim (d. 1685). The two names, Belmont and Belmonte, can be found in both branches, and it's possible the two branches are related to each other. Some members of both branches translated the name to the German SCHONENBERG or SCHOENBERG, others changed to JOSEPH or EMMANUEL. JE has a Belmont family-tree chart and many biographies; its article on "Coat of Arms" has the Belmonte family crest. The best history, linking the Sephardic and Germanic branches, is *The Belmont-Belmonte Family: A Record of 400 Years.* The American financier August Belmont (1816–1890), although born in Alzey, is not necessarily related to the above family. Relatives of the Sephardic branch include ARANYO, MONIZ, SOUZA, CORREA, SANCHES, MIRANDA, CARVALHO, CHEVALLIER, PENSO, ATIAS, MACHORA, RAFAEL, ABENATAR, MATHOS, LAPARREA, XIMENES, CURIEL, MENDES, COSTA, QUERIDO, MASCARENHAS, LANCASTRE, FONSECA, OLIVEYRA, RACHOA, ERGAS, GAON, ESCAPA, ZOUSA, PEREYRA, ALMEYDA, VAZ, NUNES and ABENDANA. Relatives on the German side include REINACH, LORCH, ELSASS, BAMBERGER, FEIST, LANDAUER, LEOPOLD, ALZEY, LAIB, PERRY, BRACH, BEHREND, STERNBERG, FRIEDENWALD, NEUBERGER and BISCHOFFSHEIM.

BELMONT-ALZEY—See BELMONT.

BELMONTE—See BELMONT.

BELZER—Related to ROKEACH.

BEMPORAD—UJ has two biographies from 19th-cent. Italy.

BENAIM—Family of North African merchants, 18th cent.; see EJ.

BENALAN—EJ has article on 9th-cent. Karaite scholar Joshua Ben'Alan.

BEN-AMMI—See RABINOWITZ.

BENAMOZEGH—JE has article on Italian Rabbi Elijah Benamozegh (1822–1900); his parents were natives of Fez, Morocco.

BENARIO—LBI has family tree beginning 1747.

BENARUS (also Benary)—JE and UJ have biographies from 19th cent. Educator Adolfo Benarus (b. 1863 in the Azores) was a grandson of David BENSABAT.

BENARY—See BENARUS.

BEN AROLOYO—See AROLLIA.

BENAS—JE has article on Englishman Baron Benas (1844–1914). Related to GOLDSCHMIDT.

BEN-ASHER—EJ has article on 10th-cent. Tiberias scribe Aaron Ben-Asher.

BENATAR—See ATTAR.

BENATTAR—See ATTAR.

BEN-AVIGDOR—JE has article on Russian Hebrew novelist Ben-Avigdor (b. 1867 near Vilna).

BENAYAH—Family of Yemenite scribes in 15th cent.; see EJ.

BENCEMERO (also Ben Zamaira)—16th-cent. Spanish name; see JE. Possibly related to BENZAMERO.

BENDA—UJ has article on French novelist Julien Benda (b. 1867).

BENDAHAN—See DAHAN.

BENDAHON—See DAHAN.

BENDAVID (also Ben-David)—JE has biographies from Turkey and Germany, 18th–19th cent.

BENDELL—UJ has one biography from 19th–20th-cent. U.S.A.

BENDEMANN—German painters, 19th cent.; see JE. LBIS has some family notes. Related to BENDIX, SCHADOW.

BENDER (also Benderly, Bendery)—JE and UJ have biographies from Germany, Ireland, South Africa and Palestine, 19th cent. Related to SAVRAN.

BENDERLY—See BENDER.

BENDERY—See BENDER.

BENDETSOHN—Russian scholar Menahem Bendetsohn of Grodno (1817–1888) was son-in-law of Reubén LIEBLING, cantor in Breslau, Germany. See JE.

BENDIG—JE has article on Meir Bendig, 15th-cent. Talmudist in Arles, France.

BENDIN—Related to PETRIKOV.

BENDISE (also Bendiseson)—LBIS has family notes.

BENDISESON—See BENDISE.

BENDIT—See BANETH.

BENDIX—Danish musicians in 19th cent.; see JE. Two Germans named Bendix took the name BENDEMANN; see UJ.

BENEDETTI—JE has article on Italian scholar Salvatore de Benedetti (1818–1891).

BENEDICKS—See BANETH.

BENEDICT—See BANETH.

BENEDICTUS—See BANETH.

BENEDIKT—See BANETH.

BENEDITE—See BANETH.

BENET—See BANETH.

BENEVENTO—EJ has article on 16th-cent. Italian cabalist Imannuel Benevento.

BEN-EZRA—JE has article on Solomon Ben-Ezra (d. 1782), chief rabbi of Smyrna, Asia Minor; he was the son of Abraham Ben-Ezra.

BENFEY—JE has article on German linguist Theodor Benfey (1809–1881), whose father had eight children.

BENGALIL (also Abengalel)—Spanish-North African family of the 13th cent.; see EJ.

BENISCH—JE has article on journalist Abraham Benisch (b. 1811 in Bohemia, d. 1878 near London).

BENJACOB—JE has article on Russian bibliographer Isaac ben Jacob Benjacob (1801–1863), born and died in Vilna area.

BENJAMIN—JE, UJ and EJ have various biographies from England, Australia, Rumania, etc. One of the earliest is Wolf Benjamin, rabbi of Chomsk, near Grodno, Russia (17th cent.). Polish architect Hillel Benjamin was born at Lasko, (18th cent.). For a family history, see ZL.

Related names include HYAMS, MEL-VILLE, TE'OMIM and de MENDES.

BEN JEHUDAH—UJ has article on Eliezer Ben Jehudah (b. 1857 in Lithuania, d. 1922 in Palestine); name was originally PERL-MAN.

BEN JUDAH—See BENJEHUDAH.

BEN-KIKI—18th-cent. Moroccan family; see EJ.

BENLOEW—JE has article on French philologist Louis Benloew (1818–1900).

BEN MEIR—EJ has article on 10th-cent. Palestinian scholar Aaron Ben Meir.

BENMOHEL—Ashkenazic name indicating descent from a ritual circumciser. JE has article on Nathan Benmohel (b. 1800 in Hamburg, d. 1869 in Dublin).

BEN-NAPHTALI—EJ has article on 9th-cent. Tiberias scribe Moses Ben-Naphtali.

BENNETT—UJ has article on engraver Solomon Bennett (1780–1841), born in Russia; originally BANETH.

BENOIT—UJ has three biographies from 19th-cent. France.

BENOLIEL—Portuguese and Moroccan name from 18th and 19th cent.; see JE and EJ.

BENREMOKH (also Rimoc, Ramukh, Re-moch, Rimokh, Raimuch)—Spanish and Moroccan family dating back to 13th cent.; see EJ. JE has article on 14th-cent. physician Astruc Raimuch.

BENSABAT—See BENARUS.

BENSADON—UJ has article on U.S. physician Joseph Bensadon (1819–1871).

BENSANCHI—See EJ article on "Politics" for a biography.

BENSAUDE—Moroccan-Portuguese family from 18th cent.; see EJ.

BENSHEIM—JE has article on German civic leader Simon Bensheim (1823–1898).

BENSIMEON—EJ has article on Jerusalem Rabbi Raphael Ben Simeon (1848–1928).

BENSUSAN—Moroccan family that dates back to 12th cent. See EJ and also *A Short History of the Bensusan Family.* UJ has an article on English novelist Samuel Bensusan (b. 1872). Related to SHOSHAN.

BENTWICH—JE and EJ have articles on English lawyer Herbert Bentwich (1856–1932). Related to YELLIN.

BENVENISTE—Old, rich and scholarly Sephardic family of Narbonne that can be traced back to 12th cent. It had branches all over Spain, Provence and parts of the Middle East; in 1900 the name was found in Bulgaria, Serbia and Vienna. Joseph ben Benveniste, who lived in Montpellier, France, c. 1190, was the grandson of Zera-hiah GERUNDI. The 17th-cent. Constantinople Rabbi Moses ben Nissim Benveniste was a grandson of Abraham ben Hananiah. See JE. Related names include NASI, MENDESIA, de SOLA and CABALL-ERIA.

BENWAISH—EJ has article on 16th-cent. Moroccan banker Abraham Benwaish.

BEN-YEHUDA—See BEN JEHUDAH.

BEN ZAMAIRA—See BENCEMERO.

BENZAMERO—Spanish-Moroccan family dating back to 13th cent.; members were in Leghorn, Italy, by 1828. See EJ. Perhaps related to BENCEMERO.

BENZAQEN—Moroccan-Spanish family traced back to 17th cent.; see EJ.

BEN ZE'EB—JE has article on grammarian Judah Lob Ben Ze'eb (b. 1764 in Cracow, d. 1811 in Vienna).

BEN ZEVI (also Ben-Zvi)—JE and UJ have articles on Russian and Pole whose names were originally SHIMSHELEVITZ and KUYAVSKY.

BENZIAN—See BENZION.

BENZION (also Benzian)—LBI has Benzian family tree beginning 1762. JE has article on 18th-cent. Galician Talmudist Benjamin Ze'eb Wolf ben Jacob ha-Levi Benzion. Related to ENDLER.

BEN ZUTA—EJ has article on 10th-cent. Karaite exegete Abu Ben Zuta.

BEN-ZVI—See BEN ZEVI.

BER—Related to JAFFE and JACOBBER.

BERAB—JE has article on Spanish Talmudist Jacob Berab (1474–1546), who died in Palestine. Related to ABULAFIA.

BERADT—UJ has article on German author Martin Beradt (b. 1881).

BERAKHAH—EJ has article on Aleppo Rabbi Isaac Berakhah (d. 1772). See also ANTIBI.

BERBI—See BEBRI.

BERCHIN—JE has article on Russian writer Jonah Borisovich Berchin (1865–1889).

BERCOVICI—See BERKOWITZ.

BERCOVITCH—See BERKOWITZ.

BERDUGO—See EJ article on *David* ben Aaron (1730–1790).

BERDYCZEWSKI—Ashkenazic name meaning "one who comes from Berdichev," Russia. JE has article on Hebrew author Micah Joseph Berdyczewski (1865–1921), son of a rabbi in Bershad, Podolia.

BERECHIAH—See KARMI.

BEREGI—UJ has article on Hungarian author Oszkar Beregi (b. 1876).

BEREK (also Berko)—JE has article on Polish Colonel Joselovich Berek (b. near Kovno, killed 1809). See also BERKOWITZ.

BEREND—See BEHREND.

BERENDSON—See BEHREND.

BERENDT—See BEHREND.

BERENICUS—See BERNICH.

BERENSON—See BEHREND.

BERENSTEIN—Dutch Rabbi Issachar Baer ben Samuel Berenstein (b. 1808) was the son of Samuel ben Berish Berenstein (b. 1767 in Hannover), whose father and grandfather, Rabbi Aryeh LOEB, were rabbis of Hannover. Aryeh Loeb was the son of Rabbi Jacob Joshua of Cracow, Lemberg and Frankfurt. See JE. Also see BERNSTEIN.

BERG—The name could come from Berg, an independent German duchy (until 1815). Jews were there at least as early as 13th cent.; in 1349 many Jews driven from Cologne settled in Berg. UJ has four biographies. See other names with the "Berg-" prefix. Related to PAGAY, LEVINE.

BERGEL (also Bergelson)—JE, EJ and UJ have biographies from 17th-cent. Germany, and 19th-cent. Hungary, Russia and Gibraltar. EJ says the Bergel family was originally from Safi.

BERGELSON—See BERGEL.

BERGER—CAJD has a family tree from Germany. JE has biographies from Austria, Germany, France, Poland and

Hungary. Also see BERG, BORGER and BURGER. Related to LEON.

BERGH—19th-cent. Dutch industrial family; see EJ.

BERGMANN (also Bergman)—LBI has a family tree beginning 1800. UJ has biographies from 19-th cent. Bohemia and Galicia. Another possible variation may be BREGMAN or BERKMAN.

BERGNER—UJ has article on actress Elisabeth Bergner (b. 1900 in Vienna).

BERGSON (also Berkson)—Warsaw family descended from Samuel ZBITKOWER; a descendant of the family is French philosopher Henri Bergson (b. 1859). See EJ. Related to LEVI, FRAENKEL, OESTERREICHER, FLATAU, PROUST.

BERGTHEIL—UJ has article on South African Jonas Bergtheil (1815–1902).

BERISH—See BAER.

BERKENTHAL (also Brezhover)—EJ has article on German-Polish writer Dov Berkenthal (1723–1805).

BERKMAN—UJ has article on author Alexander Berkman (1870–1936), born in Vilna. Another possible variation of the name may be BERGMANN.

BERKO—See BEREK.

BERKOVICH—See BERKOWITZ.

BERKOVITS—See BERKOWITZ.

BERKOWICZ—See BERKOWITZ.

BERKOWITZ (also Bercovici, Bercovitch, Berkovich, Berkovits, Berkowicz, etc.)—Ashkenazic name usually from Russia or Poland. AJA has a tree for a Berkowitz family from Philadelphia. CAJ has records of a Berkovits family. JE has article on Polish army officer Josef Berkowicz, son of Joseph BERKO. JE and UJ have other biographies from 19th-cent. Russia, Hungary, Poland, Rumania and Canada.

BERKSON—See BERGSON.

BERL—EJ has a biography in its article on "Chemistry."

BERLIN (also Berliner, Berlinerblau)—Ashkenazic name denoting one who comes from Berlin. The 18th-cent. German scholar Isaiah Berlin (1725–1799), born in Hungary, was a son-in-law of PICK and a relative of Abraham ASCH, and was scion of a famous family of scholars whose members included Yom-Tob Lip-mann HELLER and Meir ben Jacob SCHIFF; Isaiah's sister married Joseph ben Menahem STEINHART. Saul Berlin of Glogau (1740–1794), who died in London, was related to LEVIN, FRANKEL and Ezekiel LANDAU, chief rabbi of Prague. JE, UJ and EJ have numerous biographies. LBI has Berlin family trees beginning 1700 and 1738, as well as Berliner family trees beginning 1750, 1761, 1776 and 1816. Related to MAI, HENLE, SAMUDA, BALINE, MOCHIACH, BRODY, HEDIN and EPSTEIN.

BERLINER—See BERLIN.

BERLINERBLAU—See BERLIN.

BERLINGER—CAJ has a family tree and some family records.

BERMAN—See BERMANN.

BERMANN (also Berman, Baermann, Behrman, Barmann, Beerman, etc.)—Ashkenazic name derived from the German *Bär* ("bear"), a variation of the name BAER. Found mostly among German, Russian, Hungarian and Austrian families. Issachar ha-Levi Bermann (1661–1730) of Halberstadt was son of Judah LEHMANN. Baermann was a family in Frankfurt from the end of 17th cent. JE, UJ and EJ have biographies. LBIS has a Beerman family tree. Relatives include KAPLAN, KOBOR, WERTHEIMER and FISCHER.

BERN—JE has article on 19th-cent. German authors Maximilian and Olga Bern. He was born in Russia, she was born WOHLBRUCK in Vienna.

BERNAL—Spanish family name dating from Maestro Bernal, the ship physician on the first voyage of Columbus. See JE, which also has the Bernal crest in its article on "Coat of Arms."

BERNARD—Russian and German family name found from 18th cent. onward. See JE and UJ for biographies. Related to BERNHARDT, FALKENSOHN, HOROWITZ, GAD, DOMEIER, EYBESCHUTZ.

BERNAT—JE has article on French actress Julie Bernat (1827–1912). Related to FELIX.

BERNAYS—German family from Hamburg. JE has three biographies. AJA has a family tree. CAJ has a family tree from Germany and some family records.

BERND—AJA has a family tree beginning 1760. JE has one biography. See *Saga of the Bernd, Bloch and Blum Families in the U.S.A.* Related to DELLAVIE.

BERNFELD—JE and UJ have biographies from 19th- and 20th-cent. Galicia.

BERNHARD (also Bernhardt, Bernhardy)—Ashkenazic name, usually German. CAJ has a family tree from Germany, 1762–1928, related to JAFFE. Sarah Bernhardt, the actress (b. 1844), was of Dutch parentage but of German ancestry; her mother's maiden name was VAN HARD. JE, UJ and EJ have biographies. Related to SULZBERGER.

BERNHARDT—See BERNHARD.

BERNHARDY—See BERNHARD.

BERNHEIM (also Bernheimer)—Ashkenazic name found among Germans from Hamburg and French from Alsace. JE and UJ have biographies from 19th cent. AJA has a family tree. Also see *The Story of the Bernheim Family.*

BERNHEIMER—See BERNHEIM.

BERNICH (also Berenicus, Beronicus)—JE has article on Dutch poet Solomon Bernich (17th cent.).

BERNSTAMM—JE has article on Russian sculptor Leopold Bernstamm (b. 1859 in Riga).

BERNSTEIN—Ashkenazic name widely used among Germans, Russians, Poles and Hungarians. JE, UJ and EJ have numerous biographies from 19th cent. Nathan Bernstein (1836–1891) was a grandson of Solomon EGER. LBI has a family tree beginning 1648. Also see one Bernstein family history in *It Began with Zade Usher.* Related names include PORGES, ROSENTHAL, VON MISES, FALK, LOUIS, LOYEV, LEWIS, MAZUR and SINAIEFF. Also see BERENSTEIN, which may be another variation of the name.

BERNSTORFF—JE has article on 18th-cent. Danish and Prussian statesman Count Christian Bernstorff.

BEROLZHEIMER—LBI has family trees beginning 1516, 1684 and 1747.

BERONICUS—See BERNICH.

BERR—French family from Nancy, Luneville and Paris that included the first Jewish French barrister (1744). JE has four biographies. Related to EPSTEIN, ASCOLI, BING and TURIQUE.

BERSHAD (also Bershadski, Bershadsky) —Russian name taken from the town of Bershad in eastern Galicia (lower Ukraine). JE and EJ have biographies. Related to DOMOSHEVITSKY.

BERSHADSKI—See BERSHAD.

BERSHADSKY—See BERSHAD.

BERSIMSON—See BARSIMSON.

BERSOHN (also Berson)—JE and UJ have biographies from Poland and Galicia, 19th cent.

BERSON—See BERSOHN.

BERTENSOHN (also Bertenson)—JE and UJ have biographies from 19th-cent. Russia.

BERTENSON—See BERTENSOHN.

BERTHEAU—JE has article on 19th-cent. German scholar Ernest Bertheau.

BERTHEIM—UJ has article on German chemist Alfred Bertheim (1879–1914).

BERTHELOT—Related to LEMANN.

BERTHOLDI—Related to LATZKY-BERTHOLDI.

BERTINORO—JE has article on 15th-cent. Italian Rabbi Obadiah Bertinoro.

BERTONI—UJ has article on Moises Bertoni (b. 1855), descendant of a Sephardic family.

BERUSH—See BIALEH.

BESANT—JE has article on 19th-cent. English novelist Sir Walter Besant.

BESCHUTZ—LBIS has some family notes.

BESHT—See BAER.

BESREDKA—UJ has article on Russian Alexander Besredka (b. 1870).

BESSELS—JE article on "Coat of Arms" has a family crest. JE has article on German-American explorer Emil Bessels (1847–1888).

BESSIS—EJ has article on Tunisian scholar Joshua Bessis (1773–1860).

BESSO—UJ has three biographies from 19th-cent. Italy. Related to GOLDMAN.

BETERA—See BATHYRA.

BETH—Roman family; see history in VR, Vol. 1, p. 332, and Vol. 2, p. 299, 307 and 332.

BETHEL (also Beth-el, Bethelides)—Related to ANAW and JOAB.

BETHELIDES—See BETHEL.

BETTAN—UJ has article on Rabbi Israel Bettan (b. 1889 in Lithuania).

BETTAUER—EJ has article an Austro-American author Hugo Bettauer (1872–1925).

BETTELHEIM—Hungarian family originally from the town of Bethlen, whence the name, which first appeared in second half of 18th cent. JE has eight biographies. Related to GOMPERZ, KOHUT and TELLHEIM.

BETTMAN (also Bettmann)—German name. UJ has six biographies from 19th cent.

BEYFUS—Related to ROTHSCHILD.

BEYLE—Related to SOLOVEICHIK.

BEZALEL (also Bazaleel, Bazalel)—Ashkenazic name taken from the Hebrew personal name. JE has article on Russian Talmudist Joseph Bezalel (c. 1800). Related names are BACHARACH, EPHRATI, OLSCHWANGER and PERLES.

BHORUPKAR—JE has article on Indian soldier Samuel Bhorupkar of Bombay.

BIA—See BANETH.

BIACH—PD has some family records. JE has article on Austrian physician Alois Biach from Moravia.

BIAL—JE has article on Silesian violinist Rudolf Bial (b. 1834).

BIALEH—JE has article on Rabbi Zebi Hirsch Bialeh of Lemberg (17th cent.). Related to BERUSH, HERZ.

BIALIK—UJ has article on poet Hayim Bialik (b. 1873 in Russia).

BIALLOBLOTZKY—JE has article on Christian Bialloblotzky, Jewish convert to Christianity from Hannover, Germany (18th cent.).

BIBAGO (also Bibas, Bibaz)—Sephardic name. Bibas is a Spanish-Moroccan family dating from 15th cent.; see EJ. It's perhaps related to Abraham Bibago, 15th-cent. philosopher from Saragossa; see JE. A related name is BIBAS-VIVAS.

BIBAS—See BIBAGO.

BIBAS-VIVAS—See BIBAGO.

BIBAZ—See BIBAGO.

BIBIKOV—JE has article on 18th-cent. Russian statesman Dmitri Bibikov from Kiev.

BIBO (also Bibos)—AJA has tree of a family in New Mexico since 1807, traced back to Hungary in 1582. Also has Bibo family history in *The Impact of the Frontier on a Jewish Family*.

BIBOS—See BIBO.

BICHOVSKY—See BYCHOWSKY.

BICK—JE has article on Jacob Bick, Austrian author from Brody (c. 1800). Related to ROTHENBERG.

BICKELS-SPITZER—EJ has article on Zvi Bickels-Spitzer, Lemberg dramatist (1887–1917). See also SPITZER.

BICKERMANN—UJ has article on historian Elias Bickermann (b. 1897 in Russia).

BIDERMAN—See BIEDERMANN.

BIE—JE has article on German 19th-cent. professor Oskar Bie.

BIEDERMANN (also Biederman, Biderman)—JE has article on Vienna jeweler Michael Biedermann (1769–1843), whose family name was originally FREISTADT. UJ has other biographies. PD has family records. Related to DESART.

BIEGELEISEN—JE has article on Polish-Galician critic Henry Biegeleisen (1855–1934). Also see EJ. Related to KROCHMAL.

BIELEFELD—LBI has a family tree beginning 1670.

BIELINSKY—UJ has article on journalist Jacques Bielinsky (b. 1881 in Russia).

BIELITZKI—Related to DEICHES.

BIELSCHOWSKY—LBI has a family tree. UJ has an article on Albert Bielschowsky of Germany (1847–1902).

BIEN—JE and UJ have biographies from 19th-cent. Germany and U.S.A.

BIENENSTOK—JE has article on 19th-cent. writer Lev Bienenstok of Palestine and Russia.

BIERER—EJ has article on Austrian Zionist Rubin Bierer (1835–1931).

BIESENTHAL—JE has article on 19th-cent. German author Joachim Biesenthal.

BIHARI—UJ has article on Hungarian artist Sandor Bihari (1856–1906).

BIJUR—UJ has a biography from U.S.A., 19th-20th cent.

BIKAYIM—JE has biography of Meir Bikayim (18th-cent. Turkish cabalist).

BILDERSEE—UJ has a biography from U.S.A., 19th-20th cent.

BILIZ—Related to HERZL.

BILLIG (also Billigheimer, Billikopf)—UJ has biographies from England and Lithuania, 19th-20th cent. LBI has a Billigheimer family tree beginning 1765.

BILLIGHEIMER—See BILLIG.

BILLIKOPF—See BILLIG.

BIMKO—UJ has article on Polish playwright Fischel Bimko (b. 1890).

BINDER—UJ has a biography from U.S.A., 20th cent.

BINET—See BANETH.

BINETER—See BANETH.

BING (also Bingen, Binger)—Ashkenazic name taken from the town of Bingen in Hesse, Germany. JE has biographies from 17th-cent. Germany, 19th-cent. Denmark and Austria; UJ has biography from 19th-cent. France. LBI has family trees beginning 1713 and 1814. CAJ also has a family tree from Germany. For a family history, see *Eine Frankfurter jüdische Familie vom Jahre 1550 bis zur Gegenwart*. Related to DELMEDIGO, BERR, KALISCH, TUCHMANN and AUERBACH.

BINGER—See BING.

BINGER—See BING.

BINSWANGER—German name. UJ has a biography from 19th-cent. Germany-U.S.A. See *The American Descendants of Samuel Binswanger*. Related to SOLIS, LOVINGER, EGER and GOTZ.

BIRSCH-HIRSCHFELD—JE has article on 19th-cent. Prussian pathologist Felix Birsch-Hirschfeld.

BIRKHAHN—Related to LIPKIN.

BIRNBAUM (also Birnboim)—Ashkenazic name. UJ has four biographies from 19th-cent. Poland and Austria. EJ has article on Polish blackmailer Moses Birnboim (1789–1831). CAJ has Birnbaum family records; CAJD has a family tree. Related to ANSHEL.

BIRNBOIM—See BIRNBAUM.

BIRO—UJ has article on Hungarian novelist Lajos Biro (b. 1880).

BISCHITZ DE HEVES—JE has article on 19th-cent. Hungarian philanthropist Johanna Bischitz de Heves. Related to FISCHER.

BISCHOFFSHEIM—French family originally from Bischoffsheim-on-the-Tauber, Germany, which founded the Jewish community in Mayence (Mainz). JE and EJ have family trees and biographies. Related to CASSEL, GOLDSCHMIDT, BELMONT-ALZEY, D'ANVERS, MONTEFIORE, LANDSBERG, BEER, HIRSCH and DESART. See also UJ.

BISHKA—JE has article on 18th-cent. Russian Talmudist Nahman Bishka. Related to ZEDEK.

BISLICHES (also Bisseliches)—JE has article on 18th-cent. Austrian editor Mordecai Bisliches of Brody.

BISNO—See *Union Pioneer,* autobiography of U.S. labor leader Abraham Bisno (1866–1929), born in Kiev.

BISSELICHES—See BISLICHES.

BISTRITSKY (also Bistritz)—Ashkenazic name perhaps derived from the town of Banska Bystrica in Czechoslovakia. JE, EJ, UJ have biographies from Hungary and Russia, 18th and 19th cent. Related to AGMON.

BISTRITZ—See BISTRITSKY.

BITTOON (also Pittoon)—JE has article on 18th-cent. English boxer Isaac Bittoon.

BLACHSTEIN—Related to GREENHUT.

BLACK—AJA has a family tree beginning 1811. Related to LOVEMAN.

BLANC—JE has article on 18th-cent. Polish financier Piotr Blanc. Also see BLANK.

BLAND—JE has article on 18th-cent. English actress Maria Theresa Bland, born ROMANZINI of Italian parents.

BLANK—UJ has four biographies from 19th-cent. Russia, Rumania and U.S.A. See also BLANC.

BLASCHKE—UJ has article on Wilhelm Blaschke (b. 1885 in Austria).

BLASER—JE has article on Rabbi Isaac Blaser (1857–1907), from Vilna. Related to WOLK. Also see UJ.

BLASOM—Related to EPHRAIM.

BLAU—German name. JE has biographies from 19th-cent. Germany, Austria and Hungary.

BLAUSTEIN—German name meaning "blue stone." JE has two biographies from 19th-cent. Russia. See also BLOWSTEIN, BLUESTONE.

BLAUT—See PLAUT.

BLAYNEY—JE has article on 18th-cent. English Hebraist Benjamin Blayney.

BLECH—UJ has article on Leo Blech (b. 1871 in Germany)

BLEIBTREU—JE has article on Philip Bleibtreu, 18th-cent. German convert to Christianity.

BLEICHRODER—German family traced back to Samuel Bleichroder (1779–1855). JE and EJ have biographies. JE article on "Coat of Arms" has the family crest. Related to SCHWABACH. See also UJ.

BLES—JE has article on 19th-cent. communal worker David Bles, born in Holland, worked in England and Austria.

BLIN—Related to LAMBERT.

BLIND (also Blind-Cohen, Blindman)— Mathilde Blind (1841–1896), born COHEN, was related to Ferdinand Blind-Cohen, the German student who tried to kill Bismarck in 1866. See JE and UJ. EJ has article on Galician cantor Yeruham Blindman (1798–1891) of Tarnopol.

BLIND-COHEN—See BLIND.

BLINDMAN—See BLIND.

BLIOCH—See BLOCH.

BLITSTEIN—See BLITZSTEIN.

BLITZ—JE has article on 17th-cent. Amsterdam pressman Jekuthiel Blitz.

BLITZSTEIN (also Blitstein)—German name meaning "lightning stone."

BLOCH (also Block, Blioch, Blogg)—Ashkenazic name that originated as *Welsch* ("foreigner") for Alsatian Jews in Germany, then became the Slavic WALLICH and VLACH as its holders moved from Central Europe to Poland, and finally became Bloch when they migrated back to Germany. JE has a family tree from Prussia. JE, UJ and EJ have numerous biographies. AJA and LBI have family trees beginning 1650 and 1652. CAJ has a family tree from Vienna and some family records. For a family history, see JFF, No. 3; also see *Saga of the Bernd, Bloch and Blum Families in the U.S.A.* AJA has tree of a Block family of Arkansas beginning 1810. Related to WALDOW, TIKTIN, NEU, LOW, SELIG, GRATZ, RAKOWER, BALLAGI, LEO, ORGLER and PHILIPSON. Also see JE article on Posen.

BLOCK—See BLOCH.

BLOGG—See BLOCH.

BLOMBERG—Ashkenazic name probably taken from a town of the same name in Germany (there are at least five such towns). Other variations may be BLUMBERG and BLOOMBERG.

BLONDES—EJ has article on David Blondes, victim of a blood libel in Vilna in 1900.

BLOOM—UJ has one biography from 19th–20th cent. U.S.A.

BLOOMBERG—Ashkenazic name meaning "flower mountain," possibly taken from the village of the same name in Hannover, Germany. Also see BLOMBERG and BLUMBERG.

BLOOMFIELD (also Bloomfield-Zeisler)—JE has two biographies from 19th-cent. Austria. Related to ZEISLER. Also see BLUMENFELD.

BLOOMFIELD-ZEISLER—See BLOOMFIELD.

BLOOMGARDEN—UJ has article on Lithuanian poet Solomon Bloomgarden (1870–1927).

BLOOMINGDALE—UJ has article on the U.S. merchant family, which came from Bavaria in 1837.

BLOSZ—JE has article on 19th-cent. German painter Karl Blosz.

BLOWITZ—Ashkenazic name taken from Blowitz, Bohemia. JE and UJ have articles on French-English correspondent Adolf Blowitz (1825–1903), born Adolf OPPER.

BLOWSTEIN—UJ has article on poet Rachel Blowstein (1890–1931), born in Russia. A possible variation of the name is BLAUSTEIN.

BLUCHER—JE has article on Austrian Rabbi Ephraim Blucher (d. 1882 in Budapest).

BLUESTONE—UJ has article on physician Joseph Bluestone (1860–1934), born in Lithuania and descended from a scholarly family. Another possible variation of the name is BLAUSTEIN.

BLUM—JE has five biographies from 16th-cent. Germany and 19th-cent. France, Austria and Egypt. Also see *Saga of the Bernd, Bloch and Blum Families in the U.S.A.*

BLUMBERG (also Blumenberg)—UJ and JE have biographies from 19th-cent. Prussia and U.S.A. Other possible variations are BLOMBERG and BLOOMBERG.

BLUMENBERG—See BLUMBERG.

BLUMENFELD (also Blumenfeldt)—JE and EJ have biographies from 18th-cent. Russia and 19th-cent. Germany, Poland, Russia and Austria. Also see a biography in EJ article on "Psychology." CAJ has a family tree. A possible variation of the name is BLOOMFIELD. Related to ROMAN-RONETTI.

BLUMENFELDT—See BLUMENFELD.

BLUMENSTOCK—JE has article on 19th-cent. Austrian physician Leo Blumenstock, born in Cracow. Related to HALBAN.

BLUMENTHAL—German name. JE has five biographies from 19th-cent. Germany and Rumania. CAJ has records and a family tree of a Blumenthal family related to VOGEL, GOTTSCHALK, GOLDSTEIN, HEINEMANN, LOWE and SCHIFF. Another related name is SCOTT.

BLUMLEIN—See EJ article on Aaron of Neustadt. Related to ISSERLEIN.

BOAS—Dutch family in The Hague from 17th-cent.; see EJ and *Proeve eener Genealogie van der Haagsche Familie Boas.* JE also has biographies of Germans from 19th-cent. Related to GOMPERTZ, WERTHEIMER, OPPENHEIMER and KANN.

BOBELLE—PD has a family tree.

BOBTELSKY—See a biography in EJ article on "Chemistry."

BOCARA (also Bocarro)—JE has article on 19th-cent. Italian Rabbi Abraham Bocara. Related names are GRADIS and ROSALES.

BOCARRO—See BOCARA.

BOCHART—JE has article on 17th-cent. French scholar Samuel Bochart.

BOCHNER—JE has article on 17th-cent. Polish scholar Chaim Bochner, related to GANZ.

BOCK—JE has biographies from 18th-cent. in Magdeburg, Germany. For a family history, see *Die Siegburger Familie Levison*.

BODANZKY—UJ has article on conductor Arthur Bodanzky (1877–1939), born in Vienna.

BODEK—JE has two biographies from Galicia, 18th-cent. Related to MOHR. Also see EJ.

BODENHEIMER—Ashkenazic rabbinic family. See *Reshimoth Aboth*, by Markus Seckbach, which relates the family to other rabbinic families as far back as 1290. CAJ has family records, and JE has one biography from 19th-cent. Germany.

BODENSTEIN—JE has article on 19th-cent. German painter Julius Bodenstein.

BOEHM—See BOHM.

BOER—Related to VAN RIJK.

BOERNE—LBI has family trees beginning 1635 and 1665.

BOGDANOVICH—Related to JUDAH.

BOGEN—Ashkenazic name which is usually shortened from KATZENELLENBOGEN. UJ has article on educator Boris Bogen (1869–1929), born in Russia.

BOGNAR—JE has article on 19th-cent. German actress Frederike Bognar.

BOGORAZ—EJ has article on Russian writer Vladimir Bogoraz (1865–1936), also known as Nathan MENDELVICH.

BOGROV—JE has article on 19th-cent. Russian writer Grigori Bogrov.

BOGYO—UJ has article on Hungarian mathematician Samu Bogyo (1857–1928).

BOHM (also Boehm, Bohmer)—Ashkenazic name meaning "Bohemian." JE and UJ have biographies from 18th-cent. Germany and 19th-cent. Russia, Lithuania and Hungary. Related to SPEKTOR and BACHARACH.

BOHMER—See BOHM.

BOHR—UJ has a biography from 19th–20th cent. Denmark. Related to MELCHIOR.

BOINO—Related to HOMEM.

BOKANOWSKI—UJ has article on lawyer Maurice Bokanowski (1879–1928), born in France of Russian parents.

BOLAFFEY—See ABULAFIA.

BOLAFFI—See ABULAFIA.

BOLAFFIO—See ABULAFIA.

BOLAIX—See ALAISH.

BOLECHOVSKY—UJ has article on Polish interpreter Judah Bolechovsky (1723–1805).

BOLOGNA—Related to FINZI.

BONAFED—UJ has article on 15th-cent. Spanish poet Solomon Bonafed.

BONAFOS (also Bonafoux, En Bonafos)—French-Spanish family dating from 13th cent. JE has four biographies.

BONAFOUX—See BONAFOS.

BONAN—JE has article on 18th-cent. Tunisian author Isaac Bonan.

BONASTRUC—JE has article on 14th-cent. Majorcan Rabbi Isaac Bonastruc.

BONAVENTURA—JE has article on 19th-cent. Portuguese scholar Fortunato Bonaventura.

BONAVOGLIO—JE has article on 15th-cent. Sicilian physician Moses Bonavoglio. Related to HEFEZ.

BONDAVI (also Bondavin)—JE has two biographies from 14th-cent. Marseilles.

BONDAVIN—See BONDAVI.

BONDI (also Bondy)—Ashkenazic name meaning "good day"; the Hebrew variation is JOMTOB, and people with the two names are usually related to each other. Jonas Bondi (1804–1874) was a descendant of Jonathan EYBESCHUTZ. AJA and LBI have family trees beginning 1503. CAJ has some family records. JE and UJ have biographies from 18th-and 19th-cent. Austria, Germany and Bohemia. For a family history, see *Zur Geschichte der Familie Jomtob-Bondi in Prag, Dresden and Mainz.* Related to BEER, WISE, BEROLZHEIMER and WARBURG.

BONDY—See BONDI.

BONEM—Related to ITZIG.

BONET (also Bonet de Lunel)—JE has biographies from 14th-cent. Spain and France.

BONET DE LUNEL—See BONET.

BONFED—JE has article on 14th-cent. Rabbi Solomon Bonfed from Saragossa.

BONFILS—JE has article on 14th-cent. French physician Immanuel Bonfils.

BONGODA (also Bongodas)—JE has article on 14th-cent. Provençal physician Cohen Bongodas, also possibly known as Judah Nathan. Related to DURAN, CASLARI.

BONGODAS—See BONGODA.

BONGORON (also Bonjorn)—JE has article on 14th-cent. French astronomer David Bongoron.

BONHEUR—UJ has article on French painter Rosa Bonheur (1822–1899).

BONIRAC—JE has article on 14th-cent. translator Solomon Bonirac of Barcelona.

BONITO—Related to MENDES.

BONJORN—See BONGORON.

BONN—JE has article on 17th-cent. German physician Jonas Bonn, of Frankfurt.

BONNIER—Noted family in Sweden, descended from Gerhard Bonnier (1778–1862), who was born in Germany; see UJ. LBIS has a family tree and some notes. Related to RUBENSON.

BONSENIOR (also Bonsenyor)—JE has biographies from 13th-cent. Spain and 16th-cent. Provence. Related to STRUCH, NASTRUCH and ASTRUC.

BONSENYOR—See BONSENIOR.

BONVIVA—JE has article on 13th-cent. French scholar Isaac Bonviva.

BORCHARD—See BORCHARDT.

BORCHARDT (also Borchard)—German name also found in France. JE has four biographies from 19th cent. LBI has family trees beginning 1600 and 1699. LBIS has family notes.

BORCHHEIM—LBI has a family tree beginning 1655.

BORDJEL—See BURGEL.

BORG (also Borger, Burger)—JE has article on 17th-cent. Prussian cabalist Solomon Borger of Zulz. UJ has two biographies from 19th- and 20th-cent. Germany and U.S.A.

BORGER—See BORG.

BORGIL—EJ has article on 16th-cent. Turkish scholar Abraham Borgil.

BORIS—JE has article on 19th-cent. French soldier Moses Boris.

BORKUM—JE has article on 18th-cent. court Jew Kalman Borkum of Courland (Kurland).

BORN (also Borne)—JE has biographies from 18th- and 19th-cent. Germany and France. Related to BARUCH.

BORNE—See BORN.

BORNHEIM—Related to ITZIG.

BORNSTEIN—JE has articles on Germans from Breslau and Berlin, 19th cent. Related to MEISEL.

BOROCHOV—UJ has article on Russian Ber Borichov (1881–1917).

BORODAVKA (also Brodavka)—Ashkenazic name perhaps taken from the town of Brody, Galicia. JE has article on 16th-cent. Lithuanian farmer Isaac Borodavka.

BORODIN—UJ has article on Communist leader Michael Borodin (b. 1884 in Russia); originally GRUZENBERG.

BOROFSKY—See BOROWSKI.

BORONDES—CAJ has some family records.

BOROWSKI (also Borofsky)—JE has two biographies from 19th-cent. Poland and Russia.

BOSHAL (also Bostal)—JE has article on 17th-cent. Turkish Talmudist Moses Boshal.

BOSKOVITZ (also Boskowitz)—JE has two biographies from 18th-cent. Hungary and Palestine. Related to KOLIN and RAPOPORT.

BOSLANSKI (also Baslanski)—JE has article on early-19th-cent. Russian Rabbi Lipele Yom-Tov Boslanski, also known as MIRER after his hometown of Mir.

BOSTAL—See BOSHAL.

BOSTOMSKY—UJ has article on Solomon Bostomsky (b. 1891 in Lithuania).

BOSWELL—Related to GRATZ.

BOTAREL—UJ has article on 14th–15th-cent. Spanish scholar Moses Botarel.

BOTON—Spanish family which emigrated to Salonika, Turkey, in 1492. JE has a family tree and nine biographies.

BOTOSANI—CAJ has a family tree.

BOTOSHANSKY—UJ has article on journalist Jacob Botoshansky (b. 1892 in Rumania).

BOTTICHER—Related to LAGARDE.

BOTWINIK—UJ has article on writer Barnett Botwinik (b. 1884 in Russia).

BOUCHARA—Algerian family dating from 17th cent.; see EJ.

BOUDIN—UJ has article on lawyer Louis Boudin (b. 1874 in Russia).

BOUMAN—CAJ has a family tree from the Netherlands.

BOUWMEESTER—UJ has article on Dutch actor Louis Bouwmeester (1842–1925).

BOVSHOVER—UJ has article on poet Joseph Bovshover (1873–1916), born in Russia.

BOZECCHI (also Buzecchi, Bozecci, Bozecco)—Prominent Italian family since 13th cent. JE has four biographies. Related to ANAW.

BOZECCI—See BOZECCHI.

BOZECCO—See BOZECCHI.

BOZZOLO—JE has article on 16th-cent. Salonikan Talmudist Hayyim Bozzolo.

BRACH (also Brackman)—UJ has article on painter Robert Brackman (b. 1896 in Russia). Brach family is related to BELMONT. A possible variation is BROCK.

BRACKMAN—See BRACH.

BRAFMANN—JE has article on 19th-cent. Russian Jewish convert Jacob Brafmann.

BRAGADINI—Venetian family of printers traced back to 16th cent. See JE.

BRAGINSKY—UJ has article on Mark Braginsky (b. 1863 in Russia).

BRAHAM—JE has article on 18th-cent. English singer John Braham. Related to LEONI. In some cases the name is a shortening of ABRAHAM. Also see BRAHM.

BRAHINSKI—UJ has article on poet Mani Brahinski (b. 1883 in Russia).

BRAHM—JE has article on 19th-cent. German critic Otto Brahm, also known as ABRAHAMSOHN. The name is possibly a variation of BRAHAM.

BRAININ—JE has article on Russian doctor Reuben Brainin from Riga (1862–1939), whose family was in Berlin in 1900. Also see JE article on Riga (Latvia). Related to ROSENTHAL. See also BREININ.

BRAMSON—JE and UJ have biographies from 19th-cent. Lithuania.

BRANDAM—JE has article on 17th-cent. Portuguese physician Fernando Brandam.

BRANDAO—EJ has article on Portuguese soldier Ambrosio Brandao (1560–1638). The name is perhaps a variation of BRANDAM. Related to HOMEM.

BRANDEIS (also Brandes)—Family of Polish origin descended from Rabbi Judah Lowe, the MAHARAL of Prague (1525–1609), whose daughter Gittel married a Brandes. Her descendants were rabbis, physicians and soldiers through many generations, including U.S. Supreme Court Justice Louis D. Brandeis. PD also has a family tree. JE and UJ have numerous biographies. For family histories, see JFF, No. 10, or *Louis D. Brandeis: A Biographical Sketch*. Related to DARMESTETER, HA-LEVI, PASCHELES, DEMBITZ, GOLDMARK, KOHLER, DUBNOW and BRUNSCHWIG.

BRANDES—See BRANDEIS.

BRANDON—JE has biographies from 15th-cent. France and 17th-cent. Holland. Related to MOCATTA, SALVADOR.

BRANDSTADTER (also Brandstaetter)—JE has article on Galician novelist Mordecai Brandstadter (1844–1928).

BRANN—JE has two biographies from 19th-cent. Germany.

BRASCH—See BASCH.

BRASLAVSKY—Related to MOSKOVITZ.

BRAUDE—See BRODY.

BRAUDES—See BRODY.

BRAUDO—See BRODY.

BRAUN—JE has biographies from 19th-cent. Germany, Hungary and France. Related to KRETSCHMAN. See also UJ.

BRAUNSCHWEIG—Ashkenazic name that probably comes from the German duchy of Braunschweig (Brunswick), where Jews were living as early as 1241. JE has biographies from 16th-cent. Poland and Switzerland and 17th–18th-cent. Germany. Related to DEUTSCH. Also see BRUNSCHWIG.

BRAUNSTEIN—UJ has article on author Menahem Braunstein (b. 1858 in Rumania). Another possible variation of the name is BRONSTEIN.

BRAV—AJA has a family tree.

BRAVO—Sephardic name. JE has an article on 18th-cent. London financier Abraham Bravo, descendant of a Spanish-Portuguese family. Related to COSTA.

BREAL—JE has article on French philologist Michel Breal (1832–1915).

BRECHER—JE has article on Moravian physician Gideon Brecher (1797–1873), father of Adolph Brecher (1831–1894).

BREDIG—See biography in EJ article on "Chemistry."

BREGMAN—Prominent family in Grodno, Russia, 19th cent.; see JE article on Grodno. JE also has article on Russian financier Eliezer ben Moses Bregman of Grodno (1826–1896), who died in Bohemia. Another variation of the name may be BERGMAN.

BREGSTONE—UJ has article on lawyer Philip Bregstone (b. in 1866 in Russia).

BREIDENBACH—Ashkenazic name probably taken from the village of Breidenbach in Hesse-Kassel, Germany. JE has two biographies from 18th-cent. Germany.

BREIER (also Breyer)—JE has article on Austrian writer Eduard Breier (1811–1886).

Also see biography in EJ article on "Chess."

BREININ—Possibly a variation of BRAININ. CAJ has some family records.

BREISACH—PD has some family records. Related to BATOR. A possible variation is BRISAC.

BREIT—LBI has a family tree beginning 1394. Related to MUEHSAM.

BREITBART—UJ has article on Siegmund Breitbart (1883–1925), born in Poland.

BREITENSTEIN—JE has article on Austrian writer Max Breitenstein (b. 1855).

BREMER—LBI has a family tree beginning 1768. CAJ also has a family tree.

BRENNER—UJ has five biographies from U.S.A. and Russia, 19th and 20th cent.

BRENTANO (also Brentano-Cimaroli)—Family of booksellers and publishers in U.S.A. since 1853, descended from August Brentano (b. 1831 in Austria); see UJ. Related to CIMAROLI and ESKELES.

BRENTANO-CIMAROLI—See BRENTANO.

BRESLAU (also Breslauer, Breslaur, Bresler, Bressler, Bresslau, Bresselau)—Ashkenazic name taken from the city of Breslau, Prussia. JE has biographies from Germany, 17th–19th cent.; also Holland and England. Joseph ben David Breslau (1691–1752) was son-in-law of rabbi Moses ben Abraham BRODA of Bamberg. Rabbi Aryeh Lob Breslau of Rotterdam (d. 1809) had three sons, who took the name LOWENSTAMM. CAJ has a Bresselau family tree from Germany. Also see family history in *Eine Hebräische Handschrift aus Warendorf,* by Bernhard Brilling (1962). LBI has a Breslau family tree beginning 1711.

BRESLAUER (also Breslaur)—See BRESLAU.

BRESNER—JE has article on 17th–18th-cent. Austrian teacher Issac Bresner of Prague.

BRESNITZ—JE has article on 19th-cent. Austrian author Heinrich Bresnitz.

BRESSELAU—See BRESLAU.

BRESSENSDORF—German name. CAJ has family records.

BRESSLAU—See BRESLAU.

BRESSLER—See BRESLAU.

BRETT—UJ has article on Catherine Brett, a non-Jew who married Bernard HART, 1799.

BRETHOLZ (also Brettholz)—CAJ has Brettholz family records. EJ has article on Moravian historian Berthold Bretholz (1862–1936).

BRETTHOLZ—See BRETHOLZ.

BREUER—JE and UJ have biographies from Hungary and Austria, 19th cent. CAJ and PD have some family records. Related to HIRSCH.

BREYER—See BREIER.

BREZHOVER—Related to BIRKENTHAL.

BRICKNER—UJ has two biographies from U.S.A., 19th–20th cent.

BRIE—UJ has article on Argentine patriot Luis Brie (1834–1917), born in Germany.

BRIEFTREGER—Related to DORFMAN.

BRIEGER—JE and UJ have biographies from Germany, 19th cent.

BRIEL (also Brieli)—JE has article on Italian Rabbi Judah Briel of Mantua (1643–1722).

BRILIN—Ashkenazic name, perhaps a variation of BRILL. PD has family records. Related to BACHARACH.

BRILL—Ashkenazic name derived from the Hebrew acronym for Ben Rabbi Judah Lowe, indicating descent from the MAHARAL of Prague (1525–1609). JE has four biographies from 18th- and 19th-cent. Hungary and Russia. See also BRILIN. Related to LOEWE.

BRIN—UJ has article on Fanny Brin, *née* FLIGELMAN (b. 1884 in Rumania).

BRIND—UJ has article on poet Moses Brind (b. 1894 in Russia).

BRISAC—Alsatian name; possibly a variation of BREISACH. Related to DREYFUS, ENSHEIM.

BRISCK—See BRISKER.

BRISCOE—UJ has article on Irish statesman Robert Briscoe (b. 1894).

BRISKER (also Brisck, Briskie, Briszk)—Ashkenazic name derived from the town of Bresk, Russia, or Brest-Litovsk (Brisk), Poland. EJ has an article on the 19th-cent.

Transylvanian rabbinic family of Briszk. CAJ has a Brisck family tree. Also see JE article on *Moses* Isaac of Kelmy, Russia (1828–1899), whose maternal grandfather was Eliezer Brisker. Related to TREVES.

BRISKIE—See BRISKER.

BRISZK—See BRISKER.

BRITO (also de Brito)—Sephardic name. JE article on "Coat of Arms" has the family crest. Related to ABENDANA.

BROCINER—JE and UJ have biographies from 19th-cent. Rumanian family related to Josef Brociner, president of the Union of Hebrew Congregations of Rumania (1846–1918).

BROCK—Ashkenazic name, sometimes an abbreviation of Ben Rabbi Kalman, the ancestor from whom the name is taken. A possible variation is BRACH.

BROD—See BRODY.

BRODA—See BRODY.

BRODAVKA—See BORODAVKA.

BRODER—See BRODY.

BRODERSON—See BRODY.

BRODETSKY—UJ has article on mathematician Selig Brodetsky (b. 1888 in Russia). The name is perhaps a variation of BRODY.

BRODIE—See BRODY.

BRODNITZ—UJ has article on German lawyer Julius Brodnitz (1866–1936).

BRODSKI—See BRODY.

BRODSKY—See BRODY.

BROIDA (also Broido)—See BRODY.

BRODY (also Broda, Braude, Braudes, Braudy, Brodski, Brodsky, Broder, Broida, Broido, Braudo, Broderson, Brodie, Brod, possibly Brodetsky, etc.)—All variations of this Ashkenazic name indicate origin in the town or area of Brody, Galicia. The name Broda first appears in 17th-cent. Bohemia and Germany. The Brodski family is descended from the famous rabbinic family of SCHOR: Meir Schor of Brody, great-grandson of Rabbi Alexander Schor of Zolkiev, moved to Kiev about 1800, and his sons took the name Brodski ("from Brody"). Galician minstrel Berl Broder (1815–1880) was born MARGULIES. The family of German

Rabbi Simhah Broida (1824–1898) traces its ancestry to Abraham Broda, rabbi of Frankfurt, who was also an ancestor of Austrian Rabbi Heinrich Brody (b. 1868). EJ article on *Alexander* Susskind (d. 1793 in Lithuania) says he was an ancestor of the Braudes family. JE, UJ and EJ have numerous biographies. See *Mishpahat Broda*. Also see JE article on Grodno, where Benjamin Braudo (1745–1818) was rabbi. PD has Broda family records. Related to BRESLAU, BERLIN, HEDIN and LUNTZ.

BRONSTEIN—Possible variation of BRAUNSTEIN. See TROTSKY.

BROUNOFF—UJ has article on composer Platon Brounoff (1869–1924), born in Russia.

BROWN (also Browne)—UJ has biographies from Russia, England, Scotland, U.S.A. and Austria, back to 17th cent. Related to PARDO.

BROYDE—Possible variation of BRODY. JE has article on Russian scholar Isaac Broyde (b. 1867).

BRUCH—See BRUCK.

BRUCK (also Bruch, Bruckman)—Ashkenazic name that is a Hebrew acronym for Ben Rabbi Akiba, the ancestor from whom the name is derived (although not necessarily the famous Rabbi Akiba). LBI has a family tree beginning 1490. JE and UJ have biographies from 19th-cent. Russia, Austria, Hungary, Germany and U.S.A. See *The Bruck Family: A Historical Sketch*. A possible variation is BROCK or BRACH.

BRUCKMAN—See BRUCK.

BRUDNO (also Brudnoy)—UJ has article on writer Ezra Brudno (b. 1878 in Lithuania), great-grandson of Rabbi Manasseh ILIER.

BRUDO—Sephardic name. EJ has biographies from 16th-cent. Marrano family and 17th-cent. Turkish rabbi. Related to RODRIGUES, CHELEBI.

BRUEHL—German name. LBI has a family tree beginning 1849. CAJ has Bruhl family records. Related to SUSSMANN.

BRUHL—See BRUEHL.

BRUENN—Ashkenazic name probably indicating origin in the city of Brunn, Moravia. See also BRUNNER.

BRUGGEN—EJ has article on Dutch novelist Carry von Bruggen (1881–1932). Related to HAAN.

BRULL—German name. Rabbi Nehemiah Brull (b. 1843 in Moravia, d. 1891 in Frankfurt) was the grandson of the chief orthodox rabbi of Moravia, Nahum TREBITSCH. JE has four biographies from 19th-cent. Germany, Austria and Moravia. PD has some family records.

BRUNA—EJ has article on German Rabbi Israel Bruna (1400–1480).

BRUNNER—German name. JE and UJ have biographies from 19th-cent. Germany and U.S.A. LBI has a family tree beginning 1685. Also see BRUENN. Related to SOLOMON and WERTHEIMER.

BRUNSCHVIGG—See BRUNSCHWIG.

BRUNSCHWIG (also Brunschvigg, Brunswich, Brunswick, Brunswig)—German and French name. JE and UJ have biographies from 19th cent. CAJ has a Brunschwig family tree. Related to BRANDES. Also see BRAUNSCHWEIG.

BRUNSWICH—See BRUNSCHWIG.

BRUNSWICK—See BRUNSCHWIG.

BRUNSWIG—See BRUNSCHWIG.

BRUTZKUS—JE and UJ have biographies from Russia, 19th cent.

BRI—Ashkenazic name that is a Hebrew acronym for Ben Rabbi Israel, the ancestor from whom the name is taken.

BUBER—Ashkenazic name derived from the town of Bobrka, Galicia. JE has article on Galician scholar Solomon Buber of Lemberg (1827–1906).

BUBLICK—UJ has article on Gedediah Bublick (b. 1875 in Russia).

BUCHBINDER—JE has article on Austrian journalist Bernhard Buchbinder (b. 1854 in Budapest).

BUCHHEIM—JE has article on German professor Charles Buchheim (b. 1828 in Moravia, d. 1900 in London).

BUCHHOLZ—JE has article on German Rabbi P. Buchholz (1837–1892).

BUCHLER—JE and UJ have biographies from 19th-cent. Austria and Hungary. Related to NEUBAUER.

BUCHMIL—EJ has article on Russian Zionist Joshua Buchmil (1869–1938).

BUCHNER—JE has article on 18th-cent. Hebraist Wolf Buchner ha-Kohen of Brody, Galicia.

BUCHSBAUM (also Buxbaum)—Family of Jewish physicians in Frankfurt-am-Main, 17th and 18th cent., descended from Benjamin Levi Buchsbaum (1645–1715). CAJ has a Buxbaum family tree. Also see family history in MGWJ, Vol. 41 (1897), p. 128. Related to ROTHSCHILD.

BUCKSTEIN—UJ has article on novelist Abraham Buckstein, born in Russia late 19th cent. See also BUKSTEIN.

BUCURESTEANO—Ashkenazic name indicating origin in Bucharest, Rumania. JE has article on Rumanian publicist Abraham Bucuresteano (1840–1877).

BUCZACZ—Ashkenazic name derived from the town of the same name. JE has article on Galician Talmudist Abraham Buczacz (1770–1840).

BUDING (also Budinger)—JE has three biographies from Germany and Austria, 18th and 19th cent. Related to REINACH.

BUDINGER—See BUDING.

BUDKO—UJ has article on painter Joseph Budko (1888–1940), born in Poland.

BUENAHORA—Related to ORABUENA.

BUENO—Sephardic family of Spanish origin comprising many physicians and scholars. By 1900 members had settled in southern France, Italy, Holland, England and the U.S.A. The family can be traced back to 16th cent. David Bueno de Mesquita of Amsterdam, 17th cent., was married to a granddaughter of Francisco Fernandez de MORA. See JE, which has sixteen related biographies, as well as a family crest in its article on "Coat of Arms." Related to BONUS, COSTA.

BUERGER—See BURGER.

BUKARAT—EJ has article on Spanish poet Abraham Bukarat, 15th cent.

BUKSTEIN—Possible variation of BUCK-STEIN. Related to KAVEN.

BULAH—JE has two related biographies from 18th-cent. Palestine and Turkey.

BULAT—JE has two biographies from 16th-cent. Spain.

BULOFF—CAJ has some family records.

BUMSLO—See BUNZLAU.

BUNZL—See BUNZLAU.

BUNZLAU (also Bumslo, Bunzl)—Name taken from the Bohemian town of Bunzlau. JE has biography from 18th-cent. Bohemia. EJ has article on the Austro-British industrial family of Bunzl, dating from 19th cent.; PD has Bunzl family records. Related to FISHEL, LANDSOFER.

BURCHARD—Ashkenazic name. LBI has family tree beginning 1843. Related to ARON.

BURG (also Burger, Buerger)—German name. JE and UJ have biographies from Germany and Austria, 19th cent. LBI has Burger family tree beginning 1600. LBIS also has a Burg family tree. A Burger family history can be found in Die Siegburger Familie Levison. Related to SACHS, LUBLINER and PILLITZ. See also BORGER. In some cases BERGER may be a more recent variation of the name.

BURGEL (also Burgil, Bordjel)—Name of three generations of rabbis in a family in Tunis, beginning 17th cent.; see JE and EJ.

BURGER—See BURG.

BURGIN—UJ has article on author Hertz Burgin (b. 1870 in Lithuania).

BURGUNDER—Name perhaps indicating origin in Burgundy. AJA has a family tree. Related to AMBACH.

BURKAN—UJ has article on U.S. lawyer Nathan Burkan (1879–1936), born in Rumania.

BURLA—UJ has article on novelist Judah Berla (b. 1888 in Jerusalem). His family were Spanish exiles in Turkey who settled in Palestine in 18th cent.

BURROUGHS—UJ has article on U.S. lawyer Harry Burroughs (b. 1890 in Russia).

BURSTEIN—UJ has one biography from 20th-cent. U.S.A.

BUSAGLO—See BUZAGLO.

BUSAL—EJ has article on 16th-cent. Rabbi Hayyim Busal of Salonika, originally from Spain.

BUSCH—See BUSH.

BUSCHENTAL—UJ has article on German writer Lippman Buschental (1784–1818).

BUSEL—EJ has article on Zionist Joseph Busel (1891–1919).

BUSH (also Busch)—U.S. publicist Isidor Bush (1822–1898) was born in Prague; his maternal great-grandfather was Israel HONIG, first Jew raised to the nobility in Austria. See JE. AJA has his family tree beginning 1722. A separate Bush family were well-known Philadelphia merchants in 18th cent. and are related to MEARS, MYERS and GRATZ. See JE and UJ.

BUSNACH (also Busnash)—French dramatist William Busnach (b. 1832) was nephew of Fromental HALEVY. Naphtali Busnach, chief of Algerian Jews, died 1805. See JE, UJ and EJ. Related to BALRI.

BUSNASH—See BUSNACH.

BUTELBROIT—Related to GILADI.

BUTENSKY—UJ has article on sculptor Jules Butensky (b. 1871 in Poland).

BUTTENWEISER (also Buttenwieser)—German Talmudist Laemmlein Buttenweiser (1825–1901) descended from a well-known family of German rabbis. See JE and UJ.

BUTTENWIESER—See BUTTENWEISER.

BUTZEL—UJ has two biographies from U.S.A., 19th and 20th cent.

BUXBAUM—See BUCHSBAUM.

BUZAGLI—See BUZAGLIO.

BUZAGLIO (also Buzagli, Buzaglo)—JE has biographies from 18th-cent. Morocco and England.

BUZAGLO—See BUZAGLIO.

BUZECCHI—See BOZECCHI.

BYALOSTOZKY—Ashkenazic name presumably indicating origin in Bialystok, Poland. UJ has article on poet Benjamin Byalostozky (b. 1892 in Lithuania).

BYCHOWSKY (also Bichovsky)—Related to ZHIRKOVA and DUBNOW.

BYK—Ashkenazic name meaning "ox." Variations in other languages are OCHS, SCHOR, WAHL, WOHL and VOLOV, which may or may not be related to Byk. JE has article on Austrian lawyer Emil Byk (1845–1906), born in Galicia.

de la CABALLERIA (also Cavalleria)—Marrano family of Aragon, Spain, influential through its wealth and scholarship. Descended from Solomon ibn Labi de la Caballeria in 15th cent., who had nine sons. Two sons took the name PEDRO, another GONZALO; a daughter married the rich landowner Don Apres de PATERNOY, a Marrano of Verdun. EJ has a family tree chart under Cavalleria. Also see EJ. Related to BENVENISTE.

CABESSA—Moroccan family that originated in Toledo, Spain, 13th cent. Its members were in North Africa and U.S.A. by 19th cent.

CABRET (also Cabrit)—Sephardic name that came from the Spanish locality of Cabret or Cabreta. JE has article on 14th-cent. Spanish translator Jacob ben Judah Cabret.

CACERAS—See CACERES.

CACERES (also Caceras, Carceres, Carcerts, Casares, Casseras, Cazares, Caseres, De Casseres)—Sephardic family that probably came from Caceres in Spain. The family can be traced to 16th cent. in Mexico, and in 1900 family members were living in Portugal, Holland, England, Mexico, Surinam, the West Indies, Philadelphia and New York. Among those descendants are U.S. author Benjamin De Casseres (b. 1873) and Baruch SPINOZA. JE has a family tree chart and numerous biographies, and JE article on "Coat of Arms" has the family crest. Related to CARABAJAL and BAEZ.

CAEN—See COHEN.

CAESAR—UJ has two biographies from Rumania and U.S.A., 20th cent.

CAHAN (also Cahana, Cahen, Cahn, Cahun)—Russian, German and French variations of COHEN. JE has biographies from Germany, France and Lithuania, 19th cent. CAJ has Cahen family records. JE article on "Coat of Arms" has two Cahen family crests. LBI has a Cahn family tree beginning 1742; LBIS has notes of a Cahn family from Frankfurt. CAJD has a Cahn family tree from Germany. See also KAHN.

CAHANA—See CAHAN.

CAHEN—See CAHAN.

CAHN—See CAHAN.

CAHUN—See CAHAN.

CAIMIS—EJ has article on Greek journalist Moisis Caimis (1864–1929).

CAIN—See COHEN.

CAISERMAN—See KAISERMAN.

CALABRESE—Related to ANTON, JOAB, VITAL.

CALAHORA (also Calahorra)—Family of Spanish origin that lived in Cracow, Poland, from 16th cent. through 1900; see JE and UJ. Related to LOBISCH.

CALAHORRA—See CALAHORA.

CALAMANI (also Calimani)—Italian name derived from the German *Kalman,* meaning "borne by an ancestor of Joshua." See JE, which also has an article on 18th-cent. Italian Talmudist Joshua Calamani, and on Italians in Venice, 17th and 18th cent. For family history, see CB, p. 1554.

CALE—UJ has article on German poet Walter Cale (1881–1904).

CALIMANI—See CALAMANI.

CALISCH—See KALISCH.

CALM—JE has article on German author Marie Calm (1832–1887).

CALMAN-LEVY—LBI has a family tree beginning 1720; related to FUERST.

CALMANSON—EJ has article on Jacob Calmanson, physician to the Polish king, late 18th cent.

CALMER—JE has article on French baron Liefmann Calmer (1711–1784), born in Hannover. His Hebrew name was Lipmann ben Kalonymus, or "Kalman" in German, from which the name Calmer was derived.

CALNI—JE has article on 15th-cent. Turkish Rabbi Samuel Calni, son-in-law of Benjamin ben Mattathias.

CALVO—JE has article on 18th-cent. Italian physician Emanuel Calvo.

CAMERINI (also Camerino)—EJ has article on Italian literary critic Eugenio Camerini (1811–1875). Related to JOAB.

CAMMEO—EJ has article on Italian jurist Fredrico Cammeo (1872–1939).

CAMONDO—Well-known family of Jewish financiers of Spanish-Portuguese origin. Descendants were in Venice about 16th cent., in Constantinople in 18th cent., and some were in Paris in 1900. See JE; also see JE article on "Coat of Arms," which has the family crest.

CAMPANTON—JE has article on Spanish Rabbi Isaac Campanton (1360–1463). See also CANPANTON.

CAMPBELL—Related to ETTING and GOLDSMID.

CAMPEN—UJ has article on writer Michael Campen (b. 1874 in Holland).

de CAMPO—See GOMEZ.

CAMPOS—See GOMEZ.

CANDIA—JE has article on Polish poet Isaac Candia of Warsaw, early 19th cent.

CANAAN—UJ has article on English author Gilbert Canaan (b. 1884).

CANISO—Related to BARRIOS.

CANIZAL—JE has article on 15th-cent. author Jacob Canizal of Constantinople.

CANPANTON—Castilian rabbinical family of 14th cent.; see EJ. See also CAMPANTON.

CANSINO—Spanish family famous for its wealth, scholars and poets. It can be traced back to the Spanish colony at Oran, North Africa, in 13th cent. See JE; also EJ, which has a family tree. AJA has a family tree beginning 1440. Related to SASPORTAS.

CANSTATT—JE has article on German physician Karl Canstatt (1807–1850).

CANTARINI—Distinguished Italian family that lived in Padua from 16th through 19th cent. The name means "cantor." See JE. Related to CANTORI, COEN.

CANTON (also Cantoni)—JE has two biographies from Italy, 18th and 19th cent.

CANTONI—See CANTON.

CANTOR—Ashkenazic name often literally used by cantors. Moritz Cantor of Germany (b. 1829 in Mannheim) came from a family that emigrated to Holland from Portugal, another branch of that family having established itself in Russia. See JE, which also has other biographies. LBIS has some family notes. Related to HANAU. See also KANTOR.

CANTORI—16th-cent. Italian Joshua dei Cantori may have come from the CANTARINI family; see JE.

CAPADOCE (also Capadose, Capadoza)—Abraham Capadoce of Holland (1795–1874) was the son of Portuguese Jews; see JE. UJ has a Capadoza biography from 18th-cent. Holland. CAJ has a Capadose family tree, and the same family's crest can be found in JE article on "Coat of Arms." Related to COSTA.

CAPATEIRO—Sephardic name meaning "shoemaker." JE has article on 15th-cent. Portuguese traveler Joseph Capateiro.

CAPLAN—See KAPLAN.

CAPOTE—Related to MENDES.

CAPPE—Related to WOLFF.

CAPRI—JE has three biographies from 18th-cent. Italy.

CAPSALI—Family of scholars originally in Greece, 15th. cent., then in European Turkey in 15th and 16th cent. The name is taken from Cape Capsali, in the south of the Morea. See JE.

CAPUSI—EJ has article on Egyptian Rabbi Hayyim Capusi (1540–1631).

CARA—See KARA.

CARABAJAL (also Carvajal, Carabal, Caraballo, Caravajal, Carballo, Carbajal, Cavajal)—Family of Marranos in Mexico, late 16th and early 17th cent. See JE, also JE article on 19th-cent. French engineer Jules Carvallo. EJ has a family-tree chart under Carvajal. For a family history, see *La familia Carvajal* and *The Martyrdom of the Carabajal Family in Mexico, 1590–1601*. The family is related to and possibly identical with CARVALHO. Other relatives are de MATOS, de HERRERA, CACERES, ALMEIDA and ATHIAS. See also UJ.

CARABAL—See CARABAJAL.

CARABALLO—See CARABAJAL.

CARASCON—See CARRASCO.

CARASSO—JE has article on 19th-cent. Turkish traveler David Carasso.

CARAVAJAL—See CARABAJAL.

CARBAJAL—See CARABAJAL.

CARCASSONNE—French name taken from the city of the same name. JE has three biographies from 19th cent.

CARCERES—See CACERES.

CARCERTS—See CACERES.

CARDENAS—See DELGADO.

CARDINAL (also Cardineal)—JE has article on 12th–13th cent. French translator Judah Cardinal.

CARDOZO (also Cardoso, Cordozo, Cardoza)—American Sephardic family connected with the Cardozos of Amsterdam and London. Miguel Cardoso (1630–1706) was descended from Marranos in the city of Celorico, Portugal; another descendant of the family was Don Aaron Cardoza, consul for Tunis and Algiers in early 19th cent. The American branch, which includes U.S. Supreme Court Justice Benjamin Cardozo, is traced to Aaron Cardozo of London, who came to New York in 1752. JE and EJ have family trees; so do AJA and CAJ. See JE article on "Coat of Arms" for the family crest. Related to HART, CAUFFMAN, PHILLIPS, SEIXAS, NATHAN, PEIXOTTO, LIEBER, HASLEM, HOUSEMAN, GOMEZ and HOMEM.

CAREGAL—See CARREGAL.

CARIGAL—See CARREGAL.

CARILLO—JE has article on 17th-cent. Dutch educator Issac Carillo.

CARLEBACH—German name. EJ has family tree. UJ has biography from 19th-cent. Germany. CAJ has some family records. For a family history, see *The Carlebach Tradition*. Related to ADLER, STERN, ROSENAK, NEUHAUS and COHN.

CARLIN—UJ has article on editor Aaron Carlin (b. 1885 in Russia).

CARLOS—JE has article on David Carlos, 17th-cent. Spanish writer who lived in Hamburg.

CARMI—Italian family that dates from 16th cent.; see EJ. Another form of the name is CREMIEU.

CARMOLY—Eliakim Carmoly, French scholar from Sulz who died in Frankfurt in 1875, was born Behr or BAER but changed his name back to the original family name of Carmoly, which dates back to 14th cent. An Alsatian branch of the same family, noted in 18th cent., is related to RAINEAU. See JE.

CARMONA—Sephardic name derived from a city near Seville, Spain. Family of Turkish financiers in early 19th cent.; JE has three biographies.

CARO—Sephardic name. JE and UJ have biographies from 15th-cent. Spain, 18th-cent. Turkey and Prussia, and 19th-cent. Germany and Switzerland. LBIS has some family notes. AJA has the tree of a family in Illinois. Also see *Caro Family Pedigree.* Related to NAHUM, SABA, AL-BALAG, SACHSEL, SECHSEL, AMSTERDAM, MIELZINER and DELVAILLE. Also see EJ.

CARP—See KARP.

CARPI—UJ has two biographies from 18th and 19th cent.

CARRASCO (also Carascon)—JE has article on Juan Carrasco, who converted to Judaism in Madrid, 1670.

CARREGAL (also Caregal, Carigal, Carrigal, Karigal, Karigel, Karigol, Kragol)—Rabbinical family in Palestine, Holland and Barbados in 18th cent. See JE.

CARSI—See CARSONO.

CARSONO (also Carsi, Corsono)—JE has article on 14th-cent. Spanish astronomer Jacob Carsono.

CARVAJAL—See CARABAJAL.

CARVALHO—JE has article on 18th cent. Tunisian merchant Mordecai Carvalho. Related to CARABAJAL, SOLIS and BELMONTE.

CARVALLO—See CARABAJAL.

CASA—See CASE.

CASADO—Related to MENDES.

CASADIO—Related to ANAW.

CASARES—See CACERES.

CASE (also Casa, Kasa)—JE has article on 16th-cent. Polish Talmudist Joseph Case, also known as SHAPIRO. Also see EJ.

CASERES—See CACERES.

CASES (also Cazes)—Italian family from 16th-cent. Mantua, some of whom moved to Turkey and Palestine in 18th cent. JE has twelve biographies. Not necessarily related is Moroccan educator David Cazes (1851–1913); see JE.

CASHMORE—JE has article on 19th-cent. Australian social worker Michael Cashmore.

CASHWAN—UJ has article on sculptor Samuel Cashwan (b. 1900 in Russia).

CASLARI—Family originally from Caylar, France, 14th cent.; also found at the same time in Catalonia. JE has nine biographies. Related to BONGODAS, YISHARI.

CASPARI—See CASPER.

CASPARY—See CASPER.

CASPER (also Caspari, Caspary)—JE and UJ have biographies from Germany, 19th cent.

CASPI—JE has two biographies from Provence, 1297.

CASSEL—German name taken from the province of the same name. JE and UJ have biographies. LBI has family trees beginning 1782 and 1720. CAJ has some family records. Related to BISCHOFFSHEIM, ASHLEY, BEROLZHEIMER, MOUNTBATTEN, GROEDEL, and GOLDSMIT.

CASSERAS—See CACERES.

CASSIN—EJ has article on French jurist Rene Cassin (b. 1887).

CASSIRER—LBI has a family tree beginning 1857. UJ has two biographies from 19th-cent. Germany. Related to TRETZ, DURIEUX.

CASSUTO—Apparently Sephardic name. Joseph Cassuto (1803–1893) was a Portuguese rabbi born in Amsterdam who lived in Hamburg; see JE. UJ has a biography from 19th-cent. Italy.

CASTANHO—JE has article on Abraham Castanho, 17th-cent. Spanish poet who lived in Amsterdam.

CASTEL D'AJANO—JE has article on 16th-cent. Italian physician Samuel de Castel D'Ajano of Mantua.

CASTELLAZZO—Italian family in Egypt since 16th cent. Moses da Castellazzo (1467–1527) was the son of Abraham SACHS and the brother-in-law of Jacob LANDAU. See JE and EJ.

CASTELLI—JE has article on Italian scholar David Castelli (1836–1901).

CASTELLO (also Castilho, Castillo, Castelo)—JE has biographies from Holland, 17th cent., and Italy, 18th cent. AJA has a Castillo family tree beginning in 15th cent. JE article on "Coat of Arms" has the Castello family crest.

CASTELNUOVO—JE and UJ have biographies from Italy, 17th and 19th cent.

CASTELO—See CASTELLO.

CASTIGLIONI—UJ has three biographies from 19th-cent. Italy.

CASTILHO—See CASTELLO.

CASTILLO—See CASTELLO.

CASTRO(also de Castro, Crasto)—Sephardic family in Spain and Portugal, 15th cent. During the Inquisition, members dispersed to Bordeaux, Bayonne, Hamburg and Amsterdam. CAJ has a family tree. LBIS has de Castro family notes. JE article on "Coat of Arms" has the family crest. JE has twenty-five biographies. Related to MATTOS, PINTO, FEREIRA, LOPEZ-SUASSO, PENHA, MONTALTO, EZEKIAL, SIMON, OROBIO and AGUILAR.

CATALAN (also Catalano)—Italian family of Padua that dates from 13th cent. JE has five biographies. Related to LEVI.

CATARIVAS—JE has article on 18th-cent. Tunisian Talmudic scholar Shemariah Catarivas.

CATTAN—North African family that settled in Italy in the 1640s. See EJ.

CATTAUI—The foremost Jewish family in Egypt in 19th and 20th cent. See UJ and EJ. Related to ALGAZI.

CAUFFMAN—See KAUFMANN.

CAVAJAL—See CARABAJAL.

CAVALLERIA—See CABALLERIA.

CAVALLERO (also Cavagliero)—JE has biographies from 16th-cent. Provence, Italy and Africa, and 17th-cent. Turkey. Related to PEREZ.

CAVI—See family history in VR, Vol. 2, p. 288.

CAYN—CAJ has family tree beginning in 16th-cent. Germany.

CAZARES—See CACERES.

CAZES—See CASES.

CEPRANO—See JOAB.

CERF (also Cerfbeer, Cerfberr)—French variation of the German HIRSCH ("stag"); other variations, which may in some cases be related, are HERZ, HARTVIG, HARRIS and JELLINEK. The name Cerfberr or Cerfbeer, apparently the product of a union between the Cerf and BEER families, appears in Alsace and France beginning in 18th cent. See JE. Related to SINZHEIM.

CERFBEER—See CERF.

CERFBERR—See CERF.

CERVETTO—Related to BASEVI.

CHAGALL—French painter Marc Chagall (b. 1887 in Russia), was originally SHAGAL or SEGAL. See UJ and EJ.

CHAIKIN—Ashkenazic name derived from the female name Chaya. JE has article on 19th-cent. Russian Rabbi Moses Chaikin, who emigrated to Paris and London.

CHAIT—Ashkenazic name derived from the Hebrew chayyat ("tailor").

CHAJAS—See CHAJES.

CHAJES (also Chajas, Chajis)—Noted family of rabbis and scholars who migrated from Bohemia to Galicia in 17th cent. The name is derived from a maternal ancestor name Chaya. Isaac Chajes (1538–1615) was the grandfather of Jehiel ALTSCHULER; Gershon Chajes (d. 1789) was the grandson of Menaheim KROCHMAL. JE, UJ and EJ have biographies from 17th, 18th and 19th cent. Related to LAUTERBACH. See also CHAYES.

CHAJIS—See CHAJES.

CHALFAN—See HALFON.

CHALFEN—See HALFON.

CHALFIN—See HALFON.

CHALIDENKA—See It Began with Zade Usher (See Bernstein in Bibliography).

CHALIF—UJ has article on dance teacher Louis Chalif (b. 1876 in Russia).

CHANIN—See BAR ANINA.

CHANINA—See BAR ANINA.

CHAO—Important Jewish family in Kaifeng, China, 15th to 17th cent. EJ has a family tree and biographies. Also see JE.

CHAPIRO—See SPIRA.

CHAPMAN—JE has article on 19th-cent. English educator John Chapman.

CHARLAP—For family histories, see JFF, Nos. 30, 31 and 32.

CHARLEMONT—JE has article on Countess Elizabeth Jane Charlemont, 19th-cent. Irish convert to Judaism. Related to MOLYNEUX.

CHARNA (also Charnas, Charney)—UJ and EJ have biographies from 19th-cent. Russia and Lithuania. Related to NIGER, VLADECK.

CHARNAUD—Related to READING.

CHARNEY—See CHARNA.

CHAROUSEK—See biography in EJ article on "Chess."

CHARTOFF—Related to KAPLAN.

CHASANOVICH (also Chasanowich)—UJ and EJ have biographies from 19th- and 20th-cent. Russia. Pseudonym of Kasriel SCHUB. Also see CHAZANOWICZ.

CHASE—UJ has article on U.S. merchant Edward Chase (1874–1939), born in Lithuania.

CHASEISCH—JE has article on 18th-cent. German Talmudist Moses Chaseisch.

CHASKER-BURSCH—LBI has family tree beginning 1758.

CHASHKES—JE has article on 19th-cent. poet Moses Chashkes of Vilna and Odessa.

CHATZKELS—EJ has article on writer Helen Chatzkels (b. 1882 in Lithuania).

CHAVES—Portuguese name found in London and Amsterdam, 18th cent. JE has six biographies. Related to ENRIQUES.

CHAYES—UJ has biography of U.S. dentist Herman Chayes (1879–1933), born in Russia. A possible variation is CHAJES.

CHAZANOWICZ—JE has article on 19th-cent. Russian physician Joseph Chasanowicz. A possible variation is HAZZAN. Also see CHASANOVICH.

CHECHEROFSKY—Related to MUSHKIN.

CHELEBI (also Chelebi-Sinani)—See EJ article on *Abraham* ben Josiah Yerushalmi. Related to BRUDO, SINANI.

CHELM—Ashkenazic name taken from the Russian town of the same name. JE has article on Polish Rabbi Solomon Chelm (1717–1781), son-in-law of Rabbi Moses PARNAS.

CHELOUCHE—Sephardic family in Palestine from 1840.

CHERKASSKY—UJ has article on pianist Shura Cherkassky (b. 1911 in Russia).

CHERNI—UJ has article on Russian explorer Joseph Cherni (1835–1880).

CHEVALLIER—Related to BELMONTE.

CHIPIEZ—UJ has article on French architect Charles Chipiez (1835–1901).

CHIPKIN—UJ has article on U.S. educator Israel Chipkin (b. 1891 in Vilna).

CHIRINO—Spanish Marrano family, traced back to 15th cent. See EJ.

CHIZHIK—Family of Israel pioneers who came from Russia in 19th cent. EJ has two biographies.

CHMELNITSKI—EJ has article on poet Melech Chmelnitzki (1885–1946), born in Russia.

CHOMSKY—EJ has biographies from Russia and U.S.A., 19th and 20th cent.

CHORIN (also Choriner)—JE has two biographies from Hungary, 18th and 19th cent. PD has some family records.

CHORNY—JE has article on Russian traveler Joseph Judah Chorny (1835–1880).

CHOTSH—EJ has article on Polish preacher Zevi Chotsh (about 1700), grandson of Aviezer ZELIG.

CHOTZINOFF (also Chotzner)—UJ and JE have biographies from Russia, Galicia and England, 19th cent. Also see *A Lost Paradise* (New York: Knopf, 1955), autobiographoy of pianist Samuel Chotzinoff (b. 1889 in Russia).

CHOTZNER—See CHOTZINOFF.

CHOURAQUI—Family originally from Tlemcen, Algeria, 15th cent. See EJ.

CHOYNSKI—JE has article on U.S. 19th-cent. boxer Joseph Choynski.

CHRIQUI—Moroccan family. EJ has biographies beginning 18th cent. Related to SHRIKI, SARIQUE and DELEVANTE.

CHRONEGK—JE has article on German actor Ludwig Chronegk (1837–1890).

CHUDNOW—Ashkenazic name probably taken from the town of Chudnov in Volynia, Russia, southwest of Zhitomir.

CHUJOY—See biography in EJ article on "dance."

CHUMACEIRO—19th-cent. Dutch family. JE has five biographies.

CHURGIN—UJ has article on U.S. professor Pinkhos Churgin (b. 1894 in Russia).

CHURNAGOOSE—Related to MONTEFI-ORE.

CHURRIKER—JE has article on Beni-Israel soldier Abraham Churriker of India (1822–1867).

CHWISTEK—EJ has article on Polish philosopher Leon Chwistek (1884–1944).

CHWOLSON (also Khvolson)—JE and EJ have articles on Russian Orientalist Daniel Chwolson (1819–1911).

CHYET—AJA has a family tree.

CIECHANOW—EJ has article on Polish Rabbi Abraham Ciechanow (1789–1875), whose name was originally DOBRZINSKY and who married the daughter of Dan LANDAU.

CIMAROLI—Related to BRENTANO.

CITROEN—EJ has two biographies from France and Holland, 19th-20th cent.

CITRON (also Zitron)—JE has article on Russian writer Samuel Lob Citron (b. 1862). Also see UJ article on Zitron.

CIVITA—EJ has article on Italian musician David Civita, 17th cent.

CLAAR—JE has article on Austrian poet Emil Claar (b. 1842 in Lemberg).

CLAPCOTT—Related to AVIGDOR.

CLASSEN—Related to AUERBACH.

CLAVA—JE has article on 18th-cent. Spanish poet Isaiah Clava of Amsterdam.

CLAYBURG—Related to NONES.

CLEIF—JE has article on Russian Rabbi Daniel Cleif of Amsterdam (1729–1794); his son died in Russia, 1846.

CLEMENCEAU—Related to SZEPS.

COBLENZ (also Coblence)—French name taken from the town of the same name. JE has biographies from 18th and 19th cent.

COCUMBRIEL—Related to ALMOSNINO.

COEN—See COHEN.

COFFEN—See COHEN.

COHAN—See COHEN.

COHANE—See COHEN.

COHEN—The most common surname among European Jews: some 2 to 3 percent of all Jews have this name or some variation of it. The name usually indicates a family claiming descent from Aaron, the first high priest *(Kohen)*. Variations of the name include Cowen and Cowan (England); Cohan, Cohane, Cohne, Cone, Coon, Kan and Koon (U.S.A.); Cohn, Conn, KAHN and KOHN (Germany and Austria); Cahn, Cahen, Cahun, Caen, Cain and KAHN (France); Coen (Italy); Coffen (Spain); Kahin (Arab lands); and Cahan, Cahana, Kahan, Kahana, Kahane, Kagan, Kogan, Kogen, Kohan, Kohnowski and Koganowitch (Russia). Other forms are Kohne, Kohner, Cohnheim and Cohnfeld. The names Katz and Kaz are abbreviations for the Hebrew *kohen tzeddek,* "legitimate priest." In some cases variations of the name have been taken by people who are not necessarily direct descendants of Aaron (see chapter 5 above). The name is so numerous that tracing relatives with this name is virtually impossible. JE, UJ and EJ have many biographies; check all possible spellings. Family histories include *Sefer Ha-Zikaron, The Cohens of Maryland* and *Family Facts and Fairy Tales.* JE article on "Coat of Arms" has a Cohen and Cohn family crest. LBI has a Katz family tree beginning 1694. AJA has a Katz family tree from Russia. CAJ has Katz family records. Related families include BASSANO, CANTARINI, LURIA, ROTHSCHILD, MONTEFIORE, DAVIDSON, GOLDSMID, SAMUEL, LUCAS, ELIAS, MELDOLA, MINIS, HART, LEVIN, KLEEBURG, PEREZ, PALGRAVE, ANTON, BEHRENDS, MULLER, SCHULHOF, MACNIN, SPEWACK, BARNET, MOSES, ISAACS, LEVY, ABRAHAM, FLORANCE, HAYS, DAVID, PHILIPPSON, CONRAT, MOSSE, LUDWIG, ALCONIERE, CARLEBACH, KLEPFISH, GHEREA, SCHOR, LANDSBERG, SOLOWAY, MILLER, DEUTSCH, SIMONE, HECHT, FINK, GREENHUT and WERTHEIM. See also HACOHEN and HAKOHEN.

COHEN-CARLOS—See COHEN.

COHEN-LIPSCHUTZ—See COHEN.

COHEN-TANUGI—See COHEN.

COHEN-YIZHAKI—See COHEN.

COHN—See COHEN.

COHNE—See COHEN.

COHNFELD—See COHEN.

CONHEIM—See COHEN.

COHNSTEIN—JE has article on German physician Isidor Cohnstein (1841–1894).

COHON—See COHEN.

COLEMAN—UJ has article on U.S. librarian Edward Coleman (1891–1939), born in Russia. See also COLMAN.

COLLINS—JE has article on Anglo-American actress Charlotte Collins (b. 1865 in London).

COLM—UJ has article on economist Gerhard Colm (b. 1897 in Germany).

COLMAN—AJA has a family tree. Related to SCHWARTZENBERG. See also COLEMAN.

COLOGNA—UJ has article on Italian Rabbi Abram de Cologna (1755–1832), of a distinguished family.

COLOMBO—EJ has two biographies from 19th–20th-cent. Italy.

COLON (also Colonne)—JE has article on Italian Talmudist Joseph Colon (1420–1480) and French musician Jules Colonne (1838–1910). See also EJ. Related to HALFON, TREVES, TRABOT.

COLORNI—JE has two biographies from Italy, 16th and 18th cent.

COMA (also Koma)—EJ has article on 17th-cent. Vienna *dayyan* Herz Coma.

COMPIEGNE DE WEIL—See WEIL.

COMTINO—JE has article on 15th-cent. Turkish Talmudist Mordecai Comtino. Related to DELMEDIGO.

CONAT—JE has article on 15th-cent. Italian printer Abraham Conat.

CONCIO—JE has article on 17th-cent. Italian author Joseph Concio.

CONE—U.S. family founded by Herman Cone (b. 1827 in Bavaria), who arrived in U.S.A. in 1845 and married Helen GUGGENHEIM. Also see COHEN.

CONEGLIANO (also Conian, Conigliani)—Prominent family of northern Italy that can be traced to the town of Asti in 16th cent. The name is taken from the town of Conegliano. See JE and UJ. Related to PONTE.

CONFORTE (also Conforti)—Hebrew historian David Conforte (1618–1685), born in Salonika, came from a family of scholars. He married the granddaughter of Menahem de LONZANO. Turkish Talmudist Gabriel Confoto may have been David's son. See JE.

CONHEIM—Related to MORTON.

CONIAN—See CONEGLIANO.

CONIGLIANI—See CONEGLIANO.

CONITZER—LBI has family tree beginning 1789.

CONN—See COHEN.

CONQUE—JE has two biographies from 17th-cent. Palestine.

CONRAD (also Conrat, Conried)—JE, EJ and UJ have biographies from Germany and Austria, 19th cent.

CONRIED—See CONRAD.

CONS—Related to BAYLIS.

CONSIGLI (also Consiglio)—EJ has article on Italian scholar Avtalyon Consigli (1540–1616). Related to RAPOPORT.

CONSOLO—JE has two biographies from 19th-cent. Italy.

CONSTANTINIS—JE has article on Abraham Constantinis of Athens (b. 1865).

CONTENT—Related to SELIGMAN.

COOK—Related to NONES.

COON—See COHEN.

COOPER (also Coopersmith)—UJ has biographies from 17th-cent. England and Sweden, and 19th-cent. Russia. Alexander Cooper (1605–1660) was the nephew of John HOSKINS.

COPELAND—See COPLAND.

COPISAROW—UJ has article on English scientist Maurice Copisarow (1889–1959).

COPLAND (also Copeland, Coplans)—UJ has two biographies, England and U.S.A., 19th–20th cent.

COPPIO—Related to SULLAM.

CORALNIK—UJ has article on journalist Abraham Coralnik (1883–1937), born in Russia. The name is perhaps a variation of GURALNICK.

CORCHO—Related to MENDES.

CORCOS—Sephardic family which can be traced in a direct line back to late-13th-cent. Spain. Members were distinghished in Italy in 16th through 18th cent.; all Jews bearing the name Corcos from Italy are probably related. In 1900 some descendants were living in Gibraltar and Morocco. JE has a family tree and sixteen biographies. Also see family history in VR, Vol. 2, p. 106. Related to MONTEFIORE.

CORDOVA (also Cordoba)—Sephardic name taken from the city in Spain. JE has two biographies from Amsterdam and Hamburg, 17th and 18th cent.

CORDOVERO—Gedalyah Cordovero of Palestine (16th-cent. Talmudic scholar) was a nephew of Solomon ALKABIZ. 17th-cent. Polish Rabbi Aryeh Lob Cordovero was also known as TARCZINER. See JE and EJ.

CORDOZO—See CARDOZO.

CORIAT—Jewish family in 19th-cent. Morocco and U.S.A. See JE, UJ.

CORINALDI—JE has article on 18th-cent. Italian Rabbi David Corinaldi.

CORINTH—Related to BEREND.

CORONEL (also Coronel-Chacon)—Portuguese name that was early mixed with Ashkenazic families. JE has biographies from 16th-cent. Spain, 17th-cent. England, and 19th-cent. Holland and Palestine. JE article on "Coat of Arms" has the family crest.

CORREA—Sephardic name. JE has article on 17th-cent. Spanish poet Isabella Correa of Brussels, Antwerp and Amsterdam, wife of Nicholas de OLIVIER y Fullana of Majorca. See JE. Also see The Alvares Correa Families of Curaçao and Brazil. Related to BELMONTE.

CORSONO—See CARSONO.

CORTISSOS—JE has article on Spanish contractor Jose Cortissos (1656–1742), who died in London. He was fifth in direct descent from Emanuel Jose Cortisos, a 15th-cent. Spanish grandee.

CORVE—Related to BIESENTHAL.

COSIN—JE has article on Rabbi Lewi Cosin (1573–1625) of Salonika and Venice.

COSLIN—JE has article on 19th-cent. German Talmudic scholar Hayyim Coslin.

COSMANN—LBIS has some family notes.

COSTA (also Acosta, da Costa)—Sephardic family probably identical with the family of MENDES da Costa ("Mendes of the coast"). The family is a central key to

Sephardic family trees because of its wide connections to Marrano families. It can be traced to 17th cent., and there were branches in Holland, Italy and England. JE has four family trees and numerous biographies. JE article on "Coat of Arms" has the Costa and Acosta family crests. UJ has a biography of Uriel Acosta (1585–1640). Related to BRAVO, BUENO, DIAS, FERNANDEZ, GRADIS, JACHIA, LOPEZ, SILVA, SUASSO, PINTO, MESQUITA, RICARDO, BELMONTE, CAPADOSE, HENRIQUES, AGUILAR, OSORIO, VILLA-REAL, FRANCO, QUIRO, PAIBA, LINDO, MOCATTA, BELINFANTE, HOMEN and RIVERA. See also UJ and EJ. Another variation may be COTA.

COSTELLEI—See KOSTELIZ.

COTA—Sephardic name that may be a variation of COSTA. JE has article on 15th-cent. Spanish poet Rodrigo Cota, from a Marrano family. For a family history, see "B'nai Cota M'Toledot," in Hayyim Schirmann Jubilee Volume.

COUDENHOVE—JE has article on 19th-cent. Austrian author Heinrich von Coudenhove.

COURANT—EJ has article on German mathematician Richard Courant (b. 1888).

COURIEL—See CURIEL.

COURNOS—UJ has article on U.S. author John Cournos (b. 1881 in Russia). Also see his Autobiography.

COUSSERI (also Cousser)—Jewish family from Riva di Trento in northern Italy, 15th and 16th cent. The family may have come originally from Germany. The name existed in 20th-cent. Italy as CUZZERI. A poet by that name lived in 17th-cent. Padua. See JE. See family history in REJ, No. 16, p. 270.

COUTINHO (also Cuitino)—Portuguese family. In 17th and 18th cent., members lived in Amsterdam, Hamburg, Brazil and the West Indies. JE has twelve biographies. Related to SILVA.

COVICI—UJ has article on U.S. publisher Pascal Covici (b. 1888 in Rumania).

COVO (also Covos)—Family of Salonika, Turkey, originally from Covo, Italy. A branch was living in Bulgaria in 1900. JE has seven biographies dating back to 17th cent. Related to BADHAU. Also see EJ.

COWAN—See COHEN, COWEN.

COWEN—English variation of COHEN. JE has five biographies from 19th cent. related to GINGOLD, SULZER and SIMON.

CRAMER—See KRAMER.

CRASTO—See CASTRO.

CREHANGE—JE has article on French Hebraist Alexandre Crehange (1791–1872).

CREIZENACH—JE has two biographies from 19th-cent. Germany.

CREMIEU (also Cremieux, Cremieu-Foa) —French name. JE has six biographies from 18th- and 19th-cent. France. CAJ has some family records. See also UJ and EJ. Related to CARMI, FOA, KARMI, PROUST.

CRESCAS—Illustrious and learned family of France and Spain, 13th through 15th cent. French Talmudist Vidal Crescas (14th-cent.) was the brother of Don Bonifas VIDAL of Barcelona. See JE. Also see CRESQUES.

CRESKOFF—UJ has article on U.S. engineer Jacob Creskoff (b. 1900 in Russia).

CRESPIN—JE has biographies from 19th-cent. Rumania and Turkey.

CRESQUES—Probably identical with CRESCAS. UJ has article on 14th-cent. mapmaker Jehuda Cresques of Barcelona.

CRESSON—JE has article on 19th-cent. convert to Judaism Warder Cresson, born Philadelphia, died Jerusalem.

CRITZMAN—UJ has article on 19th-cent. French physician Daniel Critzman, born in Rumania.

CROISSET—UJ has article on French author Francis de Croisset (1877–1937), born in Belgium.

CROLL—UJ has article on Canadian official David Croll (b. 1900 in Russia).

CROMELIEN—AJA has a family tree beginning 1780.

CRONBACH—AJA has a family tree. Related to STEARN.

CRONEBURG—JE has article on 18th-cent. German publicist Benjamin Croneburg.

CROOL—EJ has article on 19th-cent. English educator Joseph Crool, born in Hungary.

CRUCLEANU—UJ has article on 19th-cent. Rumanian author Stefan Crucleanu.

CSEMEGI—JE and UJ have articles on Hungarian journalist Karl Csemegi (1826–1899), whose original family name was NASCH.

CSERGO—UJ has article on Hungarian writer Hugo Csergo (1877–1938).

CSILLAG—JE has two biographies from 19th-cent. Hungary.

CUENQUE—EJ has article on cabalist Abraham Cuenque (b. 1648).

CULI—JE has article on Talmudist Jacob Culi (d. 1732 in Constantinople). He was from an exiled Spanish family; his grandfather was Moses ibn HABIB.

CUNEO—Name that may come from the Italian town of the same name, which was founded by Jews in late 14th cent. See JE.

CURIEL (also Couriel)—Wealthy Marrano family that settled in the Netherlands and in Hamburg c. 16th cent. and intermarried largely with the da COSTA family. There was a branch of the family in London in 18th cent. See JE, UJ and EJ. CAJ has a family tree. JE article on "Coat of Arms" has the family crest. Related to NAJARA and VITORIA.

CURTIZ—UJ has article on movie director Michael Curtiz (b. KERTESZ in Hungary, 1889).

CUTLER—UJ has article on U.S. industrialist Harry Cutler (1875–1920), born in Russia.

CUZZERI—See COUSSERI.

CYON (also Tsion)—EJ has article on Russian physiologist Elie Cyon (1842–1912).

CZACZKES (also Tschitkis, Czatzkes)— Possible variation of CHASHKES. Related to AGNON. JE has article on 19th-cent. Russian poet Baruch Czatzkes.

CZARTORISKI—CAJ has family records.

CZATZKES—See CZACZKES.

CZECH—EJ has article on politician Ludwig Czech (1870–1942), born in Galicia.

CZELLITZER—LBI has a family tree beginning 1815.

CZERNIAKOW—EJ has article on Warsaw community leader Adam Czerniakow (1880–1942).

DA COSTA—JE and UJ have biographies. See also COSTA.

D'AGUILAR—See AGUILAR and LOUSADA.

DAHAN (also Adhan, Bendahan, Bendahon)—Name of several families originating in the Sahara regions of Morocco. See JE and EJ. Related to MONTEFIORE.

DAHLBERG—UJ has biography from 20th-cent. U.S.A.

DAHLHEIM—LBIS has family notes.

DAICHES—See DEICHES.

DAINOW—JE and UJ have biographies from Russia and England, 19th cent.

DAIXEL—UJ has article on writer Samuel Daixel (b. 1884 in Russia).

DAJAN—Related to SPEYER.

DALMBERT—JE has article on French soldier Simon Dalmbert (1776–1840).

DALPUGET—Merchant family originally from Avignon, France, which had settled in Bordeaux by the 18th cent. See JE.

DALSHEIMER—Related to FRIEDENWALD.

DAMIER—Related to MANNHEIMER.

DAMROSCH—JE and UJ have biographies from Germany and U.S.A. Also see *My Musical Life,* by Walter Damrosch (1862–1950). Related to HEIMBURG.

DAN—UJ has article on Russian journalist Fyodor Dan (1871–1947), born GURVICH.

DANGLOW—EJ has article on Australian Rabbi Jacob Danglow (1880–1962), born in England.

DANGOOR—EJ has article on Iraqi Rabbi Ezra Dangoor (1848–1930).

DANHAUSER—JE has article on French musician Adolphe-Leopold Danhauser (1835–1896).

DANIEL (also Daniels)—EJ has article on Baghdad leader Menahem Daniel (1846–1940), of Georgian origin. JE has article on Dutch communal worker D. Polak Daniels (d. 1899). LBI has a Daniel family tree beginning 1765.

DANILOWICH—Related to ELKIND.

DANIN—EJ has article on Israel pioneer Yehezkel Danin (1867–1945), born SUCHOWOLSKY in Russia. Related to YELLIN.

DANN—LBI has a family tree beginning 1627. CAJ also has a family tree. Related to LEVI, MAYER.

DANNENBAUM—LBI has a family tree beginning 1620.

DANON—Joseph Ibn Danon of Belgrade (1620–1700), who died in London, was descended from an old Spanish family which had settled at Belgrade several generations earlier. JE has five biographies from 17th-cent. Turkey, Jerusalem, Belgrade, Bosnia and Smyrna.

DANTZIG—See DANZIG.

D'ANVERS—Related to BISCHOFFSHEIM.

DANZIG (also Dantzig, Danziger)—Name derived from the Prussian city of Danzig. Abraham Danzig (b. 1747 in Danzig, d. 1820 in Vilna) was descended from a family of scholars. His great-grandfather, Jehiel MICHAEL, was rabbi in Schottland, near Danzig. See JE. UJ has biographies from Germany and Lithuania, 19th cent.

DANZIS—UJ has article on U.S. journalist Mordechai Danzis (b. 1886 in Russia).

DAPIERA (also Da Piera)—JE and EJ have biographies from 13th- and 14th-cent. Spain.

DA PONTE—See PONTE.

DARI—13th-cent. Egyptian scholar Moses Dari was a descendant of Spanish Jews who emigrated to Dara (Fez, Morocco); hence the name. See UJ.

DARMESTETER—See DARMSTADT.

DARMON (also Garmon, Jarmon, Jarmona)—North African family. EJ has biographies from 17th, 18th and 19th cent. Also see JE article on Garmon.

DARMSTADT (also Darmstadter, Darmesteter)—Ashkenazic name taken from the city of Darmstadt, Germany. JE and UJ have biographies from 18th- and 19th-cent. Germany. The Darmesteters settled in Lorraine in mid-18th cent. from the Darmstadt ghetto, and took the name Darmesteter in 1791 when French Jews were told to take surnames. See JE. Cerf

Darmesteter married Rosalie BRANDEIS in 1839. Related to HARTOG.

DARSHAN—Related to KALONYMUS, MAGGID, ZAUSMER.

DARUM—Related to HAHN.

DASCALA—Related to KANSI.

DASHEWSKI—Name probably taken from the village of Dashev near Kiev, Russia. EJ has article on Russian Zionist Pinhas Dashewski (1879–1934).

D'ASPRO—Related to EMBDEN.

DASSAULT—EJ has article on French officer Darius Dassault (b. BLOCH in 1882).

DATO—JE has article on Italian Rabbi Mordecai Dato (1527–1585).

DATTELZWEIG—German name. For a family history, see ZGJT, No. 2 (1931), p. 155.

DATTILO—Related to JOAB.

ibn DAUD—Related to ALBALIA.

DAUPHINE—Related to MONTAUBAN.

DAVID (also Davide, Davidoff, Davidon, Davidov, Davydov, Davidhof, Davidovich, Davids, Davidsohn, Davidson, etc.) —Ashkenazic name of numerous families in many countries. The prominent David family of Canada came to Montreal from Wales about 1750. JE, UJ and EJ have many biographies. CAJ has a David family tree beginning in 18th cent. AJA has a family tree related to ABRAHAM, MENDELSON and PEISER. LBIS has Davide and Davidson family notes. CAJ has Davidov family records. For David family histories, see JFF, Nos. 29, 32 and 34. Also see *Die Familie Davidson* and *It Began with Zade Usher* (See Bernstein in Bibliography). See also DAWIDSOHN. Related to SAMUEL, HAYS, MICHAELS, HART, AZULAI, DULCKEN, VEIT, COHEN, DUNNER and LIST.

DAVID (King David, c. 1040–970 B.C.E.)— Biblical king who created the empire of Judah and Israel and from whom, according to tradition, the Messiah will be descended. He was descended from Ruth the Moabitess, wife of Boaz of the family of Perez, of the tribe of Judah. See the discussion of the House of David in chapter 5 of this book, and the chart of the Davidic dynasty on pp. 56–57; also EJ

article on "David, Dynasty of." The German scholar Hermann Reckendorff tried to show that the line of David never disappeared, but passed from Zerubbabel through Hillel and certain Jewish kings in Arabia down through the ABRAVENEL family. See *Die Geheimnisse der Juden* (5 vols.), 1857. Others supposedly descended from David include RASHI, the MAHARAL of Prague, and the DAYYAN family of Syria.

DAVIDOFF—See DAVID.

DAVIDOVICH—See DAVID.

DAVIDS—See DAVID.

DAVIDSOHN (Davidson)—See DAVID.

DAVIES—AJA has a family tree beginning in New York, 1787. UJ has one biography from 19th-cent. U.S.A.

D'AVIGDOR—See ABIGDOR.

DAVILA—Sephardic name derived from the Spanish city of Avila. JE has article on Diego Davila of Castile (b. 1466 in Segovia).

DAVIN—JE has article on 14th-cent. astronomer Solomon Davin.

DAVIS—JE has seven biographies from 19th-cent. England. Related to FRANKAU, JOHNSON, JAFFE, PEIXOTTO, LEWIS and READING. See also UJ.

DAVYDOV—See DAVID.

DAWIDSOHN (also Dawison)—Influential family of Warsaw, 19th and 20th cent., that dates from Hayim Dawidsohn (1760–1854). See JE and UJ. Also see DAVID.

DAWISON—See DAWIDSOHN.

DAYAN (also Dayyan)—Hebrew name meaning "rabbinic judge." The Syrian family of Dayyan can be traced back to 10th cent. and claims descent from King David; see EJ. JE has article on 19th-cent. Turkish Rabbi Abraham Dayyan. The Dayan family of Israel began with Shemuel Dayan (b. 1891 in Russia), who married Devorah ZATOLOWSKY. See EJ.

DEBASH—Name meaning "honey"; it may be a translation of the name MILES, which was frequently borne by the Jews of Provence in the Middle Ages. See JE.

DEBEDORDO—CAJ has family records.

DE BENEDETTI—EJ has biographies from 19th- and 20th-cent. Italy.

DEBORIN—EJ has article on Russian Marxist Aram Deborin, born JOFFE in 1881.

DE CASSERES—See CACERES.

DE CHAVES—Dutch painter Aaron De Chaves (d. 1705) is mentioned in EJ article on "Artists."

DECHY—UJ has article on Hungarian geographer Mor Dechy (1851–1917).

DECKINGEN—JE has article on 16th-cent. German lexicographer Judah Deckingen.

DECSEY—JE and UJ have biographies from 19th-cent. Germany and Hungary.

DE FALK—See FALK.

DE FRECE—UJ has article on British official Walter De Frece (1870–1935).

DEGENER—PD has a family tree.

DE HAAN—EJ has article on Dutch painter Jacob De Haan (1852–1895).

DE HAAS—Dutch name said to derive from the Portuguese DIAZ. UJ has one biography from 19th-cent. England.

DEICHES (also Daiches)—Polish family dating back to 17th cent. Members were living in Russia and Austria in 1900. See JE. UJ has four biographies from 19th-cent. Lithuania. Related to ARKES, BIELITZKI and ZERNE.

DEINARD—UJ has article on author Ephraim Deinard (1846–1930), born in Russia.

DEKKER—EJ has article on Dutch writer Maurits Dekker (1896–1962).

DE KLERK—EJ has article on Dutch architect Michel De Klerk (1884–1923).

DELACRUT (also De la Crota, Delacrot)—JE has article on 16th-cent. Polish scholar Ben Solomon Delacrut.

DE LA MOTTA—Related to WOLFF.

DELANCEY—Related to FRANKS.

DE LA PENHA—UJ has article on Amsterdam-born cantor Isaac De La Penha (1866–1935), member of a famous Sephardic family.

DE LA REINA—UJ has article on 17th-cent. Cabalist Joseph De La Reina.

DELAUNAY-TERK—EJ has article on French painter Sonia TERK (b. 1885), who married Robert Delaunay and changed her name accordingly.

DELBANCO (also Del Banco)—LBIS has a family tree and notes. CAJ has family records. EJ has article on 16th-cent. Venetian Anselmo Del Banco. JE has biography from 19th-cent. U.S.A. Related to WARBURG.

DEL BENE—JE has two biographies from Italy, 16th and 17th cent.

DE LEON—See LEON.

DELEVANTE—Related to CHRIQUI.

DELGADO—Sephardic name. JE has biographies of three Marranos from 16th and 18th cent. Related to CARDENAS.

DELIATITZ—Name derived from the town of Deliatitz. JE has two biographies from 19th-cent. Russia.

DE LIEME—JE has article on Dutch Zionist Nehemia De Lieme (1882–1940).

DE LIMA—EJ has article on South African writer Joseph De Lima (1791–1858), of a Dutch family of Portuguese origin. See also LIMA.

DELINSKY—See DZIALYNSKI.

DELLA SETA—EJ has article on Italian archaeologist Alessandro Della Seta (1897–1944). Also see biography in EJ article on "Politics."

DELLA TORRE—EJ has article on Italian Rabbi Lelio Della Torre (1805–1871). Possibly related to TORRE.

DELLAVIE—Related to BERND.

DELMAR (also Lebhar)—Moroccan family of 17th and 18th cent.; later in Amsterdam. See EJ. JE article on "Coat of Arms" has the family crest.

DELMEDIGO—Family of German origin which emigrated to Crete in 14th cent. The name is Italian for "doctor." The family later returned to Germany. See JE. Related to BING and OPPENHEIM in 17th-cent. Germany, also ROFE.

DELMONTE (also Del Monte)—LBIS has family notes. EJ has article on Italian poet Crescenzo Del Monte (1868–1935).

DELOUYA (also de Loya)—Moroccan family of Spanish origin. EJ has biographies from 16th-18th cent.

DELTAS—Related to WAHL.

DE LUCENA—Family in colonial America; see EJ. AJA has a family tree beginning 1635.

DELUGTAS—See DLUGOSZ.

DELVAILLE—JE and EJ have articles on French author Albert Delvaille (b. 1870). Related to CARO.

DEL VECCHIO—One of the most ancient Italian Jewish families. EJ has biographies from 16th–18th cent.

DEMBER—See biography in EJ article on "Physics."

DEMBITZ (also Dembitzer)—JE has biographies from 19th-cent. Prussia and Galicia. Galician Rabbi Hayyim Dembitzer (1820–1892) claimed descent from Rabbi Moses ISSERLES. UJ has three biographies. Related to BRANDEIS.

DEMBO—CAJ has family records. JE has article on Russian physician Isaac Dembo (1846–1906).

DEMUTH—JE has article on 19th-cent. Austrian singer Leopold Demuth.

DENIS (also Dionis)—JE has article on Albertus Denis, one of the first members of the Portuguese community in Hamburg (1611).

DENNERY—UJ has article on French general Justin Dennery (1847–1928).

DE PASS—Family of Sephardic Jews who settled in England in 17th cent. Some members migrated to South Africa. See EJ and UJ.

DEPPING—JE has article on German-French historian Georges Depping (1784–1853).

DERENBURG (also Dernburg, Derenbourg)—French-German family originally from Derenburg, near Halberstadt, Saxony, in 18th cent. The family later moved to Offenbach, Frankfurt-am-Main and Mayence (Mainz). See JE. LBI has a Dernburg family tree.

DERI—UJ has article on Hungarian-born art historian Max Deri (b. 1878).

DERNBURG—See DERENBURG.

DERY—EJ has article on Hungarian author Tibor Dery (b. DEUTSCH in 1894).

DESART—UJ has article on Irish Senator Ellen Desart (1857–1933), daughter of Henry BISCHOFFSHEIM; her mother's maiden name was BIEDERMAN.

DE SAXE—UJ has article on Australian-born lawyer Morris De Saxe (1898–1930). See also SACHS.

D'ESCOLA—Related to KANSI.

DESMAESTRE—EJ has article on 14th-cent. Majorcan scholar Jonah Desmaestre, father-in-law of Simeon DURAN.

DE SOLA—See SOLA.

DESSAU (also Dessauer, Dessoir)—Ashkenazic name taken from the town of Dessau, Germany. JE and UJ have biographies from 18th- and 19th-cent. Germany and Hungary. LBI has Dessauer family trees beginning 1700, 1710 and 1739. CAJ has Dessauer family trees covering 1763–1961, 1715–1962, 1710–1960 and 1735–1900. Related to ITZIG, KOHLER and MENDELSSOHN.

DESSLER—EJ has article on Musar leader Elijah Dressler (1891–1954), born in Russia.

DESSOFF—JE has article on German conductor Felix Dessoff (1835–1891).

DESSOIR—See DESSAU.

DETASSICHE—CAJ has family records.

DETMOLD—JE has biographies from 18th- and 19th-cent. Germany and Austria.

DE TOLEDO—See TOLEDANO.

DETRE—UJ has article on Hungarian-born Laszlo Detre (1874–1938).

DEUTSCH (also Deutschlander, Deutschmann)—Ashkenazic name meaning "from Germany," most commonly found among Hungarians. JE, UJ and EJ have biographies. Austrian theologian Gotthard Deutsch (b. 1859) was descended from the rabbinical family of BRAUNSCHWEIG. David Deutsch (1756–1831) was the father-in-law of Meir ASH. Other relatives are ALAMAN, HATVANY-DEUTSCH, NEMTZEANU, DERY, ROSENBACH, GRIGORYEVICH and KATZ. See also DUYTSCH.

DEUTZ—Possibly a variation of DEUTSCH. JE has biographies from 18th- and 19th-cent. Germany and France. Related to DRACH.

DEVENISHKY—UJ has article on Lithuanian author Isaac Devenishky (1878–1919).

DEVIDELS—Related to SCHADOW.

DEVRIENT—LBI has family tree beginning 1669.

DEVRIES—LBI has family tree beginning 1798.

DIAMAND—See DIAMANT.

DIAMANT (also Diamand, Diamond)—UJ has biographies from 19th-cent. Galicia, Rumania and U.S.A. PD has family records. Also see *Minna Diamant, 1815–1840: Ihre Freunde und Verwandten.* Related to HERZL.

DIAMOND—See DIAMANT.

DIAS (also Diaz, Diaz de Soria)—Sephardic family in France and Amsterdam, 17th, 18th and 19th cent.; probably a predecessor of the Dutch DE HAAS family. See JE and EJ. JE also has an article on the Diaz de Soria family of Bordeaux, which is traced to 17th cent. and which derived its name from the Spanish town of Soria.

DIAZ—See DIAS.

DICK (also Dechmann, Dikstein, Dickstein)—JE and UJ have biographies from 19th-cent. Russia, Germany, Latvia, Argentina, Lithuania and U.S.A. Related to DYKAN.

DIENA—JE has biographies from 16th- and 17th-cent. Italy.

DIENEMANN (also Dienesohn)—JE and UJ have biographies from 19th-cent. Russia and Poland.

DIESENDRUCK—UJ has article on Galician-born philosopher Zevi Diesendruck (1890–1940).

DIESPECK—Related to KOHLER, LEHMANN.

DIETZ—UJ has biographies from 20th-cent. U.S.A.

DIKSTEIN—See DICK.

DILLMANN—See DILMANN.

DILLON (also Dillion)—JE has three biographies from 19th-cent. Russia. Related to LAPOWSKI.

DILMANN (also Dillmann)—Related to BEHRENDS.

DILTHEY—Related to MISCH.

DIMANSTEIN—UJ has article on Russian revolutionary Simon Dimanstein (b. 1886).

DINA—JE has article on Italian journalist Giacoma Dina (1824–1879).

DINER (also Diner-Denes)—CAJ has family records. UJ has article on Hungarian author Jazsef Diner-Denes (1857–1938).

DINESOHN—UJ has article on Polish novelist Jacob Dinesohn (1856–1919), born in Lithuania.

DINGOL—UJ has article on Russian-born writer Solomon Dingol (b. 1886).

DINIS—Related to ABOAB.

DINKELSPEIL—See family history in JFF, Nos. 3 and 4.

DINKINS—Related to MOISE.

DIONIS—See DENIS.

DIRICHLET—Related to MENDELSSOHN and ITZIG.

DISBECK—Related to KOHLER.

DISHON—Name derived from Biblical name for (1) the son of Seir and head of the aboriginal Idumean tribes and (2) the son of Anah and brother of Esau's second wife.

DISKIN—JE has article on Russian Rabbi Joshua Diskin (1818–1898).

DISPECK—JE has article on German scholar David Dispeck (18th cent.).

DISRAELI (also D'Israeli)—A wealthy Sephardic family that arrived in Venice in 1492 and came to England in 1748, changing the name from D'Israeli to Disraeli. Descendants include British Prime Minister Benjamin Disraeli, whose mother was Maria BASEVI. EJ has a family tree. JE and UJ also have biographies. For a family history, see JHSE, No. 5 (1908). JE article on "Coat of Arms" has the family crest. Related to DE LARA, TEDESCO, LEWIS, NUNEZ, de LARA, MENDEZ FURTADO, SIPRUT, LINDO, VILLA REAL and READING.

DITTEL—JE has article on Austrian surgeon Leopold von Dittel (1815–1898).

DITTENHOEFER—AJA has family tree beginning in Bavaria, 1774.

DIVEKAR—JE has two biographies from 18th- and 19th-cent. India.

DIWAN—EJ has article on Israeli emissary Judah Diwan (d. 1752).

DIX—UJ has article on clothing manufacturer Henry Dix (1850–1933), born in Russia.

DIZENGOFF—UJ has article on Tel Aviv Mayor Meier Dizengoff (1861–1936), born in Russia.

DLUGOSZ (also Delugtas)—JE has article on 17th-cent. Lithuanian poet Samuel Dlugosz.

DOB—Related to BAER and BAMBERGER.

DOBINSKA—PD has family records. Related to SCHONFELD.

DOBLIN—UJ has article on author Alfred Doblin (b. 1878 in Germany).

DOBRIN—LBI has a family tree beginning 1820.

DOBROVELICHKOVA—Related to KHERSON.

DOBROWEN—UJ has article on conductor Issai Dobrowen (b. 1894 in Russia).

DOBRUSHKIN—See DOBRUSKA.

DOBRUSKA (also Dobrushkin, Dobrzinsky)—JE and UJ have biographies from 18th-cent. Austria and 19th-cent. Russia. LBI has a family tree beginning 1715. For a family history, see JFF, No. 23. Related to CIECHANOW, FRANK and SCHOENFELD. Also see EJ.

DOBSEWITCH (also Dobsevage)—JE has article on Russian Hebraist Abraham Dobsewitch (1843–1900), died in New York.

DOCZY (also Dux)—JE has article on Hungarian poet Ludwig Doczy (1845–1918), son of Adolf Dux. Also see UJ.

DOEBLIN—LBIS has family notes.

DOKSHITZER—Name derived from the town of Dokshitzy in the government of Minsk, Russia. Related to JOLLES.

DOLARO—JE has article on Anglo-American actress Selina Dolaro (1852–1889).

DOLBIN—See biography in EJ article on "Art."

DOLFS—LBI has a family tree beginning 1725.

DOLICKI—See DOLITZKI.

DOLITZKI (also Dolicki)—JE has article on Russian poet Menahem Dolitzki (1856–1931), died in U.S.A.

DOMBOVARY—UJ has article on Hungarian lawyer Geza Dombovary (1848–1918), son of Adolf SCHULHOF.

DOMEIER—Related to BERNARD.

DOMOSHEVITSKY—Related to BERSHADSKY.

DONATH (also Donati)—JE and UJ have biographies from 19th-cent. Austria, Hungary and Italy. Related to MAY.

DONCHIN—See DON-YAHIA.

DONIN—JE has article on Nicholas Donin of 13th-cent. France.

DONNEBAUM—Family from Germany. See history in JA, Vol. I.

DONNOLO—UJ has article on Italian physician Sabbatai Donnolo (913–982).

DON-YAHIA—Russian Rabbi Yehudah Don-Yahia (1869–1941), born DONCHIN; see EJ.

DORBOLO (also Durbal)—JE has article on 12th-cent. Rabbi Isaac Ben Dorbolo, who traveled through Poland, Russia, Bohemia, France and Germany.

DORFMAN—AJA has a family tree beginning 1851. Related to BRIEFTREGER and WASSERMAN.

DORI—EJ has article on Israeli military leader Ya'akov Dori (b. DOSTROVSKY in Russia, 1899).

DORIAN—EJ has article on Rumanian writer Emil Dorian (b. 1892).

DORIS—Related to MOSESCO.

DORMIDO—JE has article on David Abravenel Dormido, born in Spain, lived in London and Amsterdam, 17th cent. Related to SOEIRA.

DORMITZER—JE has article on Austrian scholar Meir Dormitzer (d. 1743 in Prague). PD has family records.

DOSTROVSKY—See DORI.

DOUGLAS—UJ has a biography from 20th-cent. U.S.A.

DOUKHAN—UJ has a biography from 20th cent.

DOURMASHKIN—UJ has article on physician Ralph Dourmashkin (b. 1891 in Russia).

DOVE—Related to ITZIG.

DRABKIN—JE has article on Russian Rabbi Abraham Drabkin (1844–1917), who came from an old established family of Mohilev.

DRACH (also Drachman, Drachsler)—JE, UJ and EJ have biographies from 19th-cent. Italy, France, Czechoslovakia and U.S.A. PD has family records. Also see "The Drachmans of Arizona," by F. S. Fierman, in *American Jewish Archives,* Vol. 16 (November 1964), p. 135. Drachsler is perhaps a variation of DRESSLER.

DREBEN—UJ has article on U.S. soldier Sam Dreben (1878–1935), born in Russia.

DREGELY—UJ has article on Hungarian playwright Gabor Dregely (b. 1883).

DREIFUS, DREIFUSS—See DREYFUS.

DRESCHFELD—JE has article on German physician Leopold Dreschfeld (1824–1897), who died in England.

DRESDEN—Ashkenazic name taken from the city in Germany. UJ has two biographies from Holland, 19th and 20th cent.

DRESSLER—EJ has article on U.S. cardiologist William Dressler (b. 1890 in Austria). See also DRACHSLER.

DREY—UJ has one biography from 19th-cent. Moldavia.

DREYER—LBI has family trees beginning 1545 and 1735. Related to WARBURG.

DREYFOUS—See DREYFUS.

DREYFUS (also Dreifus, Dreifuss, Dreyfus-Brisac, Dreyfous)—Alsatian branch of the TREVES family, from which the name is derived. The Treves family took its name from its hometown of Treves (Trier) and traces its descent from RASHI. JE and UJ have biographies from 19th-cent. France and Switzerland. See family history in MGWJ, No. 42 (1898), p. 424. AJA has a tree for a Dreyfous family of Cincinnati and New Orleans. Related to WORMSER, LEWI, RIS and MAYER.

DREYSCHOCK—UJ has article on pianist Alexander Dreyschock (1818–1869).

DRIFZAN—Related to TREVES.

DROB—UJ has article on Rabbi Max Drob (b. 1887 in Poland).

DROBNER—EJ has article on Polish politician Boleslaw Drobner (b. 1883).

DROHOBICZER—JE has article on 19th-cent. Russian Talmudist Israel Drohobiczer.

DROIANOFF—See DRUYANOV.

DROPSIE—JE has article on Philadelphia lawyer Moses Dropsie (1821–1905).

DRUCK—UJ has article on author David Druck (b. 1883 in Latvia). Also see DRUCKER.

DRUCKER (also Druck)—Ashkenazic name that means "printer" in German. Deborah Drucker married Saul WAHL of Poland, a member of the KATZENELLEN-BOGEN family, in 16th cent. See chart on page 14 of this book. CAJ has family trees beginning 18th cent. LBIS has notes for families from Hamburg and Kassel. JE has biographies from 17th-cent. Holland and 19th-cent. Poland.

DRUYANOV (also Droianoff)—UJ has article on author Alter Druyanov (b. 1870 in Lithuania).

DUARTE—JE has article on Luis Duarte, 16th-century Chilean Marrano from Portugal, also known as Luis Noble.

DUBEC—CAJ has family records.

DUBILIER—UJ has article on U.S. engineer William Dubilier (b. 1888).

DUBIN (also Dubinsky)—UJ and EJ have biographies from 19th-cent. Poland, Russia and Latvia. Related to DUBNO.

DUBISLAV—EJ has article on German philosopher Walter Dubislav (1895–1937).

DUBLIN—UJ has article on U.S. statistician Louis Dublin (b. 1882 in Lithuania).

DUBNO (also Dubnov, Dubnow)—Russian name from the town of the same name; most Jews with a variation of this name are related in some manner. See JE. The historian Simon Dubnow (1860–1941) was a descendant of the MAHARAL of Prague (1525–1609), who was supposedly a descendant of King DAVID. See "The Genealogy of Simon Dubnow." Related families include BRANDEIS, SASSOON, BACHRACH, BICHOVSKY, RASKIN, MIRSKY, RATNER, SHERESHEVSKY, KISSIN, KAYLIN, ERLICH, PLIGET, SCHNEUERSON, JOFFIN, METALITZER, KAZHUCHIN, NISSIN, DUBIN, PERLS and MARGOLIOTH.

DUCIT—Related to SAMUEL.

DUCKESZ—CAJ has family records. EJ has article on Rabbi Eduard Duckesz (1868–1944), born in Hungary.

DUENKELSBUEHLER—LBI has a family tree beginning 1610.

DUENNER—EJ has article on Rabbi Joseph Duenner (1833–1911), born in Poland.

DUEREN—JE has article on 13th-cent. Rabbi Isaac Dueren, from the German town Düren.

DUJOVNE—EJ has article on Argentine lawyer Leon Dujovne (b. 1899 in Russia).

DUKAS—UJ has biographies from 19th- and 20th-cent. France, Germany and U.S.A.

DUKER—UJ has article on historian Abraham Duker (b. 1907 in Poland).

DUKES (also Dukesz)—JE and UJ have biographies from 19th-cent. Hungary. PD has family records. Also see DUX.

DULCKEN—See DULKEN.

DULKEN—LBI has a family tree beginning 1808. Also see Genealogy of the Dulken Family. Related to DAVID.

DUMASHEVSKI—JE has article on 19th-cent. Russian lawyer Arnold Dumashevski.

DUNNER—JE and EJ have articles on 19th-cent. Polish Rabbi Joseph Dunner, grandfather of Aaron DAVIDS.

DURAN (also Durand, Durante)—Family from Provence, 14th cent. The name means "from Oran" (Algeria). JE has fourteen biographies. Also see family tree of Moses ben Nahman Gerondi in JE. Related to BONGODA, MAESTRE, GABBAI, TAWWAH and DESMAESTRE.

DURAND—See DURAN.

DURANTE—See DURAN.

DURAW—Related to MONTEFIORE.

DURBAL—See DORBOLO.

DURIEUX—Related to CASSIRER.

DURKHEIM—JE has article on French sociologist Émile Durkheim (1858–1917).

DURLACHER—JE has article on 19th-cent. German publisher Elcan Durlacher, who lived in Paris. See family history in Nathanael Weil, Oberlandrabbiner in Karlsruhe, und seine Familie. Related to WEIL.

DUSCHAK—UJ has article on Austrian Rabbi Moritz Duschak of Moravia (1815–1890). Also see JE.

DUSCHENES—JE has article on 19th-cent. Austrian jurist Friedrich Duschenes, from Prague.

DUSCHINSKY—JE, UJ and EJ have biographies from 19th-cent. Austria and Hungary. Related to KOPPEL and WINKLER.

DUSHKIN—UJ has two biographies from Russia.

DUSHMAN—EJ has article on U.S. chemist Saul Dushman (b. 1883 in Russia).

DUX—JE has article on 19th-cent. Hungarian writer Adolf Dux. Related to DUKES.

DUVEEN—UJ has biography of English art dealer Joseph Duveen (1869–1939). See The Rise of the House of Duveen.

DUVERNOIS—UJ has article on French novelist Henri Duvernois, born SCHWABACHER in 1875.

DUWAYK—Family of rabbis in Aleppo, Syria, 18th and 19th cent. See EJ.

DUX—JE has article on 19th-cent. Hungarian writer Adolf Dux. Related to DUKES. Also see DOCZY.

DUYTSCH—Probably a variation of DEUTSCH. JE has article on Hungarian writer Christian Duytsch (18th cent.).

DWORSKY—UJ has article on philanthropist Bertha Dworsky (1860–1925), born in Russia.

DWORZACZEK—See Genealogie.

DYCHE—EJ has article on U.S. labor leader John Dyche (1867–1939), born in Lithuania.

DYER—JE and UJ have articles on U.S. community leader Isadore Dyer (1813–1888), born in Dessau, Germany, and other Dyers from Alzey, Germany. Related to OSTERMAN.

DYKAAR—UJ has article on sculptor Moses Dykaar (1885–1933), born in Lithuania.

DYKAN—EJ has article on Israeli jurist Paltiel Dykan (b. DIKSTEIN in Lithuania, 1885).

DYMOW—UJ has article on Russian writer Ossip Dymow (b. PERELMAN in 1878).

DYNOW—EJ has article on Galician scholar Zevi Dynow (1785–1841).

DYTE—JE has article on D. M. Dyte, the Englishman who saved King George III in 1800.

DZIALYNSKI—UJ has article on U.S. official Morris Dzialynski (1841–1907), born in Poland. Also see DELINSKY.

EBER (also Eberlen, Eberls, Ebers, Ebert, Eberty)—JE and UJ have biographies from Germany. See Ebert family history in *Friedrich Ebert in seiner Zeit.* Related to EPHRAIM, LEVYNSOHN and JEKELES. Also see EJ.

EBNER—UJ has article on Zionist Meir Ebner (b. 1872 in Rumania).

EBORENSIS—UJ has article on poet Flavius Eoborensis (1517–1607), from the Marrano families of ADUMIM and de ROSSI.

EBSTEIN—See EPSTEIN.

ECKMAN—UJ has article on U.S. Rabbi Julius Eckman (1805–1877), born in Poland.

ECKSTEIN—UJ has three biographies from 19th- and 20th-cent. Germany and U.S.A. CAJ has a family tree and records from Germany.

ECSERY—PD has family records.

EDEL—See EDELS.

EDELHERTZ—UJ has article on U.S. lawyer Bernard Edelhertz (1880–1931), born in Russia. Also see EDELS.

EDELMANN—JE and EJ have articles from 19th-cent. Russia and Lithuania. See also EDELS.

EDELS (also Edel, Edelson, Edelhertz, Edelmann, etc.)—Polish Rabbi Samuel Edels (1555–1631) took the name Edels from the given name of his mother-in-law, Edel, who financed his rabbinical school. A later derivation of the name is ATLAS. Samuel Edels was the son-in-law of Moses Ashkenazi HEILPRIN and an ancestor of the MARGOLIOTH family of Galicia. His son-in-law was *Moses* ben Isaac Bonems, and an 18th-cent. descendant was *Eliezer* ben Meir ha-Levi of Pinsk. See biographies in JE and EJ; also Edel biography in UJ. Samuel Edels' connections with other prominent Polish and Galician families can be traced in *Anaf Ez Aboth,* by Samuel Kahan (see Bibliography); see also *Toledot Mishpahat Schor,* by Bernard Friedberg, 1901, p. 10. Related to FALK,

HEILBRONN, KALISHER, HARIF HA-LEVI and ROSENFELD.

EDELSON—See EDELS.

EDELSTADT—UJ has article on poet David Edelstadt (1866–1892), born in Russia. Also see EDELS.

EDELSTEIN—German name meaning "precious stone." UJ has biographies from Poland, U.S.A. and Ireland. Possibly a variation of EDELS. Related to BEHREND.

EDER—UJ has article on English Zionist David Eder (1865–1936).

EDERSHEIM—JE has article on Austrian Christian missionary Alfred Edersheim (1825–1889), born of Jewish parents of Vienna.

EDINGER—JE and UJ have biographies from 19th-cent. Germany. LBI has a family tree.

EDLIN—UJ has article on U.S. writer William Edlin (b. 1878 in Russia).

EDREHI—JE has article on Moroccan cabalist Moses Edrehi (1774–1842).

EDWARDS—UJ has article on actor and composer Gus Edwards (b. 1881 in Prussia).

EFENDOPOLO—See AFENDOPOLO.

EFRATHI—See EPHRATI.

EFRATI—See EPHRATI.

EFRON—UJ has biographies from 19th-cent. Russia, Lithuania and Argentina.

EFROS—UJ has article on U.S. scholar Israel Efros (b. 1891 in the Ukraine).

EGER (also Egers, Gins, Ginsmann, Guns, Eiger, Guens, Ginz, Genz)—German family from Halberstadt, 16th cent. JE, UJ and EJ have biographies. LBI has family trees beginning 11th cent., 1572, 1600, 1609 and 1695. CAJ has an Egers family tree, related to ENGEL. See family history in *Zur Geschichte der Familie Eger-Gans-Gansmann.* Related to GANS, SCHREIBER, LEIDESDORFF, KORNFELD, SOFER, ULMAN, ZENZYMINER, BERNSTEIN, FRANKFURTER, TEMKIN, SCHLESINGER, ETTINGER, BINSWANGER, HERZBERG and BEROLZHEIMER.

EGGER—UJ has article on 19th-cent. Hungarian goldsmith David Egger.

EGOZI—JE has article on 16th-cent. Turkish Talmudist Menahem Egozi of Constantinople.

EGRA—JE has article on 18th-cent. Austrian Rabbi Meshullam Egra of Galicia.

EHINGEN—Related to JACKLIN.

EHRENBERG (also Ehrenburg)—JE, UJ and EJ have biographies from 18th- and 19th-cent. Germany and Russia. LBI has a family tree beginning 1680. Also see *Samuel Meyer Ehrenberg*, by Leopold Zunz, 1854 (in German).

EHRENFELD—Family of Hungarian rabbis descended from David Ehrenfeld (d. 1861), a son-in-law of Moses SOFER. See EJ. Related to GLAZNER and PATAI.

EHRENFEST—UJ has article on Vienna physicist Paul Ehrenfest (1880–1933). Related to AFANASIEVA.

EHRENFRIED—UJ has article on U.S. surgeon Albert Ehrenfried (b. 1880).

EHRENHAFT—UJ has article on Austrian physicist Felix Ehrenhaft (b. 1879).

EHRENKRANZ—JE has article on Galician poet Benjamin Ehrenkranz (1819–1883), who lived in Rumania and died in Constantinople.

EHRENPREIS—UJ and EJ have articles on Swedish Chief Rabbi Marcus Ehrenpreis (b. 1869 in Galicia).

EHRENREICH—JE and EJ have biographies from 19th-cent. Galicia, Italy and Hungary. Related to REGGIO.

EHRENSTAMM—Family of textile manufacturers in the Hapsburg empire, 18th and 19th cent. See EJ. LBI has a family tree beginning 1695. PD has some family records. Related to ILLOVY and KOLIN.

EHRENSTEIN—UJ has article on Vienna poet Albert Ehrenstein (b. 1886).

EHRENTHEIL—JE has article on 19th-cent. Hungarian writer Moritz Ehrentheil.

EHRENTREV—UJ has article on Hungarian Rabbi Heinrich Ehrentrev (1854–1927), who died in Munich.

EHRICH—UJ has article on U.S. antique dealer Louis Ehrich (1849–1911).

EHRLICH (also Ehrlichman, Erlich)—German name. JE and EJ have biographies from 19th-cent. Poland, Russia, Germany, Austria and Yugoslavia. LBI has family trees beginning 1600, 1737 and 1820. CAJ has family trees and records, related to HEITLER. See Ehrlichman family history in *It Began with Zade Usher* (see Bernstein in Bibliography); also see Ehrlich history in JFF, No. 34. The Erlich family is related to DUBNOW.

EHRMANN—JE has article on 19th-cent. Austrian Rabbi Daniel Ehrmann, from Bohemia.

EIBENSCHITZ—See EIBENSCHUTZ.

EIBENSCHUTZ (also Eibenschitz, Eibeschuetz, Eybeschuetz, Eybeschutz)—Family from the Moravian town of the same name, where Jews settled in 16th cent. JE, UJ and EJ have biographies from 18th-cent. Denmark and 18th–19th-cent. Germany and Hungary. Related to PERLHEFTER, OETTINGEN, SPIRA, HAKOHEN, BERNARD, JONATHANSON, BONDI, RESHEVSKY and ETTINGER.

EIBESCHUETZ—See EIBENSCHUTZ.

EICHBERG—JE has article on German violinist Julius Eichberg (d. in Boston, 19th cent.). Related to ROSEWALD, WEILLER.

EICHEL—See family history in *Stamtavlen Eichel.*

EICHELBAUM—UJ has article on Argentine novelist Samuel Eichelbaum (b. 1894).

EICHELBERG—CAJ has some family records.

EICHELGRUEN—LBI has a family tree beginning 1794, related to LOEWENSOHN.

EICHENBAUM—JE has article on Russian poet Jacob Eichenbaum (1796–1861), born in Galicia. Related to GELBER.

EICHENGRUEN—LBI has a family tree beginning 1785.

EICHENSTEIN—Related to ZHIDACHOV.

EICHHOLZ—Related to ADLER.

EICHMANN—See family history in *Stammbaum der Familie Eichmann, 1660–1931.*

EICHTHAL—JE and EJ have biographies from Germany and France, 18th and 19th cent. LBI has a family tree beginning 1744. PD has some family records. JE article on "Coat of Arms" has the family crest. Related to SELIGMANN.

EICHWALD—LBIS has some family notes.

EIDELSBERG—UJ has article on Polish-American journalist David Eidelsberg (b. 1893).

EIDLITZ—JE and EJ have biographies from Austria and Bohemia, 18th and 19th cent.

EIG—UJ has article on Russian-Israeli botanist Alexander Eig (1894–1938).

EIGENE—PD has a family tree.

EIGER—See EGER.

EILENBURG—JE has article on 16th-cent. Polish Rabbi Issachar Eilenburg, who died in Moravia.

EINAEUGLER—EJ has article on lawyer Karol Einaeugler (b. 1883 in Galicia).

EINHORN—JE and EJ have biographies from 19th-cent. Bavaria, Hungary and Russia. Related to OCHS, KOHLER, HIRSCH, SULZBERGER. Also see HORN.

EINSON—UJ has article on Russian-American-Israeli lithographer Morris Einson (1883–1936).

EINSTEIN—Ashkenazic name meaning one who works in stone construction. JE, UJ and EJ have biographies, mostly from Germany and U.S.A. LBI has family trees beginning 1754 and 1759, related to TAENZER. CAJ has a family tree from Germany. See family history in JFF, No. 28. Related to SULZBERGER.

EINZIG—EJ has article on British economist Paul Einzig (b. 1897 in Rumania).

EIS—EJ has article on Austro-Hungarian soldier Alexander von Eis (1832–1921).

EISENBAUM—UJ has article on Polish journalist Anton Eisenbaum (1791–1852).

EISENBERG—UJ and EJ have biographies from 19th- and 20th-cent. Russia, Germany and U.S.A. LBI has a family tree beginning 1770.

EISENDRATH—UJ has three biographies from 19th-cent. France and U.S.A.

EISENMAN (also Eisenmann)—UJ has biographies from 19th-cent. France and U.S.A.

EISENMENGER—CAJ has some family records.

EISENSTADT (also Aisenstadt, Eisenstadter, Eisenstaedt, Eisenstatter)—Ashkenazic name taken from the Hungarian town of the same name. JE and EJ have biographies from Poland, Germany and Hungary. LBI has a family tree beginning 1670. YIVO also has a family tree, and CAJ has some family records. See family history in *Da'at Kedoshim,* by Israel Eisenstadt. PD has some records of an Eisenstatter family. In some cases ASH is an abbreviated form of Eisenstadt. Related to HIRSCH, SHALOM, BACHARACH, GYARMATH, UNGVAR, KALLIR and LEVISON.

EISENSTEIN—JE and UJ have biographies from 19th-cent. Russia, Germany and Poland.

EISLER—JE and EJ have biographies from 19th-cent. Austria, Germany and Hungary. PD has some family records. Related to FISCHER.

EISMANN—UJ and EJ have biographies from 19th-cent. Russia.

EISNER—UJ has biographies from 19th-cent. Bavaria and U.S.A.

EISS—JE has article on 19th-cent. soldier Alexander Eiss.

EITAN—UJ has article on Polish-American writer Israel Eitan (1885–1935).

ELAZARI-VOLCANI—EJ has article on Israeli agronomist Yizhak Elazari-Volcani (1880–1925), born WILKANSKY in Lithuania.

ELB—Related to HALLE.

ELBAZ—North African family noted for its rabbis. EJ has biographies from 17th, 18th and 19th cent.

ELBE—UJ has article on 19th-cent. U.S. soldier Max Elbe.

ELBOGEN—See KATZENELLENBOGEN.

ELCAN—See ELKAN.

ELCKAN—See ELKAN.

ELEAZAR (also Alatzar, Abenalazar)—Prominent Sephardic family in Aragon during the Middle Ages. EJ has biographies from 12th, 13th and 14th cent.

ELEK—PD has family records, related to UJNEP and MALOMSZEG.

ELFAND—Ashkenazic name meaning "camel," taken from the picture on the family's house sign. The Slavic variation is GELFAND.

ELFENBEIN—EJ has article on U.S. Rabbi Israel Elfenbein (b. 1890 in Galicia).

ELHA'IK—JE has article on 18th-cent. Tunisian Rabbi Uzziel Elha'ik.

ELIANO—JE has article on Vittorio Eliano, 16th-cent. Jewish convert to Christianity. Related to LEVITA.

ELIAS—JE and UJ have biographies from 18th- and 19th-cent. Germany and England. Related to COHEN, LEVITA, SOUTHWOOD. Also see ELIASH.

ELIASBERG—JE has biographies from 19th-cent. Russia.

ELIASH—EJ has article on Israeli lawyer Mordecai Eliash (b. 1892 in Russia).

ELIASHOFF (also Eliashov)—UJ and EJ have biographies from 19th-cent. Lithuania.

ELIASON (also Eliasson)—Related to GOLDSMID. LBIS has notes of an Eliasson family.

ELIASOPH (also Eliassof)—UJ has biographies from 19th-cent. Russia and U.S.A.

ELIASSON—See ELIASON.

ELION—EJ has article on Dutch medalist Jacques Elion (1842–1893).

ELIS—See ELLIS.

ELKAN (also Elkin, Elcan, Elckan, Elken, Elkes, Elkind, Elkisch, Elkus)—JE, UJ and EJ have biographies from 18th-cent. Germany and from 19th-cent. Germany, Russia, Sweden, England, Lithuania and U.S.A. LBI has a family tree beginning 1790. CAJD has an Elken family tree from Germany. LBIS has Elkan, Elckan and Elkisch family notes. JE article on "Coat of Arms" has an Elkan family crest. Related to SOLOMON, PLAUT, MOCATTA and DANILOWICH.

ELKEN—See ELKAN.

ELKES—See ELKAN.

ELKIN—See ELKAN.

ELKIND—See ELKAN.

ELKISCH—See ELKAN.

ELKUS—See ELKAN.

ELLENBOGEN—See KATZENELLENBOGEN.

ELLENSTEIN—UJ has article on U.S. public official Meyer Ellenstein (b. 1886).

ELLERN—LBI has a family tree beginning 1600.

ELLES—See ELLIS.

ELLINGER—JE has biographies from 18th-cent. Germany and 19th-cent. Austria. Related to HOCHHEIMER.

ELLIOT—LBIS has some family notes.

ELLIS (also Elis, Elles, Ellissen)—JE has articles from 16th-cent. Poland and 19th-cent. India. Also see UJ. Related to ISRAEL, SPEYER and ELSASS.

ELLISSEN—See ELLIS.

ELLSBERG—See ELSBERG.

ELLSTATTER—See ELSTATTER.

ELMALEH—Family of rabbis and communal leaders in Turkey, Morocco and Italy. JE has biographies from 16th through 20th cent. See "Origine de la famille Elmaleh," in *Abraham Elmaleh 70th Birthday Book*. Related to GEDALIAH.

ELMAN—UJ has article on Russian violinist Mischa Elman (b. 1891).

ELNECAVE—UJ has article on journalist David Elnecave of Constantinople and Bulgaria (b. 1882).

ELOESSER—UJ has article on German author Arthur Eloesser (1870–1938). Related to LEWISOHN.

ELSASS (also Elsasser)—Related to BELMONT, ELLIS and SCHOR. Also see ELZAS.

ELSBERG (also Ellsberg)—JE and UJ have biographies from 18th-cent. Prussia and 19th-cent. U.S.A.

ELSNER—UJ has article on U.S. physician Henry Elsner (1855–1916), whose father came from Germany. CAJ has family records.

ELSENBERG—JE has article on 19th-cent. Polish teacher Jacob Elsenberg.

ELSTATTER (also Ellstatter, Ellstaetter)—UJ and JE have biography from 19th-cent. Germany.

ELTE—EJ has article on Dutch architect Harry Elte (1880–1945).

ELTZBACHER—LBI has a family tree beginning 1755. Related to HEINE.

ELYACHAR (also Elyashar)—CAJ has some family records. EJ has two biographies from Israel, 18th and 19th cent. Related to PANIGEL.

ELZAS—JE and EJ have biographies from 19th-cent. Holland, Russia, England, Germany and U.S.A. Also see ELSASS.

EMANUEL (also Emmanuel)—JE and UJ have biographies from 16th-cent. Moldavia; 18th-cent. U.S.A.; 19th-cent. England. CAJ has some family records. Related to BELMONTE, LEWIS and WHITAKER.

EMBDEN (also Emden)—German name. JE has a family tree and nine biographies beginning 17th-cent. Germany. UJ also has biographies. CAJ has an Emden family tree, and PD has Emden family records. Related to TORRE-LOMBARDINI, D'ASPRO, HEINE, VAN GELDERN, SCHIFF, LEVI, MIRELS, MOSCHELES, LEVIN, SULZBERGER, ASHKENAZI, HERSCHEL, GREENHUT and LEVINSON.

EMBER—UJ has article on U.S. scholar Aaron Ember (1878–1926), born in Russia.

EMDEN—See EMBDEN.

EMERICH (also Emmerich, Emrich)—JE and UJ have articles from 18th-cent. Prague and 19th-cent. U.S.A. LBI has an Emmerich family tree beginning 1649, related to GUMPERZ, SPEYER, ROTHSCHILD. Possibly also related to EMMERLICH.

EMIN PASHA—UJ has article on African explorer Mehmed Emin Pasha (1840–1892), born Eduard SCHNITZER in Prussia.

EMMANUEL—See EMANUEL.

EMMERICH—See EMERICH.

EMMERLICH—Possibly a variation of EMERICH. Related to WESEL.

EMOD—UJ has article on Hungarian author Tamas Emod (1888–1938).

EMRICH—See EMERICH.

EMS—LBI has a family tree beginning 1770.

EN BONAFOS—See BONAFOS.

ENDELMAN—Related to JAFFE.

ENDLER—JE has article on 18th-cent. Prague Talmudist Samuel Endler. Related to BENZION.

ENDOR—UJ has article on Brooklyn writer S. Guy Endor (b. 1901).

ENELOW—UJ has article on Russian Rabbi Hyman Enelow (1877–1934).

ENGEL—Ashkenazic name meaning "angel." JE and UJ have biographies from 19th-cent. Hungary and Russia. LBI has a family tree beginning in 1020. CAJ has a family tree and family records. PD also has some family records. Also see *The Ancestry and Descendence of Nancy Egers Engel.* Related to EGERS and NAUMANN.

ENGELBERT—JE has article on 19th-cent. German Rabbi Hermann Engelbert of Hessen.

ENGELMANN (also Engelsmann)—EJ has biographies from 19th- and 20th-cent. Hungary and Germany. Related to KOHN.

ENGELSKIRCHEN—PD has family records.

ENGELSMANN—See ENGELMANN.

ENGLANDER (also Englaender)—JE and EJ have biographies from 19th-cent. Austria. Also see EJ article on Peter Altenberg.

ENGLISCH—JE has article on 19th-cent. Austrian chess master Berthold Englisch.

ENNERY—JE has biographies from 19th-cent. France.

ENOCH—JE has article on 19th-cent. German Rabbi S. Enoch. CAJ has some family records.

ENRIQUES—See HENRIQUES.

ENRIQUEZ—See HENRIQUES.

ENSE—Related to ASSING.

ENSHEIM—JE has article on French mathematician Moses Ensheim (1750–1839). Related to METZ, BRISAC.

ENTEEN (also Entin)—UJ and EJ have article on Russian-American writer Joel Enteen, or Entin (b. 1874).

EPELTREGER—Related to EPSTEIN.

EPENSTEIN—PD has some family records. The name may be a variation of EPSTEIN.

EPHRAIM—JE, UJ and EJ have biographies beginning in 18th-cent. Germany and Italy. EJ has a family tree. LBI has a family tree beginning 1665; CAJ has family records and a family tree beginning 1776 in Germany. See family histories in JFF, Nos. 1 and 4. Related to BLASOM, FRANKEL, LEVI, HEINE, FRANKL, MIRELS, EBER, WOLFF, ITZIG, SAMSON, MOSSON, PHILLIPSON, FRIEDLAENDER, JOCHANAN, MEINHARDT, SCHMIDT and EBERTY.

EPHRATI (also Efrathi, Efrati, Ephrussi) —Hebrew name that appears in 14th-cent. Spain as Efrati and later in central Europe and Russia as Ephrati or Ephrussi. See JE and UJ for biographies. LBI has an Ephrussi family tree beginning 1792. PD has Ephrussi family records. Related to KREMER, HELLER, TEBELE and BAZALEL. Also see HA-EFRATI.

EPHRUSSI—See EPHRATI.

EPPENSTEIN—See EPSTEIN.

EPPSTEIN—See EPSTEIN.

EPSTEIN (also Ebstein, Epenstein, Eppenstein, Eppstein)—One of the oldest Slavic Jewish names, dating as far back as 1392 and taken from the town of Epstein in Styria. JE, UJ and EJ have numerous biographies, and JE has a family tree. LBI has a family tree beginning 1771. PD has records of a family related to SCHAF. See family history in *Makor Baruch.* Also see JE articles on Grodno and Pinsk. Related to LOB, ABRAHAM, AVIGDOR, NECHES, LEWIN, SIMEL, BERR, JAFFE.

ERASO—Related to de SOLA.

ERDBERG—UJ has article on Polish writer Samson Erdberg (b. 1891).

ERDOS—UJ has article on Hungarian-Italian poet Renee Erdos (b. 1879).

ERGAS—JE has article on Italian Rabbi Joseph Ergas (1685–1730). Related to BELMONTE, PINHEIRO and NAVON. Also see EJ.

ERHARD—CAJ has some family records.

ERKELES—PD has some family records.

ERLANGER—Ashkenazic name derived from the village of Klein Erdlingen, near Nordlingen—*not* from Erlangen in Bavaria. JE has three biographies from 19th-cent. France. LBI has a family tree beginning 1780. PD has some family records. JE article on "Coat of Arms" has the family crest.

ERLICH—See EHRLICH.

ERMAN (also Ermann)—EJ has article on German scholar Johann Ermann (1854–1937). Related to ITZIG. Also see UJ.

ERNST—UJ has biographies from 19th-cent. France, Moravia and U.S.A. AJA and LBI have family trees beginning 1810. Related to ALEXANDER.

ERRERA—Sephardic family that left Spain for Syria in 15th cent., then moved to Italy in 17th cent.; a branch went to Belgium in 19th cent. The name is derived from the Hebrew *irur* ("protest"). See UJ. Related to HERRERA.

ERTER—JE has article on Galician satirist Isaac Erter (1792–1851).

ERULKAR—UJ has article on Bombay physician Abraham Erulkar (b. 1887).

ESCAPA—Sephardic name. EJ has article on Turkish Rabbi Joseph Escapa (1570–1662), descended from a Spanish family. Related to BELMONTE.

ESCHELBACHER—UJ has two biographies from 18th-cent. Germany.

ESCUDERO—JE has article on 17th-cent. Spanish poet Lorenco Escudero, also known as ISRAEL and GHERPEREGRINO.

ESHKOL—EJ has article on Israeli leader Levi Eshkol (b. SHKOLNIK in Russia, 1895).

ESHNER—UJ has article on U.S. doctor Augustus Eshner (b. 1862).

ESKELES (also Eskell)—Viennese family originally from Olkusz, near Cracow, Poland. EJ has family tree and biographies beginning 18th cent. JE also has biographies. LBI has a family tree beginning 1718. JE article on "Coat of Arms" has the family crest. See family history in JFF, No. 11. Also see UJ article on Turkish diplomat Sassoon Eskell (1860–1932). Related to ITZIG, BRENTANO-CIMAROLI, WERTHEIMER and LEMBERGER.

ESKENAZI—UJ has biographies from 16th-cent. Italy and 19th-cent. Turkey. Also see ASHKENAZI.

ESOFOWICZ—UJ has biographies from 15th-cent. Russia and Poland. See also JE.

ESPERANSSA (also Esperanza)—JE has article on 17th-cent. Rabbi Gabriel Esperanssa of Safed, Palestine.

ESPERIAL—Sephardic name. JE has article on physician Samuel Esperial of Cordova, Spain.

ESPINOSA (also Spinoza)—Sephardic name taken from the town of Espino in Spain. JE has biographies from 18th-cent. Italy and 17th-cent. Holland (Spinoza). Also see biography in EJ article on "Dance." See Spinoza family history in JFF, No. 24. JE article on "Coat of Arms" has the Espinosa crest. Related to CACERES, DE CASSERES, MODIGLIANI.

ESRA—JE has article on 19th-cent. Calcutta philanthropist Elia Esra.

ESTELLA—Related to KOKHAVI.

ESTERHAZY—CAJ has some family records.

ESTEVENS—EJ has article on Danish artist David Estevens (1670–1715), of Spanish origin.

ESTROSA—See ESTRUMSA.

ESTRUMSA (also Estrosa, Estrumza)—Middle East Jewish family which takes its name from the town of Strumnitza in Macedonia and can be dated from 17th cent. JE has two biographies.

ETHAUSEN—JE has article on 17th-cent. German scholar Alexander Ethausen, of Fulda.

ETTELSON—UJ has article on U.S. lawyer Samuel Ettelson (1874–1938). Possibly a variation of EDELSON.

ETTEN—See ETTING.

ETTHAUSEN—JE has article on 18th-cent. German Rabbi Isaac Etthausen.

ETTING (also Etten)—Ashkenazic name of two prominent American families, one in New York and one in Philadelphia, apparently not related to each other. JE and UJ have numerous biographies. The Philadelphia branch is from Germany. The name is perhaps taken either from the city of Öttingen or Ettlingen. Related to MINIS, GRATZ, HAYS, SOLOMON and CAMPBELL.

ETTINGEN—See ETTINGER.

ETTINGER (also Ettingen, Oettingen, Oettinger)—Ashkenazic name taken from the city of Öttingen in Bavaria and found all over Europe. JE, UJ and EJ have biographies. CAJD has a family tree from Germany, related to HINRICHSEN and MICHEL. LBI has an Oettinger family tree beginning 1833. LBIS has Oettingen family notes. Related to RAPAPORT, ITZSCHE,

HESCHEL, NATHANSON, SCHUSTER, EYBESCHUTZ, GUENZBERG and SPEYER. Also see OTTINGER.

ETTLINGER—Ashkenazic name taken from the town of Ettlingen in Baden. An Italian variation is OTTOLENGHI. JE has a biography from 18th-cent. Germany. LBI has a family tree beginning 1733. CAJ has two family trees, one covering 1599–1930 and related to FREIMANN, HOROVITZ and PINZCOWER; the other covering 1692 to 1933 in Germany and related to Cohn, LOEWE and BAMBERGER.

ETZEL—See ITZIG.

EUCHEL—JE has article on Danish author Isaac Euchel (1756–1804), died in Berlin. Related to JOST.

EUCKEN—CAJ has some family records.

EULENBERG (also Eulenburg)—EJ has biography from 17th-cent. Poland. JE has biography from 19th-cent. Germany.

EUROPA—Related to ROSSI.

EVANS—JE has article on 19th-cent. English boxer Samuel Evans. Related to FRANKS.

EVEN SHEMUEL—EJ has article on Israeli educator Judah Even Shemuel, born KAUFMANN in Russia.

EWALD—JE has biographies from 18th-cent. Bavaria.

EWEN—UJ has two biographies from 19th-cent. Austria.

EWER—JE has article on 19th-cent. German physician Leopold Ewer.

EXTON—UJ has article on U.S. physician William Exton (b. 1876).

EYBESCHUETZ—See EIBENSCHUTZ.

EYBESCHUTZ—See EIBENSCHUTZ.

EYGES—JE has article on British anarchist Thomas Eyges (b. 1873 in Russia). See his autobiography, *Beyond the Horizon*.

EYLENBURG—EJ has article on Talmudist Issachar Eylenburg (1550–1623), born in Posen, Poland.

EYSLER—UJ has article on Austrian composer Edmund Eisler (1874–1940).

EZEKIEL—JE has biographies from 18th-cent. England and Russia, and 19th-cent. Holland and India. Related to ISRAEL,

CASTRO, HYNEMAN, SASSOON and JOHNSON.

EZOBI—JE has article on 13th-cent. Provençal poet Eliezer Ezobi.

EZOFOVICH—Related to JOZEFOWICZ.

EZRA—JE has a family tree and biographies from 18th-cent. India. Also see UJ. Related to SASSOON.

FABIAN—UJ has article on Hungarian deputy Bela Fabian (b. 1889). LBI has a family tree beginning 1773. Related to THEMAL.

FABISCH—LBI has a family tree beginning 1781. Related to HAASE.

FABRIKANT—CAJ has some family records.

FACKENHEIM—LBI has a family tree beginning 1735.

FACTOR—UJ and EJ have biographies from 19th- and 20th-cent. Russia, Poland and U.S.A. Related to FIRESTEIN.

FADENHECHT—EJ has article on Zionist Yehoshua Fadenhecht (1846–1910), born in Galicia.

FADIMAN—UJ has article on U.S. commentator Clifton Fadiman (b. 1904).

FADL—JE has article on Karaite physician Da'ud Fadl (1161–1242) of Cairo.

FAHN—UJ has article on Galician author Reuben Fahn (1878–1939).

FAHRENTHOLD—Related to FRAUENTHAL.

FAITLOVITCH—UJ has article on Polish explorer Jacques Faitlovitch (1881–1955).

FAITUSI—JE has two biographies from Tunisia, 18th cent.

FAJANS—UJ has article on Polish chemist Kasimir Fajans (b. 1887).

FALAJI—See PALAGGI.

FALAQUERA (also Palquera, Falaguera, Falaquero)—Prominent family of 13th-cent. Tudela, Spain. See EJ.

FALCO—EJ has article on Italian jurist Mario Falco (1884–1943).

FALCON—Related to GABBAI.

FALERO (also Faleiro)—JE has article on Portuguese merchant Abraham Falero (d. 1642 in Verona, Italy). Also see EJ. Related to ABOAB.

FALES—See *The Descendants of Wolf Fales; A Chronicle of the Feilchenfeld Family.* Related to FEILCHENFELD.

FALIO—Related to HERZL.

FALK (also De Falk, Falkon, Falkenau, Falkenburg, Falkland, Falkmann, Falkowitsch, Falkson, etc.)—Ashkenazic name meaning "falcon." Variations of the name are FLECKELES and WALLICH, and some people with those names are descended from Falks. JE and EJ have biographies from 16th-cent. Poland and 19th-cent. Germany, England, Hungary and Russia. Polish Talmudist Joshua Falk (d. 1614 in Lemberg) married the daughter of Israel ben Joseph EDELS (see also JE article on Bella). CAJ has a family tree beginning 1530 in Germany. AJA has a family tree beginning in 18th cent. See family history in JFF, No. 8. LBI has a Falkenau family tree beginning 1782, and a Falkson family tree beginning 1773. CAJ has a Falkmann family tree beginning 1768. Related to GOODHART, SULZBERGER, LEVY, LANDAU, LOEWENSTAMM, BERNSTEIN, BEROLZHEIMER, MAIER, FRANKENBACH, BERNARD, HEIJERMANS, THEMAL.

FALKELES—See FLECKELES.

FALKENAU—See FALK.

FALKENBURG—See FALK.

FALKENSOHN—See FALK.

FALKLAND—See FALK.

FALKMANN—See FALK.

FALKON—See FALK.

FALKOWITSCH—See FALK.

FALKSON—See FALK.

FALL—UJ has article on Czech composer Leo Fall (1873–1925).

dei FANCIULLI—Related to degli ADOLESCENTOLI.

FANO—Italian name. JE has biographies beginning 16th cent. CAJ has a family tree beginning in 19th-cent. Italy.

FANTY—LBI has a family tree beginning 1640. Related to WIESENTHAL.

FARKASCH—CAJ has a family tree from Hungary.

FAQUIN—JE has article on 14th-cent. Spanish traveler Joseph Faquin.

FARACHI (also Faragut, Fararius, Ferrarius, Franchinus)—JE has article on 13th-cent. Italian physician Moses Farachi.

FARAGUT—See FARACHI.

FARAJ—EJ has biographies from 13th-cent. Italy and 19th–20th-cent. Egypt.

FARAJI—JE has article on 17th-cent. Egyptian Rabbi Jacob Al-Faraji of Alexandria. Related to NAWANI.

FARARIUS—See FARACHI.

FARBER—Ashkenazic name meaning "painter."

FARBRIDGE—UJ has article on English author Maurice Farbridge (b. 1893).

FARBSTEIN—UJ has biographies from 19th-cent. Poland.

FARENTHOLD—Related to FRAUENTHAL.

FARHI (also Parhi, Hafari)—Family of financiers in Damascus, 18th and 19th cent.; see EJ. JE has a biography from 13th-cent. Spain.

FARIA—JE and EJ have biographies of 17th-cent. Marranos.

FARISSOL (also Perizol)—EJ has biographies from 15th-cent. France and Italy.

FARJEON—JE has article on English and New Zealand novelist Benjamin Farjeon (1838–1903). Also see UJ. Related to JEFFERSON.

FARKAS—JE has biographies from 19th-cent. Hungary.

FARRAR (also Ferrar)—JE has article on Portuguese poet Abraham Farrar (d. 1603 in Amsterdam). Related to TIRADO, LOPEZ ROSA.

FASSEL—JE has article on Austrian Rabbi Hirsch Bar Fassel (1802–1883), who died in Hungary.

FASTEN—UJ has article on zoologist Nathan Fasten (b. 1887 in Austria).

FAUDEL (also Faudel-Phillips)—JE has article on 19th-cent. London Mayor George Faudel-Phillips. JE article on

"Coat of Arms" has the family crest. Related to PHILLIPS, LEVY, LAWSON and PIRBRIGHT.

FAUST—Related to MAUCLAIR.

FAUTH—Related to SUTTON.

FAYER—JE has article on 19th-cent. Hungarian jurist Ladislaus Fayer.

FAYYUMI—JE has article on 12th-cent. Yemenite scholar Nathanael Al-Fayyumi.

FAZEKAS—UJ has article on Hungarian playwright Imre Fazekas (b. 1887).

FECHHEIMER—AJA has family trees beginning 1680 and 1797. Related to THURNAUER.

FECHNER—PD has some family records.

FEDER—JE and EJ have articles from 18th-cent. Poland and 19th–20th-cent. Germany and Czechoslovakia. Related to GUTMAN.

FEDERBUSH—UJ has article on Finnish Rabbi Simon Federbush (b. 1892 in Poland).

FEDERN—EJ has article on Austrian psychoanalyst Paul Federn (b. 1871).

FEFER—UJ has article on Ukrainian poet Isaac Fefer (b. 1900).

FEIBELMANN—AJA has a family tree beginning 1732.

FEIBES—LBI has a family tree beginning 1720, related to ITZIG and WOLFERS.

FEIERBERG—UJ has article on Russian writer Mordecai Feierberg (1874–1899).

FEIGEN (also Feigin)—UJ has article on Russian scholar Samuel Feigen (b. 1893).

FEIGENBAUM—JE and UJ have biographies from 19th-cent. Austria and Poland. LBI has a family tree beginning 1746. CAJ has some family records.

FEIGL—EJ has biographies from 19th- and 20th-cent. Czechoslovakia, Austria and Brazil.

FEILBOGEN—JE has article on Austrian Rabbi Joseph Feilbogen (1784–1869).

FEILCHENFELD—JE has article on Silesian Rabbi Gabriel Feilchenfeld (b. 1827). See *The Descendants of Wolf Fales, a Chronicle of the Feilchenfeld Family.* Related to LANDAU.

FEILER—UJ has article on German economist Arthur Feiler (1879–1942).

FEIN—Related to KLEPFISH.

FEINBERG—Ashkenazic name meaning "fine mountain" in German. EJ and UJ have biographies from 19th-cent. Russia, Prussia, Lithuania, U.S.A. and Israel. Related to BELKIND.

FEINGOLD—Ashkenazic name meaning "fine gold" in German.

FEINSTEIN—Ashkenazic name meaning "fine stone" in German. JE and UJ have biographies from 19th-cent. Russia and Poland. Also see JE article on Pruzhany, Russia, where Elijah Feinstein was rabbi from 1883.

FEIS—JE has article on 19th-cent. German merchant Jacob Feis.

FEISENBERGER—LBI has a family tree beginning 1495. Related to SCHWAB.

FEISHEL—Related to HERZL.

FEIST (also Feistel)—JE and UJ have biographies from 19th-cent. France, Germany and U.S.A. Related to BELMONT.

FEITELSON—EJ has article on writer Menahem Feitelson (1870–1912), born in Russia.

FEITS—LBIS has a family tree.

FEIWEL—JE, UJ and EJ have biographies from 18th-cent. Russia and 19th-cent. Austria. Related to WILNA, KATZENEL-LENBOGEN.

FEJER—UJ has biographies from 19th-cent. Hungary.

FEKETE—JE and UJ have biographies from 19th-cent. Hungary.

FELBERMAN—JE has article on Hungarian-British author Louis Felberman (b. 1861).

FELD—JE has biographies from 19th-cent. Hungary and Rumania. Related to ROSENFELD.

FELDMAN (also Feldmann)—JE and UJ have biographies from 19th-cent. Bavaria, Austria, Russia and Poland. Related to PALDI.

FELDSTEIN—Ashkenazic name meaning "field stone" in German.

FELEKI—JE has article on Hungarian physician Hugo Feleki (b. 1861).

FELIX—JE has biographies from 19th-cent. France and Austria. Also see EJ article on Rachel (1821–1858). Related to BERNAT.

FELLNER—UJ has article on Hungarian economist Frigyes Fellner (b. 1871). PD has family records.

FELMAN—EJ has article on Israel pioneer Aharon Feldman (1867–1893), born in Russia.

FELS—UJ has three biographies from 19th-cent. U.S.A.

FELSENSTEIN—CAJ has a family tree beginning in 18th-cent. Prague, related to LIPCHOWITZ and WEIL.

FELSENTHAL—JE has article on German-American Rabbi Bernhard Felsenthal (1822–1908). AJA has a family tree. Related to ALPINER, LEBOLD.

FENDES—Related to MELDOLA.

FENICHEL—EJ has biographies from 19th-cent. Hungary and 20th-cent. Austria.

FENYES—JE has article on Hungarian painter Adolf Fenyes (1867–1945), also known as FISCHMANN or FLEISCHMAN.

FENYO—EJ has article on Hungarian author Miksa Fenyo (b. FLEISCHMAN in 1877).

FENYVESSY—JE has article on Hungarian scribe Adolf Fenyvessy (b. 1837).

FERARU—UJ has article on Rumanian author Leon Feraru (b. 1887).

FERBER—JE, UJ and EJ have biographies from 19th-cent. Russia, Lithuania, England and U.S.A. Related to FOX.

FERDINAND—JE has article on Polish teacher Philip Ferdinand (1555–1598), who died in Holland.

FEREIRA—Related to LINDO and CASTRO.

FERENCZI—EJ has article on Hungarian psychoanalyst Sandor Ferenczi (1873–1933), born FRAENKEL.

FERME—Related to AZEVEDO and MESQUITA.

FERNANDES VILLAREAL—See FERNANDEZ.

FERNANDEZ (also Fernandes, Fernandes Villareal)—Sephardic name. Fernandes was one of the Portuguese-Jewish families expelled from the town of Dax, France, in 1684. JE and EJ have biographies of 17th-cent. Portuguese-French politician Manuel Fernandez Villareal. CAJ has a family tree. Related to VILLAREAL, COSTA, BUENO.

FERNANDO—JE has article on 19th-cent. Italian teacher Aaron Fernando.

FERNBACH—UJ has article on German architect Henry Fernbach (1829–1883).

FERNHOF—EJ has article on author Isaac Fernhof (1868–1919), born in Galicia.

FERRAR—See FARRAR.

FERRARIUS—See FARACHI.

FERRERO—Related to LOMBROSO.

FERRIZUEL—EJ has article on 12th-cent. Spanish physician Joseph Ferrizuel.

FERSTADT—UJ has article on Russian painter Louis Ferstadt (b. 1900).

FERTIG—UJ has article on U.S. lawyer Moses Fertig (b. 1887).

FERRUS—JE has article on Peter Ferrus, 15th-cent. Spanish convert to Christianity.

FESSLER—JE has article on Austrian lawyer Sigismund Fessler (b. 1845).

FEUCHTWANGER (also Feuchtwang)—UJ has biographies from 19th-cent. Germany and Moravia. LBI has family trees beginning 1786 and 1854. Also see *The Feuchtwanger Family* and *Descendants of Seligmann Feuchtwanger*. Related to LOFFLER.

FEUER—JE has article on Hungarian oculist Nathaniel Feuer (b. 1844).

FEUERBERG—EJ has article on writer Mordecai Feuerberg (1874–1899), born in Russia.

FEUERMANN—UJ has article on Galician cellist Emmanuel Feuermann (b. 1802).

FEUERRING—See biography in EJ article on "Art."

FEUERSTEIN—UJ and EJ have biographies from 19th-cent. Russia, Hungary and Czechoslovakia. Related to KAPLAN.

FEUST—JE has article on German jurist Karl Feust (1798–1872). LBI has a family tree beginning 1700. Related to BLOCH.

FEYGENBERG—EJ has article on writer Rakhel Feygenberg (b. IMRI in Russia, 1885).

FIAMETTA—JE has article on Italian Rabbi Joseph Fiametta (d. 1721).

FICHEL—JE has article on French painter Benjamin-Eugene Fichel (1826–1895). Related to SAMSON. Also see FISCHEL.

FICHER—See FISCHER.

FICHMAN—See FISCHMANN.

FIDANQUE—JE has article on English scholar Jacob Fidanque (d. 1701). AJA has a family tree beginning 17th cent. CAJ has a family tree covering 1700 to 1962.

FIEDLER—UJ has article on U.S. conductor Arthur Fiedler (b. 1894).

FIELDS—UJ has biographies from 19th-cent. U.S.A., 20th-cent. Rumania.

FIERSON—Related to GLUCK.

FIGDOR—PD has family records. Possibly a variation of ABIGDOR.

FIGO—See PIGO.

FILDERMAN—UJ has article on Rumanian lawyer Wilhelm Filderman (b. 1884).

FILENE—U.S. merchant dynasty, founded by William Filene, who came from Germany in 1848. See EJ and UJ.

FILOSOF—Related to QUERIDO.

FILIPOWSKI—JE has article on Russian editor Hirsch Filipowski (1816–1872), also known as PHILLIP.

dels FILS—See degli ADOLESCENTOLI.

FINALY—UJ has article on Hungarian philologist Henrik Finaly (1825–1898).

FINBERG—UJ has article on English art critic Alexander Finberg (1866–1939).

FINCKENSTEIN—JE has article on German poet Raphael Finckenstein (1828–1874).

FINE—EJ has two biographies from U.S.A. and England.

FINEMAN—UJ has two biographies from 19th-cent. Russia.

FINER—UJ has article on English scholar Herman Finer (b. 1898).

FINESHRIBER—UJ has article on American Rabbi William Fineshriber (b. 1880).

FINGERMAN—UJ has article on Russian-Argentine doctor Gregorio Fingerman (b. 1890).

FININBERG—EJ has article on Soviet poet Ezra Fininberg (b. 1889).

FINK (also Finkel)—Ashkenazic name meaning "finch." UJ has biographies from 19th-cent. Russia, Poland and Australia. CAJ has some family records for Fink and Finkel. Related to KAMAI and KATZ.

FINKELSTEIN—Ashkenazic name that means "a little bird stone" in German. UJ has biographies from 19th-cent. Poland and Germany. Related to FINOT.

FINLAY-FREUNDLICH—EJ has article on astronomer Erwin Findlay-Freundlich (b. 1885 in Germany). Related to FREUND-LICH.

FINN—JE has article on Russo-Polish-American chess player Julius Finn (b. 1871).

FINOT—Related to FINKELSTEIN. UJ has article on Jean Finot (1856–1922).

FINTIUS—CAJ has some family records.

FINZI—Italian family dating back to 13th cent. The name is derived from Pinehas; see EJ. JE has fifty biographies. Related to ANCONA, BOLOGNA, FORLA, RECANATI, AREZZO, TEDESCO, JOAB and LUZZATTI.

FIOR—UJ has article on Rumanian-English journalist I. H. Fior (1856–1898).

FIORENTINO—JE has article on Italian poet Solomon Fiorentino (1743–1815). Related to GALLICO.

FIORINO—JE has article on German painter Jeremiah Fiorino (1796–1847).

FIRESTEIN—Related to FACTOR.

FIRKOVICH—JE has article on Russian Karaite archaeologist Abraham Firkovich (1786–1874), from the Crimea. Related to BABOVICH.

FIRMAN—JE has article on 16th-cent. Greek Rabbi Joseph Firman. See family history in JFF, No. 20.

FIRUZ—Karaite family, probably of Persian origin, prominent from 12th through 19th cent. See EJ.

FISCHBEIN—CAJD has a family tree from Germany.

FISCHEL (also Fischell, Fischels, Fishel, Fishell, Fishelson)—Patrician family in Cracow, Poland, which came there from Bohemia in 15th cent. A probable relative, Bohemian Rabbi Meir Fischels (1703–1769), was a descendant of the MAHARAL

of Prague (1525–1609) and the son of MAR-GOLIOTH. JE, UJ and EJ have biographies from 18th-cent. Germany, Austria and Russia, and 19th-cent. U.S.A. 18th-cent. Prague Talmudist Bumsla Fischels (d. 1769) was related to FISCHER. PD has some family records. Also see Fishelson history in *It Began with Zade Usher* (see Bernstein in Bibliography). Related to FRANKEL, POLLAK, LEMEL, GOLDSTEIN, MOYZESZOWA, POWIDZKI, ZEHNER, BUNZLAU and LEVINSON. Also see EJ article on POLLACK. Another variation of the name is FICHEL.

FISCHER (also Fisher, Ficher)—JE has biographies from 18th-cent. Austria, Czechoslovakia and Hungary. LBI has a family tree. Related to MAKAI, BISCHITZ de Heves, FISCHELS, EISLER, BERMANN-FISHER and KALAHOSA.

FISCHHOF—JE has biographies from 19th-cent. Austria and Hungary. CAJ has family records. Related to AUERBACH.

FISCHMANN (also Fishman, Fichman)—JE and UJ have biographies from 19th-cent. Poland, Russia and Austria. Related to FENYES.

FISHBEIN—See FISCHBEIN.

FISHBERG—JE has article on U.S. anthropologist Maurice Fishberg (1872–1934), born in Russia.

FISHEL, Fishell—See FISCHEL.

FISHELSON—See FISCHEL.

FISHER—See FISCHER.

FISHMAN—See FISCHMANN.

FITCH—UJ has article on Austrian communal leader Louis Fitch (b. 1889).

FITZROY—Related to ROTHSCHILD.

FLATAU—JE has article on German physician Theodor Flatau (b. 1860). Related to BERGSON.

FLAUT—See PLAUT.

FLECK—JE has article on German actor Johann Fleck (1757–1801).

FLECKELES—One of the oldest Jewish families in Prague, dating at least back to 16th cent. The family was originally FALK or FALKELES, from which the name is derived. JE has three biographies. See family history in MGWJ, No. 37 (1893), p. 378; also *Der Stammbaum des R. Eleasar*

Fleckeles. Related to GANS, LOW, HESCHEL and SPITZ.

FLECKER—Related to LAUTERBACH.

FLEG—UJ has article on French writer Edmond Fleg (b. 1874 in Switzerland). See also FLEGENHEIMER.

FLEGENHEIMER—UJ has article on Swiss architect Julien Flegenheimer (1880–1938). See also FLEG.

FLEISCHER (also Fleischl, Fleischman, Fleischmann, Fleischner, Fleisher, etc.)—Ashkenazic name which means "butcher" in German. JE, UJ and EJ have biographies from 19th-cent. Austria, Hungary, Germany and U.S.A. LBI has a family tree beginning 1804. Related to LEBRECHT, FENYO, FENYES and LIVERIGHT.

FLEISCHL—See FLEISCHER.

FLEISCHMAN (Fleischmann)—See FLEISCHER.

FLEISCHNER—See FLEISCHER.

FLEISHER—See FLEISCHER.

FLEISSIG—UJ has article on Hungarian financier Sandor Fleissig (1869–1939).

FLESCH (also Flesh)—Family originally from Frankfurt-am-Main, 16th. cent., later widely distributed through Central Europe. The name is derived from the sign of a flask (*Flasche* in German) that hung on the door of the family's house. EJ mentions several generations, and JE has biographies from 18th-cent. Germany and Austria. PD has family records. See family history in *Die Familie Flesch.* Related to AUSTERLITZ, BIRNBAUM, WARBURG.

FLESH—See FLESCH.

FLETCHER—Related to AVIGDOR.

FLEXNER—JE and EJ have articles on U.S. physician Simon Flexner (1863–1946), whose father came to the U.S.A. from Bohemia.

FLISFEDER—JE has article on Russian physician D. I. Flisfeder (1850–1885).

FLIESS—UJ has article on German physician Wilhelm Fliess (1858–1928). LBI has a family tree. Related to SUSSMAN.

FLIGELMAN—Related to BRIN.

FLOERSHEIM (also Florsheim)—UJ has article on German-Swiss editor Otto Floersheim (1853–1917). CAJD has a family tree from Germany; CAJ has Florsheim family records. Related to RAUH, ROTHSCHILD, SPEYER.

FLOHR—UJ has article on Latvian chess master Salo Flohr (b. 1908).

FLORANCE—See FLORENCE.

FLORENCE (also Florance)—See JE article on Augusta, Georgia, where the first Jew was named Florence, 1825. Related to COHEN, MINIS, MONTEFIORE, NATHAN and SEIXAS.

FLORES—One of the Portuguese Jewish families expelled from Dax, France, in 1684; see JE article on Dax.

FLORENTIN—JE has biographies from 17th-cent. Italy and Salonika.

FLORIO—UJ has article on English writer John Florio (1553–1625).

FLORSHEIM—See FLOERSHEIM.

FLOWER—Related to MONTEFIORE.

FLUEGEL—UJ has article on German-American Rabbi Maurice Fluegel (1832–1911).

FOA (also Foi, Foy)—17th-cent. French family which migrated to Italy in 18th cent. JE has ten biographies. Related to MARGFOY, FRANCHETTI, SCIAMA, RODRIGUES, ZAREFATI and CREMIEU.

FOCHS—JE has article on Hungarian philanthropist Anton Fochs (d. 1874).

FOCSANEANU—CAJ has some family records.

FODOR—JE and EJ have biographies from 19th-cent. Hungary.

FOGES—JE has article on Austrian author Baruch Foges (1805–1890) of Prague.

FOHS—UJ has article on U.S. geologist Ferdinand Fohs (b. 1884).

FOI—See FOA.

FOLDES—UJ has article on Hungarian statesman Bela Foldes (b. 1848), also known as WEISZ.

FOLDI—UJ has article on Hungarian novelist Mihaly Foldi (b. 1894).

FOLIGNO—JE has article on Hananel di Foligno, 16th-cent. convert to Christianity from Rome.

FOLZ—JE has article on German playwright Hans Folz (15th cent.).

FONSECA (also Fonsequa)—Portuguese family of Amsterdam, Hamburg, London, southern France and U.S.A. JE has nineteen biographies. See family histories in KB and KS. JE article on "Coat of Arms" has the family crest. Related to ABOAB, BELMONTE and MENDES.

FONSEQUA—See FONSECA.

FONTANELLA—JE has article on 17th-cent. Italian Rabbi Israel Fontanella.

FORCHHEIMER—UJ has article on U.S. physician Frederich Forchheimer (1853–1913).

FOREMAN—UJ has article on U.S. Army officer Milton Foreman (1862–1935). Related to LEBOLD. Also see FORMAN.

FORLA—Related to FINZI.

FORMAN—UJ has article on U.S. judge Philip Forman (b. 1895).

FORMIGGINI—UJ has article on Italian writer Angelo Formiggini (1878–1938). Related to ABULAFIA.

FORMON—JE has article on 16th-cent. Turkish Talmudist Zaddik Formon.

FORMSTECHER—JE has article on German Rabbi Solomon Formstecher (1808–1889).

FORSTENHEIM—JE has article on Austrian writer Anna Forstenheim (1846–1889).

FORTI (also Fortas, Fortis)—Italian name dating from 16th cent. JE and EJ have biographies from Italy, 16th, 18th and 19th cent., and from 18th-cent. Poland. Related to HEILPRIN and PAVIA.

FORTUNA—CAJ has some family records.

FOULD (also Fuld, Fulda)—Ashkenazic name derived from the town of Fulda, Germany. Fould is a French family of bankers and politicians, beginning 18th cent.; see EJ. JE has biographies from 18th- and 19th-cent. Germany. LBI has a family tree beginning 1800. CAJ has a family tree from Germany. JE article on "Coat of Arms" has the family crest. Related to BAMBERGER, JOHLSON, SAMSON.

FOX—Ashkenazic name, often an Anglicized version taken by many Russians, Poles and Hungarians who were formerly called FUCHS. UJ has biographies from 19th-cent. U.S.A., England, Australia, Russia, Hungary and France.

FOY—See FOA.

FRAENKEL—See FRANKEL.

FRAM—UJ has article on Lithuanian poet David Fram (b. 1903), who went to Argentina.

FRANCES—JE has three biographies from 16th-cent. Italy.

FRANCHETTI—JE has two biographies from 19th-cent. Italy. Related to FOA.

FRANCHI—JE has article on Guglielmo dei Franchi, 16th-cent. convert to Christianity in Rome.

FRANCHINUS—See FARACHI.

FRANCIA—Spanish family which moved to London in 1677; some also lived in France. JE has ten biographies. Related to PINTO.

FRANCIS—Related to LURIA.

FRANCK—See FRANK.

FRANCKEL—See FRANKEL.

FRANCO—Spanish family name derived from a place near Navarre, pre-15th cent. During the inquisition the family moved to Amsterdam, Venice, Tunis and Crete. An English branch took the name LOPES and was ancestor of the barons ROBOROUGH. See JE, UJ and EJ. JE article on "Coat of Arms" has the family crest. Related to ABOAB, COSTA, MENDES.

FRANCOLM—JE has article on German educator Isaac Francolm (1788–1849).

FRANGI—JE has article on Turkish author Hayyim Frangi (1833–1903), also known as MENAHEM.

FRANK (also Franck)—Ashkenazic name meaning "Franconian." JE, UJ and EJ have biographies from 16th-cent. Poland, 18th-cent. Hungary, Austria and Galicia, and 19th-cent. France and U.S.A. LBI has a family tree beginning 1787. PD has some family records. CAJ has Franck family records. Related to FRANKL, HECHT, SULZBERGER, RAYNER, REESE, MASSARY, DOBRUSCHKA, GREENHUT, KRAUS, HAYEM and ARON.

FRANKAU—JE has article on British novelist Julia Frankau (b. 1864 in Dublin). Related to DAVIS.

FRANKEL (also Frankl, Fraenkel, Franckel)—Ashkenazic name derived from those who immigrated to Vienna from "Frankenland" (Franconia) in the West. The first Jews with the name were Moses and Aaron HELLER of Wallerstein, 16th cent. Benjamin Frankel, chief rabbi of Hanau, belonged to the KATZENEL-LENBOGEN family and was a direct descendant of Saul WAHL (1541–1617); Frankel's daughter married ADLER, and he was also related to MINZ and DRUCKER. JE, UJ and EJ have numerous biographies beginning 16th cent. LBI has family trees beginning 1508, 1641 and 1691. AJA has a tree beginning in Prague and Cleveland. CAJ has a family tree from Munich; PD also has a family tree. LBIS has Franckel family notes. For family histories, see MGWJ, No. 45 (1901), p. 205, and No. 46 (1902), p. 450; JJLG, Vol. 8 (1910), p. 201; ZGJT, No. 2 (1931), p. 67; *Forgotten Fragments of the History of an Old Jewish Family; Der goldene Tiegel der Familie Fraenkel; Neue Beiträge zur Geschichte der Familie Frankel-Spira;* and *Stammbaum der Familie Mirels-Heller-Frankel.* Related to SPIRA, WOLF, FISCHEL, MIRELS, HANAU, SCHIFF, LEVY, RITSCHEL, MEYER, BERLIN, SPEYER, TE'ONIM, EPHRAIM, MATTERSDORF, HERZBERG, HELLER, HA-LEVI, SECKEL, HOENIG, MUNK, BERGSON and FERENCZI.

FRANKEN—UJ has article on 20th-cent. U.S. writer Rose Franken.

FRANKENBERG (also Frankenburger)—JE has biographies from 17th- and 19th-cent. Germany.

FRANKENHEIM—JE has article on German physicist Moritz Frankenheim (1801–1869).

FRANKENTHAL (also Frankenthaler)—JE has article on U.S. consul Adolf Frankenthal (b. 1851 in Germany). Related to FRAUENTHAL.

FRANKFURT (also Frankfurter)—Ashkenazic name derived from city of Frankfurt-am-Main, Germany. JE has biographies from 16th-cent. Germany, 17th-cent. Poland and Holland, and 19th-cent. Germany and Austria. PD has Frankfurter family records. Related to TREVES, GUENZBERG, HIRSCH, EGER and WOLFF. Also see EJ.

FRANKL—See FRANKEL.

FRANKL-GRUN—See FRANKEL.

FRANKLIN—Family that came to England from Breslau, Germany, in 1763; next generation moved to the West Indies. JE has biographies from 19th-cent. England, Hungary, U.S.A. and Jamaica. See *Records of the Franklin Family and Collaterals.* Related to SAMUEL. Also see EJ.

FRANKO—UJ has biographies from 19th-cent. U.S.A. Related to GOLDMAN.

FRANKS—Probably a variation of FRANK. American family on both sides of the Revolutionary War, descended from Jacob Franks, who came to New York in 18th cent. An English branch is descended from Benjamin Franks (1650–1716) of Bavaria. EJ has a family tree; also see JE. See family history in *An Old New York Family.* Related to JOHNSON, SALOMON, SEIXAS, SOLOMONS, LEVY, HART, BLOCH, PHILA, DE LANCEY, HAMILTON and EVANS.

FRANZBLAU—UJ has article on U.S. educator Abraham Franzblau (b. 1901).

FRANZOS—JE has article on Austrian author Karl Franzos (1848–1904). Related to BENEDIKT.

FRAUENSTADT—JE has article on German student Christian Frauenstadt (1813–1879).

FRAUENTHAL (also Fronthall, Frankenthal, Fahrenthold)—JE and UJ have articles on Max Frauenthal (b. 1836 in Bavaria), who fought for the Confederacy with Stonewall Jackson.

FRECE—See DE FRECE.

FREDMAN—UJ has article on U.S. lawyer Joseph Fredman (b. 1895).

FREED (also Fried)—UJ has biographies from Russia, Germany and Austria, 19th and 20th cent.

FREEDLANDER—See FRIEDLAENDER.

FREEDMAN—See FRIEDMAN.

FREEHOF—UJ has article on English Rabbi Solomon Freehof (b. 1892).

FREEMAN (also Freeman-Cohen, Freiman, Freimann)—JE, UJ and EJ have biographies from 19th-cent. Poland, Russia, England, Lithuania, Germany and Canada. LBI has a Freeman family tree beginning 1740 and a Freimann tree beginning 1733. CAJ has Freimann records. Related to BELKIND and ETTLINGER. Also see FRIEMANN.

FREIBERG—U.S. family from Germany. JE has six biographies. AJA has a family tree beginning 18th cent. Related to HEINSHEIMER and PRITZ.

FREIDUS—JE has article on Latvian bibliographer Abraham Freidus (1867–1923).

FREIHEIM—JE has article on U.S. lawyer J.B. Freiheim (1848–1899), born in Bavaria.

FREIHERR—PD has some family records of a family related to DIRSZTAY and DREYFUSS.

FREIMAN (Freimann)—See FREEMAN.

FREISTADT—PD has family records from Prague and elsewhere. Related to BIEDERMANN.

FRENK (also Frenkel)—Ashkenazic name found in Hungary as early as 18th cent.; see EJ. JE and UJ have biographies from 19th-cent. Poland. Possibly a variation of FRANK or FRANKEL.

FRENSDORFF—JE has article on German scholar Solomon Frensdorff (1803–1880).

FRESCO—JE has two biographies from 18th-cent. Turkey.

FREUD (also Freudemann, Freudenberg, Freudenthal, Freudenthaler, Freudiger) —Ashkenazic names derived from the German word *Freude,* meaning "joy." JE, UJ and EJ have biographies from 17th-cent. Yugoslavia and 19th-cent. Austria, Germany and Hungary. CAJ has a Freudenberg family tree; LBI and AJA have Freudenthal family trees beginning 1787 and 1790. Related to HA-KOHEN, ARON and OBUDA.

FREUDEMANN—See FREUD.

FREUDENBERG—See FREUD.

FREUDENTHAL (also Freudenthaler)— See FREUD.

FREUDIGER—See FREUD.

FREUND—Ashkenazic name. JE has biographies from 18th- and 19th-cent. Bohemia, Austria and Germany. AJA has a family tree from Bavaria beginning 1765, related to SCHUBERT. CAJ and PD have family records. Also see biography in EJ article on "Chemistry." See also FRIEND.

FREUNDLICH—See family history in *Die Siegburger Familie Levison.* Related to FINDLAY-FREUNDLICH.

FREY—UJ has article on U.S. lawyer Abraham Frey (b. 1886).

FREYHAN—CAJ has family trees, related to HORVITZ.

FRIBOURG—UJ has article on French statesman André Fribourg (b. 1887).

FRIDBERG—See FRIEDBERG.

FRIED—See FREED.

FRIEDBERG (also Friedberger, Fridberg) —JE has biographies from 19th-cent. Germany and Poland. LBI has a family tree beginning 1503. LBI also has a Friedberger family tree beginning 1794, related to GERSTLE, and a Fridberg family tree beginning 1776, related to SCHRAGENHEIM.

FRIEDELL—UJ has article on Viennese author Egon Friedell (1878–1938), also known as FRIEDMANN.

FRIEDEMANN—See FRIEDMAN.

FRIEDENBERG—UJ has article on U.S. lawyer Albert Friedenberg (b. 1881).

FRIEDENHEIM—PD has family records.

FRIEDENTHAL—JE has two biographies from 18th-cent. Prussia.

FRIEDENWALD—Baltimore family established by Jonas Friedenwald (b. 1801 in Germany). JE has biographies and AJA has a family tree beginning 1762. Related to STERN, WEISENFELD, BELMONT, GREENBAUM, ALBORN, BAMBERGER, BAER and BEHREND.

FRIEDERIKE—Related to VARNHAGEN.

FRIEDHEIM—UJ has article on Russian pianist Arthur Friedheim (1869–1932). Related to LEMANN.

FRIEDJUNG—JE has article on Austrian journalist Heinrich Friedjung (1851–1920).

FRIEDKIN—UJ has article on U.S. publisher Israel Friedkin (1890–1939).

FRIEDLAENDER (also Friedland, Friedlander, Freedlander)—German name taken from the Duchy of Friedland in Bohemia by Jews who settled in Prague in 17th cent. LBI has family trees beginning 1475, 1650, 1712, 1776 and 1784. JE has numerous biographies, plus family trees for the

Friedland family from 17th-cent. Prague and another Friedland family from 18th-cent. Russia. CAJ has a family tree and records covering 1760 to 1912 for a Friedlander family related to LOWENHERZ. LBIS also has a Friedlander family tree. The Friedland family's relationship to other rabbinic families is traced in *Da'at Kedoshim,* by Israel Eisenstadt. Also see *Chronik der Familie Friedlander-Lowenherz, 1760–1912* and *Das Handlungshaus Joachim Moses Friedlander & Söhne zu Königsberg.* Related to AZULAI, EPHRAIM, HAGEDORN, AUERBACH, KADISH, ISSAR, ITZIG, SAMUEL, JAFFE, FROHBERG.

FRIEDLAND—See FRIEDLAENDER.

FRIEDLANDER—See FRIEDLAENDER.

FRIEDMAN (also Friedmann, Freedman, Friedemann)—JE, UJ and EJ have biographies from 19th-cent. Poland, Germany, Rumania, Hungary, England, Australia, Lithuania and U.S.A. CAJ has Friedmann family records. Related to NATHAN, HEINE, PHILLIPS, RUZHINER, GRIFF, FRIEDELL, KARLINER, KOHLER, LAUTERBACH. Also see FRYDMAN.

FRIEDRICHSFELD—JE has article on German author David Friedrichsfeld (1755–1810), who died in Amsterdam.

FRIEDSAM—Ashkenazic name meaning "peaceful" in German. UJ has article on U.S. civic leader Michael Friedsam (1858–1931).

FRIEMANN—JE has two biographies from 19th-cent. Poland. Related to ETTLINGER. Possible variation of FREEMAN.

FRIEND (also Friendly)—UJ has biographies from 19th-cent. Bohemia and U.S.A. Possible variation of FREUND.

FRIES—Related to ITZIG.

FRIESENHAUSEN—JE has article on Bavarian mathematician David Friesenhausen (b. 1828).

FRIESLANDER—CAJ has family records.

FRIGEIS—UJ has article on 16th-cent. Hungarian or Dutch physician Lazaro de Frigeis.

FRILOCK—See PRILUK.

FRIM—JE has article on Hungarian educator Jakob Frim (b. 1852).

FRISCH (also Frischman)—JE and UJ have biographies from 19th-cent. Russia, Poland and Bohemia.

FRIZIS—UJ has article on Greek war hero Mordecai Frizis (1894–1940).

FRIZZI—JE has article on Italian physician Benedetto Frizzi (1756–1844), also known as KOHEN.

FROELICH (also Frohlich, Frolich)—The name means "gay," "happy," in German. PD has some family records. Related to KRAUS.

FROHBERG—JE has article on German writer Regina Frohberg (b. 1783). Related to SALOMO, SAALING, FRIEDLANDER.

FROHLICH—See FROELICH.

FROHMAN—American theatrical family; see JE. AJA has a family tree beginning 1755.

FROMENSON—UJ has article on U.S. editor Abraham Fromenson (1874–1935).

FROMKES—UJ has article on Polish painter Maurice Fromkes (1872–1931).

FROMMER—UJ has article on Hungarian arms expert Rudolf Frommer (b. 1868).

FRONTHALL—See FRAUENTHAL.

FROSOLONI—JE has article on 18th-cent. Italian poet Isaac Frosoloni.

FRUG—JE has article on Russian writer Semion Frug (1860–1916).

FRUMKIN—JE has article on Russian author Isaac Frumkin (b. 1850). Related to BACK, LEVI, MOSES, RODKINSON and LIFSCHITZ.

FRUMMET—Related to HERZL.

FRYDMAN—Possible variation of FRIEDMAN. See family history in *Sefer Ha-yahas mi-Tshernobil ve-Rozin.*

FUBINI—JE has article on Austrian physiologist Simone Fubini (1841–1898).

FUCHS—German name meaning "fox." JE has biography from 19th-cent. Austria. Also see JE article on Grosswardein, Hungary, where Moritz Fuchs was rabbi in 19th cent. Related to FOX and JAFFE.

FUENN—Russian family from Vilna, 19th cent. JE has two biographies.

FUERST (also Furst, Fust)—JE has biographies from Germany and Poland. LBI has a family tree beginning 1550. LBIS has Furst family notes. Fust is a Hungarian variation of the name; see UJ.

FULD—See FOULD.

FULDA—See FOULD.

FULLANA—JE has article on 17th-cent. Majorcan cartographer Nicolas Fullana.

FUNARO—UJ has article on Italian doctor Roberto Funaro (b. 1883).

FUNDAM—JE has article on 18th-cent. Spanish author Isaac Fundam, who lived in Amsterdam.

FUNK—UJ has article on Polish biochemist Casimir Funk, whose family had branches in Hungary and Austria.

FUNN—UJ has article on Russian historian Samuel Funn (1818–1890).

FURST—See FUERST.

FURSTENBERG—UJ has article on wealthy Swede Pontus Furstenberg (1827–1902).

FURSTENTHAL—JE has two biographies from 18th-cent. Germany. CAJ has some family records.

FURTADO—Sephardic name. JE has biographies from 18th-cent. France. Related to HEINE and de SOLA.

FURTH—Ashkenazic name taken from the city of Furth in Germany. JE has an article on 18th-cent. German writer Meyer Furth. PD has some family records. Related to MELCHIOR.

FUST—See FUERST.

GABBAI—Family of 15th-cent. Spain which moved to Italy in 17th cent. JE has seventeen biographies. Related to YSIDRO, FALCON, DURAN, BAGDADLI. Also see UJ.

GABIROL—EJ has article on Spanish poet Solomon ibn Gabirol (1020–1057).

GABISHON—JE has article on Algerian scholar Abraham Gabishon (d. 1605), descended from a family of Granada.

GABOR—UJ has article on Hungarian novelist Andor Gabor (b. 1884).

GABRIEL—UJ has article on U.S. critic Gilbert Gabriel (b. 1890).

GABRILOVITCH—JE has article on Russian pianist Ossip Gabilovitch (b. 1878).

GAD—Related to BERNARD.

GADEN—JE has article on Daniel Gaden, 17th-cent. Russian physician to the czars, originally from Poland. Also known as YEVLEVICH, ILYIN, ZHIDOVINOV. Related to ISAYEV.

GAERTNER (also Gartner)—JE and UJ have biography from 19th-cent. Austria. Related to WARBURG.

GAGGSTATTER—AJA has a family tree beginning 1700. Related to REIS, SALOMON, STERN, KAUFMAN, NEWFIELD, ULLMAN, HART and MARX.

GAGIN—Castilian family which migrated to Morocco in 1492 and to Palestine in 18th cent. See JE.

GAGVIN—UJ has article on Israeli Rabbi Shemtob Gagvin (b. 1886).

GAI—JE has article on Italian scholar Solomon Gai of Mantua (1600–1638).

GAISMAN—UJ has article on U.S. inventor Henry Gaisman (b. 1869).

GAJARI—UJ has article on Hungarian editor Odon Gajari (1852–1919).

GAJO—JE has article on Maestro Gajo, 13th-cent. physician to Pope Nicholas IV.

GAL—UJ has article on Hungarian actor Gyula Gal (1865–1938).

GALANO—CAJ has family records.

GALANT—See GALANTE.

GALANTE (also Galant)—Italian name traced back to 16th cent., derived from *galantuomo* ("gentleman"), a tribute to the court manners of Mordecai Galante, first to bear the name. The family can be traced back to pre-Inquisition Spain; see EJ. JE has a family tree and biographies. EJ also has a biography from 19th-cent. Ukraine. Related to LEVY, HAGIS, SAGIS.

GALFAND—See GELFAND.

GALINA—JE has article on 15th-cent. Greek scholar Moses Galina.

GALIPAPA—JE has biographies from 14th-cent. Spain and 17th-cent. Rhodes and Bulgaria.

GALLEGO (also Galigo)—JE has article on poet Joseph Gallego of Amsterdam (d. 1624 in Palestine).

GALLIA—UJ has article on Hungarian jurist Bela Gallia (b. 1870).

GALLICO—Italian family of French origin, in Rome from 14th cent. See EJ and JE. Related to FIORENTINO and GRAZIANO.

GALPERIN (Galpern)—See HEILPRIN.

GALSTON—UJ has article on U.S. Judge Clarence Galston (b. 1876).

DA GAMA—JE has article on 15th-cent. German mariner Gaspard da Gama, born in Posen.

GAMBETTA—CAJ has some family records.

GAMORAN—UJ has article on Russian educator Emanuel Gamoran (b. 1895).

GANDZ—See GANS.

GANS (also Gandz, Gaunse, Gansmann) —German name taken from the picture of a goose *(Gans)* that hung over the family's door. JE, UJ and EJ have biographies from 16th-, 18th- and 19th-cent. Germany. LBI has family trees beginning 14th and 16th cent. and 1794, as well as a Gansmann family tree beginning 1600. LBIS has Gans family notes. See family history in *Zur Geschichte der Familie Eger-Gans-Gansmann.* Related to EGER, BACHARACH, FLECKELES, LUDASSY, SELIGMAN, HEINE, STEIN. Also see GANZ.

GANSMANN—See GANS.

GANSO—EJ has article on 17th-cent. Turkish Rabbi Joseph Ganso.

GANZ—Possibly a Swiss variation of GANS; see UJ. Related to BOCHNER.

GANZFRIED—JE has article on Hungarian Rabbi Solomon Ganzfried (1800–1886).

GAON—Influential Jewish family in Vitoria, Spain, 15th cent. JE has three biographies. Related to BELMONTE.

GAON of Vilna—Name applied to Elijah, the Gaon of Vilna (1720–1797), revered Talmudist. See biographies in JE, UJ and EJ. Numerous families claim a relation to him, including NECHES, PESSELES and RIVKES. See also EJ article on his son *Abraham* ben Elijah (1750–1808).

GARCIA—JE has article on 18th-cent. Spanish poet Bernardo Garcia, who lived in Amsterdam. Related to LINDO.

GARDNER—UJ has article on Russian violinist Samuel Gardner (b. 1891). Also see *An Old New York Family.*

GARFEIN—AJA has a family tree.

GARFUNKEL (also Karfunkel, Karfunkelstein)—Ashkenazic name meaning one who deals in carbuncle, a semiprecious stone. JE has Karfunkel and Karfunkelstein biographies from 18th-cent. Bohemia and 19th-cent. Silesia. LBI has Karfunkel family trees beginning 1572 and 1762. LBIS has Karfunkel family notes. A possible variation is GORFINKLE.

GARMISON—JE has article on 17th-cent. Palestinian Rabbi Samuel Garmison, born in Salonika.

GARMON—See DARMON.

GARSINO—Related to MODIGLIANI.

GART—JE has article on 15th-cent. Provençal poet Joseph Gart of Aix. The name is a translation of the Hebrew *shimroni* ("a guard"), borne by the Gard family of Avignon, to which Joseph belonged.

GARTNER—See GAERTNER.

GASCON—JE has article on 16th-cent. scholar Abraham Gascon.

GASSNER—UJ has article on U.S. painter Mordi Gassner (b. 1899).

GASTER—JE has article on scholar Moses Gaster (b. 1856 in Bucharest, d. 1939 in London).

GASTFREUND—JE has article on Galician scholar Isaac Gastfreund (1845–1880).

GATIGNO (also Gatinho, Gattegno)— Spanish family that was known in 14th cent. and was still flourishing in Turkey in 1900. The name is probably derived from the former French district of Gafines. JE has six biographies.

GATINHO—See GATIGNO.

GATTEGNO—See GATIGNO.

GATZERT—Related to KAHN.

GAUNSE—See GANS.

GAUNZ—See GUNZBURG.

GAVISON—Sephardic family that belonged to the hierarchy of Seville in 14th cent. but fled to Granada in 1391; see EJ. JE has biography of 16th–17th-cent. Egyptian scholar Meir Gavison.

GEBER—LBIS has a family tree and notes.

GEDALGE—UJ has article on French composer André Gedalge (1856–1926).

GEDALIAH (also Gediliah)—JE and EJ have biographies from 16th-cent. Salonika, 17th-cent. Italy and Palestine. Related to ELMALEH.

GEE—UJ has article on English war hero Robert Gee (b. 1876).

GEFFEN—UJ has article on South African lawyer Irene Geffen (b. 1897), related to a Lithuanian family that took the name Geffen in the 1850s. Most Lithuanians with the name Geffen are related in some way to one another.

GEGELLO—See biography from 19th-cent. Russia in EJ article on "Architecture."

GEIGER—JE has three biographies from 19th-cent. Germany. Roeschen WALLAU Geiger (1768–1856) was the mother of Rabbi Abraham Geiger (1810–1874), who married Emilie OPPENHEIM. LBI has a family tree beginning 1632. CAJ has some family records. Related to SCHIFF and WALLASE.

GEINSHEIMER—Related to GOODHART.

GEIRINGER—UJ has article on Austrian musicologist Karl Geiringer (b. 1899).

GEISMER—UJ has an article on French General Gideon Geismer (b. 1863).

GEITEL—CAJ has a family tree from Prague, 1787.

GELBER—UJ has biographies from 19th-cent. Poland and 20th-cent. Canada. CAJ has some family records. Related to EI-CHENBAUM.

GELBHAUS—EJ has article on East European writer Sigmund Gelbhaus (1850–1928).

GELDER—See GELDERN.

GELDERN (also Gelder, Van Gelder)—Family of court Jews in Düsseldorf, Germany, who came there from the village of Geldern in 17th cent.; see JE. CAJ has a Gelder family tree from the Netherlands. See family tree and history in *Stammbaum der Familie Geldern* and *Aus Heinrich Heines Ahnensaal.* Related to LIEBMANN, HEINE, SCHAUMBERG-LIPPE.

GELERTER—EJ has article on Rumanian physician Ludwig Gelerter (1873–1945).

GELFAND (also Helfand, Galfand)—Slavic variation of ELFAND.

GELHAUSER—Related to GREENHUT.

GELLER (also Gelleri)—JE and UJ have biographies from 19th-cent. Russia and Hungary. A possible variation is HELLER.

GELLMAN—UJ has article on Russian editor Leon Gellman (b. 1887). Also see *It Began with Zade Usher* (See Bernstein in Bibliography) for a family history.

GELLNER—EJ has article on Czech poet Frantisek Gellner (1881–1914).

GENAZZANO—JE has article on 16th-cent. Italian physician Elijah Genazzano.

GENIN—UJ has article on Russian painter Robert Genin (b. 1884).

GENTILI—Italian family from Gorizia, dating from 16th cent., numbering several eminent rabbis and scholars. JE has eight biographies. Hebrew variation of the name is HEFEZ; see EJ.

GENTILOMO—Related to PAVIA.

GENZ—See EGER.

GEORGE—UJ has article on German writer Manfred George (b. 1893). Also see biography in EJ article on "English Literature."

GERASI—JE has article on Turkish Talmudist Daniel Gerasi (d. 1705).

GERCHUNOFF—UJ has article on Polish writer Alberto Gerchunoff (b. 1884).

GEREB—UJ has article on Hungarian philologist Jozsef Gereb (b. 1851).

GERHARDT—EJ has article on French chemist Charles Gerhardt (1816–1856).

GERMANUS—Related to SPAETH.

GERNSBACK—UJ has article on Luxembourg publisher Hugo Gernsback (b. 1884).

GERNSHEIM—JE has article on German pianist Friedrich Gernsheim (1839–1916). Also see UJ.

GERO—JE has article on Hungarian dramatist Karl Gero (b. 1856).

GERONDI—JE has biographies from 12th- and 13th-cent. Spain. Also see JE article on *Moses* ben Nahman Gerondi. Related to NAHMANIDES.

GERONIM—Related to BASSEVI.

GEROWITSCH—UJ has article on Russian cantor Eliezer Gerowitsch (1844–1914).

GERSHENFELD—UJ has article on American bacteriologist Louis Gershenfeld (b. 1895).

GERSHENSON (also Gershenzon)—UJ has article on Russian author Michael Gershenson (1869–1925).

GERSHOM—See GERSON.

GERSHON—See GERSON.

GERSHUNI—UJ has article on Russian politician Grigory Gershuni (1870–1908).

GERSHWIN—UJ has article on U.S. composer George Gershwin (1898–1937).

GERSON (also Gershom, Gershon, Gersoni, Gersonides and Kherson)—JE has three biographies from 19th-cent. Germany and U.S.A., also 16th–17th-cent. Venice and 19th-cent. Lithuania. CAJ has a Gerson family history and records. For histories of the Prague printing family of Gersonides, see ZL, Vol. 3 (1876), p. 200, and CB, p. 2965. Related to BAUER, LOANZ, TREVES and DOBROVELICH-KOVA. Also see EJ.

GERSTEIN—JE has article on Lithuanian educator Jonah Gerstein (1827–1891).

GERSTLE (also Gerstley)—JE has article on California pioneer Lewis Gerstle (1824–1902), born in Bavaria; brother-in-law of Louis SLOSS. LBI has a family tree beginning 1810. AJA has a Gerstley family tree beginning 1670, related to MARX. Also see *Lewis and Hannah Gerstle.*

GERSTMANN—JE has article on German author Adolf Gerstmann (b. 1855).

GERTLER—UJ has article on British painter Mark Gertler (1892–1939).

GERUNDI—Related to BENVENISTE.

GESANG—UJ has article on Polish communal leader Nathan Gesang (1886–1944).

GESCHEIT—CAJ has some family records.

GEST—UJ has article on Russian theatrical producer Morris Gest (b. 1881). Related to BELASCO.

GESUNDHEIT—JE has article on Polish Rabbi Jacob Gesundheit (1815–1878) of Warsaw. Also see UJ. Related to JUKEL.

GETZ—Related to YATES.

GEWER—LBIS has family notes.

GEWITSCH—EJ has article on Austrian scribe Aaron Gewitsch (1700–1770).

GEYER—Ashkenazic name meaning "vulture"; another variation is SOKOL. Related to SONNENFELS.

GHAYYAT—JE has article on 12th-cent. poet Solomon Ghayyat.

GHAZZATI—Name derived from the town of Gaza in Palestine. JE has article on prophet Nathan Ghazzati (b. 1644 in Jerusalem, d. 1680 in Bulgaria).

GHELERTER—EJ has article on Rumanian physician Litman Ghelerter (1873–1946).

GHEREA—UJ has article on Russian-Rumanian social leader C. Dobrogeanu Gherea (1855–1920), also known as Nathan KATZ.

GHERPEREGRINO—Related to ESCUDERO.

GHEZ—Tunisian family that includes several authors. JE has biographies from 18th and 19th cent.

GHIRON (also Ghirondi)—The Ghiron and Ghirondi families are not necessarily related, although both came from Gerona, Spain. The Ghiron family left Spain in 17th cent.; JE has five biographies from 18th- and 19th-cent. Turkey. The Ghirondis settled in Padua, Italy, in late 16th cent. The family founder was also called ZARFATI ("the Frenchman"), suggesting he may have come from France. JE has four biographies. In the Middle Ages, the Ghirondi family inbred with its own relatives for several generations; see JE article on "Consanguinity."

GHOSALKER—JE has article on Beni-Israel soldier Solomon Ghosalker of India (1804–1869).

GIBBOR—JE has article on scholar Judah Gibbor of Constantinople (15th cent.).

GIBBS—UJ has article on Polish-American Judge Louis Gibbs (1880–1929).

GIDEON (also Gideon-Abudiente)—JE has article on English financier Samson Gideon (1699–1762), whose father came from Portugal and changed his name from ABUDIENTE upon his arrival in England. CAJ has a family tree from Germany. JE article on "Coat of Arms" has the family crest.

GIERKE—Related to LOENING.

GIKATILLA—Sephardic name derived from the Spanish diminutive of *chico* ("small"). JE has biographies from 11th- and 13th-cent. Spain.

GILADI—EJ has article on Bessarabian Zionist Israel Giladi (1866–1918), also known as BUTELBROIT.

GILBERT—LBI has a family tree beginning 1748.

GILDIN—UJ has article on Ukrainian poet Chaim Gildin (b. 1885).

GIMBEL—U.S. merchant family descended from Adam Gimbel (1817–1896) from Bavaria. See biographies in JE and UJ.

GINGOLD—Related to COWEN and SULZER.

GINS—See EGER.

GINSBERG—See GUNZBURG.

GINSBURG—See GUNZBURG.

GINSMANN—See EGER.

GINTZBURGER—See GUNZBURG.

GINZ—See EGER.

GINZBERG (Ginzburg)—See GUNZBURG.

GINSBURGER—See GUNZBURG.

GIOVANNI—EJ has article on Italian lute player Maria Giovanni (1470–1530).

GIRADI—Related to GERASI.

GIRBAL—JE has article on Spanish scholar Enrique Girbal (b. 1839).

GISIKO—AJA has a family tree beginning 1729 in Germany.

GISSEN—EJ has article on Israeli pioneer Avshalom Gissen (1896–1921).

GIST—Related to GRATZ.

GITELSON—UJ has article on Polish Talmudist Nehemiah Gitelson (1853–1932). AJA has a family tree. Also see *The Chronicle* of the Gitelson-Komaiko Family Association.

GLANCZ—UJ has article on Polish poet Aaron Glancz (b. 1880).

GLANS—Related to PLAUT.

GLASBERG—CAJ has some family records.

GLASER—JE has biographies from 19th-cent. Germany and Austria.

GLASNER—EJ has article on Hungarian rabbi Moses Glasner (1856–1924), a great-grandson of Rabbi Moses SOFER.

GLASS—UJ has article on English writer Montague Glass (1877–1934).

GLATSTEIN—UJ has article on Polish writer Jacob Glatstein (b. 1896).

GLATTER—UJ has article on German-Hungarian painter Gyula Glatter (1886–1927).

GLAZER—UJ and EJ have biographies from 19th-cent. Russia and Ireland. Related to HERZL.

GLAZIER—Related to SELIGMAN.

GLAZNER—Related to EHRENFELD.

GLEMBOTSKI—UJ has article on Russian writer Moses Glembotski (b. 1882).

GLICENSTEIN—UJ has article on Polish painter Enrico Glicenstein (1870–1942).

GLICKMAN—Related to YELLIN.

GLICKSON—UJ has article on Russian Zionist Moses Glickson (1878–1939).

GLICKSTEIN—See GLUCKSTEIN.

GLOGAU (also Glogauer)—Ashkenazic name taken from the town of Glogau in Silesia. JE and EJ have biographies from 18th- and 19th-cent. Austria. The Bohemian Talmudist Meir Glogauer (d. 1829 in Prague) was also called Marcus SCHLESINGER. Related to LOVY.

GLOSSMAN—UJ has article on Russian novelist Boris Glossman (b. 1893).

GLOTZ—UJ has article on French historian Gustave Glotz (1862–1935).

GLUCK (also Gluckel)—JE and UJ have biographies from 19th-cent. Austria and Rumania. AJA has a family tree. Related to PAOLI, FIERSOHN, SINGER, REVEL, RUBIN and BAIERSDORF. Also see GLUECK.

GLUCKLICH—UJ has article on Hungarian feminist Vilma Glucklich (1872–1927).

GLUCKSMANN—JE has article on Austrian author Heinrich Glucksmann (b. 1864).

GLUCKSTADT (also Glueckstadt)—UJ has article on Danish financier Isak Gluckstadt (1839–1910).

GLUCKSTEIN (also Glickstein)—Ashkenazic name that means "lucky stone" in German. English family of 18th-cent. caterers; see EJ. UJ has article on English official Samuel Gluckstein (b. 1880). Related to SALMON.

GLUCKSTHAL—UJ has article on Hungarian Senator Samu Glucksthal (1864–1937).

GLUECK—UJ has four biographies, 19th-cent. Poland. Related to TOUROFF. Also see GLUCK.

GLUECKBERG—EJ article on Cherny mentions Russian poet Alexander Glueckberg (1880–1932).

GLUECKSTADT—See GLUCKSTADT.

GLUGE—JE has article on physician Gottlieb Gluge (1812–1898), born in Westphalia.

GLUSBERG—UJ has article on Russian-Argentine author Samuel Glusberg (b. 1898).

GNESSIN (also Gniessen)—UJ has two biographies from 19th-cent. Russia.

GODCHAUX—AJA has a family tree for a U.S. family in New Orleans related to LAMM, WEIS and MAYER. Also see *The Godchaux Family of New Orleans*. French variation is GOUDCHAUX.

GODEFROI—JE has article on Dutch jurist Michael Godefroi (1818–1883).

GODFRID—UJ has article on Argentine congressman Juan Godfrid (b. 1891); a brother was born in the Ukraine.

GODINEZ—EJ has article on Spanish playwright Felipe Godinez (1585–1639).

GODOWSKY—JE has article on Russian pianist Leopold Godowsky (1870–1938).

GODSCHALK—See GOTTSCHALK.

GOETZ—See GOTZ.

GOIDO—EJ has article on Polish novelist Isaac Goido (1868–1925).

GOITEIN—JE has article on Hungarian Rabbi Baruch Goitein (d. 1842), which mentions three generations of descendants. His great-grandsons were in Copenhagen and Bavaria.

GOLD—UJ has four biographies from 19th-cent. Russia and Poland.

GOLDBAUM—JE has article on German writer Wilhelm Goldbaum (b. 1843 in Posen).

GOLDBERG (also Goldberger)—JE and UJ have biographies from 19th-cent. Poland, Russia, Lithuania, India, U.S.A. and Hungary. PD has records of a Goldberger family from Budapest. Also see "The Goldberg Brothers: Arizona Pioneers," in *American Jewish Archives*.

GOLDBLATT—JE has article on Russian painter Jacob Goldblatt (b. 1860).

GOLDBLUM—EJ has article on Polish writer Israel Goldblum. Related to MACHOL.

GOLDEN—UJ has article on German-American Judge Isadore Golden (1878–1941).

GOLDENBERG—JE has biographies from 19th-cent. Russia and Galicia.

GOLDENSON—UJ has article on Polish Rabbi Samuel Goldenson (b. 1878).

GOLDENTHAL—JE has article on Austrian Professor Jacob Goldenthal (1815–1868), born in Brody, Galicia.

GOLDENWEISER—UJ has two biographies from 19th-cent. Russia.

GOLDER—UJ has article on U.S. Congressman Benjamin Golder (b. 1891).

GOLDFADEN—JE has article on Russian poet Abraham Goldfaden (b. 1840).

GOLDFARB (also Goldforb)—UJ has articles from Poland and England, 19th cent.

GOLDFISH—Related to GOLDWYN.

GOLDFOGLE—JE has article on U.S. lawyer Henry Goldfogle (b. 1856).

GOLDFORB—See GOLDFARB.

GOLDHAMMER-SAHAWI—EJ has article on Austrian Zionist Leo Goldhammer-Sahawi (1884–1949). Related to SAHAWI.

GOLDIN (also Golding)—EJ and UJ have biographies from 19th-cent. Russia and England.

GOLDMAN (also Goldmann)—JE and UJ have biographies from 19th-cent. Poland, Germany and elsewhere. Related to BESSO, FRANKO, BAUMAN and SACHS.

GOLDMARK—JE and UJ have biographies. LBI has a family tree beginning 1799. Related to ADLER and BRANDEIS.

GOLDNER—Related to BEHREND.

GOLDSAND—UJ has article on Austrian pianist Robert Goldsand.

GOLDSCHEID—UJ has article on Austrian philosopher Rudolf Goldscheid (1870–1932).

GOLDSCHMID—See GOLDSMID.

GOLDSCHMIDT—JE has ten biographies from 19th-cent. Germany and Denmark. LBI has family trees beginning 1397, 1520, 1621, 1732, 1758, 1764, 1777 and 1812. CAJ has a family tree from Germany, 1621–1925, related to OLDENBURG; also a family tree covering 1657 to 1872. LBIS has some family notes. See family histories in JFF, Nos. 7 and 26. Also see "Die Familie Goldschmidt, Oldenburg," by Gerhard Ballin, in *Oldenburgische Familienkunde*, January 1975; *Verzeichnis der von S. B. Goldschmidt aus Frankfurt-am-Main* and *Die Siegburger Familie Levison*. JE article on "Coat of Arms" has a family crest. Related to BENAS, LIND, SCHMIDT, WARBURG, BISCHOFFSHEIM, HIRSCH, ROTHSCHILD, WORMS, SPEYER, SAMSON and AVIGDOR. English variations are GOLDSMID and GOLDSMITH; Dutch variation is GOLDSMIT; Polish variation is GOLDSZMIDT.

GOLDSMID (also Goldschmid)—Family of English financiers, descended from Uri ha-Levi of Emden, Germany, 16th cent. JE and EJ have family trees and numerous biographies. JE article on "Coat of Arms" has the family crest. Also see EJ article on D'avigdor. A family history is included in *The Cousinhood,* by Chaim Bermant. Related to COHEN, KEYSER, SALOMONS, ELIASON, SAMUEL, AVIGDOR, MONTEFIORE, MOCATTA, LUCAS, PHILIPSON, LOUSADA, STERN, PRAGER, MONTAGU, STEUART, CAMPBELL, D'AVIGDOR and WAHL. Also see GOLDSCHMIDT, GOLDSZMIDT, GOLDSMIT and GOLDSMITH, other variations of the name that are possibly related.

GOLDSMIT—Dutch variation of GOLDSCHMIDT, GOLDSMID and GOLDSMITH. See *Pedigree of the Family Goldsmit-Cassel of Amsterdam (1650–1750)*. Related to CASSEL.

GOLDSMITH—English variation of GOLDSCHMIDT, GOLDSMID and GOLDSMIT. JE has biographies from 18th–19th-cent. England and U.S.A. Aaron Goldsmith was founder of a well-known Anglo-Jewish family; see JQR, Vol. 10, p. 445. Also see *Price, Goldsmith Lowenstein and Related Families, 1700–1967.* Related to LYNDHURST, MELDOLA, de SOLA, HIRSCH, LOWENSTEIN and PRICE.

GOLDSTEIN (also Goldstone)—JE has biographies from 19th-cent. Russia, Hungary and Austria. AJA has family tree beginning 1840. LBI has family tree. CAJ has a family tree related to VOGEL, GOTTSCHALK, HEINEMANN, BLUMENTHAL, LOWE and SCHIFF. Other relatives are FISCHEL and TIETZ.

GOLDSTUCKER—JE has article on German linguist Theodor Goldstucker (1821–1872), who died in London.

GOLDSZMIDT—JE has article on Polish lawyer Joseph Goldszmidt (1846–1896). See also GOLDSCHMIDT.

GOLDWASSER (also Goldwater)—UJ has articles from 19th-cent. Poland and U.S.A.

GOLDWATER—See GOLDWASSER.

GOLDWYN—UJ has article on U.S. producer Samuel Goldwyn (b. GOLDFISH in 1882). Related to LASKY.

GOLDZIEHER (also Goldzier, Goldziher)—JE and UJ have biographies from 19th-cent. Hungary, Austria and U.S.A. LBIS has some family notes.

GOLL—UJ has article on Alsatian poet Ivan Goll (b. 1891).

GOLLANCZ—JE has biographies from 19th-cent. England and Germany.

GOLLER—UJ has article on Lithuanian-English Rabbi Izak Goller (1891–1939).

GOLLUF—EJ has article on Eleazar Golluf (d. 1389), agent of the royal family of Aragon (Spain) and an ancestor of the SANCHEZ family.

GOLODETZ—See *History of the Family Golodetz.*

GOLOMB—JE has article on Russian writer Hirsch Golomb (b. 1853 near Vilna).

GOLSCHMANN—UJ has article on French conductor Vladimir Golschmann (b. 1893).

GOLTZ—CAJ has some family records.

GOLUB—UJ has article on Polish-American educator Jacob Golub (b. 1891).

GOMBERG—UJ has article on Russian chemist Moses Gomberg (b. 1866).

GOMBINER—EJ has article on Polish Rabbi Abraham Gombiner (1637–1683).

GOMES—See GOMEZ.

GOMEZ (also Gomes, Gomez de Sosa, Gomez de Sossa)—Sephardic family descended from Isaac Gomez, a Marrano who left Madrid for Bordeaux in early 17th cent. His son went to London and later to New York, and there are many descendants in the U.S.A. JE and AJA have family trees. There was also a Portuguese family named Gomez at Antwerp in 16th cent. JE article on "Coat of Arms" has the Gomez and Gomez de Sosa crests. Related to MURCHAZO, de TOUR, de LEON, NUNEZ, CAMPOS, de LUCENA, LOPEZ, HENDRICKS, ISAACS, PEIXOTTO, HART, ALEXANDER, NATHAN, CARDOZO, SOLIS, de CAMPO, MENDES, TREBINO, USQUE, TEIXEIRA, BASURTO, WAGG and ABOAB.

GOMPEL—Related to NETTER.

GOMPERS—See GOMPERZ.

GOMPERTZ—See GOMPERZ.

COMPERZ (also Gompers, Gompertz, Gumpert, Gumpertz, Gumperz)—German name traced back to Benedictus Gomperz of the German duchy of Cleve, 18th cent. The name may come from the town of Gumpel; the family descends from Mordecai GUMPEL. Theodor Gomperz, great-grandson of Benedictus, was born 1832 in Brunn, Moravia. The Gompertz family of England, 18th and 19th cent., was descended from the Gomperz family of Emmerich, and German scholar Aaron Gumperz (1723–1769) was also called EMRICH or EMMERICH. JE, UJ and EJ have biographies. LBIS and PD have Gomperz family notes. LBI has a Gumpertz family tree beginning 1653, and a Gumperz family tree beginning 17th cent. LBIS has Gumpert family notes and CAJ has Gumpertz family records. Also see *Die Familie Gomperz.* Related to HAMELN, MONTEFIORE, WESEL, BOAS, OPPENHEIM, WERTHEIMER, ARNSTEINER, KAUFMANN, AUSPITZ, SICHROVSKY, HYNEMAN and FRAENCKEL.

GONDA—UJ has article on Hungarian lawyer Henrik Gonda (b. 1880).

GONZALEZ—UJ has article on Spanish scholar Francisco Gonzalez (1833–1917).

GONZALO—Related to de la CABALLERIA.

GOOD—UJ has article on Edward Good, Russian jeweler (b. 1881).

GOODELMAN—UJ has article on Russian sculptor Aaron Goodelman (b. 1890).

GOODHART—UJ has article on U.S. educator Arthur Goodhart (b. 1891). AJA has family tree from New Orleans, related to ROSENBAUM, FALK, LEHMAN and GEINSHEIMER.

GOODKIND—UJ has article on U.S. doctor Maurice Goodkind (1867–1939).

GOODMAN—JE has article on English preacher Tobias Goodman (d. 1825). UJ has ten biographies. AJA has a family tree from Philadelphia. Related to SALAMAN. Other variations are GUDEMANN, GUTMANN.

GORDIN—See GORDON.

GORDIS—UJ has article on Brooklyn Rabbi Robert Gordis (b. 1908).

GORDON (also Gordin)—JE and UJ have numerous biographies from 18th-cent. England, 19th-cent. Russia, Poland, etc. See *Book of the Descendants of Dr. Benjamin Lee and Dorothy Gordon.* Related to LUNTZ and LANDA.

GORELIK—UJ has article on Russian stage designer Mordecai Gorelik (1879–1942).

GORFINE—UJ has article on U.S. lawyer Emanuel Gorfine (b. 1895).

GORFINKLE—UJ has article on U.S. lawyer Bernard Gorfinkle (b. 1889). Also see GARFUNKEL.

GORIN—JE has article on Lithuanian-American journalist Bernard Gorin (b. Isaac GOIDO in 1868).

GOROCHOV—Related to ADMON.

GORWITZ—See HOROVITZ.

GOSDORFER—LBI has a family tree beginning 1503; related to BEROLZHEIMER.

GOSLAR—EJ has article on 18th-cent. Amsterdam Rabbi Naphtali Goslar.

GOTA—EJ has article on Turkish Rabbi Moses Gota (d. 1648).

GOTENDORF—JE has article on German merchant James Gotendorf (1811–1888), who came to U.S.A. and changed his name to James NATHAN.

GOTESFELD—UJ has article on Galician playwright Chone Gotesfeld (b. 1880).

GOTFRED—See "Abraham Gotfred de Meza og hans familie," in *Jodisk Samfund*.

GOTLEIB—See GOTTLIEB.

GOTTHEIL—JE has four biographies from Germany and U.S.A., 19th cent.

GOTTHEIMER—Related to GRANT.

GOTTHELFT—LBI has a family tree beginning 1698. Also see *The Gotthelft Family Tree;* it traces the family back to 1670.

GOTTLIEB (also Gotleib)—German name meaning "God, love." UJ and JE have biographies. AJA has a family tree from Colorado.

GOTTLOBER—JE has article on Russian poet Abraham Gottlober (1811–1899), son of a cantor.

GOTTSCHALK (also Godschalk, Gottschall)—JE and UJ have biographies from U.S.A., 19th cent. CAJ has a family tree and records from Germany, related to VOGEL, LOWE, GOLDSTEIN, HEINEMANN, BLUMENTHAL and SCHIFF. LBIS has some family notes. For family histories, see *Godschalk (1777–1778)* and "Note on the Jewish Ancestry of Louis Gottschalk, American Pianist and Composer." in *American Jewish Archives*.

GOTTSTEIN—JE has two biographies from 19th-cent. Germany.

GOTZ (also Goetz)—JE has article on German Rabbi Joseph Gotz (1640–1701) from Frankfurt, died in Jerusalem. Related to BINSWANGER, SCHWERIN and YATES.

GOUDCHAUX—JE has article on French statesman Michel Goudchaux (1797–1862). See also GODCHAUX.

GOUDSMIT—JE has article on Dutch jurist Joel Goudsmit (1813–1882). Also see biography in EJ article on "Dutch Literature."

GOULD—Related to MOSHEIM.

GOZHANSKY—EJ has article on Russian bundist Samuel Gozhansky (1867–1943).

GRABAU—Related to ANTIN.

GRABER—See GRAEBER.

GRABFELDER—Related to GRIFF.

GRACIA—See GRACIAN.

GRACIAN (also Gracia, Graciano)—Prominent Spanish family descended from Judah ben Barzilai. Members lived chiefly at Barcelona from 13th through 16th cent. Most used the name HEN. JE has fourteen biographies. Related to NASI and TRABOT.

GRACIANO—See GRACIAN.

GRADE—UJ has article on Russian poet Chaim Grade (b. 1910).

GRADENWITZ—LBI has a family tree beginning 1796.

GRADIS—Family of prominent merchants in southern France, around Bordeaux, 18th cent., originally from Spain. The family is said to have emigrated from Palestine to Spain after the Bar Kochba insurrection in 135 C.E. JE has a family tree and biographies. Related to BOCARRO, MENDES, RODRIGUEZ and HALEVY.

GRAEBER (also Graber)—EJ has article on Galician writer Schealtiel Graeber (b. 1856).

GRAEFENBERG—See GRAFENBERG.

GRAETKE—Related to ABRAMSON.

GRAETZ (also Graetzer, Gratz, Gratzer, Gratzner)—Ashkenazic name taken from the town of Greditz in Austrian Silesia, or from Gratz in Austria. Some members of the later prominent Philadelphia family of Gratz moved to Langendorf in 18th cent.; others came to U.S.A. in 1755. EJ has a tree for this family, which is related to SYMONS (or SIMON), MEYERS (or MEARS), ETTING, HAYS, MOSES, GIST, BOSWELL, BLOCH, JOSEPH and BUSH. JE, UJ and EJ have other biographies as well. CAJ has a Graetz family tree; AJA has the family tree of German historian Heinrich Graetz (1817–1891). LBI has a Graetzer family tree. Other relatives include MONASH and LATZ.

GRAF—UJ has two biographies from Vienna, 19th cent.

GRAFENBERG (also Graefenberg)—See *Stammbaumblätter der Familie Grafenberg*. LBI has a Graefenberg family tree beginning 1752.

GRAFTON—UJ has article on U.S. newsman Samuel Grafton (b. 1907).

GRAHL—Related to DA PONTE; see PONTE.

GRAIF—See GRIFF.

GRAJEWSKI—EJ has article on Vilna scholar Eliezer Grajewski (1843–1899).

GRALNICK (also Guralnick)—See family history in *A Link with the Future* (see Rottenberg in Bibliography).

GRANADA—EJ has article on Mexican Marrano Gabriel de Granada (b. 1629). Related to GABISHON.

GRANOVSKY—UJ has article on Russian writer Abraham Granovski (b. 1890).

GRANT—EJ has article on Irish-British financier Albert Grant (1830–1899), also known as GOTTHEIMER. AJA has a family tree.

GRAPF—See family history in *A Link with the Future* (see Rottenberg in Bibliography).

GRASSIN—CAJ has some family records.

GRATZ—See GRAETZ.

GRATZER—See GRAETZ.

GRATZNER—See GRAETZ.

GRAU—UJ has article on Moravian impresario Maurice Grau (1849–1907), who died in Paris.

GRAUBART—UJ has article on Polish-Canadian Rabbi Judah Graubart (1880–1937).

GRAUMANN—UJ has article on South African pioneer Sir Harry Graumann (1868–1938).

GRAUR—UJ has article on Rumanian editor Constantin Graur (1877–1940).

GRAY—UJ has two biographies from 19th-cent. Russia. Also known as GURARIE.

GRAYZEL—UJ has article on Russian scholar Solomon Grayzel (b. 1896).

GRAZIANI—See GRAZIANO.

GRAZIANO (also Graziani)—Name which is the Italian equivalent of Johanan. Italian Rabbi Abraham Graziano (d. 1865) probably belonged to the GALLICO family. He was a cousin of Nathanael ben Benjamin TRABOT. See biographies in JE.

GRAZOVSKI—UJ has article on Russian writer Judah Grazovski (b. 1862).

GREBER—CAJ has some family records.

GREBNITZ—Related to PERETZ.

GREEN—JE has article on English Rabbi Aaron Green (1821–1883). See also GRUN.

GREENBAUM (also Greenebaum)—German name meaning "green tree." JE has article on U.S. lawyer Samuel Greenbaum (b. 1854 in London). AJA has a family tree, related to HERZ and FRIEDENWALD, beginning 1719 in Germany. See also GRUNEBAUM. Greenebaum is a Chicago family originally from Germany; see UJ. Related to LEBOLD.

GREENBERG—UJ has biographies from 19th-cent. Russia, England, Belgium, South Africa and U.S.A.

GREENEBAUM—See GREENBAUM.

GREENFIELD—See GRUNFELD.

GREENHUT—See GRUNHUT.

GREENSFELDER—UJ has article on U.S. playwright Elmer Greensfelder (b. 1892).

GREENSTEIN (also Greenstone)—UJ has biographies from Russia and U.S.A., 19th cent. See also GRUNSTEIN.

GREENWALD—See GRUNWALD.

GREIDIKER—UJ has article on Polish merrymaker Ephraim Greidiker (18th cent.).

GREINER—UJ has article on German author Leo Greiner (1876–1928).

GRELLING—LBI has a family tree beginning 1746, related to SIMON.

GRIES—UJ has article on U.S. Rabbi Moses Gries (1868–1918).

GRIESHABER (also Grishaber, Kriegshaber)—JE has article on 18th-cent. Polish-Hungarian Rabbi Isaac Grieshaber.

GRIFF (also Graif)—AJA has a family tree beginning 18th cent., related to SECKEL, FRIEDMAN, GRABFELDER.

GRIGORYEVICH—Related to DEUTSCH.

GRILICHES—JE has biographies from Vilna, 19th cent.

GRISHABER—See GRIESHABER.

GROBARD—UJ has article on Polish critic Benjamin Grobard (b. 1892).

GRODZINSKI—Name probably derived from the city of Grodno. CAJ has some family records.

GROEDEL—LBI has family trees beginning 1782 and 1818. PD has some family records. Related to BEROLZHEIMER.

GROLLER—UJ has article on Hungarian novelist Baldwin Groller (1848–1916).

GRONAU—UJ has article on German art critic Georg Gronau (1868–1937), who died in Italy.

GRONEMANN—JE has article on German Rabbi Selig Gronemann (b. 1843).

GROPPER—UJ has article on U.S. cartoonist William Gropper (b. 1897).

GROSS (also Grosser, Grossman, Grossmann, Grosz, Groszman)—Ashkenazic name meaning "large" in German. JE and UJ have biographies from 19th-cent. Austria, Germany, Hungary and U.S.A. Austrian writer Ferdinand Gross (1849–1900) was descended from Italian ancestors; his father emigrated from Padua to Hungary, and from there to Vienna. U.S. Rabbi Louis Grossmann (b. 1863 in Vienna) was descended from a family of rabbis. Related to UJVARI.

GROSSMAN (Grossmann)—See GROSS.

GROSZ—See GROSS.

GROSZMAN—See GROSS.

GROTTE—UJ has article on Prague scholar Alfred Grotte (b. 1872). See family history in JFF, No. 9.

GROZOVSKI—JE has article on Russian Hebraist Judah Grozovski (b. 1861 near Minsk).

GRUBER—JE has article on Austrian physician Joseph Gruber (1827–1900).

GRUBY—JE has article on French physician David Gruby (1810–1898), born in Hungary.

GRUEN—See GRUN.

GRUENBAUM—See GRUNBAUM.

GRUENBERG (also Grunberg)—UJ and EJ have biographies from 19th-cent. Russia and Austria. Related to MATSNER and MINZ.

GRUENBLATT—UJ has article on Lithuanian writer Nathan Gruenblatt (b. 1886).

GRUENFELD—See GRUNFELD.

GRUENHUT—See GRUNHUT.

GRUENING—UJ has articles from 19th-cent. Germany and U.S.A.

GRUENSTEIN—See GRUNSTEIN.

GRUENWALD—See GRUNWALD.

GRUMBACH—UJ has article on French General Paul Grumbach (b. 1861).

GRUMET—Related to POLLOCK.

GRUN (also Gruen)—JE has article on Russian painter Maurice Grun (b. 1870). See biography in EJ article on "Chemistry." Also see GREEN.

GRUNBAUM (also Grunebaum, Gruenbaum)—EJ and JE have article from 19th-cent. Germany. LBI has a family tree beginning 1490, related to ELLERN. PD has Grunebaum family records. Also see GREENBAUM.

GRUNBERG—See GRUENBERG.

GRUNEBAUM—See GRUNBAUM.

GRUNEWALD—See GRUNWALD.

GRUNFELD (also Gruenfeld, Greenfield, Grunsfeld)—JE, UJ and EJ have biographies from 19th-cent. Austria, Hungary and U.S.A. LBI has a Gruenfeld family tree beginning 1766, and a Grunsfeld family tree beginning 1749. English variation of the name is GREENFIELD.

GRUNHUT (also Greenhut, Gruenhut)—JE and EJ have biographies from Germany and Hungary. German Rabbi David Grunhut (17th–18th cent.) was grandson of Simon GUNZBURG. AJA has a Greenhut family tree beginning 1290 and related to TREVES, SPIRA, LURIA, AUERBACH, ISSERLES, GUNSBERG, GELHAUSER, OPPENHEIMER, KOLON, EMDEN, HILDESHEIM, HALBERSTADT, KATZ, KLAUBER, HEIMERDINGER, LAZARUS, LIEBERMANN, LUST, BLACHSTEIN and FRANK.

GRUNSFELD—See GRUNFELD.

GRUNSTEIN (also Gruenstein)—UJ has biographies from 19th-cent. Poland and Lithuania. Also see biography in EJ article on "Chemistry." Also see GREENSTEIN.

GRUNWALD (also Greenwald, Gruenwald, Grunewald)—JE, UJ and EJ have biographies from 19th-cent. Germany, Austria, Hungary, Czechoslovakia and Sweden. CAJ has some family records. Related to ZERKOWITZ, IVANYI.

GRUSZCYNSKY—CAJ has some family records.

GRUZENBERG—CAJ has some family records. Related to BORODIN.

GUASTALLA—JE has article on Italian soldier Enrico Guastalla (1828–1903).

GUBBAY—Related to SASSOON.

GUDELSKY (also Gudelski)—See family history in *A Link with the Future* (see Rottenberg in Bibliography).

GUDEMANN—See GUTMANN.

GUEDALLA—Related to MONTEFIORE.

GUEDEMANN—See GUTMANN.

GUENZBURG—See GUNZBURG.

GUENZIG—EJ has article on Cracow Rabbi Ezriel Guenzig (1868–1931).

GUENZLER—EJ has article on Hungarian Rabbi Abraham Guenzler (1840–1910).

GUERON—JE has article on Turkish Rabbi Yakir Gueron (1813–1874), who was the sixth rabbi of Adrianople (Edirne) descended from the Gueron family.

GUETERBOCK—JE has article on German jurist Karl Gueterbock (b. 1830). LBI has a family tree beginning 1776.

GUETTA—JE has article on Talmudic scholar Isaac Guetta of Trieste (1777–1857), who died in Palestine. His ancestors went to the Middle East from Huete, Spain; his grandson was the poet David ARA of Trieste.

GUGENHEIM—See GUGGENHEIM.

GUGGENHEIM (also Gugenheim, Guggenheimer)—U.S. merchant family descended from Meyer Guggenheim (b. 1848 in Switzerland). EJ has a family tree and biographies. LBIS has some family notes. AJA has a Guggenheimer family tree. For family histories, see *The Guggenheims:*

The Making of an American Dynasty, Stammbaum der Familie Guggenheim aus Worms, Die Nachkommen des Simon Guggenheim (1730–1799) von Endingen and *Samuel Guggenheim gest. 27 Dec. 1930.* Related to MENDELSSOHN, CONE, KAHN and LANDAUER.

GUGLIELMO—JE has article on 15th-cent. Italian dancing master Benjamin Guglielmo.

GUHRAUER—JE has article on German philologist Gottschalk Guhrauer (1809–1854). CAJ has a family tree covering 1788 to 1921, related to MAZUR, KADISCH and DRUCKER.

GUINZBURG—See GUNZBURG.

GUITERMAN—UJ has article on Viennese poet Arthur Guiterman (b. 1871).

GUIZOLFI (also Giexulfis)—Zacharias de Guizolfi, 15th-cent. ruler of the Taman peninsula on the east coast of the Black Sea, was a descendant of Simone de Guizolfi, a Genoese Jew who, by marriage with the Princess Bikhakhanim, became ruler of the peninsula (under the protection of the Genoese republic) in 1419. See JE.

GULAK—UJ has article on Latvian scholar Asher Gulak (1881–1940).

GUMBERT—Related to SPEYER.

GUMPEL—Mordecai Gumpel (17th cent.) is an ancestor of the GOMPERZ family; see JE. Also see "Die Hamburger Familie Gumpel und der Dichter Heinrich Heine" in *Zeitschrift für die Geschichte der Juden.* Related to OPPENHEIM and SAMSON.

GUMPERT—See GOMPERZ.

GUMPERTZ—See GOMPERZ.

GUMPERZ—See GOMPERZ.

GUMPLOWICZ—UJ has article on Polish political scientist Ludwig Gumplowicz (1838–1909).

GUMPRECHT—LBIS has some family notes. Related to WARBURG.

GUNDELFINGER—See GUNDOLF.

GUNDERMANN—LBI has a family tree beginning 1739.

GUNDERSHEIMER—Related to AMBACH.

GUNDOLF (also Gundelfinger)—UJ has article on German historian Friedrich Gundolf (1880–1931).

GUNSBERG—See GUNZBURG.

GUNSBURG—See GUNZBURG.

GUNZ—See GUNZBURG.

GUNZBURG (also Gunzburger, Ginsberg, Ginsburg, Gintzburger, Ginzberg, Ginzburg, Ginsburger, Guenzburg, Guinzburg, Gunsberg, Gunsburg, Gunz, etc.)—Ashkenazic family name traced back to the town of Gunzburg, Bavaria. The family's progenitor came there from Ulm in Württemberg and called himself Simeon Ulma-Gunzburg (d. 1586). ULM, ULMA and ULLMAN are supposed to be branches of the Gunzburg family; another variation is GAUNZ. When the Jews of Russia and Austria were ordered to take family names (c. 1800), many took this name even though they are not related to the original Gunzburg family; see JE. But EJ article on Guenzburg traces some Russians and East Europeans with this name back to the original family. CAJ has a family tree for Gunzburg (1544–1902) and Gunzburger (from Germany), as well as some records for Ginzberg and Ginsburger families. LBI has a Ginsburg family tree. LBIS has Gunzburg family notes. JE article on "Coat of Arms" has the Gunzburg family crest. For family histories, see BJGL, Vols. I, 2 and 3; also *Toledot Mishpahat Gunzburg* and *Zur Genealogie der Familie Gunzburg.* The family is linked to other prominent families in *Da'at Kedoshim,* by Israel Eisenstadt. Related to ROSENTHAL, ROSENBERG, WARBURG, HIRSCH, SASSOON, GUTMANN, JAFFE, OETTINGEN, KLIACHKO, GREENHUT and EGER. Also see JE article on Pinsk.

GUNZENHAUSER—UJ has article on 15th-cent. German printer Azriel Gunzenhauser, also known as ASHKENAZI.

GUNZIG—UJ has article on Polish Rabbi Israel Gunzig (1868–1931).

GURALNICK—See family history in *A Link with the Future* (see Rottenberg in Bibliography). Also see CORALNICK.

GURARIE—See GRAY.

GUREWICZ—See HOROVITZ.

GURLAND—JE has article on Russian writer Jonah Gurland (1843–1890).

GURVICH—See HOROVITZ.

GURWICZ—See HOROVITZ.

GUSIKOW—EJ has article on Russian musician Joseph Gusikow (1802–1837).

GUTAH—JE has article on author Zerahiah Gutah (d. 1647 in Cairo).

GUTENBERG—UJ has article on German scientist Beno Gutenberg (b. 1889).

GUTERBOCK—JE has biographies from 19th-cent. Germany.

GUTFREUND—EJ has article on Czech sculptor Otto Gutfreund (1889–1927).

GUTH—CAJ has a family tree from Germany.

GUTHEIM—UJ has article on German Rabbi James Gutheim (1817–1886).

GUTMACHER—UJ has article on German Rabbi Elijah Gutmacher (1796–1874).

GUTMAN—See GUTMANN.

GUTMANN (also Gutman, Guttmann, Gutzmann, Gudemann, Guedemann)—Ashkenazic name derived from the German *gut,* meaning "good." JE and EJ have biographies from 18th- and 19th-cent. Austria, Germany, Poland and Hungary. LBI has family trees beginning 1600, 1756, 1760, 1784 and 1807. PD has Gutmann family records; CAJ has Gudemann family records. Related to FEDER, GUNZBURG and GELSE. The name may be a predecessor of GOODMAN.

GUTT—UJ has article on Belgian finance minister Camille Gutt (b. 1884).

GUTTEREZ—Related to HENRIQUES.

GUTTMACHER—EJ has article on Polish Rabbi Elijah Guttmacher (1795–1874), of Posen.

GUTTMANN—See GUTMANN.

GUTZMANN—See GUTMANN.

GUVAN—LBIS has some family notes.

GUZIKOV—JE has article on Russian musician Michael Guzikov (1806–1837), descended from a family of talented musicians.

GYARMATH—Related to EISENSTADT.

HAAN—UJ has article on Dutch writer Jacob Haan (1881–1924). Related to BRUGGEN. See also HAHN.

HAARBLEICHER—JE has article on German author Moses Haarbleicher (1797–1869).

HAAS (also Haase)—JE and UJ have biographies from 18th-cent. Bohemia and 19th-cent. Germany, Moravia and U.S.A. Simhah Haas of Bohemia (1710–1768) was the father-in-law of Solomon DUBNO. CAJ has a Haas family tree beginning in 17th-cent. Germany, and Haase family records. U.S. lawyer Arthur Garfield HAYS (b. 1881) was originally Haas. See family history in JFF, No. 24. Also see DE HAAS.

HABER (also Haberkasten, Habermann)—Ashkenazic name derived from the town of Habern in Bohemia. 16th-cent. Polish Rabbi Kalman Haberkasten was father-in-law of Solomon LURIA. JE and UJ have biographies from 18th- and 19th-cent. Germany. LBI has Haber family trees beginning 1768 and 1801. JE article on "Coat of Arms" has the Haber family crest. Related to HERZL, LAUTERBACH and KROCHMAL.

HABERKASTEN—See HABER.

HABERMANN—See HABER.

HABIB (also Habiba)—Sephardic name. JE and EJ have biographies from Spain and Portugal, 14th, 15th and 16th cent. Moses Ibn Habib (Palestine, 17th cent.) married the daughter of Jacob HAGIZ. Related to CULI.

HABILLO—Elish Habillo of Venice (18th cent.) was descended from a prominent Palestinian family; see JE, which also has biographies from 17th-cent. Palestine and 15th-cent. Spain.

HABSBURGER—See family history in JFF, No. 23.

HABSHUSH—EJ has article on Yemenite writer Hayyim Habshush (d. 1899).

HACHUEL—JE has article on Moorish woman martyr Sol Hachuel (d. 1834 in Fez, Morocco).

HACKENBURG (also Hachenburger)—UJ has article on U.S. merchant William Hackenburg (1837–1918). LBI has a Hachenburger family tree beginning 1700. Related to TELLER and ALLEN.

HACKER—UJ has article on U.S. historian Louis Hacker (b. 1899).

HACOHEN (also Ha-Kohen)—Variation of COHEN. EJ has article on Russian writer Mordecai Hacohen (1856–1936). Related to EYBESCHUTZ, BACHARACH, TORRE, KAHANA, FREUDEMANN, HARIF HA-LEVI, ARONSON and SOPHER.

HADAMARD—JE has biographies from 19th-cent. France.

HADASSI—Name that may mean "native of Edessa" (in Turkey). JE has article on 12th-cent. scholar Judah Hadassi of Constantinople.

HADDAD—JE has article on scholar Isaac Haddad (d. 1755 on Gerba, an island near Tunis).

HADIDA—JE has article on 15th-cent. Spanish Talmudist Abraham Hadida.

HA-EFRATI—EJ has article on Silesian poet Joseph Ha-Efrati (1770–1804), also called TROPPLOWITZ. Also see EPHRATI.

HAETZYONI—EJ has article on German Zionist Yehudah Haetzioni (1868–1938).

HAFARHI—See FARHI.

HAFFKINE—JE has article on bacteriologist Waldemar Haffkine (1860–1930), born in Odessa.

HAGEDORN—UJ has biography from 19th-cent. U.S.A. AJA has family tree beginning 1753, related to FRIEDLANDER, SOLOMON and ROSENBAUM.

HAGEGE—JE has article on Tunisian Rabbi Abraham Hagege (d. 1880).

HAGELBERG—LBI has family tree, related to AUERBACH and EHRLICH.

HAGEN—UJ has article on German banker Louis Hagen (1855–1932), who converted to Catholicism.

HAGENOW—LBI has a family tree beginning 1806, related to JACOBSON. Also see HAGUENAU.

HAGER—Related to VIZHNITZ.

HAGIN—JE has article on 13th-cent. English Tosafist Berechiah de Nicole, a member of the Hagin family.

HAGIS—See HAGIZ.

HAGIZ (also Hagis)—Spanish Jews who lived in Fez, Morocco, and Constantinople in 17th cent. See JE. Related to HABIB, HAYYUN and GALANTE.

HAGOZER—EJ has article on 13th-cent. circumcisers Gershom and Jacob Hagozer, father and son.

HAGUENAU (also Haguenauer)—Name taken from the Alsatian town of Hagenau. UJ has article on French Rabbi J. Haguenau, grandfather of French Rabbi Isaac LEVY. Related to TRENEL. Also see HAGENOW.

HAHLO (also Hallo)—Name probably derived from the German town of Halle in Saxony. CAJ has a family tree from Germany. UJ has article on German art historian Rudolf Hallo (b. 1896). See family history in *Geschichte der Familie Hallo.* Related to SAMSON. Also see HALLE.

HAHN—Ashkenazic name from the German word for "rooster." JE has biographies from 16th-, 17th- and 19th-cent. Germany. Rabbi Joseph Hahn (d. 1637) was the son of SELIGMANN; the family name came from the family house, called "Zum roten Hahn"—the Red Rooster. His grandson was Joseph ben Moses KOSMAN, son-in-law of Moses Reiss DARUM. LBI has a family tree beginning 1755. LBIS has some family notes. Also see biography in EJ article on "Politics." Related to NORDLINGEN. A possible variation is HAAN.

HAHNEMANN—Ashkenazic name derived from the female name Hannah.

HAIDA—JE has biographies from 17th and 18th-cent. Germany and Bohemia. Abraham Haida of Prague (17th cent.) was also known as LEMBERGER.

HAIM—JE has article on 19th-cent. Serbian author Israel Haim.

HAINDORF—JE has article on German writer Alexander Haindorf (1784–1862).

HAJEK—UJ has article on Hungarian physician Marcus Hajek (1861–1941), who married Gisela SCHNITZLER.

HAKAN (also Hakim)—JE and EJ have articles on Egyptian Rabbi Samuel Hakan, or Hakim (1480–1547).

HAKHAM—EJ has article on Iraqi scholar Simon Hakham (1843–1910).

HAKIM—See HAKAN.

HA-KOHEN—See HACOHEN.

HALASZ—JE and UJ have biographies from 19th-cent. Hungary.

HALAYO—JE has article on David Halayo.

HALBAN—JE has article on Austrian statesman Heinrich Halban (1846–1902),

born BLUENSTOCK in Cracow. He married a sister of Victor ADLER.

HALBERSTADT (also Halberstaedter)—Ashkenazic name taken from the town of Halberstadt in Saxony. JE has three biographies from 18th-cent. Germany. LBI has a family tree beginning 1754. Related to ROTHSCHILD, SCHIFF and GREENHUT.

HALBERSTAM—Austrian scholar Solomon Halberstam (1832–1900), born in Cracow, has eminent rabbis on both his parents' sides. See EJ; also see family tree in his book, *Siah Yizhaki.*

HALBERTHAL—UJ has article on Rumanian writer Avrum Halberthal (b. 1881); his pseudonym was HALBERT.

HALDEMAN—UJ has article on U.S. author Emanuel JULIUS (b. 1889), who took his wife's name to become HALDEMAN-JULIUS.

HA-LEVI (also Halevi)—See LEVI.

HALEVY—French variation of LEVI. JE has five biographies from 18th- and 19th-cent. France. Composer Jacques Halevy (1799–1862) came from Bavaria, where his family name had been Levi. Polish historian Isaac Halevy was born RABINOWITZ in 1847; see UJ. Related to BUSNACH, LEVINSON.

HALFAN—See HALFON.

HALFNAUS—See HALFON.

HALFON (also Chalfin, Chalfen, Halfan, Halfnaus, Chalfan)—Ashkenazic name that means "moneychanger" in Hebrew. Family of printers in Italy, 15th–16th-cent.; see CB, p. 2813. JE has biographies from Italy and from 18th–19th-cent. Moravia and Tripoli. CAJ has Halfon family records. Related to JAFFE and COLON. Also see HALPHEN.

HALFORD—JE has article on British soldier George Halford (1878–1900).

HALIC (also Helic, Halicz)—Family of Jewish printers in Cracow that dates back to 16th cent.; see UJ. Also see EJ article on Anshel of Cracow.

HALKIN—UJ has article on poet Simon Halkin (b. 1899 in Russia).

HALL—Related to MONTEFIORE.

HALLE (also von Halle)—Ashkenazic name taken from the Prussian town of Halle in Saxony. Another variation is

HAHLO. JE has article on German translator Aaron Halle (1754–1835), born in Halle. LBI has family trees beginning 1736, 1763, 1860. AJA has a family tree beginning 1680, related to ELB, LUEBKE. LBIS has a family tree and notes. Related to HEINE and WOLFSOHN.

HALLGARTEN—UJ has article on German philanthropist Charles Hallgarten (b. 1838).

HALLO—See HAHLO.

HALMI—UJ has article on Hungarian chemist Gyula Halmi (b. 1879).

HALPER—See HEILPRIN.

HALPERIN—See HEILPRIN.

HALPERN—See HEILPRIN.

HALPERT—UJ has article on Russian painter Samuel Halpert (b. 1884).

HALPHEN—Variation of HALFON. JE has two biographies from 19th-cent. France. Related to ROTHSCHILD.

HALTERN—JE has article on German writer Joseph Haltern (d. 1818).

HAM—CAJ has a family tree from Germany.

HAMBERGER—See HAMBURGER.

HAMBOURG—See HAMBURGER.

HAMBRO—JE has article on German-English businessman Joseph Hambro (1780–1848), who died in London.

HAMBURGER (also Hamburg, Hamberger, Hambourg)—Ashkenazic name meaning one who comes from Hamburg, Germany. JE has biographies from Germany, England and Prague, 17th, 18th and 19th cent. Mordecai Hamburger (1660–1730), born in Hamburg, died in London, married the daughter of Gluckel von HAMELN. LBI has a family tree beginning 1600. CAJ has family records. LBI also has a Hamburg family tree beginning 1772. UJ has Hambourg biographies from 19th-cent. Russia. See Hamburger family history in JHSE, No. 3 (1937), p. 57. Also see HOMBERG.

HAMDI—EJ has article on Yemenite hymnologist Levi Hamdi (1861–1930).

HAMELN—German diarist Gluckel von Hameln (1646–1724) was born in Hamburg and died in Metz; her husband, Hayyim Hameln, came from the Prussian town of the same name. She wrote an autobiography; see JE and EJ. LBI has a family tree beginning 1560. Also see *Die Kinder des Hildesheimer Rabbiners: Samuel Hameln.* Related to GOMPERTZ, KRUMBACH-SCHWAB, BAIERSDORF, BEHRENDS, LIEBMANN and HAMBURGER.

HAMILTON—Related to FRANKS.

HAMIZ—EJ has article on Venetian physician Joseph Hamiz (d. 1676).

HAMMERSCHLAG (also Hammerslough) —JE has article on 17th-cent. Moravian cabalist Joseph Hammerschlag. Related to BEHREND and ROSENWALD.

HAMMERSLOUGH—See also HAMMERSCHLAG.

HAMMERSTEIN—JE has article on U.S. theatrical manager Oscar Hammerstein (b. 1848 in Berlin).

HAMON—Ancient family originally from Spain, which settled in Turkey and produced several physicians. JE has six biographies from 16th cent. and later.

HANAN—JE has article on 18th-cent. Turkish Rabbi Isaac Hanan.

HANANIA (also HANANIAH)—Name probably taken from the Biblical Chenaniah, a Levite of the family of Izharites. See JE article on *Moses ha-Levi ha-Nazir,* son-in-law of 17th-cent. Talmudist Abraham Ibn Hananiah. Related to BENVENISTE.

HANAU (also Hannaux, Hanno, Hanauer) —Ashkenazic name taken from the town of Hanau in Hesse-Nassau, Germany. JE has biographies from Germany, 17th, 18th and 19th cent., and 19th-cent. France. Rabbi Zebi Hirsch Hanau (1662–1740) came from the FRANKEL family. LBI has a family tree beginning 1700. Related to ROTHSCHILD, MUNZENBERG, CANTOR, SCHIFF, ROSENBERG and LEBRECHT.

HANAUER—See HANAU.

HANBURY—JE has article on 19th-cent. English actress Lily Hanbury.

HANDALI—EJ has article on 17th-cent. Turkish Rabbi Joshua Handali. Related to KYRA.

HANDEL—CAJ has some family records.

HANINA—See BAR ANINA.

HANKIN—EJ has article on Ukrainian Zionist Yehoshua Hankin (1864–1945). Related to BELKIND.

HANNAUX—See HANAU.

HANNELES—JE has article on 16th-cent. Rabbi Judah Hanneles (named after his mother, Hannah). Also see EJ article on *Eliakim* Goetz.

HANNO—See HANAU.

HANNOVER (also Hanover)—Ashkenazic name taken from the Prussian city of Hannover. JE has biographies from 17th-cent. Germany and Russia. CAJ has some Hannover family records. Related to JOSEPH.

HANOVER—See HANNOVER.

HANSEN—LBIS has some family notes.

HANSLICK—UJ has article on music teacher Eduard Hanslick (b. 1825 in Prague). See family histories in JFF, Nos. 21, 30 and 31.

HANTKE—UJ has article on Zionist Arthur Hantke (b. 1874 in Berlin).

HANTOS—UJ has article on economist Elemer Hantos (b. 1881 in Budapest).

HARARI—Name given in the Middle Ages to certain Jews in France, Italy and the Middle East; it means "of the mountain." JE has article on 13th-cent. French poet Judah Harari.

HARASZT—Related to JELLINEK.

HARBURGER—Ashkenazic name taken from the German town of Harburg, south of Hamburg. JE has article on German jurist Heinrich Harburger (b. 1851).

HARBY—Family living in southern U.S.A. since 18th cent. JE has eight biographies, and AJA has a family tree beginning 18th cent. Related to LYON.

HARDEN—JE has article on German author Maximilian Harden (b. WITKOWSKY in 1861).

HARDOON—UJ has article on philanthropist Silas Aaron (b. 1847 in Turkey).

HARF—Related to REICHER.

HARIF (also Harif Ha-Levi)—Polish rabbinical family of 16th through 19th cent.; see EJ. Related to EDELS, HA-KOHEN, MARGOLIOTH, KREMNITZER, HOROVITZ and MARCUS. Also see JE and UJ. Some members are mentioned in *Anaf Ez Aboth,* by Samuel Kahan, which relates many East European rabbinic families.

HARIRI—Families of Karaites in Kurdistan from 17th cent. See EJ.

HARIZI—UJ has a biography from 12th-cent. Spain.

HARKAVY—Russian family believed to have descended from Mordecai JAFFE (1530–1612). Its immediate ancestor was Joseph of Turetz (d. 1778), who lived in the province of Minsk. JE has sixteen biographies. Also see *Stammbuch der Familie Harkavy.* Related to ROMM.

HARMATI—UJ has article on composer Sandor Harmati (b. 1892 in Budapest).

HARRACH—CAJ has family records.

HARRIS (also Harrison, Harrisse)—Variation of the German HIRSCH ("stag"); other variations are HERZ, HARTVIG, CERF and JELLINEK. JE and UJ have biographies from 19th-cent. U.S.A., England and France. AJA has a family tree from Dallas, Texas. LBI has a family tree beginning 1833 in U.S.A. See *Moss-Harris Pedigree Chart* and *The Family of Isaac and Rebecca Harris.* Related to MOSS.

HARROW—UJ has article on chemist Benjamin Harrow (b. 1888 in England).

HARRWITZ—See HOROVITZ.

HARSELANI—JE has article on 10th-cent. Karaite scholar Abraham al-Harselani of Babylonia.

HART—Several families of this name, of English origin, settled in U.S.A. and Canada in 18th cent. Ephraim Hart (b. 1747 in Bavaria, d. 1825 in New York) came from the family of HIRZ; he married Frances NOAH. JE has nineteen biographies from U.S.A. and Canada, and five from England, Australia and Germany; the earliest is Aaron Hart (b. 1670 in Breslau, d. 1756 in England). EJ has a family tree. AJA has a tree for a Hart family of Memphis, Tenn. Related to LEON, COHEN, SEIXAS, JUDAH, DAVID, SALOMON, JOSEPH, SAMUEL, LEVY, GOMEZ, CARDOZO, BRETT, NOAH, WAGG, FRANKS and GAGGSTATTER.

HARTGLASS—UJ has article on Zionist Maximilian Hartglas (b. 1883 in Poland).

HARTIG—LBI has a family tree beginning 1726.

HARTMAN (also Hartmann)—JE and UJ have biographies from 18th- and 19th-cent. Germany, Austria and Hungary.

HARTOG (also Hartogh, Hartogensis)—Dutch name. JE has eight biographies from 19th cent. CAJ has a family tree from Germany and Holland, 1720–1959, related to LEYSER. Other relatives are MOSS and DARMESTETER.

HARTOGENSIS—See HARTOG.

HARTOGH—See HARTOG.

HARTT—UJ has article on Canadian deputy Maurice Hartt (b. 1892 in Rumania).

HARTVIG (also Hartwig, Hartvigson)—German variation of HIRSCH ("stag"); other variations are HERZ, HARRIS, CERF and JELLINEK. JE has two biographies from 19th-cent. Denmark. See family history in *Levin Marcus Hartvigs efterkommende.*

HARTVIGSON—See HARTVIG.

HARTWIG—See HARTVIG.

HARTZELL—See *Herzog and Lambert Genealogy.* The HERZOG family in this book later became Hartzell.

HAREUBENI—CAJ has some family records.

HARZFELD—See HERZFELD.

HASAN—EJ has article on 11th-cent. Yemenite Abu Hasan.

HASDAI—Sephardic name. JE has several biographies from Spain, 10th through 13th cent.

HASENCLEVER—UJ has article on German playwright Walter Hasenclever (b. 1890).

HASID—Related to JAFFE.

HASLEM—Related to CARDOZO.

HASON—JE has two biographies, one from 16th-cent. Turkey.

HASSAN—Spanish-Moroccan family in Granada from 1287. See EJ.

HASSLER—JE has article on U.S. musician Simon Hassler (1832–1901), born in Bavaria.

HAST—JE has article on London cantor Marcus Hast (b. 1840 in Warsaw).

HATCHEVALL—Related to MONTEFIORE.

HATSEK—JE has article on Hungarian cartographer Ignaz Hatsek (b. 1828).

HATVANY (also Hatvany-Deutsch)—UJ has article on Hungarian industrial family, originally DEUTSCH. Related to MADARASSY-BECK.

HAUPT—CAJ has some family records.

HAUSDORF—EJ has article on Silesian Zionist Azriel Hausdorf (1823–1905).

HAUSEN (also Hauser, Hausner)—JE and UJ have biographies from 18th-cent. Denmark, 19th-cent. Hungary and Poland. Related to MEYER.

HAUSER—See HAUSEN.

HAUSNER—See HAUSEN.

HAUSSMANN (also Houseman)—JE has two biographies from 19th-cent. Germany. Related to CARDOZO.

HAVAS—JE and UJ have biographies from Hungary, 19th cent.

HAVELBURG—CAJ has some family records.

HAVER—Syrian family of rabbis, beginning in 16th cent. See EJ.

HAYEM—JE has three biographies from France, 19th cent. Related to FRANCK.

HAYES—CAJ has some family records.

HAYIM—UJ has biography from 17th-cent. Poland.

HAYON—EJ has article on Bosnian cabalist Nehemiah Hayon (1655–1730).

HAYS—Dutch family that emigrated to America in early 18th cent. JE has a family tree and numerous biographies. Also see *Records of the Myers, Hays and Mordecai Families from 1707 to 1913.* Related to ETTEN (or ETTING), LEVY, GRATZ, SARZEDAS, JACOBS, MINIS, WOOD, MEYERS, POST, PEIXOTTO, HERSHFIELD, ZEMANSKY, SULZBERGER, TOURO, DAVID, SOLIS, ADOLPHUS, MEARS, JUDAH, MICHAEL, COHEN, MORDECAI, MYERS and HAAS.

HAYYAT—JE has article on 15th–16th-cent. Spanish cabalist Judah Hayyat.

HAYYIM—JE has biographies from 13th-cent. Spain, 16th-cent. Constantinople, 17th-cent. Smyrna, 18th-cent. Amsterdam. Related to JAFFE and TREVES.

HAYYON—JE has two biographies from 17th–18th-cent. Turkey and Palestine. Possibly related to HAYYUN.

HAYYOT—See HAYYUT.

HAYYUJ—JE has article on Spanish scholar Judah Hayyuj (b. 950 in Morocco), lived in Cordova.

HAYYUN—Sephardic name. JE has biographies from 15th through 18th cent., from Portugal, Bosnia and Palestine. Related to MEDINA and HAGIZ. Perhaps a variation of HAYYON.

HAYYUT (also Hayyot)—JE and UJ have article on Polish Rabbi Menahem Hayyut (or Hayyot) (d. 1636 in Vilna), descended from a pious Provençal family. His grandson Isaac Hayyut died near Lemberg, Galicia, 1726.

HAZAI—UJ has article on Hungarian General Samu Hazai (b. 1851).

HAZAK—JE has article on Italian Rabbi Jacob Hazak (1689–1782).

HAZAN—See HAZZAN.

HAZAZ—UJ has article on writer Hayim Hazaz (b. 1898 in Russia).

HAZKUNI—JE has article on Galician Talmudist Abraham Hazkuni (b. 1627 in Cracow, d. in Syria).

HAZZAN (also Hazan)—Middle Eastern rabbinical family, probably of Spanish origin. The name is derived from the office of overseer *(hazzan),* which an ancestor held. In 1900, members were living in Spain, Smyrna, Alexandria and other eastern Mediterranean cities. JE has a family tree and fourteen biographies, plus two articles on apparently unrelated people from Speyer, 11th cent., and Volhynia, 16th cent. Related to HORWITZ, QUERIDO, ACAN, ALGAZI and PALAGGI. A possible variation is CHAZANOWICZ.

HECHIM—Related to HOCHHEIMER.

HECHT—Ashkenazic name meaning "pike" in German, taken from the picture on the family's house sign. The Hecht family in Boston came from Heinstadt, Germany, in 19th cent. JE has five biographies from Germany and U.S.A. Related to TELLER and KATZ.

HECKSCHER (also Hekscher)—Ashkenazic name taken from the town of Höxter on the Weser River, Germany. JE has biographies from Germany, 17th, 18th and 19th cent. LBIS has a family tree and notes. CAJ has records and a family history. Related to MELCHIOR.

HEDIN—UJ has article on Swedish explorer Sven Hedin (b. 1865). His maternal great-grandfather was Aaron BRODY or Aaron BERLIN. See family history in JFF, No. 27.

HEFEZ—Related to BONAVOGLIO and GENTILI.

HEFTMAN—UJ has article on poet Joseph Heftman (b. 1888 in Poland). His pseudonyms were YOSIPPON and IMMANUEL.

HEIDENHAIN—See HEIDENHEIM.

HEIDENHEIM (also Heidenhain)—JE and EJ have biographies from 18th- and 19th-cent. Germany.

HEIDRICH—CAJ has some family records.

HEIDT—CAJ has a family tree from Prague.

HEIFETZ—UJ has article on Russian violinist Jascha Heifetz (b. 1901).

HEIJERMANS—UJ has article on Dutch writer Hermann Heijermans (1864–1924); pen name Samuel FALKLAND.

HEILBORN—See HEILPRIN.

HEILBRON—See HEILPRIN.

HEILBRONER—See HEILPRIN.

HEILBRONN—See HEILPRIN.

HEILBRUNN—See HEILPRIN.

HEILBUT (also Heilbuth)—JE has articles from 18th-cent. Germany and 19th-cent. France. LBIS has a family tree and notes. Related to WARBURG.

HEILIGMAN—Related to POLLOCK.

HEILPERIN—See HEILPRIN.

HEILPERN—See HEILPRIN.

HEILPRIN (also Halpern, Heilbronn, Heilbrunn, Heilperin, Heilbron, Heilbroner, Heilperin, Heilpern, Heilborn, Halperin, Helpern, Alpron, Galpern, Heilprun, Galperin, Halper, Helpern)—German name derived from the town of Heilbronn in Württemberg. All Jews with variations of this name are not necessarily related; many Jews of Austria, Germany and Russia indiscriminately assumed these names when ordered to take family names (c. 1800). However, there are four distinct branches of the Heilprin name. JE has charts for three branches; many Heilprins in Russia claimed (1900) descent from the fourth branch. The oldest branch dates back to Zebulon Heilprin, 16th cent., whose son Moses of Brest-Litovsk was the father-in-law of Samuel EDELS. Another branch descends from Lithuanian Rabbi Jehiel Heilprin (1660–1746), a descendant of Solomon LURIA, who traced his genealogy back through RASHI (1040–1105). A Heilprin branch is also related to the BAAL SHEMTOB, founder of Hasidism. See numerous biographies in JE, most from Poland, Russia and Germany. Also see EJ article on *Abraham* ben Hayyim of Lublin, Poland (d. 1762), a grandson of ISSER, whose son married FORTIS. CAJ has a Heilprin family tree. LBI has a Heilbrunn family tree beginning 1683. LBIS has notes of a Heilbron family from Posen. CAJ has Halpern family records. Relationships to other prominent rabbinical families can be traced in *Anaf Ez Aboth,* by Samuel Kahan, and *Da'at Kedoshim,* by Israel Eisenstadt. Relatives include KATZENELLENBOGEN, HURWITZ, HOROVITZ, JAFFE, WAHL, HENNIGSON, ORNSTEIN, KAMINSKI, EPSTEIN and RAPHAEL. Also see JE article on Pinsk, Russia, where Samuel Halpern was rabbi.

HEIM—JE has article on Austrian jurist Michael Heim (b. 1852).

HEIMANN—UJ has article on German writer Moritz Heimann (b. 1868). LBI has a family tree beginning 1815, related to FACKENHEIM. CAJ has some family records.

HEIMBURG—Related to DAMROSCH.

HEIMERDINGER—See HEMERDINGER.

HEINE—The family of German poet Heinrich Heine can be traced to Isaac Heine of Hannover (17th cent.). JE has a family tree and other biographies. LBI has Heine family trees beginning 1614, 1682, 1722, 1745. JE article on "Coat of Arms" has the family crest. Also see *Heinrich Heines Stammbaum väterlicherseits; Aus Heinrich Heines Ahnensaal;* and *Heinrich Heines Berliner Verwandte und deren Vorfahren.* Related to GANS, POPERT, NEUWIED, von GELDERN, HALLE, FRIEDMAN, OPPENHEIMER, FURTADO, EMBDEN, MIRAT, ROCCA, MENDELS-SOHN, EPHRAIM, KAULLA, MICHEL, BEHREND, BEROLZHEIMER.

HEINEFETTER—JE has two biographies from 19th-cent. Germany. Related to STOCKL.

HEINEMANN (also Heinmann, Hyneman) —JE has biographies from 19th-cent. Germany. CAJ has a family tree, related to VOGEL, GOTTSCHALK, GOLDSTEIN, BLUMENTHAL, LOWE and SCHIFF. Hyneman is a U.S. family of remote Spanish and modern German origin that came to U.S.A. in 18th cent.; see JE. Its relatives include LOWENGRUND, RHINE, GUMPERT and EZEKIEL. Other related names are SALOMON and HELLMAN.

HEINMANN—See HEINEMANN.

HEINSHEIMER—AJA has a family tree. Related to WERTHEIMER and FREIBERG.

HEISCHELL—JE article on "Coat of Arms" has the family crest.

HEISE—See HEYSE.

HEITLER—JE has article on Austrian physician Moritz Heitler (b. 1847 in Hungary).

HEKSCHER—See HECKSCHER.

HELBO—Related to KARA.

HELD—JE has article on French actress Anna Held (b. 1880), who married Florenz ZIEGFELD Jr. CAJ has some family records.

HELEN—Viennese family. See family history in MGWJ, Vol. 42 (1898), p. 366.

HELFAND—See GELFAND.

HELFMAN—EJ has article on Russian revolutionary Hessia Helfman (1855–1882).

HELFY—UJ has article on Hungarian patriot Ignac Helfy (b. 1830).

HELIC—See HALIC.

HELIN—JE has article on Polish Talmudist Jacob Helin (1625–1700), grandson of Solomon LURIA and son-in-law of Lob HELLER of Satanov.

HELIOT—French family whose ledger has been published by Isidore Loeb; see JE, Vol. 8, p. 290.

HELLER—Polish Rabbi Yom-Tob Lipmann Heller (1579–1654) was born in Bavaria and died in Cracow. He wrote an autobiography and was the ancestor of Russian Rabbi Jehiel Heller (1814–1861). See JE, which also has seven biographies from 19th-cent. Austria, Russia and Hungary. AJA has a family tree beginning 1780. See family histories in *Heller Family Tree; Stammbaum der Familie Mirels-Heller-Frankel;* and *The Descendants of Emanuel Straus and Fanny Heller Straus.* Also see UJ article on *Jacob* Joseph Hakohen. Related to MIRELS, FRANKEL, STRAUS, HELIN, KLEMPERER, MINKOVSKY, SPITZER, BERLIN, EPHRATI, KORNER, MARGOLIS, MANDELBAUM and HUTZLER. A possible variation is GELLER.

HELLMAN (also Helman)—LBI has a family tree beginning 1609. Related to SELIGMAN, SCHIFF, HEINMAN, BACH, KATZENELLENBOGEN, WAHL.

HELMAN—See HELLMAN.

HELPERN—See HEILPRIN.

HELPHAND—UJ has article on Russian journalist Alexander Helphand (b. 1867).

HELTAY (also Heltai)—JE has article on Hungarian deputy Franz Heltay (b. 1861).

HEMENT—JE has article on French educator Felix Hement (1827–1891).

HEMERDINGER (also Heimerdinger)—JE has article on French jurist Michel Hemerdinger (1809–1880). Related to GREENHUT.

HEN—Related to GRACIAN.

HENDLE—JE has article on French statesman Ernest Hendle (1844–1900). Also see HENLE.

HENDRICKS—See HENRIQUES.

HENGSHULER—Related to ROTHSCHILD.

HENGSTENBERG—JE has article on German scholar Ernst Hengstenberg (1802–1869).

HENIKSTEIN—JE has article on Austrian general Alfred Henikstein (1810–1882).

HENLE—JE has four biographies from 18th- and 19th-cent. Germany. See family history in MGWJ, No. 62 (1918), p. 223. Related to OTTENHEIMER, LEVI, BERLIN and LEBOLD.

HENNIGSON—LBI has a family tree beginning 1800.

HENOCH (also Henochs)—JE has biographies from 16th-cent. Palestine and 19th-cent. Germany.

HENRIK—PD has family records.

HENRIQUES (also Henriquez, Hendricks, Enriquez, Enriques)—American family connected with families of the same name in London and Amsterdam, of Sephardic origin. It's descended from Jacob Henriques, who settled in Jamaica in early 18th cent. JE has family trees and biographies for both Henriques and Hendricks families. Also see its articles on Spanish poetess Isabella Henriquez (d. 1680), who settled in Amsterdam, and the Enriquez family, 15th-cent. Marranos who may be ancestors of Henriques. LBIS has a Henriques family tree. JE article on "Coat of arms" has the Enriques family crest. Also see *Stamtavlen Henriques, 1725–1948.* Related to QUIXANO, GUTTEREZ, LEON, MESQUITA, MELDOLA, MENDES, COSTA, WARBURG, ABOAB, de SOLA, CHAVES, GOMEZ, LOPEZ, LEVY, ISAACS, JUDAH, NATHAN and numerous others in U.S.A.

HENRIQUEZ—See HENRIQUES.

HENRY—JE has three biographies from 19th-cent. England and U.S.A. AJA has a family tree. Related to LYON, LINDO and de SOLA.

HENSCHEL (also Hensel)—Ashkenazic name derived from the female name Hannah. JE has three biographies from Germany, 18th and 19th cent. Also see biography in EJ article on "Art." Related to MENDELSSOHN and ITZIG.

HENSEL—See HENSCHEL.

HEPNER (also Heppner)—JE has article on German-American journalist Adolf Hepner (b. 1846 in Posen). CAJ has Heppner family records.

HERBERT—UJ has biographies from Poland and Rumania, 19th cent.

HERBST—EJ has article on Bulgarian Zionist Karl Herbst (1865–1919).

HERCZEG (also Herczeghy)—UJ has biographies from Hungary, 19th cent.

HERCZEL—See HIRSCH.

HERLITZ—UJ has article on historian Georg Herlitz (b. 1885 in Germany). CAJ has some family records.

HERMALIN—UJ has article on writer David Hermalin (b. 1865 in Rumania).

HERMAN (also Hermann)—JE and UJ have biographies from 19th-cent. Germany and Hungary. Related to LEBRECHT. Also see HERRMANN.

HERON—Related to MONTEFIORE.

HERRERA (also de Herrera)—JE has article on Spanish cabalist Alonzo de Herrera (d. 1631 in Holland). He may be descended from the famous Spanish commander Fernandez Gonzalo de Cordova. Related to ERRERA and CARABAJAL.

HERRMAN (also Herrmann)—JE and UJ have biographies from U.S.A., France, Czechoslovakia and England, 19th cent.

HERSCH—See HIRSCH.

HERSCHBERG—See HIRSCHBERG.

HERSCHEL—See HIRSCHEL.

HERSCHELL—See HIRSCHEL.

HERSCHMAN—See HIRSCHMANN.

HERSHFIELD—See HIRSCHFELD.

HERSTEIN—UJ has article on painter Adolf Herstein (b. 1869 in Poland).

HERTZ—See HERZ.

HERTZBERG—See HERZBERG.

HERTZKA—See HERZ.

HERTZVELD—See HERZFELD.

HERXHEIMER—JE has article on German Rabbi Salomon Herxheimer (1801–1884).

HERZ (also Hertz, Hertzka, Herzl)—Ashkenazic name that means "stag" in German; variations in other languages are HARTWIG, HARRIS, CERF and JELLINEK, although these are not necessarily related. JE has biographies from 18th- and 19th-cent. Germany, Austria, France, Denmark and Hungary. EJ article on Theodor Herzl (1860–1904) contains his ancestry. CAJ has Hertz family tree. LBIS has notes of a Hertz family related to HILDESHEIM. LBI has a Herzl family tree beginning 1761. For family histories, see JFF, Nos. 6, 15 and 27; also *The Descendants of Anschel Herz of Bonn; Zur Geschichte der Familie Herz in Weilburg; Fünfhundert Jahre Familiengeschichte, 1430–1930;* and *Theodor Herzls väterliche und mütterliche Vorfahren.* Related to SARONY, de LEMOS, ROTHSCHILD, BIALEH, OPPEN-

HEIM, ARNSTEIN, von LAEMEL, LEIDESDORFER, GREENBAUM, KAHN, LEBOLD, BEREND, MOSES, DIAMANT, ABELES, HABER, BILIZ, FEISHEL, FALIO, SIMON, FRUMMET, SHALOM and GLAZER.

HERZBERG (also Herzberg-Frankel, Hertzberg)—JE has biographies from Galicia and Russia, 19th cent. Related to FRANKEL.

HERZENSTEIN—JE has two biographies from Russia, 19th cent.

HERZFELD (also Hertzveld, Harzveld)—JE has biographies from Germany and Holland, 18th and 19th cent. Also see biography in EJ article on "Dutch Literature." CAJ has Herzfeld family records. Related to STEGMANN, SIMMONS, STADTHAGEN, POSTRELKO, LOWENSTAMM and HIJMANS.

HERZOG—JE has article on Austrian writer Jacob Herzog (b. 1842). LBI has a family tree beginning 1768. Also see *Herzog and Lambert Genealogy;* this Herzog family later became HARTZELL. Related to SULZBERGER and MAUROIS.

HES—LBI has a family tree beginning 1742.

HESCHEL—EJ has article on Lithuanian Talmudist Abraham Heschel (d. 1664). Related to MUNZ, FLECKELES and ETTINGER.

HESS (also Hesse, Hessen)—Ashkenazic name meaning one from the district of Hessen or Hesse, Germany. JE and UJ have biographies from 18th-cent. Germany and 19th-cent. Germany, France and Russia. German educator Michael Hess (1782–1860) was the son of Michael Hess KUGELMANN. German socialist Moses Hess (1812–1875) had a Polish grandfather. Related to SAMUEL.

HESSBERG—JE has article on U.S. lawyer Albert Hessberg (b. 1856).

HESSE—See HESS.

HESSEN—See HESS.

HEVESI (also Hevesy)—JE and UJ have biographies from 19th-cent. Hungary.

HEYDEMANN—JE has article on German archaeologist Heinrich Heydemann (1849–1889).

HEYDENFELDT—JE has article on U.S. jurist Solomon Heydenfeldt (1816–1890).

HEYDENREICH—See *Handbuch der Genealogie,* by Eduard Heydenreich.

HEYMAN (also Heymann, Heymans)—JE and EJ have biographies from 19th-cent. Germany, Holland and Sweden. LBIS has a family tree and notes from Göteborg, Sweden. LBI has Heymann family trees beginning 1790 and 1804.

HEYMANS—See HEYMAN.

HEYSE (also Heise)—EJ has article on German author Paul Heyse (1830–1914). Related to ITZIG.

HICHENBERG—CAJ has a family tree from Germany.

HICKL—EJ has article on Moravian Zionist Max Hickl (1873–1924).

HIGGER—UJ has article on Rabbi Michael Higger (b. 1898 in Lithuania).

HIJMANS—Related to HERTZVELD.

HILAROWICZ—Related to NUSBAUM.

HILBERG—JE has article on Austrian philologist Isidor Hilberg (b. 1852 in the Ukraine).

HILBERT—Related to JUDAH.

HILDESHEIM (also Hildesheimer)—Ashkenazic name derived from the German town of Hildesheim in the province of Hannover. JE has biographies from Germany, 17th and 19th cent. CAJ has some Hildesheimer family records. Related to GREENHUT, HERTZ and HIRSCH.

HILF—UJ has article on U.S. writer Mary Hilf (b. 1874 in Russia). See her autobiography, *No Time for Tears.*

HILFERDING—UJ has article on German statesman Rudolf Hilferding (b. 1877 in Vienna).

HILFSTEIN—UJ has article on physician Chaim Hilfstein (b. 1877 in Cracow).

HILLEL—The Talmudic authority Hillel I, or Hillel the Great, was born in Babylonia c. 70 B.C.E. and died in Jerusalem c. 10 C.E. According to tradition, he is descended from King David through David's son Shephatiah. Another tradition holds that Hillel's grandson Gamaliel the Elder was the great-grandfather of Johanan ha-Sandalar of 2nd-cent. Egypt, who was in turn the ancestor (thirty-three generations removed) of RASHI (1040–1105). This descendance (see chart on page 12)

was apparently dreamed up in 17th-cent. Italy, and serious scholars say it is total nonsense. Nevertheless, numerous Jews use it to claim descent from Hillel and King David. One claim worth considering is that of Ben Meir, Palestinian rabbi of 9th and 10th cent., whose family traced its descent to Hillel; see UJ article on Ben Meir. Also see ABRAVANEL.

HILLER—JE has two biographies from 19th-cent. Germany.

HILLION—See AYLLON.

HILLMAN—UJ has article on labor leader Sidney Hillman (b. 1887 in Lithuania). AJA has notes on his family.

HILLQUIT—JE has article on U.S. lawyer Morris Hillquit (1869–1933), born in Riga. See his autobiography, *Loose Leaves from a Busy Life.*

HILSNER—CAJ has some family records.

HIMMELBLAU—German name meaning "sky-blue."

HINDUS—UJ has article on writer Maurice Hindus (b. 1891 in Russia).

HIPP—CAJ has some family records.

HIRSCH (also Hersch, Hirschel, Hirschl, Herczel, Herschell, etc.)—Ashkenazic name meaning "stag" in German; other variations, not necessarily related, are HERZ, CERF, HARRIS and JELLINEK. JE, UJ and EJ have numerous biographies from 18th- and 19th-cent. Austria, France, Germany, Hungary, England, Lithuania and U.S.A. LBI has family trees beginning 1708, 1765, 1783, 1787 and 1816. LBIS has a family tree and notes from Stockholm, related to LAZARUS. AJA has family trees from Cincinnati and Memphis. JE article on "Coat of Arms" has the family crest. A Hirsch family is related to major Ashkenazic rabbinical families in *Reshimoth Aboth,* by Markus Seckbach. See family histories in JJLG, 1926, and *Die Familie von Hirsch auf Gereuth.* Related to HILDESHEIMER, GOLDSCHMIDT, BISCHOFFSHEIM, WEHLE, WERTHEIMER, FRANKFURTER, KUHN, EISENSTADT, EINHORN, GUNZBURG, MENDELSON, SELIGMAN, BIESENTHAL, BREUER, SZTERENYI, LOVINGER, WEINBERGER, GOLDSMITH, LOEB, LEVIN, WARBURG, EMDEN and WAHL. Also see HIRSHEL, HIRSCHS.

HIRSCHBEIN—UJ has article on poet Perez Hirschbein (b. 1880 in Russia).

HIRSCHBERG (also Herschberg)—JE and UJ have biographies from 19th-cent. Germany and Poland. LBI has a family tree beginning 1884. CAJ has some family records. Related to JAFFE. Also see HIRSZENBERG.

HIRSCHEL—See HIRSCH.

HIRSCHENSOHN (also Hirschenson)—JE has article on Talmudist Isaac Hirschensohn of Palestine (b. 1844 in Russia). Related to LICHTENSTEIN and POOL.

HIRSCHFELD (also Hirschfelder, Hirschfeldt, Hershfield)—JE and UJ have biographies from 19th-cent. Germany, Poland, Austria, England and U.S.A. LBI has family trees beginning 1767, 1771, 1780, 1817 and 1829. Related to AUERBACH, ARON, EHRLICH, HAYS, THORSCH and WAHL. Another variation of the name may be HERZFELD. Also see HIRSZFELD.

HIRSCHHORN—Ashkenazic name taken from the town of Hirschhorn on the Neckar River, Germany. Also see HIRSZHORN.

HIRSCHKAHN—UJ has article on Russian writer Zvi Hirschkahn (b. 1886).

HIRSCHL—See HIRSCH.

HIRSCHLAFF—LBIS has family notes.

HIRSCHLAND—LBI has a family tree beginning 1545. Also see *Die Familie Hirschland*.

HIRSCHLER—JE has article on Hungarian oculist Ignaz Hirschler (1823–1891).

HIRSCHMANN (also Herschman)—JE has article on French composer Henri Hirschmann (b. 1873). Related to MANNHEIMER. Also see HIRSHMAN.

HIRSCHS—LBIS has a family tree. Also see HIRSCH.

HIRSCHSPRUNG—19th-cent. Danish family; see JE.

HIRSHEL—EJ has article on Austrian functionary Meyer Hirshel (d. 1674). See also HIRSCH.

HIRSHMAN—JE has article on Russian oculist Leonard Hirshman (b. 1839). Also see HIRSCHMANN.

HIRSZENBERG—JE has article on Polish painter Samuel Hirszenberg (b. 1866). The name is a Polish variation of HIRSCHBERG.

HIRSZFELD—Polish variation of HIRSCHFELD. UJ has article on Polish bacteriologist Ludwik Hirszfeld (b. 1883).

HIRSZHORN—Polish variation of HIRSCHHORN. UJ has article on Polish author Samuel Hirszhorn (b. 1889).

HIRSZOWICZ—EJ has article on 18th-cent. Polish merchant Abraham Hirszowicz.

HIRZ—Related to HART.

HITZIG—See ITZIG.

HLADIK—JE has article on 13th-cent. Bohemian Talmudist Abraham Hladik.

HOCHHEIM (also Hechim, Hochheimer)—Bavarian family of Hochheimer is named for its original home in Hochheim, Germany. It dates to 18th cent. and has some members in U.S.A. American Rabbi Henry Hochheimer was born 1818 in Ansbach, Germany; his maternal grandfather was Meyer ELLINGER. JE has six biographies.

HOCHMUTH—JE has article on Hungarian Rabbi Abraham Hochmuth (1816–1889).

HOCHSCHILD—UJ has article on Bolivian executive Mauricio Hochschild (b. 1881 in Germany).

HOCHSTADTER (also Hochstaedter, Hochstetter)—JE has article on German Rabbi Benjamin Hochstadter (1810–1888). LBI has a Hochstaedter family tree beginning 1760, related to EDINGER. Another related name is KAHN.

HOCK—JE has article on Austrian writer Simon Hock (1815–1887), born in Prague. Related to VEITH.

HODARA—UJ has article on Turkish author Menahem Hodara (1869–1926).

HOENIGSBURG—A Bohemian-Austrian family traced back to 18th cent. Also known as KAPP. See EJ.

HOFF—LBIS has some family notes.

HOFFA (also Hoffer)—JE and UJ have biographies from Germany and Hungary, 19th cent.

HOFFER—See HOFFA.

HOFFMANN (also Hoffman, Hofmann, Hofmannsthal)—JE and UJ have biographies from 18th- and 19th-cent. Germany, Hungary, Austria, Lithuania, Czechoslovakia and U.S.A. Merchant Isaak Hofmann (b. 1759 in Prague, d. 1849 in Vienna) was the grandfather of Hugo Hofmannsthal; see UJ. LBI has a Hofmann family tree beginning 1802, related to APPEL. PD has Hofmannsthal family records. JE article on "Coat of Arms" has a Hoffmann family crest. See Hoffman family history in *Die Siegburger Familie Levison.* See Hofmann family history in ZGJT, No. 2 (1931). See Hofmannsthal family history in JFF, No. 19.

HOFHEIMER—UJ has article on U.S. merchant Nathan Hofheimer (1848–1921), born in Germany. Also see *The Descendants of Moses Son of Naphtali of Hofheim, or Moses Hofheimer, 1781–1962.*

HOFMANN—See HOFFMANN.

HOFMANNSTHAL—See HOFFMANN.

HOFSTADTER—UJ has article on U.S. lawyer Samuel Hofstadter (b. 1894 in Poland).

HOFSTEIN—UJ has article on poet David Hofstein (b. 1889 in Russia).

HOGA—EJ has article on Polish translator Stanislau Hoga (1791–1860).

HOHEB—Related to de SOLA.

HOHENSTAUFEN—See family history in JFF, No. 23.

HOHENTHAL—Related to JONAS.

HOLDHEIM—JE has article on German Rabbi Samuel Holdheim (1806–1860). CAJ has some family records.

HOLITSCHER—JE and UJ have biographies from 19th-cent. Hungary.

HOLLAENDERSKI—See HOLLANDER.

HOLLANDER (also Hollaenderski)—Ashkenazic name meaning "one who comes from Holland." JE has biographies from Poland, Germany and U.S.A., 19th cent. CAJ has some family records.

von HOLTEN—Related to SAMSON.

HOLTZ (also Holz)—LBI has a Holz family tree beginning 1773, related to THEMAL. CAJ has some family records.

HOLZBERG—Related to SOLOVEICHIK.

HOLZMANN—JE has article on Austrian historian Michael Holzmann (b. 1860 in Moravia).

HOMBERG (also Homburg, Homburger)—JE has article on Austrian educator Herz Homberg (1749–1841), born near Prague. CAJ has some family records. LBI has a Homburger family tree beginning 1694. CAJD has a family tree from Germany. Related to HESSE. The name is a possible variation of HAMBURGER.

HOMEM (also Homen)—Sephardic name. JE and UJ have articles on Portuguese martyr Antonio Homem (d. 1624). His father was Vaez BRANDAO, his mother was a granddaughter of Nunez CARDOZO, and his grandfather was Moses BOINO. Related to ACOSTA and NUNEZ.

HOMIYOTH—JE has article on Berosh Homiyoth, pen name of Naphtali NEUMANOVITZ.

HOND—UJ has article on Dutch Rabbi Meijer de Hond (b. 1882).

HONIG (also Honigman, Honigsmann)—Ashkenazic name meaning "honey" in German. JE and UJ have biographies from 18th- and 19th-cent. Austria, Germany, Rumania and Galicia. PD has some family records. JE article on "Coat of Arms" has the family crest. Related to BUSH and FRANKEL.

HONOR—UJ has article on U.S. educator Leo Honor (b. 1894 in Russia).

HOPF—LBI has a family tree beginning 1794, related to TUCHMANN.

HORE-BELISHA—See BELISHA.

HORN (also Hornbostel, Hornthal)—JE and UJ have biographies from 18th–19th-cent. Germany and Austria. Also see EJ article on Ignaz EINHORN.

HORODENKER—JE article on *Nahman* ben Simhah of Bratzlav refers to his great-grandfather, Rabbi Nahman Horodenker.

HORODEZKY—UJ has article on author Samuel Horodezky (b. 1871 in Russia), a direct descendant of Rabbi Israel the BAAL SHEMTOB, founder of Hasidism.

HOROVIC—See HOROVITZ.

HOROVICZ—See HOROVITZ.

HOROVITZ (also Horowitz, Horwitz, Hurwitz, Horowicz, Horvitz, Hurwitz, Hurvitz, Gurvich, Gurewicz, Gurwicz, Gorwitz, Hourwitz, Harrwitz, Urwicz, etc.)—Ashkenazic name derived from the Bohemian town of Horovice, from which this Levite family emigrated in 15th cent. The name is traced back to Isaiah ben Moses ha-Levi Horowitz. Subsequent forms of the name depend on where members of the family settled; Russian forms, for example, are Gorwitz, Gurwicz and Gurewicz. From 16th cent. onward, Horovitz was a prominent and widely related rabbinical family. Phinehas Horowitz (b. 1731 in Poland, d. 1805 in Frankfurt-am-Main) was descended from a long line of rabbinical ancestors; he married the daughter of Joel HEILPERN. Shabbetai Horowitz (1590–1660) married the daughter of Moses HARIF of Lublin; Isaiah Horowitz (1555–1630) married the daughter of Abraham MAUL of Vienna. JE, UJ and EJ have extensive biographies from 16th cent. onward. LBI has a Horovitz family tree beginning 1733. CAJ has a Horovitz family tree covering 1599–1930, related to ETTLINGER and FREIMANN. PD has Horowitz family records. CAJ has a Horvitz family tree, related to FREYHAN. The family's relationships to other prominent rabbinical families in Eastern Europe can be traced in *Anaf Ez Aboth,* by Samuel Kahan. For family histories, see ZGJT, No. 2 (1931); also *Toledot Mishpahat Hurwitz* and *Directory and Genealogy of the Horowitz-Margareten Family.* Also see EJ article on *Eliezer* ben Jacob ha-Levi; JE articles on Pinsk, Grodno and Posen; UJ article on *Jacob Isaac* of Lublin; and EJ article on *Abraham* Hayyim (1750–1816). Related to MEYERSON, HAZZAN, SCHIFF, HEILPRIN, POCHAPOVSKY, LEWINSOHN, KATZENELLENBOGEN, BERNARD, HUBERT, KROCHMAL, WAHL, MARGARETEN and DAN.

HOROWICZ—See HOROVITZ.

HOROWITZ—See HOROVITZ.

HORSCHETZKY—JE has article on Austrian physician Moritz Horschetzky (1788–1859).

HORT—EJ has article on New Zealand Jewish pioneer Abraham Hort (1790–1869).

HORVITZ—See HOROVITZ.

HORWITZ—See HOROVITZ.

HOS—UJ has article on Zionist leader Dov Hos (1894–1941), born in Russia.

HOSCHANDER—UJ has article on archaeologist Jacob Hoschander (1874–1933), born in Austria.

HOSCHEL—UJ has article on Polish Rabbi Abraham Hoschel (1765–1825).

HOSHKE—JE has article on Rabbi Reuben Hoshke of Prague (d. 1673).

HOSKINS—Related to COOPER.

HOURWICH—See HOROVITZ.

HOURWITZ—See HOROVITZ.

HOUSEMAN—See HAUSSMANN.

HOXTER—CAJ has a family tree from Germany.

HOZIN—EJ has article on Iraqi Rabbi Zedekiah Hozin (1699–1773).

HUARTE de SAN JUAN—EJ has article on Sephardic author Juan Huarte de San Juan (1529–1589) of Navarre.

HUBERMANN—UJ has article on violinist Bronislaw Hubermann (b. 1882 in Poland).

HUBERT—UJ has article on inventor Conrad Hubert (1860–1928), born HOROWITZ in Russia.

HUBNER—Galician name; see UJ.

HUBSCH (also Huebsch)—Meaning "pretty" in German. JE has article on U.S. preacher Adolph Hubsch (1830–1884), born in Hungary, descended from the JAFFE family.

HUDSON—Related to SCHIFF.

HUGO—Related to BERNSTEIN.

HUHNER—UJ has article on U.S. lawyer Leon Huhner (b. 1871 in Germany).

HULDSCHINER (also Huldschinsky)—UJ has article on novelist Richard Huldschiner (1872–1931), born in Germany. LBI has a Huldschinsky family tree beginning 1864, related to ARNHOLD.

HULDSCHINSKY—See HULDSCHINER.

HUNTERBERG—UJ has article on U.S. author Max Hunterberg (b. 1883 in Russia).

HUREWITZ—See HOROVITZ.

HURST—UJ has article on U.S. author Fannie Hurst (b. 1889).

HURTADO de MENDOZA—JE article on "Coat of Arms" has the family crest.

HURVITZ—See HOROVITZ.

HURWITZ—See HOROVITZ.

HUSAIN—JE has article on 16th-cent. Talmudist Immanuel Husain.

HUSIK—UJ has article on U.S. philosopher Isaac Husik (1876–1939), born in Russia.

HUSS—Related to THON.

HUSSAKOF—UJ has article on U.S. zoologist Louis Hussakof (b. 1881 in Russia).

HUSSERL—UJ has article on German philosopher Eduard Husserl (1859–1938).

HUSSY—Related to ROSENSTOCK.

HUTH—JE has article on German scholar Georg Huth (1867–1906).

HUTZLER—AJA has a family tree beginning 18th cent., related to HELLER, WOMBACHER. Also see family history in *Hutzler.*

HUVOS—UJ has article on Hungarian economist Jozsef Huvos (1838–1914).

HYAMS (also Hyamson)—JE and UJ have biographies from Russia, England, U.S.A. and India, 19th cent. Related to BENJAMIN.

HYE—CAJ has a family tree from Austria, beginning 19th cent.

HYMAN (also Hymans)—UJ has six biographies from Holland, Belgium and U.S.A., 19th and 20th cent. Related to PHILLIPS.

HYMERVITCH—Related to LIST.

HYNEMAN—See HEINEMANN.

IBN ABBAS—EJ has article on 13th-cent. Spanish writer Judah Ibn Abbas.

IBN AL-BARQULI—13th-cent. Babylonian family; see EJ.

IBN ALFAKHAR—Family originally from Spain, 12th cent. See EJ.

IBN DANA—See ABENDANA.

IBN DAUD—See ALBALIA.

IBN EZRA—EJ has article on Spanish poet Abraham Ibn Ezra (1089–1164).

IBN GHAYYAT—Family of poets from Lucena, 11th cent. See EJ.

IBN MENASHEH—See family history in *Jose Millas-Vallicrosa commemorative book.* Also see ABENMENASSE.

IBN SHOSHAN—Family of Toledo, Spain, in 12th cent.; see EJ. Related to SASSOON.

IBN WAQAR—13th-cent. Castilian family; see EJ.

IBN YAHYA—See family history in *Sefer Dibre ha-Yamim.* Also see JACHIA.

IDELSOHN—UJ has biographies from Russia and Lithuania, 19th and 20th cent.

IGEL—See IGLAUER.

IGLAUER (also Igel)—Name derived from the town of Iglauer, Moravia. JE and UJ have biographies from Austria and U.S.A., 19th–20th cent. LBI has an Iglauer family tree beginning 1805, related to TUCHMANN.

IGNACE—UJ has article on French deputy Eduard Ignace (1862–1924).

IGNOTUS—UJ has article on Hungarian writer Hugo Ignotus (b. 1869).

IGRA—EJ has article on Hungarian Rabbi Moses Igra (1752–1802).

IGUDICH—Related to JUDAH.

IKLE—LBIS has a family tree.

ILIER—Related to BRUDNO.

ILIOWIZI—JE has article on U.S. Rabbi Henry Iliowizi (b. 1850 in Russia).

ILLESCOS—JE has article on 14th-cent. Bible commentator Jacob di Illescos.

ILLOVY—See ILLOWY.

ILLOWAY—See ILLOWY.

ILLOWY (also Illovy, Illoway)—U.S. Rabbi Bernhard Illowy (1814–1871), born in Bohemia, was descended from a family of Talmudists first known in 17th-cent. Bohemia. His son was Henry Illoway. See JE, UJ and EJ. Related to EHRENSTAMM.

ILNA'E—EJ has article on Lithuanian philosopher Eliezer Ilna'e (1885–1929), also known as SCHOENBAUM.

ILYIN—Related to GADIN.

IMBER—JE has article on Austrian poet Naphtali Imber (1856–1909), born in Galicia.

IMRI—Related to FEYGENBERG.

dels INFANZ—See degli ADOLESCENTOLI.

INFELD—UJ has article on physicist Leopold Infeld (b. 1898 in Poland).

INSELBUCH—UJ has article on Rabbi Elias Inselbuch (1866–1936), born in Poland.

INSLER—UJ has article on Galician lawyer Abraham Insler (1894–1938).

INSTONE—UJ has article on English industrialist Samuel Instone (1878–1937).

IOFAN—See JOFAN.

IOFFE—See JAFFE.

IRAQI—Yemenite-Indian family name dating from 18th cent. EJ has three biographies.

ISAAC (also Isaaci, Isaacks, Isaacs, Isaacsohn, Isak, etc.)—JE, UJ and EJ have numerous biographies, beginning with Jacob Isaac of Poland (d. 1510), and German writer Johann Isaac (1515–1577). LBI has Isaac family trees beginning 1787 and 1808. LBIS also has an Isaac family tree. AJA has an Isaacs family tree beginning 1750. CAJ has Isak family records. Isak family histories can be found in JFF, Nos. 22 and 23. Related to LANDAU, BATTISTA, LELOV, ALTSCHULER, HAROLD, AZULAI, LEO, MONTEFIORE, GOMEZ, BARNATO, SOLOMON, MARKS, READING and COHEN.

ISAACI—See ISAAC.

ISAACKS—See ISAAC.

ISAACS—See ISAAC.

ISAACSOHN (Isaacson)—See ISAAC.

ISAK—See ISAAC.

ISAYEV—Related to GADEN.

ISBITZKI—UJ has article on labor leader Joseph Isbitzki (1876–1928), born in Lithuania.

ISCANDARI—Family of Talmudists in Egypt, 17th and 18th cent. See EJ.

ISCOVESCU—JE has article on Rumanian painter Barbu Iscovescu (1816–1854).

ISIDOR—JE has article on French Rabbi Lazard Isidor (1813–1888), grandson of Hirsch KATZENELLENBOGEN.

ISLER—JE has article on German philologist Meyer Isler (1807–1888). CAJ has family records.

ISRAEL (also Israeli, Israels, Israelsohn, Israelson, etc.)—Eastern Mediterranean family of rabbis and authors prominent in Alexandria, Jerusalem and Rhodes, 18th cent. See JE and UJ, which also have un-related biographies from 17th-cent. Russia, 18th-cent. Germany and Egypt, and 19th-cent. Holland, Latvia and U.S.A. JE also has Israeli biographies from 14th-cent. Spain, and 9th- and 10th-cent. Egypt. LBIS has Israel family notes. AJA has an Israel family tree (Midshipman Joseph Israel) beginning 1692. Related to MONTEFIORE, ESCUDERO, MELDOLA, EZEKIAL, SAMUEL, KRESPIN, ELLIS and MOSKOWITZ.

ISRAELI—See ISRAEL.

ISRAELS—See ISRAEL.

ISRAELSOHN (Israelson)—See ISRAEL.

ISSACHAR—Related to BAER and KAHANA.

ISSAR—See ISSERLES.

ISSER—See ISSERLES.

ISSERL—See ISSERLES.

ISSERLEIN (Isserlin)—See ISSERLES.

ISSERLES (also Issar, Isser, Isserl, Isserlein, Isserlin)—Ashkenazic rabbinic name derived from ISRAEL. Polish Rabbi Moses Isserles (1520–1572) was the son-in-law of Shalom SHEKNA, rabbi of Lublin, and was related to Solomon LURIA and Meir KATZENELLENBOGEN. See JE, UJ and EJ. Israel Isserlein, German Talmudist of 14th and 15th cent., was the nephew of Aaron BLUMLEIN. CAJ has an Isserl family tree from Cracow, Poland, beginning 16th cent. Related to AUERBACH, DEMBITZER, SHAKNA, LICHTENFELD, MENDELSSOHN, TEITELBAUM, MEISELS, WULFF, GREENHUT, LEVINSON, MORPURGO, MINTZ, HEILPRIN and FRIEDLAND. Also see JE articles on relatives *Moses* ben Isaac Bonems and *Naphtali* ben David.

ISTEL—UJ has article on musicologist Edgar Istel (b. 1880 in Germany).

ISTRUMSA—EJ has article on Greek Rabbi Hayyim Istrumsa (18th–19th cent.).

ITALIA—UJ has article on 17th-cent. Dutch engraver Shalom Italia.

ITELSON—UJ has article on scholar Gregor Itelson (1852–1926), born in Russia.

ITTINGA—Related to ORNSTEIN.

ITZIG (also Hitzig)—German family dating from 18th cent. EJ has a family tree; JE has eighteen biographies. LBI has family trees beginning 1200, 1500, 1609, 1720 and

1679. See family history in JFF, No. II. Related to BARTHOLDY, MENDELSSOHN, FRIEDLANDER, ESKELES, LEVI, BONEM, BORNHEIM, OPPENHEIM, OPPENFELD, ARNSTEIN, JAFFE, LEVY, DESSAU, WULF, KUGLER, HEYSE, BAYER (or BAEYER), RIBBECK, ERMAN, ETZEL, DOVE, SALOMON, HENSEL, DIRICHLET, SAALING, ROTHSCHILD, PEREIRA, FRIES, EPHRAIM, and WOLFERS.

ITZSCHE—Related to ETTINGER.

IVANYI-GRUNWALD—UJ has article on Hungarian painter Bela Ivanyi-Grunwald (1867–1940). Related to GRUNWALD.

IZBICA-RADZYN—EJ has article on 19th-cent. Hasidic dynasty.

JABALI—JE has article on 10th-cent. Karaite scholar Abu al-Tayyib al Jabali, also known as Samuel ben MANSUR.

JABEZ—JE has biographies from 15th-cent. Spain and Portugal and 16th-cent. Turkey. Related to ASHKENAZI.

JABOTINSKY—UJ has article on writer Vladimir Jabotinsky (1880–1940), born in Russia.

JACHIA—Portuguese family descended from *Yahya* ibn Ya'isch, 11th cent. See JE article on Yahya; also CB, p. 3059; and JFF, No. II. Also see IBN YAHYA. Related to COSTA.

JACKLIN (also Jaecklin)—JE has article on 14th-cent. financier Jacob Jacklin of Ulm. Related to EHINGEN.

JACKS—See JACOBS.

JACKSON—JE and UJ have biographies from 19th-cent. England and U.S.A. AJA has a family tree beginning 1787.

JACOB (also Jacobs, Jacks, Jacobi, Jacobke, Jacobovich, Jacobowitz, Jacobowsky, Jacobsen, Jacobsohn, Jacobson, Jacobsson, Jacobsthal, Jacoby, Jacobber, etc.)—Family name that can be found as early as 12th cent. (in England) and 14th cent. (in France and Austria). JE, UJ and EJ have numerous biographies for all variations of the name. CAJ has a Jacob family tree from Germany and Denmark, covering 1620 to 1924 and related to UNNA, PHILIPP and MICHAEL. LBI has Jacobi family trees beginning 1767 and 1786, one of which is related to WITKOW-

SKI. AJA has a Jacobi family tree from New York and South Carolina, beginning 1790. LBIS has Jacobowitz and Jacobsson family notes. AJA has a Jacobs family tree from Prussia, beginning 1828, related to JACKS; and a Jacobson family tree beginning 1879, related to MUSHKIN and KROSKAL. CAJ has Jacoby family records. See family history in *Geschichte der Familie Unna (Hamburg-Kopenhagen)*. Related to ARCHIVOLTI, AUERBACH, OPPENHEIMER, BER, LANDAU, ROSENTHAL, d'AVIGDOR, PHILLIPS, HAYS, NONES, MELCHIOR, SAMSON. Also see JACUBOVIC.

JACOR—Related to ROMANIN.

JACQUES—JE has article on Austrian deputy Heinrich Jacques (1831–1894). Related to NONES.

JACUBOVICH—CAJ has family records. See also JACOB.

JADASSOHN—JE has two biographies from Germany, 19th cent.

JADKONSKY—CAJ has a family tree from Germany.

JADLOWKER—UJ has article on singer Hermann Jadlowker (b. 1878 in Latvia).

JAECKEL—LBI has a family tree beginning 1757.

JAECKLIN—See JACKLIN.

JAFFA—See JAFFE.

JAFFE (also Jaffa, Jaffin, Joffe, Joffin, Ioffe)—Widespread rabbinic family whose branches in Italy, Russia, Austria, Germany, U.S.A. and Britain all descend from Mordecai Jaffe of Prague (1530–1612) and his uncle Moses Jaffe, who traced their ancestry to Samuel ben Elhanan, great-grandson of RASHI (1040–1105). The name is Hebrew for "beautiful." JE has 132 biographies; UJ and EJ have numerous articles as well. LBI has a family tree beginning 1650. CAJ has a family tree from Germany covering 1762 to 1928 and related to BERNHARD. PD has family records. See family history in CB, p. 2919; also *Der Schweriner Oberrabiner Mordechai Jaffe, seine Ahnen und Nachkommen.* Related to ITZIG, SINGER, MEIER, MARGOLIES, SCHLESINGER, ROSENTHAL, WALLERSTEIN, SABA, KALMANKES, ABRAHAM, ZALMAN, ASHKENAZI, SIRKES, BACH, WAHL, EPSTEIN, GUNZBURG, ABERL, HALFON, ZUNDEL, LAIT, DAVIS,

OPPERT, ENDELMAN, BER, SILBERSTROM, KEIDANY, HAYYIM, MEYER, FUCHS, MAMROTH, ZUTA, WALSH, LOB, HARKAVY, MEYERBEER, ASCHER, KALONYMUS, FRIEDLANDER, BAUKSER, RIESSER, GINZBERG, HEILPRIN, SERED, AARON, LANDAU, WOLF, WEKSLER, KALMAN, ZEDEK, MARGOLIOTH, LEWINSTEIN, MASKILEISON, HASID, BACHARACH, PREHNER, ABELE, RABINOWITZ, HUBSCH, ROSENBERG, SOLOVEICHIK, RAGOLER, PLUNGIAN, OLSCHWANGER, SCHAFFER, KOOK and DEBORIN. Also see JE article on *Moses* ben Issachar (Moravia, 17th cent.), a nephew of Mordecai Jaffe.

JAFFIN—See JAFFE.

JAGEL—JE has two biographies from Italy, 17th cent.

JAMA—EJ has article on 12th-cent. North African scholar Samuel Ibn Jama.

JAMAL—EJ has article on Yemenite Solomon Jamal (d. 1666).

JAMES—JE has article on English actor David James (1839–1893), also known as BELASCO. Related to MONTEFIORE.

JAMPEL—UJ has article on Rabbi Siegmund Jampel (b. 1874 in Galicia).

JANNER—CAJ has some family records.

JANOSI—PD has some family records.

JANOWER (also Janowski, Janowsky)—JE and UJ have biographies from Poland and Russia, 19th and 20th cent. Also see JE article on Pinsk, and EJ article on "Chess."

JANOWSKI (Janowsky)—See JANOWER.

JAPHET—UJ has article on German composer Israel Japhet (1818–1892).

JARAY—UJ has article on sculptor Sandor Jaray (b. 1870 in Rumania).

JARCHO—UJ has article on physician Julius Jarcho (b. 1882 in Russia).

JARE—Italian family traced back to 15th cent. The name means "God-fearing." See JE, which has six biographies.

JARETZKI—UJ has article on U.S. lawyer Alfred Jaretzki (1861–1925).

JARMON (Jarmona)—See DARMON.

JARNO—JE has article on Hungarian actor Josef Jarno (b. 1866), also known as COHEN.

JAROSLAW (also Jaroslawski)—Ashkenazic name derived from the town of Jaroslav, Galicia. JE has article on 18th-cent. tutor Aaron Jaroslaw of Lemberg, Galicia. AJA has a Jaroslawski family tree beginning 1796 in Posen.

JASINOWSKI (also Jassinowsky)—Ashkenazic name probably derived from the city of Jassy, Rumania. UJ and EJ have biographies from Russia, 19th cent.

JASTREMSKI—UJ has article on U.S. soldier Leon Jastremski (1843–1911).

JASTROW—JE has biographies from 19th-cent. Germany and U.S.A., 18th-cent. Poland. CAJ has some family records.

JASZI—Ashkenazic name probably taken from the town of Jassy, Rumania. UJ has article on Hungarian professor Oscar Jaszi (b. 1875).

JAVAL—French 19th-cent. family of physicians and authors; see JE.

JAVETZ—See JAWITZ.

JAVID—UJ has article on Turkish statesman Mahmad Javid Bey (1876–1926), born into a family of Jews who converted to Mohammedanism in 17th cent.

JAVITS—See JAWITZ.

JAWETZ—See JAWITZ.

JAWITZ (also Javetz, Javits, Jawetz)—UJ has articles from 15th-cent. Portugal and 19th-cent. Poland; EJ has a biography from 18th-cent. Turkey.

JAWLIKAR—JE has article on 19th-cent. India soldier Samuel Jawlikar.

JAZKAN—UJ has article on journalist Samuel Jazkan (1874–1937), born in Lithuania.

JEANRENAUD—Related to MENDELSSOHN.

JEFFERSON—Related to FARJEON.

JEHIEL—Related to DAVIDSOHN and PERLES.

JEHUDA—Family in 13th-cent. Germany. See histories in CB, p. 2415 (with family tree), and ZL, p. 613.

JEITELES (also Jeitteles)—Austrian family traced back to the first half of 18th cent. EJ has a family tree; JE has six biographies.

JEKELES—Family of Cracow businessmen traced back to 16th cent.; see EJ. Related to EBERLS.

JELIN—See JELLINEK.

JELLINEK (also Jelin)—Ashkenazic variation of HIRSCH ("stag"); other variations, not necessarily related, are HERZ, HARTVIG, HARRIS and CERF. JE has biographies from 18th-cent. Austria and Germany and 19th-cent. Russia. Also see biography in EJ article on "Chemistry." Related to HARASZT.

JENER—JE has article on Polish Rabbi Abraham Jener (1806–1876).

JEREMIAS—CAJ has family records.

JERUSALEM (also Jerusalimski)—UJ and EJ have biographies from 19th cent. Related to KOTANYI.

JERWITZ—Related to SCHREIBER.

JESHURUN—See JESURUN.

JESI—JE has article on Italian engraver Samuel Jesi (1789–1853).

JESSEL—JE has article on English master of the rolls Sir George Jessel (1824–1883). JE article on "Coat of Arms" has the family crest. Related to BELMONT.

JESSNER—UJ has article on theater manager Leopold Jessner (b. 1878 in Germany).

JESSURUN—See JESURUN.

JESURUN (also Jeshurun, Jessurun)—Family of Spanish exiles found in Amsterdam and Hamburg, 16th cent. JE has eight biographies. LBI has a Jessurun family tree beginning 1748. Related to PINA, MELDOLA, LOBATO and de SOLA.

JEWELL—JE has article on English circus owner Jacob Jewell (d. 1884).

JEWNIN—JE has article on Russian Talmudist Abraham Jewnin of Grodno (d. 1848).

JEZOWER—UJ has article on author Ignatz Jezower (b. 1878 in Poland).

JHIRATKAR—JE has article on Indian soldier Solomon Jhiratkar (b. 1818).

JILOVSKY—UJ has article on artist George Jilovsky (b. 1884 in Prague).

JITTA—UJ has article on Dutch professor Daniel Jitta (b. 1854).

JIZFAN—EJ has article on Yemenite author Judah Jizfan (d. 1837).

JOAB—Family traced back to Aaron ben Samuel ha-Nasi in 10th-cent. Rome. JE has a family tree and fifty biographies. Related to BETHEL, FINZI, ROFE, NAKDAN, CALABRESE, CEPRANO, TRIOUFO, RECANATI, DATTILO, CAMERINO.

JOACHIM (also Joachimsen, Joachimsthal)—JE has biographies from Germany, Hungary and U.S.A., 19th cent. PD has some family records. Related to VAMBERY.

JOACHIMSEN—See JOACHIM.

JOACHIMSTHAL—See JOACHIM.

JOCHANAN—Related to EPHRAIM.

JOCHELSON—JE has article on Russian explorer Waldemar Jochelson (1856–1937), born in Vilna.

JOEL—JE has biographies from Germany and England, 19th cent. LBI has a family tree beginning 1830, related to ARON. PD has family records. JE article on "Coat of Arms" has the family crest. See family history in JFF, No. 34.

JOFAN (also Iofan)—UJ has article on architect Boris Jofan (b. 1891 in Russia).

JOFFE—See JAFFE.

JOFFIN—See JAFFE.

JOGICHES—EJ has article on Polish socialist Leon Jogiches (1867–1919).

JOHLSON (also Jolson)—German writer Joseph Johlson (1777–1851) was also known as Fulda; see JE. U.S. singer Al Jolson was born Asa YOELSON in Russia, 1886; see UJ.

JOHNSON—Texas and Ohio family descended from David Israel Johnson of 18th-cent. England; see JE, which has seven biographies. Also see *The Ancestry of Rosalie Morris Johnson.* Related to EZEKIEL, ABRAHAM, DAVIS, FRANKS, JONAS, MORRIS.

JOLLES—JE has article on Galician and Russian author Zechariah Jolles (1814–1852). Related to DOKSHITZER and LIPSCHUTZ.

JOLOWICZ—EJ and UJ have biographies from Germany and England, 19th cent.

JOLSON—See JOHLSON.

JOMTOB—Ashkenazic name meaning "good day" in Hebrew; translated by one branch to BONDI. See *Zur Geschichte der*

Familie Jomtob-Bondi in Prag, Dresden und Mainz.

JONA—See JONAH.

JONAH (also Jona)—EJ has biographies from 16th-cent. Egypt and 17th-cent. Palestine.

JONAS (also Jonasson)—JE has biographies from 19th-cent. Germany, France and U.S.A. LBIS has a family tree and notes, related to Jonasson, JOHNSON, MEYERSON and PHILIPSON. LBI has family trees beginning 1700, 1760 and 19th cent. Other relatives are BONN, HOHENTHAL, SEIXAS, JUDAH, MIREL, FUERST, STEINHEIMER.

JONASSON—See JONAS.

JONATHANSON—JE has two biographies from 18th-cent. Russia. Related to EYBESCHUTZ.

JONES—JE has biographies from 18th–19th-cent. England and U.S.A.

JOSAPHAT—Related to REUTER.

JOSEF—See JOSEPH.

JOSEFFY—See JOSEPH.

JOSELEWICZ—EJ has article on Polish Colonel Berek Joselewicz (1770–1809). Also see JOSEPH.

JOSEPH (also Josephi, Josephs, Josephson, Josephsson, Josephtal, Josephsthal, Josephthal, Josef, Joseffy)—Prominent Canadian family of Joseph is descended from Naphtali Joseph of 18th-cent. Holland; there are also branches traced to 18th-cent. Russia and Germany. See JE and UJ, which have numerous other biographies under all variations of the name. LBI has a Josephson family tree beginning 1766, related to MARC; a Josephtal family tree beginning 1638, related to BEROLZHEIMER; and a Josephsthal family tree beginning 1657. CAJ has records of the Josephi and Josef families. LBIS has a Josephson family tree and notes, as well as Josephsson family notes. AJA has a Joseph family tree beginning 1800 and related to SELIG and SCHWARZCHILD. JE article on "Coat of Arms" has Josephs family crest. Also see tree in *Stammbaum der Familie Josephthal,* which traces descendants of Lazarus Josephthal of Ansbach (b. 1657). Related to HART, SOLOMONS, de SOLA, MOSES, HANNOVER, GRATZ, LEVI, SASSOON, BELMONTE and MELDOLA. Also see JOSELEWICZ, JOZEFOWICZ.

JOSEPHI—See JOSEPH.

JOSEPHS—See JOSEPH.

JOSEPHSON—See JOSEPH.

JOSEPHSSON—See JOSEPH.

JOSEPHTAL (Josephsthal, Josephthal)—See JOSEPH.

JOSHUA—CAJ has some family records. Related to LANDAU and DUBNO.

JOSSA—JE has article on Russian engineer Grigori Jossa (1800–1874).

JOST—JE has article on German historian Isaac Jost (1793–1860). CAJ has some family records. Related to EUCHEL and WOLF.

JOURDAN—LBI has family trees beginning 1782 and 1819.

JOZEFOWICZ—Family of Lithuanian financiers in 16th cent., also known as EZOFOVICH. See EJ. Also see JOSEPH.

JSAK—Family of Cracow printers, 17th cent. See CB, p. 2952.

JUDA—See JUDAH.

JUDAH (also Juda)—U.S. family in Newport, R.I., from 17th cent., also in Jamaica and Surinam; JE has twenty-five biographies. Also a Russian family from Grodno, 16th cent.; JE has fourteen biographies. LBI has a Juda family tree beginning 1753. The American Judah family is related to HILBERT, SEIXAS, LEVY, HENDRICKS, JONAS, HART, CORREA and HAYS. The Russians are related to BOGDANOVICH and IGUDICH.

JUDD (also Judkiewicz)—JE has article on U.S. manufacturer Max Judd (b. 1851 in Cracow).

von JUDE (also von Judemann)—See family history in JFF, No. 22.

JUDSON—UJ has article on U.S. writer Solomon Judson (b. 1879 in Russia).

JUKEL—UJ has article on Polish Rabbi Reb Jukel (1816–1878), born GESUNDHEIT.

JULIUS—UJ and EJ have biographies from 18th- and 19th-cent. Germany and U.S.A. LBIS has some family notes. Related to HALDEMAN.

JULLUS—CAJ has some family records.

JUNG—UJ has biographies from Italy, Austria, Hungary, 19th–20th cent.

JUNGREIS—EJ has article on Hungarian Rabbi Asher Jungreis (1806–1872).

JUSTER—UJ has article on Rumanian historian Jean Juster (1886–1916).

JUSTO—JE has article on 17th-cent. cartographer Jacob Justo, also known as ZADDIK.

JUTROSINSKY—LBI has a family tree.

JUWEL—JE has article on 19th-cent. Galician scholar Moses Juwel.

KABAK—UJ has article on writer Aaron Kabak (1880–1914), born in Lithuania.

KABIR—EJ has article on Iraqi official Abraham Kabir (b. 1885).

KABISI—JE has article on 16th-cent. Turkish printer Abraham Kabisi.

KABOS—JE and UJ have biographies from Hungary, 19th cent.

KACZER—UJ has article on Hungarian author Illes Kaczer (b. 1877).

KADELBURG—JE has article on German actor Gustav Kadelburg (b. 1851).

KADISCH (also Kadish)—JE has article on 19th-cent. Hungarian teacher Zerah Kadisch. CAJ has a family tree covering 1788–1921, related to MAZUR, GURAUER and DRUCKER. Another related name is FRIEDLAND.

KADISH—See KADISCH.

KADOORIE—UJ has article on merchant Ellis Kadoorie (1865–1922).

KAEMPF—JE has article on Austrian Rabbi Saul Kaempf (b. 1818 in Poland, d. 1892 in Prague).

KAFAH—EJ has article on Yemenite scholar Yihye Kafah (1850–1932).

KAFKA—UJ has two biographies from Prague, 19th and 20th cent.

KAGAN (also Kaganovich, Kaganovsky, Kogan, Koganowitch, Kogen, etc.)—Russian variation of COHEN. UJ has biographies from 19th-cent. Russia and Poland.

KAGANOVICH—See KAGAN.

KAGANOVSKY—See KAGAN.

KAHAN—Russian variation of COHEN.

KAHANA—Russian variation of COHEN.

KAHANE—See COHEN.

KAHANOV—Probably a Russian variation of COHEN. EJ has article on Jerusalem Talmudist Moses Kahanov (1817–1883).

KAHANOVITSCH—Russian variation of COHEN.

KAHIN—See COHEN.

KAHLER—UJ has biographies from 19th- and 20th-cent. Prague. PD has some family records.

KAHN—German name derived from the sign of a boat (Kahn) on the family's door. JE has biographies from 19th-cent. Germany, France and Belgium. LBIS has some family notes. AJA has three family trees. Also see Die Familie Kahn von Sulzburg/Baden. Related to COHEN, BRUCKMAN, SCHIFF, WERTHEIMER, KOHN, OPPENHEIMER, ADLER, WEIL, HERZ, HOCHSTETTER, LEMANN, MARX, GATZERT, ROSENGART, LOEW. Also see CAHN.

KAHNSHTAM—EJ has article on Polish educator Aharon Kahnshtam (1859–1921).

KAHRSTADT—CAJ has some family records.

KAIDANOVER (also Keidany)—JE has article on Polish Rabbi Aaron Samuel Kaidanover (1614–1676), related to COHEN. Other related names are KIRCHHAHN and JAFFE. Also see KOIDONOVER.

KAISAR—See KAISER.

KAISER (also Kaisar, Kaiserman, Caiserman)—UJ and JE have biographies from 19th-cent. Hungary, Lithuania, Rumania and U.S.A. Also see KAYSER.

KAISERMAN—See KAISER.

KALAFRI—Related to POSNER.

KALAHORA—LBI has a family tree beginning 1495.

KALA'I—Turkish-Crimean-Italian family dating from 16th cent. JE has four biographies. Related to MATTITHIAH.

KALAZ (also Khallas)—Name meaning "collector of trades." JE has article on 16th-cent. Algerian moralist Judah Kalaz.

KALCHMANN—CAJ has a family tree from Germany.

KALICH—See KALISCH.

KALIFA—JE has article on 17th-cent. Moroccan poet Moses Kalifa. Related to BEDERSI.

KALIR—JE has article on 10th-cent. Italian poet Eleazar Kalir.

KALISCH (also Kalish, Calisch, Kalich, Kalischer, Kalisher, Kalisker, Kolisch, Kolischer)—Ashkenazic name derived from the town of Kalisz (Kalisch) in Poland, where Jews have lived since 13th cent. JE, UJ and EJ have biographies, from 17th-cent. Poland, 18th-cent. Germany, and other European countries in 19th cent. LBIS has a Kalisch family tree related to Kalischer and KREMNITZER. LBI has a Kalischer family tree beginning in 17th cent. CAJ has Kalischer family records. Related to LINDAU, BING, LEHMANN, EDELS, LIPKIN, WARKA, TUCKER, RAGOLER, WAHL and PICON.

KALISCHER—See KALISCH.

KALISH—See KALISCH.

KALISHER—See KALISCH.

KALISKER—See KALISCH.

KALLEN—UJ has article on U.S. philosopher Horace Kallen (b. 1882 in Germany).

KALLIR—JE and UJ have biographies from Hungary, 18th cent., and Galicia, 19th cent. LBI has a family tree beginning 1792. Related to EISENSTADT.

KALLMES—LBI has a family tree beginning 1550.

KALLO (also Kallos)—EJ and UJ have biographies from 18th- and 19th-cent. Hungary.

KALMAN (also Kalmankes)—Ashkenazic name meaning "borne by an ancestor of Joshua." UJ has article on Hungarian composer Imre Kalman. Also see CALMER and CALAMANI. Related to JAFFE.

KALOMITI—JE has article on 15th-cent. Turkish scholar Abraham Kalomiti.

KALONYMUS—Prominent family from 8th-cent. Italy and 10th-cent. Germany. JE has a family tree and twelve biographies. LBI also has a family tree, related to ULLSTEIN. Also see JE articles on Da-

vid ben Jacob Meir, David ben Kalonymus, David Kalonymus of Naples, and Mayence (Mainz), and see EJ article on Eleazar ben Judah of Worms. Related to SALTMAN, DARSHAN and JAFFE.

KALUSHINER—UJ has article on poet Joseph Kalushiner (b. 1893 in Poland).

KAMAI—Related to FINKEL.

KAMAIKY—UJ has article on U.S. newspaper publisher Leon Kamaiky (b. 1864 in Lithuania). He was the son-in-law of Kasriel SARASOHN. A possible variation of the name may be KOMAIKO.

KAMANKER—JE has article on 18th-cent. Polish scholar Moses Kamanker.

KAMBIL—See KAMNIAL.

KAMELHAR—EJ has article on Galician Rabbi Jekuthiel Kamelhar (1871–1937).

KAMENEV (also Kameniav)—UJ has article on Russian Leo Kamenev (1883–1936). Related to STONE.

KAMENKA—EJ has article on Ukrainian Hassid Zevi Kamenka (d. 1781).

KAMENSKY—See KAMINSKI.

KAMINER—JE has article on Russian physician Isaac Kaminer (1834–1901), who died in Switzerland. Related to KAUEN.

KAMINKA—JE has article on Russian scholar Armond Kaminka (b. 1866), who lived in Austria and Germany.

KAMINSKI (also Kaminsky, Kamensky)—UJ has biographies from Russia and Poland, 19th cent. Related to HALPERN, MELMAN and TURKOV.

KAMNIAL (also Kambil)—JE has article on 11th-cent. Spanish physician Abraham Kamnial.

KAMNITZER—Related to HARIF HA-LEVI.

KAN—See COHEN.

KANDEL—UJ has biographies from 19th- and 20th-cent. Rumania.

KANDT (also Kant)—UJ has article on German scientist Richard Kandt (1876–1918). CAJ has some Kant family records.

KANITZ—JE has two biographies from 19th-cent. Hungary. PD has some family records. Related to SIDON.

KANN—German name that originated with Levites who lived under the sign of the jug (*Kanne* in German), an emblem of Levite duties. JE has biographies from 18th-cent. Germany and 19th-cent. France. CAJ has a family tree from Germany and Holland, covering 1595 to 1966; also a tree for a Kann family of Frankfurt-am-Main, related to HORWITZ. Other related names are BOAS, SPEYER and WERTHEIMER.

KANSI—JE has article on 14th-cent. French astronomer Samuel Kansi, also known as D'Escola or D'Ascala.

KANT—See KANDT.

KANTOR (also Kantorovitch, Kantorowicz)—Ashkenazic name, probably indicating an ancestor who was a cantor. JE and UJ have biographies from 19th-cent. Russia and Poland. LBI has a Kantorowicz family tree beginning 1831. LBIS has Kantorowicz family notes. See also CANTOR.

KANTOROVITCH—See KANTOR.

KANTOROWICZ—See KANTOR.

KAPILOVITCH—UJ has article on poetess Leah Kapilovitch (b. 1898 in Russia).

KAPLAN (also Kaplansky, Kaplun-Kogan, Caplan)—JE and UJ have biographies from 19th-cent. Russia and Poland. AJA has a family tree, related to YAFFE, SOLOMON, CHARTOFF, RABINOWITZ, MARKELL, BERMAN and FEUERSTEIN.

KAPLANSKY—See KAPLAN.

KAPLUN-KOGAN—See KAPLAN.

KAPOSI—JE has biographies from 16th-cent. Egypt and 19th-cent. Austria. Related to KOHN.

KAPP (also Kappel, Kapper, Koppel, Koppelmann, Kopperl, Koppleman)—JE and UJ have biographies from 19th-cent. Russia, England, Austria, and Germany. LBI has a Kapp family tree. Also see tree in *Stammtafel Koppel,* tracing a family related to THURNAUER. Other related names are HOENIGSBURG, MUKDONI, ALTENKUNSTADT and DUSCHINSKY.

KAPPEL—See KAPP.

KAPPER—See KAPP.

KAPUZATO—EJ has article on 15th-cent. Salonikan Rabbi Moses Kapuzato.

KARA (also Cara)—JE has five biographies from 11th-cent. France and 15th-cent. Bohemia. Related to HELBO.

KARABACEK—UJ has article on Austrian Josef von Karabacek (1845–1918).

KARACSONY (also Karaczewski)—UJ and EJ have biographies from 19th-cent. Hungary and Russia.

KARACZEWSKI—See KARACSONY.

KARDOS—UJ has article on educator Albert Kardos (1861–1924).

KAREH—EJ has article on Yemenite scholar Solomon Kareh (1804–1885).

KAREIS—JE has article on Austrian electrician Josef Kareis (b. 1837).

KARESKI—CAJ has some family records.

KARFF—UJ has article on chess player May Karff (20th cent.).

KARFUNKEL—See GARFUNKEL.

KARFUNKELSTEIN—See GARFUNKEL.

KARGAU—JE has article on 18th-cent. German Talmudist Mendel Kargau.

KARGER—UJ has article on U.S. journalist Gustav Karger (1866–1924), born in Berlin. Also see family history in *Familienblätter zur Erinnerung an unseren verewigten Vater Raphael J. Karger.*

KARIGAL—See CARREGAL.

KARIGEL—See CARREGAL.

KARIGOL—See CARREGAL.

KARINTHY—UJ has article on Hungarian author Frigyes Karinthy (1888–1938).

KARL—CAJ has some family records.

KARLIN (also Karliner)—Dynasty of Zaddikim in Karlin, Lithuania, beginning 18th cent.; also known as PERLOV. See EJ. Related to FRIEDMANN.

KARMAN—JE has article on Hungarian educator Moritz Karman (1843–1915), also known as KLEINMANN.

KARMI (also Carmi)—French family of the Middle Ages. JE has sixteen biographies. Related to BERECHIAH. Another variation of the name is CREMIEUX.

KARNIOL—UJ has article on cantor Alter Karniol (1855–1925), born in Russia.

KARP (also Carp, Karpeles, Karpf, Kars)—Ashkenazic name taken from the picture of a carp on a family's door. JE, UJ and EJ have biographies from 18th-cent. Austria and 19th-cent. Rumania, Austria and Bohemia.

KARPELES—See KARP.

KARPF—See KARP.

KARPOV—UJ has article on Russian chemist Lev Karpov (1879–1921).

KARS—See KARP.

KARSUNSKY—See family in *It Began with Zade Usher* (see Bernstein in Bibliography).

KASA—See CASE.

KASABI—JE has article on 17th-cent. Turkish Talmudist Joseph Kasabi.

KASAS—UJ has article on Russian author Ilya Kasas (1832–1912).

KASHER—UJ has article on Rabbi Menahem Kasher (b. 1895 in Poland).

KASKEL (also Kaskele)—17th-cent. family of German court Jews who moved to Poland in 18th cent. See EJ.

KASOVICH—JE has article on U.S. farmer Israel Kasovich (b. 1858 in Russia). See his autobiography, *The Days of Our Years.*

KASPE (also Kaspi)—EJ has biography from 13th–14th-cent. Spain. UJ has biography from 19th-cent. Russia-U.S.A.

KASPI—See KASPE.

KASS—Name perhaps derived from the German district of Kassel (Cassel). CAJ has a family tree covering 1838 to 1963, related to BALLIN.

KASSAB—See KASZAB.

KASSEL—Name probably taken from the German district of Kassel (Cassel). UJ has article on novelist David Kassel (1881–1935), born in Russia.

KASSOVSKY—UJ has article on scholar Hayim Kassovsky (b. 1872 in Jerusalem).

KASSOWITZ—UJ has article on Austrian physician Max Kassowitz (1842–1913). PD has records of a family from Prague.

KASTAN—UJ has article on German journalist Isidor Kastan (1840–1931).

KASVAN—UJ has article on writer Avner Kasvan (1837–1898), born in Russia. His son moved to Rumania.

KASZAB (also Kassab)—UJ has article on Hungarian industrialist Aladar Kaszab (1868–1929).

KATONA—UJ has article on Hungarian painter Nandor Katona (1864–1932).

KATSCHER—JE has article on Hungarian writer Bertha Katscher (b. 1860), also known as UNGAR, KELLNER and KOLLE.

KATTINA—EJ has article on 19th-cent. Russian author Jacob Kattina.

KATZ—See COHEN.

KATZENELLENBOGEN (also Katzenelenbogen, Katzenelnbogen, Ellenbogen, Elbogen, Bogen, etc.)—Rabbinical family descended from twelve Jews who settled at the town of Katzenelenbogen in Hesse-Nassau, Germany, in 1312, with thousands of descendants and huge family connections throughout Europe and America. The name was first used after the family moved to Padua, Italy, by Meir Katzenellenbogen (1482–1565); two generations later the family was in Poland. Because of the length of the name, it has often been shortened to Ellenbogen, Bogen, etc. See family tree on page 14 of this book; also tree in JE. LBI has family trees beginning 14th cent., 1482, 1325, 1480 and 1525. LBIS has a family tree and notes. PD has a family tree. CAJ has family records covering 1800–1821. *Eileh Toledot: These Are the Generations* traces the family in an unbroken line from 1969 back to 14th cent. *Records of the Samuel Family* contains valuable information. Relationships with other prominent rabbinic families are traced in *Anaf Ez Aboth,* by Samuel Kahan, and *Da'at Kedoshim,* by Israel Eisenstadt. Also see family histories in JFF, Nos. 4 and 16, and *Genealogische Übersicht über einige Zweige der Nachkommenschaft des Rabbi Meir Katzenellenbogen von Padua.* PD has an Elbogen family tree and CAJ has Elbogen family records. For an Ellenbogen family history, see *Hevel ha-Kesef.* Related to MINZ, HOROWITZ, AUERBACH, SCHOR, HEILPRIN, HELMAN, TREVES, LURIA, WAHL, LEIBERMAN, POPPERS, LEVINSON, ISIDOR, ISSERLES, CAPSALI, PADUA, KLATZKO, SLONIK, SAMUEL and LEVY. Also see JE article on Kholm (Chelm).

KATZENELNBOGEN—See KATZENELLENBOGEN.

KATZENELSON—See KAZENELSON.

KATZENSTEIN—UJ has biographies from 19th-cent. Germany. CAJ has some family records.

KATZER—See KAZ.

KATZIZNE—UJ has article on poet Alter Katzizne (b. 1885 in Lithuania).

KATZMAN (also Kazman, Kazmann)—UJ has article on Russian chemist Boris Kazman (1874–1933). Related to WEIZMANN. Also see COHEN.

KATZOWICH—UJ has article on writer Israel Katzowich (1859–1934), born in Lithuania. The name is a variation of KATZ, in turn a variation of COHEN.

KAUDERS—JE has article on Prague Rabbi Samuel Kauders (1762–1838). Related to ARNSTEIN.

KAUFFMAN (also Kauffmann, Kaufman, Kaufmann, Kaufman-Cosla, Cauffman) —Ashkenazic name that means "merchant" in German. JE, UJ and EJ have biographies from 17th-cent. Poland and 19th-cent. Germany, Russia, Austria, Hungary and Rumania. LBI has Kauffmann family trees beginning 1693 and 1818, related to MILCH, MUGDAN and STERNHEIMER. CAJ has a Kaufmann family tree beginning 1800 and some family records. Other relatives are GAGGSTATTER, KROTOSCHIN, GOMPERZ, EVEN SHEMUEL, PASTERNAK, CARDOZO and PHILLIPS.

KAUFMAN (Kaufmann)—See KAUFFMAN.

KAULLA (also Kaula)—Family in Württemberg, Germany, from the end of 18th cent.; originally from Stuttgart. See JE and UJ. LBI has family trees beginning 1740. PD has Kaula and Kaulla family records. JE article on "Coat of Arms" has the family crest. Related to AUERBACHER, HEINE, SAMSON and ELTZBACHER.

KAUN—UJ has two biographies from 19th–20th-cent. Russia, Germany and U.S.A.

KAUVAR—UJ has article on U.S. Rabbi Charles Kauvar (b. 1879 in Vilna).

KAVEN—AJA has a family tree, related to BUKSTEIN, POSNER, SEGAL and KAMINER.

KAYLIN—Related to DUBNOW.

KAYSER—JE and UJ have biographies from 19th-cent. France and Germany. LBI has a family tree beginning 1760, related to ARON. Also see KAISER.

KAYSERLING—German family of 19th cent.; see JE. Related to ALNAQUA and NEUMAN.

KAYTON—AJA has a family tree beginning 19th-cent. Germany; the family's name was originally KOETHEN.

KAZ—Jewish family name in 16th-cent. Prague, presumably a variation of KATZ and therefore of COHEN.

KAZAZ—EJ has article on Karaite scholar Elijah Kazaz (1832–1912) from the Crimea.

KAZENELSON (also Katzenelson, Kaznelson)—JE and UJ have biographies from 19th-cent. Russia.

KAZHUCHIN—Related to DUBNOW.

KAZIMIERZ—Hasidic dynasty from Plonsk, Russia, 19th cent. See EJ.

KAZIN—EJ has article on Aleppo Rabbi Judah Kazin (1708–1783).

KAZMAN (Kazmann)—See KATZMANN.

KAZNELSON—See KAZENELSON.

KECSKEMETI—UJ has biographies from Hungary and Rumania, 19th and 20th cent.

KEHIMKAR—EJ has article on Indian historian Hayim Kehimkar (1830–1909).

KEHLMAN—Related to WOHLLERNER.

KEIDANY—See KAIDANOVER.

KEILER—LBI has a family tree beginning 1573.

KEITH—Ashkenazic name derived from the Hebrew chayyat, for "tailor."

KELE—Related to ROTHSCHILD.

KELEMEN—UJ has article on Hungarian deputy Sam Kelemen (1862–1916).

KELEN—UJ has article on Hungarian cartoonist Imre Kelen (b. 1895).

KELIN—See KOLIN.

KELLER (also Kellermann, Kellermeister, Kellner)—JE and UJ have biographies from 19th-cent. Galicia, Germany and Austria. CAJ has Keller family records. Related to WEILL and KATSCHER.

KELLERMANN—See KELLER.

KELLERMEISTER—See KELLER.

KELLIN—See KOLIN.

KELLNER—See KELLER.

KELMER—Related to RAGOLER.

KELSEN—UJ has article on law professor Hans Kelsen (b. 1881 in Prague).

KELTER—JE has article on U.S. athlete Arthur Kelter (b. 1869).

KEMENY—UJ has article on Hungarian author Ferenc Kemeny (19th–20th cent.).

KEMPNER—JE has four biographies from 19th-cent. Germany and Poland. LBI has a family tree beginning 1755. Related to RABINOWITSCH.

KEPES—UJ has article on Hungarian physician Gyula Kepes (d. 1924).

KERN—UJ has two articles from 19th- and 20th-cent. Austria and U.S.A.

KERTESZ—See CURTIZ.

KESSEL—UJ has article on writer Joseph Kessel (b. 1898 in Argentina).

KESSLER—See KESZLER.

KESTENBERG—UJ has article on musician Leo Kestenberg (b. 1882 in Hungary). CAJ has some family records.

KESZLER (also Kessler)—UJ has article on Hungarian critic Jozsef Keszler (1845–1927).

KETT—Related to ROTHSCHILD.

KEYSER (also Keysor)—Moritz CHRISTIANI (b. 1690 in Altorf, d. 1740 in Prague) is descended from the Keyser family of Schleusingen, Bavaria. See JE. JE and UJ also have biographies from 19th-cent. England and U.S.A. Related to GOLDSMID and SAMUEL.

KEYSOR—See KEYSER.

KHALLAS—See KALAZ.

KHARASCH—UJ has article on chemist Morris Kharasch (b. 1895 in Russia).

KHARIK—UJ has article on poet Izi Kharik (b. 1898 in Russia).

KHERSON—See GERSON.

KHIN—JE has article on Russian author Rachel Khin (b. 1863).

KHLOPLIANKIN—UJ has article on Soviet official Ivan Khopliankin (b. 1890).

KHURILKAR—JE has article on 19th-cent. Indian soldier Joseph Khurilkar.

KHVOLSON—See CHWOLSON.

KIEFER—CAJ has family records.

KIMCHI—See KIMHI.

KIMHI (also Kimchi)—Family of scholars which originated in 11th-cent. Spain and spread to Italy, Turkey, Syria and England. JE has thirty-four biographies. Also see UJ. See family histories in MGWJ (1884), p. 552, and (1885), p. 382; also *Abraham Elmaleh 70th Birthday Book*, p. 126. Related to PEREZ, MEHLER.

KINDERFREUND—JE has article on Polish scholar Aryeh Kinderfreund (1798–1873).

KINDERMANN—Related to REICHER.

KIPNIS—JE and UJ have biographies from 19th- and 20th-cent. Russia. See *Partial Autobiography*, by Russian-born U.S. businessman Sam Kipnis.

KIRALFY—JE has article on Hungarian composer Imre Kiralfy (b. 1845).

KIRCHHAHN—See KAIDANOVER.

KIRCHHEIM—JE has article on German scholar Raphael Kirchheim (1804–1889).

KIRIMI—Name derived from the town of Kirim (also Sulehat) in the Crimea. JE has article on 14th-cent. Crimean Rabbi Abraham Kirimi.

KIRKISANI—Name derived from Circassia. JE has a biography from 10th cent.

KIRSANOV—UJ has article on Russian poet Semen Kirsanov (b. 1906).

KIRSCHBAUM—JE has article on Austrian physician Eliezer Kirschbaum (1797–1860), born in Galicia. See family history in *A Link with the Future* (see Rottenberg in Bibliography).

KIRSCHBRAUN—EJ has article on Polish Zionist Elijah Kirschbraun (1882–1931).

KIRSCHNER—UJ has article on German cantor Emanuel Kirschner (1857–1938).

KIRSCHSTEIN (also Kirstein)—JE and UJ have biographies from Poland and Germany, 19th–20th cent.

KIRSTEIN—See KIRSCHSTEIN.

KISCH (also Kish)—Distinguished family that came to Prague from Chiesch, Bohemia, in 16th cent. In 1900, descendants were spread throughout Europe. JE has four biographies. CAJ has a family tree and records from Prague covering 17th through 20th cent. CAJ also has a Kish family tree from France. See family history in JFF, No. 29. Related to KRAUS and ARNDT.

KISH—See KISCH.

KISLING—UJ has article on painter Maurice Kisling (b. 1891 in Poland).

KISS—UJ has two biographies from 19th–20th-cent. Hungary. Related to KLEIN and KOBOR.

KISSIN—Related to DUBNOW.

KISSINGER—Name derived from the Bavarian resort town of Kissingen, where Jews first settled in 17th cent.

KISTEMAEKERS—UJ has article on French writer Henry Kistemaekers (1872–1938), born in Belgium.

KITSEE (also Kitssee, Kittseer)—U.S. inventor Isador Kitsee (1845–1931), born in Vienna, was a descendant of Maimonides; see UJ. JE has article on Hungarian Talmudist Michael Kittseer (1775–1845). Related to KOHUT.

KITSSEE—See KITSEE.

KITTSEER—See KITSEE.

KITZINGER—JE has article on 16th–17th-cent. author Jacob Kitzinger. LBI has a family tree beginning 1870, related to JAFFE.

KLAAR—JE has article on Austrian writer Alfred Klaar (b. 1848 in Prague).

KLABIN—Brazilian family from Lithuania, 19th cent.; see EJ.

KLACZKO (also Klatzko)—One of the leading Jewish families of Vilna, 19th cent. JE has biographies from France and Lithuania. Russian Rabbi Mordecai Klatzko (1797–1883), born in Vilna, was surnamed MELTZER and was a descendant of Meir KATZENELLENBOGEN of Padua. Related to MINZ.

KLAPP—See KLAPPER.

KLAPPER (also Klapp, Klopfer, etc.)—Ashkenazic name meaning "a gossip" in German. JE and UJ have Klapp biographies from Austria and Rumania, 19th cent.

KLATZKIN—UJ has article on writer Jacob Klatzkin (b. 1882 in Russia).

KLATZKO—See KLACZKO.

KLAUBER (also Klauberia)—Related to GREENHUT and LURIA.

KLAUS (also Klausner)—Ashkenazic name indicating (in German) the rabbi of a secret worship meeting. LBI has a family tree beginning 1630. JE has Klausner biographies from 14th-cent. Austria and 19th-cent. Russia. CAJ has Klausner family records. Also see EJ article on Aaron of Neustadt (d. 1421), brother-in-law of Abraham Klausner. Related to STEINITZ.

KLAUSNER—See KLAUS.

KLEE—UJ has article on Zionist Alfred Klee (b. 1875 in Berlin).

KLEEBERG—JE has two biographies from 19th-cent. Germany and U.S.A. Related to COHEN.

KLEEREKOPER—CAJ has some family records.

KLEIBER—UJ has article on conductor Erich Kleiber (b. 1890 in Vienna).

KLEIN—Ashkenazic name that means "small" in German. JE has fourteen biographies from 19th-cent. Germany, England, Hungary, Austria, France and U.S.A. See family history in A Link with the Future (see Rottenberg in Bibliography). Related to NEMES and KISS.

KLEINBERG—Related to LEVINTHAL.

KLEINLERER—UJ has article on lawyer Davide Kleinlerer (b. 1899 in Poland).

KLEINMANN—UJ has a biography from 19th–20th-cent. Russia. Related to KARMAN.

KLEINPENNIG—CAJ has a family tree.

KLEMENTEVNA—Related to SLUTSKAYA.

KLEMPERER—JE has three biographies from 19th-cent. Germany and Austria. Austrian Rabbi Guttmann Klemperer (1815–1882) was descended on his mother's side from Yom-Tob Lipmann Heller. PD has some family records.

KLEPFISH—EJ has article on Polish Rabbi Samuel Klepfish (1820–1902). Related to KAHANA, MIKLISHANSKY, FEIN and YADKOVSKI.

KLERK—UJ has article on Dutch architect Michel de Klerk (1884–1923).

KLETZKIN—Name probably taken from the Russian town of Kletzkin in the government of Minsk; Jews were there from 16th cent. UJ has a biography of publisher Borys Kletzkin (1875–1937), born in Russia.

KLEY—JE has two biographies from 18th- and 19th-cent. Germany.

KLIACHKO—Related to GUENZBURG.

KLINGER—PD has some family records. Related to BUCHBINDER.

KLOMPUS—CAJ has some family records.

KLOPFER—See KLAPPER.

KLOTZ—JE has article on French journalist Louis Klotz (b. 1868), of Alsatian descent.

KLUGER—JE has article on Polish Rabbi Solomon Kluger (1783–1869).

KLUMEL—UJ has article on Zionist leader Meier Klumel (1869–1935), born in Latvia.

KNEFLER—JE has article on U.S. soldier Frederick Knefler (b. 1833 in Hungary).

KNINA—CAJ has a family tree from Czechoslovakia, 1724–1886.

KNIZSHNIK—UJ has article on poet Zelda Knizshnik (b. 1869 in Vilna).

KNOLLER—CAJ has a family tree from Germany.

KNOPF—UJ has article on U.S. financier Samuel Knopf (1862–1932), born in Poland.

KNOX—UJ has article on U.S. author Israel Knox (b. 1906 in Russia).

KOBER (also Kobler, Kobner, Kobor, Kobrin)—Name possibly derived from the Russian town of Kobryn in the government of Grodno; Jews were there from 16th cent. JE and UJ have biographies from 18th-cent. Russia and 19th-cent. Austria, Germany, Galicia, Hungary and Russia. Hungarian author Tamas Kobor was born BERMANN in 1867; he was brother-in-law of Jozsef KISS.

KOBLER—See KOBER.

KOBNER—See KOBER.

KOBOR—See KOBER.

KOBRIN—See KOBER.

KOCH—UJ has article on U.S. official Joseph Koch (1844–1902).

KODER—UJ has article on Samuel Koder (b. 1869 in India); married Esther RAHABI.

KOENEN—JE has article on Dutch historian Hendrik Koenen (1809–1874).

KOENIG (also Konig)—JE and UJ have biographies from 19th-cent. Hungary, Chile and U.S.A.

KOENIGSBERG (also Konigsberg, Konigsberger)—Name probably derived from Königsberg, in East Prussia. JE and UJ have biographies from 19th–20th-cent. Germany, Poland and U.S.A. CAJ has some Konigsberger family records. Related to JOSEPHS.

KOENIGSWARTER—See KONIGSWARTER.

KOERNER—EJ has article on Grodno Rabbi Moses Koerner (1766–1836).

KOETHEN—See KAYTON.

KOGAN—See KAGAN.

KOGANOWITCH—See KAGAN.

KOGEN—See KAGAN.

KOHAN—See COHEN.

KOHEN—German variation of COHEN. Family of printers in 16th-cent. Germany, related to KAZ. Other related names are SPIRA, KAIDANOVER, FRIZZI, LISSER, SCHIFF and SOLAL.

KOHLBERG—LBI has family trees beginning 1545, 1717. Related to LOEWENSTEIN.

KOHLER—Rabbi Kaufmann Kohler of Bavaria (19th cent.), descended from a family of rabbis; his maternal great-great-grandfather was David DISBECK. See JE and UJ. AJA has this family's tree beginning 1611 in Germany, related to DISPECK, DESSAU, NETTER, LOEWENMAYER, AUB, HERZ, BAIERSDORFER, FRIEDMANN, NEWHOUSE, OPPENHEIMER, BRANDEIS, BERMANN, MAINZER and MANN. CAJ has some family records. Also related to EINHORN and SULZBERGER.

KOHN (also Kohne, Kohner, Kohnowski)—German variations of COHEN. JE, UJ and EJ have numerous biographies. LBI has a family tree beginning 1771. AJA has a family tree beginning 1744 in Bohemia, related to BALOG, KAHN, WODITZKA, ROSENWASSER, RUZICKA, SAPHIR, LOWY, STEINER, URBACH, WINTERNITZ,

SINGER and POLLACK. Other related names are KAHANA, KAPOSI, WERTHEIMER and KUNFI.

KOHNE—See KOHN.

KOHNER—See KOHN.

KOHNOWSKI—See KOHN.

KOHNSTAMM—LBI has a family tree beginning 1650.

KOHUT—JE has biographies from 19th-cent. Hungary and U.S.A. of Jews descended from a family of rabbis, including among their ancestors KITSSEE and PALOTA. Also see UJ, and JE article on Grosswardein, Hungary. Related to BETTELHEIM.

KOIDONOVER—EJ has article on Minsk Talmudist Aaron Koidonover (1614–1676). Also see KAIDANOVER.

KOIGEN—UJ has article on philosopher David Koigen (1879–1939), born in Russia. The name is a possible variation of KOGAN and thus of COHEN.

KOKABI—JE has article on German physician Joseph Kokabi of 17th–18th-cent. Ferrara.

KOKESCH—EJ has article on Austrian Zionist Ozer Kokesch (1860–1905).

KOKHAVI—EJ has article on 14th-cent. Avignon Talmudist David Kokhavi.

KOKISOW—Noted Karaite family in Poland and the Crimea, 18th, 19th and 20th cent. See UJ.

KOL—UJ has article on Dutch socialist Henri Kol (1852–1925).

KOLAR—UJ has article on conductor Victor Kolar (b. 1888 in Hungary).

KOLEKTAR—JE has article on Anglo-Indian soldier Moses Kolektar (b. 1842).

KOLIN (also Kelin, Kellin)—Name taken from the town of Kolin in Bohemia, where Jews first settled in 14th cent. The family descends from Rabbi Samuel Kolin of that town (1720–1806); see EJ. Related to EHRENSTAMM, BOSKOVITZ, LOW. Also see KOLLINSKY.

KOLISCH (Kolischer)—See KALISCH.

KOLLE (also Koller)—UJ has biographies from 19th–20th-cent. Hungary, Bohemia and U.S.A. Related to KATSCHER.

KOLLINSKY—Possibly a variation of KOLIN. Weimar family traced back to early 19th cent. See family tree in JA, No. 1.

KOLODNY—CAJ has some family records.

KOLON—Related to GREENHUT.

KOMA—See COMA.

KOMAIKO—See The Chronicle (see Gitelson in Bibliography). Related to GITELSON. A possible variation is KAMAIKY.

KOMPERT—JE has article on Austrian author Leopold Kompert (1822–1886).

KON—UJ has article on 20th-cent. Polish industrialist Oskar Kon.

KONIG—See KOENIG.

KONIGSBERG (Konigsberger)—See KOENIGSBERG.

KONIGSTEIN—JE has article on Austrian oculist Leopold Konigstein (b. 1850).

KONIGSWARTER (also Koenigswarter)—Family from Bohemia, 18th cent.; one branch has been in France since 19th cent. See JE. LBI has Koenigswarter family trees beginning 1740. PD has Konigswarter family records. See family history in Toledot Bet Konigswarter. Related to SAMSON and WERTHEIMER.

KONT (also Konti)—UJ has biographies from 19th-cent. Austria and Hungary.

KOOK (also Kuk)—UJ has article on Rabbi Abraham Kook (1864–1935), born in Latvia, a descendant of Mordecai JAFFE.

KOON—See COHEN.

KOOPMAN—See family history in JFF, No. 26.

KOPELIOWITZ—Related to ALMOG.

KOPELOFF—UJ has article on writer I. Kopeloff (1858–1933), born in Russia.

KOPLIK—JE has article on U.S. physician Henry Koplik (b. 1858).

KOPPEL—See KAPP.

KOPPELMANN—See KAPP.

KOPPERL—See KAPP.

KOPPLEMAN—See KAPP.

KORACH—CAJ has a family tree from Italy.

KORAH—EJ has article on Yemenite scholar Hayyim Korah (1824–1914).

KORANYI—JE has article on Hungarian doctor Friedrich Koranyi (1828–1913).

KORCH—See KORCH.

KORDA—UJ has biographies from Hungary, 19th and 20th cent.

KOREFF (also Koref)—JE and UJ have biographies from 18th- and 19th-cent. Germany. See family history in JFF, No. 29.

KOREIN—UJ has article on Hungarian communal leader Dezso Korein (b. 1870).

KORETZER—Name taken from the Russian town of Koretz, Volhynia. Related to SPIRA.

KORKIS—EJ has article on Galician Zionist Abraham Korkis (1865–1921).

KORMENDI—UJ has article on Hungarian author Ferenc Kormendi (b. 1900).

KORN—JE and UJ have biographies from 19th-cent. Germany, Hungary, Galicia and U.S.A.

KORNER—JE has article on 18th-cent. Russian author Moses Korner, a grandson of Yom-Tob Lipmann HELLER.

KORNFELD—JE and UJ have biographies from 18th- and 19th-cent. Austria, Hungary and U.S.A. PD has some family records. Related to EGER.

KORNGOLD—UJ has article on composer Erich Korngold (b. 1897 in Austria).

KORNIK (also Kurnik)—JE has article on German Rabbi Meir Kornik (d. 1826).

KOROSI—JE has article on Hungarian statistician Joseph Korosi (1844–1926).

KORTNER—UJ has article on actor Fritz Kortner (b. 1892 in Vienna).

KOSCH—JE has article on German physician Raphael Kosch (1803–1872).

KOSMAN—Related to HAHN.

KOSMINSKY—JE has article on 19th-cent. Austrian Marks Kosminsky.

KOSSARSKI—JE has article on German poet Julius Kossarski (1812–1879).

KOSTELIZ (also Costellez)—JE has article on Egyptian Rabbi Abigdor Kosteliz (1572–1659).

KOSTERLITZ—CAJ has some family records.

KOTANYI—Related to JERUSALEM.

KOTIK—UJ has article on writer Ezekiel Kotik (1847–1921), born in Russia.

KOTINSKY—UJ has article on entomologist Jacob Kotinsky (b. 1873 in Russia).

KOTSK—EJ has article on Lublin Hasid Menahem of Kotsk (1787–1859).

KOUSSEVITZKY—UJ has article on conductor Serge Koussevitzky (b. 1874 in Russia).

KOVES—JE has article on Hungarian painter Joseph Koves (1853–1917).

KOVNER (also Kowner)—Name taken from Lithuanian city of Kovno, where Jews first settled in 15th cent. JE and UJ have biographies from Vilna, 19th cent.

KOWALSKY—EJ has article on Polish Rabbi Judah Kowalsky (1862–1925).

KOWNER—See KOVNER.

KOZIENICE—EJ has article on Polish Hasid Israel Kozienice (1733–1814).

KRACAUER—See KRAKAUER.

KRACKOWIZER—See KRAKAUER.

KRAFFT—See KRAFT.

KRAFT (also Krafft)—UJ has article on Louis Kraft (b. 1891 in Moscow). CAJ has Krafft family records.

KRAGOL—See CARREGAL.

KRAKAUER (also Kracauer, Krackowizer) —Name derived from the city of Cracow (or Krakow), in Galicia, Poland. UJ has biographies from 19th-cent. Germany and Austria. Also see biography in EJ article on "Art."

KRAKENBERGER—LBI has a family tree beginning 1785.

KRAMER (also Cramer, Kremer)—Ashkenazic name meaning "merchant." JE has biography of Moses Kramer, 17th-cent. Lithuanian Talmudist. CAJ and PD have family records. CAJ has a Cramer family tree from Germany, 18th and 19th cent. Related to PINCZOW, RAFF and EPHRATI.

KRAMSZTYK—JE has two biographies from Poland, 19th cent.

KRANTZ—See KRANZ.

KRANZ (also Krantz)—UJ has article on preacher Jacob Kranz (1741–1804), born in Lithuania. Also known as ROMBRO.

KRASA—UJ has article on composer Hans Krasa (b. 1899 in Prague).

KRASNOPOLSKI—JE has article on Austrian jurist Horace Krasnopolski (b. 1842).

KRASS—UJ has article on U.S. Rabbi Nathan Krass (b. 1880 in Russia).

KRAUS (also Krauss, Krausz, Krause)—JE has six biographies from 19th-cent. Austria. AJA has a family tree beginning 18th cent., related to ADLER, BACHMAN, FROELICH, RICE, LAUER, FRANK and NATHAN. Other related names are NEWSALT and KISCH. Also see UJ.

KRAUSHAR (also Kraushaar, Krausharowa)—JE has article on Polish jurist Alexander Kraushar (1843–1931).

KRAUSKOPF—JE has article on U.S. Rabbi Joseph Krauskopf (1858–1923), born in Prussia.

KRAUSS—See KRAUS.

KRAUSZ—See KRAUS.

KRAYN—EJ has article on German painter Hugo Krayn (1885–1919).

KREININ—EJ has article on Byelorussian civic leader Meir Kreinin (1866–1939).

KREISLER—UJ has article on violinist Fritz Kreisler (b. 1875 in Vienna).

KREMENETZKY—See KREMNITZER.

KREMER—See KRAMER.

KREMNITZER (also Kremenetzky)—Name derived from the Polish town of Kremenetz, where Jews first settled in 15th cent. JE, UJ and EJ have articles from 17th-cent. Poland and 19th-cent. Russia. Related to KALISCH.

KREMSER (also Kremsier)—JE has biographies from 17th-cent. Germany and Poland, and 18th–19th-cent. Germany. Related to von ADLERSTHAL.

KREPLAK—UJ has article on writer Jacob Kreplak (b. 1885 in Poland).

KREPPEL—UJ has article on journalist Jonas Kreppel (b. 1874 in Galicia).

KRESPIN (also Krispin)—JE and EJ have biographies from 18th and 19th cent. Related to ISRAEL.

KRETSCHMAN—Related to BRAUN.

KREYN—UJ has article on composer Alexander Kreyn (b. 1883 in Russia).

KRIEGSHABER—See GRIESHABER.

KRINSKY—Ukrainian name meaning "one who cultivates flowers." The name may also be derived from the district of Kerensk in the former Russian government of Pensa.

KRISHABER—UJ has biography from 19th-cent. Hungary. Also see GRIESHABER.

KRISPIN—See KRESPIN.

KRISTELLER—UJ has article on German physician Samuel Kristeller (1820–1900).

KRISTIANPOLLER—Well-known rabbinical family in Galicia. See UJ.

KROCH (also Krock, Korch)—Family in Prague prior to 18th cent. See EJ.

KROCHMAL—JE has biographies from 17th-cent. Poland and Moravia. UJ has article on Nahman Krochmal (1785–1840) of Galicia, father-in-law of Nathan HOROWITZ. Related to ASHKENAZI, BIEGELEISEN, CHAJES, HABERMANN.

KROHN—See KRON.

KROL—UJ has two biographies from Russia, Poland and U.S.A., 19th–20th cent.

KRON (also Krohn)—JE and UJ have biographies from 19th-cent. Russia and Germany.

KRONACHER (also Kronecker, Kronik)—JE has biographies from 19th-cent. Germany. LBI has a family tree beginning 1725. CAJ has a family tree, 1725–1960.

KRONECKER—See KRONACHER.

KRONENBERG—JE has two biographies from 19th-cent. Poland and Russia.

KRONENGOLD—CAJ has family records from 1881 to 1889.

KRONER—JE and UJ have biographies from Germany, 19th cent.

KRONFELD—UJ has two biographies from Austria and U.S.A., 20th cent.

KRONIK—See KRONACHER.

KRONTHAL—LBI has family trees beginning 1694 and 1775. See family histories in JFF, Nos. 22, 23 and 24. Related to PERL.

KROTOSCHIN (also Krotoshinsky)—UJ has article on U.S. soldier Abraham Krotoshinsky (b. 1892 in Poland).

KUBINSKY—PD has family records.

KRUMBACH—Related to HAMELN.

KRUMENAU—Related to OPPENHEIM.

KRUPNIK—UJ has article on writer Baruch Krupnik (b. 1889 in Poland).

KRUSKAL—AJA has a family tree beginning 1879, related to JACOBSON.

KRYSA—JE has article on 18th-cent. Galician Frankist Judah Krysa.

KUBELSKY—UJ has article on U.S. comedian Jack Benny (b. Kubelsky in 1894).

KUFFNER—PD has family records.

KUGEL (also Kugelmann, Kugler)—UJ has article on Rumanian physician Leopold Kugel (1838–1915), born in Hungary. Related to HESS and ITZIG.

KUGELMANN—See KUGEL.

KUGLER—See KUGEL.

KUH—JE has biographies from 18th-cent. Germany and 19th-cent. Austria.

KUHAYL—EJ has article on Yemenite pseudo-Messiah Shukr Kuhayl (1840–1864).

KUHN—JE has biographies from 19th-cent. Germany and Austria. See a family history in *The Ancestry of Rosalie Morris Johnson.* Related HIRSCH, MORRIS and OPPENHEIM.

KUK—See KOOK.

KUKIZOW—Russian Karaite family dating from 17th cent. See EJ.

KULAKOFSKY—Related to MUSHKIN.

KULBAK—UJ has article on poet Moses Kulbak (b. 1896 in Lithuania).

KULISCHER (also Kulisher)—JE and UJ have biographies from 19th-cent. Russia.

KULKA (also Kulke)—JE has biographies from 19th-cent. Austria.

KULP—CAJD has a family tree. Also see *The Kulp Family: A Genealogy,* a detailed history of a family originally from Frankfurt-am-Main. Related to SPEYER.

KUN—UJ has two biographies from 19th-cent. Hungary. Related to KOHN.

KUNFI—UJ has article on Hungarian socialist Zsigmund Kunfi (1879–1929), born KOHN. Also see EJ.

KUNITZER—JE has article on Hungarian Rabbi Moses Kunitzer (d. 1837), a descendant of the MAHARAL of Prague (1525–1609).

KUNOS—JE has article on Hungarian scholar Ignatz Kunos (b. 1861).

KUNSTADT—EJ has article on Hungarian Rabbi Ignaz Kunstadt (1838–1909). LBI has a family tree beginning 1790.

KUPCHIK—UJ has article on U.S. chess master Abraham Kupnik (b. 1892 in Russia).

KUPERNIK—JE has article on Russian Abraham Kupernik (1821–1893).

KURANDA—JE and UJ have biographies from 19th-cent. Austria.

KURNIK—See KORNIK.

KURREIN—JE has article on Austrian Rabbi Adolf Kurrein (b. 1846 in Moravia). CAJ has family records from 1905.

KURSHEEDT—UJ has article on U.S. broker Israel Kursheedt (1766–1852), born in Germany, son-in-law of Gershom SEIXAS.

KURTZ (also Kurtzig, Kurz)—UJ has biographies from 19th-cent. Russia and Austria. See family history in *Ostdeutsches Judentum: Tradition einer Familie (Kurtzig).*

KURTZIG—See KURTZ.

KURZ—See KURTZ.

KURZWEIL—See "Past Shock," in *Newsday* (Long Island, N.Y.) *Sunday Magazine,* Sept. 19, 1976, regarding a Kurzweil family from Dobromil, Galicia.

KUSEL—JE has article on German jurist Rudolph Kusel (1809–1880). JE article on "Coat of Arms" has the family crest.

KUSHIN—UJ has article on U.S. builder Nathan Kushin (b. 1884 in Russia). See his autobiography, *Memoirs of a New American.*

KUSHNIROV—UJ has article on poet Aaron Kushnirov (b. 1898 in Russia).

KUSSMAN—UJ has article on writer Leon Kussman (b. 1884 in Latvia).

KUTNER (also Kuttner)—JE has biographies from 19th-cent. Germany. PD has family records. CAJ has Kuttner family records from 1846.

KUTTOWER (also Kutower)—JE has article on Polish Rabbi Abraham Kuttower (d. 1760 in Jerusalem), brother-in-law of Israel the BAAL SHEMTOB.

KUYAVSKY—Related to BEN-ZVI.

KWARTIN—UJ has article on cantor Savel Kwartin (b. 1874 in Russia).

KWITKO—UJ has article on poet Leib Kwitko (b. in Russia, late 19th cent.).

KYRA—UJ has article on Turkish Jewess Esther Kyra (1530–1600), of Spanish descent, widow of Elijah HANDALI.

LABAND—UJ has article of German professor Paul Laband (1838–1918).

LABANOWSKI—Karaite family in 17th-cent. Lithuania. See EJ.

LABATT—JE has biographies from 19th-cent. Sweden and U.S.A. LBIS has some family notes.

LABI—Turkish family of rabbis, dating from 16th cent. and descended from a Spanish family of scholars. JE has four biographies.

LA BOETIE—EJ has article on French humanist Etienne La Boetie (1530–1563).

LABOSCHIN—UJ has article on painter Siegfried Laboschin (b. 1868 in Poland).

LACHMANN—UJ has three biographies from 19th-cent. Germany and Russia. LBI has a family tree beginning 1832. Related to MOSSE.

LACHOWER—UJ has article on critic Fishel Lachower (b. 1883 in Poland).

LACK—See family history in You Can't Live All Your Life: A Story About Fannie Lack.

LACKENBACHER—PD has some family records.

LADENBURG—Family of German financiers and scholars dating from Moses Ladenburg of Ladenburg, Baden, mid-18th cent. See UJ. LBI has a family tree beginning 1762, related to DREYFUSS. See family history in Ladenburg: Familie und das Mannheimer Bankhaus Wilhelm H.

Ladenburg & Söhne. Related to PRINGS-HEIM and SAMSON.

LADIER—JE has article on Russian Rabbi Dob Bar Ladier (1770–1834), who came from Liady, the probable source of his name.

LAEMEL (also Laemmle, Lemel, Lemle, Lammlin, Lamlein, Lammel, Lemmlein)—EJ and UJ have biographies from 18th–19th-cent. Austria and 19th-cent. Germany. JE has article on Asher Lemmlein of 16th-cent. Venice. PD has Lamel family records. Related to HERZ and FISCHEL. JE article on "Coat of Arms" has the Lammel crest.

LAFER—UJ has article on Brazilian industrialist Horacio Lafer (b. 1893), of Lithuanian parents.

LAGARDE—German Paul Lagarde (1827–1891) was born BOTTICHER but took the name of his mother's family.

LAGARTO—JE and UJ have articles on 17th-cent. South American Rabbi Jacob Lagarto, of Dutch parents.

LAGUNA—JE has article on 17th-cent. Spanish poet Daniel Laguna, born in Portugal of Marrano parents.

LAIB—Related to BELMONT.

LAIT—Related to JAFFE.

LAJTA—UJ has article on Hungarian architect Bela Lajta (1875–1920).

LAKATOS—UJ has article on Hungarian author Laszlo Lakatos (b. 1882).

LAKOS—UJ has article on Hungarian painter Alfred Lakos (b. 1870).

LAMBERT—JE has article on French scholar Mayer Lambert (b. 1863), a descendant of Gershom Ulf ASHKENAZI and Elijah BLIN of 16th-cent. Worms. LBI has a family tree beginning 1699, related to HERZOG. Another related name is ROTH-SCHILD. For family history, see Herzog and Lambert Genealogy.

LAMDAN—UJ has article on poet Isaac Lamdan (b. 1899 in Russia).

LAMEGO—Related to MOCATTA.

LAMEL—See LAEMEL.

LAMLEIN—See LAEMEL.

LAMM—UJ has article on literary critic Martin Lamm (b. 1880 in Sweden). LBIS has a family tree and notes. Related to GODCHAUX.

LAMMEL—See LAEMEL.

LAMMLIN—See LAEMEL.

LAMPORT—UJ has biographies from Poland and U.S.A., 19th–20th cent.

LAMPRONTI—JE has article on Italian Rabbi Isaac Lampronti (1679–1756), whose great-grandfather came to Italy from Constantinople in 16th cent.

LANCASTRE—Related to BELMONTE.

LANCZY—JE and UJ have biographies from 19th-cent. Hungary.

LANDA—UJ has article on English writer Linda Landa (1881–1941), sister of Samuel GORDON.

LANDAU (also Landauer)—Ashkenazic name taken from the city of Landau in western Germany. It is found largely among Polish Jews, who probably were expelled from that city in mid-16th cent. The name itself was used as a Jewish family name as early as 1480. From the end of 16th cent. onward, the descendants of the original Landau family were in Poland, especially the western part of Podolia (annexed by Austria in 1772). In various cases the name Landau was taken by Jews who had no connection with the original emigrants from Germany. JE has a family tree and fourteen related biographies, plus three unrelated biographies from 19th-cent. Russia and Germany. LBI has a Landau family tree beginning 1545, and Landauer family trees beginning 1690 and 1776. CAJ has a Landau family history written 1951, other Landau records beginning 1744, and Landauer family trees from Germany, 1833–1939 and 1690–1936. AJA has a family tree from 17th-cent. Germany. Also see Landau family histories in *B'nai Landau Lemishpahatim* and *Ma'alot ha-Yuhasin*. See Landauer family history in *Family Tree of Elias and Karoline Landauer (Hurben-Krumbach-Munich)*. Related to JOSHUA, ISAAC, JACOBKE, POLAK, ROTHSCHILD, FEILCHENFELD, JAFFE, BERLIN, CASTELLAZZO, BASCHKO, CIECHANOW, AVIGDOR, FALK, POPPER, BOZIAN, WORMS, BAUER, BELMONT, OBERDORFER, LEVINGER, LEVI, WORG, GUGGENHEIMER and MARGOLIOTH.

LANDAUER—See LANDAU.

LANDE—LBI has a family tree beginning 1780, related to GANS.

LANDER—See family history in *It Began with Zade Usher* (see Bernstein in Bibliography).

LANDESBERG (also Landesberger)—See LANDSBERG.

LANDESCO—UJ has article on U.S. banker Alexander Landesco (b. 1880 in Russia).

LANDESMANN—See LANDMAN.

LANDMAN (also Landesmann, Landsman, Landmann)—UJ has article on U.S. Rabbi Isaac Landman (b. 1880 in Russia). LBI has a Landmann family tree beginning 1748. JE has article on Austrian poet Heinrich Landesmann (1821–1902), brother-in-law of Berthold AUERBACH.

LANDOWSKA—UJ has article on pianist Wanda Landowska (b. 1877 in Warsaw).

LANDSBERG (also Landsberger, Landesberg, Landesberger)—Russian family of scholars and philanthropists, traced back to Abraham Landsberg (1756–1831) of Kremenetz, who had six sons. Others with variations of the name include Joseph Landsberger (b. 1848 in Posen), a descendant of Aryeh LOB (d. 1737 in Posen). See JE and UJ. CAJ has Landsberg family records; PD has Landesberger family records. See family history in *B'nai Shlomo*. Also see JE articles on Pinne, Germany, and Grosswardein, Hungary. Related to BISCHOFFSHEIM, POSNER, BAMBERGER, KATZ.

LANDSBERGER—See LANDSBERG.

LANDSHUT (also Landshuth)—JE has article on German Leser Landshuth (1817–1887), born in Posen. CAJ has Landshut and Landshuth family records. See family history in *Neumark, Westpreussen und die Familie Landshut*.

LANDSMAN—See LANDMAN.

LANDSOFER—JE has article on Bohemian Talmudist Jonah Landsofer (1678–1712), also known as BUNZLAU or BUMSLO.

LANDSTEINER—UJ has article on pathologist Karl Landsteiner (b. 1868 in Vienna).

LANG—UJ has biographies from Lithuania, Palestine and U.S.A., 19th and 20th cent. LBI has a family tree beginning 1749. PD has some family records.

LANGENSCHWARZ—JE has article on German Maximilian Langenschwarz (1801–1860).

LANGER (also Langerman and Langner) —UJ has biographies from 19th-cent. Germany, U.S.A., South Africa, Wales and Czechoslovakia.

LANGERMAN—See LANGER.

LANGNER—See LANGER.

LANGSTEDTER—Related to LEBRECHT.

LANGSTEIN—UJ has article on physician Leopold Langstein (1876–1933), born in Vienna.

LANIADO—Sephardic family, dating back to 16th cent., which settled in Italy and the East. JE has four biographies.

LANIATORE—See LEVI.

LANTZ—UJ has article on German industrialist Lazare Lantz (1823–1909).

LAPAPA—JE has article on Eastern Rabbi Aaron Lapapa (d. 1674).

LAPARA—See LAPARREA.

LAPARREA (also Lapara)—Related to BELMONTE.

LA PEYRERE—EJ has article on French theologian Isaac La Peyrere (1596–1676).

LAPIDOT—EJ has article on Vilna Zionist Alexander Lapidot (1819–1906).

LAPIN—UJ has article on poet Berl Lapin (b. 1888 in Russia).

LAPOWSKI—AJA has a family tree, related to DILLON.

LAQUEUR—JE and UJ have biographies from Germany and France, 19th cent.

de LARA—Name taken by the Spanish family Cohen de Lara, whose members settled in Amsterdam, Hamburg, London and U.S.A. JE has ten biographies dating from 16th cent. onward. Related to DISRAELI, MENDEZ DA COSTA, RUSSELL. Also see COHEN.

LARIN—EJ has article on Russian economist Yuri Larin (1882–1932), also known as Mikhail LURYE.

LARRIMORE—UJ has article on French actress Francine Larrimore (b. 1898), whose mother's maiden name was ADLER.

L'ARRONGE—JE and UJ have articles on German Adolf L'Arronge (1838–1908), whose father's name was AARON or ARONSOHN.

LASALLE—See LASSALLE.

LASAR—PD has some family records.

LASCH (also Lash)—JE has article on German teacher Gershon Lasch (1803–1883).

LASCOFF—UJ has article on U.S. pharmacologist Leon Lascoff (b. 1867 in Vilna).

LASERON (also Laserson)—UJ has article on jurist Max Laserson (b. 1887 in Latvia). LBIS has Laseron family notes.

LASERSON—See LASERON.

LASH—See LASCH.

LASK (also Laskar, Lasker, Lasker-Schuler, Laski)—JE and UJ have Lasker and Laski biographies from 19th-cent. Germany, England and U.S.A. UJ has article on Galician philosopher Emil Lask (1875–1915). CAJ has Lask family records. Related to LAZARUS, ROSENSOHN, SCHULER.

LASKAR—See LASK.

LASKER—See LASK.

LASKI—See LASK.

LASSALLE (also Lasalle)—JE and UJ have biographies from 19th-cent. Germany and France. LBI has a Lassalle family tree. See family histories in AJF, Vol. 2, p. 27, and MGWJ, Vol. 62 (1918), p. 270. Related to LASSEL.

LASSAR—JE has article on German Oscar Lassar (1849–1907).

LASSEL—See LASSALLE.

LASSEN (also Lasson)—JE has biographies from 19th-cent. Germany and Denmark. Related to LAZARUSSOHN and WARBURG.

LASSON—See LASSEN.

LASZ (also Laszlo)—JE has biographies from 19th-cent. Hungary. Related to LAUB.

LATAS—See LATTES.

LATES—See LATTES.

LATIF—EJ has article on Spanish philosopher Isaac Latif (1210–1280).

LATTAS—See LATTES.

LATTEINER—JE has article on German playwright Joseph Latteiner (b. 1853 in Rumania).

LATTES (also Lates, Lattas, Latas)—Family living in Cuneo, Italy, continuously from 16th cent. at least until 1900. The name seems to have originated in Lattes, a small town near Beziers, France. See JE, which has eighteen biographies beginning in 13th cent. Probably unrelated is Isaac ·de Lattes, grandson of Immanuel, son of Rabbi Eliezer ben Immanuel of Tarascon, Provence, 14th cent.; see JE article on *David* ben Isaac. Also see family history in VR, No. 2, p. 104.

LATZ—AJA has a family tree beginning 1851 in Germany, related to GRAETZ, GRATZ, GRATZER and GRATZNER.

LATZKO—UJ has article on Hungarian author Adolf Latzko (b. 1876). PD has some family records.

LATZKY-BERTHOLDI—UJ has article on editor Jacob Latzky-Bertholdi (1881–1940), born in Russia. Related to BERTHOLDI.

LAUB—JE has article on Austrian violinist Ferdinand Laub (1832–1875), also known as LASZLO.

LAUCHHEIMER—JE has article on U.S. naval officer Charles Lauchheimer (1859–1920).

LAUER—Related to LAUTERBACH and KRAUS.

LAUFER—UJ has article on scholar Berthold Laufer (1874–1934), born in Germany.

LAUTENBURG—JE has article on Hungarian theater manager Sigmund Lautenburg (1852–1918).

LAUTERBACH—Family from Galicia, traced back to 1800. JE has two biographies from U.S.A. and Galicia, 19th cent. See *Chronicle of the Lauterbach Family.* Related to CHAJES, SUSSMAN, LAUER, HABER, SCHORR, FRIEDMANN, FLECKER and MANDEL.

LAWANI—EJ has article on 15th-cent. Yemenite scholar Da'ud Lawani.

LAWAT—EJ has article on Ukrainian Hasid Abraham Lawat (1835–1890).

LAWRENCE—JE has article on English surgeon John Lawrence (1828–1870).

LAWSON—JE has article on English publisher Lionel Lawson (1823–1879). Related to FAUDEL-PHILLIPS.

LAZAR—UJ has two biographies from 19th-cent. Hungary.

LAZARD—International bankers from France, 19th cent.; see EJ.

LAZARE—JE has article on French author Bernard Lazare (1865–1903). CAJ has some family records.

LAZAREANU—EJ has article on Rumanian author Barbu Lazareanu (b. 1881).

LAZAREVITCH—Related to ZINBERG.

LAZARSFELD—UJ has article on psychologist Paul Lazarsfeld (b. 1901 in Vienna).

LAZARUS (also Lazarussohn)—JE and UJ have biographies from 19th-cent. Germany. LBI has a family tree beginning 1790. AJA has family trees beginning 1757 and 1808, related to SOLOMONS, YATES and GREENHUT. CAJ has a family tree. LBIS also has a family tree and notes, related to HIRSCH and LASKAR. Other relatives include SAMUEL, STEINTHAL, REMY, STURMHOEFEL and LASSON.

LAZARUSSOHN—See LAZARUS.

LEAVITT—UJ has article on teacher Ezekiel Leavitt (b. 1880 in Russia).

LEBENSBAUM—UJ has article on poet Rose Lebensbaum (b. 1887 in Poland).

LEBENSOHN—See LEVENSON.

LEBENSTEIN—Related to HELLER.

LEBERT—JE has biographies from 19th cent. Germany. Related to LEWY, LEVY.

LEBHAR—Related to DELMAR.

LEBLANG—UJ has article on theatrical financier Joseph Leblang (1874–1931).

LEBOLD—AJA has a family tree from Chicago, beginning in 18th-cent. Bavaria, related to GREENEBAUM, HERZ, FELSENTHAL, HEYMANN, FOREMAN, HENLE,

GUTMANN, STIEFEL and FREUDEN-THALER.

LEBRECHT—AJA has a family tree beginning Germany, 1700, related to STRAUS, FLEISCHER, HANAUER, HERMANN, SIMON, TUCHNER and LANGSTEDTER. LBI also has a family tree beginning 1700.

LECACHE—UJ has article on French writer Bernard Lecache (b. 1892).

LECHNICH—Related to ROTHSCHILD and SPEYER.

LEDERER—JE has biographies from 19th-cent. Austria and Hungary.

LEDERMANN—LBI has family trees beginning 1700 and 1714.

LEE—JE and UJ have biographies from 19th-cent. England and Galicia. See a family history in *Book of the Descendants of Dr. Benjamin Lee and Dorothy Gordon*. Related to GORDON.

LEESER—JE has article on U.S. Rabbi Isaac Leeser (1806–1868), born in Germany, a nephew of Zalma REHINE.

LEEUW—JE has article on Dutch Talmudist Jacob de Leeuw (1811–1883).

LEFKOWITZ—Ashkenazic name derived from LOB or LOEWE, for "lion." UJ has two biographies from 19th-cent. Germany and Hungary.

LEFMANN—JE has article on German philologist Salomon Lefmann (b. 1831), from a family of old Westphalian settlers.

LEFSCHETZ—See LIPSCHUTZ.

LEFTWICH—UJ has article on writer Joseph Leftwich (b. 1892 in Holland).

LEHFELD—See LEHFELDT.

LEHFELDT (also Lehfeld)—UJ has article on physicist Robert Lehfeldt (1868–1927), born in England. Related to ADLER.

LEHMAIER—Related to SELIGMAN.

LEHMANN (also Lehman, Leman, Lemann, Lemans)—JE, UJ and EJ have biographies from 19th-cent. Germany, Poland and France. French Rabbi Joseph Lehmann (b. 1843) was a descendant of Swabian rabbis and also of Rabbi David DIESPECK. JE has article on Dutch educator Moses Lemans (1785–1832). LBI has a Lehmann family tree beginning 17th cent. AJA has a Lehmann family tree beginning 1832 in Germany, and a Lehman

family tree. LBIS has a Leman family tree and notes. CAJ has records of a Lehmann family from Germany, related to LEHRFELD. AJA also has a Lemann family tree, related to BERTHELOT and FRIEDHEIM. Also see family histories in *Der polnische Resident Berend Lehmann* and *The Lemann Family of Louisiana*. Related to BAUER, FRANKEL, BERMANN, KALISCH, WERTHEIMER, KAHN.

LEHR (also Lehrer, Lehrs)—Ashkenazic name derived from the German verb *lehren*—"to teach." UJ has biographies from 19th-cent. Poland and Germany. LBI has a family tree beginning 1774.

LEHREN—Dutch family whose name is derived from Lehrensteinfeld, a village in Württemberg, Germany. JE has three biographies from 19th cent.

LEHRER—See LEHR.

LEHRFELD—CAJ has family records from Germany, related to LEHMANN.

LEHRMAN—UJ has article on English Rabbi Simon Lehrman (b. 1900).

LEHRS—See LEHR.

LEIB—Related to LEVINSON.

LEIBERMANN—See LIEBERMAN.

LEIBOWITZ (also Liebowitz, Libowitz)—UJ has article on U.S. Judge Samuel Leibowitz (b. 1893 in Rumania).

LEICHTENTRITT—UJ has article on musicologist Hugo Leichtentritt (b. 1874 in Posen).

LEIDESDORF (also Leidesdorff, Leidesdorfer)—JE, UJ and EJ have biographies from 19th-cent. Austria and Hungary. William Leidesdorff (b. 1802 in Hungary, d. 1848 in California) was related to the EGER and SOFER (SCHREIBER) families. Leidesdorfer was a Viennese family of 18th and 19th cent., related to HERZ. LBI has a Leidesdorf family tree beginning 1749; PD has family records. AJA has a Leidesdorff family tree beginning 1755 in Germany, related to MAGNUS and SUSSKIND. LBIS has Leidesdorff family notes. Also related to WERTHEIMER.

LEIMDORFER—JE has article on Hungarian Rabbi David Leimdorfer (1851–1922).

LEINER—Dynasty of Polish Hasidim, begun by Mordecai Joseph Leiner (1802–1854). See UJ.

LEIPZIG—Ashkenazic name derived from the city of Leipzig, Germany. UJ has biographies from England and Sweden, 19th and 20th cent.

LEISERSON—UJ has article on U.S. economist William Leiserson (b. 1883 in Estonia).

LEITMERITZ—JE has article on 17th-cent. German Benjamin Leitmeritz.

LEITNER—JE has article on Professor Gottlieb Leitner (b. 1841 in Budapest, d. 1899 in Bonn).

LEIVICK—Pseudonym of Russian poet Leivick HALPER (b. 1888). See UJ.

LEKERT—EJ has article on Lithuanian bootmaker Hirsch Lekert (1880–1902).

LEKHNO—EJ has article on Crimean scholar David Lekhno (d. 1735), whose family name indicates his Polish origin.

LELOV (also Lelow)—Hasidic dynasty in Poland, beginning 18th cent.; related to ISAAC. See EJ.

LELOW—See LELOV.

LEMAN—See LEHMAN.

LEMANN—See LEHMAN.

LEMANS—See LEHMAN.

LEMBERG (also Lemberger)—Ashkenazic name taken from the city of Lemberg (now Lwow) in Galicia. JE has article on 17th-cent. author Judah Lemberger. Also see JE article on *Moses* ben Aaron. PD has some Lemberger family records. Related to ESKELES and HAIDA.

LEMEL—See LAEMEL.

LEMLE—See LAEMEL.

LEMMLEIN—See LAEMEL.

LEMON—JE and UJ have articles on Dutch physician Hartog Lemon (d. 1823), also known as ROFE (a name which suggests Sephardic ancestry). His daughter married J. LITTWAK of Amsterdam.

de LEMOS—JE article on "Coat of Arms" has the family crest. Related to HERZ.

LEMPERT—UJ has article on U.S. surgeon Julius Lempert (b. 1891 in Poland).

LENDVAI—UJ has article on Hungarian composer Erwin Lendvai (b. 1882).

LENEL—UJ has article on German professor Otto Lenel (1849–1935). LBI has a family tree beginning 1500.

LENGFELD—JE has article on U.S. chemist Felix Lengfeld (b. 1863).

LENGYEL—UJ has two biographies from Hungary and U.S.A., 19th–20th cent.

LENKEI—UJ has article on Hungarian playwright Henrik Lenkei (b. 1863).

LEO—JE and UJ have articles from 19th-cent. Poland and England. Poet Friedrich Leo (1820–1898), born in Poland, was the nephew of August BLOCH. AJA has a family tree, related to LEWIS, SIMSON and ISAACKS.

LEON (also Leao, de Leon)—Spanish-Portuguese family which in 1900 had branches in Italy, Holland, Germany, England, southern France, the eastern Mediterranean, the West Indies and Surinam. JE has twenty related biographies, beginning 16th cent., plus five other biographies of Leons who are apparently not related to this family—from 13th-cent. Spain, 15th- and 16th-cent. Italy, and 19th-cent. U.S.A. JE article on "Coat of Arms" has the family crest. Jacob Judah Leon (1603–1675) took the name TEMPLO; see UJ. Also see JE article on Dax, France, where the Leon family was among the Jews expelled in 1684. Related to MONTEFIORE, GOMEZ, MEDICI, NONES, HENDRICKS, HART, HENRIQUES and MOISE.

LEONE (also Leoni, Leonini)—EJ has biographies from 18th-cent. England and 19th-cent. Italy. Related to AZULAI, BRAHAM and LOEB.

LEONI—See LEONE.

LEONINI—See LEONE.

LEOPOLD—Related to BELMONT.

LERMA—JE has article on 16th-cent. Spanish Talmudist Judah Lerma.

LERNER—JE has three biographies from 19th-cent. Russia and Germany. CAJ has some family records. Related to MUNK and MUNKACSI.

LERT—Related to BAUM.

LESMAN—See LESMIAN.

LESMIAN (also Lesman)—EJ has article on Polish poet Boleslaw Lesmian (1878–1937).

LESSER—JE has five biographies from 19th-cent. Germany and Poland.

LESSING—UJ has article on German philosopher Theodor Lessing (1872–1933). Related to LEVINSON.

LESSMANN—JE has article on German historian Daniel Lessmann (1784–1831).

LESTSCHINSKY—UJ has article on pamphleteer Jacob Lestschinsky (1876–1935), born in Russia. CAJ has family records from 1832–1872.

LETTERIS—JE has article on Austrian scholar Meir Letteris (1800–1871), descended from a family of printers originally from Amsterdam. For a family history beginning 1544, see CB, p. 3064.

LEUBSDORF—See family history in *Die Siegburger Familie Levison.*

LEVAILLANT—UJ has article on French administrator Isaie Levaillant (1845–1911). Related to TORRES.

LEVALD—See LEWALD.

LEVANDA (also Lewanda)—JE has article on Russian author Lev Levanda (1835–1888). Also see LEWANDOWSKI.

LEVAY—UJ has article on Hungarian economist Henrik Levay (1826–1901).

LEVEN—JE has two biographies from 19th-cent. France. CAJ has some family records. Also see UJ article on Elizabeth STERN.

LEVENE—See LEVINE.

LEVENFISH—See biography in EJ article on "Chess." Related to LOEWENFISH.

LEVENSON (also Levinson, Levinsohn, Lebensohn, Levinson-Lessing)—JE has biographies from 19th-cent. Russia and Denmark. Russian scholar Isaac Levinsohn (1788–1860) was the son of Judah LEVIN, who was a grandson of Jekuthiel SOLOMON. Judah's father married a daughter of Zalman COHEN. AJA has a family tree from Galicia that traces back through Saul WAHL to HILLEL and King DAVID, related to HALEVY, REIZES, LEIB, LUBLINER, WEIL, ISSERLES, ASHKENASI, MIRELS, EMDEN, RAPPOPORT, KATZENELLENBOGEN and FISHEL. The name of this family tree is *Isaac Levinson's Genealogy.* Other related names are BANK, LESSING and MICHAILISHKER.

LEVENTHAL—See LEVINTHAL.

LEVENTRITT—JE has article on U.S. lawyer David Leventritt (b. 1845).

LEVERSON—EJ has article on English novelist Ada Leverson (1865–1936), related to BEDDINGTON. Another related name is SCHIFF.

LEVERTIN—JE has article on Swedish poet Oskar Levertin (b. 1862). LBIS has a family tree and notes.

LEVETUS—JE has article on English writer Celia Levetus (1819–1873), daughter of Joseph MOSS.

LEVI—One of the most common Jewish names, traditionally taken by Levites—male descendants of Levi (excluding descendants of Aaron). See chapter 5. Other forms of the name are LEVY, LEWI, HALEVI and HALEVY. JE has twenty-four biographies. EJ has a family tree, and LBI has family trees beginning 1300, 1498, 1627, 1754 and 1792. JE article on "Coat of Arms" has Halevi family crest. Also see *Stammtafel und Register der Nachkommenschaft der Samuel Alexander Levi aus Frankfurt-am-Main* and *Autobiografia di un padre di famiglia.* The name is so widespread that the name is unlikely to indicate a family relationship by itself. Related to WERTHEIMER, LANIATORE, CATALAN, EMBDEN, FRUMKIN, ITZIG, JOSEPH, JUDAH, LOMBROSO, MONTEFIORE, SELIGMAN, WORMS, ABOAB, BERGSON, HENLE, ARPA, EPHRAIM, OPPENHEIMER, BERLINGER, ELLINGER, LANDAUER, BRANDEIS, WITZENHAUSEN, FRANKEL and SOLOVEICHIK.

LEVIAS—JE has article on U.S. scholar Caspar Levias (b. 1860 in Russia).

LEVIN—Ashkenazic name most likely derived from LOEWE, although in some cases it may come from LEVI. Hirschel Levin (1721–1800) was also called LOBEL and LYON; he was a nephew of Jacob EMDEN. JE has eleven biographies, and JE article on "Coat of Arms" has the family crest. CAJ has family records. Another variation of the name is LEWIN. Related to HERSCHEL, LEVINSOHN, OLSCHWANG, ROBERT, VARNHAGEN, ASSER and WEINSTOCK.

LEVINE (also Levene)—For probable derivation, see LEVIN. UJ has biographies from Russia, U.S.A. and Argentina, 19th and 20th cent. Related to PHILLIPS, WINSTOCK, ROSENTHAL, BERG. Also see LHEVINNE.

LEVINGER—See LOEWE.

LEVINSKI—CAJ has some family records.

LEVINSOHN—See LEVENSON.

LEVINSON—See LEVENSON.

LEVINSON-LESSING—See LEVENSON.

LEVINSTEIN—See LOEWE.

LEVINTHAL—See LOEWE.

LEVISOHN—See LEVISON.

LEVISON (also Levisohn)—Name derived from LEVI. JE and UJ have biographies beginning 18th cent. LBI has a family tree. Also see *Die Siegburger Familie Levison.* Also see LEWISOHN.

LEVITA (also Lewita, Lewite, Levitan)— Poet Elijah Levita (1468–1549) was born in Germany, died in Venice; see JE. UJ has two biographies from 19th-cent. Russia and Germany. CAJ has a family tree from Germany. Related to BATTISTA, ELIANO, ELIAS.

LEVITAN—See LEVITA.

LEVITZKI—UJ has article on pianist Mischa Levitzka (1898–1941), born in Russia. Related to ADLER.

LEVNER—EJ has article on Russian writer Israel Levner (1862–1916).

LEVONTIN—UJ has article on Palestinian colonist Zalman Levontin (1856–1940).

LEVY—English, American and French variation of LEVI, although the spelling is found in other countries as well; usually indicates a Levite. JE has forty-one biographies, plus a tree of the family of Benjamin Levy of Philadelphia (18th cent.). LBI has family trees beginning 1521 and 1773. JE article on "Coat of Arms" has a Levy crest. Related to HART, ITZIG, MACHADA, de SOLA, LUMLEY, NONES, PHILLIPS, WOLFF, SEIXAS, ELBOGEN, LEBERT, GALANTE, MOISE, FRANKEL, FAUDEL-PHILLIPS, LINDO, HENDRICKS, HAYS, HAGENAU, LIEBERT, MANUEL, POLOCK, RODENBERG, SALAMANSOHN, WALEY, YULEE, FRANKS, FALK, ZBITKOWER, COHEN and LEVY-ALVARES.

LEVY-ALVAREZ—See LEVY.

LEVYNSOHN—Related to EBERS.

LEVYSOHN—Variation of LEVY. JE and UJ have biographies from 19th-cent. Germany and Denmark.

LEWALD (also Levald)—JE and UJ have biographies from 18th- and 19th-cent. Germany. LBI has a family tree beginning 1700, related to SPIERO. LBIS has notes. Other related names are MIELZINER and STAHR.

LEWANDA—See LEVANDA.

LEWANDOWSKI—JE has article on German composer Louis Lewandowski (1823–1894). LBI has a family tree beginning 1818. Also see LEVANDA.

LEWEK—See LEWKO.

LEWENTHAL—See LOEWE.

LEWENZ—LBI has a family tree beginning 1852, related to ARNHOLD.

LEWES—Related to MANHEIMER.

LEWI—Variation of LEVI. JE has article on U.S. physician Joseph Lewi (1820–1897), born in Bohemia. AJA has a family tree beginning 1783 in Germany, related to RESIK, SCHWARZ, DREIFUS, POPPER and MACK. Another related name is WOLFF.

LEWIN—See LOEWE.

LEWINSKY—See LOEWE.

LEWINSOHN—See LOEWE.

LEWINSTEIN—See LOEWE.

LEWIS—Probably a variation of LEVI. JE has six biographies from 19th-cent. England and U.S.A. AJA has a family tree beginning 18th cent., related to LEO. Other related names are SELIGMAN, DISRAELI, EMANUEL, PHILIPSON, DAVIS and TEMPLE.

LEWISOHN—JE has article on U.S. merchant Leonard Lewisohn (1847–1902), born in Germany. AJA has a family tree, related to ELOESSER.

LEWISOHN (also Lewysohn, Lewyson)— JE has three biographies from 19th-cent. Germany and U.S.A. AJA has a Lewisohn family tree, related to ELOESSER. CAJ has Lewyson family records. Also related to RAUNHEIM and SELIGMAN. See also LEVISON and LEVI.

LEWITA—See LEVITA.

LEWITE—See LEVITA.

LEWKO—EJ has article on wealthy Cracow Jew Jordanis Lewko (d. 1395).

LEWKOWITSCH—See LEFKOWITZ.

LEWY—Ashkenazic name derived either from LEVI or from LOEWE. JE has biographies from 19th-cent. Germany and Denmark. AJA has a family tree. See JE article on Pinne, Poland. Related to LEBERT.

LEWYSOHN—See LEWISOHN.

LEWYSON—See LEWISOHN.

LEUWY—See LOEWE.

LEYA—LBIS has some family notes.

LEYSER—CAJ has a family tree from Germany and Holland, 1720–1959.

LHEVINNE—UJ has article on pianist Josef Lhevinne (b. 1874 in Russia). See also LEVINE.

LIBAN—CAJ has some family records.

LIBERMAN (Libermann)—See LIEBERMAN.

LIBIN—UJ has article on writer Solomon Libin (b. 1872 in Russia).

LIBOSCHUTZ—See LIPSCHUTZ.

LIBOWITZ—See LEIBOWITZ.

LIBSCHITZ—See LIPSCHUTZ.

LICHENHEIM—LBI has a family tree beginning 1838, related to ARON.

LICHT—UJ has article on U.S. poet Michael Licht (b. 1893 in Russia).

LICHTENBERG—JE has biographies from 19th-cent. Hungary and U.S.A.

LICHTENFELD—JE has article on Polish author Gabriel Lichtenfeld (1811–1887), a descendant of Moses ISSERLES. Related to PERETZ.

LICHTENSTADT (also Lichtenstadter)—JE and UJ have biographies from 19th-cent. Russia, Bohemia and Germany. See family history in ZGJT, Vol. 2 (1931), p. 147.

LICHTENSTEIN—JE and UJ have biographies from 19th-cent. Germany, Hungary, Russia, Lithuania, Poland and U.S.A. Also see *The Virginia Lichtensteins.* Related to ADLER, HIRSCHENSOHN. Also see LICHTSTEIN.

LICHTEIM—UJ has biographies from 19th- and 20th-cent. Germany.

LICHTSCHEIN—JE has article on Hungarian Rabbi Ludwig Lichtschein (d. 1886).

LICHTSTEIN—Possible variation of LICHTENSTEIN. JE has two biographies from 18th- and 19th-cent. Poland.

LIDZBARSKI—UJ has article on philologist Mark Lidzbarski (1868–1928), born in Poland.

LIEBEN—Ashkenazic name taken from the town of Lieben, near Prague. UJ has four biographies from 19th–20th cent. Austria and Bohemia. PD has some family records. See family history in *Fünfzig Jahre eines Wiener Hauses.* Related to AUSPITZ.

LIEBENBERG—PD has some family records.

LIEBER—Related to AUSPITZ and CARDOZO.

LIEBERMAN—See LIEBERMANN.

LIEBERMANN (also Lieberman, Leibermann, Liberman, Libermann)—JE and UJ have biographies from Russia, Germany, Austria, Hungary, Galicia, Poland, South Africa, England and U.S.A., beginning 17th cent. LBI has a family tree beginning 1748. LBIS has some family notes. Also see JE article on Posen, Poland. Related to GREENHUT and KATZENELLENBOGEN.

LIEBERT—UJ has article on philosopher Arthur Liebert (b. 1878 in Berlin), originally LEVY. LBIS has some family notes.

von LIEBIG—See family history in JFF, No. 27.

LIEBLING—JE and UJ have biographies from Germany, 19th cent. Related to BENDETSOHN.

LIEBMAN—See LIEBMANN.

LIEBMANN (also Liebman)—UJ has biographies from Germany, 17th, 18th and 19th cent. Jost Liebmann (1640–1702) married Esther SCHULHOF; their daughter married Aaron WOLF. Liebmann's descendants include BEER and MEYERBEER. Also see EJ article on *Aaron* ben Isaac Benjamin Wolf. PD has some family records. See family tree in *Stammtafeln der von Liebmann-Schwarzschild (1555–94) abstammenden Familien.* Related to VAN GELDERN, HAMELN.

LIEBOWITZ—See LEIBOWITZ.

LIEBRECHT—JE has article on German folklorist Felix Liebrecht (1812–1890).

LIEBREICH—JE has two biographies from 19th-cent. Germany.

LIEFMANN—See LIPMANN.

LIEME—UJ has article on Dutch Zionist Nehemia de Lieme (1882–1940).

LIEPMANN—See LIPMANN.

LIFSCHITZ—See LIPSCHUTZ.

LIFSHITZ—See LIPSCHUTZ.

LIGETI—UJ has article on Hungarian sculptor Miklos Ligeti (b. 1871).

LILIEN—JE has article on Austrian artist Ephraim Lilien (b. 1874 in Galicia). CAJ has some family records. Related to SAMSON.

LILIENBLUM—JE has article on Russian scholar Moses Lilienblum (1843–1910), born in Kovno.

LILIENFELD—CAJ has a family tree from Germany.

LILIENTHAL—JE has two biographies from 19th-cent. Germany and U.S.A. LBI has a family tree beginning 1630. CAJ has some family records. See *The Lilienthal Family Record.* Related to SELIGMAN.

LIMA (also De Lima)—JE and EJ have articles on 17th-cent. Lithuanian scholar Moses Lima. Related to SAMSON and de SOLA.

LIMBURG—See biography in EJ article on "politics."

LIND—Related to GOLDSCHMIDT.

LINDAU (also Lindauer)—JE and UJ have biographies from Germany, 18th, 19th and 20th cent. LBI has a family tree beginning 1685. Related to KALISCH and SULZBERGER.

LINDEN—PD has some family records.

LINDERER—UJ has article on German writer Robert Linderer (1824–1886). CAJ has some family records.

LINDNER—Related to MOSKOWITZ.

LINDO—One of the oldest and most esteemed Sephardic families of London. It can be traced back to Isaac Lindo (d. 1712). JE has a family tree and six biographies. Related to ABARBANEL, FEREIRA, MATTOS, MOCATTA, COSTA, NORSA, LYON, ALOOF, LEVY, HENRY, GARCIA, ALEXANDER and DISRAELI.

LINETZKI—JE has article on Russian humorist Isaac Linetzki (1839–1915).

LINIK—CAJ has some family records.

LINZ—CAJ has some family records.

LION—See LYON.

LIPCHITZ—See LIPSCHUTZ.

LIPCHOWITZ—CAJ has a family history beginning 18th cent., related to FELSENSTEIN and WEIL.

LIPINER—JE has article on Austrian poet Siegfried Lipiner (1856–1903) from Jaroslav, Galicia.

LIPKIN—Russian family that takes its name from Dob Bar Lipkin, rabbi of Plungian (first half of 18th cent.). JE has a family tree and two biographies. Israel Lipkin (d. 1883) was also known as Israel SALANTER. Relatives include BIRKHAHN, GOLDBERG, KALISCHER and RABINOWITZ.

LIPMAN—See LIPMANN.

LIPMANN (also Lipman, Lippmann, Liefmann, Liepmann)—Ashkenazic name that may have come from the northwest German principality of Lippe, where Jews first settled in 14th cent. JE and UJ have biographies from 19th-cent. Germany, France, Austria and U.S.A. JE also has an article on Yom-Tob Lipmann-Muhlhausen, of 14th–15th-cent. Austria. Also see JE article on Coblenz, (or Koblenz), Germany. Related to MANN, PINCUS, SONNENFELS, SPIRA, SAMSON. Also see LIPPE.

LIPPE—JE and UJ have biographies from 19th-cent. Galicia and Rumania. Also see LIPMANN.

LIPPMANN—See LIPMANN.

LIPSCHITZ—See LIPSCHUTZ.

LIPSCHUTZ (also Lipschitz, Lupschutz, Libschitz, Lifschitz, Lifshitz, Liboschutz, Luboschutz, Lefschetz, Lipchitz, etc.)—Family of Polish and German rabbis. The name is derived from Liebeschitz, a town in Bohemia. JE, UJ and EJ have numerous biographies from 16th cent. onward, although all are not necessarily related. See family history in ZGJD, Vol. 1 (1929), p. 200. Also see JE article on Pinsk. Related to TEITELBAUM, JOLLES, FRUMKIN, ROKEACH, LOW, MUSHKIN, AUERBACH and NEMENOFF.

LIPSON—UJ has article on English economist Ephraim Lipson (b. 1888).

LIPTAI—UJ has article on Hungarian writer Imre Liptai (1876–1927).

LISBONNE—JE has article on French lawyer Eugene Lisbonne (1818–1891).

LISHANSKY—EJ has article on Ukrainian Zionist Yosef Lishansky (1890–1917).

LISKER—JE has article on 17th-cent. Russian Rabbi Abraham Lisker.

LISMAN—Related to POCHAPOVSKY.

LISSACK—JE has article on English writer Morris Lissack (1814–1895), born in Posen.

LISSAUER—JE and UJ have biographies from 19th-cent. Germany. LBI has a family tree beginning 1722.

LISSER—JE has two biographies from 18th-cent. Poland. Related to KOHEN (of Lemberg), LIWA and TOCKELS.

LIST—UJ has article on singer Emanuel List (b. 1891 in Vienna). AJA has a family tree beginning 1861.

LITMAN—UJ has article on economist Simon Litman (b. 1873 in Russia).

LITTAUER (also Litthauer)—JE has biographies from Poland and U.S.A., 19th cent.

LITTEN—UJ has biography of German professor Fritz Litten (b. 1873).

LITTHAUER—See LITTAUER.

LITTWAK—See LITWACK.

LITVINOFF—UJ has article on Russian statesman Maxim Litvinoff (b. 1876).

LITWACK (also Littwak, Littwack, Litwakov)—Ashkenazic name usually meaning "from Lithuania." JE has article on Dutch mathematician Juda Litwack (1760–1836), born in Poland. UJ has article from 19th-cent. Russia. The name was also the pseudonym of journalist Hayim HELFAND. Related to LEMON.

LITWAKOV—See LITWACK.

LIUKHOVETSKY—Related to MAISKY.

LIUZZI—UJ has article on Italian composer Fernando Liuzzi (1884–1941).

LIVERIGHT—Related to FLEISHER.

LIVINGSTON—AJA has a family tree from Prussia and New York, beginning 1837. Related to MINIS.

LIWA—Related to LISSER.

LOANS (also Loanz)—German family name since 15th cent. German cabalist Elijah Loans (1564–1636) was a descendant of RASHI (1040–1105) and also related to the BAAL SHEMTOB. See JE and EJ. Other relatives include LURIA, LUNTZ, WORMSER and GERSHOM.

LOB—See LOEB.

LOBATO (also Lobatto)—Marrano family which lived in Amsterdam from 16th cent. JE has four biographies. AJA has some family notes. Related to PINA and JESHURUN.

LOBISCH—See LOEB.

LOBO—JE has article on 17th-cent. Spanish poet Moses Lobo of Amsterdam.

LOCKER—UJ has article on Zionist Berl Locker (b. 1877 in Galicia).

LOEB (also Lob, Loebel, Lobel, Lobisch)—Ashkenazic name meaning "lion"; another variation is LOEWE. JE, UJ and EJ have biographies beginning in 16th-cent. Germany and Poland. LBI has a Loeb family tree; CAJ has a Lob family tree and Lobel family records. Related to BERENSTEIN, SCHIFF, SELIGMAN, SIMON, LEONI, HIRSCH, AUERBACH, BACHARACH, MARGOLIOTH, EPSTEIN, LANDSBERGER, JAFFE, WARBURG, LEVIN and CALAHORRA.

LOEBEL—See LOEB.

LOEFFLER—CAJ has some family records. Related to FEUCHTWANGER. Also see LOFFLER.

LOEN—CAJ has some family records.

LOENING—German family originally named LOEWENTHAL. UJ has five biographies from 19th and 20th cent. Related to GIERKE.

LOESKE—UJ has article on German botanist Leopold Loeske (1865–1935).

LOESER—LBI has a family tree beginning 1811, related to PLAUT.

LOEVE—See LOEWE.

LOEVE-VEIMARS—See LOEWE.

LOEVINGER—See LOEWE.

LOEVINSON—See LOEWE.

LOEWE (also Loew, Loewen, Loewenberg, Loewenfeld, Loewenfisch, Loewengart, Loewenherz, Loewenmayer, Loewenstam, Loewenstamm, Loewenstein, Lewinstein, Levinstein, Levinger, Loevinger, Levinthal, Lewenthal, Lewin, Lewinsky, Lewinsohn, Leuwy, Loewenthal, Loewi, Loewit, Loewy, Lovinger, Lovinson, Lovy, Low, Lowe, Lowenberg, Lowenfeld, Lowengard, Lowengrund, Lowenherz, Lowenmaier, Lowenrosen, Lowenstamm, Lowenstein, Lowenthal, Lowi, Lowinger, Lowinsohn, Lowisohn, Lowy)—Ashkenazic name meaning "lion" in German; another variation is LOEB. While all names with the Loewe stem are certainly not related to one another, they can all be traced to the original Loewe, as may some other names such as LEVIN. In some cases the name was taken by Jews who claimed descent from Judah Lowe, the MAHARAL of Prague; this is known to be the case for the Low family; see JFF, Nos. 6, 11 and 12, and CAJ Low family trees from Hungary, Russia and Germany. CAJ has family trees for Loewe (related to ETTLINGER and BAMBERGER), Lowe (related to VOGEL, SCHIFF, GOTTSCHALK, GOLDSTEIN, HEINEMANN and BLUMENTHAL), Lowenherz (covering 1760–1912; related to FRIEDLANDER), Lowenstein (from Germany and Pakistan), and Levinger (Hungary). CAJ also has records for Leuwy and Loev. LBI has family trees for Loewen (beginning 1747), Loewenstein (beginning 1784), Levinstein (beginning 1772), Loewi (beginning 1746), Loewy (beginning 1794, related to PROSKAUER), Loevinson (beginning 1770) and Loewenthal (beginning 1670 and 1700). AJA has a Lowenstein family tree. PD has family records for Lowenrosen, Lowenstamm and Lowenthal. See Loewenthal family history in JFF, No. 14. Also see *Price, Goldsmith, Lowenstein and Related Families, 1700–1967; Chronik der Familie Lowenstein-Porta; The Descendants of Moritz Lowenthal of Ladenburg; The Loevinger Family of Laupheim, Pioneers in South Dakota; Die Familie Loewengart (in Württemberg); Geschichte der Familien Valentin, Loewen und Manheimer-Behrend;* and *Chronik der Familie Friedlander-Lowenherz, 1760–1912.* Related to BRILL, ASHKENAZI, FALK, JAFFE, HURVITZ, TERRIS, EPSTEIN, KLEINBERG, BINSWANGER, LANDAUER, RAFF, SULZER, LOENING, SCHWAB, BEER, SCHULHOF, KAHN, SINGER, KELIN, KOLLIN, BACHARACH, SCHOMBERG, FLECKELES, BLOCH, LIPSCHITZ, MUNZ, MAYERHYNEMAN, FRIEDLANDER, HERTZVELD, BRESLAU, KAHANA, MOSSE, KATZ, PRICE, LYONS, GOLDSMITH, PORTA, AUERBACH, METZLER and KOHN.

LOEWEN—See LOEWE.

LOEWENBERG—See LOEWE.

LOEWENFELD—See LOEWE.

LOEWENFISH—See LOEWE.

LOEWENGART—See LOEWE.

LOEWENHERZ—See LOEWE.

LOEWENMAYER—See LOEWE.

LOEWENSTAM (Loewenstamm)—See LOEWE.

LOEWENSTEIN—See LOEWE.

LOEWENTHAL—See LOEWE.

LOEWI—See LOEWE.

LOEWIT—See LOEWE.

LOEWY—See LOEWE.

LOFFLER—UJ has article on criminologist Alexander Loffler (1866–1929). Also see LOEFFLER.

LOHNER—UJ has article on author Fritz Lohner (b. 1883 in Bohemia).

LOHNSTEIN—LBI has a family tree.

LOITMAN—Related to BARRON.

LOLLI—JE has two biographies from 19th-cent. Italy.

LOMBROSO (also Lumbroso, Lumbrozo) —Sephardic family from Portugal; in Italy and America, 17th cent.; France and Tunis, 18th cent. See biographies in JE and UJ. Related to MOCATTA, LEVI and FERRERO.

LOMZER—Related to WASSERZUG.

LONDON (also Londoner)—Name presumably taken from the city of London, although the name can be found in Lithuania as far back as 1661. See biographies in UJ and EJ; also *Shades of My Forefathers.* Related to NEWSALT.

LONGO—JE has article on 16th-cent. Turkish poet Saadia Longo.

LONNERSTAEDTER—LBI has a family tree beginning 1790.

LONSANO—Related to CONFORTE.

LONSCHEIN—EJ has article on U.S. builder Sam Lonschein (b. 1885 in Rumania). See his autobiography, *My 83 Years.*

LONZANO—JE has biographies from 16th-cent. Palestine, 18th-cent. Austria. Related to CONFORTE, NEUMANN.

LOPATIN—Ashkenazic name probably taken from the town of Lopatyn, near Brody, Galicia.

LOPES—See LOPEZ.

LOPES-DUBEC—See LOPEZ.

LOPEZ (also Lopes, Lopes-Dubec, Lopez Rosa, Lopez Suasso)—Spanish name for "wolf." JE and UJ have biographies beginning in 16th-cent. England. Lopes-Dubec was a Sephardic family active in France, 18th and 19th cent. Lopez Rosa was a 17th-cent. Portuguese family. JE article on "Coat of Arms" has the Lopez and Lopez-Suasso family crests. Related to FRANCO, COSTA, MOISE, RIVERA, GOMEZ, SEIXAS, HENDRICKS, de SOLA, NUNEZ, MENDEZ, MONTAIGNE, AMES, FARRAR and CASTRO.

LORBEERBAUM—See UJ article on *Jacob* ben Jacob Moses of Lissa, Poland (19th cent.), a member of the Lorbeerbaum family and great-grandson of Zebi Hirsch ASHKENAZI.

LORIA—See LURIA.

LORCH—Related to BELMONT.

LORJE—See LURIA.

LORKI—EJ has article on Joshua Lorki, Spanish convert to Christianity (d. 1419).

LORONHA—See NORONHA.

LORSCH—Related to TELLER.

LOSADA—See LOUSADA.

LOSER—LBIS has some family notes.

LOSINSKI—UJ has article on historian Samuel Losinski (b. 1874 in Russia).

LOTH—UJ has article on U.S. communal worker Moritz Loth (1832–1913), born in Austria. AJA has a family tree beginning 1860 in Slovakia, related to STRASSBURGER.

LOTHAR—UJ has article on Hungarian author Rudolf Lothar (b. SPITZER in 1865).

LOTMAR—UJ has article on law professor Philipp Lotmar (1850–1922), born in Germany.

LOUIS—UJ has article on English engineer Henry Louis (1855–1939). AJA has tree beginning 1778, related to POLLACK and BERNSTEIN.

LOUISSON—UJ has article on New Zealand official Charles Louisson (1854–1924), born in London.

LOUPPES—Related to MONTAIGNE.

LOURIE—See LURIA.

LOUSADA (also Losada)—Sephardic family in Jamaica that claims to be descended from Spanish grandees; JE has a family tree, and JE article on "Coat of Arms" has the family crest. Related to BARROW, D'AGUILAR, GOLDSMID, WILLS, WOLSELY, TARD, MOCATTA and MONTEFIORE.

LOVEMAN—JE has article on U.S. poet Robert Loveman (b. 1864). AJA has family tree beginning 1811 in Hungary, related to BLIACH.

LOVINSON—See LOEWE.

LOVY—See LOEWE.

LOW—See LOEWE.

LOWE—See LOEWE.

LOWENBERG—See LOEWE.

LOWENFELD—See LOEWE.

LOWENGARD—See LOEWE.

LOWENGRUND—See LOEWE.

LOWENHERZ—See LOEWE.

LOWENMAIER—See LOEWE.

LOWENROSEN—See LOEWE.

LOWENSTAMM—See LOEWE.

LOWENSTEIN—See LOEWE.

LOWENTHAL—See LOEWE.

LOWI—See LOEWE.

LOWINGER—See LOEWE.

LOWINSOHN (Lowisohn)—See LOEWE.

LOWY—See LOEWE.

de LOYA—See DELOUYA.

LOZOVSKY—UJ has article on Russian commissar Solomon Lozovsky (b. 1878).

LOZOWICK—UJ has article on U.S. architect Louis Lozowick (b. 1892 in Russia).

LUBARSCH (also Lubarsky)—UJ and JE have biographies from 19th-cent. Germany and Russia.

LUBARSKY—See LUBARSCH.

LUBETZKY—EJ has article on French Rabbi Judah Lubetzky (1850–1910).

LUBIN—UJ has four biographies from Poland and U.S.A., 19th and 20th cent. Related to WEINSTOCK and POLLACK.

LUBITSCH—UJ has article on movie producer Ernst Lubitsch (b. 1892 in Germany).

LUBLIN (also Lubliner, Lublinsky)—Ashkenazic name taken from the city of Lublin, Poland, where Jews first settled in 14th cent. JE and EJ have biographies from 19th-cent. Germany and Poland. Polish Talmudist Meir Lublin (1558–1616) was related to SHAPIRO; see EJ. LBIS has some family notes. LBI has a family tree beginning 1838 and related to SEGALL. Other relatives are LEVINSON and SPIRA.

LUBLINER—See LUBLIN.

LUBLINSKY—See LUBLIN.

LUBOSCHUTZ—See LIPSCHUTZ.

LUCA—UJ has article on poet Abraham Luca (b. 1879 in Rumania).

LUCAS—JE and UJ have biographies from 19th- and 20th-cent. England, Germany and U.S.A. Related to GOLDSMID, MONTEFIORE, COHEN and MOCATTA.

LUCCA—UJ has article on Austrian singer Pauline Lucca (1841–1908), niece of Samuel LUCKA.

de LUCENA—UJ has article on Abraham de Lucena of New York (d. 1670). Related to GOMEZ.

LUCKA—UJ has article on Samuel Lucka (1803–1891), born in Prague. Related to LUCCA.

LUDASSY—JE has article on Hungarian journalist Moriz Ludassy (1825–1885). Related to GANS.

LUDO—UJ has article on Rumanian writer J. Ludo (b. 1897).

LUDVIPOL—EJ has article on Odessa journalist Abraham Ludvipol (1865–1921).

LUDWIG—UJ has biographies from Germany, Russia and U.S.A., 18th and 19th cent. Related to COHN.

LUEBKE—Related to HALLE.

LUEGER—CAJ has some family records.

LUFT—LBI has a family tree beginning 1775. LBIS has some family notes.

LUIDOR—EJ has article on Galician writer Joseph Luidor (d. 1921).

LUKACS (also Lukas)—UJ has two biographies from Hungary, 19th cent. PD has some family records, related to LESSNER.

LUKAS—See LUKACS.

LUMBROSO (Lumbrozo)—See LOMBROSO.

LUMLEY—JE has article on British director Benjamin Lumle (1811–1875), born in Canada; related to LEVY.

LUNA—Related to NASI.

LUNCZ—JE has article on Russian editor Abraham Luncz (1854–1918).

LUNEL—Name found as early as 18th cent.; see EJ. UJ has article on author Armand Lunel (b. 1892 in France).

LUNGE—UJ has article on German chemist Georg Lunge (1839–1923).

LUNIETZ—EJ has article on Ukrainian preacher Gedaliah Lunietz (d. 1785).

LUNTESCHUTZ—UJ has article on painter Jules Lunteschutz (1822–1893), born in France.

LUNTZ—Family from Worms, Germany, descended from LOANS; one branch of the family called itself RABINOWITZ in 18th cent. Related to LURIE, BRAUDO, NAHUM and GORDON. See JE.

LUPERIO (also Lupercio)—JE has article on 17th-cent. Spanish apologist Isaac Luperio.

LUPERCIO—See LUPERIO.

LUPO—Rumanian variation of WOLF.

LUPSCHUTZ—See LIPSCHUTZ.

LURIA (also Loria, Lurie, Lourie, Lurye, Lorje)—Russian family with branches elsewhere in Europe that traces its descent from Solomon SPIRA (14th cent.), a descendant of RASHI (1040–1105). The name apparently comes from the Italian town of

Loria, near Bassano, although some historians say the name is derived from the Loire Valley in France. See family tree on page 13 of this book; see UJ for a discussion of the Luria genealogy. JE, UJ and EJ have several biographies beginning 16th cent. An excellent discussion of the family's descent is found in *Eileh Toledot* (in English). Also see *Mishpahat Luria,* and *Die Familie Lourie (Luria).* Related to FRANCIS, KLAUBERIA, KALONYMUS, KLAUBER, de SOLA, HEILPRIN, HELIN, ISSERLES, COHEN, LOANS, HABERKASTEN, AUERBACH, GREENHUT, LUNTZ, LARIN.

LURIE—See LURIA.

LURJE—See LURIA.

LURYE—See LURIA.

LUSCHE—Related to WALLICH.

LUSITANO (also Lusitanus)—Related to MONTALTO and USQUE.

LUST—Related to GREENHUT.

LUSTGARTEN—Ashkenazic name meaning "pleasure garden" in German.

LUTTER—Ashkenazic name derived from the town of Kaiserslautern in Bavaria.

LUXEMBURG—UJ has article on revolutionary Rosa Luxemburg (1871–1919), born in Russia.

LUZKI (also Lutzki, Lucki)—UJ has biographies from the Crimea and Galicia, 17th and 19th cent.

LUZZATTI (also Luzzatto)—Italian family dating from 16th cent., descended from a German who migrated to Italy from Lausitz, Germany; hence the name. JE and UJ have biographies. CAJ has some family records. See family histories in *Die Familie Luzzatto* and in *Autobiografia di S.D. Luzzatto.* Also see AJF, Vol. 1, p. 4. Related to MORPURGO, SEGRE and FINZI.

LUZZATTO—See LUZZATTI.

LVOVITCH—See LWOW.

LWOW (also Lvovitch, Lwuw)—Name derived from the city of Lwow (formerly Lemberg), Galicia. UJ has biographies from 18th and 19th cent. See family history in MGWJ, Vol. 72 (1928), p. 487. Related to MARCUS.

LWUW—See LWOW.

LYNDHURST—Related to GOLDSMITH.

LYON (also Lyons, Lion)—Variation of the names LOEB and LOEWE. JE has biographies from 18th-cent. Poland and England, 19th-cent. Holland, Surinam and U.S.A. CAJ has a Lion family tree from Germany, 1779–1967. LBIS has Lion family notes. Related to HARBY, HENRY, LINDO, D'AVIGDOR, LEVIN, MOISE, WAHL, NATHAN and WEINSTEIN.

LYONS—See LYON.

MAADEN—CAJ has a family tree from Amsterdam, 1804–1857.

MA'ARAI—Moroccan family in 13th cent.; see JE.

MAARSEN (also Maarssen)—JE and UJ have articles from 17th- and 19th-cent. Holland. Also see family history in CB, p. 3001.

MAAS (also Maass)—JE has biographies from 18th-cent. France and 19th-cent. England. LBI has a family tree beginning 1516, related to MOLL. CAJ has a Maass family tree from Germany.

MACCOBY—EJ has article on Polish Zionist Hayyim Maccoby (1858–1916).

MACHADO—Name of Jews who emigrated from Portugal to Mexico and the West Indies in 17th cent. JE has eight biographies, and JE article on "Coat of Arms" has the family crest. Related to NUNEZ, PHILLIPS, MOSES, SEIXAS, Uriah P. LEVY, NOAH and ARNSTEIN.

MACHAUT—EJ has article on Denis de Machaut, 14th-cent. Parisian convert to Christianity.

MACHIEL (also Machiels, Machiels-Clinbourg)—CAJ has a Machiel family tree beginning 1804 in Amsterdam, and a Machiels family tree, also from Amsterdam. JE article on "Coat of Arms" has the Machiels-Clinbourg crest.

MACHINI—CAJ has some family records.

MACHLUP—JE has article on Hungarian merchant Adolf Machlup (1833–1895).

MACHOL—AJA has a family tree beginning 1831 in Germany, related to GOLDBLUM.

MACHORA—See MACHORRO.

MACHORRO (also Machora, Machorre, Maczoro, Magoro)—Sephardic family in Brazil, Germany, Holland, Hungary and Italy. JE has biographies from 17th cent. onward. Related to BELMONTE.

MACHT—UJ has article on U.S. physician David Macht (b. 1882 in Russia).

MACKOWSKY—UJ has article on art historian Hans Mackowsky (b. 1871 in Berlin).

MACNIN—Moroccan family dating from 18th cent., also known as COHEN. See EJ.

MADARASSY-BECK—Family of Hungarian economists descended from Mendel BECK in 18th cent. Related to HATVANY. See UJ.

MADURO—AJA has a family tree from Curaçao.

MAERZROTH—Related to BARACH.

MAESTRE—Related to DURAN.

MAGGID (also Magidoff)—Russian historian and genealogist Hillel Maggid (1829–1903), also known as STEINSCHNEIDER, was a descendant of Saul WAHL (Poland, 1541–1617); see JE. Moses DARSHAN was also known as Maggid; see UJ.

MAGIDOFF—See MAGGID.

MAGINO—JE has article on 16th-cent. French silk manufacturer Meir Magino of Venice.

MAGNES—See MAHNUS.

MAGNIN—AJA has a family tree beginning 1842 in Holland.

MAGNUS (also Magnes)—JE has eight biographies from 18th- and 19th-cent. England and Germany. LBI has a family tree beginning 1712, and another covering four generations. LBIS has a family tree and notes. CAJ has records for Magnus (related to ISLER, LILIEN and MOSSE) and for Magnes. Related to EMANUEL, MONTEFIORE, SAMSON, LEIDESDORFF.

MAGYAR (also Magyar-Mannheimer)—Ashkenazic name that means "Hungarian." UJ has article on painter Gusztav Magyar-Mannheimer (1859–1937). Related to MANNHEIMER and ROBERT.

MAHARAL of Prague—Nickname given to the great rabbi known variously as Lowe Judah, Judah Lowe and Lowe ben Bezalel (1525–1609), a reputed descendant of King David. His descendants include

BRILL, DUBNOW, KUNITZER, BRANDEIS and the family of Leopold LOW (1811–1875).

MAHLER—JE has three biographies from 19th-cent. Austria.

MAI—German printer Joseph Mai (1764–1810) was son-in-law of Isaiah BERLIN, rabbi of Breslau. See JE.

MAIER—JE has article on German Rabbi Joseph von Maier (1797–1873). LBI has a family tree beginning 1794.

MAIMI—EJ has article on Solomon Maimi (d. 1497), rabbi in Portugal.

MAIMON—UJ has a biography from 13th-cent. Egypt; JE has biographies from 18th- and 19th-cent. Russia and Lithuania.

MAIMONIDES—EJ has article on Spanish scholar Moses Maimonides (1135–1204).

MAINZ (also Mainzer)—Name taken from the German city of Mainz (formerly Mayence). LBI has a family tree beginning 1622. Related to KOHLER.

MAISEL—EJ has article on Polish Talmudist Elijah Maisel (1821–1912).

MAISKY—UJ has article on Soviet diplomat Ivan Maisky (b. 1884); originally LIUKHOVETSKY.

MAISON—JE has article on Bavarian merchant Karl Maison (1840–1896).

MAJER-LEONARD—LBI has a family tree beginning 1756.

MAJOR—JE has biographies from 16th-cent. Turkey and 19th-cent. Hungary.

MAKAI—Hungarian poet Emil Makai (1871–1901) was the son of Rabbi Anton FISCHER. The name probably comes from the town of Mako, where Fischer was rabbi 1864–1896. See JE.

MAKOWER—Name taken from Mako, Hungary. UJ has four biographies from England, Germany and Poland, 19th and 20th cent.

MAKSHAN—JE has article on 16th-cent. Bohemian Talmudist Samuel Makshan.

MALACHI—Related to SILVA.

MALAKH—EJ has article on Russian Shabbatean Hayyim Malakh (1650–1717).

MALAMUD (also Malamut)—UJ has two biographies from 19th-cent. Russia. Also see MELAMED.

MALBIM—JE has article on Russian Rabbi Meir Malbim, son-in-law of Rabbi Hayyim AUERBACH.

MALCA (also Malka, Malkah)—Moroccan family from 14th cent. See EJ.

MALDONADO de SILVA—EJ has article on Francisco Maldonaldo de Silva, Marrano martyr of Peru (1592–1639).

MALECH—Poet Leib Malech (1894–1936) was born SALZMAN in Poland; see UJ.

MALEKAR—JE has article on India soldier Moses Malekar (b. 1830).

MALINA—See MOLINA.

MALINOVSKI—Related to TROKI.

MALISOFF—UJ has article on U.S. chemist William Malisoff (b. 1895 in Russia).

MALKA (Malkah)—See MALCA.

MALKI—JE has biographies from 17th-cent. Rhodes and Palestine. Rabbi Ezra Malki of Rhodes was brother-in-law of Hezekiah de SILVA.

MALKIN—UJ has article on U.S. pianist Manfred Malkin (b. 1884 in Russia).

MALLER—UJ has article on U.S. educator Julius Maller (b. 1901 in Lithuania).

MALTER—JE has article on U.S. Rabbi Henry Malter (1867–1925), born in Galicia.

MALVANO—JE has article on Italian diplomat Giacomo Malvano (1841–1922).

MAMROTH—UJ has article on German financier Paul Mamroth (b. 1859). LBI has a family tree beginning 1800. Related to JAFFE.

MANASSE (also Manasseh)—JE and UJ have biographies from 19th-cent. Salonika and Germany. Related to MASSENA.

MANCROFT—UJ has article on British official Arthur Mancroft (b. 1872).

MANDEL (also Mandell, Mandl, Mendel, Mendels)—Ashkenazic name from the first name Mandel (meaning "almond"), Mendel was a prominent Hungarian family which flourished in Buda in late 15th and early 16th cent. Zechariah Mendel (1707–1746), rabbi of Grodno, was the son of Aryeh Lob ben Nathan Nata of Slutsk (d. 1729). See JE and UJ, which also have biographies from 19th-cent. Hungary, Germany and France. PD has records of a Mandel family related to THEBEN. See Mandel family history in JFF, No. 5. Also see JE article on Grodno, and EJ article on "Politics." Related to ROTHCHILD (not Rothschild), LAUTERBACH, ADLER, NEANDER and VISHNITZ.

MANDELBAUM—UJ has article on U.S. Judge Samuel Mandelbaum (b. 1886 in Poland). LBI has family trees beginning 1816 and 1837. Related to HELLER.

MANDELKERN—JE has article on Russian poet Solomon Mandelkern (1846–1902).

MANDELL, MANDELLI, MANDELLO— See MANDEL.

MANDELSHTAM—See MANDELSTAMM.

MANDELSTAMM (also Mandelshtam)— JE and UJ have biographies from 19th-cent. Russia.

MANDL—See MANDEL.

MANE—LBI has a family tree beginning 1849, related to GUTMANN.

MANES—UJ has article on insurance executive Alfred Manes (b. 1877 in Germany).

MANHEIM—See MANNHEIM.

MANHEIMER—See MANNHEIM.

MANI—JE has article on Turkish Rabbi Elijah Mani (d. 1899 in Palestine). Related to YELLIN.

MANIEVICH—UJ has article on Russian painter Abraham Manievich (b. 1883).

MANIN—UJ has article on Italian patriot Daniele Manin (1804–1857).

MANKIEWICZ—UJ has article on U.S. professor Frank Mankiewicz (1872–1941), born in Berlin.

MANN—UJ has three biographies from Galicia and U.S.A., 19th and 20th cent.

MANNE—JE has article on Russian poet Mordecai Manne (1859–1886).

MANNER—See MANNHEIM.

MANNHEIM (also Mannheimer, Manheim, Manheimer, Manner)—Ashkenazic name taken from the village of Monheim in Swabia—not from the city of Mannheim in Baden. JE and UJ have biographies from Germany, Hungary and France, 19th cent. LBI has a Mannheimer family tree beginning 1525 and a Manheimer family tree beginning 1772. LBIS has notes on the Mannheimer and Manheimer families. PD has records for the Manheim family (related to DIAMANT) and the Mannheim family. A Manheimer family history can be found in *Geschichte der Familien Valentin, Loewen und Manheimer-Behrend* (see Valentin in Bibliography). Related to SCHIFF, DAMIER, HERSCHMAN, MANNER, MAGYAR-MANNHEIMER, LEWES, BEHREND and VALENTIN.

MANNHEIMER—See MANNHEIM.

MANOR—PD has some family records.

MANSH—UJ has article on Galician communal worker Philip Mansh (1838–1890).

MANSI—Related to ANAW.

MANSUR (also Mansurah)—EJ has article on Yemenite scholar Saadiah Mansurah (19th cent.). Related to JABALI.

MANSURAH—See MANSUR.

MANTINO—JE has article on Italian physician Jacob Mantino (d. 1516), whose parents left Tortosa, Spain, in 1492.

MANUEL—JE and UJ have biographies from 19th-cent. France. Educator Eugene Manuel (1823–1901) was grandson of the famous Paris *hazzan* LOVY, and brother-in-law of Ernest LEVY-ALVARES. Related to SEIXAS and LEVY.

MAOR-KATAN—LBIS has some family notes.

MAPLESON—Related to NATHAN.

MAPU—JE has article on Russian novelist Abraham Mapu (1808–1867), born near Kovno.

MARAGOWSKY—UJ has article on U.S. cantor Jacob Maragowsky (b. ROWNER in Russia, 1856).

MARAM (also Marum)—See "Der Name Maram (Marum)" in *Forschung aus Judentum.* LBIS has some Marum family notes.

MARBURG (Marburger)—See MORPURGO.

MARC—See MARK.

MARCELLO—JE has article on Italian musician Benedetto Marcello (1686–1739).

MARCIN—UJ has article on U.S. writer Max Marcin (b. 1879 in Germany).

MARCK—See MARK.

MARCKWALD—UJ has article on German chemist Willy Marckwald (b. 1864). See family history in *Fünfhundert Jahre Familiengeschichte, 1430–1930* (see Herz in Bibliography).

MARCUS—See MARKUS.

MARCUSE—See MARKUS.

MARCZALI—JE has article on Hungarian historian Heinrich Marczali (1856–1940), son of Marczali-Morgenstern. Related to MORGENSTERN.

MARDOS—Related to SUNDELES.

MAREES—UJ has article on painter Hans von Marees (1837–1887), born in Germany; his name was originally REINHARD and his mother's maiden name was SUSSMANN.

MAREK—UJ has article on Russian historian Peter Marek (1862–1920), born in Lithuania. Related to MEYSL.

MARETZEK—JE has article on Austrian impresario Max Maretzek (b. 1821 in Moravia, d. 1897 in U.S.A.).

MARGALIOT (Margalioth)—See MARGOLIOTH.

MARGARETEN—See *Directory and Genealogy of the Horowitz-Margareten Family* (see Horowitz in Bibliography). Related to HOROWITZ.

MARGARITA—See MARGOLIOTH.

MARGFOY—Related to FOA.

MARGOLIES—See MARGOLIOTH.

MARGOLIN—See MARGOLIOTH.

MARGOLIOT—See MARGOLIOTH.

MARGOLIOTH (also Margulies, Margolis, Margolin, Margolies, Margoliot, Margoliouth, Margoliuth, Margoshes, Margaliot, Margarita, Morgulis)—Polish family of Talmudic scholars that traces its descent from RASHI (1040–1105) on one side and from SCHOR and Samuel EDELS on the other. The name means "pearl" in Hebrew and may have been taken from the female given name, "Perle." Virtually all Jews with some variation of the name, and whose ancestors came from eastern Galicia, are descended from this family, and many other Jews with the name are related as well. JE has a family tree and twenty-four biographies, beginning with Samuel Margolioth in 16th cent. *Anaf Ez*

Aboth, by Samuel Kahan, traces the family back to Prague in 15th cent. JE, UJ and EJ have numerous biographies. Judah Lob Margolioth (d. 1811 in Frankfurt-an-der-Oder) was a grandson of Rabbi Mordecai JAFFE. Meir Margolioth (d. 1790 in Galicia) was a nephew of Aryeh AUERBACH; his daughter married Naphtali HERZ. Russo-Polish Rabbi Isaac Margolis (1842–1887) was a descendant of Yom-Tob Lipmann HELLER of Prague. CAJ has Margulies family records. The definitive Margolioth family history is *Ma'alot ha-Yuhasin,* by Ephraim Zalman Margolioth (1762–1828), published in 1900 by his grandson, A.B. KROCHMAL. Also see Margulies history in *A Link with the Future* (see Rottenberg in Bibliography). Related families include LOB, OTTO, HARIF ha-LEVI, FISCHELS, DUBNO, LANDAU, BRODY, BRODER and RABBINOWITZ.

MARGOLIS—See MARGOLIOTH.

MARGOLIUTH—See MARGOLIOTH.

MARGOLOUTH—See MARGOLIOTH.

MARGOSHES—See MARGOLIOTH.

MARGULIES—See MARGOLIOTH.

MARHAZE—Related to GOMEZ.

MARIANSKY—See family history in *A Link with the Future* (see Rottenberg in Bibliography).

MARICH—See MARIK.

MARIK (also Marich)—Spanish name dating from 15th cent. See JE.

MARINI—JE has article on Italian Rabbi Solomon Marini (d. 1670).

MARINOV—UJ has article on U.S. writer Jacob Marinov (b. 1869 in Russia).

MARIX—JE has article on U.S. naval commander Adolph Marix (1848–1919), born in Saxony.

MARK (also Marc, Marck)—JE and UJ have biographies from France, 18th–19th cent., and Lithuania, 19th–20th cent. LBI has a Marc family tree beginning 1657, related to MAYER, and a Marck family tree beginning 1725. Another related name is LEWI. Also see MARKS.

MARKELL—Related to KAPLAN.

MARKENS—JE has article on U.S. writer Isaac Markens (b. 1846).

MARKISH—UJ has article on poet Peretz Markish (b. 1895 in Russia).

MARKON—UJ has article on scholar Isaak Markon (b. 1875 in Russia).

MARKOVICH (also Markowitz)—UJ has article on physician Jacob Markowitz (b. 1901 in Rumania). Related to DUBNO.

MARKOWITZ—See MARKOVICH.

MARKREICH—Ashkenazic name that is apparently a Hebraized version of the town of Leer in eastern Frisia. LBI has a family tree beginning 1598.

MARKS—JE and UJ have biographies from 18th–19th-cent. England, U.S.A. and South Africa. AJA has some family trees. Related to NONES, AYRTON, ISAACS and SIEFF. Also see MARK, MARX.

MARKUS (also Marcus, Marcuse, Markusewich)—JE and UJ have biographies from Germany, Hungary and England beginning 17th cent. The German physician Moses Marcus (1730–1786), born in Hungary, was the son of Rabbi Moses LWUW (called Moses HARIF) and grandson of Rabbi Mordecai MOCHIAH; see UJ. LBI has Marcus family trees beginning 1690 and 1832. LBIS has Marcus and Marcuse family trees. CAJ has a Marcuse family tree from Posen, and Markus and Marcus family records. PD also has Marcus family records. AJA has general information about a Marcus family. Related to ROBERT, SZALIT, BLOCH, SEIBERLING.

MARKUSEWICH—See MARKUS.

MARLI—JE has article on 16th–17th-cent. Italian Talmudist Samuel Marli.

MARMER (also Marmor, Marmorek, Marmorstein, Marmur)—JE and UJ have biographies from 19th-cent. Hungary, Galicia, Lithuania and Russia.

MARMOR—See MARMER.

MARMOREK—See MARMER.

MARMORSTEIN—See MARMER.

MARMUR—See MARMER.

MARNER—Related to BERNSTEIN.

MARON (also Maroni)—LBI has a Maron family tree beginning 1841, related to ARNHOLD. UJ has article on Italian Rabbi David Maroni (1810–1888).

MARONI—See MARON.

MARPURCH—See MORPURGO.

MARR—UJ has article on German actor Heinrich Marr (1797–1871).

MARROT—Related to SASSOON.

MARSCHAK (also Marshak)—UJ has two biographies from 19th-cent. Russia.

MARSHAK—See MARSCHAK.

MARSHALL—UJ has two biographies from U.S.A., 19th–20th cent.

MARSHUETZ (also Marschuetz)—AJA has a family tree from Bavaria.

MARTEAU—UJ has article on violinist Henri Marteau (1874–1934), born in France.

MARTOS—UJ has article on Hungarian author Ferenc Martos (1875–1938).

MARTOV—UJ has article on Russian revolutionary Julius Martov (1873–1923), born ZEDERBAUM.

MARULI—Related to POTCHI.

MARUM—See MARAM.

MARWITZ—LBI has a family tree beginning 1854, related to ARNHOLD.

MARX—JE has seven biographies from 19th-cent. Germany and France. Karl Marx (1818–1883), a descendant of KATZENELLENBOGEN, married Jenny WESTPHAL. EJ traces the name back as far as 1795. AJA has family trees beginning 1713 and 1750. The Marx family's relation to other major Ashkenazic rabbinic families is traced in *Reshimoth Aboth,* by Markus Seckbach. CAJ has some family records. JE article on "Coat of Arms" has a Marx family crest. Related to AGNON, SCHUBACH, GERSTLEY, GAGGSTATTER and KOHN. Other possible variations are MARK and MARKS.

MASACH—Family of Toledo, Spain; see history in Zunz GL, p. 425.

MASCARENHAS—Related to BELMONTE.

MASCHKOWSKI—LBIS has some family notes.

MASE—UJ has article on Russian Rabbi Jacob Mase (1860–1924).

MASHA'IRIAL—Iraqi family from 13th cent.; see EJ.

MASHIAH—JE has article on 10th-cent. Karaite scholar Hasun ben Mashiah of Egypt or Babylonia.

MASIE—EJ has article on Byelorussian physician Aaron Masie (1858–1930).

MASKILEISON—JE has two biographies from 18th–19th-cent. Russia. Abraham Maskileison (1788–1848) was a descendant of Rabbi Israel JAFFE of Shklov.

MASLIANSKY—JE has article on Russian preacher Zebi Masliansky (b. 1856 near Minsk). Related to PERSKIE.

MASLOV (also Maslow)—UJ has article on journalist Peter Maslov (b. 1867 in Russia).

MASNUT—EJ has article on 13th-cent. Aleppo Talmudist Samuel Masnut.

MASSARAN—See MASSARANI.

MASSARANI (also Massarano, Massaran)—Italian family known since 15th cent.; it came from Massarano, a small town near Novara in Piedmont. JE mentions ten members; related to ROSSI. EJ has an article on 16th-cent. Italian choreographer Jacchino Massarano, perhaps related.

MASSARANO—See MASSARANI.

MASSARY—UJ has article on actress Fritzi Massary (b. 1882 in Vienna). Related to FRANK.

MASSEL—JE has article on Russian Hebraist Joseph Massel (b. 1850 near Vilna).

MASSENA—UJ has article on French Marshal André Massena (1758–1817), born MANASSE.

MASTBOIM (also Mastbaum)—UJ has article on writer Yoiel Mastboim (b. 1882 in Russia).

MASTOW (also Mastov)—See family history in *It Began with Zade Usher* (see Bernstein in Bibliography).

MAT—JE has article on Galician Rabbi Moses Mat (1550–1606).

MATALON—Name derived either from the city of Toulon, France, or from the Italian town of Mataloni. JE has two biographies from 16th-cent. Turkey.

MATHOS—Related to BELMONTE.

MATIASSON—LBIS has some family notes.

MATKAH—EJ has article on 13th-cent. Spanish writer Judah Matkah.

de MATOS—Related to CARABAJAL. Also see MATTOS.

MATSNER—Related to GRUENBERG.

MATTERSDORF—JE has article on Hungarian Rabbi Joab Mattersdorf (d. 1807), father-in-law of Isaac ben Lippmann FRANKEL.

MATTITHIAH—Related to KAKA'I.

MATTOS—Possible variation of de MATOS. JE article on "Coat of Arms" has the family crest. Related to LINDO, MOCATTA, CASTRO.

MATTUCK—UJ has article on Rabbi Israel Mattuck (b. 1883 in Lithuania).

MA'TUK—One of the oldest Jewish families in Baghdad. EJ has article on 18th-cent. Baghdad astronomer Sulayman Ma'tuk. See family history in JQR, No. 17, p. 415. Related to YAHUDA.

MATZ—UJ has biographies from Lithuania and U.S.A., 19th and 20th cent.

MATZEL—JE has article on Hungarian soldier Asher Matzel (1763–1842).

MAUCLAIR—UJ has article on French writer Camille Mauclair (b. FAUST in 1872).

MAUL—Related to HOROWITZ.

MAUREY—UJ has article on French dramatist Max Maurey (b. 1868).

MAURICE—JE and UJ have articles on French theatrical director Charles Maurice (1805–1896), son of Maurice SCHWARTZENBERGER.

MAUROGONATO—JE has article on Italian legislator Isacco Maurogonato (1817–1892), who came from a prominent family in Ferrara. His father was Israel PESARO, but he took the name Maurogonato for one of his mother's relatives.

MAUROIS—UJ and EJ have articles on French writer André Maurois (b. Émile HERZOG in 1885).

MAUSCHBERGER—JE has article on 18th-cent. Bible scholar Leopold Mauschberger.

MAUTHNER (also Mautner)—JE has four biographies from 19th-cent. Austria and Germany. LBI has a family tree beginning 1817.

MAVROGHENI—CAJ has some family records.

MAX—UJ has article on actor Edouard Max (1869–1924), born in Rumania.

MAXIMON—See MAXIMOWSKI.

MAXIMOWSKI (also Maximon)—EJ has article on Galician essayist Shalom Maximowski (1881–1933).

MAY—Ashkenazic name taken from the town of Mayen in the Rhineland. A family of merchants named May flourished in the Tyrol in 16th, 17th and 18th cent.; one branch went to Poland. The family is related to DONATI and BASSEVI; see UJ. JE also has three biographies, including 16th-cent. Polish Rabbi Isaac May of Lublin. LBI has family trees beginning 1653, 1685 and 1844, related to GUMPERTZ and REIS. CAJ has a family tree from Hamburg, covering 1650 to 1962, related to RUBEN. PD has records of a May family from Innsbruck, Austria. See a family history in JFF, No. 14. Related to WOLFF. Also see MAYER.

MAYBAUM—JE has article on German Rabbi Siegmund Maybaum (b. 1844 in Hungary).

MAYER (also Mayerman, Mayersohn, Mayerson)—Ashkenazic name probably taken from the town of Mayen in the Rhineland. JE and UJ have biographies from 18th- and 19th-cent. Belgium, France, Germany, Austria, Rumania and U.S.A. LBI has family trees beginning 1627, 1762, 1766, 1781 and 1807, related to LEVI, DREYFUSS and MARC. AJA has a family tree beginning 1832, related to STEINER and GODCHAUX, and a tree beginning 1800, related to REIS, LOWENGARD, LOWENBERG and SALOMON. LBIS has a family tree; CAJ has family trees from Germany and family records. CAJ also has Mayersohn family records. Mayerman is a family of rabbis in Morocco and Algeria; see EJ. JE article on "Coat of Arms" has a Mayer family crest. For Mayer family histories, see JFF, Nos. 30 and 31; also *Memoir and Genealogy of the Ferdinand and Jette Steiner Mayer Family, 1832–1971; Aunt Sister's Book; Aus der Geschichte der Familie Ascher Mayer;* and *Die Siegburger Familie Levison.* Related to SCHIFF, SELIGMAN, PHILIPSON, TELLER. Also see MAY.

MAYERMAN—See MAYER.

MAYERSOHN (Mayerson)—See MAYER.

MAYO—JE has article on Smyrna Rabbi Raphael Mayo (d. 1810).

MAZE (also Mazer)—UJ has two biographies from Russia-U.S.A.-Canada, late 19th cent.

MAZEH—EJ has article on Russian Zionist Jacob Mazeh (1859–1924).

MAZER—See MAZE.

MAZLIAH—JE has article on Italian cabalist Judah Masliah (d. 1728). His genealogy is traced back to Abraham ben Samuel of Padua, who married in 1530. Judah's son was a brother-in-law of Isaiah BASSANI.

MAZUR—CAJ has a family tree covering 1788 to 1921, related to KADISCH, GUHRAUER and DRUCKER.

McIVER—Related to MONTEFIORE.

MEARS—UJ has articles from 18th-cent. America, 19th-cent. Russia. Related to GRATZ, HAYS and BUSH.

ME'ATI—Family of translators in Rome, 13th and 14th cent. The name is the Hebrew equivalent of Cento ("hundred" in Italian), the town of the family's origin. JE has three biographies.

MECKAUER—LBI has a family tree beginning 1805.

MECKLER—UJ has article on U.S. editor David Meckler (b. 1891 in Lithuania).

MEDELSHEIM—CAJ has some family records.

MEDEM—UJ has article on socialist Vladimir Medem (1879–1923), born in Latvia.

MEDGYES—UJ has article on Hungarian painter Ladislas Medgyes (b. 1892).

MEDICI—UJ has article on 17th-cent. Italian convert Paolo Medici, also known as SEBASTIANO; born LEON.

MEDINA (also Medini)—Prominent family, mostly in Turkey and Egypt in 16th and 17th cent. The name is probably taken from one of two Spanish cities named Medina. Samuel Medina (1505–1589) was the grandfather of Samuel HAYYUN. JE has a family tree and ten biographies, plus five other Medina and Medini biographies, apparently unrelated, including one from 18th-cent. England and one from

19th-cent. Palestine. Related to MONTEFIORE.

MEDINI—See MEDINA.

MEHLER—LBI has a family tree beginning 1540, related to BACHMEHLER. Another related name is KIMHI.

MEHLSACK—Name derived from the German name for the town of Samilia, Poland. EJ has article on Polish Talmudist Eliakim Mehlsack (1780–1854). Also see SAMILER.

MEHRING—UJ has article on poet Walter Mehring (b. 1896 in Berlin).

MEIDNER—UJ has article on painter Ludwig Meidner (b. 1884 in Germany). LBIS has some family notes.

MEIER—See MEYER.

MEIEROVICS—See MEYER.

MEINEK—JE has article on 18th-cent. German scholar Moses Meinek.

MEINHARD (also Meinhardt)—UJ has article on theatrical director Carl Meinhard (b. 1875 in Czechoslovakia). Related to EPHRAIM.

MEIR—UJ has article on Palestinian Rabbi Jacob Meir (1856–1939). Related to MUNK and OLSCHWANGER. Also see MEYER.

ME'IRI—JE has article on Provençal Talmudist Menahem Me'iri (1249–1306), whose Provençal name was Don Vidal SOLOMON.

MEISACH—JE has article on Russian author Joshua Meisach (b. 1848 near Kovno).

MEISEL (also Meisels, Meysels, Meisl, Meysl, Meusel, Meussl)—Bohemian family famous chiefly through Mordecai Meisel (1528–1601), "primate of Prague," also known as MAREK or Meusel. His family originally came from Cracow, and he married the daughter of Isaac ROFE. See JE, UJ and EJ, which have numerous biographies. EJ says some family members were descended from Moses ISSERLES. CAJ has Meisel, Meisels and Meisl family records. Related to BORNSTEIN.

MEISL—See MEISEL.

MEISSNER—UJ has article on Czech political leader Alfred Meissner (b. 1871).

MEISTER—UJ has article on U.S. author Morris Meister (b. 1895 in Poland).

MEISTERLIN (also Meisteri)—Jewish family of Styria and Vienna, 14th and 15th cent. See UJ.

MEITNER—UJ has article on physicist Lise Meitner (b. 1878 in Vienna).

MEKHLIS—UJ has article on Soviet commissar Lev Mekhlis (b. 1889 in Russia).

MEKLENBURG—Ashkenazic name derived from the territory of Mecklenburg in northern Germany, where Jews first settled in 13th cent. UJ has article on German Rabbi Jacob Meklenburg (1785–1865), born in Poland.

MELAMED—EJ has biographies from 15th-cent. Spain. UJ has a biography from 19th-cent. Lithuania and U.S.A. Also see MALMUD.

MELCHETT—UJ has article on English industrialist Alfred Melchett (1868–1930), son of Ludwig MOND.

MELCHIOR—Family originally from Hamburg, with branches there and in Denmark and England. See JE and UJ. LBIS has some family notes. For genealogy and history, see *Stamtavlen Melchior* and *Moses & William G. Melchior, 1761–1961*. Related to BALLIN, ROSBACH, FURTH, UNNA, HECKSCHER, TRIER, JACOBSEN, BOHR, RAPHAEL and VOGUE.

MELDOLA—Ancient Sephardic family whose genealogy can be traced through sixteen generations without a break to Isaiah Meldola of Toledo, Spain (b. 1282). One branch took the name MONTALTO in Portugal. Descendants were living in U.S.A. and Canada in 1900. JE has a family tree and twenty-three biographies. Related to AZUBI, HENRIQUES, SENIOR, PARDO, SARPHATY, AGUILAR, ABIATHAR, ABULAFIA, FENDES, OSORIO, JESURUN, ISRAEL, da SILVA, WALLACK, de SOLA, MENDES, JOSEPH, SUASSO, SAMUEL, GOLDSMITH, COHEN, PISA and POOL.

MELLER—UJ has biographies from Hungary, 19th and 20th cent.

MELLI—Family of Italian scholars and rabbis that dates from the 15th cent. The name is derived from the village of Melli in the province of Mantua. JE has five biographies from 15th, 16th and 17th cent.

MELLO (also Melo)—JE has article on Rabbi David Melo (b. 1550 in Spain, d. in Amsterdam). Related to ABENATAR.

MELMAN—Related to KAMINSKI.

MELO—See MELLO.

MELOL (also Melul)—JE has article on 18th-cent. Italian translator Moses Melol.

MELRICH—LBIS has some family notes.

MELTZER—UJ has article on U.S. physician Samuel Meltzer (1851–1920). Related to KLATZKO.

MELUL—See MELOL.

MELVILLE—JE has article on English author Lewis Melville (b. Lewis BENJAMIN in 1874).

MENAHEM—Related to FRANGI.

MENDEL—See MANDEL.

MENDELS—See MANDEL.

MENDELSBURG—JE has article on Russian teacher Leon Mendelsburg (1819–1897).

MENDELSOHN—See MENDELSSOHN.

MENDELSON—See MENDELSSOHN.

MENDELSSOHN (also Mendelsohn, Mendelson, Mendelsson)—German family known for the scholar and the musician, descended from Moses ISSERLES, according to tradition. JE has a family tree beginning 1700, and thirteen biographies. EJ also has a family tree. LBI has family trees beginning 16th cent., 1729, 1740 and 1748. See family histories in ZGJD, Vol. I (1929), p. 200; *"New Light on the Family of Felix Mendelssohn,"* in *Hebrew Union College Annual;* and "Die Familie Mendelssohn," in *Abraham unser Vater*. JE also has biographies for Mendelson and Mendelsohn families from 18th- and 19th-cent. Poland and Germany. Moses Mendelson (d. 1861 in Hamburg) was related to Samson Raphael HIRSCH. Other related names are BARTHOLDY, GUGENHEIM, ITZIG, MEYER, VEIT, SCHLEGEL, HEINE, DIRICHLET, JEANRENAUD, HENSEL, NEANDER, SALOMON, ARNSTEIN, SEELIGMAN, DESSAU, DAVID.

MENDELSSON—See MENDELSSOHN.

MENDELVICH—Related to BOGORAZ.

MENDES (also Mendez, Mendesia, Mendez da Costa, Mendez Furtado)—

Sephardic name of at least two main families: 1) a family that emigrated from Spain to Portugal and later settled in Holland, England and U.S.A. JE has nine biographies, beginning 16th cent.; 2) an old Spanish family that remained in Spain after the expulsion of 1492. Descendants went to France, Holland, Italy and Turkey in 16th and 17th cent.; one branch fled from Spain to the West Indies in 1786. JE has a family tree and eight biographies for this branch, whose relatives include PEREIRA, da COSTA, GOMEZ, VAEZ, OSORIO, SOLA, SESPEDES, QUIROS, HENRIQUES, SOARES, CASADO, MORRO, BONITO, GRADIS, FONSEQUA, NUNES, CORCHO, NETTO and NASI. CAJ has family records from Barbados. JE article on "Coat of Arms" has a Mendes and Mendez family crest. Other relatives include CORONEL, MELDOLA, POOL, MIGUEZ, MICAS, MOCATTA, ABENAES, ABENDANA, BENJAMIN, FRANCO, BENVENISTE, de LARA, DISRAELI and WILLIAMS.

MENDESIA—See MENDES.

MENDEZ—See MENDES.

MENDEZ da COSTA—See MENDES.

MENDEZ FURTADO—See MENDES.

MENDL—See MANDEL.

MENDLIN—Probably a variation of MANDEL. JE has article on Russian economist Jacob Mendlin (b. 1842).

MENDONCA—UJ has article on Brazilian journalist Hypolito Mendonca (1774–1823).

MENDOZA—JE has article on English pugilist Daniel Mendoza (1763–1836). Related to ISAACS.

MENES—UJ has article on historian Avrohom Menes (b. 1897 in Poland).

MENGS—JE has biographies from 18th-cent. Holland and Austria.

MENKEN—American family whose earliest known member was Solomon Menken (b. 1787 in Prussia, d. 1853 in Cincinnati). He married the daughter of Benjamin MORANGE. See JE, UJ and EJ. Related to THEODORE.

MENKO—CAJ has family tree from Holland covering 1742 to 1960.

MENZ (also Menzel)—JE has article on 18th-cent. Rabbi Abraham Menz of Frankfurt-am-Main. PD has some Menzel family records. Related to MOOS.

MENZEL—See MENZ.

MERARI—JE has article on 17th-cent. Venetian poet Moses Merari.

MERCADO—UJ has article on communal leader Charles de Mercado (1863–1909), born in the British West Indies.

MERESHIN—UJ has article on writer Abraham Mereshin (b. 1880 in Russia).

MERLIN—French family. See history in *Une famille lorraine: Les Merlin de Thionville.*

MERRICK—UJ has article on English actor Leonard Merrick (1864–1939), descended from a Jewish family named MILLER.

MERTON—UJ has article on German financier Wilhelm Merton (1848–1916), born MOSES. Related to SELIGMAN.

MERX—CAJ has family records.

MERZBACH (also Merzbacher)—UJ has four biographies from Germany and U.S.A., 19th and 20th cent. LBIS has a Merzbach family tree, related to SYMONS. LBI has Merzbacher family trees beginning 1730 and 1845, related to JAFFE.

MESA—See MEZA.

MESHORER—Related to BASS.

MESQUITA—Castilian family whose members found their way to Holland, England and America during the Inquisition. JE mentions eight names from 17th and 18th cent. JE article on "Coat of Arms" has the family crest. Related to COSTA, FERME, AZEVEDO and HENRIQUES.

MESSEL—UJ and EJ have biographies from 18th- and 19th-cent. Germany and England. The family is ancestor of Anthony ARMSTRONG-JONES. Also related to SELIGMAN.

MESSER—Italian name derived from *maestro,* the title given to physicians. JE has article on 15th-cent. Italian physician and Rabbi Leon Messer of Mantua.

MESSING—Prussian family whose members settled in U.S.A., 19th cent. JE has five biographies.

MESTEL—UJ has article on poet Yankev Mestel (b. 1884 in Galicia).

METALITZER—Related to DUBNOW.

METCHNIKOFF—UJ has article on French biologist Elie Metchnikoff (1845–1916), born in Russia.

METZ—Name probably derived from the Alsatian city of Metz, where Jews settled as early as 3rd century C.E. JE has article on 19th-cent. German scholar Isaac Metz. CAJ has a family tree from Amsterdam. Related to ENSHEIM.

METZGER (also Metzker)—Ashkenazic name meaning "butcher" in German. UJ has article on U.S. writer Yud Metzker (b. 1901 in Galicia). Related to SCHIFF.

METZKER—See METZGER.

METZLER—JE has article on Austrian contralto Pauline LOWY (b. 1853), who married Ferdinand Metzler and took the name Metzler-Lowy.

METZON—See family history in *Mine Forfaeder.*

MEUSEL—See MEISEL.

MUESSL—See MEISEL.

MEYER (also Meyers, Meier, Meyerowitz, Meierovics, Meyerson, Myer, Myers, Myerson, Meir)—Ashkenazic name taken from the Hebrew word for "wise" or "scholarly." JE, UJ and EJ have numerous biographies from 18th- and 19th-cent. Denmark, France, Germany, Poland, Rumania, England, U.S.A. and Russia. CAJ has a Meyer family tree. CAJ also has Meyers family archives covering 1818 to 1857, related to JACOBY, and Meier family records. CAJD has a Meyer family tree from Germany, related to LOB. LBI has Meyer family trees beginning 1680, 1747, 1780, 1797, 1862 and 1875, related to FACKENHEIM, MUEHSAM and WOLLMAN. LBIS has a Meyer family tree, related to HAUSEN. See family history in *The Ancestors of Emil Louis Meyer and Helen Levy Meyer of Hannover, Germany;* also *Records of the Myers, Hays and Mordecai Families from 1707 to 1913.* The relationship of a Meyer family to other major rabbinic Ashkenazic families is traced in *Reshimoth Aboth,* by Markus Seckbach. Related to JAFFE, MENDELSSOHN, FRANKEL, TRIER, EHRENBERG, MIREL, RAFF, de SOLA, BUSH, HOROWICZ and MEYER-LOEVINSON.

MEYEROWITZ—See MEYER.

MEYERS—See MEYER.

MEYERBEER—German composer Giacomo Meyerbeer (1791–1864), born Jacob BEER, was a descendant of Jost LIEBMANN. See JE and UJ. LBI has family trees beginning 1392, 1500, 1670 and 1677. Related to JAFFE and RICHTER.

MEYERHOF—UJ has article on physiologist Otto Meyerhof (b. 1884 in Germany). LBI has a family tree beginning 1742, related to MARKREICH.

MEYER-LOEVINSON—LBI has a family tree beginning 1794, related to MEYER.

MEYERSON—See MEYER.

MEYERSTEIN—UJ has biographies from 19th- and 20th-cent. England and Germany.

MEYER-SUST—LBI has a family tree beginning 1657. Related to SUST.

MEYLER—CAJ has a family tree from the Netherlands, 1720 to 1959.

MEYROWITZ—UJ has article on conductor Selmar Meyrowitz (b. 1875 in Germany).

MEYSELS—See MEISEL.

MEYSL—See MEISEL.

MEYUHAS—Oriental family which gave several rabbinical writers to Jerusalem and Constantinople. JE and EJ have biographies from 17th, 18th and 19th cent.

MEZA (also Mesa)—A family of Amsterdam with several distinguished rabbis. JE has six biographies from 18th- and 19th-cent. Holland and Denmark.

MEZAH—EJ has article on Lithuanian writer Joshua Mezah (1834–1917), also known as SEGAL.

MEZEI (also Mezey)—JE has three biographies from 19th-cent. Hungary. CAJ has some family records.

MEZO—UJ has article on Hungarian athlete Ferenc Mezo (b. 1885).

MEZOFI—UJ has article on Hungarian deputy Vilmos Mezofi (b. 1870).

MHUSHILKAR—JE has article on 19th-cent. India soldier Reuben Mhushilkar.

MICAS—Related to MENDES.

MICHAEL (also Michaeli, Michaelis, Michaels, Michaelsen, Michel, Michelson)—JE, UJ and EJ have biographies from 18th- and 19th-cent. Germany, U.S.A., Latvia and Denmark. EJ also has article on German soldier Jud Michel (d. 1549). Financier Simon Michel (d. 1719 in Vienna), also known as PRESSBURG, was an ancestor of Heinrich HEINE. LBI has a Michael family tree beginning 1675, and Michaelis family trees beginning 1655 and 1800. LBIS has Michael family notes. CAJ has a Michaelis family tree from Germany and Michaeli family records. PD has Michel family records. Also see family history in *Familie Michael (Hamburg), 1620–1924*. Related to HAYS and PRZLUBSKA.

MICHAELI—See MICHAEL.

MICHAELIS—See MICHAEL.

MICHAELS—See MICHAEL.

MICHAELSEN—See MICHAEL.

MICHAILISHKER—Related to LEBENSOHN.

MICHEL (Michelson)—See MICHAEL.

MICHELSTAEDTER—EJ has article on Italian poet Carlo Michelstaedter (1887–1910).

MICHOLLS—Related to MONTEFIORE.

MIDLOURSKY—UJ has article on 19th-cent. physician J. F. Midloursky, born in Russia.

MIDDLEMAN—JE has article on 19th-cent. English Rabbi Judah Middleman.

MIELZINER—JE and UJ have articles on U.S. Rabbi Moses Mielziner (1828–1903), born near Posen; married Rosette LEVALD of Copenhagen. His mother was born Rachel CARO, a descendant of Joseph Caro of Toledo and Safed.

MIESES (also Mises)—Family of German and Galician scholars of 18th and 19th cent. See JE and UJ. CAJ has some family records. Also see *Toledot Fabius Mieses*.

MIGUEZ—Related to MENDES.

MIKLISHANSKY—Related to KLEPFISH.

MIKLOS—UJ has article on Hungarian editor Andor Miklos (1880–1933).

MILAN—UJ has article on German-born soldier Gabriel Milan (1631–1689), brother-in-law of Joshua ABENSOUR.

MILCH—UJ has two biographies from 19th- and 20th-cent. Poland and Germany. LBI has family trees beginning 1774 and 1818.

MILES—Related to DEBASH.

MILHAU—JE has two biographies from 18th-cent. France. Related to MOSCAT.

MILLAO—Related to ABENSUR.

MILLAUD—JE and UJ have biographies from 19th-cent. France.

MILLER—UJ has eight biographies from 19th- and 20th-cent. U.S.A., Russia and England. Related to MERRICK and KATZ.

MILLIN—UJ has two biographies from Lithuania and South Africa, 19th and 20th cent.

MILMAN—JE has article on English historian Henry Milman (1791–1868).

MINDEN—JE has two biographies from 18th-cent. Germany and Poland. Lob Minden (d. 1751) was also known as Judah SELICHOWER.

MINERBI—JE has article on Italian diplomat Hirschel de Minerbi (b. 1838), descendant of a wealthy Jewish family of Trieste.

MINIKES—UJ has article on writer Chaim Minikes (1867–1932), born in Lithuania.

MINIR—Family of scholars in Tudela, Italy, with members also in the eastern Mediterranean. JE has six biographies, beginning 14th cent.

MINIS—U.S. family especially prominent in the South. Its founder, Abraham Minis, went from England to Georgia in 1733. JE has a family tree and ten biographies. Related to POLLACK, COHEN, HAYS, LIVINGSTON, ETTING, FLORANCE and TOBIAS.

MINKIN—UJ has article on Rabbi Jacob Minkin (b. 1885 in Poland).

MINKOVSKY (also Minkowski)—UJ has four biographies from Lithuania, Russia and Poland, 19th and 20th cent. JE has article on Russian cantor Phinehas Minkovsky (b. 1859), a descendant of Yom-Tob Lipmann HELLER.

MINKOWSKI—See MINKOVSKY.

MINOR—JE has article on Russian Rabbi Solomon Minor (1827–1900) of Vilna.

MINSKI (also Minsky)—Name taken from the Russian city of Minsk, where Jews first settled in 16th cent. JE has article on Russian poet Nikolai Minski (b. WILENKIN in 1855). Related to WENGEROFF.

MINTZ—See MINZ.

MINZ (also Mintz, Munz)—Ashkenazic family of rabbis and scholars that can be traced back to 15th cent. The name is derived from the city of Mayence (Mainz) in Germany. Descendants were in Germany, Italy and Russia from 16th cent. onward. JE has a family-tree chart and biographies. Moses Mintz (15th cent.), German Talmudist, was a son of Israel ISSERLEIN; see EJ. Moses Munz (or Minz) (1750–1831) was brother-in-law of Moses Joshua HESCHEL and was related by marriage to Moses SOFER. See family tree on page 14 of this book. CAJ has some Munz family records. Da'at Kedoshim, by Israel Eisenstadt, traces the family's relationships with other rabbinic families. Also see family history in JFF, No. 37, and see JE articles on Mayence (Mainz) and Padua. Related to KATZENELLENBOGEN, GRUNBERG, KLATZKO, WAHL, LOW and POCHAPOVSKY.

MINZESHEIMER—Related to SULZBERGER.

MIRANDA—Italian family name originally taken from the town of Miranda, near Oporto, Portugal. UJ has article on early U.S. settler Isaac Miranda (d. 1733). Related to BELMONTE.

MIRAT—Related to HEINE.

MIREL—See MIRELS.

MIRELS (also Mirel, Mirles)—Rabbi Meshullam Mirels (1620–1706) was father of a large family ramified throughout Poland and Lithuania. His daughter Sarah was the wife of Zebi Ashkenazi and mother of Jacob EMDEN. Meshullam Mirels' father's name was NEUMARK. JE has biographies from 17th and 18th cent. AJA has a Mirel family tree from Cincinnati, related to JONAS, MEYER and SALOMON. See Stammbaum der Familie Mirels-Heller-Frankel. Related to SPIRA, EPHRAIM, LEVINSON, HELLER, FRANKEL.

MIRER—Related to BOSLANSKI.

MIRES—JE has article on French financier Jules Mires (1809–1871).

MIRKES (also Mirkin)—Ashkenazic name derived from the female name Miriam. JE has article on 18th-cent. Lithuanian Talmudist Solomon Mirkes.

MIRKIN—See MIRKES.

MIRLES—See MIRELS.

MIRSKY—Related to DUBNOW.

MISCH—UJ has two biographies from Germany and U.S.A., 19th–20th cent. Related to DILTHEY.

MISCHAKOFF—UJ has article on violinist Mischa Mischakoff (b. 1895 in Russia).

MISES—See MIESES.

MITCHELL—AJA has a family tree beginning 1821 in Posen, Germany. JE has article on three Mitchell brothers from Cracow, Galicia, who settled in Little Rock, Arkansas, in 1838. Related to OFFENBACH.

MITTWOCH—UJ has article on scholar Eugen Mittwoch (b. 1876 in Germany).

MITZ—Related to SALOMONS.

MITZKUN—JE has article on Russian Hebraist David Mitzkun (1836–1887).

MIZRAHI—Eastern Mediterranean family including some well-known rabbinical authors. The name means "an Oriental," and is used by many Persian Jews who have settled in Turkey. There are two branches of the family, one from Jerusalem and one from Constantinople. JE and EJ have biographies beginning in 14th cent.

MOCATTA—English family of Sephardic origins, originally named LUMBROZO in Spain. It can be traced back to 17th cent. JE has a family tree and five biographies. JE article on "Coat of Arms" has the family crest. Related to LINDO, XIMENES, MATTOS, LAMEGO, LOUSADA, BRANDON, COSTA, MONTEFIORE, NAHON, SCHLOSS, ELKIN, GOLDSMID, LUCAS and MENDES. Also see UJ.

MOCH—UJ has three biographies from France, 19th and 20th cent.

MOCHIAH—Related to MARCUS and BERLIN.

MOD'AI—Family of Turkish authors. JE has three biographies from 18th and 19th cent.

MODEL (also Modell)—JE and EJ have articles on Marx Model of Germany

(17th–18th cent.), whose family came from Öttingen, Bavaria. LBI has a family tree beginning 1699. See family history in JJLG, Vol. 8 (1910), p. 202. Related to OPPENHEIMER.

MODENA—Italian family presumably named for the city of Modena in central Italy. JE and EJ have biographies beginning 16th cent. Also see EJ article on *Aaron* Berechiah (d. 1639), a cousin of Leone Modena.

MODERN—EJ has article on Hungarian Rabbi Judah Modern (1819–1893).

MODIANO—JE has article on Turkish Rabbi Joseph Modiano (18th cent.), whose family originally came from Modena, Italy; hence the name.

MODIGLIANI—JE and UJ have biographies from 19th-cent. Italy. Artist Amedeo Modigliani (1884–1920) was descended from SPINOZA through his mother, whose maiden name was GARSINO.

MODON (also Modona)—JE has biographies from Italy, 17th, 18th and 19th cent.

MODONA—See MODON.

MODZHITZ—Hasidic dynasty in Poland, 19th cent. See EJ.

MOELLIN—See MOLLN.

MOGULESKO—JE has article on U.S. comedian Sigmund Mogulesko (b. 1858 in Bessarabia).

MOHACSI—UJ has article on Hungarian author Jeno Mohacsi (b. 1886).

MOHILEWER—Name taken from the Russian city of Mohilev (or Moghilef) on the Dnieper, where Jews first settled in 1522. JE has article on Russian Rabbi Samuel Mohilewer (1824–1898).

MOHL—UJ has article on engineer Emanuel Mohl (b. 1883 in Russia).

MOHOLY-NAGY—UJ has article on painter Ladislaus Moholy-Nagy (b. 1895 in Hungary).

MOHR—See MUHR.

MOISE—U.S. family descended from 18th-cent. Abraham Moise, who was born in Alsace and emigrated to the West Indies. JE has fifteen biographies. See *Moise Family of South Carolina*. Related to

MOSES, LOPEZ, LEVY, LYON, LEON, WOLFE and DINKINS.

MOISSAN—EJ has article on French chemist Henry Moissan (1852–1907).

MOISSEIFF—UJ has article on U.S. engineer Leon Moisseiff (b. 1872 in Latvia).

MOLCHO (also Molko)—UJ has article on Portuguese Marrano Solomon Molcho (1500–1532).

MOLIN—See MOLLN.

MOLINA (also Malina, Molinas)—JE has article on 16th-cent. Egyptian Rabbi Isaac Molina, born in Italy.

MOLK—EJ has article on U.S. oilman Isador Molk (b. 1898 in Lithuania). See his autobiography, *The Making of an Oilman*.

MOLKO—See MOLCHO.

MOLL—JE has article on German physician Albert Moll (b. 1862). LBI has a family tree beginning 1516.

MOLLN (also Molin, Moellin)—Family from Mayence (now Mainz), Germany. The name is personal, not for a place. JE has two biographies from 14th cent. EJ has article on German-Austrian Talmudist Jacob Moellin (1360–1427), also known as SEGAL.

MOLNAR—UJ has article on Hungarian writer Ferenc Molnar (b. NEUMANN in 1878).

MOLO—JE has article on 17th-cent. Dutch financier Francisco Molo.

MOLODOWSKY—UJ has article on poet Kadia Molodowsky (b. 1894 in Poland).

MOLYNEUX—Related to CHARLEMONT.

MOMBACH—JE has article on musician Julius Mombach (b. 1813 in Germany, d. 1880 in England).

MOMBERT—UJ has article on poet Alfred Mombert (1872–1942), born in Germany.

MOMMSEN—CAJ has some family records.

MONASCH (also Monash)—UJ has article on Australian engineer John Monash (1865–1931), related to Heinrich GRAETZ. LBIS has Monasch family notes.

MOND—JE, UJ and EJ have biographies from England and Germany, 19th and

20th cent. Related to MELCHETT and READING.

MONIES—JE has article on Danish artist David Monies (1812–1894).

MONIN—UJ has article on writer Jose Monin (b. 1895 in Russia).

MONIS (also Moniz)—JE has article on American scholar Judah Monis (1683–1764), who may have been born in Algiers. Related to BELMONTE.

MONNICKENDAM—UJ has article on Dutch painter Martin Monnickendam (b. 1874).

MONSANTO—Related to de SOLA.

MONSOWIZ—CAJ has some family records.

MONTAGU (also Montague)—The Montagu family of 19th-cent. England is descended from the families of MOSES and SAMUEL; see JE. JE article on "Coat of Arms" has the family crest. Also related to GOLDSMID, SPIELMANN, SWAYTHLING and WAHL.

MONTAIGNE—UJ has article on French essayist Michel de Montaigne (1533–1592). His mother's maiden name was de LOUPPES and her father was LOPEZ, a descendant of Mayer PACAGON of Spain.

MONTALTO—JE has article on 16th–17th-cent. Portuguese physician Filotheo Montalto, who may have been the brother of Amatus LUSITANUS. Related to CASTRO and MELDOLA.

MONTAUBAN—Related to DAUPHINE.

MONTEFIORE (also Montefiori)—English family whose name is derived from a town of the same name in Italy (there are three such towns, and the town of the family's origin isn't known). The family was at Ancona, Italy, in 1630. JE has extensive family trees beginning 17th cent.; EJ also has a family tree. JE also has fifteen biographies. JE article on "Coat of Arms" has the family crest. CAJ has Montefiori family records. See family history in *The Cousinhood,* by Chaim Bermant. Related to OLIVETTI, ALVARES, MEDINA, MOCATTA, ISRAEL, HERON, BENDAHON, GUEDALLA, HATCHEVALL, ABRAHAM, LEON, ISAACS, JAMES, FLORANCE, CHURNAGOOSE, WEINBAUM, VENTINA, SOMERSOLL, SWART, DURAW, CORCOS, SOLOMONS, ROTHSCHILD, HALL, SEBAG, GOLDSMID, GOMPERTZ, WALEY, LUCAS, DAVIDSON, SICHEL, FLOWER, YORKE, SPIELMANN, LOUSADA, MAGNUS, McIVER, ATATORA, BEDDINGTON, MICHOLLS, LEVI, SAMUEL, COHEN, SALOMONS, BARROW.

MONTEUX—UJ has article on French conductor Pierre Monteux (b. 1875).

MONTEZINOS—JE and UJ have articles from 17th and 19th cent.

MONTI—Related to ZARFATI.

MONTORO—JE has article on Spanish poet Anton de Montoro (1404–1477), related to Juan de BAENA.

MONZON—JE has two biographies from 16th-cent. Turkey and Morocco.

MOOS—JE has article on German otologist Solomon Moos (1831–1895). AJA has a family tree, related to SCHLESINGER and MENZ. Also see *History of the Family Moos.*

de MORA—Related to BUENO.

MORAIS—Italian family that came there after fleeing Portugal during the Inquisition. JE has two biographies from 19th-cent. U.S.A., descendants of the original family. Related to WEIL.

MORALI—CAJ has family records from Algiers, 1896–1946.

MORANGE—Related to MENKIN.

MORAWCZYK—Family of Polish scholars in the 16th and 17th cent., originally from Moravia. JE has three biographies.

MORAWITZ—EJ has article on Austrian banker Karl Morawitz (1846–1914).

MORDECAI—Family of German origin that came to U.S.A. in second half of 18th cent. See JE and UJ. Also see *Records of the Myers, Hays and Mordecai Families from 1707 to 1913,* and "Some Notes on the Mordecai Family," in *Virginia Magazine of History.* Related to RUSSELL, MYERS, HAYS.

MORDELL—UJ has three biographies from 19th–20th-cent. Lithuania and U.S.A.

MORDO—JE has article on physician Lazare Mordo (1744–1823) of Corfu.

MORENO (also Morenu)—Proper name adopted as a family name by Spanish-Portuguese Jews. Families with this name were in Bayonne, London and Hamburg in 17th cent., and also in Turkey in 1900. JE has four biographies; JE article on "Coat of Arms" has a family crest. Related to HENRIQUEZ, PAZ and SHALOM.

MORENU—See MORENO.

MORGAN—Related to SINGER.

MORGENSTERN—JE has two biographies from 19th-cent. Germany. Related to ARENDT, BAUER and MARCZALI.

MORGENTHAU—UJ has two biographies from German and U.S.A., 19th and 20th cent. Related to NAUMBURG.

MORGULIS—See MARGOLIOTH.

MORHANGE—See ALKAN.

MORITZ—JE has article on U.S. engineer Albert Moritz (b. 1860).

MORLEY—UJ has article on author Edith Morley (b. 1875 in London).

MOROSINI—JE has article on Italian Giulio Morosini (1612–1687), descended from a wealthy family that traced its ancestry back to Nehemiah.

MORPURGO—An Austro-Italian family whose name is derived from the town of its origin, Marburg, in Styria. The family is said to be descended from Rabbi Israel ISSERLEIN (15th cent.) and is also known as MARBURG, MARBURGER and MARPURCH. JE and UJ have biographies beginning 17th cent. Samson Morpurgo (1681–1740) was the father of Moses SHABBETHAI. JE article on "Coat of Arms" has the family crest. LBI has a family tree beginning 1761. CAJ has family records, related to GRASSIN. Also see *La Famiglia Morpurgo di Gradisca, 1585–1885*. Related to REGGIO, LUZZATTO and PAPO.

MORRIS (also Morrison)—JE and UJ have biographies from 19th-cent. Germany, U.S.A. and Jamaica. See *The Ancestry of Rosalie Morris Johnson, Daughter of George Calvert Morris and Elizabeth Kuhn*. Related to ROBERTS, WARBURG, VOGEL.

MORRISON—See MORRIS.

MORRO—Related to MENDES.

MORROS—Movie producer Boris Morros was born 1895 in Russia; see UJ.

MORSE—JE has two biographies from 19th-cent. Germany and U.S.A.

MORTARA—JE and UJ have biographies from Italy, 19th cent.

MORTEIRA (also Mortera)—JE has article on Dutch Rabbi Saul Morteira (1596–1660), of Portuguese descent. Related to PARDO.

MORTON—JE has two biographies from 19th-cent. U.S.A. and England. Related to CONHEIM.

MORWITZ—JE has article on U.S. physician Edward Morwitz (1815–1893), born in Prussia.

MOSCAT—Related to MILHAU.

MOSCATI—See MOSCATO.

MOSCATO (also Moscati)—JE has article on 16th-cent. Italian Rabbi Judah Moscato. CAJ has Moscati family records.

MOSCHKOWITZ—See MOSKOWITZ.

MOSCHELES—JE has two biographies from 19th-cent. England and Austria. Ignaz Moscheles (1794–1870) married Charlotte EMDEN. Also related to ROTT.

MOSCHIDES—See JE article on Tobias COHN.

MOSCONI (also Moskoni)—JE has article on Bulgarian scholar Judah Mosconi (b. 1328).

MOSCOVITCH—See MOSKOWITZ.

MOSE—Related to RUBINO.

MOSEB—German family name; see history in ZL, p. 107.

MOSELY—JE has article on English financier Alfred Mosely (b. 1855).

MOSEN—See MOSES.

MOSENTHAL—JE and UJ have biographies from Germany, Austria and South Africa, 19th cent. See family history in JFF, No. 37.

MOSER—JE has article on German merchant Moses Moser (1796–1838).

MOSES (also Mosen, Mosessohn)—JE has biographies from Germany, Russia and Indian, 18th and 19th cent. Banker Silas Moses of India (b. 1845) was related to the SASSOON family. LBI has family trees beginning 1600 and 1757. PD has some family records. Also see family tree from Amsterdam in CB, p. 2993. Related to PHILLIPS, NATHAN, MACHADO, JOSEPH, MONTAGU, GRATZ, FRUMKIN, HERTZ, LEVY, MOSSE, MERTON, BARDACH, COHEN and WIERSBOLOWSKY. French variation of the name is MOISE.

MOSESCO—UJ has article on U.S. editor Lillian Mosesco (b. DORIS in Rumania).

MOSESSOHN—See MOSES.

MOSHEIM—UJ has article on German actress Grete Mosheim (b. 1905); married GOULD.

MOSKONI—See MOSCONI.

MOSKOVITCH—See MOSKOWITZ.

MOSKOVITZ—See MOSKOWITZ.

MOSKOWITZ (also Moskovitch, Moskovitz, Moschcowitz, Moscovitch)—UJ has biographies from 19th-cent. Russia, Hungary, Rumania, Argentina and U.S.A. Related to BRASLAVSKY, LINDNER and ISRAELS.

MOSLER—JE has article on U.S. painter Henry Mosler (1841–1920). Related to SALZER.

MOSS—JE has two biographies from 19th-cent. U.S.A. AJA has a family tree beginning 18th-cent. England. Also see *Moss-Harris Pedigree Chart*. Related to HARTOG, LEVETUS, HARRIS.

MOSSE—Name traced to Marcus MOSES (1807–1865) of Germany, who changed his family name to Mosse. He is related to COHN, LOWENSTEIN and LACHMANN. JE has three biographies from 19th-cent. Germany and France. LBI has family trees beginning 1700, 1767 and 1786, related to WITKOWSKI. CAJ has family records, related to ISLER, MAGNUS and LILIEN.

MOSSERI—Family in Egypt, said to have come from Italy about 1750; see EJ.

MOSSINSON—UJ has article on Russian educator Benzion Mossinson (1878–1942).

MOSSNER—UJ has article on German General Walther von Mossner (1846–1932), related to RIESE.

MOSSIRI—JE has article on Turkish Rabbi Hayyim Mossiri (d. 1800 in Jerusalem).

MOSSON—Related to EPHRAIM.

MOSZKOWSKI—Name probably taken from the city of Moscow. JE has article on German pianist Moritz Moszkowski (1854–1935).

MOTAL—JE has two biographies from 16th- and 17th-cent. Turkey.

MOTKE—UJ has article on Lithuanian jester Chabad Motke (d. 1875).

MOTOT—JE has two biographies, from 14th-cent. Spain and 15th-cent. Lombardy.

MOTTA—JE has two biographies from U.S.A., 18th and 19th cent.

MOTTL—EJ has article on German conductor Felix Mottl (1856–1911).

MOTZKIN—UJ has article on Russian Zionist Leo Motzkin (1867–1933), who died in Paris.

MOUNTBATTEN—Related to CASSEL.

MOUTET—UJ has article on French socialist Marius Moutet (b. 1876).

MOVSHOVITZ—CAJ has some family records.

MOYZESZOWA—Related to FISHEL.

MUDAWWAR—JE has two biographies from the Middle East, 12th cent.

MUEHSAM—See MUHSAM.

MUELHAUSEN (also Muhlhausen)—EJ has article on 14th–15th-cent. Bohemian scholar Yom-Tob Muhlhausen. Also known as LIPMANN-Muhlhausen.

MUELLER—See MULLER.

MUGDAN—LBI has a family tree beginning 1790.

MUGNON—JE has article on Spanish scholar David Mugnon (d. 1629 in Venice).

MUHLFELD—JE has article on French novelist Lucien Muhlfeld (1870–1902).

MUHLHAUSEN—See MUELHAUSEN.

MUHLMANN—UJ has article on Russian singer Adolf Muhlmann (b. 1866).

MUHR (also Mohr)—JE and EJ have biographies from Germany, Galicia and U.S.A. See family history in *Abraham Muhr: Ein Lebensbild*. Related to BODEK.

MUHSAM (also Muehsam)—Name conferred by Frederick the Great in 1784 on Pinkus SELIGMAN PAPPENHEIM as a token of the trouble *(Mühe)* he went to in saving the life of a Prussian officer. JE has a biography from 19th-cent. Austria. LBI has Muehsam family trees beginning 1394, 1747, 1785, and 1840, related to JAFFE. Also see family history in *Geschichte des Namens Muhsam.*

MULDER—JE has article on Dutch educator Samuel Mulder (1792–1862), born SCHERJVER; his brother-in-law was H. A. WAGENAAR.

MULHAUSEN—See MUELHAUSEN.

MULLER (also Mueller)—JE and EJ have biographies from 19th-cent. Galicia, Germany and Hungary. CAJ has family records from Hungary, 1851, related to HERSCHEL. Another related name is COHEN (in Austria).

MUNDLAK—UJ has article on Polish painter Regina Mundlak (b. 1887).

MUNELES—CAJ has some family records.

MUNI—UJ has article on U.S. actor Paul Muni, born WEISENFREUND.

MUNIUS—JE has article on French Rabbi Moses Munius (1760–1842).

MUNK—JE has four biographies from 19th-cent. Germany and France. See family histories in MGWJ, No. 55, p. 349, and ZGJD, No. 1 (1929), p. 141. Also see EJ article on FRANKEL, and *Die Identität der Familien Theomim und Munk.* Other relatives are LERNER, MUNKACSI, MEIR and THEOMIM.

MUNKACSI—Name taken from the Hungarian city of Munkacs. JE has article on Hungarian philologist Bernhard Munkacsi (1860–1937), descendant of a famous rabbinical family. His ancestors include R. Joseph STATHEGEN, Joseph Lasch LERNER, and Gabriel and Ezekiel BANTH. Also see MUNK.

MUNSTERBURG—JE has article on U.S. psychologist Hugo Munsterburg (1863–1916), born in Prussia.

MUNZ—See MINZ.

MUNZENBERG—Related to HANAU.

MURANYI—JE has article on Hungarian lawyer Armin Muranyi (1841–1902).

MURCHAZO—Related to GOMEZ.

MUSA—JE has article on Spanish physician Hayyim ibn Musa (1390–1460).

MUSHKIN—AJA has a family tree of a Milwaukee family beginning in 18th-cent. Russia, related to LIPSHITZ, JACOBSON and KULAKOFSKY.

MUSSAFIA—JE has biographies from 17th-cent. Spain and Holland, and 19th-cent. Austria and Bosnia.

MUSSINA—Related to PHILIPSON.

MUTNIK (also Mutnikovich)—EJ has article on Lithuanian Zionist Abraham Mutnik (1868–1930).

MUTNIKOVICH—See MUTNIK.

MUTTERPERL—See PERLMUTTER.

MUYAL—EJ has article on Moroccan diplomat Abraham Muyal (1847–1885).

MYER—See MEYER.

MYERS—See MEYER.

MYERSON—See MEYER.

MYSH—JE has article on Russian jurist Mikhail Mysh (b. 1846 in Koretz).

MYSLBEK—UJ has article on Prague sculptor Josef Myslbek (1848–1922).

NAAMIAS—Sephardic family of Toledo, Spain. See Zunz GL, p. 429.

NAAR—Sephardic family in Amsterdam, 17th cent., and later in West Indies and U.S.A. See JE and UJ. AJA has a family tree beginning 1832. Related to PEIXOTTO.

NA'ARI—See NAGARI.

NABARRO—See NAVARRO.

NABOKOV—UJ has article on Russian composer Nicolas Nabokov (b. 1903).

NABON (also Navon)—Turkish family which produced several rabbinical writers from 17th cent. onward. It had several branches, including one at Jerusalem and one at Constantinople. See JE and EJ. Related to ERGAS and AZULAI.

NACHAMSON (also Nachimson, Nakimson)—UJ has article on Russian-German editor Miron Nachimson (b. 1880), also known as SPECTATOR. Also see *Always Be Good to Each Other: The Story of the Nachamsons.*

NACHEZ (also Naschitz)—UJ has article on Tivador Nachez, Hungarian-Swiss composer (1855–1930).

NACHIMSON—See NACHAMSON.

NACHMAN (also Nachmanovich, Nach-manowicz, Nachmanson)—LBIS has some family notes. Nachmanovich was a wealthy family in Lwow, Poland, from 16th cent. onward; see EJ. UJ has biography of Swedish scholar Ernst Nachmanson (b. 1877).

NACHOD—JE and UJ have biographies from 19th-cent. Germany.

NACHTLICHT—UJ has article on Moravian architect Leo Nachtlicht (b. 1872).

NADAI—UJ has article on Hungarian artist Pal Nadai (b. 1881).

NADEL (also Nadelman)—Ashkenazic name often used by tailors; its literal meaning is "needle." UJ has biographies from Russia, Germany and Poland, late 19th cent. Also see NADLER.

NADIR—UJ has article on Polish writer Moishe Nadir (b. 1885), also known as Isaac REISS.

NADJARA—UJ has article on Palestinian poet Israel Nadjara (1555–1628). Also see NAJARA.

NADLER—UJ has article on Austrian finance expert Marcus Nadler (b. 1895). Also see NADEL.

NADSON—JE has article on Russian poet Simon Nadson (1862–1886).

NAFUSI—See NIFOCI.

NAGAR—See NAJARA.

NAGARA—See NAJARA.

NAGARI (also Na'ari)—JE has article on philosopher Moses Nagari of Rome (c. 1300). His family was also known as ADOLESCENTOLI.

NAGAWKER—JE has two biographies from 19th-cent. India.

NAGDELA (also Nagrela)—JE has article on Spanish statesman Abu Nagdela (1031–1066). Also see JE article on *Samuel* ha-Nagid.

NAGLER—Ashkenazic name often used by carpenters; derived from the German *Nagel* ("nail"). UJ has article on Polish-American labor official Isadore Nagler (b. 1895).

NAGRELA—See NAGDELA.

NAGY—UJ has article on Hungarian author Endre Nagy (1877–1938).

NAHAWENDI (also Nahawandi)—EJ has article on 9th-cent. Karaite scholar Benj. Nahawendi.

NAHM—UJ has article on Kentucky banker Max Nahm (b. 1864).

NAHMANI—JE has article on 18th-cent. Italian Talmudist Samson Nahmani.

NAHMANIDES—See JE article on *Moses ben Nahman Gerondi*. Related to GERONDI.

NAHMIAS—One of the most ancient and prominent Jewish families of Toledo, Spain. Its oldest known member is Joseph Nahmias, son-in-law of Joshua ben Isaac ibn SAIDUM, who was living in 1112. See JE, which mentions twenty-six members from 12th through 17th cent. Related to ABENDANA.

NAHMOLI—JE has article on 18th-cent. Talmudist Joseph Nahmoli, father-in-law of Isaac ibn SHANGI.

NAHON—Family of rabbis of Morocco and Portugal from 16th cent. onward; see EJ. Related to MOCATTA.

NAHOUM-EFFENDI—See NAHUM.

NAHUM (also Nahoum-Effendi)—JE, UJ and EJ have biographies from 17th-cent. Turkey and 19th-cent. Galicia, Egypt and Turkey. Related to CARO and LUNTZ.

NAIDITSCH—UJ has article on Russian Zionist Isaac Naiditsch (b. 1868).

NAJAR—Family of Spanish refugees in Algeria and Tunis in 14th cent. Not related to the NAJARA family, although some Najara family members spell their name Najar.

NAJARA (also Najar, Nijar, Nagar, Nagara)—Middle Eastern family originally from Najera, Spain. In 1900, members were found in Algiers, Tunis, Damascus, Gaza, etc. JE has nine biographies. Related to CURIEL. A possible variation is NADJARA.

NAJDUS—EJ has article on Yiddish poet Leib Najous (1890–1918), born in Poland.

NAKDAN—See JOAB.

NAKIMSON—See NACHAMSON.

NAMIER—UJ has article on Russian historian Lewis Namier (b. 1888).

NAPHTALI—UJ has article on German economist Fritz Naphtali (b. 1888).

NAPRAVNIK—UJ has article on Bohemian-Russian conductor Eduard Napravnik (1839–1916).

NAQUET—JE has article on French chemist Alfred Naquet (1834–1916). Also see VIDAL.

NARBONI—Name derived from the city of Narbonne in southern France, where the Jews were expelled in 13th cent. JE has article on 12th-cent. French Rabbi David Narboni. Also see JE article on Narbonne.

NAROL—JE has article on French Rabbi Moses Narol (d. 1659). His father was Eleazar KOHEN, who came from Narol, Galicia.

NASATIR—UJ has article on U.S. consular official Abraham Nasatir (b. 1904).

NASCH—Related to CSEMEGI.

NASCHER—JE has article on Hungarian writer Sinai Nascher (1841–1901).

NASCHITZ—See NACHEZ.

NASI (also Nassi, Nassy)—Sephardic family that fled from Spain to Portugal. Members were found in Turkey in 16th cent., in Surinam in 17th cent., and in Brazil in 18th cent. See JE, UJ and EJ. Also see *The House of Nasi,* and "Nasi Family of Basia Settled in Calcutta," in JQR, Vol. 17, p. 423. Related to LUNA, MENDEZ, BENVENISTE, MENDES, MENDESIA and GRACIA.

NASSAU—Ashkenazic name presumably taken from the German district of Nassau. JE has article on Austrian journalist Adolf von Nassau (b. 1834).

NASSI—See NASI.

NASSY—See NASI.

NASTRUCH—Related to BONSENYOR.

NATAF—JE has article on 18th–19th-cent. Tunisian Rabbi Isaac Nataf.

NATAN—See NATHAN.

NATANSON—See NATHANSON.

NATHALIE—JE has article on French actress Zaive Nathalie (1816–1885).

NATHAN (also Nathans, Natan)—U.S. family in New York since 18th cent. JE and EJ have family trees and biographies. LBI has a family tree beginning 1503. See history of another Nathan family in *Mar-*

cus M. Nathan, København, 1859–1959. Related to SEIXAS, LYONS, MOSES, HENDRICKS, MAPLESON, FLORANCE, FRIEDMAN, WOLFF, SOLIS, BONGODAS, PEIXOTTO, GOMEZ, GOTENDORF, CARDOZO, SAMUEL, ABRAHAMS, TREU, AVIGDOR, KRAUS and RUSSELL.

NATHANSEN—See NATHANSON.

NATHANSOHN—See NATHANSON.

NATHANSON (also Natanson, Nathansen, Nathansohn)—JE and UJ have biographies from 18th-cent. Denmark and Russia, and 19th-cent. Denmark and Poland. LBIS has a family tree and notes. See a family history in *It Began with Zade Usher* (see Bernstein in Bibliography). Related to RABINOWITZ and ETTINGER.

NATONEK—UJ has article on Hungarian Zionist Josef Natonek (1813–1892).

NAUMANN—See NEUMANN.

NAUMBOURG—See NAUMBURG.

NAUMBURG (also Naumbourg)—JE has biographies from 18th-cent. Bavaria and 19th-cent. France. AJA has a family tree beginning 1612, related to WEHLE. LBI has a family tree beginning 1612. Also related to MORGENTHAU. Also see NOMBERG.

NAVARRA—See NAVARRO.

NAVARRE—See NAVARRO.

NAVARRO (also Nabarro, Navarra, Navarre)—Sephardic name presumably taken from the kingdom of Navarre in France. JE and UJ have biographies from 14th-cent. Portugal, 17th-cent. Italy and 19th-cent. England. Related to BASSANI.

NAVON—See NABON.

NAVON BEY—UJ has article on Palestinian financier Joseph Navon Bey (1852–1934). Also see NABON.

NAWAWI—Related to FARAJI.

NAWI—Iraqi rabbinical family beginning 18th cent. See EJ.

NAZIMOVA—UJ has article on Crimean actress Alla Nazimova (b. 1879).

NAZIR—JE has article on Isaac Nazir, 17th-cent. founder of cabalism in Palestine.

NEANDER—JE has article on Johann Neander (1789–1850), born MENDEL, German historian who converted to Christianity. See family history in JFF, No. 33. Related to MENDELSSOHN.

NECHE (also Neches)—Prominent family in Grodno, Lithuania, 19th cent.; see JE article on Grodno. Solomon Neches of Jerusalem (b. 1891) was descended from Elijah the GAON of Vilna; see EJ. Related to EPSTEIN.

NECHES—See NECHE.

NEGRIN—See NIGRIN.

NEGRO—See YAHYA.

NEHAMA—JE has article on Turkish Rabbi Judah Nehama (1825–1899).

NEIDUS—UJ has article on Yiddish poet Leib Neidus (1890–1918), born in Russia.

NEIGRESHL—UJ has article on Galician poet Mendel Neigreshl (b. 1903).

NEILSON—JE has article on English actress Julia Neilson (b. 1868), related to TERRY.

NEISSER—JE has article on German dermatologist Albert Neisser (1855–1916). LBI has a family tree beginning 1766.

NELSON—UJ has article on German philosopher Leonard Nelson (1882–1927).

NEMENOFF—Related to LUBOSCHUTZ.

NEMENYI—JE has article on Hungarian lawyer Ambrosius Nemenyi (b. NEUMANN in 1852).

NEMES—UJ has article on Hungarian art dealer Marcel Nemes (1866–1930), born Moses KLEIN.

NEMIROV—See NIEMIROWER.

NEMNO—CAJ has some family records.

NEMOY—UJ has article on Russian scholar Leon Nemoy (b. 1901).

NEMTZEANU—UJ has article on Rumanian poet Barbu Nemtzeanu (1886–1919), born DEUTSCH.

NEPI—JE has article on Italian physician Graziano Nepi (1759–1836).

NEROL—Related to BACHARACH.

NETIRA—See EJ article on *Abraham* ben Netira of Baghdad (10th cent.).

NETO—UJ has article on 17th-cent. Rabbi Isaac Neto of Surinam. Also see NETTO, NIETO.

NETTER—Ashkenazic name taken from the town of Nidda in Hesse, Germany. JE has three biographies from 19th-cent. France. LBI has family trees beginning 1777. CAJ has some family records. Related to GOMPEL and KOHLER. Also see NOETHER.

NETTI—UJ has article on Bohemian musician Paul Netti (b. 1889).

NETTO—Related to MENDES. See also NETO, NIETO.

NETZLER—Related to TRIVALE.

NEU—Related to BLOCH.

NEUBAUER—JE has article on Hungarian and English librarian Adolf Neubauer (1831–1907). Related to BUCHLER. Also see NEUGEBAUER.

NEUBERG—See NEUBURGER.

NEUBERGER—See NEUBURGER.

NEUBURGER (also Neuberg, Neuberger, Newburger, Newburgh, etc.)—JE and UJ have biographies from 19th-cent. Germany, Austria and U.S.A. LBI has a family tree beginning 1770. Related to BELMONT.

NEUDA—JE has article on Austrian Rabbi Abraham Neuda (1812–1854), related to SCHMIEDL.

NEUFELD (also Newfield)—JE and UJ have biographies from 19th-cent. Poland, Hungary and U.S.A.

NEUGASS—Related to NEWMAN.

NEUGEBAUER—Possible variation of NEUBAUER. JE has article on Hungarian writer Ladislaus Neugebauer (b. 1845).

NEUHAUS (also Neuhof, Newhouse)—Related to CARLEBACH, OPPENHEIMER and KOHLER.

NEUHOF—See NEUHAUS.

NEUMANN (also Neuman, Naumann, Neumanovitz, Newman)—JE and UJ have biographies from 18th-cent. Germany and Hungary, 19th-cent. Austria, Russia, England and U.S.A. Related to BAMBERGER, LONZANO, NEMENYI, MOLNAR, KAYSERLING, ENGEL, NEUGASS and HOMIYOTH.

NEUMANOVITZ—See NEUMANN.

NEUMARK (also Newmark)—JE has article on German Talmudist Mirels Neumark (d. 1706). UJ has two biographies from 19th-cent. U.S.A. CAJD has a family tree from Germany covering 1696 to 1908. PD has some family records. Related to ASHKENAZI, MIRELS and ROSENTHAL.

NEUMEGEN—JE has article on Leopold Neumegen (1787–1875), English educator born in Posen.

NEUMEYER (also Newmyer, etc.)—UJ has biographies from 19th-cent. Germany and U.S.A.

NEURATH—JE has article on Austrian economist Wilhelm Neurath (b. 1840).

NEUSCHOTZ—UJ has article on Rumanian philanthropist Jacob de Neuschotz (1819–1888).

NEUSTADT (also Neustaedter, Neustatter) —Ashkenazic name taken from Neustadt in Germany. JE and UJ have biographies from 19th-cent. Germany, Galicia and U.S.A. LBI has a family tree beginning 1615. CAJ has family records from 18th cent.

NEUSTAEDTER—See NEUSTADT.

NEUSTATTER—See NEUSTADT.

NEUWIED—Related to HEINE.

NEUWEIDEL—JE has article on Russian scholar Elias Neuweidel (1821–1886).

NEUWIRTH—CAJ has some family records.

NEVAKHOVICH—JE has article on Russian writer Lob Nevakhovich (d. 1831).

NEWBURGER—See NEUBURGER.

NEWBURGH—See NEUBURGER.

NEWCORN—UJ has article on Galician lawyer William Newcorn (b. 1868).

NEWFIELD—See NEUFELD.

NEWHOUSE—See NEUHAUS.

NEWMAN—See NEUMANN.

NEWMARK—See NEUMARK.

NEWMYER—See NEUMEYER.

NEWSALT—AJA has a family tree written in 1870, related to KRAUSE and LONDONER.

NEY—UJ has article on Hungarian opera singer David Ney (1843–1900). LBI has a

family tree beginning 1680, related to STERN.

NEYMARCK—JE has article on French economist Alfred Neymarck (1848–1921).

NIEDERLANDER—JE has article on 16th-cent. Austrian scribe Abraham Niederlander, also known as SOFER and SCHREIBER.

NIEGO—UJ has article on Turkish communal leader Joseph Niego (b. 1864).

NIEHEIMER—Related to RANSOHOFF.

NIEMIROWER (also Nemirov)—Name presumably taken from a Russian city or town of Nemirov (there are several). UJ has article on Galician Rabbi Jacob Niemirower (1871–1939), who died in Rumania and whose family can be traced back five generations in Jassy, Rumania.

NIEROP—JE has two biographies from Holland, 19th cent.

NIETO—JE has biographies from 17th- and 18th-cent. Portugal, England and Italy. JE article on "Coat of Arms" has a family crest. Also see NETO and NETTO.

NIFOCI (also Nafusi)—EJ has article on 14th-cent. Majorcan astronomer Isaac Nifoci.

NIGER—UJ has article on Samuel Niger (b. 1883), pseudonym of CHARNEY.

NIGRIN (also Negrin)—JE has two biographies from Palestine, 16th and 17th cent.

NIJAR—See NAJARA.

NIKITIN—EJ has article on Russian scholar Victor Nikitin (1839–1908).

NIKOLAEVICH—Related to NISSELOVICH.

NIKOVA—See biography in EJ article on "Dance."

NIMZOWITSCH—UJ has article on Latvian-Danish chess master Aron Nimzowitsch (1887–1935).

NIN—Related to TRILLINGER.

NIRENSTEIN—UJ has article on U.S. lawyer Samuel Nirenstein (b. 1899).

NISSE—UJ has article on Bertram Nisse of England, 19th–20th-cent.

NISSELOVICH (also Nikolaevich)—UJ has article on Russian jurist Lazar Nisselovich (1862–1913).

NISSENBAUM—See NUSSBAUM.

NISSIM (also Nissim-Oglu)—JE has biographies from 18th-cent. Turkey and 19th-cent. India. Related to ANISIMOV and TROKI.

NISSIN—JE has article on Swedish singer Henriette Nissin (1819–1879). Related to SALOMAN and DUBNO.

NIZER—UJ has article on British-American lawyer Louis Nizer (b. 1902).

NIZZA—JE has article on 17th-cent. Venetian Rabbi Solomon Nizza.

NOAH—JE has article on U.S. politician-writer Mordecai Noah (1785–1851). Related to HART, MACHADO and PHILLIPS.

NOBEL (also Noble)—UJ has article on Hungarian-German Rabbi Nehemia Nobel (1871–1922). CAJ has some family records. Related to DUARTE.

NOBLE—See NOBEL.

NOETHER (also Neter)—Family of 19th-cent. German mathematicians; see EJ. LBI has a family tree beginning 1686, related to ROSENTHAL. Another variation of the name is NETTER.

NOLA—JE has two biographies from 16th-cent. Italy.

NOMBERG—UJ has article on Polish writer Hirsch Nomberg (1874–1924). The name may be a variation of NAUMBURG.

NONES—Sephardic family in America, descended from Benjamin Nones, who came to Philadelphia from Bordeaux, France, in 1777. JE has a family tree; AJA has a family tree beginning 1680. Related to LEVY, MARKS, LEON, CLAYBURG, JACQUES, ANDREWS, COOK, ABRAHAMS, JACOBS. The family might perhaps be related in the distant past to NUNEZ.

NORDAU—JE has article on Austrian philosopher Max Nordau (1849–1923), born in Budapest; related to SUDFELD. PD has some family records.

NORDEN—JE and UJ have biographies from 19th-cent. England, Australia and Germany.

NORDHEIM (also Nordheimer)—JE and UJ have biographies from 19th-cent. Germany and U.S.A.

NORDLINGEN—Related to HAHN.

NORONHA (also Loronha)—EJ has article on Fernao de Noronha (1470–1540), Marrano colonizer of Brazil.

NORRIS—Related to SOLIS.

NORSA—Related to LINDO.

NORZI—Name derived from the town of Norcia in Italy. JE has ten biographies from Italy, beginning 15th cent.

NOSSBAUM—See NUSSBAUM.

NOSSIG—JE has article on Austrian author and sculptor Alfrid Nossig (b. 1864).

NOTKIN—JE has article on Russian financier Nathan Notkin (d. 1804).

NOTOVICH—JE has article on Russian journalist Osip Notovich (b. 1849).

NOVA—UJ has article on U.S. Judge Algernon Nova (b. 1881).

NOVEIRA—JE has article on 18th-cent. Italian Rabbi Menahem Noveira.

NOVOMINSKI—Related to OLGIN.

NOWAKOWSKI—UJ has article on Russian composer David Nowakowski (1848–1921).

NOZIERE—UJ has article on French critic Fernand Noziere (1874–1931).

NUNES—See NUNEZ.

NUNEZ (also Nunes, Nunez de Lara)—Marrano family dating from 15th cent. JE has ten biographies. Related to RODRIGUES, LOPEZ, HOMEM, MACHADO, GOMEZ, PEREYRA, ABENDANA, MENDES, PHILLIPS, ALMEYDA, PINA, BELMONTE, VAIS, VAEZ and DISRAELI. Perhaps related to NONES.

NUROK—UJ has article on Latvian Rabbi Mordecai Nurok (b. 1879).

NUSBAUM—See NUSSBAUM.

NUSSBAUM (also Nusbaum, Nossbaum, Nissenbaum)—German name derived from the sign of a nut tree *(Nussbaum)* on the family's door. JE and UJ have biographies from 19th-cent. Russia, Poland, Bavaria and U.S.A. LBI has a family tree beginning 1833. CAJ has some family records. Related to ROSENWALD, OPPENHEIMER.

NUSSINOV—UJ has article on Russian critic Isaac Nussinov (b. 1889).

NYARI—JE has article on Hungarian art critic Alexander Nyari (b. 1861).

NYBURG—UJ has article on U.S. lawyer Sidney Nyburg (b. 1880).

NYMWEGEN—Related to ARNSTEIN.

OAKES—See OCHS.

OBEDIENTE—See ABUDIENTE.

OBERDORFER—UJ has article on U.S. soldier Eugene Oberdorfer (b. 1896). Related to LANDAUER.

OBERMANN—UJ has article on Polish scholar Julian Obermann (b. 1888).

OBERMAYER (also Obermeyer)—UJ has two biographies from 19th-cent. Germany and U.S.A. PD has some family records.

OBERNAUER—UJ has article on U.S. attorney Harold Obernauer (b. 1887).

OBERNDORF (also Oberndoerffer, Oberndorffer)—UJ has article on U.S. psychiatrist Clarence Oberndorf (b. 1882). LBI has an Oberndoerffer family tree beginning 1760. Related to WILMERSDORFFER.

OBERNECK (also Obernik, Obornik)—EJ has article on Austrian Talmudist Judah Obernik (d. 1520). JE and UJ have biographies from 18th-cent. Austria and 19th-cent. Germany.

OBUDA—Related to FREUDIGER.

OCHS (also Oakes)—German name meaning "ox." Other variations in various languages, not necessarily related, are SCHOR, BYK, WAHL, WOHL and VOLOV. JE has biographies from 19th-cent. Germany and U.S.A. LBI has a family tree beginning 1728, related to DUENKELS-BUEHLER. LBIS has some family notes. Related to EINHORN, SULZBERGER, WISE.

ODETS—UJ has article on U.S. playwright Clifford Odets (b. 1906).

OELSNER—UJ has article on English scholar Herman Oelsner (1871–1923).

OESTERREICHER (also Osterreicher, Ostriker, Oestreicher)—Ashkenazic name indicating origin in Austria (Österreich). UJ has article on Austro-Hungarian physician Joseph Oesterreicher (1756–1832). LBI has an Oestreicher family tree begin-

ning 1761. Related to BERGSON and RAKOVS.

OETTINGEN (Oettinger)—See ETTINGEN.

OFEN—See ALT-OFEN.

OFFENBACH—Name taken from the German town of Offenbach in Hesse; Jews first settled there in 17th cent. JE has article on French composer Jacques Offenbach (1819–1880), born in Cologne; married Hermina MITCHELL, a Catholic.

OFFICIAL—Franco-German family of 13th cent.; see EJ.

OFFNER (also Ofner)—UJ has biographies from 19th-cent. Bohemia, Austria and U.S.A.

OFNER—See OFFNER.

OISTRAKH—UJ has article on Russian violinist David Oistrakh (b. 1908).

OKO—UJ has article on Russian-American author Adolf Oko (b. 1883).

OLDEN—UJ has three biographies from 19th-cent. Germany. Related to OPPEN-HEIM.

OLDENBURG—Name taken from the grand duchy of Oldenburg in northern Germany; Jews first settled there in the Middle Ages. LBI has a family tree beginning 1621, related to GOLDSCHMIDT-OLDENBURG.

OLGIN—UJ has article on Russian lecturer Moissaye Olgin (1878–1939), also known as NOVOMINSKI.

OLINSKY—UJ has article on Russian painter Ivan Olinsky (b. 1878).

OLIVEIRA—See OLIVEYRA.

OLIVEN—LBI has a family tree beginning 1730.

OLIVETTI—Italian industrial family of 19th cent.; see EJ. Related to MONTEFI-ORE.

OLIVEYRA (also Oliveira, Olivier)—Sephardic name. JE has article on Portuguese author Solomon de Oliveyra of Amsterdam (d. 1708). JE article on "Coat of Arms" has an Oliveira family crest. Related to BELMONTE, CORREA and de SOLA.

OLIVIER—See OLIVEYRA.

OLLENDORF (also Ollendorff)—JE has two biographies from 19th-cent. France.

OLLESHEIMER—LBI has a family tree beginning 1823.

OLMO—JE has article on Italian Rabbi Jacob Olmo (1690–1757). Related to ANAW.

OLSCHKI—Italian-German-Swiss family of editors, 19th cent. See UJ.

OLSCHWANG (also Olschwanger)—JE has two biographies from 19th-cent. Russia. Related to BAZALEEL, JAFFE, LEVIN and MEIR.

OLSHAUSEN—JE has article on German scholar Justus Olshausen (1800–1882).

OLTARSH—UJ has article on U.S. architect David Oltarsh (1883–1940).

ONDERWIJZER—JE has article on Dutch Rabbi Abraham Onderwijzer (1863–1934).

ONKENEIRA—JE has article on 16th-cent. Turkish poet Isaac Onkeneira.

ONODI—UJ has article on Hungarian doctor Adolf Onodi (1857–1919).

OPATOSCHU (also Opatoshu, Opatovsky, Opatow)—UJ has article on Joseph Opatoshu (b. 1887), Russian writer also known as Opatovsky. JE has article on 16th-cent. Moravian Rabbi Samuel Opatow. CAJ has Opatoschu family records.

OPATOVSKY—See OPATOSCHU.

OPATOW—See OPATOSCHU.

OPET—JE has article on German writer Otto Opet (b. 1866).

OPPE—See OPPENHEIM.

OPPENFELD—Related to ITZIG.

OPPENHEIM (also Oppenheimer)—Ashkenazic name taken from the German town of Oppenheim in Rhein-Hessen; Jews first settled there in 13th cent. JE and UJ have numerous biographies from Germany, Austria and England, beginning 17th cent. AJA has an Oppenheim family tree beginning 1600, related to COHEN and AUERBACH, and an Oppenheimer family tree beginning in 18th cent., related to GREENHUT, KOHLER, JACOB, KAHN and KUHN. LBI has Oppenheim family trees beginning 1556, 1633, 1676 and 1825, related to KAULLA, GROSSMAN and OPPE, and Oppenheimer family trees beginning 1397, 17th cent., 1650, 1713, 1745, 1770, 1778, 1807 and 1876, related to FRAENKEL, JAFFE, MEYERHOF, REIS, CAHNER, HESS,

KATZ, SONDHEIMER, HECHT, HERZ, NOSSBAUM, NEUHOF and SCHIFF. PD has Oppenheim and Oppenheimer family records. CAJ has Oppenheim family records. LBIS has Oppenheimer family notes. JE article on "Coat of Arms" has both Oppenheim and Oppenheimer family crests. See a family history in *Die Siegburger Familie Levison.* Related to WEISS, BEHRENDS, GUMPEL, BACHRACH, GEIGER, SCHIFF, SPEYER, DELMEDIGO, ROTHSCHILD, ITZIG, TE'ONIM, KRUMENAU, OLDEN, SCHWARTZ, WOLFF, GOMPERZ, TAUFFENBERGER, HEINE, WERTHEIMER, WARBURG, SUSS, BOAS and MODEL.

OPPER—JE and UJ have articles on U.S. cartoonist Frederick Opper (1857–1937). Related to BLOWITZ.

OPPERT—JE has three biographies from 19th-cent. Germany. Related to JAFFE.

OPPLER—UJ has four biographies from 19th-cent. Germany. PD has some family records. Related to SAMSON.

ORABUENA (also Buenahora)—Spanish family from Navarre in 14th and 15th cent. JE has eight biographies.

ORBACH—See AUERBACH.

ORDRONAUX—UJ has article on French privateer Jean Ordronaux (1778–1841).

ORENSTEIN (also Ornstein)—Ashkenazic name taken from the town of Arnstein in Bavaria. JE and UJ have biographies from 19th-cent. Russia, Galicia, Austria and England, including one descendant of 17th-cent. Rabbi Joel SIRKES. Related to ETTINGER, WAHL, ITTINGA and HALPERIN. Also see ARNSTEIN.

ORGELBRAND—UJ has article on Polish publisher Samuel Orgelbrand (1810–1868).

ORGLER—AJA has a family tree beginning 1650, Germany and U.S.A., related to BLOCH and GRATZ.

ORLIK—UJ has article on Prague painter Emil Orlik (1870–1932).

ORLOFF—UJ has two biographies from 19th-cent. Russia.

ORMANDY—UJ has article on conductor Eugene Ormandy (b. 1899 in Hungary).

ORMODY DE ORMOD—UJ has article on Hungarian economist Vilmos Ormody de Ormod (1838–1932).

ORNITZ—UJ has article on U.S. author Samuel Ornitz (b. 1891).

ORNSTEIN—See ORENSTEIN.

OROBIO—Related to CASTRO and SIMON.

OROSDI—Related to SCHNABEL.

ORSHANSKY—JE has article on Russian author Ilya Orshanski (1846–1875).

ORSKA—UJ has article on Russian-Austrian actress Daisy Orska (1894–1930).

ORTA—EJ has article on Marrano scientist Garcia de Orta (1500–1568).

ORTEGA—UJ has article on Spanish author Manuel Ortega (b. 1888).

ORTLEPP—Related to PHILLIPS.

ORVIETO—UJ has article on Italian author Angelo Orvieto (b. 1869).

OSBORN—UJ has article on German art historian Max Osborn (b. 1870).

OSER—JE has biographies from 18th- and 19th-cent. Austria. CAJ has a family history.

OSIMO—JE has article on Italian physician Marco Osimo (1818–1881).

OSIRIS—JE has article on French philanthropist Daniel Osiris (1825–1908).

OSOFSKY—Related to ASSAF.

OSORIO—Related to ABENDANA, COSTA, MELDOLA, MENDES and de SOLA.

OSSOWETZKY—EJ has article on Ukrainian Zionist O. Ossowetzky (1858–1929).

OSTERBERG—JE has article on U.S. engineer Max Osterberg (b. 1869 in Frankfurt-am-Main). LBI has a family tree beginning 1786.

OSTERMAN—Related to DYER.

OSTERREICHER—See OESTERREICHER.

OSTRIKER—See OESTERREICHER.

OSTROGORSKI (also Ostrogski)—Ashkenazic name taken from the Galician town of Ostrog. JE has article on Russian economist Moisei Ostrogorski (1854–1917). CAJ has Ostrogski family records from 17th and 18th cent.

OSTROLENK—UJ has article on Polish-American economist Bernhard Ostrolenk (b. 1887).

OSTROPOLER (also Ostropoli)—JE and EJ have biographies from 17th- and 18th-cent. Poland and Russia. Also see UJ article on *Jacob* Joseph Hakohen.

OSTROWSKI (also Ostrowsky)—UJ has two biographies from 19th-cent. Russia.

OSVAT—UJ has two biographies from 19th-cent. Hungary.

OSZTERN—UJ has article on Hungarian scholar Salamon Osztern (b. 1879).

OTTENBERG—UJ has article on U.S. doctor Reuben Ottenberg (b. 1882).

OTTENHEIMER—JE has article on German poet Henriette Ottenheimer (1807–1883). Related to HENLE.

OTTENSOOSER (also Ottensoser, Ottensosser)—JE and EJ have biographies from 18th- and 19th-cent. Germany.

OTTERBOURG—UJ has article on German-American diplomat Marcus Otterbourg (1827–1893).

OTTINGEN—See OTTINGER.

OTTINGER (also Ottingen)—JE has biographies from 17th-cent. Poland and 18th-cent. Germany. See also ETTINGER.

OTTO—Related to MARGOLIOTH.

OTTOLENGHI (also Ottolengo)—Italian name derived from the German town of Ettlingen in Baden, where the family presumably originated. JE has nine biographies from 16th- and 18th-cent. Italy.

OULIF—JE has article on French lawyer Charles Oulif (1794–1867).

OUMANSKY—UJ has article on Russian journalist Constantin Oumansky (b. 1902).

OUNGRE—UJ has article on Belgian colonist Louis Oungre (b. 1880).

OVADIA—UJ has article on Turkish-American Rabbi Nissim Ovadia (1890–1942).

OVARY—JE has article on Hungarian historian Leopold Ovary (1833–1919).

PACAGON—Related to MONTAIGNE.

PACHECO—EJ has article on early American merchant Rodrigo Pacheco (d. 1749). CAJ has some family records.

PACHT—UJ has article on Austrian-American lawyer Isaac Pacht (b. 1890).

PACIFICI (also Pacifico)—UJ and EJ have biographies from 19th-cent. Italy and Gibraltar.

PADAWER (also Padover, Padva)—French family whose name is derived from Padua, Italy, its original home. The family later migrated to Poland before moving to France.

PADOA (also Padovani, Padover, Padua, Padway)—All variations of this name indicate origin in Padua, Italy. JE and UJ have biographies from 19th-cent. Italy, England, Austria and Russia. Russian Rabbi Jacob Padua (d. 1854) was related to KATZENELLENBOGEN.

PADOVANI—See PADOA.

PADOVER—See PADOA.

PADUA—See PADOA.

PADWAY—See PADOA.

PAEFF—UJ has article on Russian sculptor Bashka Paeff (b. 1893).

PAGAY—JE has three biographies from 19th-cent. Austria. Related to BERG.

PAGEL—JE has article on German medical writer Julius Pagel (1851–1912).

PAGGI—JE has article on Italian Hebraist Angelo Paggi (1789–1867).

PAIBA—See PAIVA.

PAIVA (also Paiba, Payba)—Spanish Marrano family with members in Amsterdam and Mexico in 17th cent. JE has three biographies. Related to COSTA.

PAKE—AJA has a family tree from Mobile, Alabama, related to UNGER.

PAKULLY—Related to SCHOTTLANDER.

PALACHE (also Palaggi, Falaji, Pallache)—Moroccan and Turkish family whose name first appeared in Spain as Palyaj; see EJ. JE has biographies from 16th and 18th cent. JE article on "Coat of Arms" has a family crest. Related to HAZZAN.

PALAGGI—See PALACHE.

PALAGYI—Hungarian family which changed its name from SILBERSTEIN in 19th cent. See JE.

PALDI—UJ has article on Russian artist Israel Paldi (b. FELDMAN in 1893).

PALEY—JE and UJ have biographies from Lithuania and U.S.A., 19th–20th cent.

PALGRAVE—JE has five biographies from 18th cent. Related to COHEN and TURNER.

PALITSCHINETZKI—JE has article on Russian scholar Joseph Palitschinetzki (1805–1886).

PALITZ—UJ has article on Latvian financier Clarence Palitz (b. 1887).

PALLACHE—See PALACHE.

PALLENBERG—UJ has article on Viennese-Czech actor Max Pallenberg (1877–1934).

PALLIERE—UJ has article on French writer Alme Palliere (b. 1875).

PALOTA—Related to KOHUT.

PALQUERA—See FALAQUERA.

PALYI—UJ has article on Hungarian publicist Ede Palyi (b. 1865).

PAM—UJ has two biographies from Bohemia and U.S.A., 19th cent.

PAN—JE has article on 16th-cent. German authoress Taube Pan, related to PIZKER.

PANET (Paneth)—See BANETH.

PANIGEL—UJ and EJ have biographies from 19th–20th-cent. Bulgaria and Israel. Related to ELYASHER.

PANKEN—UJ has article on U.S. Judge Jacob Panken (b. 1879 in Russia).

PANN—UJ has article on Latvian painter Abel Pann (b. 1883), also known as PFEFFERMANN.

PANOFSKY—UJ has article on German art historian Erwin Panofsky (b. 1890).

PANSIERI—See PANZIERI.

PANZIERI (also Pansieri)—Name originating in Portugal, 16th cent.; also found later in Turkey and Italy. JE has nine biographies.

PAOLI—JE has article on Austrian poet Beth Paoli (1814–1894); related to GLUCK.

PAP—UJ has two biographies from 19th-cent. Hungary. Related to KOHN.

PAPERNA—EJ has two biographies from 19th-cent. Italy and Russia.

PAPO—JE and EJ have biographies from 19th-cent. Bulgaria and 18th-cent. Italy. Italian Rabbi Samuel Papo (1708–1774) was the father-in-law of Samson MOR-PURGO.

PAPPENHEIM (also Pappenheimer)—German name derived from the Bavarian town of Pappenheim, where Jews first settled in 14th cent. JE and UJ have biographies from 18th-cent. Silesia and 19th-cent. Germany, Hungary and U.S.A. Bertha Pappenheim of Germany (1859–1936) was a descendant of GLUCKEL of Hameln; see EJ. Related to MUHSAM.

PARDO—Sephardic family whose name is derived from the Spanish *prado* ("meadow"). The name first appears in Amsterdam in 16th cent. A branch in America from 17th cent. onward was known as BROWN or BROWNE. JE, UJ and EJ have biographies. CAJ has some family records. JE article on "Coat of Arms" has the family crest. Related to AZULAI, MELDOLA and MORTEIRA.

PARENTE—JE article on "Coat of Arms" has the family crest.

PARENZO—Family of printers in 16th- and 17th-cent. Venice, probably of German origin. See JE and EJ.

PARHI—See FARHI.

PARHON—JE has article on 12th-cent. Spanish writer Solomon Parhon.

PARIENTE—Moroccan family of Spanish origin. See EJ.

PARISER—Related to SOLOVEICHIK.

PARISH-ALVARS—JE has article on English composer Elias Parish-Alvars (1810–1849), who died in Vienna.

PARKER—UJ has article on U.S. writer Dorothy Parker (b. ROTHSCHILD in 1893).

PARLAGHY—UJ has article on Hungarian artist Vilma Parlaghy (1864–1923).

PARNAS—UJ and EJ have articles from 19th-cent. Galicia and Lithuania.

PARSI—JE has article of 15th-cent. Portuguese mathematician Joseph Parsi.

PARSONNET—UJ has article on Russian doctor Aaron Parsonnet (b. 1889).

PAS—JE article on "Coat of Arms" has a family crest.

PASCAL—See PASCHELES.

PASCH—See PASCHELES.

PASCHELES (also Pascal, Pasch, Paschkis)—JE and UJ have biographies from 19th-cent. Germany, England and Austria. Related to BRANDEIS.

PASCHKIS—See PASCHELES.

PASCIN—EJ has article on painter Jules Pascin (1885–1930), born PINCUS in Bulgaria.

PASHA—JE has article on Turkish army surgeon Jacques Pasha (1850–1903).

PASMANEK—UJ has article on Russo-French writer Dan Pasmanek (1869–1930).

PASS—JE has two biographies from 19th-cent. South Africa.

PASSI—EJ has article on 16th-cent. Turkish statesman David Passi, born in Portugal.

PASSIGLI—JE has article on Italian physician Ugo Passigli (b. 1867).

PASSOVER—UJ has article on Russian jurist Alexander Passover (1840–1910).

PASTERNACK—See PASTERNAK.

PASTERNAK (also Pasternack)—UJ and EJ have biographies from 19th-cent. Russia and Poland.

PASTOR (also Pasztor)—UJ has article on Hungarian author Arpad Pasztor (b. 1877). Related to STOKES.

PASZTOR—See PASTOR.

PAT—EJ has article on labor leader Jacob Pat (born 1890 in Russia).

PATAI—EJ has article on Hungarian writer Jozsef Patai (b. 1882); married Edith EHRENFELD.

PATERNOY—See de la CABALLERIA.

PATO—See PATTO.

PATTI—Related to STRAKOSCH.

PATTO (also Pato)—Spanish family name from 17th cent. See JE.

PAUCKER—UJ has article on Rumanian editor Simon Paucker (b. 1864.)

PAULLI—JE has article on Danish religious fanatic Holger Paulli (1644–1714).

PAULY—UJ has article on Hungarian soprano Rose Pauly (b. 1895). LBI has a family tree beginning 1672.

PAVIA—Italian family dating from 8th-cent. JE has three biographies. Related to FORTIS and GENTILOMO.

PAVIETI—Related to POGGETTI.

PAYBA—See PAIVA.

PAZ—JE has article on Portuguese Marrano Duarte de Paz (died 1541). Related to MORENO.

PEARLMAN—See PERLMAN.

PECHENIK—See *The Pechenik Family.*

PECK—UJ has article on U.S. doctor Samuel Peck (b. 1900).

PECKELSHEIMER—Related to RANSO-HOFF.

PEDET—AJA has a family tree.

PEDRO—See de la CABALLERIA.

PEEL—CAJ has some family records.

PEERCE—UJ has article on U.S. tenor Jan Peerce (b. PERELMUTH in 1904).

PEGI—See BAGI.

PEINE—LBIS has some family notes.

PEISER (also Peyser)—Family from Peisern, Poland, 17th cent. JE has biographies from Poland and U.S. LBIS has some Peyser family notes. Related to DAVID.

PEIXOTTO—American Sephardic family that came from Spain and Holland in 17th cent. JE has fourteen biographies. Related to PIPSOTO, CARDOZO, PICCIOTTO, HAYS, SEIXAS, GOMEZ, DAVIS, NATHAN, PHILLIPS and NAAR.

PEKELIS—UJ has article on Russian sociologist Alexander Pekelis (b. 1902).

PELS—Ashkenazic name taken from the town of Pilica (or Pils) in Poland.

PELTIN—JE has article on Polish author Samuel Peltin (1831–1896).

PELTZ—UJ has article on Rumanian novelist Jacob Peltz (b. 1899).

PENHA—Related to DE LA PENHA, CASTRO and VAZ DIAS.

PENIEL—JE has article on scholar Solomon Peniel.

PENSO—Spanish-Turkish family name of 17th cent. JE has six biographies. See family histories and trees in KB, p. 86, and *The Belmont-Belmonte Family.* Related to BELMONTE.

PERAHYA—EJ has two biographies from Salonika, 17th cent. Perhaps a variation of PEREIRA.

PEREFERKOVICH—JE has article on Russian author Nahum Pereferkovich (1871–1940).

PEREIRA (also Pereire, Pereyra)—Spanish-Dutch family traced back to 17th cent.; the French variation is Pereire. JE has biographies. PD has family records, related to ARNSTEIN. JE article on "Coat of Arms" has the family crest. See family history in article by Abraham Yaari in *Isaias Press* commemorative book (1953). Related to ITZIG, POOL, AGUILAR, RODRIGUES, PINTO, QUITINO, NUNEZ, BELMONTE and ABENDANA. Also see PEYRERE.

PEREIRE—See PEREIRA.

PERELMAN (Perelmann)—See PERLMAN.

PERELMUTH—See PEERCE.

PEREMYSHLYANY—Name derived from the Galician city of Przemysl. EJ has article on Galician Rabbi Meir Peremyshlyany (1780–1850).

PERES—See PEREZ.

PERETZ—JE has two biographies from 19th-cent. Poland and Russia. Related to GREBNITZ, ZEITLIN, LICHTENFELD and RINGELHEIM. Also see PERITZ.

PEREYRA—See PEREIRA.

PERES (also Perez)—Marrano family name, with branches in Central and South America. JE has fifteen biographies. See a family history in *The Peres Family.* Related to CAVALLERO, COHEN, KIMHI and SHEMAIAH.

PERGAMENT (also Pergamenter)—JE and EJ have biographies from Russia and Austria, 19th cent.

PERGOLA—EJ has article on Italian Rabbi Raphael de la Pergola (1876–1923).

PERITZ—UJ has article on German scholar Ismar Peritz (b. 1863). The name is perhaps a variation of PERETZ.

PERIZOL—See FARISSOL.

PERL—See PERLES.

PERLA—See PERLES.

PERLBACH—JE has article on German historian Max Perlbach (1848–1921).

PERLE—See PERLES.

PERLES (also Perl, Perla, Perle, Perls)—Family of scholars and writers from Hungary and Bohemia. The name is derived from *Perle,* German for "pearl." The family from Prague is descended from the MAHARAL of Prague (1525–1609); that connection is traced in *Megilath Yuhasin.* JE and EJ have biographies from Austria, Hungary and Poland, beginning 17th cent. CAJ has some family records. Related to JEHIEL, BAZALEEL, SCHEFFTEL, ALTSCHUL and DUBNOW.

PERLHEFTER—JE and EJ have articles on 17th-cent. Bohemian Rabbi Issachar Perlhefter, who was born EYBESCHUETZ but took his wife's surname.

PERLMAN (also Pearlman, Perelman, Perelmann)—Ashkenazic name meaning either "dealer in pearls" or "husband of Pearl." UJ and JE have biographies from 19th-cent. Russia and Poland. Related to BEN JUDAH, BEN JEHUDAH and DYMOW. Also see JE article on Minsk, Russia.

PERLMUTTER (also Mutterperl)—Ashkenazic name that probably indicates a dealer in mother-of-pearl. UJ and EJ have biographies from Hungary and Poland, 18th–19th cent. See history in *La famille Perlmutter.*

PERLOV—Related to KARLIN.

PERLROTT-CSABA—UJ has article on Hungarian painter Vilmos Perlrott-Csaba (b. 1880).

PERLS—See PERLES.

PERLZWEIG—UJ has two biographies from 19th-cent. England and Russia.

PERRY—Related to BELMONT.

PERSITZ—EJ has article on Israeli publisher Shoshanah Persitz (b. ZLATOPOLSKI in Russia, 1893).

PERSKI (also Perskie, Persky)—UJ and EJ have biographies from 19th-cent. Russia and U.S.A. Related to MASLIANSKY.

PERSOV—EJ has article on Russian writer Shmuel Persov (b. 1890).

PERUGIA—Related to ROTHSCHILD and SASSOON.

PERUTZ—EJ has biographies from Austria and England, 19th–20th cent.

PESAHSON—EJ has article on Russian bund leader Isaac Pesahson (b. 1876).

PESANTE (also Pizante)—JE has article on 16th-cent. Turkish scholar Moses Pesante.

PESARO—JE and EJ have biographies from 14th-cent. Germany and 19th-cent. Italy. Related to MAUROGONATO.

PESELES—See PESSELES.

PESOA—Related to PHILLIPS.

PESSELES (also Peseles, Pessels)—JE and EJ have articles on 18th-cent. Vilna scholar Joseph Pesseles, related to Elijah, the GAON of Vilna. LBI has a Pessels family tree beginning 1708.

PETERDI—UJ has article on Hungarian poet Andor Peterdi (b. 1881). Related to VARNAI.

PETERFI—UJ has article on Hungarian biologist Tibor Peterfi (b. 1883).

PETLIURA—CAJ has some family records.

PETRIKOV—Related to BENDIN.

PETSCHEK—Bohemian industrial family from Prague, 19th cent. See UJ.

PETTELMAN—CAJ has some family records.

PEVSNER (also Pevzner)—EJ has four biographies from Russia, Germany and England, 19th and 20th cent.

PEYRERE—Probably a variation of PEREIRA. UJ has article on French scholar Isaac de la Peyrere (1594–1676).

PEYSER—See PEISER.

PFANN—Related to SCHIFF.

PFEFFERMANN—Related to PANN.

PFEIFFER—UJ has article on Hungarian chemist Ignac Pfeiffer (b. 1867).

PFLAUM—Ashkenazic name taken from the town of Pflaumloch.

PFORZHEIMER—UJ has article on U.S. civic worker Carl Pforzheimer (b. 1879).

PHIEBIG (also Pheibush)—LBI has a family tree beginning 1639, related to SPIR.

PHEIBUSH—See PHIEBIG.

PHILA—Related to FRANKS.

PHILADELPHIA—UJ has article on English physicist Jacob Philadelphia (b. 1720).

PHILIP—See PHILIPP.

PHILIPP (also Philip, Phillip)—UJ has article on Hungarian pianist Edmond Philipp (b. 1863). CAJ has a family history. LBIS has some Philip family notes. See family history in *Geschichte der Familie Unna (Hamburg-Kopenhagen)*. Related to JACOB and UNNA. Also see FILIPOWSKI.

PHILIPPE—JE has three biographies from 19th-cent. France.

PHILIPPI—UJ has article on German dramatist Felix Philippi (1851–1921).

PHILIPPS—See PHILLIPS.

PHILIPPSON—See PHILIPSON.

PHILIPSEN—See PHILIPSON.

PHILIPSON (also Philippson, Philipsen, Phillipson, Philipsson)—JE and UJ have biographies from Germany, England and U.S.A. beginning 18th cent. LBIS has a Philipson family tree and notes, also Philipsson and Philippson family notes. LBI has a Philippson family tree beginning 1518. CAJ has some Philippson family records. See family histories in *The Philipsons: The First Jewish Settlers in St. Louis, 1807–1858* and *Familien Philipsen i Pilestraede*. Related to ARNSWALDE, COHN, MUSSINA, BLOCK, PRIETTO, LEWIS, MAYER, GOLDSMID, JONAS.

PHILIPS—See PHILLIPS.

PHILLIP—See PHILIPP.

PHILLIPS (also Philipps, Philips)—U.S. family, prominent in New York and Philadelphia, descended from Jonas Phillips, who emigrated from Germany to England in 1751 and came to America in 1756. The family name was originally PHEIBUSH. JE has a family tree and fourteen biographies of this family, which is related to MACHADO, NUNEZ, PESOA, LEVY, SEIXAS, MOSES, CAUFFMAN, NOAH, SOLOMON, JACOBS, FRIEDMAN, LEVINE and HYMAN. JE also has seven other biographies, from 18th-cent. Poland and 19th-cent. England, Jamaica and U.S.A. AJA has a family tree beginning in 18th-cent. Bohemia. CAJ has Philips family records from Germany, 1779 to 1884. Other relatives are FAUDEL,

PIRBRIGHT, PEIXOTTO, CARDOZO, BARNERT, ORTLEPP and WAHL.

PHILLIPSON—See PHILIPSON.

PHOEBUS—UJ has biography from 15th-cent. Germany. Related to BACHARACH.

PIASTRO—UJ has article on Crimean violinist Mishel Piastro (b. 1891).

PIATELLI—Related to ANAW.

PIATIGORSKAIA—See PIATIGORSKY.

PIATIGORSKY (also Piatigorskaia)—UJ has two biographies from Russia, 19th and 20th cent.

PIATNITSKY—UJ has article on Russian author Osip Piatnitsky (b. 1882).

PICA—PD has some family records.

PICARD—EJ has two biographies from 19th-20th-cent. Germany, U.S.A. and Israel.

PICCIOTTO—Family in Italy from 18th cent. Also, Haim Picciotto (b. 1806 in Aleppo, d. 1879 in London) came from an ancient eastern Mediterranean family that still has members living in Syria. See JE, UJ and EJ. Related to PEIXOTTO.

PICHEL—UJ has article on U.S. actor Irving Pichel (b. 1891).

PICHIO—See PIGO.

PICHLER—JE has article on Austrian painter Adolf Pichler (b. 1834 near Pressburg).

PICHO—See PICHON.

PICHON (also Picho)—JE has biographies from 14th-cent. Spain and 17th-cent. Turkey.

PICK (also Picker, Pickart)—Name originating in Picardy, Italy. JE and UJ have biographies from 19th-cent. England, Austria and Germany. CAJD has a family tree from Germany. LBIS has a family tree. PD has some family records. Related to BERLIN and POCHAPOVSKY.

PICKER—See PICK.

PICKART—See PICK.

PICON—UJ has article on U.S. actress Molly Picon (b. 1898); related to KALICH.

PICQUIGNY—Related to WETZLER.

PIERLEONI—Noble Roman family of Jewish origin which converted to Christianity in 11th cent. See JE.

PIETOSI—Related to ANAW.

PIGO (also Figo)—Italian family of rabbis. JE has biographies from 16th-cent. Turkey and 17th-cent. Italy. Also see JE article on Azariah *Figo* of Venice (1579–1647).

PIJADE—EJ has article on Yugoslav revolutionary Mosa Pijade (b. 1890).

PIKES—JE has article on 16th-cent. German Rabbi Abraham Pikes.

PIKLER—19th-cent. Hungarian family. UJ has three biographies.

PILDERWASSER—Related to WEISSER.

PILICHOWSKI—UJ has article on Leopold Pilichowski (1869–1933), Polish painter who died in London.

PILLITZ—JE has article on 19th-cent. Hungarian Rabbi Daniel Pillitz (pen name Theodore Burger).

PILNIAK—UJ has article on Russian writer Boris Pilniak (b. 1894), also known as VOGAU.

PIMENTEL—JE has article on 18th-cent. Spanish poet Sara Pimentel, who lived in England. JE article on "Coat of Arms" has the family crest.

PIMIENTA—UJ has article on Fray Pimienta (1688–1720), Spanish priest from the West Indies who converted to Judaism.

PINA (also de Pinna)—Portuguese Marrano family that escaped to Amsterdam, also known as JESHURUN. JE has two biographies from 16th and 17th cent. Related to de SOLA, LOBATO and NUNES.

PINANSKI (also Pinansky)—UJ has article on U.S. Judge Abraham Pinanski (b. 1887).

PINCAS—See PINCUS.

PINCHERLE—UJ has article on Italian pediatrician Maurizio Pincherle (1879–1939).

PINCUS (also Pincas, Pinkus, Pinhas, Pinkas)—UJ and EJ have biographies from 19th- and 20th-cent. Germany, Hungary, Israel and U.S.A. LBI has a Pinkus family tree, related to FRAENKEL, GRAETZER and POLKE. Other relatives are LIPMAN and PASCIN.

PINCZOW—JE has three biographies from 17th–18th-cent. Poland. Rabbi Joseph Pinczow was a descendant of Rabbi Jacob POLLAK, and son-in-law of Rabbi Moses KRAMER of Vilna. Also see PINZCOWER.

PINE (also Pnie)—Name taken from the town of Peine, Hannover. JE has article on 14th-cent. German translator Samson Pine.

PINEL—Related to USQUE.

PINELES—EJ has two biographies from Galicia, 19th and 20th cent.

PINELO—See family history in *Los Leon Pinelo*.

PINERO (also Pinheiro)—JE has article on English dramatist Arthur Pinero (1855–1934), descended from a Sephardic family. Moses Pinheiro of 17th-cent. Italy was brother-in-law of Joseph ERGAS; see JE.

PINES—JE and EJ have biographies from 18th–19th-cent. Russia. Rabbi Elijah Pines was a descendant of the families of Jacob POLLAK and Judah Lob PUCHOWITZER. Yehiel Pines (1843–1913) was related to RIVLIN and the father-in-law of YELLIN.

PINHAS—See PINCUS.

PINHEIRO—See PINERO.

PINKAS—See PINCUS.

PINKHOF—JE has article on Dutch physician Herman Pinkhof (b. 1863).

PINKUS—See PINCUS.

de PINNA—See PINA.

PINNE—See PINNER.

PINNER (also Pinne)—Name taken from the Polish town of Pinne, near Posen. JE and UJ have biographies from 19th-cent. Germany and Poland. PD has some Pinne family records.

PINSKER (also Pinski)—Name taken from the town of Pinsk, Russia. JE and UJ have biographies from Russia, Poland and Galicia, 18th and 19th cent. Dob Bar Pinsker of Poland (18th cent.) was a descendant of Nathan SPIRA of Cracow.

PINSKI—See PINSKER.

PINSON—UJ has article on U.S. writer Koppel Pinson (b. 1904 in Lithuania).

PINTERS—LBIS has some family notes.

PINTHUS—UJ has article on German critic Kurt Pinthus (b. 1886). LBI has a family tree beginning 1744.

PINTO (also de Pinto)—Portuguese family. Some members were in Italy and Syria in 16th cent., in Holland in 17th cent., and in Brazil and U.S.A. in 18th cent. See JE. JE article on "Coat of Arms" has the family crest. Related to TORRE, COSTA, CASTRO, FRANCIA, PEREYRA and VITAL.

PINZCOWER—CAJ has a family history covering 1599 to 1930, related to ETTLINGER, FREIMANN and HOROVITZ. Also see PINCZOW.

PIPERNO—JE has article on Italian economist Settimio Piperno (b. 1834).

PIPSOTO—Related to PEIXOTTO.

PIRBRIGHT—JE has article on English statesman Henry Pirbright (1840–1903), who married TEDESCO and PHILLIPS. JE article on "Coat of Arms" has the family crest. Related to FAUDEL-PHILLIPS and WAHL.

PIRES—See PYRRHUS.

PIROGOV—JE has article on Russian physician Nikolai Pirogov (1810–1881).

PISA—Italian family deriving its name from the city of Pisa; it can be traced back to 15th cent., and is descended from the da SINAGOGA family of Rome. See JE and EJ, which have biographies from 16th through 19th cent. Also see *La famiglia da Pisa.* Related to ANAW and MELDOLA.

PISK—UJ has article on Viennese composer Paul Pisk (b. 1893).

PISKO—UJ has article on U.S. philanthropist Seraphine Pisko (1861–1942).

PISARRO—Family of painters in the West Indies, originally from Portugal and France. See JE and UJ.

PISTINER—UJ has article on Austrian labor leader Jacob Pistiner (1882–1930).

PITLUCK—AJA has a family tree from St. Joseph, Mo.

PITTOON—See BITTOON.

PIZA—AJA has a family tree beginning 18th cent.

PIZKER—Related to PAN.

PIZZIGHETONE—JE has article on 16th-cent. Italian Talmudist David Pizzighettone.

PJURKO—JE has article on Russian Hebraist Abraham Pjurko (b. 1853).

PLACZEK—JE has two biographies from 19th-cent. Hungary and Austria. CAJ has some records. Also see PLATZEK.

PLANKENSTERN—Related to WETZLER.

PLATT—UJ has article on U.S. lawyer Samuel Platt (b. 1874).

PLATZEK—UJ has article on U.S. Judge Marx Platzek (1854–1932). The name is perhaps a variation of PLACZEK.

PLAU—AJA has a family tree beginning 1726, Sweden.

PLAUT (also Blaut, Flaut)—EJ has biographies from 19th–20th-cent. Hungary, Germany and U.S.A. AJA has a family tree beginning in 18th-cent. Germany, related to GLANS and KATZ. LBI has family trees beginning 1675 and 1843. Some Plauts have been traced back to 12th cent.; contact Elizabeth Plaut, 46 Ridelle Avenue, Toronto 10, Ont., Canada.

PLESSNER—JE has two biographies from 19th-cent. Germany. CAJ has some family records.

PLETSCH—JE has article on 14th–15th-cent. German physician Solomon Pletsch.

PLIGET—Related to DUBNOW.

PLOTKE (also Plotkin)—JE and EJ have biographies from 19th-cent. Germany and Canada. Also see *Struggle for Justice,* autobiography of Canadian farmer Abe Plotkin (19th cent.).

PLOTKIN—See PLOTKE.

PLOTNIKOFF—UJ has article on Russian conductor Eugene Plotnikoff of Odessa (b. 1877).

PLOTZ (also Plotzki)—Ashkenazic name taken from the government of Plock (or Plozk) in Russian Poland. UJ and EJ have biographies from 19th-cent. Poland and U.S.A.

PLUMER—UJ has article on British Viscount Herbert Plumer (1857–1932).

PLUNGIAN (also Plunigansky)—Name taken from the town of Plungian in the government of Kovno, Russia; Jews were first in the town in 18th cent. JE has article on Russian Hebraist Mordecai Plungian (1814–1884), a descendant of Mordecai JAFFE.

PLUNIGANSKY—See PLUNGIAN.

PNIE—See PINE.

PNIOWER—UJ has article on German philologist Otto Pniower (1859–1932).

PO—UJ has article on Russian sculptress Lina Po (b. 1900).

POCHAPOVSKY—AJA has a family tree beginning 1800 in White Russia, related to PICKER, LISMAN, MINTZ, HURWITZ. The name of this family tree is *Descendants of Velvel Pochapovsky*.

POCHOWITZER (also Puchowitzer)—JE has article on 17th-cent. Russian Rabbi Judah Pochowitzer (or Puchowitzer). Related to PINES. Also see PUKHOVITSER.

PODELL—UJ has article on Russian-American lawyer David Podell (b. 1884).

PODIEBRAD—JE has article on Austrian writer David Podiebrad (1816–1882).

PODOLSKY—UJ has article on U.S. writer Edward Podolsky (b. 1902).

PODRO—CAJ has some family records.

POEL—14th-cent. Catalonian astronomer Jacob Poel may have been the father of *David* Bonet Bonjorn. See JE.

POGANY—UJ has article on Hungarian official Jozsef Pogany (b. 1886).

POGGETTI—JE has article on 16th–17th-cent. Italian Rabbi Jacob Poggetti, also called PAVIETI.

POGORELSKY—JE has article on Russian physician Messola Pogorelsky (b. 1862).

POHL—UJ has article on Moravian actor Max Pohl (1855–1935). LBIS has some family notes. Also see POLLINI.

POKI—EJ has article on 16th-cent. scholar Judah Poki of Constantinople, a nephew of Elijah BASHYAZI. Related to BAGI.

POLACCO—See POLLAK.

POLACEK (also Polatschek, Polachek)—Name which probably implies combined Polish and Czech descent. UJ and EJ have biographies from Russia, U.S.A. and Czechoslovakia, 19th and 20th cent. CAJ has Polatschek family records.

POLACHEK—See POLACEK.

POLACK—See POLLAK.

POLAK—See POLLAK.

POLANYI—EJ has two biographies from 19th–20th-cent. Hungary and Austria.

POLATSCHEK—See POLACEK.

POLEYEFF—UJ has article on Russian Rabbi Moses Poleyeff (b. 1888).

POLGAR—UJ has article on Austrian critic Alfred Polgar (b. 1875).

POLIAKOFF—Russian-French family in 19th cent. UJ has three biographies. Also see POLYAKOV.

POLIER—UJ has article on U.S. Judge Justine Polier (b. 1903).

POLITZER—JE has article on Austrian otologist Adam Politzer (1835–1920), born in Hungary.

POLKE—LBI has a family tree beginning 1776, related to FRAENKEL, GRAETZER and PINKUS.

POLL—UJ has article on German-Swedish physician Heinrich Poll (1877–1939).

POLLACK—See POLLAK.

POLLAK (also Polacco, Polack, Polak, Pollack, Pollock, Polock)—Ashkenazic name implying origin in Poland. Many rabbis claim descent from Rabbi Jacob Pollak (1460–1541), creator of the study of *pilpul* (dialectic). He married the daughter of Moses FISCHEL. JE, UJ and EJ have numerous biographies from 19th-cent. Poland, Austria, Holland, England, Hungary and Germany; Polacco is an Italian variation of the name. PD has records of a Pollak family related to PARNAU and PARNEGG. LBIS has some Pollak family notes. LBI has a Pollack family tree beginning 1772. Related to LANDAU, STUDENZKI, PINCZOW, MINIS, ZEHNER, KOHN, LEVY, BARNETT, SULZBERGER, ULTON, LUBIN, GRUMET, SOBOL.

POLLEGAR (also Pulgar, Policar)—EJ has article on 14th-cent. Spanish scholar Isaac Pollegar.

POLLINI—UJ has article on German impresario Bernhard Pollini (1838–1897), born Baruch POHL.

POLLITZER—JE and UJ have biographies from 19th-cent. Europe.

POLLOCK—See POLLAK.

POLLONAIS—JE has two biographies from 19th-cent. France.

POLOCK—See POLLAK.

POLOTSK—Name taken from the town of Polotsk, Poland, where Jews first settled in 16th cent. JE has article on 18th-cent. Polish commentator Phinehas Polotsk.

POLYA—UJ has article on Hungarian economist Jakab Polya (1844–1897).

POLYAKOV—Family of Russian bankers and railroad constructors, 19th cent.; see EJ. Also see POLIAKOFF.

POMERANTZ—EJ has article on Polish poet Berl Pomerantz (b. 1900).

POMERIA—See POMIS.

POMIS—An old Italian family which claimed descent from King David, and is also supposed to be descended from the POMERIA family, one of the four Jewish families brought from Jerusalem to Rome by Titus after the Temple destruction in 70 C.E. The family lived in Rome until 1100, then scattered throughout Italy. See JE. Related to ALATINO and ANAW.

PONTE (also Da Ponte)—JE and UJ have articles on Lorenzo Ponte (or Da Ponte), Italian-American writer (b. CONEGLIANO in Italy 1749, d. in New York 1838); married Nancy GRAHL.

PONTREMOLI—JE has biographies from Turkey and Italy, 18th and 19th cent. Also see biography in EJ article on "Architecture."

POOL—UJ has biographies from 19th-cent. England and Palestine. Related to MELDOLA, MENDES, PEREIRA, SOLA and HIRSCHENSON.

POPERT—Ashkenazic name taken from the town of Boppard on the Rhine. LBIS has some family notes. Related to HEINE.

POPPELAUER—LBIS has some family notes.

POPPER (also Poppers, Popper Bozian)—Ashkenazic name which originated in Frankfurt-am-Main. Popper was a family of Bohemian entrepreneurs in 17th and 18th cent. Polish merchant Wolf Popper Bozian (d. 1625) married a daughter of Judah LANDAU. See JE and EJ for details, as well as biographies of others with the name from 19th-cent. Austria, Hungary and U.S.A. PD has family records, related to ARTBERG and EDL. Also related to KATZENELLENBOGEN and LEWI.

POPPER BOZIAN—See POPPER.

POPPERS—See POPPER.

PORGES (also Porjes)—The prominent 18th–19th-cent. Bohemian family Porges von Portheim was related to the SPIRA family; see JE, which also has other biographies from 17th-cent. Bohemia and Palestine and 19th-cent. Germany. Moses Porges (b. in Prague, 17th cent.) was related to HOROWITZ. PD has some family records. JE article on "Coat of Arms" has a family crest. See family tree in *Stammbaum der Familien Porges* (this is the original Porges family of Portheim). Also related to BERNSTEIN.

PORJES—See PORGES.

PORTALEONE—Family of northern Italy that dates back to 14th cent. JE has five biographies from 14th to 17th cent. Also see article by Vittore Colorni on p. 169 of *S.H. Margulies Memorial Book*. Related to the SOMMO (or SOMMI) family.

de PORTELLA—Family of courtiers in 13th cent. Aragon, Spain. EJ has biographies.

PORTEN—LBI has a family tree beginning 1884, related to JAFFE.

PORTIS—UJ has article on U.S. physician Sidney Portis (b. 1884).

PORTNER—LBI has a family tree beginning 1847, related to JAFFE.

PORTNOFF (also Portnoy)—UJ and EJ have biographies from 19th-cent. Russia, Germany and Lithuania.

PORTNOY—See PORTNOFF.

PORTO—Italian family that is a predecessor of the RAPOPORT family. JE and EJ have biographies from 16th- and 17th-cent. Italy. Also see EJ article on Porto-Rafa.

PORTRAPA—See RAPOPORT.

PORTUGALOV—JE has article on Russian physician Benjamin Portugalov (1835–1896).

POSENER—See POSNER.

POSNANSKI (also Poznanski, Poznansky)—Name taken from the city of Poznan (formerly Posen) in Poland. Some Jews were there as early as 11th cent.; others came from Germany in 13th cent. Posnanski was a family of Polish scholars in 19th and 20th cent.; see EJ. EJ and JE have two other biographies from Poland and Russia, 19th cent. Related to SAVOIR.

POSNER (also Posener, Pozner)—Ashkenazic name taken from the city of Posen (now Poznan) in Poland; see above entry. JE, UJ and EJ have biographies from 17th-, 18th- and 19th-cent. Germany, Poland, Hungary and Russia. Rabbi Solomon Posner (1778–1863) was the son of Rabbi Joseph LANDSBERG and the nephew of Ze'eb KALAFRI. Rabbi David Posner (17th cent.) was the son of Naphtali SHPITZ. CAJ has some family records. Also see *The Posner Family Tree*.

POSSART—JE has two biographies from 19th-cent. Germany.

POST—Related to HAYS.

POSTAL—UJ has article on U.S. editor Bernard Postal (b. 1905).

POSTRELKO—Original name of Abraham HARZFELD; see UJ.

POTCHI—JE has article on 16th-cent. Constantinople scholar Moses Potchi. He belonged to the MARULI family, a name his son adopted.

POTOCKI (also Potofsky, Potoski)—Name which may be taken from the Polish town of Potok. JE and EJ have biographies from 18th-cent. Poland and 19th-cent. Russia. Related to ROSE.

POTOFSKY—See POTOCKI.

POTOSKI—See POTOCKI.

POVISHNOFF—UJ has article on Russian pianist Leff Povishnoff (b. 1891).

POWIDZKI—Related to FISCHEL.

POZNANSKI (Poznansky)—See POSNANSKI.

POZNER—See POSNER.

PRADO—JE and EJ have articles on 17th-cent. Marrano and a German. Also see PARDO.

PRAG—See PRAGER.

PRAGER (also Prag)—Name taken from the city of Prague. JE and EJ have biographies from 19th-cent. Germany and England. LBI has a family tree beginning 1503. CAJ has some family records, covering 1868 to 1908. Also see JE article on *Moses* ben Menahem. Related to MONTAGU.

PRATO—UJ has article on Italian Rabbi David Prato (b. 1882).

PREGEL—UJ has article on Russian-French poet Sophie Pregel (b. 1900).

PREGER—EJ has article on playwright Jacob Preger (1887–1942), born in Russia.

PREHNER—Related to JAFFE.

PREMSLA—Name taken from the Galician city of Przemysl. JE has article on 16th–17th-cent. Galician grammarian Shabbethai Premsla.

PRENOWITZ—UJ has article on Russian writer Joseph Prenowitz (1871–1938).

PRERAU (also Prerauer)—Ashkenazic name taken from the town of Prerau in Moravia, where Jews first settled in 14th cent. JE has article on 18th–19th-cent. Moravian Hebraist Benjamin Prerau. LBI has a Prerauer family tree beginning 1814.

PRESS—JE and EJ have biographies from Russia and Israel, 19th–20th cent.

PRESSBURGER (also Pressburg)—Name taken from the city of Pressburg (now Bratislava) in Slovakia. LBI has a family tree beginning 1630. Related to MICHEL.

PRESSER—EJ has article on Dutch historian Jacob Presser (b. 1899).

PRESSMAN—UJ has article on U.S. attorney Lee Pressman (b. 1906).

PREUSS—Ashkenazic name derived from Preussen, the German word for Prussia. EJ has two biographies from 19th- and 20th-cent. Germany.

PREYER—CAJ has some family records.

PRIBRAM (also Przibram)—JE has two biographies from 19th-cent. Austria.

PRICE—JE has article on English journalist Julius Price (b. 1858). See *Price, Goldsmith, Lowenstein and Related Families, 1700–1967*. Related to GOLDSMITH and LOWENSTEIN.

PRIDEAUX—JE has article on English scholar Humphrey Prideaux (1648–1724).

PRIETTO—Related to PHILIPSON.

PRIJS—EJ has article on historian Joseph Prijs (b. 1889 in Germany).

PRILUK (also Frilock, Purlik, Prylucki, Przyluk)—JE and EJ have biographies from 17th-cent. Poland and 19th-cent. Russia.

PRIMO—JE has article on Samuel Primo (1635–1708), born in Jerusalem.

PRINCE—UJ has article on German-American official Leopold Prince (b. 1880). Also see PRINS and PRINZ.

PRINGSHEIM—JE has article on German botanist Nathaniel Pringsheim (1823–1894); UJ has three biographies. LBI has a family tree beginning 1700, related to LEDERMANN. Also related to LADENBURG.

PRINS—EJ has two biographies from Holland, 18th and 19th cent. Also see PRINCE and PRINZ, which may be variations.

PRINZ—UJ has article on 19th-cent. Hungarian theologian Gyula Prinz. Also see PRINCE and PRINS.

PRITZ—Related to FREIBERG.

PROBST—EJ has article on bibliographer Menahem Probst (1881–1941), born in Galicia.

PROCHOWNIK—UJ has article on 9th-cent. Polish-Jewish hero Abraham Prochownik. See a family history in JFF, No. 6.

PROSER—JE has article on Russian Hebraist Moses Proser (b. 1840 near Kovno).

PROSKAUER—Ashkenazic name possibly taken from the Russian town of Proskurov in the government of Podolia. UJ has five biographies from 19th-cent. Germany. LBI has family trees, related to FRAENKEL, POLKE, GRAETZER.

PROSSNITZ (also Prosstitz)—Ashkenazic name taken from the Moravian town of Prossnitz, where Jews first settled in 15th cent. after being exiled from Olmutz in 1454. JE and EJ have biographies from 18th- and 19th-cent. Galicia and Hungary.

PROSSTITZ—See PROSSNITZ.

PROUST—EJ has article on French writer Marcel Proust (1871–1922), whose mother's maiden name was WEIL or WEILL. Related to BERGSON and CREMIEUX.

PROVENÇAL (also Provenzale)—Name taken from Provence in France. EJ has four biographies from 14th- and 15th-cent. France and Italy.

PROVENZALE—See PROVENÇAL.

PRYLUCKI—See PRILUK.

PRZEDBORZ—Hasidic dynasty founded by the Polish Rabbi Isaiah of Przedborz (d. 1830). See EJ.

PRZIBRAM—See PRIBRAM.

PRZLUBSKA—Related to MICHELSON.

PRZYLUK—See PRILUK.

PRZYSUCHA—EJ has article on Polish holy man Jacob Przysuchba (1766–1814).

PSANTIR—JE has article on Rumanian writer Jacob Psantir (1820–1901).

PUCHER—JE has article on Polish Rabbi Solomon Pucher (1829–1899).

PUCHOWITZER—See POCHOWITZER.

PUGLIESE—EJ has article on Italian soldier Emanuele Pugliese '(b. 1874).

PUKHACHEWSKY—EJ has article on Israel pioneer Michael Pukhachewsky (1863–1947), born in Russia.

PUKHOVITSER—EJ has article on scholar Judah Pukhovitser (1630–1700) of Lithuania, Poland and Germany. Also see POCHOWITZER.

PULITZER—JE has article on U.S. journalist Joseph Pulitzer (1847–1912), born in Budapest.

PUMPIANSKI—JE has article on Russian Rabbi Aaron Pumpianski (1835–1893).

PURJESZ—UJ has four biographies from 19th-cent. Hungary.

PURLIK—See PRILUK.

PYKE—JE has article on English barrister Lionel Pyke (1854–1899).

PYRRHUS—EJ has article on Portuguese Marrano poet Didacus Pyrrhus (1517–1607), originally PIRES.

QUASTEL—UJ has article on English biochemist Juda Quastel (b. 1899).

QUERIDO—Jacob Querido (b. in Salonika, d. 1690 in Alexandria) was the son of Jacob FILISOF and brother-in-law of *Shabbetai* Zebi. Another Jacob Querido (Smyrna, 17th cent.) was the son-in-law of Joseph HAZZAN. See JE and EJ; also EJ article on Dutch novelist Israel Querido (1872–1932). Related to BELMONTE.

QUETSCH—JE has article on Austrian Rabbi Solomon Quetsch (1798–1856).

QUIRO (also Quiros)—Related to COSTA and MENDES.

QUITINO—Related to PEREYRA.

QUITTNER—UJ has article on Hungarian architect Zsigmond Quittner (1857–1918), related to VAGFALVA.

QUIXANO—Related to HENRIQUES.

RAAB—Name probably taken from the Hungarian town of Raab (Györ in Hungarian), where Jews have lived since 15th cent. EJ has article on Israel pioneer Judah Raab (1858–1948), born in Hungary.

RABBA—EJ has article on 16th-cent. Italian preacher Menaham Rabba.

RABBINER—Ashkenazic name indicating descent from a rabbi. JE has article on Russian Rabbi Mordecai Rabbiner (1758–1830), descended on his mother's side from Mordecai JAFFE.

RABBINO—Related to RICCHI.

RABBINOVICZ (Rabbinowicz, Rabbinowitz)—See RABINOWITZ.

RABE—JE has article on German translator Johann Rabe (1710–1798). The name is also a variation of RAPOPORT.

RABENER—JE has article on Austrian Hebraist Mattithiah Rabener (b. 1826 in Lemberg).

RABI—EJ has article on U.S. physicist Isidor Rabi (b. 1898 in Austria-Hungary).

RABIN—Family of scholars descended from Israel Rabin (b. 1882 in Russia). See UJ and EJ. Also see RABINOWITZ.

RABINOFF—See RABINOWITZ.

RABINOVICH (Rabinovitch, Rabinovitz, Rabinowicz, Rabinowitsch)—See RABINOWITZ.

RABINOWITZ (also Rabbinowicz, Rabbinovicz, Rabinowitz, Rabinoff, Rabinovich, Rabinovitch, Rabinovitz, Rabinowicz, Rabinowitsch, etc.)—Ashkenazic name indicating descent from one or more rabbis. JE, UJ and EJ have numerous biographies, all from 19th-cent. Russia. CAJ has Rabinowitz family records. See family histories in *Nine Generations: 200 Years Memoirs of Our Family* and *It Began with Zade Usher* (see Bernstein in Bibliography). Related to ARONOWITSCH, ZAAR, BRODSKI, KAPLAN, BEN-AMMI, KEMPNER, NATHANSOHN, HALEVY,

RASHKES and MARGOLIN. Another variation of the name may be RABIN.

RABON—EJ has article on poet Israel Rabon (1900–1943), born in Poland; also known as RUBIN.

RABOY—UJ has article on Russian-Polish author Isaac Raboy (1882–1944).

RACCAH—Tripoli Rabbi Mas'ud Raccah (1690–1768) was descended from the Raccah family of Venice; his son-in-law was Nathan ADADI. See JE and EJ.

RACHLIS—Ashkenazic name probably derived from the female name Rachel. Many families of this name come from Chmielnik, Russia.

RACHMIEL—LBIS has some family notes.

RACHOA—Related to BELMONTE.

RADEK—UJ has article on Galician publicist Karl Radek (1885–1939); born SOBELSOHN.

RADIN—EJ has three biographies from Poland and U.S.A., 19th and 20th cent.

RADITZ—UJ has article on Russian painter Lazar Radnitz (b. 1887).

RADNER—JE has article on Russian writer David Radner (1848–1901) of Vilna.

RADO—JE and EJ have biographies from 19th–20th-cent. Hungary. Related to RODER.

RADOMSKO (also Radomsk)—EJ has article on Polish holy man Solomon of Radomsko (1803–1866).

RADOS—UJ has article on Hungarian mathematician Gusztav Rados (b. 1862), who converted to Christianity.

RADOSHITSER—EJ has article on Polish Rabbi Issachar Radoshitser (1765–1843).

RADZIWILL—CAJ has some family records.

RAFAEL—Related to BELMONTE. Also see RAPHAEL.

RAFES—EJ has article on Russian bund leader Moses Rafes (1883–1942).

RAFF—AJA has a family tree beginning 1699 in Germany, related to MEIER, ULLMANN, ROWE, ROSENBERG, KRAMER and LEVINGER.

RAFFALOVICH—EJ has two biographies from 19th–20th-cent. Russia.

RAGOLER—JE has two biographies from 18th- and 19th-cent. Lithuania and Russia. Rabbi Elijah Ragoler (1794–1849), also known as Elijah KALISHER, was descended from Mordecai JAFFE through Zebi Hirsch ASHKENAZI; see JE. Another related name is KELMER.

RAGSTATT—JE has article on 17th-cent. German Friedrich Ragstatt, born WEIL.

RAHABI—JE has article on 18th-cent. Indian candlemaker David Rahabi. Related to KODER and ROTENBURG.

RAHAMIM—JE has article on Turkish writer Nissim Rahamim (d. 1828 at Smyrna).

RAHMER—JE has article on German Rabbi Moritz Rahmer (1837–1904).

RAIMUCH—See BENREMOKH.

RAINEAU—Related to CARMOLY.

RAINER—UJ has article on Austrian actress Luise Rainer (b. 1912).

RAISA—UJ has article on Polish soprano Rosa Raisa (b. 1893).

RAISIN—UJ has two biographies from 19th-cent. Poland.

RAISMAN—UJ has article on British civil servant Sir Abraham Raisman (b. 1892).

RAISZ—EJ has article on U.S. geographer Erwin Raisz (b. in Hungary).

RAIZISS—UJ has article on Russian chemist George Raiziss (b. 1884).

RAJK—See REICH.

RAJPURKAR—EJ has article on Indian soldier Joseph Rajpurkar (1834–1905) of Bombay.

RAKOSI—EJ has article on Hungarian Communist dictator Matyas Rakosi (b. 1892).

RAKOUS—UJ has article on Bohemian author Vojtech Rakous (1862–1935), also known as OSTERREICHER.

RAKOWER—JE has article on Polish Rabbi Joseph Rakower (d. 1707), also known as BLOCH.

RAKOWSKI—JE has article on Austrian author Abraham Rakowski (b. 1855 in Galicia).

RALL—EJ has article on writer Yisrael Rall (1830–1893), born in Galicia.

RAMBACH—See RAMBERT.

RAMBERT—EJ has article on British ballet teacher Marie Rambert (b. RAMBACH in Warsaw, 1888).

RAMUKH—See BENREMOKH.

RANDEGGER—JE has article on Austrian educator Maier Randegger (1780–1853), born at Randegg.

RANGER—JE has article on English financier Morris Ranger (1830–1887), born in Germany.

RANK—UJ has article on Viennese psychoanalyst Otto Rank (1884–1939), born ROSENFELD.

RANSCHBURG—JE and EJ have biographies from 18th- and 19th-cent. Germany and Hungary.

RANSOHOFF—JE has article on U.S. physician Joseph Ransohoff (1853–1921). AJA has a family tree from Cincinnati, beginning 1800, related to NIEHEIMER and PECKELSHEIMER.

RAPA—See RAPOPORT.

RAPAPORT—See RAPOPORT.

RAPEE—UJ has article on Budapest conductor Erno Rapee (b. 1891).

RAPHAEL (also Raphaelowitz, Raphaelson, Raphaely, Raphall)—JE, UJ and EJ have biographies from 16th-cent. Italy, 18th-cent. Sweden and 19th-cent. Poland, U.S.A. and England. LBIS has Raphael family notes. CAJ has some Raphaelowitz family records. Related to HEILPERN, MELCHIOR and RICCHI. Also see RAFAEL.

RAPHAELOWITZ—See RAPHAEL.

RAPHAELSON—See RAPHAEL.

RAPHAELY—See RAPHAEL.

RAPHALL—See RAHPAEL.

RAPIPORT—See RAPOPORT.

RAPOPORT (also Rapaport, Rappaport, Rappert, Rapperport, Rappe, Rapa, Rappoort, Rapiport, etc.)—Widespread rabbinical family whose members were known to be living in eighty cities in Europe and Asia in 1900. The names Rapa and Rappe are traced to Mainz, Germany, in 1450, and later became RABE in Germany. The various branches of this family all claim a common *Kohenitic* origin from Rabbi Menahem Rapa ha-

Kohen of Porto, Italy, who married into the PORTO family in 16th cent. and changed his name to Rapoport ("Rapa of Porto"). Another branch of the family called itself Portrapa. See JE, UJ and EJ. Over the centuries, members of the family intermarried with the most prominent Ashkenazic rabbinical families; these relationships are traced in *Anaf Ez Aboth,* by Samuel Kahan, and *Da'at Kedoshim,* by Israel Eisenstadt. One branch of the family took the name WARSCHAUER in 1818. Also see JE articles on Pinsk, Grodno and Przemysl; UJ article on Cohen; and EJ article on Porto-Rafa. PD has Rapaport family records. UJ traces the name Rapaport back to Galicia in 16th cent. Related to SCHRENZEL, KATZENELLENBOGEN, ETTINGER, SILVA, LEISELS, CONSIGLIO, BOSKOVITZ and LEVINSON.

RAPPAPORT—See RAPOPORT.

RAPPE—See RAPOPORT.

RAPPERPORT—See RAPOPORT.

RAPPERT—See RAPOPORT.

RAPPOLD—UJ has article on U.S. soprano Marie Rappold (b. WINTEROTH in 1905).

RAPPOLDI—JE has article on Austrian violinist Edouard Rappoldi (b. 1839).

RAPPOPORT—See RAPOPORT.

RASCHKOW—JE has two biographies from 19th-cent. Germany.

RASCHPITZ (also Raschwitz)—JE has article on 17th-cent. scholar Hayyim Raschpitz of Prague.

RASCHWITZ—See RASCHPITZ.

RASHI—The name is an acronym for Rabbi Solomon ben Isaac (*Reb* Shlomo Yitzhaki), the revered Talmudic commentator of Troyes, France (1040–1105). Several Ashkenazic rabbinical families claim descent from him, including TREVES, LURIA, KATZENELLENBOGEN, HEILPRIN, LOANS, and the ZARFATI family of Morocco. While their claims are certainly possible, no family can trace its ancestry back to Rashi in an unbroken line. See the chart on page 12 of this book. A table worked out in 17th-cent. Italy purports to show Rashi's descent from Hillel the Great and King David through Johanan ha-Sandalar of 2nd-cent. Egypt, but the chart is apparently totally spurious

(see page 11 of this book). For more discussion of Rashi's ancestors and descendants, see *Rashi,* by M. Liber, 1905, and *Eileh Toledot (These Are the Generations),* by N. Rosenstein, 1969. Both books are in English.

RASHKES—Related to RABBINOWITZ.

RASKAI—UJ has article on Hungarian urologist Dezso Raskai (b. 1866).

RASKIN—UJ has two biographies from 19th-cent. Russia. Related to DUBNOW.

RATH—EJ has article on Russian Talmudist Meshullam Rath (b. 1875).

RATHAUS—JE and UJ have biographies from 19th–20th-cent. Russia and Poland.

RATHENAU—EJ has two biographies from 19th–20th-cent. Germany. CAJ has some family records; LBIS has notes.

RATISBONNE—Ashkenazic name taken from the Bavarian city of Ratisbon (now Regensburg), where Jews were living before the Christian era. JE has two biographies from 19th-cent. France.

RATNER—JE has two biographies from 19th-cent. Russia. Also see JE article on Grodno, Russia. Related to DUBNOW.

RATSHESKY—UJ has article on U.S. civic official Abraham Ratshesky (1864–1943), related to SHUMAN.

RAU (also Rauh)—UJ and EJ have biographies from 19th–20th-cent. France, Germany, Israel and U.S.A. Related to FLOERSHEIM.

RAUH—See RAU.

RAUNHEIM—JE has article on U.S. engineer Saly Raunheim (1838–1904), born in Germany; brother-in-law of LEWISOHN.

RAUSUK—JE has article on Hebrew poet Samson Rausuk (b. 1793 in Lithuania, d. 1877 in London).

RAVA—UJ has article on Italian governor Maurizio Rava (1878–1935).

RAVAGE—UJ and EJ have articles on Rumanian-American journalist Marcus Ravage (b. REVICI in 1884). See his autobiography, *An American in the Making.*

RAVAYA—Family of courtiers in 13th-cent. Spain. See EJ.

RAVENNA—UJ has two biographies from 19th-cent. Italy.

RAVICH—UJ has article on Russian-American urologist Abraham Ravich (b. 1888).

RAVID (also Ravidowitz, Rawidowicz)—UJ has two biographies from 19th–20th-cent. Russia and Poland.

RAVIDOWITZ—See RAVID.

RAVITZ—See RAWICZ.

RAWICZ (also Ravitz)—JE and EJ have biographies from 19th–20th-cent. Germany and Russia. LBI has Rawicz family trees beginning 1725 and 1755.

RAWIDOWICZ—See RAVID.

RAWNITZKI—JE has article on Russian author Joshua Rawnitzki (1859–1944), born in Odessa.

RAY—EJ has article on French photographer Man Ray (b. 1890).

RAYNAL—JE has article on French statesman David Raynal (1841–1903).

RAYNER—JE has two biographies from Germany and U.S.A., 19th cent. Related to FRANK.

RAYSS—EJ has article on Israeli botanist Tscharna Rayss (b. 1890 in Russia).

RAZOVSKY—UJ has article on U.S. immigration expert Cecilia Razovsky (b. 1891); related to DAVIDSON.

RAZUMNI—UJ has article on Russian cantor Solomon Razumni (1866–1904).

READING—UJ has biographies from 19th–20th-cent. England and Australia. Related to ISAACS, DAVIS, MENDOZA, DISRAELI, CHARNAUD and MOND.

REBENSTEIN—Related to BERNSTEIN.

REBUSH—UJ has article on Russian producer Roman Rebush (b. 1895).

RECANATI—Italian family deriving its name from the city of Recanati. JE has a family tree and eleven biographies, from 13th through 18th cent. Related to FINZI, JOAB and YAHYA.

RECHNITZ—LBI has a family tree beginning 1785.

RECHT—UJ has article on Bohemian lawyer Charles Recht (b. 1887).

RECKENDORF—JE has article on German scholar Hermann Reckendorf (1825–1875).

REDDINGE—JE has article on 13th-cent. English preacher Robert Reddinge.

REDLICH—JE has article on Polish engraver Henry Redlich (1840–1884). PD has some family records.

REE—JE has five biographies from 17th- and 18th-cent. Germany and Denmark.

REED—UJ has article on Philadelphia actress Florence Reed (b. 1883).

REESE—UJ has article on Chicago philanthropist Michael Reese (1815–1878), related to FRANK.

REEVE—JE has article on English actress Ada Reeve (b. 1870).

REGGIO—Name taken from the Italian city of Reggio (there are two: one on the Strait of Messina, where Jews first came in 4th cent., the other in the province of Reggio, where Jews arrived in 15th cent. The latter is the more likely source of the name). JE has four biographies from 18th- and 19th-cent. Italy. Related to EHRENREICH and MORPURGO.

REH—UJ has article on Austrian educator Frank Reh (b. 1887).

REHFISCH (also Rehfuss)—JE and UJ have two biographies from 18th–19th-cent. Germany.

REHFUSS—See REHFISCH.

REHINE—EJ has article on U.S. merchant Zalma Rehine (1757–1843), born in Prussia. Related to LEESER.

REICH—JE has three biographies from 19th-cent. Germany and Hungary. See also RAJK.

REICHARD—UJ has article on Hungarian author Zsigmond Reichard (1863–1916).

REICHENBACH—LBI has a family tree beginning 1825. LBIS has some family notes.

REICHENHEIM—JE has article on German manufacturer Leonhard Reichenheim (1814–1868). LBIS has some family notes.

REICHER (also Reicherson, Reichert)—Ashkenazic name indicating German origin. JE and UJ have biographies from 19th-cent. Germany, Austria and U.S.A. Related to KINDERMANN and HARF.

REICHERSON—See REICHER.

REICHERT—See REICHER.

REICHINSTEIN—See biography in EJ article on "Chemistry."

REICHLER—UJ has article on Austro-American Rabbi Max Reichler (b. 1885).

REIDER—UJ has article on Russian philologist Joseph Reider (b. 1886).

REIF—JE has article on Galician poet Abraham Reif (1802–1859).

REIFENBERG—UJ has article on German chemist Adolf Reifenberg (b. 1899).

REIFMANN—JE has article on Russian author Jacob Reifmann (1818–1895).

REIK—UJ has article on Vienna psychoanalyst Theodor Reik (b. 1889).

REILING—Related to SEGHERS.

REINACH—German family which emigrated to France in first half of 19th cent. JE has four biographies, all from 19th cent. JE article on "Coat of Arms" has the family crest. CAJ has some family records. Related to BELMONT and BUDING.

REINER—UJ has two biographies from 19th-cent. Hungary.

REINES—JE has two biographies from 19th-cent. Russia. Isaac Reines (b. 1839 near Minsk) was a descendant of Saul WAHL. CAJ has some family records.

REINFELD—UJ has article on U.S. chess master Fred Reinfeld (b. 1910).

REINGANUM—UJ has article on German lawyer Max Reinganum (1798–1878).

REINHARD—See REINHARDT.

REINHARDT (also Reinhard, Reinhart)—UJ has biographies from 19th-cent. Hungary and Austria, and 20th-cent. U.S.A. Related to MAREES.

REINHART—See REINHARDT.

REINITZ—UJ has article on Hungarian economist Max Reinitz (b. 1851).

REINMANN—EJ has article on Galician traveler Salomon Reinmann (1815–1880).

REINOWITZ—JE has article on Jacob Reinowitz (b. 1818 in Poland, d. 1893 in London).

REINWALD—CAJ has some family records.

REIS (also Reiss)—UJ has biographies from 19th-cent. Poland, Germany and Galicia. LBI has family trees beginning 1670 and 1780, related to HAROLD. LBIS has some family notes from Sweden. Related to GAGGSTATTER, MAYER, NADIR and SCHIFF. Also see RIESS.

REISCHER—JE has article on Austrian Rabbi Jacob Reischer (d. 1733), who married a daughter of Rabbi Simon SPIRA.

REISEN (also Rejzin)—19th-cent. Russian family of writers; UJ has three biographies.

REISENBERG—UJ has article on Russian pianist Nadia Reisenberg (b. 1904).

REISS—See REIS.

REITLINGER—JE has article on French jurist Frederick Reitlinger (b. 1836). PD has some family records.

REITMAN—UJ has article on U.S. physician Ben Louis Reitman (1879–1942).

REITZENBERGER—LBI has a family tree beginning 1800, related to TUCHMANN.

REITZES—PD has some family records.

REIZENSTEIN—CAJD has a family tree from Germany.

REIZELES—See REIZES.

REIZES (also Reizeles)—17th-cent. Polish family; see EJ. Related to LEVINSON.

REJZIN—See REISEN.

RELGIS—UJ has article on Rumanian poet Eugene Relgis (b. 1895).

REMAK—JE has two biographies from 19th-cent. Germany.

REMENYI—JE has article on Hungarian violinist Eduard Remenyi (1830–1898).

REMOCH—See BENREMOKH.

REMOS—EJ has article on Majorcan physician Moses Remos (1406–1430).

REMY—Related to LAZARUS.

RENARD—CAJ has some family records.

RENAUD—UJ has article on French opera singer Maurice Renard (1861–1933).

RENNER-RUBEN—LBI has a family tree beginning 1650.

RESHEVSKY—UJ has article on Polish chess master Samuel Reshevsky (b. 1911), a descendant of J. EYBESCHUTZ.

RESIK—Related to LEWI.

RESNICK—UJ has article on Russian-Argentinian journalist Salomon Resnick (b. 1895). Also see REZNIKOFF.

RESSLER—UJ has article on Polish author Benjamin Ressler (b. 1901).

RETHI—See RETHY.

RETHY (also Rethi and Reti)—JE and UJ have biographies from 19th–20th-cent. Hungary and Czechoslovakia.

RETI—See RETHY.

RETTIG—Ashkenazic name meaning "radish" (*Rettich* in German).

REUBENI (also Reuveni)—UJ has article on 16th-cent. visionary David Reubeni, who was born in Arabia and died in Spain.

REUCHLEIN—CAJ has some family records.

REUTER—German-French news-service founder Baron Paul von Reuter (1821–1899), was born Israel JOSEPHSTHAL, a descendant of the JOSAPHAT family. See EJ. JE article on "Coat of Arms" has the Reuter family crest.

REUVENI—See REUBENI.

REVAI—JE has article on Hungarian deputy Mor Revai (1860–1926).

REVEL—UJ has article on Lithuanian-American scholar Bernard Revel (1885–1940). Related to GLUECK.

REVERE—JE has article on Italian dramatist Giuseppe Revere (1812–1889).

REVESZ—UJ has two biographies from 19th-cent. Hungary.

REVICI—See RAVAGE.

REVUSKY—UJ has article on Russian journalist Abraham Revusky (b. 1889).

REWALD—CAJ has some records. LBIS has family notes.

REYNER—UJ has article on U.S. civic official Harry Reyner (b. 1893).

REZNIK—See REZNIKOFF.

REZNIKOFF (also Reznik)—UJ has two biographies from Russia and U.S.A., 19th–20th cent. See a family history in *Family Chronicle.* Also see RESNICK.

RHEINGANUM—Related to SCHIFF.

RHEINHOLD—JE has article on German sculptor Hugo Rheinhold (1853–1900).

RHEINSTEIN—UJ has article on U.S. engineer Alfred Rheinstein (b. 1889).

RHEINSTROM—UJ has article on German-French jurist Henry Rheinstrom (b. 1884).

RHINE—Related to HYNEMAN.

RHINEWINE—UJ has article on Polish-Canadian journalist Abraham Rhinewine (1887–1932).

RHODES—UJ has article on Italian author Solomon Rhodes (b. 1895).

RIAZANOV—UJ has article on Russian revolutionary David Riazanov (b. 1870).

RIBALOW—UJ has article on Russian writer Menachem Ribalow (b. 1899).

RIBARY—UJ has article on Hungarian lawyer Geza Ribary (1889–1942).

RIBBECK—Related to ITZIG.

RIBEIRO—Portuguese Marrano family dating from 15th cent. See EJ. Related to SANCHEZ.

RIBERA—See RIVERA.

RIBKAS (also Ribkes)—JE has article on Russian Talmudist Moses Ribkas (d. 1671 in Vilna). The name means "son of Rebecca." His family came from Prague.

RIBKES—See RIBKAS.

RICARDO—JE has article on English political economist David Ricardo (1772–1823), whose family moved from Italy to Holland in early 18th cent.; two generations later, one branch moved to London. JE article on "Coat of Arms" has the family crest. Related to COSTA.

RICCHI—JE has article on Italian Rabbi Immanuel Ricchi (1688–1743), also known as RAPHAEL. His maternal uncle was Jedidiah RABBINO.

RICE—JE has three biographies from 19th-cent. Germany and U.S.A. Related to KRAUS.

RICHARDS (also Richardson)—UJ has biographies from 19th–20th-cent. Lithuania, U.S.A., England and South Africa. CAJ has some Richards family records.

RICHARDSON—See RICHARDS.

RICHE—UJ has article on Polish-American realtor Aaron Riche (b. 1885).

RICHETTI—JE has article on 17th-cent. Rabbi Joseph Richetti, who was born in Safed and died in Italy.

RICHMAN—JE has article on U.S. educator Julia Richman (1855–1912).

RICHTER—Ashkenazic name meaning "rabbinic judge." UJ has article on German philosopher Raoul Richter (1871–1912), related to MEYERBEER. LBI has a family tree beginning 1823. LBIS has some family notes.

RICIUS—EJ has article on German apostate Paulus Ricius (d. 1541).

RIDBAZ—JE has article on Russian Rabbi Jacob Ridbaz (b. 1845 near Grodno); also known as WILLOWSKI.

RIDER—UJ has article on U.S. engineer John Rider (b. 1900).

RIEGELMAN—UJ has article on U.S. lawyer Harold Riegelman (b. 1892).

RIEGER—JE has article on German Rabbi Paul Rieger (1870–1939).

RIEMANN—JE has article on Solomon Riemann (d. 1873 in Vienna).

RIES—See RIESS.

RIESMAN—See RIESS.

RIESE—See RIESS.

RIESS (also Ries, Riesman, Riese, Riesser)—JE and UJ have biographies from 18th-cent. Germany and 19th-cent. Germany, Poland, Holland and Russia. Lazarus Riesser (1763–1828) was the son-in-law of SUSSKIND. LBIS has some Riess family notes. Related to TOCKELS, MOSSNER, JAFFE, SILBER, WAHL. Also see REIS.

RIESSER—See RIESS.

RIETI—Italian family whose name comes from the city of Rieti and which can be traced back to 14th cent. JE has a family tree and mentions numerous members from 14th through 17th cent. Also see VR, Vol. 2, p. 74.

RIFKIND—UJ has article on Russian-American Judge Simon Rifkind (b. 1901). Also see RIVKES.

RIGLER—UJ has article on U.S. doctor Leo Rigler (b. 1896).

RIMOC (Rimokh)—See BENREMOKH.

RIMOS—JE has article on poet Moses Rimos (1406–1430), who died in Palermo, Sicily.

RINDSKOPF—CAJD has a family tree from Germany, related to PHILIPS.

RING—JE has article on German novelist Max Ring (1817–1901), born in Galicia.

RINGEL—UJ has article on Polish Zionist Michael Ringel (1880–1939).

RINGELBLUM—CAJ has some family records.

RINGELHEIM—Related to PERETZ.

RINGER—UJ has article on Russian physician Adolph Ringer (b. 1883).

RINTEL—JE has article on Australian Rabbi Moses Rintel (1823–1880), born in Scotland.

RIQUETTI—JE has article on 17th-cent. scholar Joseph Riquetti of Safed.

RIS—See family history in *Die Nachkommen des Rabbiner Raphael Ris*. Related to DREIFUS.

RITSCHEL—Related to FRANKEL.

RITT—UJ has article on U.S. mathematician Joseph Ritt (b. 1893).

RITTENBERG—UJ has biographies from 19th-cent. Russia and Hungary.

RITTER—Galician name. JE has two biographies from 19th-cent. Germany. PD has some family records.

RITTERBAND—Related to SOLIS.

RITTNER—UJ has article on Galician professor Edward Rittner (b. 1845).

RITZWOLLER—See a family history in *It Began with Zade Usher* (see Bernstein in Bibliography).

RIVERA (also Ribera)—Spanish family whose members settled in Mexico in 17th-cent. and later came to U.S.A. JE has two biographies from 18th-cent. U.S.A. Related to ACOSTA and LOPEZ.

RIVKES (also Rivkin, Rivkind)—JE and UJ have biographies from 18th-cent. Lithuania and 19th-cent. Russia and Poland. Rabbi Moses Rivkes was the maternal uncle of *David* ben Aryeh Loeb of Lida, Lithuania, and was also related to Elijah, the GAON of Vilna (1720–1797). Also see RIFKIND.

RIVKIN (Rivkind)—See RIVKES.

RIVLIN—Family originally from Vilna which has been in Israel at least seven generations. See family histories in *Sefer ha-Hem Lemhishpahat Rivlin* and *Yosef Rivlin Memorial Volume.* See article in EJ, also JE article on *Riga,* Latvia. Related to PINES.

ROBACK—UJ has article on Russian author A. A. Roback (b. 1890).

ROBBIO—JE has article on 17th-cent. Talmudist Mordecai Robbio of Italy.

ROBERT (also Roberts)—UJ and EJ have biographies from 18th- and 19th-cent. Germany and Hungary. Related to LEVIN, MARCUS, TORNOW, VARNHAGEN, MORRISON and MAGYAR.

ROBERTS—See ROBERT.

ROBINSON—UJ has five biographies from 19th-cent. Russia, Lithuania, Rumania and England.

ROBLES—JE has article on 17th-cent. English Marrano Antonio da Robles, born in Portugal. AJA has a family tree. Related to WOLFF and SASSO.

ROBOROUGH—Related to FRANCO.

ROCAMORA—JE has article on Spanish physician Isaac de Rocamora (1600–1684), who died in Amsterdam.

ROCCA—UJ has article on Italian publicist Enrico Rocca (b. 1895). Related to HEINE.

ROCK—UJ has article on U.S. lawyer Lillian Rock (b. 1896).

ROCKER—UJ has article on Austro-American stockbroker Louis Rocker (b. 1894).

RODA RODA—UJ has article on Slovenian humorist Alexander Roda Roda (b. Ladislaus ROSENFELD in 1872).

RODENBERG—JE has article on German poet Julius Rodenberg (b. LEVY in 1831 at Rodenberg in Hesse).

RODER—JE has article on German composer Martin Roder (1851–1895). Also see RADO.

RODGERS—UJ has article on U.S. composer Richard Rodgers (b. 1902).

RODKINSON—Related to FRUMKIN.

RODOLF—UJ has article on South African merchant Samuel Rodolf (1812–1882).

RODRIGUES (also Rodriguez)—Sephardic family that is said to have emigrated (with the GRADIS family) from Palestine at the time of the Bar Kochba insurrection (135 C.E.) and settled first in Portugal and later in Spain. Many Jews with the name Rodriguez were martyred by the Spanish Inquisition in 17th and 18th cent. JE mentions numerous people in Spain, Portugal, Italy, Amsterdam, Hamburg, France, from 15th cent. on. Also see EJ article on *Amatus* Lusitanus (1511–1568). JE article on "Coat of Arms" has a Rodriguez family crest. Related to SALVADOR, PEREIRE, FOA, NUNEZ and BRUDO.

RODRIGUEZ—See RODRIGUES.

RODZINSKI—UJ has article on Dalmatian conductor Artur Rodzinski (b. 1894).

ROEDELSHEIM (also Rudelsheim)—Name probably taken from the Prussian town of Rodelheim, near Frankfurt-am-Main, where Jews first settled in 13th cent. JE has article on 18th-cent. Dutch scholar Eleazar Roedelsheim, probably of German descent. Related to AMELANDER.

ROEST—JE has article on Dutch bibliographer Meyer Roest (1821–1890).

ROFE—Sephardic name meaning "doctor." JE has two biographies from 14th-and 15th-cent. Italy. Daniel ben Samuel ha-Rofe, rabbi at Tivoli, Italy, was grandson of 14th-cent. Roman poet Daniel ben Judah. Related to DELMEDIGO, AUERBACH, JOAB, LEMON, MEISEL and MEYSL.

ROGERS—UJ has article on U.S. composer Bernard Rogers (b. 1893).

ROGOFF—UJ has article on Russian-American writer Harry Rogoff (b. 1882).

ROHEIM—UJ has article on Hungarian ethnologist Geza Roheim (b. 1891).

ROHLING—CAJ has some family records.

ROITMAN—UJ has article on Russian cantor David Roitman (b. 1884).

ROIZMAN—UJ has article on Russian author Matvei Roizman (b. 1896).

ROJAS—UJ has article on 16th-cent. Spanish lawyer Fernando de Rojas.

ROJOK—See a family mentioned in *It Began with Zade Usher* (see Bernstein in Bibliography).

ROKACH—See ROKEACH.

ROKEACH (also Rokach, Rokeah)—Ashkenazic name that means "spice merchant" in Hebrew. UJ has biographies from Galicia and Israel, 19th–20th cent. CAJD has a family tree from Germany. Also see JE article on Pinsk, Russia. Related to BAK, BELZER, LIPSCHITZ.

ROKEAH—See ROKEACH.

ROLLAND—CAJ has some family records.

ROLLE—Related to JASTROW.

ROLNIK—UJ has article on Polish poet Joseph Rolnik (b. 1879).

ROMAN—JE has article on writer Jacob Roman (b. 1570 in Constantinople, d. 1650 in Jerusalem), of Spanish descent.

ROMANELLI—JE has article on Italian poet Samuel Romanelli (1757–1814).

ROMANER (also Romanin, Romano)—Names derived from the city of Rome, Italy. JE has biographies from Italy, 14th, 17th, 18th and 19th cent. Related to JACOR.

ROMANIN—See ROMANER.

ROMANO—See ROMANER.

ROMAN-RONETTI—EJ has article on Rumanian author Moise Roman-Ronetti (1847–1908), also known as BLUMENFELD.

ROMANZINI—Related to BLAND.

ROMBERG—JE has article on German physician Moritz Romberg (1795–1873).

ROMBRO—UJ has article on Jacob Rombro, also known as KRANZ.

ROME—UJ has article on U.S. composer Harold Rome (b. 1908).

ROMI—JE has biographies from 10th–11th and 17th cent.

ROMM—Family of printers and publishers in Vilna. The family came there from Grodno in 18th cent. and moved to New York in late 19th cent. JE mentions six members. Related to HARKAVY.

RONA (also Ronai)—JE and EJ have three biographies from 19th-cent. Hungary.

RONAI—See RONA.

RONALD—UJ has article on English conductor Landon Ronald (1873–1938), son of Henry RUSSELL.

RONGY—UJ has article on Lithuanian surgeon Abraham Rongy (b. 1878).

RONSBURG—Name taken from the city of Ronsperg in Bohemia. JE has article on Bohemian Rabbi Bezalel Ronsburg (1760–1820), who took the formal surname ROSENBAUM.

RONSHEIM—AJA has a family tree beginning 1750 in Germany.

ROPSHITSER—EJ has article on Galician Hasid Naphtale Ropshitser (1760–1827).

ROQUEMARTINE—JE has article on 14th-cent. French scholar David Roquemartine, born in the city of the same name.

ROSALES—JE has article on Italian physician Jacob Rosales (1588–1662), son of Fernando BOCARRO. Also see ROSANES.

ROSALSKY—UJ has article on U.S. Judge Joseph Rosalsky (1877–1937).

ROSANES (also Rosanis)—Family originally from Rosas, a Spanish seaport. Its members emigrated to Portugal in 15th century and later to Turkey, Austria and Russia. This family may be related to ROSALES. JE has seven biographies from Turkey, Russia, Bulgaria and Galicia, 17th, 18th and 19th cent. See family tree in *La Genealogie de la famille Rosanes*.

ROSANOFF—UJ has article on Russo-American chemist Martin Rosanoff (b. 1874).

ROSBACH—Related to MELCHIOR.

ROSE—JE, UJ and EJ have biographies from 19th-cent. Poland and Rumania. Related to POTOSKI and ROSENBERG.

ROSEBERRY—JE has article on English philanthropist Hannah Roseberry (1851–1890), born ROTHSCHILD.

ROSELLO—JE has article on 16th-cent. scholar Mordecai Rosello of Spain and France, also known as RUSCELLI.

ROSEMAN—AJA has a family tree beginning 1684.

ROSEN—JE has two biographies from 19th-cent. Poland and Russia. Also see a family mentioned in *It Began with Zade Usher* (see Bernstein in Bibliography).

ROSENAK—UJ has article on Hungarian Rabbi Leopold Rosenak (1869–1923). Related to CARLEBACH.

ROSENAU—JE has two biographies from 19th-cent. Germany and U.S.A.

ROSENBACH (also Rosenbacher)—JE has three biographies from 19th-cent. Germany, Bohemia and U.S.A. Related to DEUTSCH.

ROSENBACHER—See ROSENBACH.

ROSENBAUM—Ashkenazic name meaning "rose tree" in German. UJ has six biographies. LBI has family trees beginning 1660, 1748, 1776, 1790, related to MARKREICH and HALBERSTADT. See family histories in *The Rosenbaums of Zell* and *Familientafel der Nachkommen*. Related to AMBACH, GOODHART, HAGEDORN, RONSBURG and ZELL.

ROSENBERG—JE and UJ have numerous biographies from 19th-cent. Hungary, Germany and Russia. Russian-American writer Abraham Rosenberg (b. 1838 in Pinsk) was descended from the JAFFE family. LBI has a family tree beginning 1668. PD has some family records. Also see JE article on Grosswardein, Hungary, where Alexander Rosenberg was rabbi. Related to BEHREND, BAKST, HANAUER, GUNZBURG, RAFF, ROTT, ROSE.

ROSENBLAT—See ROSENBLATT.

ROSENBLATT (also Rosenblat)—JE and UJ have biographies from 19th-cent. Poland, Russia and Galicia.

ROSENBLOOM (also Rosenblum)—UJ has biographies from 19th-cent. Russia, Poland, Scotland and U.S.A. CAJ has some Rosenblum family records.

ROSENBUSCH—EJ has article on German geologist Karl Rosenbusch (1836–1914).

ROSENCRANTZ (also Rosenkranz)—UJ has article on U.S. doctor Esther Rosencrantz (b. 1896). Related to GOLDBERG.

ROSENDALE—JE has article on U.S. lawyer Simon Rosendale (1842–1937).

ROSENFELD—JE and UJ have numerous biographies from 18th–19th-cent. Russia, Poland, Denmark, Galicia, Germany and U.S.A. LBI has family trees beginning 1756 and 1781. AJA has a family tree beginning 1741 in Russia, related to SHAPIRO, EDELSON and WEINSTEIN. See a family history in *Descendants of Joshua, 1741–1971*. Also see JE article on Grosswardein, Hungary, where a Joseph Rosenthal was rabbi. Also related to RANK and RODA RODA.

ROSENGARDT (Rosengart)—See ROSENGARTEN.

ROSENGARTEN (also Rosengardt, Rosengart)—Ashkenazic name meaning "rose garden" in German. UJ has two biographies from 19th-cent. Russia and Germany. LBI has a Rosengardt family tree beginning 1803. Related to KAHN.

ROSENGOLTS—See ROZENGOLTS.

ROSENHAIN—JE has two biographies from 19th-cent. Germany.

ROSENHAUPT—JE has article on German cantor Moritz Rosenhaupt (1841–1900).

ROSENHEAD—UJ has article on English mathematician Louis Rosenhead (b. 1906).

ROSENHEIM—See biography in EJ article on "Chemistry." Related to SULZBERGER.

ROSENKRANZ—See ROSENCRANTZ.

ROSENMAN—UJ has article on U.S. Judge Samuel Rosenman (b. 1896), of Polish parentage.

ROSENSOHN (also Rosenson)—UJ has biographies from 19th cent. Related to LASKER.

ROSENSTEIN—JE has article on German physician Samuel Rosenstein (b. 1832).

ROSENSTOCK—UJ has two biographies from 19th–20th cent. Poland and Germany. Related to HUSSY.

ROSENTHAL (also Rosenthaler)—JE, UJ and EJ have more than twenty biographies from 18th–19th-cent. Poland, Germany, England, Austria, Hungary and U.S.A. One Rosenthal family in Russia, descended from Solomon of Wirballen (a town on the Prussian frontier), came from Skud and was surnamed SKUDSKI; this family is related to BRAININ, JACOBOVICH and SOLOWEITSCHIK. Leon Rosenthal (1817–1887), born in Vilna, was the son-in-law of Samuel NEUMARK. LBI has a family tree beginning 1706. AJA has a Rosenthal family tree from Germany and Philadelphia, beginning 1790, related to LEVINE; and a Rosenthaler family tree beginning 1803 in Bavaria. CAJ and PD have Rosenthal family records. See a family tree in *Zur Geschichte der Juden im Gebiet* and *Toledot Mishpahat Rosenthal*. Related to BERNSTEIN, JAFFE, ROZSAVOLGYI, SELIGMAN, GUNZBURG.

ROSENTHALER—See ROSENTHAL.

ROSENWALD—UJ has three biographies from 19th-cent. Germany. AJA has a family tree beginning 1740 in Bavaria. Related to HAMMERSLOUGH and NUSBAUM.

ROSENWASSER—AJA has a tree of a Cleveland family beginning 1756. Related to KOHN.

ROSENZWEIG—JE has two biographies from 19th-cent. Germany and Russia. LBI has a family tree beginning 1746. See family history in JFF, No. 33. Related to AGAI.

ROSEWALD—JE has article on U.S. singer Julie Rosewald (b. 1847 in Stuttgart), daughter of Moritz EICHBERG and sister of a Mrs. WEILLER. Related to FRIEDENWALD.

ROSEWATER—JE has three biographies from 19th-cent. Bohemia and U.S.A. AJA has a family tree from Nebraska beginning 1865.

ROSIN (also Rosing, Rosinger)—JE and UJ have biographies from 19th-cent. German, Russia and Hungary. Also see *My Life and Message,* autobiography of Hungarian-born U.S. Rabbi Samuel Rosinger (b. 1877).

ROSING—See ROSIN.

ROSINGER—See ROSIN.

ROSKILL—Related to SAMSON.

ROSMER—Related to BERNSTEIN.

ROSNOSKY—JE has article on U.S. merchant Isaac Rosnosky (1846–1907), born in Prussia.

ROSS—UJ has article on U.S. boxer Barney Ross (b. ROZOVSKY in 1909).

ROSSDALE—UJ has article on U.S. politician Albert Rossdale (b. 1878).

ROSSELLI—UJ has article on Italian anti-Fascist leader Carlo Rosselli (1899–1937), who died in France.

ROSSHEIM—UJ has article on U.S. lawyer Irvin Rossheim (b. 1887).

ROSSI—Italian family known in 14th through 17th cent., descended from an old Jewish family which, according to tradition, was brought to Rome by Titus from Jerusalem when the Temple was destroyed in 70 C.E. JE has four biographies. Also see VR, Vol. 1, p. 396. Related to AZARIA, EBORENSIS, EUROPA and MASSARANI.

ROSSLER—UJ has article on Viennese novelist Carl Rossler (b. 1864).

ROSTE—Related to WALLICH.

ROSTEN—UJ has article on Polish-American writer Leo Rosten (b. 1908).

ROTENBERG (Rotenburg)—See ROTHENBERG.

ROTH—JE has three biographies from 19th-cent. Germany, Austria and Switzerland. AJA has a family tree.

ROTHAFEL—UJ has article on American Samuel Rothafel (1882–1936).

ROTHBAND—UJ has article on British communal leader Sir Henry Rothband (19th cent.).

ROTHCHILD—CAJ has some family records. Related to MANDEL.

ROTHENBERG (also Rotenberg, Rotenburg, Rothenburg, Rottenberg, Rutenberg, Ruttenberg, etc.)—Ashkenazic name originating in Germany, with two possible sources: 1) a city in Germany with some variation of the name "Rothenberg"—there are a dozen such cities, and the best-known of them, Rothenburg-on-the-Tauber, is the least likely because the Jews were banished there in 1520 and did not return until 1875; 2) descendants of Meir of Rothenburg (1215–1293)—his relatives went to Alsace when he was imprisoned there, and members of his family were there for centuries; others of his descendants with some variation of the name Rothenburg were found at Prague. See "La Famille de Meir de Rothenburg," by Neubauer, in REJ, Vol. 12, page 91. Also see JE and EJ. Rotenburg was a family in Cochin that originated in Frankfurt, 18th cent.; see EJ. Also see JE article on Grodno, Russia, where Mordecai Susskind Rothenberg was rabbi from 1681 to 1691, and JE article on *Meir* of Rothenburg. The name Rottenberg appears frequently among Jews who moved from Germany to Hungary. See family history in *A Link with the Future* (see Rottenberg in Bibliography). Related to BICK and RAHABI.

ROTHENBURG—See ROTHENBERG.

ROTHENSTEIN—Family of 19th-cent. British artists; see UJ.

ROTHER—LBI has a family tree beginning 1765.

ROTHMANN—See a family tree in *Stammbaum der Familie Rothmann.*

ROTHSCHILD—Celebrated family of financiers descended from Moses Rothschild of 16th-cent. Frankfurt-am-Main. JE has an extensive family tree; EJ also has a family tree. LBI has family trees beginning 1546, 1730 and 1803. The name is derived from the red shield painted on the family's door. Family histories include *The Rothschilds: A Family Portrait; The Rothschilds: A Family of Fortune;* "The Rise of the House of Rothschild," in JQR, Vol. 20, p. 385; *Die Familie Rothschild; Das Haus Rothschild in der Zeit seiner Blüte, 1830–1871; Les Rothschilds: Une famille de financiers juifs au 19ème siècle;* and *The Cousinhood,* by Chaim Bermant, which traces the family's links with other prominent British families. A Max Rothschild, apparently unrelated, was one of the first modern Jewish settlers in Athens, Greece, 1833; see JE article on Athens. Related to COHEN, MONTEFIORE, ROSEBERRY, HENGSHULER, KELE, WEZLAR, SCHEYER, HANAU, BUCHSBAUM, LECHNICH, KETT, HALBERSTADT, OPPENHEIM, STIBEL, ZUNZ, COHN, SHAMES, SCHNAPPER, HERZ, GOLDSCHMIDT, LANDAU, FLORSHEIM, WORMS, STERN, SICHEL, BEYFUS, FITZROY, YORKE, WEISSWEILER, PERUGIA, BEHRENS, ANSPACH, EPHRUSSI, HALPHEN, LAMBERT, SASSOON, ITZIG, ADLER and STADTHAGEN. JE article on "Coat of Arms" has the family crest.

ROTHSCHILD-EMMERICH—LBI has a family tree beginning 1649.

ROTHSTEIN—CAJ has some family records.

ROTHWELL—UJ has article on British conductor Walter Rothwell (1872–1927).

ROTT—JE has article on Austrian actor Moritz Rott (1797–1860), also known as ROSENBERG. He was a nephew of Ignaz MOSCHELES.

ROTTEMBOURG—Possible variation of ROTHENBERG. EJ has article on French Army officer Henri Rottembourg (1769–1836).

ROTTEN—CAJ has some family records.

ROTTENBERG—See ROTHENBERG.

ROTTENSTREICH—UJ has article on Galician Zionist Fishel Rottenstreich (1875–1938).

ROUKHOMOVSKY—UJ has article on Russian engraver Israel Roukhomovsky (1860–1934), who died in Paris.

ROVIGO—EJ has article on Italian cabalist Abraham Rovigo (1650–1713).

ROVNER—See ROWNER.

ROWE—JE has article on U.S. economist Leo Rowe (b. 1871). Related to RAFF.

ROWNER (also Rovner)—Name taken from the Russian city of Rovno. Related to MARAGOWSKY.

ROZENGOLTS (also Rosengolts)—UJ has article on Russian revolutionary Arkadii Rozengolts (1889–1938).

ROZMARIN—UJ has article on Polish Zionist Harry Rozmarin (b. 1886).

ROZOVSKI (also Rozovsky, Rozowski)—UJ and EJ have biographies from 19th-cent. Russia and Lithuania. Also see ROSS.

ROZOWSKI—See ROZOVSKI.

ROZSA—UJ has article on Hungarian author Dezso Rozsa (b. 1885).

ROZSAHEGYI—UJ has article on Hungarian actor Kalman Rozsahegyi (b. 1873).

ROZSAVOLGYI—JE has article on Hungarian composer Markus Rozsavolgyi (1787–1848), also known as ROSENTHAL.

ROZSAY—JE has article on Hungarian physician Joseph Rozsay (1815–1885).

RUBASHOV—UJ has article on Polish Zionist Shneur Rubashov (b. 1889).

RUBEN (also Rubenovitz, Ruben-Renner, Rubens, Rubenson)—UJ has biographies from 19th-cent. Sweden, Lithuania and U.S.A. LBIS has Ruben and Rubenson family notes. LBI has a Ruben-Renner family tree beginning 1650. Also see Rubens biography in EJ article on "English Literature." Related to WARBURG and BONNIER.

RUBENOVITZ—See RUBEN.

RUBEN-RENNER—See RUBEN.

RUBENS—See RUBEN.

RUBENSON—See RUBEN.

RUBENSTEIN—See RUBINSTEIN.

RUBIN—JE and UJ have biographies from 19th-cent. Galicia, Rumania and Denmark. See family history in *A Link with the Future* (see Rottenberg in Bibliography). Related to ABRAMSON, GLUECK and RABON.

RUBINER—UJ has article on U.S. Judge Charles Rubiner (b. 1898).

RUBINO (also Rubinov)—UJ has biographies from 19th-cent. Germany and Russia. Related to MOSE and SPEYER.

RUBINOW—See RUBINO.

RUBINSTEIN (also Rubenstein)—JE and UJ have biographies from 19th-cent. Russia, Austria, Canada and U.S.A. CAJ has some family records.

RUBINYI—UJ has article on Hungarian linguist Mozes Rubinyi (b. 1881).

RUBIO—EJ has article on 18th-cent. Palestinian *hakham* Mordecai Rubio.

RUBO—JE has two biographies from 19th-cent. Germany.

RUBY—UJ has article on U.S. Judge Israel Ruby (b. 1888).

RUDELSHEIM—See ROEDELSHEIM.

RUEDENBERG—UJ has article on German physicist Reinhold Ruedenberg (b. 1883).

RUEFF—JE has article on French merchant Jules Rueff (b. 1854 in Paris).

RUELF (also Rulf)—EJ has article on German Rabbi Isaac Ruelf (1831–1902).

RUKEYSER—UJ has two biographies from 19th-cent. U.S.A.

RULF—See RUELF.

RUMPLER—UJ has article on Austrian auto constructor Eduard Rumpler (1872–1940).

RUMSCH—JE has article on Russian teacher Isaac Rumsch (1822–1894).

RUNKEL—JE has article on German Rabbi Solomon Runkel (d. 1426).

RUPPIN—UJ has article on Prussian agronomist Arthur Ruppin (1876–1943).

RUSCELLI—See ROSELLO.

RUSSELL—JE and UJ have biographies from 19th cent. English composer Henry Russell (1812–1900) married de LARA.

AJA has a family tree from Winder, Georgia. Related to NATHANS and MORDECAI.

RUTENBERG (Ruttenberg)—See ROTHENBERG.

RUTTKAY-ROTHAUSER—UJ has article on Hungarian playwright Miksa Ruttkay-Rothauser (1863–1913).

RUZHINER—UJ and EJ have articles on Ukrainian Hasid Israel Ruzhiner (1797–1851), also known as FRIEDMAN. EJ has his family tree.

RUZICKA—Related to KOHN.

RYMANOWER—EJ has article on Russian Hasid Menahem Rymanower (b. 1815).

RYNARZEWSKI—CAJ has some family records.

RYPINS—UJ has article on U.S. educator Stanley Rypins (b. 1891).

RYSKIND—UJ has article on U.S. journalist Morrie Ryskind (b. 1895).

SA'ADI—17th-cent. Yemenite family. See EJ.

SAALING—Related to FROHBERG and ITZIG.

SAALSCHUTZ—JE has two biographies from 19th-cent. Germany.

SABA—EJ has article on Spanish cabalist Abraham Saba (d. 1508). Related to CARO and JAFFE.

SABATH—UJ has article on Bohemian-American politician Adolph Sabath (b. 1866).

SABBADINI—UJ has article on Trieste educator Salvatore Sabbadini (b. 1873).

SABER—UJ has article on South African pioneer Samuel Saber (d. 1919).

SABIN—UJ has article on London organist Wallace Sabin (1860–1937).

SABSOVICH—JE has article on U.S. politician Hirsch Sabsovitch (b. 1860 in Russia).

SACERDOTE—JE has article on Italian poet Donato Sacerdote (1820–1883).

SACHAR—UJ has article on U.S. writer Abram Sachar (b. 1899).

SACHER—UJ and EJ have articles on British Zionist Harry Sacher (b. 1881), brother-in-law of Israel SIEFF.

SACHS (also Sacks)—Ashkenazic name which has four possible sources: 1) the French pet form of "Isaac"; 2) indicating origin in Saxony; 3) a variation of the Hebrew or Czech ZAK; 4) a surname adopted by Jewish refugees from Stendal and Speyer, from the Hebrew initials for "the holy seed of Stendal (or Speyer)." JE and UJ have biographies from 19th-cent. Germany, Russia and U.S.A. LBI has family trees beginning 1700, 1759, 1760, 1789, 1807. LBIS has a family tree and notes, related to TAUSK. CAJ has some family records. See family histories in JFF, Nos. 10, 26, 27, 35 and 36. Related to BURG, CASTELLAZZO and GOLDMAN. Also see SAX and DE SAXE.

SACHSEL—Related to CARO.

SACK—See SAK.

SACKE—UJ has article on South African pioneer Henry Sacke (1856–1933), born in Lithuania.

SACKHEIM—JE has two biographies from 18th- and 19th-cent. Russia and Lithuania. Tobiah Sackheim (d. 1822) was a descendant in the sixth generation of Israel ben Shalom of Rosinoi (d. 1659). Also see SAKHEIM.

SACKLER—UJ has article on Galician playwright Harry Sackler (b. 1883), related to SCHREYER.

SACKS—See SACHS.

SACKUR—UJ has article on German chemist Otto Sackur (1880–1914).

SAENGER (also Sanger)—JE and UJ have biographies from 19th-cent. Germany, Lithuania and U.S.A.

SAFIR—UJ has article on U.S. biologist Shelley Safir (b. 1890).

SAFRAN (also Safrin)—EJ and UJ have biographies from 19th- and 20th-cent. Russia and Rumania.

SAFRIN—See SAFRAN.

SAGIS—Spanish-Turkish family known in 16th cent.; see EJ. Related to GALANTE.

SAHAWI—See GOLDHAMMER.

SAHULA—UJ has article on Spanish poet Isaac Sahula (1244–1281).

SAIDUM—Related to NAHMIAS.

SAINEANU—UJ has article on Rumanian folklorist Lazar Saineanu (1850–1929), born SCHIEN.

SAITSCHIK—UJ has article on Lithuanian-Swiss writer Ruben Saitschik (1868–1938).

SAJO—JE has article on Hungarian author Aladar Sajo (b. 1869).

SAK (also Sack)—15th-cent. European name which is an acronym of *zera kodesh* ("descendants of martyrs"). UJ has biographies from 15th cent., also 19th–20th-cent. Germany and U.S.A.

SAKALL—UJ has article on Hungarian comedian S.Z. Sakall (b. 1885).

SAKEL—UJ has article on Galician physician Manfred Sakel (b. 1900).

SAKHAROFF—See biography in EJ article on "Dance."

SAKHEIM—UJ has article on Latvian writer Arthur Sakheim (1887–1931). LBI has a family tree beginning 1660. Also see SACKHEIM.

SAKOLSKI—UJ has article on U.S. economist Aaron Sakolski (b. 1880).

SALAMAN—See SOLOMON.

SALAMON—See SOLOMON.

SALANT (also Salanter)—JE has article on Rabbi Samuel Salant of Jerusalem (b. 1816 in Bialystok, Russia); he took his wife's name. The name Salanter is related to LIPKIN.

SALANTER—See SALANT.

SALE—UJ has three biographies of 19th-cent. Kentucky family.

SALEM—JE has two biographies from 18th-cent. Turkey and 19th-cent. China.

SALEMFELS—PD has some family records.

SALFELD—JE has article on German Rabbi Siegmund Salfeld (1843–1926).

SALGO—JE has article on Hungarian psychiatrist Jacob Salgo (b. 1849).

SALIH—18th-cent. family in Yemen; see EJ.

SALIN—Related to SCHIFF.

SALKIND (also Salkinson)—Lithuanian poet Solomon Salkind of Vilna (d. 1868) was the father of Isaac Salkinson (d. 1883). See JE.

SALKINSON—See SALKIND.

SALMAN—See SALMON.

SALMON (also Salman)—19th-cent. British family related to TAAROA, the Tahitian royal family. See UJ. Related to GLUCKSTEIN and TOCKELS.

SALMONY—UJ has article on German art historian Alfred Salmony (b. 1890).

SALMSON—LBIS has some family notes.

SALOMAN—See SOLOMON.

SALOMO—Related to FROHBERG.

SALOMON—See SOLOMON.

SALOMONE—See SOLOMON.

SALOMONS—See SOLOMON.

SALOMONSEN—See SOLOMON.

SALOMONSOHN—See SOLOMON.

SALTEN—See SALZ.

SALTMAN—Related to KALONYMUS.

SALUS—UJ has article on Bohemian poet Hugo Salus (1866–1929).

SALUSQUE—Related to USQUE.

SALVADOR—London family originally named RODRIGUEZ. JE has three biographies from England, France and U.S.A., 18th–19th cent. AJA has a family tree. JE article on "Coat of Arms" has the family crest. Related to BRANDON.

SALVENDI—EJ has article on Prussian Zionist Adolf Salvendi (1837–1914).

SALZ (also Salzer, Salzman, Salzmann, Salten)—Ashkenazic name meaning "salt" in German. UJ has biographies from 19th–20th-cent. Hungary and Bohemia. AJA has a family tree of a Cincinnati family from Germany, beginning 1765, related to MOSLER. Also related to MALECH.

SALZER—See SALZ.

SALZMAN (Salzmann)—See SALZ.

SAMAMA—EJ has article on Tunisian scholar Nessim Samama (1805–1873).

SAMBARI—JE has article on Egyptian Joseph Sambari of Alexandria (1640–1703).

SAMEGAH—JE has article on Turkish Talmudist Joseph Samegah (d. 1629 in Venice).

SAMELSOHN—JE has article on German ophthalmologist Julius Samelsohn (1841–1899).

SAMFIELD—UJ has article on Bavarian Rabbi Max Samfield (1844–1915).

SAMILER—JE has article on Russian Talmudist A. G. Samiler (1780–1854), also known as MEHLSACK and SMIELER.

SAMINSKY—UJ has article on Russian composer Lazare Saminsky (b. 1882).

SAMMTER—JE has article on German Rabbi Asher Sammter (1807–1887).

SAMOILOVICH—UJ has article on Russian explorer Rudolph Samoilovich (b. 1884).

SAMOSCZ—JE has article on German author David Samoscz (1789–1864).

SAMPAYO—Portuguese-Dutch family. JE article on "Coat of Arms" has the family crest. Related to BELMONT and TEIXEIRA.

SAMPSON—See SAMSON.

SAMPTER—UJ has article on U.S. poet Jessie Sampter (1883–1938).

SAMSON (also Sampson, Samsonschen)—Ashkenazic family whose pedigree is considered the most extensive in Jewish genealogy, according to UJ. The family is descended from Samson GUMPEL (d. 1767 in Wolfenbüttel, Germany). LBI has family trees beginning 1697, 1765 and 1813, related to KANTOROWICZ and MARKREICH. LBIS has a family tree and notes. CAJ has some family records. See family histories in JFF, No. 25; also Die Genealogie einer jüdischen Familie in Deutschland: Die Geschlecht Samson aus Wolfenbüttel and Stammbaum der Samsonschen Familie. Related to FICHEL, WARBURG, JACOBSON, STERK, WERTHEIM, KAULLA, GERNSHEIM, SALOMONSON, GOLDSCHMIDT, WEINTHAL, FOULD, KONIGSWARTER, LADENBURG, WOLFKEHL, BASSERMAN, EPHRAIM, LIMA, ASCHROTT, STERN, OPPLER, LIPPMANN, SPEYER, HAHLO, STRASSMANN, von HOLTEN, ROSKILL, MAGNUS, LILIEN and von STOSCH.

SAMSONSCHEN—See SAMSON.

SAMTER—UJ has article on German-Bohemian banker Adolf Samter (1840–1883).

SAMUDA—18th-cent. Spanish-Portuguese-English family. JE has six biographies. Related to d'AGUILAR, BERLIN.

SAMUEL (also Samuels, Samuelson, Samuely)—JE has more than fifty biographies from 17th-cent. Poland, 18th-cent. England, and 19th-cent. Germany and India, plus a family tree of the Samuel-YATES family of England. This family can be traced back to Saul WAHL of Poland (1541–1617), a descendant of the KATZENELLENBOGEN family. JE article on "Coat of Arms" has three Samuel family crests. See family histories in AJF, Vol. 2 (1916), p. 39; also *Records of the Samuel Family,* which traces the connection with Saul Wahl; *The Samuel Family of Liverpool and London from 1755 Onwards;* and *The Cousinhood,* by Chaim Bermant. Related to MONTEFIORE, SOFER, MONTAGU, WORMS, DAVID, SEIBEL, WEINER, KEYSER, ABRAHAMS, MELDOLA, de SOLA, COHEN, HART, SPIELMAN, ISRAEL, HESS, GOLDSMID, NATHAN, LAZARUS, FRIEDLANDER, BEARSTED, FRANKLIN, VAHL, DUCIT and SOLIS.

SAMUELS—See SAMUEL.

SAMUELSON—See SAMUEL.

SAMUELY—See SAMUEL.

SAMULON—See family history in JFF, No. 18.

SAMUN—JE has article on 18th-cent. Italian Talmudist Joseph Samun.

SANCHES—See SANCHEZ.

SANCHEZ (also Sanches)—JE has article on Antonio Sanchez (1699–1783), Marrano court physician in Russia who died in Paris. Related names are BELMONTE, GOLLUF and RIBEIRO.

SANCHO (also Sandje, Shangi)—15th-cent. Oriental Jewish family. JE has five biographies. Related to NAHMOLI.

SANDELS (also Sandelson)—LBIS has a family tree. UJ has article on British writer David Sandelson (b. 1889).

SANDELSON—See SANDELS.

SANDERS—JE has article on German writer Daniel Sanders (1819–1897), related to VEIT.

SANDGROUND—UJ has article on South African scientist Jack Sandground (b. 1899).

SANDJE—See SANCHO.

SANDLER—Ashkenazic name that means "cobbler" in German.

SANDOR—JE has article on Hungarian merchant Paul Sandor (1860–1936).

SANDZER—EJ has article on Austrian Talmudist Hayyim Sandzer (d. 1783).

SANGER—See SAENGER.

SANIELEVICI—UJ has article on Rumanian critic Heric Sanielevici (b. 1871).

SAN MINIATO—Related to ANAW.

SANTANGEL—UJ has article on Luis de Santangel, 16th-cent. Marrano in Queen Isabella's court.

SANTILLANA—UJ has article on North African theologian David Santillana (1855–1931).

SANUA—JE has article on Egyptian publicist James Sanua (b. 1839).

SAPHIR (Saphire)—See SPIRA.

SAPIR—See SPIRA.

SAPOSS—UJ has article on Russian economist David Saposs (b. 1886).

SARAGOSSI—JE has article on 15th-cent. Talmudist Joseph Saragossi, from Spain.

SARASOHN—JE and UJ have biographies of Polish-American journalist Kasriel Sarasohn (1835–1905), father-in-law of Leon KAMAIKY.

SARAVAL—Italian family in 16th-cent. Venice. JE has six biographies.

SARBO—UJ has article on Hungarian neurologist Arthur Sarbo (b. 1867).

SARCINO—See SARSINO.

SARFATI (Sarfaty)—See ZARFATI.

SARIQUE—See CHRIQUI.

SARKO (also Zarko, Zarik)—JE has articles on 15th-cent. Italian poet Joseph Sarko and 16th-cent. Greek writer Judah Zarko.

SARLOUIS—UJ has article on Dutch Rabbi Lodewijk Sarlouis (b. 1884).

SARMAD—JE has article on 17th-cent. Persian poet Mohammed Sarmad.

SARMIENTO—Spanish-English family. See JE, which also has two family crests in its article on "Coat of Arms."

SARONY—Related to HERZ.

SARPHATI (Sarphaty)—See ZARFATI.

SARSINO (also Sarcino)—JE has article on 17th-cent. Italian Rabbi Jacob Sarsino.

SARUG (also Saruk)—JE has article on 16th-cent. Italian cabalist Israel Sarug.

SARUK—See SARUG.

SARZEDAS—Related to HAYS.

SASON—Family in 16th-cent. Salonika. JE has four biographies.

SASPORTAS—Spanish family of whom the earliest known member was in Oran, Algeria, in 16th cent. JE has four biographies. Related to CANSINO.

SASSLOWER—JE has article on 17th-cent. Russian scholar Jacob Sasslower.

SASSO—UJ has article on Costa Rican civic worker Alfredo Sasso (b. 1897). Related to ROBLES.

SASSON—EJ has article on Ottoman scholar Aaron Sasson (1550–1626).

SASSOON—Sephardic family descended from the IBN SHOSHAN family of 12th-cent. Toledo Spain, and claiming descent from King David. Prominent branches developed in India and England. JE and EJ both have family trees and biographies. See family histories in *The Sassoon Dynasty; The Sassoons;* and "The Sassoon Family in Bombay," in JQR, Vol. 17, p. 423. The family's relationships to other prominent English families are traced in *The Cousinhood,* by Chaim Bermant. Related to MARROT, JOSEPH, EZEKIEL, BEER, GUNZBURG, PERUGIA, GUBBAY, DUBNOW, ROTHSCHILD, MOSES, YELLIN and EZRA.

SASULY—UJ has article on Austro-American statistician Max Sasuly (b. 1888).

SATANOW—Ashkenazic name taken from the Galician town of Satanov. JE has article on Polish-German poet Isaac Satanow (1733–1805).

SATENSTEIN—UJ has article on Lithuanian executive Louis Satenstein (b. 1874).

SATZ—UJ has article on Polish actor Ludwig Satz (b. 1891).

SAUDEK—UJ has article on Bohemian physiologist Robert Saudek (1880–1935).

SAVAGE—UJ has article on Lithuanian lawyer Leon Savage (b. 1888).

SAVETSKY—See a family history in *It Began with Zade Usher* (see Bernstein in Bibliography).

SAVOIR—UJ has article on Polish-French playwright Alfred Savoir (1884–1934), born POZNANSKI.

SAVRAN—18th-cent. Hasidic dynasty; see EJ. Related to SOLOMON and BENDERY.

SAX—JE has article on Russian-English engineer Julius Sax (1824–1890). Also see SACHS.

SAXL—UJ has two biographies from 19th-cent. Austria.

SAYCE—JE has article on English archaeologist Archibald Sayce (b. 1846).

SCAZZOCCHIO—See family history in VR, Vol. 2, p. 98.

SCHAAP—UJ has article on U.S. merchant Michael Schaap (b. 1874).

SCHAAR—PD has some family records.

SCHACH—Ashkenazic name which is an acronym indicating descent from Shabbetai Cohen. EJ has article on German Zionist Fabius Schach (1868–1930).

SCHACHTER (also Shachter)—UJ has article on Hungarian surgeon Miksa Schachter (1859–1917), Rumanian Rabbi Jacob Shachter (b. 1887).

SCHADOW—18th-cent. German family descended from Johann Gottfried Schadow, a sculptor. See family history in JFF, No. 18. Related to DEVIDELS, BENDEMANN, d'ALTON and WOLFF. Also see SHADOVSKY.

SCHAEFER (also Schaeffer)—LBI has a Schaefer family tree beginning 1693, related to KAUFFMAN, and a Schaeffer family tree beginning 1824. Also see SCHAFFER.

SCHAF—Related to EPSTEIN.

SCHAFFER—UJ has two biographies from 19th–20th-cent. Russia and U.S.A. Related to JAFFE. Also see SCHAEFER.

SCHAFFGOTSCH—CAJ has some family records.

SCHAFIER—CAJ has some family records.

SCHAFIROFF—See SPIRA.

SCHAIER—CAJ has some family records.

SCHAIKEWITZ—JE has article on Russian novelist Nahum Schaikewitz (b. 1849).

SCHAMES (also Shames)—EJ has article on U.S. baker Morris Schames (b. 1881 in Poland). See his autobiography, *25 Years with the Jewish Bakers*. Shames is related to ROTHSCHILD.

SCHANZER—UJ has article on Italian statesman Carlo Schanzer (b. 1865 in Vienna).

SCHAPIRA—See SPIRA.

SCHAPIRO—See SPIRA.

SCHARFENBERG—CAJD has a family tree from Germany.

SCHARFFENECK—Related to WORMS.

SCHARFSTEIN—UJ has article on Ukrainian author Zevi Scharfstein (b. 1884).

SCHARRER—UJ has article on British pianist Irene Scharrer (b. 1885).

SCHARTENBERG—CAJ has some family records.

SCHATZ (also Shatz, Shatzkes)—Hebrew acronym derived from *shaliach tzibbur,* meaning one who leads the congregation in prayers. JE and EJ have biographies from 19th-cent. Russia. Related to ANIN.

SCHAUMBERG-LIPPE—Related to van GELDERN.

SCHAY (also Shaye)—LBI has a family tree beginning 1515, related to WUERZBURGER. Another related name is AUSPITZ.

SCHAZKI—CAJ has some family records.

SCHECHTER—Ashkenazic name derived from the Hebrew *shochet* ("butcher"). JE has article on Rabbi Solomon Schechter (b. 1847 in Rumania).

SCHEFFTEL—See SHEFTALL.

SCHEFTELOWITZ—See SHEFTALL.

SCHEID—JE has article on French writer Elie Scheid (1841–1922).

SCHEIN—Related to SAINEANU.

SCHEINDLINGER—JE has article on Polish Rabbi Samuel Scheindlinger (d. 1796).

SCHELER—EJ has article on German philosopher Max Scheler (1874–1928).

SCHENCK (also Schenk, Schenker)—Russian-American movie-producing family from 19th-cent.; see UJ. JE and UJ also have biographies from 19th–20th-cent. Poland and Hungary. PD has some Schenk family records.

SCHENK—See SCHENCK.

SCHENKER—See SCHENCK.

SCHER—See SHER.

SCHERESCHEWSKI (also Shereshevsky)—JE has three biographies from 19th-cent. Russian. Related to DUBNOW.

SCHERJVER—Related to MULDER.

SCHERMAN (also Schermann)—UJ has biographies from 19th–20th-cent. Poland and Canada.

SCHERZER—CAJ has some family records.

SCHEUER—JE has article on 18th-cent. German Talmudist Jacob Scheuer, related to UTIZ. CAJ has some family records.

SCHEY—JE has article on Hungarian merchant Philipp Schey (1798–1881). PD has some family records.

SCHEYER—LBIS has some family notes. Related to ROTHSCHILD.

SCHICK (also Schueck, Schuck, Shklover)—JE, UJ and EJ have biographies from 19th-cent. Lithuania and Sweden. LBIS has some Schuck family notes. For family histories, see JFF, Nos. 13 and 14, and *Der Stammbaum der Familie Schick.*

SCHIE—LBI has a family tree beginning 1751.

SCHIFF—Priestly family from Frankfurt-am-Main, descended from Zedek Schiff, 14th cent. The family was originally named KAHN, which is German for the boat painted on the family's house sign, but this later was changed to *Schiff* ("ship"). JE has a family tree and seven biographies. LBI has family trees beginning 1627 and 1716. LBIS has some family notes, and PD has some family records. See "Two Branches of the Schiff Family in

Frankfurt," in JQR, Vol. 10, p. 450, and Vol. XI, p. 385. Also see UJ article on Cohen for a discussion of the evolution of the family name. Related to OPPENHEIM, GLOGAU, MANNHEIM, BERLIN, EMBDEN, RHEINGANUM, PFANN, ZUNZ, HANAU, WOLF, FRANKEL, KOHEN, WURTZBURG, METZGER, SALIN, DREYFUS, MAYER, ADLER, SCHWARTSCHILD, VOGEL, HALBERSTADT, WOHL, REISS, LOEB, HORWITZ, HELLMAN, CAHN, GEIGER, LEVERSON and HUDSON.

SCHIFFER (also Schiffers)—JE has biographies from 19th-cent. Russia, Poland and Germany.

SCHILDER—UJ has article on Viennese psychiatrist Paul Schilder (1880–1940).

SCHILDKRAUT—UJ and EJ have biographies from 19th-cent. Turkey, Austria and U.S.A. See also *My Father and I,* autobiography of Joseph Schildkraut, U.S. theatrical figure (b. 1896 in Vienna).

SCHILL—See SCHILLER.

SCHILLER (also Schill, Schiller-Szinessy) —Galician name. AJA has a family tree. JE has biographies from 19th-cent. France, Hungary and England.

SCHILLINGER—UJ has article on Russian composer Josef Schillinger (b. 1895).

SCHINDLER—JE has article on German-American author Solomon Schindler (1842–1915).

SCHIPPER—UJ has article on German scholar Jacob Schipper.

SCHITLOWSKY—See ZHITLOWSKY.

SCHLANGER—Ashkenazic name taken from the town of Schonlanke.

SCHLAPRINGER—PD has some family records.

SCHLEGEL—Dorothea MENDELSSOHN married Friedrich Schlegel; see UJ article on Philipp VEIT.

SCHLESINGER (also Schloessinger)—Ashkenazic name meaning "from Silesia." JE has biographies from 19th-cent. Germany, Austria and Hungary. LBI has family trees beginning 1707, 1784, and 1780, related to BIELEFELD. CAJD has a family tree from Germany, 1600–1936. CAJ, PD and LBIS all have family notes or records. Related to JAFFE, GLOGAUER, SULZ-

BERGER, EGER, SZENES, MOOS. Also see JE article on Pinne, Poland.

SCHLETTSTADT—JE has article on 14th-cent. German Rabbi Samuel Schlettstadt, from Alsace.

SCHLIPPENTOCH—CAJ has some family records.

SCHLOESSINGER—See SCHLESINGER.

SCHLONSKY—UJ has article on Russian editor Abraham Schlonsky (b. 1900).

SCHLOSS—UJ has two biographies. AJA has a family tree beginning 1801, related to LEVY. CAJ and LBIS have records and notes. Related to MOCATTA and SELIGMAN.

SCHLOSSBERG—UJ has article on Russian labor leader Joseph Schlossberg (b. 1875).

SCHMELKES—JE has article on Austrian physician Gottfried Schmelkes (b. 1807 in Prague, d. 1870 in Switzerland).

SCHMIDT—Related to GOLDSCHMIDT and EPHRAIM. Also see SCHMIT.

SCHMIEDL—JE has article on Austrian Rabbi Adolf Schmiedl (b. 1821). Related to NEUDA.

SCHMIT—UJ has article on Russian painter Menachem Schmit (b. 1896). A possible variation is SCHMIDT.

SCHNABEL—Ashkenazic name taken from Schnabelwaid in Bavaria. JE has two biographies from 19th-cent. Austria. PD has some records of a Schnabel family related to OROSDI.

SCHNAPPER—LBI has a family tree beginning 1714. Related to ROTHSCHILD.

SCHNEERSON—A Hasidic family that founded the Lubavich movement. EJ has a family tree. See a family history in *Toledot Mishpahat ha-rav mi-Ladi.* Related to ALEXANDROW, SEGAL, SLONIM.

SCHNEIDER—Ashkenazic name meaning "tailor" in German. UJ has two biographies from 19th-cent. Poland and Russia. CAJ has some family records. Related to ALEXANDER.

SCHNEUERSON—See SCHNEURSOHN.

SCHNEURSOHN (also Schneuerson, Shneur)—UJ has biography of Russian poet Zalman Shneur (b. 1887). CAJ has

Schneursohn family records. Related to DUBNOW, SZERENCSES.

SCHNITZER (also Schnitzler)—Ashkenazic name meaning "carver" in German. JE has biographies from 19th-cent. Germany, Austria and Hungary. See UJ article on *Emin* Pasha. Related to HAJER.

SCHNURMANN—JE has article on Russian-English scholar Nestor Schnurmann (b. 1854).

SCHOCKEN—UJ has article on German merchant Salmann Schocken (b. 1877).

SCHOEN—Ashkenazic name meaning "beautiful" from the German *schön.* UJ has article on Austrian educator Max Schoen (b. 1888).

SCHOENBAUM—Related to ILNA'E.

SCHOENFELD—See SCHONFELD.

SCHOENFLIES—LBI has a family tree beginning 1667. UJ has article on German mathematician Arthur Schoenflies (1853–1928).

SCHOENHACK (also Schonhak)—EJ has article on Polish writer Joseph Schoenhack (1812–1870).

SCHOENHEIMER—UJ has article on German chemist Rudolf Schoenheimer (1897–1941).

SCHOFMANN—UJ has article on Russian writer Gershom Schofmann (b. 1880).

SCHOLEM—UJ has article on German philologist Gershom Scholem (b. 1897).

SCHOMBERG—British family which went to England from Cologne in 17th cent. JE has four biographies from 18th cent. Related to LOW.

SCHONBERG—See SCHONENBERG.

SCHONENBERG (also Schonberg)—UJ has biographies from 17th-cent. Portugal and 19th-cent. Austria. Related to BELMONT and BELMONTE.

SCHONFELD (also Schoenfeld)—JE has article on Hungarian Hebraist Baruch Schonfeld (1778–1852). A Schoenfeld family is related to DOBRUSCHKA.

SCHONHAK—See SCHOENHACK.

SCHOR (also Schorr, Shor, Schoor, Schur, Shore, etc.)—Polish and Galician rabbinical family that traces its descent to Joseph ben Isaac Bekhor Shor, a poet of 12th-

cent. Orleans, France. The name means "ox"; variations in other languages, some of which are related, are OCHS, BYK, WAHL, WOHL and VOLOV. The family is related to many of the most prominent Ashkenazic rabbinical families, including WAHL, KATZENELLENBOGEN, MARGOLIOTH and EDELS. JE has biographies from 16th- and 19th-cent. Poland and Galicia. One branch of the family came from Brody, Galicia, and called itself BRODSKI; another branch took the name WOLOWSKI. See JE articles on these two families. The family's relationship to other rabbinic families is traced in *Anaf Ez Aboth,* by Samuel Kahan. See family histories and genealogies in *Toledot Mishpahat Schor* and *Ateret Tiferet Israel;* the latter book contains an imperfect genealogy of Israel Schor (1823–1889). PD has some Schur family records. Also see JE article on *Joseph* ben Isaac Bekor Shor, EJ article on Joseph *Bekhor* Shor, UJ article on *Joseph* Bechor Shor, and JE article on Grodno, Russia, where Ephraim Solomon Shor (d. 1614) was rabbi. Related to ELSASSER, LAUTERBACH, KATZ.

SCHORR—See SCHOR.

SCHOSSBERGER—JE has article on Hungarian merchant Simon Schossberger de Torna (1796–1874). PD has some family records.

SCHOTT (also Schottlaender, Schottlander)—JE has three biographies from 18th- and 19th-cent. Germany. Julius Schottlander (b. 1835) was brother-in-law of Louis PAKULLY. LBI has a Schottlaender family tree.

SCHOTTLAENDER (Schottlander)—See SCHOTT.

SCHOTZ—UJ has article on Estonian sculptor Benno Schotz (b. 1891).

SCHOUR—UJ has article on Russian professor Isaac Schour (b. 1900).

SCHRAMECK—UJ has article on French statesman Abraham Schrameck (b. 1867).

SCHRECKER—UJ has article on Viennese philosopher Paul Schrecker (b. 1889).

SCHREIBER (also Schriber)—JE and EJ have biographies from 18th- and 19th-cent. Germany, Austria and U.S.A. Rabbi Moses Schreiber (1763–1839) was also known as Moses SOFER; he married Sarah JERWITZ, and his descendants officiated for generations as rabbis in Pressburg (now Bratislava) and other Slovakian towns. LBI has a family tree beginning 1735. PD has some family records. See a family history in *Ketov zot Zikaron.* Related to EGER, LEIDESDORFF and SPITZER.

SCHREINER—JE has two biographies from 19th-cent. Galicia and Hungary.

SCHRENZEL—EJ has article on Galician scholar Moses Schrenzel (1838–1912) of Lemberg. Related to RAPOPORT.

SCHREYER (also Shrier)—JE and EJ have biographies from Hungary and Galicia, 19th cent. Related to SACKLER.

SCHRIBER—See SCHREIBER.

SCHTEINGART—UJ has article on Latvian physician Mario Schteingart (b. 1893).

SCHUB (also Shub)—Hebrew acronymic name taken from *shocket ubodek* ("slaughterer and examiner"). Related to CHASANOVICH.

SCHUBACH—Related to MARX.

SCHUBART—Related to AMBACH.

SCHUBERT—Related to FREUND.

SCHUCK (Schueck)—See SCHICK.

SCHUELEIN—UJ has article on German painter Julius Schuelein (b. 1881).

SCHUELLER (also Schuler)—UJ has article on Austrian official Richard Schueller (b. 1870). Related to LASKER.

SCHUHL—JE has article on French Rabbi Moise Schuhl (b. 1845).

SCHULBAUM—JE has article on Austrian scholar Moses Schulbaum (b. 1835 in Galicia). His mother was descended from Hakam Zebi.

SCHULER—See SCHUELLER.

SCHULHOF (also Schulhoff)—JE has biographies from 17th-, 18th- and 19th-cent. Austria. Also related to COHEN, DOMBOVARY, LIEBMANN and LOEW.

SCHULMAN (also Schulmann and Shulman)—JE has biographies from 19th-cent. Germany, Russia, U.S.A. and Holland.

SCHULTE—See SCHULTZE.

SCHULTZ—See SCHULTZE.

SCHULTZE (also Shultz, Schulte, Schultz, Schulz)—Galician name, taken from the German word for "steward" or "overseer." UJ has article on Canadian Judge Samuel Shultz (1865–1917).

SCHULZ—See SCHULTZE.

SCHUR—See SCHOR.

SCHUSTER—Ashkenazic name that means "cobbler" in German. One family traces itself back to 1607, when Jacob ETTINGEN took Schuster as his family name; see UJ. JE has article on English physicist Arthur Schuster (b. 1851 in Germany). CAJ has some family records from Germany, 1790.

SCHWAB (also Schwabach, Schwabacher, Schwaben)—Ashkenazic name meaning "from Swabia" in German. JE has biographies from 19th-cent. Germany, France and Moravia. LBI has a Schwab family tree beginning 1495. CAJ has Schwabach and Schwaben family records. PD also has Schwabach family records. Related to HAMELN, LOEW, BLEICHRODER and DUVERNOIS.

SCHWABACH—See SCHWAB.

SCHWABEN—See SCHWAB.

SCHWADRON (also Shvadron)—EJ has article on Galician Rabbi Shalom Shvadron (1835–1911).

SCHWALBE—JE has article on German anthropologist Gustav Schwalbe (b. 1844).

SCHWARTZ—See SCHWARZ.

SCHWARTZBART—See SCHWARZBART.

SCHWARTZCHILD—See SCHWARZSCHILD.

SCHWARTZENBERG (also Schwartzenberger, Schwarzenberg)—AJA has a family tree. CAJ has some Schwarzenberg records. Related to COLMAN and MAURICE.

SCHWARTZSCHILD—See SCHWARZSCHILD.

SCHWARZ (also Schwartz)—Ashkenazic name meaning "black." JE and UJ have numerous biographies from 19th-cent. Austria, Germany, Hungary, France, Palestine. U.S.A. Rumanian humorist Moses Schwartz (1812–1870) was also known as CELIBI; see UJ. CAJ has records of Schwarz families from Hungary and Portugal, and of a Schwartz family from

France, 1876 to 1952. Related to LEWI and OPPENHEIM.

SCHWARZBART (also Schwartzbard, Schwarzbart)—The name means "black beard" in German. UJ has article on Polish official Izak Schwarzbart (b. 1888). CAJ has Schwartzbard and Schwarzbart family records.

SCHWARZCHILD—See SCHWARZSCHILD.

SCHWARZENBERG—See SCHWARTZENBERG.

SCHWARZFELD—CAJ has some family records. JE has four biographies of a Rumanian family prominent in 19th cent.

SCHWARZMAN (also Schwarzmann, Shwartzman)—UJ and EJ have biographies from 19th-20th-cent. Russia. Related to SHESTOV.

SCHWARZSCHILD (also Schwartzschild, Schwartzchild, Schwarzchild)—Ashkenazic name taken from the black shield painted on a family's front door. LBI has family trees beginning 1490 and 1555. LBIS has some family notes. UJ has article on German astronomer Karl Schwarzchild (1873–1916). See family tree in *Stammtafeln der von Liebmann-Schwarzschild (1555–94) abstammenden Familien.* Also see a Schwarzchild family history in JFF, No. 18. Related to LIEBMANN, SCHIFF and JOSEPH.

SCHWEID—UJ has article on Polish actor Mark Schweid (b. 1891).

SCHWEIGER—UJ has article on Hungarian Rabbi Lazar Schweiger (b. 1872).

SCHWEITZER—The name means "Swiss" in German. EJ has article on Hungarian soldier Eduard von Schweitzer (1844–1920). LBI has a family tree beginning 1724.

SCHWERIN—Ashkenazic name probably derived from a German town of the same name (there are two: one near Mecklenburg, the other on the Warthe River in Posen province, now Poznan, in Poland). JE has article on Hungarian Rabbi Gotz Schwerin (1760–1845). LBI has a family tree beginning 1780, related to KANTOROWICZ. Another related name is GOETZ.

SCHWIMMER—UJ has article on Hungarian dermatologist Erno Schwimmer (1837–1898).

SCHWOB—JE has article on French journalist Marcel Schwob (1867–1905).

SCIAMA—Related to FOA.

SCOTT—JE has article on English author Charles Scott (1803–1866), born BLUMENTHAL.

SEBAG—Family prominent in North Africa after 16th cent.; see EJ. JE has article on English teacher Solomon Sebag (1828–1892). Related to MONTEFIORE.

SEBASTIANO—Related to MEDICI.

SEBESTYEN—UJ has article on Hungarian author Karoly Sebestyen (b. 1872).

SEBLITZKY—See STEBLICKI.

SEBOK—UJ has article on Hungarian author Zsigmond Sebok (1861–1916).

SECHSEL—Related to CARO.

SECKBACH—Ashkenazic rabbinic family. See *Reshimoth Aboth,* by Markus Seckbach.

SECKEL—Ashkenazic name which is a diminutive form of Isaac. Related to FRANKEL and GRIFF.

SEDBON—JE has article on 18th-cent. Tunisian Rabbi Joseph Sedbon.

SEE—Family of Alsatian origin. JE has eight biographies, all from 19th-cent. See family history in ZS, Vol. 3, p. 212.

SEEGEN—JE has article on Austrian Josef Seegen (b. 1822).

SEELER—UJ has article on German director Moriz Seeler (1888–1941).

SEELIG—See SEELIGMANN.

SEELIGMANN (also Seelig, Seeligman, Seeligson)—Seeligman von Eichthal was an 18th-cent. German industrial family; see UJ, which also has a Seeligson biography from 19th-cent. Texas. LBIS has a Seelig family tree. Related to MENDELSSOHN. A possible variation of the name is SELIGMAN.

SEELIGSON—See SEELIG.

SEGAL (also Segall, Segel, Siegel, etc.)—Ashkenazic name which is an acronym for the Hebrew *segan leviyyah* ("assistant, or member, of the Levites"). JE and UJ have biographies from 18th-cent. Russia and 19th-cent. Rumania, Germany and U.S.A. LBI has a Segall family tree beginning 1734. PD has some Siegel family records. Related to KARP, CHAGALL, MEZAH, MOELLIN, SCHNEERSOHN and KAVEN.

SEGALL—See SEGAL.

SEGELMESSI—JE has article on 14th-cent. African liturgist Judah Segelmessi.

SEGHERS—UJ has article on German writer Anna Seghers (b. REILING in 1900).

SEGOVIA—Related to ALGAZI.

SEGRE (also Segri)—Italian family of scholars. JE has fourteen biographies from the 16th-, 17th-, and 18th-cent. See a Segri family history in VR, Vol. 2, p. 274. Related to LUZZATO.

SEGRI—See SEGRE.

SEIBEL—Related to SAMUEL.

SEIBERLING—JE has article on Russian educator Joseph Seiberling (d. 1882); he was the son of Isaac MARKUSEWICH.

SEIDEL—UJ has article on Russian violinist Toscha Seidel (b. 1900).

SEIDLIN—UJ has article on Russian educator Joseph Seidlin (b. 1892).

SEINSHEIMER—AJA has a family tree beginning 1830.

SEIXAS—American Sephardic family whose founder came to America from Portugal in 1730. JE has a family tree and five biographies. Related to FRANKS, MANUEL, JUDAH, LEVY, MACHADO, LOPEZ, JONAS, SOLOMONS, FLORENCE, NATHAN, PHILIPPS, CORDOZO, PEIXOTTO, HART, KURSHEEDT and SUTTON.

SEKLES—UJ has article on German composer Bernhard Sekles (1872–1934).

SELDEN—JE has article on English jurist John Selden (1584–1654).

SELICHOWER (also Selchow, Selkowe)—Name taken from the town of Selichow, Poland. Related to MINDEN.

SELIG—Related to BLOCH and JOSEPH.

SELIGMAN (also Seligmann)—American family originally from Bavaria, traced back to Abraham Seligman (1715–1775). JE has an extensive family tree and six biographies. LBI has a Seligmann family tree beginning 1628, related to LIPMANN and HERZFELD. PD has Seligmann family records. JE article on "Coat of Arms" has a Seligmann family crest (under Weliner).

Also see *The Family Register of the Descendants of David Seligman* and *The Story of the Seligmans*. Relatives include STEINHARDT, STETTHEIMER, WEDELES, CONTENT, LEHMAIER, HELLMAN, WASSERMANN, GLAZIER, ARNOLD, BEER, LILIENTHAL, LOEB, WALTER, SPIEGELBERG, LEVI, MESSEL, MERTON, KIRSCH, LEWIS, WILENKIN, SCHLOSS, SELIGSBERG, MAYER, BEDDINGTON, ROSENTHAL, STERN, GANS, UHLFELDER, LEWISOHN, MUHSAM, HAHN, WILDA and EICHTHAL. A possible variation of the name is SEELIGMAN.

SELIGSBERG—See SELIGMAN.

SELIGSOHN—JE has two biographies from 19th-cent. Russia and Poland.

SELIKSOVICH—UJ has article on Lithuanian scholar George Seliksovich (1863–1926).

SELKE—Related to BAIERSDORF.

SELKOWE—See SELICHOWER.

SELLO—LBI has a family tree beginning 1780.

SELMAN—See family history in *The Selmans*.

SELOVE—Usually abbreviation of YOSELOVICH.

SELTMANN—UJ has article on Hungarian historian Rezso Seltmann (1889–1930).

SELTZER—CAJ has some family records.

SELVER—UJ has article on Czech writer Paul Selver (b. 1888).

SEMAN—UJ has article on Polish-American educator Philip Seman (b. 1881).

SEMANA—See SHEMANA.

SEMARJAH—14th-cent. Roman family. See family tree in VR, Vol. 1, p. 450.

SEMEL—UJ has article on Galician merchant Bernard Semel (b. 1878).

SEMIATITSCH—JE has article on 17th–18th-cent. Lithuanian Talmudist Gedaliah Semiatitsch.

SEMKOVSKY—UJ has article on Russian journalist Semen Semkovsky (b. 1882).

SEMON—JE has two biographies from 19th-cent. Germany and England.

SENATOR—JE has article on German doctor Herman Senator (1834–1911). CAJ has some family records.

SENDER—UJ has article on German deputy Toni Sender (b. 1888). Related to SAFRIN.

SENEOR—EJ has article on Spanish courtier Abri Seneor (1412–1493).

SENESH—See SZENES.

SENIOR—JE has biographies from 15th-cent. Segovia and 18th-cent. Germany. CAJ has some family records. Related to MELDOLA and de SOLA.

SEPHARDI—Related to ANKAVA.

SEQUIRA—JE has article on English physician Isaac Sequira (1738–1816), born in Lisbon.

SERED—Related to JAFFE.

SERENI—Ancient Roman family still living in Italy today; see EJ.

SERERO—Family of Spanish scholars who moved to Fez, Morocco, during the Inquisition. See EJ.

SERFADI—Related to SHURRABI.

SERKES—See SIRKES.

SERKIN—See SIRKES.

SERUSI—Tunisian and Libyan diplomatic family of the 17th, 18th and 19th cent.; see EJ.

SERUYA—Moroccan family of 15th cent. See EJ.

SERVI—JE has article on Italian Rabbi Flaminio Servi (1841–1904).

SESPEDES—Related to MENDES.

SESSO—See biography from 15th-cent. Italy in EJ article on "Art."

SETZER—UJ has article on Russian writer Samuel Setzer (b. 1882).

SEVITZKY—UJ has article on Russian conductor Fabien Sevitzky (b. 1893); also known as KOUSSEVITZKY.

SFEJ—JE has article on Rabbi Abraham Sfej (d. 1784 in Amsterdam), born in Tunis.

SFORNO—Italian family with many distinguished rabbis and scholars. JE has eight biographies from 15th, 16th and 17th

cent. See family history in VR, Vol. 2, p. 80.

SHABAZI—EJ has article on 17th-cent. Yemenite poet Salem Shabazi.

SHABBETHAI—Related to MORPURGO.

SHACHTER—See SCHACHTER.

SHADOVSKY—Journalist Israel Shadovsky was born 1876 in Lithuania; see EJ article on Victor *Shulman.* Also see SCHADOW.

SHAG—EJ has article on Hungarian rabbi Abraham Shag (1801–1876); also known as ZWEBNER.

SHAGAL—See CHAGALL.

SHAKNA (also Shekna)—JE has article on Polish Talmudist Shalom Shakna (1510–1558), father-in-law of Moses ISSERLES. Also see UJ article on *Baruch* Yavan.

SHALAL—JE has article on Egyptian Isaac Shalal (d. 1525 in Jerusalem).

SHALEM—EJ has article on Salonikan scholar Samuel Shalem (d. 1760).

SHALIT—See SZALIT.

SHALKOVITZ—UJ has article on Russian writer Abraham Shalkovitz (1862–1921).

SHALOM—JE has article on Italian scholar Abraham Shalom (d. 1492). Related to EISENSTADT, HERZL and MORENO.

SHALOWITZ—UJ has article on Russian-American lawyer Aaron Shalowitz (b. 1892).

SHAMES—See SCHAMES.

SHANGI—See SANCHO.

SHAPERA—See SPIRA.

SHAPIRA—See SPIRA.

SHAPIRO—See SPIRA.

SHARABI—EJ has article on Jerusalem cabalist Shalom Sharabi (1720–1777).

SHARFMAN—UJ has article on Russian economist Isaiah Sharfman (b. 1886).

SHATTON—See SZATENSZTEJN.

SHATZ—See SCHATZ.

SHATZKES—See SCHATZ.

SHAVITCH—UJ has article on Russian conductor Vladimir Shavitch (b. 1888).

SHAYE—See SCHAY.

SHEFFIELD—UJ has article on German physician Hermann Sheffield (b. 1871).

SHEFTAIL—See SHEFTALL.

SHEFTALL (also Sheftail, Sheftel, Scheff-tel, Scheftelowitz)—U.S. family originally from Portugal, prominent in Georgia in 18th and 19th cent. See JE and UJ, which also have unrelated biographies from 19th-cent. Germany. AJA has a family tree beginning 1783. See also "Some Notes on the Early History of the Sheftalls of Georgia," in *Publications of the American Jewish Historical Society*, Vol. 17 (1909), p. 167. Schefftel is related to PERLES.

SHEFTEL—See SHEFTALL.

SHEFTMAN—A family by this name is included in *It Began with Zade Usher* (see Bernstein in Bibliography).

SHEIKH—EJ has article on Yemenite philanthropist Abraham Sheikh.

SHEIN—JE has article on Russian ethnographer Pavel Shein (1826–1900).

SHEINKIN—EJ has article on Russian Zionist Menaham Sheinkin (1871–1924).

SHEKNA—See SHAKNA.

SHEMAIAH—Related to PEREZ.

SHEMANA (also Semana)—Prominent scholarly family of 19th-cent. Tunis. JE has four biographies.

SHEPHERD—Related to TOBIAS.

SHEPS—UJ has article on Polish writer Elias Sheps (b. 1892).

SHER (also Scher)—Ashkenazic name meaning "shears," often used by tailors. A family by this name is included in *It Began with Zade Usher* (see Bernstein in Bibliography).

SHERESHEVSKY—See SCHERESCHEWSKI.

SHERTOK—UJ has article on Ukrainian Zionist Moshe Shertok (b. 1894).

SHESTAPOL—EJ has article on Russian Hasid Wolf Shestapol (1832–1872).

SHESTOV—UJ has article on Russian-French philosopher Lev Shestov (1866–1938), also known as SCHWARZMANN.

SHEUERMAN—Related to ADLER.

SHILLMAN—UJ has article on Irish communal worker Bernard Shillman (b. 1892).

SHIM'ON—EJ has article on 12th-cent. Moroccan poet Joseph Shim'on.

SHIMONOWITZ—UJ has article on Russian poet David Shimonowitz (b. 1886).

SHIMSHELEVITZ (also Shimshelewitz, Shimshi)—See family history in *Megilat Yuhasin*. Also see UJ article on *Ben* Zevi, a relative.

SHIMSHI—See SHIMSHELEVITZ.

SHINDOOKH—EJ has article on 18th-cent. Nasi of Baghdad Moses Shindookh.

SHINWELL—UJ has article on British M.P. Emanuel Shinwell (b. 1884).

SHIPER—UJ has article on Polish deputy Ignac Shiper (b. 1884).

SHISKES—JE has article on Polish scholar Saul Shiskes (d. 1797 in Vilna).

SHKLOVER—See SHKLOVSKI.

SHKLOVSKI (also Shklover)—Name taken from the Russian town of Shklov, where Jews first settled in early 16th cent. JE has article on Russian journalist Isaac Shklovski (b. 1865). Shklover is also a variation of SCHICK.

SHKOLNIK—See SKULNIK.

SHNEUR—See SCHNEURSOHN.

SHOLAL—See SOLAL.

SHOMER—See family history in *Yesterday*.

SHOR (Shore)—See SCHOR.

SHOSHAN—Related to BENSUSAN. Also see IBN SHOSHAN.

SHOSHKES—UJ has article on Polish writer Henry Shoshkes (b. 1891).

SHPITZ—See SPITZ.

SHRIER—See SCHREYER.

SHRIKI—See CHRIQUI.

SHRIMSKI—JE has article on New Zealand politician Samuel Shrimsk (1828–1902), born in Posen.

SHTIF—UJ has article on Russian philologist Nochum Shtif (1879–1933).

SHUB—See SCHUB.

SHULLAM—JE has article on 16th-cent. physician Samuel Shullam, of Spanish descent.

SHULMAN—See SCHULMAN.

SHULSINGER—EJ has article on *hazzan* Bezalel Shulsinger (1779–1873), born in Russia.

SHULTZ—See SCHULTZE.

SHUMAN—JE has article on U.S. merchant Abraham Shuman (b. 1838 in Prussia), whose daughter married RAT-SHESKY.

SHURER—EJ has article on journalist Haim Shurer (b. 1895 in Russia).

SHURRABI—JE has article on Indian *hakam* Shelomo Shurrabi (d. 1856 in Bombay). His maternal grandfather was Meyer SERFADI.

SHUSSLOWITZ—JE has article on 19th-cent. Russian scholar Judah Shusslowitz.

SHVADRON—See SCHWADRON.

SHWARTZMAN—See SCHWARZMAN.

SIBONI—Family of rabbis in Morocco, 18th and 19th cent. See EJ.

SICHEL—JE has two biographies from 19th-cent. France and Germany. CAJ has some family records. Related to MONTEFIORE and ROTHSCHILD.

SICHER (also Sicherman)—EJ has article on Czech Rabbi Gustav Sicher (b. 1880). A Sicherman family from Slovakia (then Hungary) is included in *A Link with the Future* (See Rottenberg in Bibliography).

SICHROVSKY—EJ has article on Austrian railroad entrepreneur Heinrich von Sichrovsky (1794–1866), father-in-law of Theodor GOMPERZ. PD has some family records.

SID (also Sidi)—Common family name among eastern Mediterranean Jews. JE has biographies from 15th-cent. Egypt, 18th-cent. Bulgaria and 19th-cent. Serbia.

SIDI—See SID.

SIDIS—UJ has article on Ukrainian psychologist Boris Sidis (1867–1923).

SIDON—JE has article on Hungarian Rabbi Simon Sidon (1815–1891). His father's name was KANITZ, after the town in Moravia. PD has some family records.

SIEBENBERGER—JE has article on Russian Hebraist Isaac Siebenberger (d. 1879 in Warsaw).

SIEFF—See SIFF.

SIEGEL—See SEGAL.

SIEGHART—UJ has article on Austrian financier Rudolf Sieghart (1866–1937).

SIENIAWSKI—CAJ has some family records from Poland, 1689 to 1740.

SIESBY—JE has two biographies from 19th-cent. Denmark.

SIFF (also Sieff)—Ashkenazic name taken from the Hebrew *ze'eb* ("wolf"); also see WOLF. EJ has article on British industrialist Israel Sieff (b. 1889), brother-in-law of Simon MARKS and Harry SACHER.

SIGMAN—EJ has article on U.S. labor leader Morris Sigman (1880–1931), born in Russia.

SIK—UJ has article on Hungarian poet Sandor Sik (b. 1889).

SIKILI—Name taken from Sicily. EJ has article on 13th–14th-cent. Rabbi Jacob Sikili.

SILBER—See SILVER.

SILBERBUSCH—UJ has article on Polish writer David Silberbusch (1854–1936).

SILBERFARB—EJ has article on Russian writer Moses Silberfarb (1876–1934).

SILBERG—EJ has article on Israeli Judge Moshe Silberg (b. 1900 in Lithuania).

SILBERGLEIT—Silesian family of 19th cent. UJ has two biographies.

SILBERMAN (Silbermann)—See SILVERMAN.

SILBERSTEIN (also Silverstein)—Ashkenazic name meaning "silver stone" in German. JE has biographies from 19th-cent. Hungary, Germany, Russia and U.S.A. LBI has a family tree, related to EHRLICH and AUERBACH. Another related name is PALAGI.

SILBERSTROM—Related to JAFFE.

SILBERT—UJ has article on Russian painter Ben Silbert (1893–1939).

SILKIN (also Silkiner)—EJ and UJ have biographies from 19th–20th-cent. Lithuania, U.S.A. and England.

SILMAN—EJ has article on writer Kadish Silman (1880–1937), born in Lithuania.

SILVA—Sephardic family name. JE has six biographies from 17th–18th-cent. Portugal, Holland, Brazil, Peru and Italy. Italian author Hezekiah Silva (1659–1698) was the son-in-law of Mordecai MALA-

CHI. Related to COSTA, COUTINHO, MALKI and MELDOLA.

SILVEIRA—See SILVEYRA.

SILVER (also Silber)—UJ and EJ have biographies from 19th-cent. Russia, Lithuania, etc. Related to RIESSER.

SILVERBERG—UJ has article on German industrialist Paul Silverberg (b. 1876).

SILVERMAN (also Silberman, Silbermann)—JE, EJ and UJ have biographies from 19th-cent. Lithuania, Hungary, Germany, Russia, England and U.S.A.

SILVERSTEIN—See SILBERSTEIN.

SILVEYRA (also Silveira)—JE has two biographies from 17th-cent. Spain, France and Holland.

SIMA—UJ has article on Russian artist Marion Sima (b. 1902).

SIMCHONI—EJ has article on scholar Jacob Simchoni (1884–1926), born SIMCHOWITZ in Poland.

SIMCHOWITZ—JE has article on Russian Rabbi Samuel Simchowitz (d. 1896). Also see SIMCHONI.

SIMEL—Related to EPSTEIN.

SIMHAH—Related to ALMOSNINO.

SIMMEL—UJ has article on German philosopher Georg Simmel (1858–1918).

SIMMONS—JE has article on English Rabbi Laurence Simmons (1852–1900), who married a daughter of Professor HERZFELD of Germany.

SIMON (also Simons, Simoni, Simonis, Simonsen, Simonssohn, Simon-Veit, etc.)—JE and UJ have biographies from 17th-, 18th- and 19th-cent. Belgium, France, Germany, England, Holland, Denmark and U.S.A. Sir John Simon of England (1818–1897) was descended from the OROBIO family (related to CASTRO). English authoress Rachel Simon (1823–1899) was the daughter of Simeon SALAMAN and Alice COWEN. LBI has Simon family trees beginning 930, 1655, 1732, 1782 and 1818, related to GRELLING; also Simon-VEIT family trees beginning 1669 and 1758; a Simoni family tree beginning 1827, related to PHILIPPSON; and a Simonssohn family tree beginning 1730, related to BLOCH. LBIS has a Simonis family tree. CAJD has a family tree from Germany, related to MAYER. See family histories in

Stiftungs-Urkunde betreffend die Moritz Simonsche Familien-Stiftung; Stammbaum der Familie Michael Simons; and *Jacob Simonsen und Frau Rose, geb. Hahn, und ihre Vorfahren.* Other related names include BELMONT, GRATZ, LOEB, HERZL, LEBRECHT.

SIMONE—EJ has article on Czech journalist André Simone (b. KATZ in 1895).

SIMONI—See SIMON.

SIMONIS—See SIMON.

SIMONS—See SIMON.

SIMONSEN—See SIMON.

SIMONSSOHN—See SIMON.

SIMON-VEIT—See SIMON.

SIMONYI—JE has article on Hungarian linguist Sigmund Simonyi (1853–1919).

SIMSON—Early New York family, from 18th cent. onward. See EJ, which also has three unrelated biographies from 19th–20th-cent. Germany. JE article on "Coat of Arms" has a family crest. Related to LEO.

DA SINAGOGA (also de Synagoga)—Related to ANAW and PISA.

SINANI—Related to CHELEBI.

SINGER (also Singerman)—Ashkenazic name indicating a soloist or officiating minister in a synagogue. JE has eight biographies from 19th-cent. Hungary, Austria, Germany and England; EJ has biography from Argentina, 19th–20th cent. LBI has family trees beginning 1719 and 1836, related to SUSSMANN. AJA has a family tree that traces the Singer and MORGAN families from Reb Menahem MENDEL of Kotzk. Related to GLUECK, JAFFE, KOHN, LOW and VEIT.

SINGERMAN—See SINGER.

SINIGAGLIA—Italian family from the town of Sinigaglia. JE has a small family tree and five biographies from 17th and 18th cent.

SINKO—EJ has article on Yugoslav author Ervin Sinko (b. Franjo SPITZER in 1898).

SINTZHEIM—See SINZHEIM.

SINZHEIM (also Sintzheim)—JE has article on French Rabbi Joseph Sinzheim (1745–1812), brother-in-law of Herz CERF-

BEER. PD has some Sinzheim family records; CAJ has some Sintzheim family records. Also related to AUERBACH.

SIPRUT—See SIPRUTINI.

SIPRUTINI (also Siprut)—EJ has article on 18th-cent. Dutch cellist Emanuel Siprutini. Siprut family is related to DISRAELI.

SIRILLO—JE has article on 15th–16th cent. Spanish Talmudist Solomon Sirillo.

SIRKES (also Sirkis, Serkes, Serkin, Syrkin)—Ashkenazic name derived from the female name Sarah. JE has article on Polish Rabbi Joel Sirkes (1561–1640) and on his descendant, Russian jurist Maximilian Syrkin (b. 1858). UJ has biographies from 19th–20th-cent. Russia and Czechoslovakia. CAJ has Sirkis family records. AJA has a Syrkin family tree. Also see UJ and EJ articles on *David* ben Samuel ha-Levi (1586–1667), a relative. Other relatives include JAFFE.

SIRKIS—See SIRKES.

SIRMAY—UJ has article on Hungarian composer Albert Sirmay (b. 1880); also known as SZIRMAI.

SIROTA—EJ has article on *hazzan* Gershon Sirota (1874–1943), born in Russia.

SISKIND—See SUSSKIND.

SITBON—Prominent family in 18th-cent. Tunis. See EJ.

SKALLER—See family history in *The Family History of Nicholas Paul Alexander.*

SKLAR—UJ has article on Lithuanian chemist Samuel Sklar (b. 1897).

SKLIANSKY—UJ has article on Russian physician Efraim Skliansky (1892–1925).

SKOSS—UJ has article on Russian scholar Solomon Skoss (b. 1884).

SKREINKA—JE has article on Hungarian scholar Lazar Skreinka (19th cent.).

SKUDSKI—Name taken from the Russian town of Shkud in the government of Kovno; Jews first settled there in 1725. Related to ROSENTHAL.

SKULNIK (also Shkolnik)—UJ has article on Polish actor Menashe Skulnik. Shkolnik is related to ESHKOL.

SKUTECZKY—JE has article on Hungarian painter Damianus Skuteczky (1850–1921).

SLATKINE—EJ has article on bibliographer Menahem Slatkine (b. 1875 in Russia).

SLAWSON—EJ has article on U.S. social worker John Slawson (b. 1896 in Russia).

SLIOSBERG (also Sliozberg)—UJ has article on Russian-French lawyer Henry Sliosberg (1863–1937).

SLOCHOWER—UJ has article on Austrian educator Harry Slochower (b. 1900).

SLOMAN (also Slomann)—JE and UJ have biographies from 19th-cent. England and Denmark.

SLOMOVITZ—UJ has article on Russian-Polish editor Phillip Slomovitz (b. 1896).

SLONIK—Name taken from Salonika, Greece. JE has article on Polish Talmudist Benjamin Slonik (1550–1619), an ancestor of Ezekiel KATZENELLENBOGEN.

SLONIM (also Slonimski, Slonimsky)—Name taken from the Russian town of Slonim in the government of Grodno; Jews were there in 16th cent. or earlier. JE, UJ and EJ have biographies from 18th- and 19th-cent. Poland and Russia. Slonim was a Hasidic dynasty in 19th–20th-cent. Poland; Slonimsky was a family of scientists in 18th–19th-cent. Poland. See family history in *Toledot Mishpahat ha-rav mi-Ladi.* Related to SCHNEERSOHN, STERN, WENGEROFF, VENGEROV.

SLONIMSKI (Slonimsky)—See SLONIM.

SLOSS—Related to GERSTLE.

SLOT—UJ has article on South African physician Gerald Slot (b. 19th cent.).

SLOTKI—EJ has article on scholar Israel Slotki (b. 1884 in Jerusalem).

SLOUSCHZ (also Sloucz, Slouzsch)—JE has two biographies from 19th-cent. Russia. CAJ has Sloucz and Slouzsch family records.

SLOUZSCH—See SLOUSCHZ.

SLUCKI (also Slutzki)—JE and EJ have biographies from 19th-cent. Russia and Poland.

SLUSZ—CAJ has some family records.

SLUTSKAYA—UJ has article on Russian revolutionary Vera Slutskaya (1874–1917); also known as KLEMENTEVA.

SLUTZKI—See SLUCKI.

SMALLENS—UJ has article on Russian-American conductor Alexander Smallens (b. 1889).

SMILANSKY—UJ has article on Russian novelist Moshe Smilansky (b. 1874).

SMIELER—See SAMILER.

SMITH—UJ has five biographies from 19th-cent. England.

SMOLAR—UJ has article on Ukrainian journalist Ber Smolar (b. 1897).

SMOLENSKIN—Name taken from the Russian city of Smolensk, where Jews first settled in 1489. JE has article on Russian writer Peter Smolenskin (1842–1885). Related to TEMKIN.

SMUSHKEVICH—UJ has article on Lithuanian army officer Iakov Smushkevich (b. 1902).

SNAPPER—UJ has article on Dutch physician Isadore Snapper (b. 1889).

SNEERSOHN—EJ has article on proto-Zionist Hayyim Sneersohn (1834–1882).

SNOW (also Snowman)—JE and UJ have two biographies from 19th–20th-cent. England.

SOARES—Related to MENDES.

SOAVE—JE has article on Italian Hebraist Moses Soave (1820–1882).

SOBEL (also Sobol, Sobelsohn)—According to one source, all Jews from Hungary with this name are somehow related to each other. EJ and UJ have biographies from 19th–20th-cent. Russia and U.S.A. See a family history in *A Link with the Future* (see Rottenberg in Bibliography). Related to POLLOCK and RADEK.

SOBELSOHN—See SOBEL.

SOBERNHEIM—JE has article on German physician Joseph Sobernheim (1803–1846).

SOBESKI—UJ has article on Polish art historian Michael Sobeski (b. 1877).

SOBOL—See SOBEL.

SOCHACZEW—EJ has article on Polish Rabbi Abraham Sochaczew (1839–1910).

SOCOLOW—See SOKOL.

SOEIRA—JE has article on Samuel Soeira (b. 1625 in Amsterdam, d. 1657 in London), who took the family name of his mother. He was the nephew of Manuel DORMIDO.

SOFER—JE has article on Hungarian Rabbi Hayyim Sofer (1821–1886). EJ has a family tree. Also see JE article on DESSAUER. Other related names are SCHREIBER, NIEDERLANDER, SAMUEL, MUNZ, BLUMENFELDT, LEIDESDORFF, EGER, GLASNER and EHRENFELD.

SOKOL (also Sokolnikov, Sokoloff, Sokolov, Sokolow, Socolow)—Ashkenazic name meaning "vulture"; another variation, not necessarily related, is GEYER. JE and UJ have biographies from 19th–20th cent. Russia. Russian journalist Nahum Sokolow (1859–1936) was a descendant of Nathan SHAPIRA.

SIKOLNIKOV—See SOKOL.

SOKOLOFF (Sokolov, Sokolow)—See SOKOL.

de SOLA—Sephardic family whose earliest known members lived in Toledo and Navarre in 8th and 9th cent. Descendants were living in Holland, England, Canada, U.S.A. and Curaçao in 1900. JE has an extensive family tree and thirty-four biographies, from 9th through 18th cent. Relatives include JOSEPH, MELDOLA, MENDES, LOPEZ, BENVENISTE, ALVAREZ, OLIVEIRA, HENRIQUEZ, FURTADO, HOHEB, TORRES, MONSANTO, LIMA, SENIOR, de PINNA, LEVY, HENRY, ERASO, MYER, LURIA, JESSURUN, OSORIO, SAMUEL, ASHER, GOLDSMITH, BELAIS and POOL.

SOLAL (also Sholal)—North African family from 13th cent. See EJ, which also has an article on Egyptian scholar Isaac Sholal (d. 1524). Related to KOHEN.

SOLDI—JE has article on French engraver Emile Soldi (1846–1906).

SOLIS (also da Solis, de Solis)—Spanish and Portuguese family, some of whose members escaped to the Netherlands, France, England, U.S.A. and the West Indies. The U.S. branch is descended from Solomon Solis and his wife, born Isabel da FONSECA, who moved from Spain to Amsterdam in 17th cent. JE has a family tree and eight biographies from the 15th, 17th, 18th and 19th cent. Relatives include

GOMEZ, BINSWANGER, CARVALHO, HAYS, NATHAN, NORRIS, RITTERBAND, SAMUELS, SARFATY, VALENTINE and many more in U.S.A.

SOLLEDER—CAJ has some family records.

SOLMSEN—UJ has article on German philologist Felix Solmsen (1865–1911). The name may be a variation of SOLOMONSEN.

SOLMSSON—See SOLOMON.

SOLOMON (also Salomon, Solomons, Salaman, Salamon, Saloman, Salomons, Salomone, Salomonsen, Salomonsohn, Salomonson, etc.)—JE, UJ and EJ have numerous biographies beginning 18th cent., from Germany, England, Denmark, Australia, U.S.A., Canada, Sweden, Fiji, Poland. The English family of Salomons is descended from 18th-cent. London resident Solomon Salomons; see JE, which also has the family crest in its article on "Coat of Arms." JE also has article and family tree on the U.S. family descended from Revolutionary War–era financier Haym Salomon (1740–1785). AJA also has a Haym Salomon genealogy covering 1649 to 1920 and related to ANDREWS, GAGGSTATTER, MAYER and MIREL. LBI has Salomon family trees beginning 1763, 1815 and 1838, related to ARON. LBIS has some notes on the Saloman and Salomonsen families. Salomonsohn was a family of 18th-cent. German bankers; see JE. Also see family history in *Records of My Family.* Relatives include PHILLIPS, BRUNNER, ME'IRI, LEVINSOHN, ISAACS, ELKAN, ETTING, SAVRAN, ABRAMSON, HAGEDORN, KAPLAN, LAZARUS, FRANKS, SEIXAS, JOSEPH, MONTEFIORE, SIMON, GOODMAN, NISSEN, FRANKS, HART, HEINEMANN, ADAM-SALOMON, ITZIG, MENDELSSOHN, MITZ, GOLDSMID, WALEY, LEVY and SOLMSEN.

SOLOMONS—See SOLOMON.

SOLOVEICHIK (also Soloweitschik, Solovyev)—Ashkenazic name meaning "nightingale." JE and UJ have biographies from 19th-cent. Russia and Lithuania. EJ has a family tree. Related to SHAPIRA, BEYLE, HA-LEVI, HOLZBERG, PARISER and ROSENTHAL.

SOLOVYEV—See SOLOVEICHIK.

SOLOWAY—Related to KATZ.

SOLOWEITSCHIK—See SOLOVEICHIK.

SOLTES—UJ has article on Polish writer Mordecai Soltes (b. 1893).

SOMARY—UJ has article on Austrian economist Felix Somary (b. 1881).

SOMEKH—JE has article on Baghdad Rabbi Abdallah Somekh (1813–1889).

SOMERSOLL—Related to MONTEFIORE.

SOMLO (also Somlyo)—UJ has two biographies from 19th–20th-cent. Hungary.

SOMLYO—See SOMLO.

SOMMER—UJ has article on Austrian General Emil von Sommer (1866–1940).

SOMMO (also Sommi)—EJ has article on Italian dramatist Judah Sommo (1527–1592). Related to PORTALEONE.

SOMOGYI—UJ has article on Hungarian editor Bela Somogyi (1868–1920).

SONCINO—15th-cent. Italian printing family, from the town of the same name. JE has five biographies; EJ has a family tree. CAJ has some family records. See a family history in CB, p. 3053.

SONDER—Related to WEIL.

SONNE (also Sonnemann)—UJ and JE have biographies from 19th-cent. Poland and Germany.

SONNEMANN—See SONNE.

SONNENFELD—See SONNENFELS.

SONNENFELS (also Sonnenfeld)—18th-cent. Austrian family; JE has three biographies. LBI has a family tree beginning 1680. CAJ has family records, 18th–19th-cent.; PD also has some records. See family history in ZGJT, Vol. 3 (1933), p. 224, and JFF, No. 13 (1928). JE article on "Coat of Arms" has the family crest. JE also has a Sonnenfeld biography from 19th-cent. Hungary. Related to WIENER, LIPMANN and GEYER.

SONNENSCHEIN (also Sonneschein)—Ashkenazic name meaning "sunshine" in German. UJ has article on English linguist Edward Sonnenschein (1851–1929). JE has biography from 19th-cent. Hungary-U.S.A.

SONNENTHAL—JE has article on Austro-Hungarian actor Adolf Sonnenthal (1834–1909). PD has some family records.

SONNESCHEIN—See SONNENSCHEIN.

SONNINO—JE has article on Italian politician Sidney Sonnino (1849–1922), born in Egypt.

SOPHER—AJA has a family tree, related to HACOHEN.

SORANI—JE has article on Italian jurist Ugo Sorani (b. 1850).

SORAUER—UJ has article on German botanist Paul Sorauer (1839–1916).

SORS—UJ has article on Hungarian artist Ivan Sors (b. 1895), also known as STERN.

SORSBY—UJ has two biographies from 19th-cent. England.

SOS—UJ has article on Hungarian editor Endre Sos (b. 1905).

SOSA—Portuguese family dating back to the mid-16th cent. JE has four biographies.

SOSSNITZ—JE has article on Russian Talmudist Joseph Sossnitz (1837–1910).

SOUSA DE MACEDO—UJ has article on Marrano author Antonio Sousa de Macedo (1606–1682). Also see SOUZA.

SOUTHWOOD—UJ has article on Polish-English publisher Baron Southwood (b. 1873), also known as ELIAS.

SOUTINE—UJ has article on Russian painter Chaim Soutine (b. 1894).

SOUZA (also Zousa)—Related to BELMONTE. Also see SOUSA de MACEDO.

SOYER—19th-cent. Russian writing family. UJ has three biographies.

SPADA—CAJ has family records from 1600 to 1938.

SPAETH—JE has article on Johann Spaeth of Venice, also known as GERMANUS, convert to Judaism (d. 1701 in Amsterdam).

SPANIER—JE has article on German writer Meyer Spanier (b. 1864). LBI has family trees beginning 16th cent. and 1676, related to FRAENKEL. LBIS has some family notes.

SPANJAARD—See family history in *Die Familie Spanjaard*.

SPATZ—LBI has a family tree beginning 1794.

SPECTATOR—Related to NACHIMSON.

SPECTOR (also Spektor)—Russian name meaning "inspector," used by Hebrew teachers to enable them to live in zones otherwise forbidden to Russian Jews. JE has two biographies from 19th-cent. Russia. CAJ has Spektor family records. A Spector family is included in *It Began with Zade Usher* (see Bernstein in Bibliography). Related to BOHMER.

SPEIER—See SPEYER.

SPEISER—UJ has article on Galician scholar Ephraim Speiser (b. 1902).

SPEKTOR—See SPECTOR.

SPERBER—UJ has article on Bukovinan scholar Alexander Sperber (b. 1897).

SPEWACK—UJ has article on Russian journalist Samuel Spewack (b. 1899); related to a COHEN family from Hungary. Also see SPIVAK.

SPEYER (also Speier)—German family from the town of Speyer, 16th cent. Another form of the name is SPIRA. Branches were known in England, Holland and U.S.A. in 1900. JE has a family tree and eight biographies. LBI has a family tree. Also see genealogy in *Stammtafeln der Familie Speyer*. Related to KULP, OPPENHEIM, STRAUS, FLORSHEIM, KANN, STERN, CAHN, HAMBURG, OETTINGER, FRANKEL, DAJAN, EMRICH, SAMSON, LECHNICH, TRAUMANN, ADLER, GUMPERTZ, GOLDSCHMIDT, STRUMPFLUG, RUBINO, ELLISSEN and GUMBERT.

SPICKLER—JE has article on German musician Max Spicker (1858–1912).

SPIEGEL—JE and UJ have biographies from 19th-cent. Hungary, Austria, Germany, Bohemia and U.S.A. AJA has a family tree from Chicago, beginning 1828. CAJ has some family records.

SPIEGELBERG—Early family in New Mexico, originally from Germany. UJ has five biographies. Related to SELIGMAN.

SPIELMAN—See SPIELMANN.

SPIELMANN (also Spielman)—Ashkenazic name meaning "player" in German. 19th-cent. English family; see JE and UJ. Isidore Spielmann (1854–1925) was a nephew of Samuel MONTAGU. See *The Early History of the Spielmann Family*. Also see biography in EJ article on "Chess." Related to MONTEFIORE and SAMUEL.

SPIERO—See SPIRA.

SPINGARN—UJ has two biographies from 19th–20th-cent. U.S.A.

SPINKA—EJ has article on Hasidic Rabbi Joseph Spinka (1838–1909), related to ZEVI.

SPINOZA—See ESPINOSA.

SPIR—See SPIRA.

SPIRA (also Spir, Spire, Spiro, Saphir, Sapir, Schapira, Schapiro, Shapera, Shapira, Shapiro, Spiero, etc.)—Ashkenazic name indicating descent from ancestors in the Bavarian town of Speyer. Many Jews with a variation of this name share a common ancestry, although they are not necessarily descended from Solomon Spira (14th cent.), a descendant of RASHI (1040–1105) and ancestor of the LURIA family. Variations of the name Spira were found in Bavaria, Bohemia and Poland in 17th cent., and in Russia beginning in 18th cent. See various biographies in JE, UJ and EJ. LBI has a Spira family tree beginning 1630, related to KAULLA and PRESSBURGER; a Spir family tree beginning 1639; and a Spiero family tree beginning 1700. PD has some Spiro family records. See a Spira family history in *Neue Beiträge zur Geschichte der Familie Frankel-Spira*. For a history of a Prague family of printers named Spira, descended from Jehiel Michael in 15th cent., see CB, p. 2629. For a Spira family history from Jungbunzlau, see *Jüdische Centralblatt*, by Grunwald, Vol. 7 (1888), p. 78. Also see JE articles on Riga, Latvia, and Grodno, Russia, the latter regarding 19th-cent. Rabbi Moses Shapiro, a son-in-law of Isaac of Slonim. Related names include LUBLIN, KOHEN, EYBESCHUTZ, PORGES, FRANKL, MIRELS, RESICHER, PINSKER, ASKENAZI, SCHAFIROFF, KORETZER, LIPMANN, FRANKEL, GREENHUT, KOHN, SOKOLOW, SOLOVEICHIK, CASE and ROSENFELD.

SPITZ—See SPITZER.

SPITZER (also Spitz, Shpitz)—Ashkenazic name taken from the town of Spitz in Austria. JE has biographies from 17th-cent. Moravia, 18th-cent. Hungary and 19th-cent. Austria, Hungary and France. Hungarian Rabbi Samuel Spitzer (1839–1896) was a descendant of Rabbi Yom-Tob HELLER; Benjamin Spitzer (d. 1893) was a son-in-law of Moses SCHREIBER. See family histories in JA, Vol. I, No. 3, p. 16; also *Die Nachkommen von Moses (Josef) Zweig*. Related to LOTHAR, SINKO, ZWEIG, FLECKELES, WOLF, POSNER and BICKELS-SPITZER.

SPIVACK—See SPIVAK.

SPIVAK (also Spivack)—UJ has four biographies from 19th–20th-cent. Russia. A Spivak family is included in *It Began with Zade Usher* (See Bernstein in Bibliography). Another variation of the name is SPEWACK.

SPRINGER—PD has some family records.

SPRINZENSTEIN—PD has some family records.

SRAFFA—UJ has article on Italian lawyer Angelo Sraffa (b. 1865).

STADTHAGEN (also Stathegen)—JE has article on German Rabbi Joseph Stadthagen (d. 1715), related to ASHKENAZI, BONN, HERZFELD AND ROTHSCHILD. Also related to MUNKACSY.

STAHL—JE has two biographies from 19th-cent. Germany.

STAHR—Related to LEWALD.

STALMASTER—UJ has article on U.S. Judge Irvin Stalmaster (b. 1897 in Russia).

STAMMBAUM—Related to ABRAHAM.

STAMPFER—EJ has article on Hungarian Rabbi Jehoshua Stampfer (1852–1908). CAJ has some family records.

STANCA—UJ has article on Rumanian physician Stefan Stanca (1865–1898), born STEIN.

STAND—UJ has article on Austrian deputy Adolf Stand (1870–1919), born in Galicia.

STANISLAVSKI—JE has article on Russian author Simon Stanislavski (b. 1850).

STARGARDT—LBIS has a family tree and notes.

STARK—UJ has article on U.S. cantor Edward Stark (1863–1918).

STARR—Related to STRENG.

STASSEVITCH—UJ has article on violinist Paul Stassevitch (b. 1894 in Russia).

STATHEGEN—See STADTHAGEN.

STAUB—JE has article on German jurist Hermann Staub (1856–1904).

STAURIANU—CAJ has some family records.

STEARN—Related to CRONBACH.

STEBLICKI (also Seblitzky)—JE has article on Joseph Steblicki (1726–1807), German convert to Judaism.

STECKERL (also Steckler)—JE has article on U.S. jurist Alfred Steckler (1856–1929). LBI has a Steckerl family tree.

STECKLER—See STECKERL.

STEFANN—UJ has article on Austrian music critic Paul Stefan (b. 1879).

STEG—See family history in *Denk ich an Deutschland in der Nacht: Die Geschichte des Hauses Steg.*

STEGMANN—Related to HERZFELD.

STEIMAN—EJ has article on Latvian poet Beynush Steiman (1897–1919).

STEIN—JE has biographies from 19th-cent. Germany and Hungary. LBI has family trees beginning 1700, 1756 and 1766, related to APPEL and KOHN. AJA has a family tree from Philadelphia, beginning 1795. Related names include GANS, STANCA and THALBERG.

STEINACH—UJ has article on Austrian physiologist Eugen Steinach (b. 1861). His family's name was ULLMANN until 1813.

STEINBACH—JE has two biographies from 19th-cent. Austria.

STEINBERG—JE has biographies from 19th-cent. Russia and Hungary. See family tree in *Genealogie de la famille Steinberg,* which traces a Steinberg family from 14th cent. onward.

STEINDAL—LBIS has some family notes.

STEINDLER—UJ has article on surgeon Arthur Steindler (b. 1878 in Vienna).

STEINDORFF—JE has article on German scholar Georg Steindorff (b. 1861).

STEINER—JE and UJ have biographies from 19th-cent. Germany, Austria and Czechoslovakia. AJA has a family tree beginning 1832, related to MAYER. Another related name is KOHN.

STEINFELD—JE has article on Australian statesman Emanuel Steinfeld (1827–1893), born in Silesia.

STEINHARDT (also Steinhart)—Ashkenazic name taken from the town of Steinhart in Bavaria. JE and UJ have biographies from 18th- and 19th-cent. Germany. Related to BERLIN and SELIGMAN.

STEINHART—See STEINHARDT.

STEINHAUS (also Steinhausen)—UJ has two biographies from 19th–20th-cent. Germany and Poland.

STEINHEIM—JE has article on German-Swiss physician Solomon Steinheim (1789–1866). LBI has a family tree beginning 1789. See family history in *Salomon Ludwig Steinheim, Gedenheim.*

STEINHERZ—CAJ has some family records.

STEINITZ—JE has two biographies from 19th-cent. Germany and Bohemia. LBI has family trees beginning 1751 and 1796. LBIS has some family notes.

STEINMAN—UJ has two biographies from 19th–20th-cent. Galicia and U.S.A.

STEINMETZ—UJ has article on U.S. scientist Charles Steinmetz (1865–1923), born in Germany.

STEINSCHNEIDER—JE has article on Austrian scholar Moritz Steinschneider (1816–1907). Related to MAGGID.

STEINTHAL—JE and UJ have biographies from 19th-cent. Germany. Hayim Steinthal (1823–1899) was the brother-in-law of Moritz LAZARUS. LBI has a family tree beginning 1720. See a family history in *Fünfhundert Jahre Familiengeschichte, 1430–1930.*

STEKEL—UJ has article on psychoanalyst Wilhelm Stekel (1868–1940), born in Vienna.

STERK—Related to SAMSON.

STERN (also Sterne)—JE and UJ have biographies from 18th-cent. Russia and Poland, 19th-cent. Germany, Latvia and Hungary. LBI has family trees beginning 17th cent., 1807, 1829, 1860. AJA has a family tree from Germany, Delaware and Philadelphia, related to BAMBERGER, FRIEDENWALD and GAGGSTATTER. CAJ and PD have some family records. See a family tree in *Stammtafel der Familie Abraham Stern;* also see family histories in JFF, Nos. 13 and 32. Related to GOLDSMID, WANDSWORTH, SPEYER, SELIGMAN, SAMSON, SLONIMSKY, LEVEN, SORS, CARLEBACH, WEIL, SZTERENYI.

STERNBERG—UJ has two biographies from 19th–20th-cent. Germany and Russia. LBI has a family tree beginning 1762. LBIS has some family notes. CAJD has a family tree from Germany, related to ADLER and SPIER. Another related name is BELMONT.

STERNE—See STERN.

STERNER—JE has article on English artist Albert Sterner (b. 1863).

STERNHARZ—EJ has article on Russian Hasid Nathan Sternharz (1780–1845).

STERNHEIM (also Sternheimer)—UJ has article on dramatist Carl Sternheim (1878–1943), born in Germany. LBI has a Sternheimer family tree beginning 1640.

STERNHELL—Related to ADLER.

STETTAUER (also Stettenheim, Stettheimer, Stettiner)—Ashkenazic names probably taken from the district of Stettin in Pomerania, where Jews first settled in 13th cent. UJ and JE have biographies from 19th–20th-cent. Germany. LBI has a Stettauer family tree beginning 1821. Stettheimer is related to SELIGMAN.

STETTENHEIM—See STETTAUER.

STETTHEIMER—See STETTAUER.

STETTINER—See STETTAUER.

STEUART—Related to MONTAGU.

STEUER (also Steuerman)—UJ has biographies from Hungary, Rumania and U.S.A., 19th–20th cent.

STEUERMAN—See STEUER.

STEUSS—Wealthiest Jewish family in Vienna prior to 1421. See UJ.

STIASSNY—JE has article on Austrian architect Wilhelm Stiassny (b. 1842).

STIBEL—See STIEBEL.

STIEBEL (also Stibel)—LBIS has some family notes. Stibel is related to ROTHSCHILD. Also see STYBEL.

STIEDRY—UJ has article on conductor Fritz Stiedry (b. 1883 in Vienna).

STIEFEL—Related to LEBOLD.

STIEGLITZ (also Stiglitz)—JE has three biographies from 18th-cent. Germany. LBI has family trees beginning 1710 and 1770, related to MARC. See family history in D. Stieglitz aus Arolsen, ihre Vorfahren

und Nachkommen. Stiglitz is a family of Russian barons of Jewish origin who came from Germany in 18th cent.; see UJ.

STIER—JE has article on German Rabbi Josef Stier (b. 1844 in Hungary).

STIGLITZ—See STIEGLITZ.

STILLER—JE has article on Hungarian physician Bertalan Stiller (1837–1922).

STILLING—JE has two biographies from 19th-cent. Germany.

STIX—AJA has a family tree beginning 1750.

STOCKL—Related to HEINEFETTER.

STOERK—See STORK.

STOKES—UJ has article on writer-artist Rose Stokes (1879–1933), born in Poland. Related to WIESLANDER.

STOKVIS—JE has article on Dutch physician Barend Stokvis (1834–1902).

STOLIAR (also Stoliarsky)—UJ has two biographies from 19th–20th-cent. Russia and Argentina.

STOLPER—UJ has article on economist Gustav Stolper (b. 1888 in Vienna).

STONE—UJ has six biographies from 19th–20th-cent. U.S.A., Lithuania and Russia. Seymour Stone (b. 1877) was the son of David KAMENIAV.

STORA—Algerian family dating from 15th cent.; see EJ. CAJ has some family records.

STORK (also Stoerk)—JE has article on Austrian scientist Karl Stork (1832–1869), born in Hungary. PD has some Stoerk family records.

von STOSCH—Related to SAMSON.

STOSSEL—UJ has article on painter Oscar Stossel (b. 1879 in Austria). Related to BANETH.

STRAKOSCH—JE has two biographies from 19th-cent. Austria and Hungary. PD has some family records. Related to PATTI.

STRANSKY—UJ has article on conductor Josef Stransky (1872–1936), born in Bohemia.

STRASBURGER (also Strassburger)—Name probably taken from the Alsatian city of Strassburg (or Strasbourg), where

Jews have lived since 1st cent., C.E. UJ has article on botanist Eduard Strasburger (1844–1912), born in Poland. Related to LOTH.

STRASCHUN—See STRASHUN.

STRASCHUNSKY—See STRASHUN.

STRASHUN (also Straschun, Straschunsky)—JE and UJ have biographies from 19th-cent. Russia and Latvia.

STRASSBURGER—See STRASBURGER.

STRASSER—PD has some family records.

STRASSMAN—Related to SAMSON.

STRAUCHER—UJ has article on attorney Benno Straucher (b. 1854 in Austria). CAJ has some family records.

STRAUS (also Strauss, Strausz, Strouse)—U.S. family originally from Otterberg, Germany, 18th cent.; there was also a Hungarian branch in 19th cent. See JE. JE also has other biographies from 19th-cent. Hungary, France, Germany. Also see UJ for a Strausz biography. LBI has Straus family trees beginning 1470 and 1815, and a Strauss family tree beginning 1658. AJA has a Straus family tree from Richmond, Virginia, related to HELLER. CAJD has a Strauss family tree from Germany. PD has some records of a Strauss family of Pressburg (Bratislava). See family histories in *The Descendants of Emanuel Straus and Fanny Heller Straus* and *Verzeichnis der von Hirsch Herz Straus aus Frankfurt-am-Main.* Related to SPEYER, HELLER and LEBRECHT.

STRAUSS (Strausz)—See STRAUS.

STREIT—UJ has article on writer Shalom Streit (b. 1889 in Galicia).

STRELISK (also Strelisker, Strelitz)—JE and EJ have biographies from 19th-cent. Russia, Austria and Rumania. Strelitz is related to ARNSTEIN.

STRELITZ—See STRELISK.

STRELSIN—UJ has article on U.S. industrialist Alfred Strelsin (b. 1898 in Russia).

STRENG—AJA has a family tree beginning 1817, from Louisville and Pittsburgh; related to LEVI and STAIR.

STRETYN—EJ has article on Galician Hasid Judah Stretyn (d. 1854).

STRICH (also Stricker)—UJ has biographies from 19th–20th-cent. Germany, Moravia and Hungary.

STRICKER—See STRICH.

STRNAD—UJ has article on Austrian architect Oscar Strnad (1879–1935).

STROM—Related to WARBURG.

STROUSBERG—JE has article on German industrialist Bethel Strousberg (1823–1884).

STROUSE—See STRAUS.

STRUCH (also Struck)—JE has article on German painter Hermann Struck (b. 1876). Struch is related to BONSENYOR.

STRUCK—See STRUCH.

STRUMPFLUG—Related to SPEYER.

STRUMZA—See ESTRUMSA.

STRUNSKY—UJ has article on U.S. editor Simeon Strunsky (b. 1879 in Russia).

STRUPP—UJ has article on jurist Karl Strupp (1886–1940), born in Germany.

STUCKHART—LBI has a family tree beginning 16th cent., related to FRAENKEL.

STUDENZKI—JE has article on 19th-cent. Polish physician Moses Studenzki, related to POLAK.

STURM—Ashkenazic name taken from the town of Szrem in Poland.

STURMDORF—UJ has article on U.S. gynecologist Arnold Sturmdorf (1862–1934), born in Vienna.

STURMHOEFEL—Related to LAZARUS.

STYBEL—UJ has article on merchant Abraham Stybel (b. 1885 in Poland). Also see STIEBEL.

SUAREZ—19th-cent. Egyptian banking family, of Spanish descent. See EJ.

SUASSO—Spanish family which had branches in Holland and England in 17th cent. JE has five biographies. JE article on "Coat of Arms" has the family crest. Related to COSTA, MELDOLA and TEIXEIRA.

SUBBOTIN—EJ has article on Russian economist Andrey Subbotin (1852–1906).

SUBER—LBIS has some family notes.

SUCHOSTAVER—JE has article on Galician teacher Mordecai Suchostaver (1790–1880).

SUCHOWOLSKY—Related to DANIN.

SUDFELD—Related to NORDAU.

SUESS—EJ has article on Austrian geologist Eduard Suess (1831–1914).

SUKEINIK—UJ has article on archaeologist Eleazar Sukenik (b. 1889 in Poland).

SULLAM—JE has article on Italian poet Sara Sullam (1592–1641), born COPPIO.

SULTANSKY—JE has article on Mordecai Sultansky (1785–1878), who died in the Crimea.

SULZBACH (also Sulzbacher)—JE and UJ have biographies from Germany and U.S.A., 19th–20th cent.

SULZBACHER—See SULZBACH.

SULZBERGER—American and German family which derives its name from the town of its origin, Sulzburg, near Regensburg in Bavaria. The family can be traced back to Eliezer Sulzberger (b. c. 1600). JE has a family tree and mentions twelve members. LBI has a family tree beginning 1570. Relatives include ADLER, AUB, BAYERSDORFER, BERNHARDT, EMDEN, FRANK, FALK, EINSTEIN, EINHORN, HAYS, HERZOG, KOHLER, LINDAUER, LOWENMAIER, POLLOCK, OCHS, MINZESHEIMER, ROSENHEIM, SCHLESINGER and WASSERMANN.

SULZER—Ashkenazic name taken from the town of Sollstadt. JE has article on Austrian cantor Salomon Sulzer (1804–1890), whose family was named LOEWY prior to 1813. Related to COWEN and GINGOLD.

SUMBAL—EJ has article on Moroccan diplomat Samuel Sumbal (d. 1782).

SUMMERFIELD—UJ has article on English jurist Woolfe Summerfield (b. 1897).

SUNDEL—See SUNDELES.

SUNDELES (also Sundel)—JE has article on 16th-cent. Polish scholar Zebi Sundeles, son-in-law of Mordecai MARDOS.

SUPINO—UJ has two biographies from 19th–20th-cent. Italy.

SURE—UJ has article on U.S. chemist Barnett Sure (b. 1891 in Lithuania).

SURGUN—EJ has article on Dutch East Indian merchant Isaac Surgun (1701–1791).

SUSAN—EJ has article on Moroccan Rabbi Issachar Susan (1510–1580) of Fez.

SUSMANN—See SUSSMANN.

SUSMANOVITZ—See SUSSMANN.

SUSS—Related to OPPENHEIMER.

SUSSKIND (also Siskind)—Ashkenazic name meaning "sweet child" in German. JE has article on German Alexander Susskind (d. 1307). Related to LEIDESDORFF, RIESSER and ROTHENBERG.

SUSSMANN (also Sussman, Susmann, Susmanovitz)—Ashkenazic name meaning "sweet man" in German. JE has four biographies from 18th-cent. Poland, Holland and Germany and 19th-cent. England. LBI has Sussmann family trees beginning 1755 and 1774, related to SCHOLEM, and a Susmann family tree beginning 1801, related to MARKREICH. CAJ has some Susmanovitz family records. Related to AUERBACH, LAUTERBACH and MAREES.

SUST—See MEYER-SUST.

SUTRO—JE has four biographies from 19th-cent. Germany, England and U.S.A.

SUTTON—AJA has a family tree, related to FAUTH and SEIXAS.

SUWALSKI—Name probably taken from the Polish city of Suwalki. EJ has article on writer Isaak Suwalski (1863–1913) of Kolno.

SUZIN—EJ has article on Jerusalem Rabbi Solomon Suzin (d. 1835).

SVAB—JE has article on Hungarian Karl Svab (d. 1829).

SVERDLOV—UJ has article on Russian Communist Iakov Sverdlov (1885–1919).

SWART—Related to MONTEFIORE.

SWARZENSKI—UJ has article on art historian Georg Swarzenski (b. 1876 in Germany).

SWAYTHLING—UJ has article on English banker Baron Swaythling (1832–1911), born Samuel MONTAGU.

SWIREN (also Zwirn)—UJ has article on U.S. Rabbi David Swiren (b. 1889 in Poland).

SYKES—UJ has article on U.S. Judge Philip Sykes (b. 1884 in Lithuania).

SYLVA—Portuguese family. JE article on "Coat of Arms" has the family crest. Also see SILVA.

SYLVESTER—JE has article on English mathematician James Sylvester (1814–1897).

SYMMONS—UJ has article on English Judge Alexander Symmons (1862–1923).

SYMONS—Related to GRATZ and MERZBACH.

de SYNAGOGA—See da SINAGOGA.

SYRKIN—See SIRKES.

SZABO—UJ has two biographies from 19th–20th-cent. Hungary.

SZABOLCSI—UJ has three biographies from 19th–20th-cent. Hungary. Related to WEINSTEIN.

SZALARDY—UJ has article on Hungarian welfare worker Mor Szalardy (1851–1914).

SZALIT (also Shalit)—UJ has article on painter Rahel Szalit (b. MARCUS in Lithuania, 1896).

SZANA—UJ has article on Hungarian physician Sandor Szana (1868–1926).

SZANTO—Name probably taken from the town of Szanto, Hungary. JE has two biographies from 19th-cent. Hungary and Austria.

SZARVADY—UJ has article on French publicist Frigyes Szarvady (1822–1882), born in Hungary.

SZASZY—UJ has article on Hungarian jurist Gusztav Szaszy-Schwarz (1858–1920). PD has records of the Szaszy family, related to SCHWARZ.

SZATENSZTEJN (also Shatton)—UJ has article on Polish official Wladyslaus Szatensztejn (b. 1893).

SZATMARI—UJ has article on Hungarian deputy Mor Szatmari (1856–1931).

SZEGO—UJ has article on mathematician Gabriel Szego (b. 1895 in Hungary).

SZEKELY—UJ has two biographies from Hungary and Transylvania, 19th–20th cent.

SZELL—UJ has article on conductor Georg Szell (b. 1897 in Hungary).

SZEMERE—UJ has article on Hungarian educator Samu Szemere (b. 1881).

SZENDE—UJ has article on Hungarian sociologist Pal Szende (1879–1930), a nephew of Ignac ACSADY.

SZENES (also Senesh)—JE has article on Hungarian painter Philip Szenes (b. 1864). Related to SCHLESINGER.

SZENKAR—UJ has article on conductor Eugen Szenkar (b. 1891 in Budapest).

SZEP (also Szeps)—UJ has two biographies from 19th–20th-cent. Hungary and Galicia. Austrian journalist Moritz Szeps (1834–1902) was father-in-law of CLEMENCEAU and ZUCKERKANDL.

SZERENCSES—JE and UJ have articles on Hungarian official Emerich Szerencses (d. 1526), originally named Zalman SHNEUR.

SZERESZOWSKI—UJ has article on Polish banker Raphael Szerezsowski (b. 1869).

SZIGETI—UJ has article on violinist Joseph Szigeti (b. 1892 in Hungary).

SZILAGYI—UJ has article on Hungarian poet Geza Szilagyi (b. 1875).

SZILASI—JE has article on Hungarian philologist Moriz Szilasi (1854–1905).

SZILI—JE has article on Hungarian ophthalmologist Adolf Szili (b. 1848).

SZIRMAI—See SIRMAY.

SZOLD—JE has two biographies from 19th-cent. Hungary and U.S.A. PD has some family records. Also see *The Szolds of Lombard Street.*

SZOLLOSI—UJ has article on Hungarian author Zsigmond Szollosi (b. 1872).

SZOMAHAZY—UJ has article on Hungarian journalist Istvan Szomahazy (1866–1927).

SZOMORY—UJ has article on Hungarian author Dezso Szomory (b. 1869).

SZONDI—UJ has article on neurologist Lipot Szondi (b. 1897 in Hungary).

SZTERENYI—UJ has article on Hungarian Jozsef Szterenyi (1861–1939), son of STERN, grandson of HIRSCH.

SZWARC—UJ has article on painter Marek Szwarc (b. 1892 in Poland).

SZYK—UJ has article on painter Arthur Szyk (b. 1894 in Poland).

TAAROA—Tahitian royal family which was interspersed with Jews. See UJ article on SALMON.

TABAK—EJ has article on Hungarian Solomon Tabak (1832–1908).

TABORI—JE and UJ have biographies from 19th–20th-cent. Hungary.

TACHAU—CAJ has a family history.

TAGLICHT—UJ has article on Rabbi Israel Taglicht (b. 1862 in Slovakia).

TAIKOS—JE has article on 18th-cent. German scholar Gedaliah Taikos.

TAIROFF—UJ has article on Russian theater director Alexander Tairoff (b. 1885).

TAITAZAK—Prominent Spanish family that moved to Salonika after 1492. JE has four biographies from 15th- and 16th-cent. Salonika.

TAKU—EJ has article on 13th-cent. Dachau Tosafist Moses Taku.

TAL—JE has article on Dutch Rabbi Tobias Tal (1847–1898).

TALKAR—JE has two biographies from 19th-cent. India.

TALMEY—UJ has article on U.S. physician Max Talmey (1869–1941), born in Russia.

TAM—JE has article on 15th-cent. Portuguese-Turkish Rabbi Jacob Tam.

TAMAKH—EJ supplemental volume has article on Spanish philosopher Abraham Tamakh (d. 1393).

TAMAR—Related to TEITELBAUM.

TAMARIN—Russian family that claims to have come into Judaism via the Khazar conversion (8th cent.) and to have taken its name from Tamara, queen of Georgia in 13th cent. This family is included in *A Link with the Future* (see Rottenberg in Bibliography).

TANDLER—UJ has article on Professor Julius Tandler (1869–1936), born in Moravia.

TANG—JE has article on 18th-cent. English author Abraham Tang.

TANNENBAUM—JE and UJ have biographies from 19th–20th-cent. Prussia, Austria and Hungary. Related to KATZ.

TANSMAN—UJ has article on composer Alexander Tansman (b. 1897 in Poland).

TANUJI—JE has article on 16th-cent. Egyptian Rabbi Ishmael Tanuji.

TANZER—JE has article on Austrian rabbi Aaron Tanzer (b. 1871 in Hungary). CAJ has some family records.

TARCZINER—See TORCZYNER.

TARD—Related to LOUSADA.

TARKLIS (also Terkel, Terk, Tuerkel)—Name meaning "from Turkey." Related to DELAUNAY-TERK.

TARNOFF—Name probably taken from the Galician town of Tarnow.

TARNOPOL—Name taken from the Galician city of Tarnopol. UJ has article on Russian reformer Joachim Tarnopol (1810–1900).

TARONJI Y CORTEZ—UJ has article on Majorcan poet Jose Taronji y Cortez (1847–1890), who may be a descendant of Raphael TERONGI (d. 1691).

TARRASCH—JE has article on German doctor Siegbert Tarrasch (1862–1934).

TARTAKOWER—UJ has two biographies from 19th–20th-cent. Galicia and Russia.

TAUB—Ashkenazic name from *Taube,* meaning "dove" in German.

TAUBENHAUS—UJ has article on U.S. plant pathologist Jacob Taubenhaus (1884–1937), born in Palestine.

TAUBENSCHLAG—UJ has article on U.S. law professor Rafael Taubenschlag (b. 1881 in Galicia).

TAUBER—UJ has article on tenor Richard Tauber (b. 1892 in Austria). CAJ has some family records.

TAUBES—JE has article on Rumanian Rabbi Aaron Taubes (1787–1852) born in Lemberg, Galicia.

TAUBLER—UJ has article on historian Eugen Taubler (b. 1879 in Poland).

TAUFFENBERGER—Related to OPPENHEIMER.

TAUSIG—See TAUSSIG.

TAUSK—See TAUSSIG.

TAUSSIG (also Tausig, Tausk)—JE, UJ and EJ have biographies from 19th-cent. U.S.A., Austria, Czechoslovakia and Poland. CAJ and PD have some family records. LBIS has a Tausk family tree, related to SACHS. Other relatives include BEER and AUSTERLITZ.

TAUWITZ—JE has article on German composer Eduard Tauwitz (1812–1894).

TAVUS (also Tawus)—EJ has article on 16th-cent. Persian translator Jacob Tavus.

TAWIL—See EJ article on *Abraham* ben Mordecai Ha-Levi, a relative.

TAWIOW—EJ has article on Russian author Israel Tawiow (1858–1920).

TAWRIZI—EJ has article on Karaite physician Judah Tawrizi (d. 1646).

TAWUS—See TAVUS.

TAWWAH—JE has article on 16th-cent. Algerian scholar Abraham Tawwah, related to DURAN.

TAYYIB—Tunisian family dating back to 17th cent. JE has four biographies.

TCHERNIAKOW—UJ has article on Polish martyr Adam Tcherniakow (1881–1942).

TCHERNOWITZ—UJ has article on author Chaim Tchernowitz (b. 1871 in Lithuania).

TEBELE—See JE article on *Moses* Judah Lob ben Samuel (d. 1889), father-in-law of Rabbi David Tebele of Minsk, Russia. Related to EPHRATI.

TEDESCHI—See TEDESCO.

TEDESCO (also Tedeschi)—The name means "German" in Italian. JE has biographies from 19th-cent. Italy, Austria and Russia. Related to DISRAELI, FINZI and PIRBRIGHT. Also see TODESCO.

TEEP—Related to WARBURG.

TEGLIO—Related to ALEGRE.

TEHINA—JE has article on zealot leader Abba Tehina.

TEICHHOLZ—CAJ has some family records.

TEITEL—UJ has article on Russian Judge Jacob Teitel (1850–1940).

TEITELBAUM—JE and UJ have articles on Galician Hasid Moses Teitelbaum, who signed his name TAMAR and claimed descent from Moses ISSERLES. Also related to LIPSCHUTZ.

TEIXARA—See TEIXEIRA.

TEIXEIRA (also Teixara, Texeira, Teixeyra)—Noble Portuguese Marrano family whose name was originally SAMPAYO. In 1900, members were in Hamburg, London, Holland, Vienna and Venice. See JE, which has three biographies beginning 17th cent. Also see family histories in JFF, Nos. 17 and 29, and AJF, 1912, p. 5. JE article on "Coat of Arms" has the family crest. Related to ABOAB, GOMEZ and SUASSO.

TEIXEYRA—See TEIXEIRA.

TELCS—JE has article on Hungarian sculptor Eduard Telcs (b. 1872).

TELLER—JE and EJ have biographies from 17th-cent. Bohemia and 19th-cent. Hungary. A Bavarian Teller family is traced in *Teller Family in America, 1842–1942*. Related to ANATHAN, GOLDBERG, HACKENBURG, HECHT, LORSCH and MAYER.

TELLHEIM—Related to BETTELHEIM.

TELTSCHER—PD has some family records.

TEMERLS—JE has article on German Talmudist Jacob Temerls (d. 1667 in Vienna), also known as ASHKENAZI.

TEMKIN—UJ has article on Polish poet Mordecai Temkin (b. 1891), a descendant of Perez SMOLENSKIN and Abraham EGER.

TEMPLE—Related to LEWIS.

TEMPLER—JE has article on Austrian theologian Bernhard Templer (b. 1865).

TEMPLO—EJ has article on Dutch Rabbi Judah Templo (1603–1675). Related to LEON.

TENCZER—JE has article on Hungarian author Paul Tenczer (1836–1905).

TENENBAUM—UJ has article on U.S. physician Joseph Tenenbaum (b. 1887 in Poland).

TE'OMIM (also Theomim, Theomin)—Family in 16th-cent. Poland and 17th-cent. Bohemia. JE has eight biographies. PD has Theomim family records. See family histories in MGWJ, Vol. 55 (1911), p. 355, and *Die Identität der Familien Theomim und Munk*. Also see EJ article on FRANKEL. Other relatives are MUNK, OPPENHEIM, BENJAMIN, ZUNZ and ZINZ.

TEPPER—UJ has article on painter Joseph Tepper (b. 1886 in Russia).

TERK—See TARKLIS.

TERKEL—See TARKLIS.

TERNI—JE has two biographies from 18th-cent. Italy.

TERONGI—JE has article on Majorcan martyr Raphael Terongi (d. 1691). He may be the ancestor of TARONJI; see UJ.

TERQUEM—JE has article on French mathematician Olry Terquem (1782–1862).

TERRACINO—JE has four biographies from 17th-cent. Italy.

TERRAMARE—PD has some family records.

TERRIS—Related to LEWIN.

TERRY—Related to NEILSON.

TETIEVSKY—See *It Began with Zade Usher* (see Bernstein in Bibliography).

TEUTSCH—LBI has family trees beginning 1590 and 1725. Also see *Geschichte der Juden der Gemeinde Venningen— Familie Teutsch von 1590–1936.*

TEWELES—JE has article on Austrian dramatist Heinrich Teweles (1856–1927), born in Prague.

TEXEIRA—See TEIXEIRA.

THALBERG—EJ has article on Geneva pianist Sigismund Thalberg (1812–1870), related to STEIN.

THALMESSINGER—UJ has article on U.S. merchant Meyer Thalmessinger (1829–1906), born in Germany. LBI has a family tree beginning 1772.

THAUSING—UJ has article on Austrian art historian Moritz Thausing (1838–1884).

THEBEN—JE has article on Koppel Theben, president of the Jews of Pressburg (d. 1799 in Prague). PD has some family records. See family history in JFF, No. 5. Related to MANDL.

THEILHABER—UJ has article on author Felix Theilhaber (b. 1884 in Germany).

THEMAL—LBI has a family tree beginning 1773.

THEMANS—CAJ has a family tree from the Netherlands, 1745 to 1956.

THEODOR (also Theodore)—JE has article on German Rabbi Julius Theodor (1849–1923). Related to MENKEN.

THEOMIM (Theomin)—See TE'OMIM.

THIBAULT—UJ has article on French writer Anatole France, born Anatole Thibault. His maternal grandmother was Jewish.

THIEL—UJ has article on Swedish banker Ernst Thiel (b. 1859). LBIS has some family notes.

THOMAS—JE has article on German actor Emile Thomas (b. 1836).

THOMASHEFSKI (also Thomashefsky)— JE has article on U.S. actor Boris Thomashefsky (1866–1939), born in Kiev, Russia.

THON—UJ has five biographies from 19th–20th-cent. Galicia. Henryka Thon married HUSS.

THOREK—UJ and EJ have articles on U.S. surgeon Max Thorek (b. 1880 in Hungary). See his autobiography, *A Surgeon's World.*

THORMAN—JE has article on Simson Thorman from Bavaria, the first Jew in Cleveland, Ohio, 1837; see JE article on Cleveland.

THORSCH—LBI has family trees beginning 1771, 1809, 1829 and 1861.

THURNAUER—Related to FECHHEIMER and KOPPEL.

TIBBON—French family dating back to 12th cent.; see EJ. Related to ANATOLI.

TIETZ (also Tietze)—JE and UJ have biographies from 19th–20th-cent. Germany and Austria. See a family history in *Hermann Tietz: Geschichte einer Familie.*

TIKTIN (also Tiktiner, Tiktinski)—Name taken from the Polish town of Tiktin. JE has biographies from 16th-cent. Austria, 18th-cent. Russia and Silesia, and 19th-cent. Lithuania. CAJ has some family records. Related to BLOCH.

TIKTINER—See TIKTIN.

TIKTINSKI—See TIKTIN.

TINNEY—AJA has a family tree in Utah, traced back to King DAVID.

TIOMKIN—EJ has article on Russian Zionist Vladimir Tiomkin (1861–1927).

TIRADO—JE has article on 16th-cent. scholar Jacob Tirado of Amsterdam. Related to FARRAR.

TISCHEBOW—Ashkenazic name, common in Riga, Latvia; taken from *tisha b'Av,* "the ninth of Ab."

TISCHLER—UJ has article on Austrian-American painter Victor Tischler (b. 1890).

TISHBI—JE has article on 16th-cent. Karaite scholar Judah Tishbi, from Belgrade.

TIVOLI—EJ has article on Italian painter Serafino da Tivoli (1826–1890). Related to ANAW.

TOBENKIN—UJ has article on U.S. journalist Elias Tobenkin (b. 1882 in Russia).

TOBIAS—UJ has article on English novelist Lily Tobias, born SHEPHERD. Another related name is MINIS.

TOCH—UJ has three biographies from 19th–20th-cent. Austria and U.S.A.

TOCKELS—JE has article on German Talmudist Mordecai Tockels (d. 1743), also known as LISSER. Related to RIES and SALMAN.

TODESCO (also Todesko)—JE has article on Austrian financier Austrian Todesco (1792–1844). PD has Todesco and Todesko family records. Related to WORMS. Also see TEDESCO.

TOKATYAN—UJ has article on tenor Armand Tokatyan (b. 1898 in Bulgaria).

TOLEDANO (also de Toledo)—Spanish family name taken from the city of Toledo, Spain, where Jews first settled in 6th cent. In 1900, family members were found living in Salonika, Jerusalem, Turkey, Africa, Holland and England. JE has nineteen biographies beginning in 16th cent. See family history in Zunz GL, p. 440.

de TOLEDO—See TOLEDANO.

TOLLER—UJ has article on socialist Ernst Toller (1893–1939), born in Germany.

TOLNAI—UJ has article on Hungarian publisher Simon Tolnai (b. 1867).

TOMASHOV—JE has article on 17th-cent. Polish Rabbi Jacob Tomashov.

TORCZYNER (also Tarcziner)—UJ has article on Bible scholar Harry Torczyner (b. 1886 in Poland). Related to CORDOVERO.

TORDESILLAS—JE has article on 14th-cent. Spanish controversialist Moses Tordesillas.

TORNAI (also Tornay)—UJ has article on Hungarian painter Gyula Tornai (1861–1928). PD has some family records.

TORNOW—Related to ROBERT.

TOROK—UJ has article on Hungarian dermatologist Lajos Torok (b. 1863).

TORRE (also Torre-Lombardini)—JE has article on Italian rabbi Hillel Torre (1805–1871), related to HA-KOHEN and TREVES. Other related names are EMBDEN, DELLA TORRE and PINTO.

TORRES—UJ has biographies from 15th-cent. Spain and 19th–20th-cent. France. Henry Torres (b. 1891) was a grandson of Isaie LEVAILLANT. Related to de SOLA.

de TOUR—Related to GOMEZ.

TOURO—JE has article on U.S. philanthropist Judah Touro (1775–1854). See also *The Touro Family in Newport*. Related to HAYS.

TOUROFF—UJ has article on writer Nisson Touroff (b. 1877 in Russia). Related to GLUECK.

TOWNE—See biography in EJ article on "Art."

TRABOT (also Trabotti, Trabotta)—Italian family dating from 15th cent. JE has nineteen biographies. Related to COLON, GRACIANO, GRAZIANO, AZRIEL and ZARFATI.

TRABOTTA (Trabotti)—See TRABOT.

TRACHTENBERG (also Trajtenberg)—JE has article on Russian jurist Herman Trachtenberg (1839–1895). CAJ has some Trajtenberg family records.

TRAJTENBERG—See TRACHTENBERG.

TRANI—Spanish family traced back to 15th cent., descended from an Italian family dating from 12th cent. See UJ and JE.

TRAUB (also Traube, Traubel)—*Traube* means "grape" in German. JE has biographies from 19th-cent. Germany and U.S.A. LBIS has some Traub family notes.

TRAUBE—See TRAUB.

TRAUBEL—See TRAUB.

TRAUGOTT—LBIS has a family tree and notes.

TRAUMANN—Related to SPEYER.

TREBINO (also Tremino)—JE has article on Tomas Trebino, martyr burned in Mexico or Lima, 1649. Related to GOMEZ.

TREBITSCH (also Trebitz)—Ashkenazic name taken from the Austrian town of Trebisch. JE and UJ have biographies from 18th- and 19th-cent. Austria and 19th-cent. Hungary. CAJ has some family records. Related to BRULL.

TREFOUSE—See TREVES.

TREFUS—See TREVES.

TREMELLIUS—JE has article on Italian Hebraist John Tremellius (1510–1580).

TREMINO—See TREBINO.

TRENEL—JE has article on French Rabbi Isaac Trenel (1822–1890).

TREU—UJ has article on German painter Marquard Treu (1712–1796), born NATHAN.

TREUENWART—PD has some family records.

TREVES (also Trefus, Trevis, Trivash, Tribas, Trefouse)—Family which derives its name from Trier (Treves), Germany, the town of its origin. The name later evolved into DREYFUS. This is one of the few families that can authentically claim descent from RASHI (1040–1105). Rabbi Joseph Treves of Marseilles, 14th cent., was a descendant of Judah Sir Leon of Paris (1166–1224), a great-great-great-grandson of Rashi. Joseph had three sons, and a daughter who married Samuel SPIRA, ancestor of the LURIA and KATZENELLENBOGEN families. (See charts on pages 13 and 14.) JE has a family tree beginning in 13th-cent. Italy and forty-one biographies, beginning in 14th-cent. France and 15th-cent. Germany, Greece and Poland. PD has some family records. See family histories and trees in *Eileh Toledot*, by N. Rosenstein, 1969 (in English), "The Treves Family in England: A Genealogical Sketch," in the *Jewish Chronicle;* and VR, Vol. 2, p. 261. JE article on "Coat of Arms" has a family crest. Related to TORRE, DRIFZAN, ZARFATI, FRANKFURT, HAYYIM, COLON, BRISKER, ASHKENAZI, VESOUL, GERSHON and GREENHUT. A possible variation is TRIWOSCH.

TREVINO de SOBREMONTE—EJ has article on Mexican martyr Thomas Trevino de Sobremonte (1592–1649).

TREVIS—See TREVES.

TRIBAS—See TREVES.

TRIEBER—UJ has article on U.S. jurist Jacob Trieber (d. 1927), born in Germany.

TRIER—Danish family dating from 18th cent., probably deriving its name from the German city of Trier. JE has five biographies. LBI has a family tree beginning 1807. LBIS has some family notes. Related to BALLIN, MELCHIOR and MEYER.

TRIESCH—JE has article on Austrian dramatist Fredrich Triesch (b. 1845).

TRIESTE—Name probably taken from the city of Trieste. JE has article on Italian merchant Gabriel Trieste (1784–1860).

TRIETSCH—UJ has article on Zionist writer David Trietsch (1870–1935), born in Germany.

TRILLINGER—JE has article on 17th-cent. Austrian Rabbi Eliezar Trillinger, also known as NIN. Related to YOSPA.

TRIOUFO—Related to JOAB.

TRIVALE—UJ has article on essayist Ion Trivale (1889–1917), born NETZLER in Rumania.

TRIVASH—See TREVES.

TRIWOSCH—JE has article on Russian writer Joseph Triwosch from Vilna (b. 1856). The name is perhaps a variation of TREVES.

TROKENHEIM—UJ has article on Polish Senator Jacob Trokenheim (b. 1879).

TROKI—Ashkenazic name taken from the town of Troki, Russia, in 16th cent. JE has six biographies. Related to MALINOVSKI and NISSIM.

TROPPLOWITZ—Related to HA-EFRATI.

TROTSKY—Russian Communist Leon Trotsky (1879–1940) was born BRONSTEIN.

TRUMPELDOR—UJ has article on Zionist leader Joseph Trumpeldor (1880–1920), born in Russia.

TRUNK—UJ has article on writer J. J. Trunk (b. 1887 in Poland).

TRUSKER—UJ has article on Polish Senator Adolf Trusker (b. 1871).

TSANIN—CAJ has some family records.

TSCHERIKOWER—CAJ has some family records.

TSCHERNIKOWSKI—UJ has article on poet Saul Tschernikowski (b. 1875).

TSCHLENOW—UJ has article on Zionist leader Jehiel Tschlenow (1864–1918), born in Lithuania.

TSCHITKIS—See CZATZKES.

TSION—See CYON.

TUCH (also Tuchmann, Tuchner, Tuck, Tucker, etc.)—Ashkenazic name taken from the town of Touque in France. JE and UJ have biographies from 19th–20th-cent. France, England and Russia. LBI has a Tuchmann family tree beginning 1774. Relatives include KALISH and LEBRECHT.

TUCHMANN—See TUCH.

TUCHNER—See TUCH.

TUCHOLSKY—UJ has article on satirist Kurt Tucholsky (1890–1935), born in Berlin.

TUCK (Tucker)—See TUCH.

TUERKEL—See TARKLIS.

TUGEL—See biography in EJ article on "Dance."

TUGENDHOLD—JE has two biographies from 18th- and 19th-cent. Russia.

TULL—JE has article on Hungarian artist Edmund Tull.

TUNKEL—UJ has article on writer Joseph Tunkel (b. 1881 in Russia).

TUR—JE has article on Russian Hebraist Naphtali Tur (d. 1885), who lived in Warsaw.

TURIQUE—Related to BERR.

TURKOV—Related to KAMINSKI.

TURNER—Related to PALGRAVE.

TUROCZI-TROSTLER—UJ has article on Hungarian educator Jozsef Turoczi-Trostler (b. 1888).

TURTELTAUB—Ashkenazic name meaning "turtle dove" in German, JE has article on Austrian physician Wilhelm Turteltaub (b. 1816).

TUSKA—Active U.S. family which came from Germany in 19th cent. See UJ.

TUWIM—UJ has article on Polish poet Julian Tuwim (b. 1894). CAJ has some family records.

TVERSKY (Twerski)—See TWERSKY.

TWERSKY (also Tversky, Twerski)—Name taken from Tveria (Tiberias) in Israel. See family history in *Sefer Ha-yahas mi-Tshernobil ve-Rozin.* Also see EJ and UJ articles on *David* of Talna and *David ben Mordecai* (Russia, 1808–1882), a relative. Related to FRYDMAN.

TYGEL—UJ has article on U.S. writer Zelig Tygel (b. 1890 in Poland).

UCEDA—JE has article on 16th-cent. Palestinian Rabbi Samuel Uceda.

UDELL—Ashkenazic variation of the name Judah.

UFENHEIMER—LBIS has some family notes.

UGOLINO—JE has article on Italian Blaisio Ugolino (b. 1700).

UHLFELDER—LBI has a family tree beginning 1712. Related to SELIGMAN.

UJVARI—UJ has article on Hungarian author Peter Ujvari (1869–1931), son of Wolf GROSZMAN.

ULIF—Related to ASHKENAZI.

ULLMAN—See ULLMANN.

ULLMANN (also Ullman, Ulm, Ulma, Ulman, Ulmann)—Ashkenazic name usually taken from the German city of Ulm in Württemberg, where Jews were living before the Christian era. JE and UJ have biographies from 19th-cent. Hungary, Germany, France and U.S.A. CAJ has Ullman family records; PD has Ullmann family records. Related to GUNZBURG, GAGGSTATTER, AMBACH, RAFF, STEINACH.

ULLSTEIN—Family of publishers in Berlin. UJ has biographies from 19th–20th-cent. Germany and U.S.A. LBI has family trees beginning 1503 and 1792, related to KALONYMUS.

ULM (Ulma)—See ULLMANN.

ULMAN (Ulmann)—See ULLMANN.

ULTON—Related to POLLOCK.

UMANI—Related to ANAW.

UNGAR—See UNGER.

UNGER (also Ungar, Ungvar)—Ashkenazic name indicating Hungarian origin. JE, UJ and EJ have biographies from 19th-cent. Hungary, Austria and Germany. Related to EISENSTADT, KATSCHER, PAKE and WEISS.

UNGVAR—See UNGER.

UNNA—JE has article on German physician Paul Unna (1850–1929). LBIS has a family tree, and CAJ has some family records. See a family history in *Geschichte der Familie Unna (Hamburg-Kopenhagen)*. Related to JACOB, MELCHIOR and PHILIPP.

UNSHLIKHT—UJ has article on Revolutionary Iosif Unshlikht (b. 1879 in Poland).

UNTERBERG—UJ has article on U.S. manufacturer Israel Unterberg (1863–1934), born in Lithuania.

URBACH—A variation of AUERBACH. UJ has article on physician Erich Urbach (b. 1893 in Prague). Related to KOHN.

URBINO—Italian family traced back to the city of the same name, 14th cent. JE has seven biographies.

URDANG—UJ has article on pharmacist George Urdang (b. 1882 in Germany).

URI—AJA has a family tree beginning 1819, related to WALLERSTEIN.

URWICZ—See HOROVITZ.

URY—JE and UJ have biographies from 19th–20th-cent. Alsace and Germany.

USISHKIN (also Ussishkin)—JE has article on Russian Zionist Michael Usishkin (1863–1941).

USQUE—Spanish family which took its name from its town of Huesca and which migrated to Portugal and Italy in 15th cent. JE has three biographies. Related to GOMEZ, LUSITANO, PINEL and SALUSQUE.

USSISHKIN—See USISHKIN.

UTIZ—Related to SCHUER.

UZAN—North African family dating from 18th cent. See EJ.

UZIEL—Family name found primarily in Spain, 15th cent., and in North Africa and Italy thereafter. JE has seven biographies.

VADAS—UJ has article on Hungarian attorney Lipot Vadasz (1861–1924).

VAEZ—Portuguese family living in Lisbon, 16th cent. JE has seven biographies. Related to MENDES and NUNES.

VAGFALVA—Related to QUITTNER.

VAGO—UJ has article on Hungarian official Bela Vago (b. 1891).

VAHL—See WAHL.

VAIS—Related to NUNES.

VAJDA—UJ has article on Hungarian writer Ernest Vajda (b. 1886).

VALABREGUE—Well-known family of southern France which dates back to 14th cent.; also known as AULBREGUE. See UJ. JE has article on French dramatist Albin Valabregue (1853–1936).

VALENSI—Sephardic family that left Spain in 15th cent. and went to Marrakesh, Tunis, Venice and U.S.A. The name is probably taken from the Spanish city of Valencia, where Jews first settled in Moorish times.

VALENTIN (also Valentine, Vallentin, Vallentine)—JE has articles from 19th-cent. Germany and England. LBI has family trees beginning 1430 and 1683. CAJ has some family records, 1810 to 1883. See family history in *Geschichte der Familien Valentin, Loewen und Manheimer-Behrend*. Related to MANHEIMER, SOLIS and VALETTI.

VALENTINE—See VALENTIN.

VALERIO—JE has article on 16th-cent. Greek author San Valerio.

VALERIUS—UJ has article on 17th-cent. Italian physician David Valerius.

VALERO—Sephardic family originally from Constantinople; in Jerusalem from 19th cent. See EJ.

VALETTI—UJ has article on German actress Rosa Valetti (1878–1937), born VALLENTIN.

VALI (also Valle)—JE has article on 18th-cent. Italian Rabbi Moses Vali.

VALLE—See VALI.

VALLENTIN (Vallentine)—See VALENTIN.

VALLS—JE has article on Spanish Marrano Raphael Valls (d. 1691).

VALOBRA—UJ has article on Italian scientist Sansome Valobra (b. 1883).

VAMBERY—JE and UJ have articles on Hungarian scholar Arminius Vambery (1832–1913), whose family name was WAMBERGER, originally BAMBERGER. He married Cornelia ARANYI, niece of Joseph JOACHIM.

VAN DEN BERGH—Dutch family of industrialists. UJ has five biographies from 19th and 20th cent.

VAN GELDERN—Related to EMBDEN.

VAN HARD—Related to BERNHARDT.

VAN OVEN—English 18th-cent. family, originally from the Dutch town of Oven. JE has three biographies. Related to BASAU.

VAN PRAAG (also Van Praagh)—JE and UJ have biographies from 19th–20th-cent. Holland and England.

VAN RAALTE—EJ has article on Dutch lawyer Eduard Van Raalte (1841–1921).

VAN RIJK—UJ has article on Dutch actress Esther Van Rijk (1853–1937), who married Henri de BOER.

VAN STRAALEN—JE has article on English Hebraist Samuel Van Straalen (1845–1902), born in Holland.

VARGA—UJ has article on Hungarian economist Evgenii Varga (b. 1897).

VARNAI—UJ has article on Hungarian poet Zseni Varnai (b. 1881), who married Andor PETERDI.

VARNHAGEN—UJ has article on German socialite Rahel Varnhagen von Ense (1771–1833), born LEVIN, later FRIEDERIKE. Related to ASSER and ROBERT.

VARSHAVSKI—See WARSCHAUER.

VAZ—Related to BELMONTE.

VAZ DIAS—Dutch family of Marrano descent that can be traced back to 1760. See UJ. Related to PENHA.

VAZONYI (also Vazsonyi)—JE and UJ have biographies from 19th–20th-cent. Hungary.

VECCHIO—Italian family dating from the time of the Second Temple (70 C.E.). JE has five biographies.

VECINHO (also Vizino)—JE has article on 15th-cent. Portuguese scientist Joseph Vecinho.

VEGA—JE has article on 16th-cent. Rabbi Judah Vega from Amsterdam.

VEIGELSBERG—JE has article on Hungarian publicist Leo Veigelsberg (1846–1907).

VEIL—See WEIL.

VEINGER—EJ has article on Russian and Polish scholar Mordecai Veinger (1892–1929).

VEIT (also Veitel, Veith)—JE and EJ have biographies from 18th-cent. Germany and 19th-cent. Austria. LBI has family trees beginning 1669 and 1758, related to SIMON. CAJ has Veit and Veitel family records. Related to DAVID, HOCK, MENDELSSOHN, SANDERS and SINGER.

VEITEL—See VEIT.

VEITH—See VEIT.

VELASCO—See BELASCO.

VELTWYCK—EJ has article on German apostate Gerard Veltwyck (d. 1555).

VENETIANER (also Veneziani)—Name probably derived from Venice, Italy. JE has biographies from 19th-cent. Hungary, Italy and France.

VENEZIANI—See VENETIANER.

VENGEROV (Vengerova)—See WENGEROFF.

VENTINA—Related to MONTEFIORE.

VENTURA (also Venture)—Family name in 16th-cent. Italy and Greece; the name Venture appears in 18th-cent. France. JE has eleven biographies.

VENTURE—See VENTURA.

VEPRIK—UJ has article on composer Alexander Veprik (b. 1899 in Russia).

VERA Y ALARCON—JE has article on 17th-cent. Spanish martyr Lope de Vera y Alarcon.

VERBLOVSKI—JE has article on 19th-cent. Russian jurist Gregori Verblovski.

VERCELLI—CAJ has some family records.

VEREA—UJ has article on poet Adrian Verea (b. 1876 in Rumania).

VERVEER (also Verweer)—Dutch painting family of 19th cent. JE has two biographies.

VERWEER—See VERVEER.

VESOUL—Related to TREVES.

VESZI—JE has article on Hungarian editor Joseph Veszi (1858–1939).

VIDA—UJ has article on Hungarian deputy Jeno Vida (b. 1872).

VIDAL (also Vidal-Naquet)—Portuguese family. JE article on "Coat of Arms" has the family crest. JE also has article on French financier Samuel Vidal-Naquet (b. 1859). Related to CRESCAS and NAQUET.

VIDAS—JE has article on 15th-cent. Spanish scholar Samuel Vidas.

VIERFELDER—LBI has a family tree beginning 1693.

VIERTEL—UJ has article on U.S. writer Berthold Viertel (b. 1884 in Vienna).

VIGDER (Vigdor)—See ABIGDOR.

VIGDOROWITZ—See ABIGDOR.

VIGDORTSHIK—See ABIGDOR.

VILLA-REAL—Family of Portuguese notables; see EJ. Related to COSTA, DISRAELI and FERNANDEZ.

VINAWER—EJ has article on Russian lawyer Maxim Vinawer (1862–1926).

VINER—UJ has article on economist Jacob Viner (b. 1892 in Canada).

VINSHNUPSKY—Family from Suwalki, Poland, is mentioned in *A Link with the Future* (see Rottenberg in Bibliography).

VISONTAI—UJ has article on Hungarian lawyer Soma Visontai (1854–1925).

VISSER—UJ has article on Dutch Judge Lodewijk Visser (1871–1942).

VITABO—Roman family; see history in VR, Vol. 2, p. 262.

VITAL—Italian family dating from 16th cent.; JE has six biographies. Also see UJ. Hayim Vital was also known as CALABRESE. Related to PINTO.

VITERBI—See VITERBO.

VITERBO (also Viterbi)—UJ and EJ have biographies from 17th- and 19th-cent. Italy. CAJ has some Viterbi family histories.

VITKIN—EJ has article on Russian Zionist Joseph Vitkin (1876–1912).

VITORIA—EJ has article on Marrano prelate Francisco de Vitoria (d. 1592), related to ABOAB and CURIEL.

VIVANTE—See VIVANTI.

VIVANTI (also Vivante)—UJ has biographies from 19th–20th-cent. Italy. CAJ has some family records.

VIVES—EJ has article on Spanish humanist Juan Vives (1492–1540). Also see ABEN-VIVES.

VIZHNITZ—Hasidic dynasty in 19th-cent. Russia; see EJ. Related to HAGER and MENDEL.

VIZINO—See VECINHO.

VLADECK—UJ has article on U.S. socialist Baruch Vladeck (1886–1938), born CHARNEY in Russia.

VOGAU—Related to PILNIAR.

VOGEL—JE has article on London agent Sir Julius Vogel (1835–1899), who also lived in New Zealand. Related to MORRIS and SCHIFF.

VOGELSTEIN—German rabbinic family from 19th-cent. Bohemia; see JE. LBI has a family tree beginning 1729.

VOGUE—UJ has article on French historian Charles Vogue (1829–1916), born MELCHIOR.

VOLOV—See WAHL.

VOLOZHINER—EJ has article on Russian Rabbi Hayyim Volozhiner (1749–1821).

VOLPE—Ashkenazic name taken from Wolpia in Poland. UJ has article on U.S. conductor Arnold Volpe (1869–1940), born in Lithuania. Another variation of the name is WOLPER.

VOLTERRA—JE and UJ have biographies from Italy, 15th, 18th and 19th cent. CAJ has some family records.

VOLYNSKY—See biography in EJ article on "Dance."

VON ADLERSTHAL—Related to KREMSER.

VON HALLE—Related to WARBURG.

VON HONIG—Related to WOLFF.

VON MISES—Related to BERNSTEIN.

VOORSANGER—JE has article on U.S. Rabbi Jacob Voorsanger (1852–1908), from Amsterdam.

VORONOFF—UJ has article on surgeon Serge Voronoff (b. 1866 in Russia).

VOS—See biography in EJ article on "Politics."

VOSS—Related to WARBURG.

VOZNITSYN—EJ has article on Russian sailor Alexander Voznitsyn (d. 1738).

VRIES (also Vriesland)—UJ has three biographies from 19th–20th cent. Holland.

VRIESLAND—See VRIES.

WAAGENAR—See WAGENAAR.

WACHSTEIN—UJ has article on Austrian historian Bernhard Wachstein (1868–1935), born in Galicia.

WACHTEL—UJ has article on painter William Wachtel (b. 1875 in Galicia).

WAGENAAR (also Waagenaar)—EJ has article on Dutch Rabbi Lion Wagenaar (1855–1930). CAJ has some Wagenaar family records. Related to MULDER. A variation of the name may be WAGNER.

WAGG—UJ has article on Alexander Wagg of Germany (1719–1803), who married Rachel GOMEZ; his mother's maiden name was HART.

WAGHALTER—Family of musicians, traced back to the Polish violinist Laibisch Waghalter (1790–1868), descendant of a Spanish family. See UJ.

WAGNER—UJ has article on Danish sculptor Siegfried Wagner (b. 1874 in Germany). CAJ has a family history. Also see WAGENAAR.

WAHL (also Vahl, Wohl)—Ashkenazic name meaning "ox." Variations in other languages, some of which are related, are OCHS, SCHOR, BYK and VOLOV. Polish and Russian Jews with this name can probably trace their ancestry to Saul Wahl (1541–1617) of the KATZENELLEN-BOGEN family, a prominent Polish citizen and, according to some accounts, king of Poland for a one-day interim period. Saul married Deborah DRUCKER and had five sons and six daughters, and their grandchildren married SCHOR, BEINOS, KALISHER and DELTAS. A Wohl family of Lithuania was descended from Saul Wahl; other descendants include LYON, HIRSCH-

FELD, BARNETT, HERSCHEL, PIRBRIGHT, PHILLIPS, GOLDSMID, MONTAGUE, SAMUEL, ADLER, FRANKEL, VAHL, RIESSER, WOLK, MINZ, HOROWITZ, AUERBACH, HEILPRIN and HELMAN. See *Records of the Samuel Family;* also family history in JFF, Nos. 4 and 6. JE and EJ have biographies from Poland and Germany. LBI has a family tree beginning 1617, related to EGER and LEIDESDORF. PD has Wahl and Wohl family records. JE article on "Coat of Arms" has a Vahl family crest. Also see JE article on Kholm. Other relatives are JAFFE, MAGGID, REINES, MUNZ, ORNSTEIN, LEVINSON and SCHIFF.

WAHLTUCH—JE has two biographies from 19th-cent. Russia.

WAHREN—LBIS has a family tree and notes.

WAHRMANN—JE has four biographies from 18th-cent. Hungary and 19th-cent. Russia. PD has some family records.

WAIFE—Related to GOLDBERG.

WAINER—UJ has article on Argentine official Jacobo Wainer (b. 1896).

WAKRULKAR—JE has article on Indian soldier Solomon Wakrulkar (b. 1838).

WAKSMAN—UJ has article on U.S. microbiologist Selman Waksman (b. 1888 in Russia). Also see WAXMAN.

WALDBERG—PD has some family records.

WALDEN—JE has article on Polish Talmudist Aaron Walden (1835–1912).

WALDENBERG—JE has article on German physician Louis Waldenberg (1837–1881).

WALDES—UJ has article on industrialist Heinrich Waldes (1884–1941), born in Prague.

WALDMAN—UJ has article on U.S. welfare worker Morris Waldman (b. 1879 in Hungary). CAJ has some family records.

WALDOW—Related to BLOCH.

WALDSTEIN—JE and UJ have biographies from 19th–20th-cent. U.S.A. and Lithuania. Related to WALSTON.

WALDTEUFEL—JE has article on French composer Emile Waldteufel (b. 1837).

WALEY—Name of an English family originally called LEVY. JE and UJ have biographies from 19th-cent. England. JE article on "Coat of Arms" has the family crest. Related to MONTEFIORE and SALOMONS.

WALK—Ashkenazic name which is a variation of WOLF.

WALKOWITZ (also Walkomitz)—UJ and EJ have biographies from 19th–20th-cent. Russia.

WALLACH (Wallack)—See WALLICH.

WALLASE (also Wallau)—18th-cent. *dayyan* Lazer Wallase was the maternal grandfather of Abraham GEIGER. See EJ article on Nathan ben Simeon *Adler.*

WALLAU—See WALLASE.

WALLERSTEIN—JE and UJ have biographies from 18th-cent. Germany, 19th-cent. Bohemia. CAJ has some family records. Related to JAFFE and URI.

WALLICH (also Wallach, Wallack, Wlach) —Ashkenazic name derived from WELSCH ("foreign"), applied to Alsatian Jews in Germany. When they moved on to Poland, this became Wallich, Wallach, Wloch and in some cases FALK; for those who later returned to Germany, the name evolved still further, to BLOCK. JE has seven biographies and a family tree beginning 16th-cent. Germany. LBIS has some family notes. See Wallach family histories in JFF, Nos. 33 and 34; also *Die Familie Wallich.* Related to LUSCHE, ROSTE and MELDOLA.

WALPOLE—Related to WOLFF.

WALSH—Related to JAFFE.

WALSRODE—CAJ has a family tree beginning in 16th-cent. Germany, related to COHEN.

WALSTON—UJ has article on author Charles Walston (1856–1927), born WALDSTEIN.

WALT—UJ has article on U.S. writer Abraham Walt (1872–1938), born in Russia.

WALTER—UJ has article on conductor Bruno Walter (b. 1876 in Berlin). Related to SELIGMAN.

WALTOFF—UJ has article on U.S. physician De Dayne Boris Waltoff (b. 1865 in Lithuania). See his autobiography, *Live Links.*

WALZER—AJA has a family tree from Stratford, Conn.

WAMBERGER—See VAMBERY.

WANDSWORTH—JE has article on English banker Lord Sidney Wandsworth (b. 1845), related to STERN. JE article on "Coat of Arms" has the family crest.

WANEFRIEDEN—JE has article on 18th-cent. Amsterdam preacher Eliakim Wanefrieden.

WANNEH—EJ has article on mid-17th-cent. Yemenite cabalist Isaac Wanneh.

WARBURG—Family originally from Germany which has spread throughout the world since 17th cent. JE has a family tree and twenty-eight biographies. LBI has a family tree, related to SCHIFF. LBIS has a family tree and notes. See family histories in JFF, No. 29; also *The Warburgs: The Story of a Family* and *Stamm- und Nachfahrentafeln der Familie Warburg.* Related to SAMSON, LOB, HEILBUT, GUNZBURG, GUMPRECHT, RUBEN, DELBANCO, VON HALLE, HENRIQUES, BONDY, GOLDSCHMIDT, FLESH, ABRAHAM, LASSEN, DREYER, MORRIS, STROM, GARTNER, HERSCHEL, VOSS, OPPENHEIMER and TEEP.

WARKA—Hasidic dynasty in Poland from 19th cent., related to KALISH. See EJ.

WARNER—UJ has article on the Warner brothers, movie producers who came to U.S.A. from Poland, late 19th cent. Related to WORMS.

WARRENS—JE has article on Swedish poet Rosa Warrens (1821–1878).

WARSCHAUER (also Warshauer, Warshaur, Warshaw, Warshawski, Warszawiak, Varshavski)—Ashkenazic name indicating origin in Warsaw. JE, UJ and EJ have biographies from 19th–20th-cent. Russia, Poland and England. Related to RAPOPORT.

WARSHAUER (Warshaur)—See WARSCHAUER.

WARSHAW—See WARSCHAUER.

WARSHAWSKI—See WARSCHAUER.

WARSZAWIAK—See WARSCHAUER.

WARTENEGG von WERTHEIMSTEIN— Austrian family from 18th cent. onward. See EJ. JE article on "Coat of Arms" has the family crest.

WASKER—JE has article on Indian soldier Solomon Wasker (d. 1850).

WASSERMAN (also Wassermann)—UJ and EJ have biographies from 19th–20th-cent. Germany. LBI has Wassermann family trees beginning 1635, 1720, 1760 and 1807. PD has some Wasserman and Wassermann family records. Related to DORFMAN, SELIGMAN and SULZBERGER.

WASSERTRILLING—JE has article on 19th-cent. Austrian Hebraist Hermann Wassertrilling.

WASSERVOGEL—UJ has article on U.S. Judge Isidor Wasservogel (b. 1871 in Hungary).

WASSERZUG—JE has article on Polish and English composer Haim Wasserzug (1822–1882), also known as LOMZER. Also see EJ. See family history in JJLG, Vol. 9.

WATERMAN—UJ has article on U.S. physician Sigismond Waterman (1819–1899), born in Germany.

WATTERS—UJ has three biographies from 19th–20th-cent. Germany and U.S.A.

WAWELBERG—JE has article on Russian banker Hippolite Wawelberg (1844–1901).

WAXMAN—UJ has two biographies from 19th–20th-cent. Russia and U.S.A. Also see WAKSMAN.

WEBER—UJ has article on U.S. artist Max Weber (b. 1881 in Russia).

WEBSTER—See a family history in *We Remember: Saga of the Baum-Webster Family Tree, 1842–1964.*

WECHSELMANN—JE has article on Hungarian architect Ignaz Wechselmann (1828–1903).

WECHSLER (also Weksler)—Ashkenazic name meaning "moneychanger" in German. UJ has article on U.S. physician Israel Wechsler (b. 1886 in Rumania). AJA has a family tree from New York, beginning 1795. Related to JAFFE.

WEDELES—Related to SELIGMAN.

WEHLE (also Wehli)—LBI has family trees, related to PERLMANN. PD has some Wehle and Wehli family records. See family history in ZGJT, Vol. 3 (1933), p. 113 (from Prague). Related to HIRSCH and NAUMBURG.

WEHLI—See WEHLE.

WEICSELBAUM (also Weixelbaum)—JE has article on Austrian physician Anton Weicselbaum (b. 1845).

WEIDNER—EJ has article on Vienna and Italian physician Paulus Weidner (1525–1585), also known as ASHKENAZI. PD has some family records.

WEIGEL—EJ has article on Polish martyr Catherine Weigel (1460–1539). Related to ZALUSZOWSKA.

WEIGERT—JE has article on German pathologist Karl Weigert (1845–1904). LBI has family trees beginning 1700, related to MAMROTH and PRINGSHEIM.

WEIL (also Weill, Weyl, Weille, Weiler, Weilen, Veil, Compiegne de Weil, De Veil)—Family name from Germany and Alsace (France). The Weil family of southern Germany traces its descent from Meir of Rothenburg (1215–1293), and most people with a variation of this name may share a common origin. JE has numerous biographies from 18th–19th-cent. Germany and France. Also see JE article on Meir of Rothenburg. LBI has Weil family trees beginning 1750, 1756, 1792 and 1806, related to ARON and PLAUT; also Weill family trees beginning 1790. AJA has a Weil family tree beginning 1777 and a Weill family tree from Oakland, Calif. CAJ has Weill family records and PD has Weilen family records. *Weil–De Veil: A Genealogy, 1360–1956* traces the descendants of Juda Weil in an unbroken line through seventeen generations. For other family histories, see *Strangers in the Land: The Story of Jacob Weil's Tribe; Het Geslacht de Weille; Nathanael Weil, Oberlandrabbiner in Karlsruhe und seine Familie;* and *Ahnentafel der Kinder des Nathan Weill in Kippenheim.* JE article on "Coat of Arms" has a crest of Weil von Weilen, an 18th-cent. Austrian family. Related to MORAIS, RAGSTATT, BROD, PROUST, SONDER, DURLACHER, STERN, KELLERMEISTER, EICHBERG and ROSEWALD.

WEILEN—See WEIL.

WEILER—See WEIL.

WEILHEIMER—PD has some family records.

WEILL (Weille, Weiller)—See WEIL.

WEINBAUM—Related to MONTEFIORE.

WEINBERG (also Weinberger)—JE and UJ have biographies from 19th–20th-cent. Russia, Germany, Bohemia and U.S.A. PD has some family records. A Weinberger family from Slovakia is related to HIRSCH. Also see WEINSBERG.

WEINBERGER—See WEINBERG.

WEINER—JE has five biographies from 19th-cent. Germany, Belgium and Russia. AJA has a family tree. Related to SAMUEL. In some cases the name may be derived from WIENER.

WEINGARTEN (also Weingaertner)—JE and EJ have biographies from 19th-cent. France and Poland.

WEINGAERTNER—See WEINGARTEN.

WEININGER—UJ has article on Austrian philosopher Otto Weininger (1880–1903).

WEINKOP—CAJ has some family records.

WEINLAUB—LBI has a family tree beginning 1850.

WEINMANN—EJ has article on Bohemian industrialist Jacob Weinmann (1852–1928).

WEINREICH—UJ has article on author Max Weinreich (b. 1894 in Latvia).

WEINSBERG—Ashkenazic name taken from the town of Weinberg, Hohenzollern. CAJ has some family records from 15th-cent. Germany. Also see WEINBERG.

WEINSTEIN—Ashkenazic name meaning "wine stone" in German. UJ has article on U.S. technician Louis Weinstein (1881–1930), born in Russia. Related to ROSENFELD and SZABOLCSI.

WEINSTOCK—UJ has article on U.S. author Harris Weinstock (1854–1922), born in London, half brother of David LUBIN.

WEINTHAL—UJ has article on author Leo Weinthal (b. 1865 in South Africa, d. 1930 in London).

WEINTRAUB—The name means "wine grape." UJ has article on cantor Shlomo Weintraub (b. 1781 in Russia, d. 1829 in Galicia).

WEIS—See WEISS.

WEISBACH—UJ has article on art historian Werner Weisbach (b. 1873 in Berlin).

WEISENFELD—PD has some family records. Related to FRIEDENWALD.

WEISENFREUND—UJ has article on actor Paul MUNI (b. Muni Weisenfreund in Austria, 1895).

WEISL—See WEISS.

WEISS (also Weis, Weisz, Weisl, Wiesel) —Ashkenazic name meaning "white" in German. JE and UJ have biographies from 18th-cent. Austria and 19th–20th-cent. France, Russia, Hungary and U.S.A. LBI has a family tree beginning 1700. PD has some Weiss and Weisl family records. See a family history in *Autobiography of Julius Weiss,* U.S. merchant (1826–1909), born in Germany. Related to WEISSFELD, UNGVAR, DEUTSCH, OPPENHEIM, GODCHAUX, FOLDES and FRIEND.

WEISSBERG—JE has article on Russian writer Isaac Weissberg (1841–1904).

WEISSELBERGER—UJ has article on Austrian public official Salomon Weisselberger (1867–1931).

WEISSENBERG—JE has article on Russian physician Samuel Weissenberg (1867–1928).

WEISSER—UJ has article on U.S. cantor Samuel Weisser (b. PILDERWASSER in Russia, 1888).

WEISSFELD—Related to WEISS.

WEISSMAN (also Weissman-Chajes)—JE has two biographies from 19th-cent. Austria. Related to CHAJES.

WEISSWEILER (also Weisweiler)—PD has some Weisweiler family records. Related to ROTHSCHILD.

WEISZ—See WEISS.

WEIXELBAUM—See WEICSELBAUM.

WEIZMANN—UJ has article on chemist and Zionist Chaim Weizmann (1874–1952), born in Poland; married Vera KAZMAN.

WEKSLER—See WECHSLER.

WELING—Bavarian family from 19th cent., also known as SELIGMANN. See JE. JE article on "Coat of Arms" has the family crest.

WELLENSTEIN—PD has some family records.

WELLESZ—UJ has article on composer Egon Wellesz (b. 1885 in Vienna).

WELSH (also Weltsch)—Ashkenazic name meaning "foreign," first applied to Alsatian Jews in Germany. It is a forerunner of WALLICH and BLOCH. JE and EJ have biographies from Russia and Prague, 19th–20th-cent. CAJ has some family records from Czechoslovakia. PD also has some family records.

WELTNER—UJ has article on Hungarian author Jakob Weltner (1873–1936).

WELTSCH—See WELSH.

WENDLAND—EJ has article on German scholar Paul Wendland (1864–1915). Related to WOHLBRUCK.

WENGER (also Wengeroff)—UJ has biographies from 19th–20th-cent. Russia. Related to MINSKY, SLONIMSKY and VENGEROVA.

WERBEL (also Werbelowsky, Werber)—JE, UJ and EJ have biographies from 19th- and 20th-cent. Galicia, Prussia and Austria.

WERBELOWSKY—See WERBEL.

WERBER—See WERBEL.

WERFEL—UJ has article on writer Franz Werfel (b. 1890 in Prague).

WERNE—See WERNER.

WERNER (also Werne)—JE and UJ have biographies from 19th–20th-cent. Poland.

WERNIKOVSKI—JE has article on Russian Talmudist Judah Wernikovski (1823–1901).

WERTHEIM (also Wertheimer, Wertheimber)—Ashkenazic name taken from the town of Wertheim in Baden. JE and UJ have biographies from 17th-cent. Austria and 19th-cent. Austria, Hungary, England and U.S.A. LBI has Wertheimer family trees beginning 17th cent., 1721, 1738, and 1770, related to FRAENKEL; and a Wertheimber tree beginning 1588. AJA has a Wertheimer tree from Dayton, Ohio, and Denver, Colo., beginning 1815. PD and CAJ have Wertheimer family records. See Wertheimer family history in JFF, Nos. 7, 8, 9 and 10. Also see *Samson Wertheimer, der Oberhoffactor und Landes-Rabbiner, 1658–1724; Verzeichnis der Nachkommen des Leopold und der Rosa Wolf, 1800–1866;* and AJF (1912), p. 12. JE article on "Coat of Arms" has the Wertheimer family crest. Related to SAMSON, KATZ, OPPENHEIM, OPPENHEIMER, KANN, BERMANN, BEHRENS, ESKELES, KOHN, HIRSCH, LEVI, KONIGSWARTER, LEHMANN, KAHN, BRUNNER, LEIDESDORFER, GOMPERZ, ARNSTEIN, BOAS and WOLF.

WERTHEIMBER (also Wertheimer) —See WERTHEIM.

WERTHER—PD has some family records.

WESEL (also Wessel, Wessely, Wesslig)—JE and UJ have biographies from 17th-cent. Germany, 18th-cent. Germany and 19th–20th-cent. Austria and Russia. CAJ has some Wessely family records. PD has some Wesslig family notes.

WESSEL—See WESEL.

WESSELY—See WESEL.

WESSLIG—See WESEL.

WESTERFELD—LBI has a family tree beginning 1783.

WESTHEIM (also Westheimer)—UJ has article on art critic Paul Westheim (b. 1879 in Germany). AJA has a Westheimer family tree, related to HEINSHEIMER.

WESTPHAL—Related to MARX.

WETTACH—UJ has article on Swiss clown Adrien Wettach (b. 1880), known as "Grock."

WETTSTEIN—EJ has article on Polish historian Feivel Wettstein (1858–1924).

WETZLAR (also Wetzler, Wezlar)—Ashkenazic name taken from the Hessian town of Wetzlar, where Jews first settled in 12th cent. UJ and EJ have biographies beginning 16th-cent. Austria. See family history in *Das Testament der Baronin Eleonora Wetzlar von Plankenstern;* also *Die Descendenz des Karl Abraham Freiherrn von Wetzlar,* by Paul Diamant, in AJF, Vol. 1 (1913). PD has some family records. Related to PICQUIGNY, PLANKENSTERN and ROTHSCHILD.

WETZLER—See WETZLAR.

WEYL—See WEIL.

WEZLAR—See WETZLAR.

WHITAKER—Related to EMANUEL.

WIDAL—JE has article on French physician Fernand Widal (1862–1929).

WIENER—Ashkenazic name meaning "from Vienna." UJ has six biographies from 19th–20th-cent. Germany, England,

Poland, Belgium and U.S.A. Related to SONNENFELS. A possible variation is WEINER.

WIENIAWSKI—JE has two biographies from 19th-cent. Russia.

WIENSKOWITZ—LBI has a family tree beginning 1774, related to HALBERS.

WIERNIK (also Wiernikorski)—JE and EJ have biographies from 19th–20th-cent. Russia.

WIERNIKORSKI—See WIERNIK.

WIESEL—See WEISS.

WIESENFELD—Related to FRIEDEN-WALD.

WIESENTHAL—LBI has a family tree beginning 1781.

WIESLANDER—Related to STOKES.

WIESNER—JE and UJ have biographies from 19th–20th-cent. Prague and Austria. PD has some family records.

WIGA—JE has article on 16th-cent. Polish preacher Judah Wiga.

WIGODA—See WIGODER.

WIGODER—See genealogy of Myer Joel Wigoder in *Sefer Zikaron*.

WIHL—JE has article on German poet Ludwig Wihl (1807–1882), died in Brussels.

WIJSENBEEK—UJ has article on psychoanalyst Caroline Wijsenbeek (b. 1884 in Holland).

WILCZYNSKI—JE has article on German-American mathematician Ernest Wilczynski (b. 1876).

WILDA—JE and UJ have biographies of German jurist Wilhelm Wilda (1800–1856), born SELIGMANN.

WILDENBRUCH—CAJ has some family records.

WILDENSTEIN—UJ has article on art historian Georges Wildenstein (b. 1892 in Paris).

WILDMANN—EJ has article on Polish Rabbi Isaac Wildmann (1789–1853).

WILE—Related to WATTERS.

WILENKIN—JE has article on Russian bureaucrat Gregory Wilenkin (b. 1864). Related to MINSKI and SELIGMAN.

WILENSKY—UJ has two biographies from 19th–20th-cent. Russia and U.S.A.

WILENTZ—UJ has article on U.S. lawyer David Wilentz (b. 1895 in Russia).

WILHELM—CAJ has some family records.

WILKANSKY—Related to ELAZARI-VOL-CANI.

WILLIAMS—Related to MENDEZ DA COSTA.

WILLOWSKI—EJ has article on Lithuanian Talmudist Jacob Willowski (1845–1913). Related to RIDBAZ.

WILLS—Related to LOUSADA.

WILLSTATTER (also Willstaetter)—UJ has article on chemist Richard Willstatter (1872–1942), born in Germany. LBI has a Willstaetter family tree beginning 1720, related to APPEL.

WILMERSDOERFER (also Wilmersdorffer)—JE has article on Bavarian financier Max von Wilmersdorffer (1824–1903). LBI has a Wilmersdoerfer family tree beginning 1730. Related to OBERNDORFFER.

WILNA—Ashkenazic name taken from the city of Vilna, Lithuania, where Jews first settled in 14th cent. EJ has article on Rabbi Jacob Wilna of Vilna (d. 1732). Related to FEIWEL and KAHANA.

WIMPFHEIMER—Ashkenazic name derived from a town or district in Germany named Wimpfen. There are at least three such places: Wimpfen in Hessen, Wimpfen am Berge and Wimpfen in Thal. The word *Heim* is German for "home" and thus the name literally means one whose home is in Wimpfen.

WINAWER—JE and UJ have biographies from 19th–20th-cent. Russia, Poland and France.

WINDMUEHL-COHN—See WINDMUELLER.

WINDMUELLER (also Windmuller, Windmuehl-Cohn)—LBI has a Windmuehl-Cohn family tree beginning 1706, and a Windmueller tree beginning 1690. CAJ has Windmuller family records, 1763–1866. See a family history in *Chronik der Familie Windmuller*.

WINDMULLER—See WINDMUELLER.

WINKLER—JE, UJ and EJ have biographies beginning 17th-cent. Vienna, also 19th-cent. Poland and Rumania. LBI has a family tree beginning 1795, related to TUCHMANN. See family history in REJ, Vol. 20 (1890), p. 275. Also related to DUSCHINSKY.

WINKOOP—CAJ has some family records.

WINSTOCK—AJA has a family tree, related to LEVINE and LEVIN.

WINTER—JE and UJ have biographies from Hungary and Czechoslovakia, 18th, 19th and 20th cent. PD has some family records, related to WIGMAR.

WINTERFELD—UJ has article on German composer Max Winterfeld (b. 1879); his pseudonym was Jean Gilbert.

WINTERNITZ—JE has two biographies from 19th-cent. Austria. Related to KOHN.

WINTEROTH—Related to RAPPOLD.

WINTERSTEIN—JE and UJ have biographies from 19th-cent. Austria and Prague.

WISCHNITZER—UJ has article on historian Mark Wischnitzer (b. 1882 in Poland). CAJ has some family records.

WISE—JE and UJ have articles from 19th-cent. U.S.A. Rabbi Stephen Wise (b. 1874 in Hungary) was a grandson of Joseph WEISS. Related to BONDI and OCHS.

WISHNIPOLSKY—This family is included in *It Began with Zade Usher* (see Bernstein in Bibliography).

WISLICKI—UJ has article on Polish politician Waclaw Wislicki (1882–1935).

WISSOTZKY—JE has article on Russian philanthropist Kalonymus Wissotzky (1824–1904).

WITCOWSKY—See WITKOWSKI.

WITKOWSKI (also Witcowsky, Witkowsky)—UJ and EJ have biographies from 19th–20th-cent. Russia, Germany and U.S.A. Witkowsky was the original name of Maximilian HARDEN. LBI has a family tree beginning 1737. Also see a family tree in *Stammbaum der Familie J. L. Jacobi;* and *Forgotten Pioneer,* a biography of U.S. peddler Morris Witcowsky (1862–1948), born in Russia. Related to JACOBI and WITTING.

WITKOWSKY—See WITKOWSKI.

WITTELSHOFER—JE has article on Austrian physician Leopold Wittelshofer (1818–1889), born in Hungary.

WITTGESTEIN—PD has some family records.

WITTING—UJ has article on German banker Richard Witting (1856–1923), born WITKOWSKI.

WITTLIN—UJ has article on Polish writer Jozef Wittlin (b. 1896).

WITTMANN—JE has article on Hungarian physicist Franz Wittmann (b. 1860).

WITZENHAUSEN—Dutch printer Uri Witzenhausen (1613–1715) was the son of HALEVI; see UJ article on *Uri* Phoebus. CAJ has some family records. See *Family Tree of Rabbi Moshe Witzenhausen, Ancestors and Descendants.*

WIX—PD has some family records.

WLACH—See WALLICH.

WODIAMER—See WODIANER.

WODIANER (also Wodiamer)—JE has six biographies from 19th-cent. Hungary. The name is descended from Samuel WOIDZISLAW, who came to Hungary from Bohemia about 1750. PD has some Wodiamer family records. Also see UJ.

WOGUE—JE has two biographies from 19th-cent. France.

WOHL—See WAHL.

WOHLAUER—LBI has a family tree beginning 1789, related to SACHS.

WOHLBRUCK—UJ has article on actress Olga Wohlbruck (1867–1913), who married BERN and WENDLAND.

WOHLLERNER—JE has article on Austrian writer Jetty Wohllerner (1813–1891), related to KEHLMANN.

WOHLWILL—LBI has a family tree beginning 1799.

WOIDZISLAW—See WODIANER.

WOLF (also Wolfe, Wolfes, Wolff, Wolffe, Woolf, Wulf, Wulff)—Ashkenazic name meaning "wolf," often indicating an ancestor whose first name was Wolf. Variations in various languages, some possibly related, are WOLK, WALK, LUPO (Rumanian), LOPEZ (Spanish) and SIFF (Hebrew). JE and UJ have numerous biographies from 18th-cent. Denmark,

America and Germany, and 19th-cent. Austria, South Africa, England, Russia and Sweden. LBI has Wolf family trees beginning 1659, 1786 and 1808, a Wolfes family tree beginning 1650, and Wolff family trees beginning 1681 and 1800. CAJ has some Wolf family records. CAJD has a Wolf family tree from Germany. PD has some Wolf family records, related to SPITZER, and also some Wolff family records. See Wolf family history in JFF, No. 5; also *Four Generations; Die Familie Wolf: Verzeichnis der Nachkommen des Leopold und Rosa Wolf; Chronik der Familie Wolf; Geschichte der Familie Wolfes aus Mehle bei Hildesheim;* and *Aus der Heimat Mendelssohns: Moses Benjamin Wulff und seine Familie, die Nachkommen des Moses Isserles.* Related to JOST, JAFFE, FRANKEL, BEER, SCHIFF, LIEBMANN, WOLFTHORN, WERTHEIMER, MOISE, ROBLES, LEVY, de la MOTTA, VON HONIG, CAPPE, WALPOLE, OPPENHEIM, MAY, LEWI, SCHADOW, EPHRAIM, FRANKFURTER, ARNSTEIN, ITZIG and IS-SERLES.

WOLFE—See WOLF.

WOLFENSTEIN (also Wolffenstein)—JE has article on Russian writer Martha Wolfenstein (b. 1869). LBI has a Wolffenstein family tree beginning 1759, related to PLAUT.

WOLFERS—LBI has a family tree beginning 1720.

WOLFES—See WOLF.

WOLFF (Wolffe)—See WOLF.

WOLFFENSTEIN—See WOLFENSTEIN.

WOLFFING—CAJ has some family records.

WOLFFSOHN (Wolffson)—See WOLF-SOHN.

WOLFFSTEIN—LBI has a family tree beginning 1817.

WOLFKEHL—See WOLFSKEHL.

WOLFLER—JE has article on Austrian physician Bernard Wolfler (b. 1816).

WOLFNER—JE has article on Hungarian deputy Theodore Wolfner (b. 1864). PD has some family records.

WOLFOVSKY—UJ has article on author Menaham Wolfovsky (b. 1893 in Russia).

WOLFSFELD—UJ has article on German painter Erich Wolfsfeld (b. 1884).

WOLFSKEHL (also Wolfkehl)—UJ has article on German poet Karl Wolfskehl (b. 1869), descendant of a family of financiers. Related to SAMSON.

WOLFSKY—LBIS has some family notes.

WOLFSOHN (also Wolfson, Wolffsohn, Wolffson)—JE and UJ have biographies from 19th–20th-cent. Germany, Lithuania, Rumania, Honduras and U.S.A. Also see JE article on Pinsk, Russia. Related to HALLE.

WOLFSON—See WOLFSOHN.

WOLFTHORN—UJ has article on painter Julie Wolfthorn (b. WOLF in Germany, 1868).

WOLK—Ashkenazic name, a variation of WOLF. U.S. Rabbi Samuel Wolk (b. 1902 in Lithuania) was a descendant of Saul WAHL; his aunt Rose Wolk married Isaac BLASER. See UJ.

WOLKOWISKI—EJ has article on Russian merchant Jehiel Wolkowiski (1819–1903).

WOLLEMBORG—JE has article on Italian economist Leone Wollemborg (1859–1932).

WOLLHEIM—JE and UJ have biographies from 19th- and 20th-cent. Germany.

WOLLSTEIN—LBIS has some family notes.

WOLOWSKI (also Wolofsky)—A Polish branch of the SCHOR family which changed its name in late 17th cent. after some of its members converted to Christianity. See JE. Also see *Journey of My Life,* autobiography of Canadian publisher Harry Wolofsky (b. 1876 in Poland).

WOLPER—JE has article on Russian educator Michael Wolper (b. 1852). Also see VOLPE.

WOLSELY—Related to LOUSADA.

WOLSKY—See a family history in *Yizkor.*

WOLWOFF—See *I Yield to Destiny,* autobiography of U.S. cantor Israel Wolwoff (b. 19th cent. in Russia).

WOOD—Related to HAYS.

WOOLF—See WOLF.

WORG—Related to LANDAUER.

WORMS (also Wormser, de Worms)—English-German family descended from Aaron Worms of Frankfurt-am-Main, 18th cent.; Austrian and French branches appeared in 19th cent. The name is taken from the German town of Worms, where Jews first settled in 10th cent. Sekel Wormser of Germany (1768–1847) was a descendant of Elijah LOANS. JE has a family tree and ten biographies. UJ also has biographies. CAJ has Worms and Wormser family records. PD has Worms family records, related to Lord PIRBRIGHT. Also see *Genealogical History of the Family de Worms*. JE article on "Coat of Arms" has the family crest. Related to SAMUEL, LANDAUER, MORRISON, WARNER, SCHARFFENECK, LEVI, ADLER, GOLDSCHMIDT, ROTHSCHILD, TODESCO, DREIFUS and BAMBERGER.

WORMSER—See WORMS.

WOYSLAVSKY—UJ has article on writer Zvi Woyslavsky (b. 1890 in Poland).

WRESCHNER—UJ has article on psychologist Arthur Wreschner (1866–1932), born in Germany.

WUERZBURGER—See WURZBURGER.

WULF (Wulff)—See WOLF.

WULMAN—UJ has article on physician Leon Wulman (b. 1887 in Russia).

WUNDERBAR—JE has article on Russian author Reuben Wunderbar (1812–1868).

WUNDERLICH—UJ has article on professor Frieda Wunderlich (b. 1884 in Germany). LBI has a family tree.

WURTZBURG—See WURZBURGER.

WURZBURGER (also Wuerzburger, Wurtzburg)—Ashkenazic name taken from the Bavarian city of Würzburg, where Jews first settled in 11th cent. JE has article on U.S. journalist Julius Wurzburger (1819–1876), born in Germany. LBI has Wuerzburger family trees beginning 1689 and 1730. Wurtzburg family is related to SCHIFF.

WYSBER—JE has article on Hungarian journalist Ludwig Wysber (b. 1817).

XIMENES—JE has two biographies from 18th-cent. England. JE article on "Coat of Arms" has two family crests. Related to BELMONTE and MOCATTA.

YADKOVSKI—Related to KLEPFISH.

YAFFE—A variation of JAFFE. Related to KAPLAN.

YAHUDA—UJ has article on scholar Abraham Yahuda (b. 1877 in Jerusalem), descended from a Sephardic family which traced its origin back to the Geonim of Babylonia. Related to MA'TUK. Also see YEHUDAH.

YAHUDI—EJ has article on Bukharan poet Yusuf Yahudi (1688–1755).

YAHYA—Portuguese family in the Middle Ages, which later moved to Italy and Turkey. JE has a family tree and thirty-three biographies. Related to NEGRO and RECANATI.

YA'ISH—JE has article on 13th-cent. Spanish representative David Ya'ish. Related to ALGAZI.

YAKHINI—EJ has article on Constantinople cabalist Abraham Yakhini (1617–1682).

YAKOBOVITS—Related to AKAVYA.

YAMPOLSKY—A family by this name is included in *It Began with Zade Usher* (see Bernstein in Bibliography).

YARCHO—EJ has article on Argentine physician Noe Yarcho (1862–1912).

YARMOLINSKY—UJ has article on U.S. author Avraham Yarmolinsky (b. 1890 in Russia).

YASSER—UJ has article on musician Joseph Yasser (b. 1893 in Poland).

YATES—Prominent English family of 18th and 19th cent. JE has two biographies. See *The History and Genealogy of the Jewish Families of Yates and Samuel of Liverpool*. Related to ABRAHAMS, GETZ, GOETZ, LAZARUS and SAMUEL.

YEHUDAH—Related to YELLIN.

YELLIN—UJ and EJ have biographies from 19th–20th-cent. Jerusalem, Poland and U.S.A. EJ has a family tree. David Yellin (1864–1941) was a descendant of the SASSOON family. Related to DANIN, GLICKMAN, PINES and YEHUDAH.

YERUSHALMI—Name indicating origin in Jerusalem. JE has article on 16th-cent. scholar Solomon Yerushalmi, of unknown origin, also known as ASHKENAZI.

YEVLEVICH—Related to GADEN.

YEZIERSKA—UJ has article on U.S. novelist Anzia Yezierska (b. 1885 in Poland). See his autobiography, *Red Ribbon on a White Horse.*

YISHARI—Related to CASLARI.

YIZHAKI—JE has two biographies from 16th-cent. Turkey. Related to AZULAI.

YOELSON—See JOLSON.

YOFFEY—19th-cent. Russian family; see EJ. The name is probably a variation of JAFFE.

YORKE—Related to MONTEFIORE and ROTHSCHILD.

YORK-STEINER—UJ has article on author Heinrich York-Steiner (1859–1934), born in Hungary.

YOSELOVICH (also Yoselowitz)—Ashkenazic name meaning "son of Joseph" and indicating an ancestor by that name. One abbreviated form is SELOVE.

YOSELOWITZ—See YOSELOVICH.

YOSPA—Related to TRILLINGER.

YOUNG—Related to BEHREND.

YSIDRO—Related to GABBAI.

YULEE (also Yuly)—JE and UJ have articles on West Indian politician David Yulee (1811–1886), son of Moses LEVY. EJ has Yuly biographies beginning in 17th cent. Morocco. Related to ABEN.

YULY—See YULEE.

YUSHKEVICH—UJ has article on author Semion Yushkevich (1868–1927), born in Russia.

ZAAR—UJ has article on writer Isaac Zaar (b. RABINOVICH in Lithuania, 1885).

ZABLUDOWSKI—JE has two biographies from 19th-cent. Russia.

ZABOTINSKY—UJ has article on Argentine dentist Alejandro Zabotinsky (1880–1941), born in Russia.

ZACHUTH—See ZACUTO.

ZACK—UJ has article on painter Leon Zack (b. 1892 in Russia).

ZACUTH—See ZACUTO.

ZACUTO (also Zachuth, Zacuth, Zacutus)—Spanish and Portuguese family name. JE and EJ have biographies from 15th-cent. Spain, 16th–17th-cent. Portugal. Also see EJ article on *Zacutus* Lusitanus. Related to ALVARES.

ZACUTUS—See ZACUTO.

ZADDIK—Related to JUSTO.

ZADKINE—UJ has article on sculptor Ossip Zadkine (b. 1890 in Russia).

ZAGAJSKI—UJ has article on industrialist Mieczyslaus Zagajski (b. 1895 in Poland).

ZAHALON—Spanish family. JE has five biographies from 16th cent.

ZAK—Ashkenazic name with several sources: 1) an acronym of *zera kedoshim*, Hebrew for "the seed of martyrs"; 2) a Czech word for "schoolboy"; 3) in some cases, a variation of SACHS. UJ has article on painter Eugen Zak (1884–1926), born in Russia of Polish parents.

ZALINSKI—JE has two biographies from 19th-cent. Poland and U.S.A.

ZALKIND—Related to ZEMLIACHKA.

ZALMAN—Related to JAFFE.

ZALUDKOWSKI—UJ has article on U.S. Rabbi Elias Zaludkowski (1890–1943), born in Poland.

ZALUSZOWSKA—Related to WEIGEL.

ZAMENHOF—JE has article on Lazarus Zamenhof, inventor of Esperanto (b. 1859 in Russia). CAJ has some family records.

ZAMOSC—See ZAMOSZ.

ZAMOSZ (also Zamosc)—JE and EJ have biographies from 17th-cent. Poland and 18th-cent. Germany. Related to BEHR.

ZANGWILL—JE has two biographies from 19th-cent. England. Related to AYRTON.

ZAPPERT—JE has four biographies from 17th-cent. Austria and 19th-cent. Hungary. CAJ has family records from 18th and 19th cent. PD has some family records.

ZAREFATI (Zarfathi) See ZARFATI.

ZARFATI (also Zarefati, Zarfathi, Sarfaty, Sarphati, Sarphaty)—French and Eastern family dating from 13th cent. The name is Oriental for "French." JE and UJ have biographies. One branch of the family, descended from RASHI (1040–1105) through his grandson Rabbenu Tam, settled in Morocco. See family histories in MGWJ (1873), p. 282, and in KS, p. 212. Also see JE article on *Moses* ben Jacob of 15th-16th-cent. Russia, father-in-law of Abraham Zarfati. JE also has a biography from 19th-cent. Holland of Samuel Sarphaty. Related to FOA, MONTI, TREVES, TRABOT, TRABOTTI, GHIRONDI, SOLIS and MELDOLA.

ZARIK—See SARKO.

ZARISKI—UJ has article on mathematician Oscar Zariski (b. 1899 in Poland).

ZARKO—See SARKO.

ZARZA—See ZARZAL.

ZARZAL (also Zarza, Zarzar)—14th-cent. Spanish family. JE has three biographies.

ZARZAR—See ZARZAL.

ZATOLOWSKY—Related to DAYAN.

ZAUSMER (also Zausner)—JE has two biographies from 16th-cent. Poland. Also see *Unvarnished,* autobiography of U.S. labor leader Philip Zausner (b. 1884 in Poland).

ZAUSNER—See ZAUSMER.

ZAYYAH—EJ has article on Jerusalem Rabbi Joseph Zayyah (16th cent.).

ZBARAZER—See EHRENKRANZ.

ZBITKOWER—EJ has article on Warsaw merchant Joseph Samuel Zbitkower (1730–1801), husband of Judith LEVY and great-grandfather of Henri BERGSON.

ZDEKAUER—PD has some family records.

ZEBI—See JE article on *Moses* ben Abraham ha-Kadosh (17th-cent. Lithuania). Related to AZULAI.

ZEDEK—JE has article on Austro-English scholar Joseph Zedek (1827–1903). Related to BISHKA.

ZEDERBAUM—JE and UJ have articles on Russian journalist Alexander Zederbaum (1816–1893), born in Poland; grandfather of Julius MARTOV.

ZEDNER—JE has article on German librarian Joseph Zedner (1804–1871). Related to ALNAQUA.

ZEEBI—JE has article on Palestinian Talmudist Israel Zeebi (1651–1731). Related to AZULAI.

ZEHNER—Related to FISCHEL and POLLACK.

ZEISEL (also Zeisler, Zeissl)—JE has biographies from 19th-20th-cent. Austria.

ZEISLER—See ZEISEL.

ZEISSL—See ZEISEL.

ZEITLIN—JE has three biographies from 18th-cent. Russia. Related to PERETZ.

ZELAZOWSKA—JE has article on Catherine Zelazowska (1460–1540), royal Polish convert to Judaism.

ZELIG—Related to CHOTSH.

ZELIQZON—UJ has article on philologist Leon Zeliqzon (b. 1858 in France).

ZELL—Related to ROSENBAUM.

ZELLERBACH—EJ has biography from 19th-cent. Bavaria.

ZELLERMAYER—Family in U.S.A. For a chart of descendants, contact Eric Schwartz, 32 Strawberry Street, Philadelphia, Pa. 19106.

ZELMAN—JE has article on Austro-Italian poet Samuele Zelman (1808–1885), from Trieste.

ZEMACH—UJ has three biographies from 19th-20th-cent. Poland and U.S.A.

ZEMAH—JE has article on 17th-cent. Portuguese cabalist Jacob Zemah, who died in Jerusalem.

ZEMANSKY—Related to HAYS.

ZEMLIACHKA—UJ has article on Russian official Samoilova Zemliachka (b. ZALKIND in 1876).

ZEMLINSKY—UJ has article on composer Alexander Zemlinsky (1872–1941), born in Vienna.

ZEMURRAY—UJ has article on U.S. executive Samuel Zemurray (b. 1877 in Russia).

ZENTLER—UJ has article on industrialist Micu Zentler (b. 1873 in Rumania).

ZENZYMINER—Related to EGER.

ZEPIN—UJ has article on U.S. Rabbi George Zepin (b. 1878 in Russia).

ZERBONI—CAJ has some family records.

ZERFFI—JE has article on Hungarian journalist Gustav Zerffi (b. 1820).

ZERKOWITZ—Austrian authoress Sidonie Zerkowitz (b. 1852 in Moravia) married GRUNWALD; See JE article on Grunwald-Zerkowitz.

ZERNE—Related to DEICHES.

ZEROR—JE has article on Algerian Rabbi Raphael Zeror (1681–1737).

ZEVI—Related to SPINKA.

ZEYER—EJ has article on Czech poet Julius Zeyer (1841–1901).

ZHIDACHOV—Hasidic dynasty from 19th cent., related to EICHENSTEIN. See EJ.

ZHIDOVINOV—Related to GADEN.

ZHIRKOVA—UJ has article on Russian author Yelizaveta Zhirkova (b. 1888); married BYCHOWSKY.

ZHITLOWSKY (also Schitlowsky)—UJ has article on writer Chaim Zhitlowsky (1865–1943), born in Russia.

ZIDEK—EJ has article on Czech scholar Pavel Zidek (1413–1471).

ZIEGFELD—Related to HELD.

ZIEGLER—JE has article on Austro-Hungarian Rabbi Ignaz Ziegler (1861–1948). CAJ has some family records from Hungary and Germany.

ZIELENZIGER—LBI has a family tree beginning 1701, related to GRUNSFELD. LBIS has some family notes.

ZIELONKA—UJ has article on U.S. Rabbi Martin Zielonka (1877–1938), born in Germany.

ZIFRONI—Old Roman Jewish family; see UJ article on *Immanuel* ben Solomon.

ZIGELBOJM—UJ has article on Polish official Samuel Zigelbojm (1894–1943).

ZILBERCWEIG—UJ has article on writer Zalmen Zilbercweig (b. 1894 in Poland).

ZILBERTS—UJ has article on composer Zavel Zilberts (b. 1881 in Russia).

ZILBOORG—UJ has article on psychiatrist Gregory Zilboorg (b. 1890 in Russia).

ZILZER—JE has article on Hungarian painter Antal Zilzer (b. 1861).

ZIMAND—UJ has article on U.S. writer Savel Zimand (b. 1893 in Rumania).

ZIMBALIST—UJ has article on violinist Efrem Zimbalist (b. 1889 in Russia).

ZIMBLER—A family of this name is included in *It Began with Zade Usher* (see Bernstein in Bibliography).

ZIMMER (also Zimmern)—JE has two biographies from 19th-cent. England and Bavaria.

ZIMMERN—See ZIMMER.

ZIMMERSPITZ—CAJ has some family records from Poland, 1809 to 1862.

ZINBERG—UJ has article on historian Israel Zinberg (1873–1943), born LAZAREVITCH in Russia.

ZINGHER—UJ has article on U.S. official Abraham Zingher (1885–1927), born in Rumania. The name is a possible variation of SINGER.

ZINOVIEV—UJ has article on Russian propagandist Grigorii Zinoviev (1883–1936).

ZINZ—Related to TE'OMIM.

ZIPPER (also Zippert)—UJ has article on Zionist Gerschon Zipper (1868–1920), born in Galicia. LBI has a Zippert family tree, related to WITKOWSKI.

ZIPPERT—See ZIPPER.

ZIPSER—JE has article on Hungarian Rabbi Maier Zipser (1815–1869).

ZIRELSON—UJ has article on Russian Rabbi Judah Zirelson (1859–1941).

ZIRNDORF—JE has article on German-American poet Heinrich Zirndorf (b. 1829 in Bavaria, d. 1893 in Cincinnati).

ZISOOK—Polish form of Isaac.

ZITRON—See CITRON.

ZIVIER—UJ has article on German historian Ezechiel Zivier (1868–1925).

ZLATOPOLSKI—Related to PERSITZ.

ZLOCISTI—UJ has article on writer Theodor Zlocisti (b. 1874 in Poland).

ZLOTNIK—UJ has article on Rabbi Judah Zlotnik (b. 1887 in Poland).

ZOFFANY—UJ has article on 18th-cent. painter John Zoffany.

ZOLD—UJ has article on Hungarian General Morton Zold (b. 1865).

ZOLLER—UJ has article on Polish Rabbi Israele Zoller (b. 1881).

ZOLLSCHAN—UJ has article on physician Ignaz Zollschan (b. 1877 in Austria).

ZOMBER—JE has article on Polish scholar Bernhard Zomber (1821–1884).

ZON—UJ has article on forester Raphael Zon (b. 1874 in Russia).

ZONDEK—UJ has article on physician Bernard Zondek (b. 1891 in Germany).

ZORACH—UJ has article on U.S. sculptor William Zorach (1887–1926), born in Lithuania. See his autobiography, *Art Is My Life.*

ZOREF—JE has article on Rabbi Samuel Zoref of Posen (d. c. 1710).

ZOUSA—See ZOUZA.

ZOX—JE has article on Australian Ephraim Zox (1837–1899), born in London.

ZSOLNA—PD has some family records.

ZSOLT—UJ has article on novelist Bela Zsolt (b. 1895 in Hungary).

ZUCKER—JE has two biographies from 19th-cent. Germany.

ZUCKERKANDL—JE and UJ have articles on Austrian anatomist Emil Zuckerkandl (b. 1849), who married the daughter of Moritz SZEPS.

ZUCKERMANDEL—The name means "sweet almond." JE has article on German Rabbi Moses Zuckermandel (b. 1836).

ZUCKERMANN (also Zukerman, Zuckerman)—JE has biographies from 18th–19th-cent. Germany and Russia. CAJ has some family records.

ZUCKOR—See ZUKOR.

ZUCROW—See biography in EJ article on "Aeronautics."

ZUENZ—See ZUNZ.

ZUKERMAN—See ZUCKERMANN.

ZUKERTORT—JE has article on chess player Johannes Zukertort (b. 1842 in Poland, d. 1888 in London).

ZUKOR (also Zuckor)—UJ has article on film producer Adolf Zukor (b. 1873 in Hungary). See his autobiography, *The Public Is Never Wrong.*

ZUMOFF—See *Our Family: A History of Five Generations, 1831–1956.*

ZUNDEL—Related to JAFFE.

ZUNSER—See ZUNZ.

ZUNTZ—See ZUNZ.

ZUNZ (also Zuenz, Zunser, Zuntz)—Ashkenazic name derived from Zons, a place on the Rhine. The genealogy of German scholar Leopold Zunz (1794–1886) can be traced back in an unbroken line for three centuries. See JE, which also has biographies from 18th- 19th- and 20th-cent. Poland, Germany and Russia. See family histories in MGWJ, Vol. 38 (1894), p. 481; also *Die Familie Zunz; Dr. Leopold Zunz und seine Frankfurter Ahnen;* and *Yesterday.* Related to BEHRENS.

ZUPNIK—JE has article on Galician writer Aaron Zupnik (b. 1850).

ZURIEL—JE has article on 17th-cent. mathematician Moses Zuriel.

ZUSSIA—See EJ article on *Abraham Joshua* (d. 1825).

ZUTA—Related to JAFFE.

ZWAAB—CAJ has some family records.

ZWEBNER—Related to SHAG.

ZWEIFEL—JE has two biographies from 19th-cent. Germany and Russia.

ZWEIG—UJ has two biographies from 19th–20th-cent. Germany. See family history and six family trees in *Die Nachkommen von Moses (Josef) Zweig.* Related to SPITZER.

ZWIRN—See SWIREN.

ZYDOWSKY—See family history in JFF, No. 6.

Bibliography

For one reason or another, many of the books listed here have no single author. Thus I've listed books according to title rather than author.

JEWISH FAMILY HISTORIES

What follows is a list of Jewish family history books, published publicly or privately, which I have come across in libraries or through word of mouth (as much publishing information as possible has been included). Because many such books are circulated only among family members, I have no doubt missed many of them. Also, because these books are almost always printed in limited quantities, it may be difficult for you to find them. To help solve this problem, I've tried to indicate in parentheses after each entry the name of at least one library where I found the particular book mentioned. You may, of course, be able to find the book at other places than the one or two I've mentioned. Where these locations are abbreviated, they refer to the following:

AJA—American Jewish Archives, Cincinnati
AJHS—American Jewish Historical Society, Waltham, Mass.

CAJ—Central Archives for the History of the Jewish People, Jerusalem
HUC—Hebrew Union College Library, Cincinnati
JTS—Jewish Theological Seminary Library, New York
LBI—Leo Baeck Institute library, New York
NYPLG—New York Public Library, Genealogy division
NYPLJ—New York Public Library, Jewish Division
PGS—Pennsylvania Genealogical Society, Philadelphia
YIVO—YIVO Institute for Jewish Research, New York

Multiple-Family Histories and Genealogies

Americans of Jewish Descent, by Malcolm H. Stern (Cincinnati: Hebrew Union College Press, 1960). 307 pp. of genealogical charts for Jewish families that were in U.S.A. before 1840.

Anaf Ez Aboth, by Samuel Kahan (Cracow, 1903). Numbered charts and biographies showing the interrelationships of the Ashkenazic rabbinic families Horowitz, Heilprin, Rapoport, Margulies, Schor, Katzenellenbogen and many others. In Hebrew. (HUC)

The Cousinhood, by Chaim Bermant (New York: Macmillan, 1972). An account of the intermarried English-Jewish aristocracy that includes the families Cohen, Rothschild, Goldsmid, Samuel and Sassoon. 466 pp. with pictures and family trees.

Da'at Kedoshim, by Israel Eisenstadt (St. Petersburg, 1898). Histories of Ashkenazic rabbinical families Eisenstadt, Bacharach, Ginzburg, Heilprin, Horowitz, Minz, Friedland, Katzenellenbogen and Rapoport. In Hebrew. (HUC)

The Grandees, by Stephen Birmingham (New York: Harper & Row, 1971). Sephardic families in the United States. 368 pp.

"Our Crowd," by Stephen Birmingham (New York: Harper & Row, 1971). German families of New York. 404 pp.

Reshimoth Aboth: Eine Ahnentafel von 27 Generationen bis zum Jahre 1290, by Markus Seckbach (1936). General information on major Ashkenazic rabbinical families, easy to follow, in chart form. Includes Seckbach, Mayer, Auerbach, Hirsch, Marx, Bodenheimer and others. (HUC)

Individual-Family Histories and Genealogies

(listed by family, according to the primary family in each book)

Aboab—*Die Familie Aboab,* by Leopold Loewenstein (Pressburg: A. Alkalay & Sohn, 1905). (HUC)

Abrahamsen—*Abraham Elias af Haus-esterhousmere (Familien Abrahamsen),* ed. by Josef Fischer (Copenhagen, 1918). (CAJ)

Adler—*The Family of Max and Sophie R. Adler,* by Robert Adler (Chicago, 1972). (AJA, AJHS)

Alexander—*Notes on the Alexander Family of South Carolina and Georgia and Connections,* by Henry Aaron Alexander (Atlanta, 1954). (HUC)

Alexander—*The Family History of Nicholas Paul Alexander,* by Ulrich Skaller (London, 1972). 34 pp. (YIVO)

Almosnino—*La Famille Almosnino,* by Eliakim Carmoly (Paris: Dondey, 1850). 31 pp. (HUC)

Altschuler—*The Altschuler Family Tree,* by Ralph Straunch (New York, 1975. Descendants of Moses and Sarah Altschuler. (YIVO)

Alvares Correa—*The Alvares Correa Families of Curaçao and Brazil,* by H. M. Alvares Correa (Paris, 1965). 60 pp. (AJHS)

Andriesse—"Het Geslacht Andriesse," in *Gens Vostra,* Nos. 8, 9 and 10 (Amsterdam, 1975), pp. 237–246 and 292–298. In Dutch. (CAJ)

Anschel—*The Descendants of Herz Anschel of Bonn,* by Siegfried Auerbach (London, 1964). (AJA)

Arnstein—*Die Familie Arnstein,* by Max Grunwald (1911). 19 pp. (LBI)

Arye—"Chronicle of the Family Arye of Samokov, Bulgaria," in *Jews in Bulgaria,* pp. 193–211 (1963). (YIVO)

Asch—*Zur Familiengeschichte Asch, 1713–1913,* by Adolf Berliner (Berlin, 1913). 16 pp. (YIVO)

Auer—*The Auer Family Tree,* by Stanley Klein (Cincinnati: 1966). (HUC)

Auerbach—*The Auerbach Family: The Descendants of Abraham Auerbach,* by Siegfried Auerbach (London: Perry Press, 1957). (CAJ)

Auspitz—*Fünfzig Jahre eines Wiener Hauses,* by J. Winter (1927).

Babicz—*Babicz Family of Warsaw.* (YIVO)

Bacharach—*R. Jair Chaim Bacharach,* by David Kaufmann (Trier; 1894). (YIVO)

Baer—see Behr.

Baerwald—*Geschichte des Hauses Baerwald* (Nakel, 1893). 112 pp. (YIVO)

Ball—*Jüdisches Leben einst und jetzt,* by Kurt Ball-Kaduri (1961). (LBI)

Ballin—*Die Familie Ballin,* by Oscar Ballin (Gandersheim, 1913). 74 pp. (CAJ and YIVO)

Bamberger—*The Descendants of Rabbi Seligmann Bar Bamberger, the "Würzburger Rav" (1807–1878)* (Jerusalem: Wahrman Books, 1964). 196 pp. in English, 14 pp. in Hebrew. (LBI)

Baum-Webster—*We Remember: Saga of the Baum-Webster Family Tree, 1842–1964,* by Lawrence Crohn (New York: 1964). (AJA)

Beer—*Urkundliches von Michael Beer und über seine Familie,* by Paul Hoffman (1908). (LBI)

Behr—*The Behr Tree (1683–1949),* by Arnold Levy (Taunton, England: Wessex Press, 1949). 130 pp. (YIVO)

Behrend—see Valentin.

Belmont—*The Belmont-Belmonte Family: A Record of 400 Years,* by Richard Gottheil (New York, 1917). 244 pp.; 100 copies printed. A definitive and well-researched history of the well-known Sephardic-German family, written by a Columbia University history professor. (PGS)

Bensusan—*A Short History of the Bensusan Family,* by A. D. Bensusan (Johannesburg, 1935). (HUC)

Bernd—*Saga of the Bernd, Bloch and Blum Families in the U.S.A.,* by Helen Frank (1961). (AJHS)

Bernheim—*The Story of the Bernheim Family,* by Isaac Bernheim (Louisville, 1910). (AJHS)

Bernstein—*It Began with Zade Usher: The History and Record of the Families Bernstein, Loyev (Lewis) and Mazur,* by Yaffa Draznin (Los Angeles: JAMY Publications, 1972). Traces numerous families back to Russia and Galicia, as early as 1785. (NYPLG)

Bibo—*The Impact of the Frontier on a Jewish Family,* by F. S. Fierman (El Paso: Texas Western College Press, 1961). 32 pp. (HUC)

Bing—*Eine Frankfurter jüdische Familie vom Jahre 1550 bis zur Gegenwart,* by Elias Ullmann (Frankfurt, 1880). 49 pp. (HUC and YIVO)

Binswanger—*The American Descendants of Samuel Binswanger,* by Myer Solis-Cohen (Philadelphia, 1957). (AJA)

Bloch—see Bernd.

Blum—see Bernd.

Boas—*Proeve eener genealogie van der Haagsche familie Boas,* by D. S. van Zuiden (The Hague, 1939). In Dutch. (HUC)

Bock—see Levison.

Bondi—*Zur Geschichte der Familie Jomtob-Bondi in Prag, Dresden und Mainz,* by Jonas Marcus Bondi (Frankfurt, 1921). (CAJ and YIVO)

Brandeis—*Louis D. Brandeis: A Biographical Sketch,* by Jacob de Haas (New York: Bloch Publishing Co., 1929). The author, a close friend of Brandeis, mentions the judge's ancestors on both sides.

Broda (Braude)—*Mishpahat Broda,* by Azriel Meir Broda (Warsaw, 1938). (YIVO)

Bruck—*The Bruck Family: A Historical Sketch,* by Alfred J. Bruck (London and New York, 1946). 306 manuscript pages. (LBI)

Burger—see Levison.

Carabajal—*The Martyrdom of the Carabajal Family in Mexico, 1590–1601,* by George A. Kohut (Portland, Ore., 1904). (HUC)

Carlebach—*The Carlebach Tradition: The History of My Family,* by Naphtali Carlebach (1973). (AJHS)

Caro—*Caro Family Pedigree,* by Abraham Caro (New York, 1928–1929). (HUC)

Carvajal—*La familia Carvajal,* by A. Toro (Mexico City, 1944). (HUC)

Cohen—*The Cohens of Maryland,* by Aaron Baroway (Baltimore, 1924). (HUC)

Cohen—*Family Facts and Fairy Tales,* by Evelina Gleaves Cohen (Wynnewood, Pa., 1953). Traces a Cohen family of Philadelphia back to Westphalia, 1745. (PGS)

Cohen—*Sefer Ha-Zikaron,* by Baruch Cohen (New York, 1920). (AJHS)

Correa—see Alvares.

Cota—"B'nai Cota M'Toledot" (History of the Sons of Cota), by Francisco Cantera Burgos, in *Hayyim Schirmann Jubilee Volume,* ed. by Schraga Abramson (1970), pp. 319–45.

Davidsohn—*Die Familie Davidsohn,* by E. N. Frank (1924). (YIVO)

Diamant—*Minna Diamant, 1815–1840: Ihre Freunde und Verwandten,* by Paul J. Diamant (Tel Aviv: Olamenu, 1964). 102 pp. (LBI and CAJ)

Dubnow—"The Genealogy of Simon Dubnow," by S. A. Horodetzky, in *YIVO Annual of Jewish Social Science,* Vol. 6 (1951). Traces the historian's ancestry back to the Maharal of Prague and beyond. (YIVO)

Dulken—*Genealogy of the Dulken Family.* (CAJ)

Duveen—*The Rise of the House of Duveen,* by James H. Duveen (London and New York, 1957). 252 pp. (HUC)

Dworzaczek—*Genealogie,* by Wladimierz Dworzaczek (Warsaw, 1959). In Polish. (CAJ)

Ebert—*Friedrich Ebert in seiner Zeit* (Bremen, 1965). (CAJ)

Eger—*Ketov zot Zikaron,* by Benjamin Schreiber (New York, 1957). Eger and Schreiber families. 350 pp. In Hebrew. (HUC)

Eger—See Gans.

Eichel—*Stamtavlen Eichel,* by Josef Fischer (Copenhagen, 1909). In Danish. (CAJ)

Eichmann—*Stammbaum der Familie Eichmann, 1660–1931,* by Ruelf (Detmold, 1931). 34 pp.

Ellenbogen—*Hevel ha-Kesef,* by Meyer Ellenbogen (Brooklyn, 1937). (AJHS)

Elmaleh—"Origine de la famille Elmaleh," by Abraham Galante, in *Abraham Elmaleh 70th Birthday Book* (1959), p. 22 and pp. 56 ff. In Hebrew and French.

Engel—*The Ancestry and Descendence of Nancy Egers Engel,* by J. H. Richter (Washington, 1954). (HUC)

Epstein—*Makor Baruch,* by Baruch Epstein (1954). (AJHS)

Feilchenfeld—*The Descendants of Wolf Fales: A Chronicle of the Feilchenfeld Family,* by Walter Fales (New York, 1947). (LBI)

Feuchtwanger—*Descendants of Seligmann Feuchtwanger,* by Martin Feuchtwanger (Tel Aviv: Edition Olympia, 1952). (CAJ)

Feuchtwanger—*The Feuchtwanger Family,* by Ludwig F. Toby (Tel Aviv: Olympia, 1952). 157 pp. (HUC)

Fleckeles—*Der Stammbaum des R. Eleasar Fleckeles,* by David Kaufmann (Breslau, 1893). 16 pp. (HUC)

Flesch—*Die Familie Flesch,* by Heinrich Flesch (Brunn, 1914). 68 pp. (HUC)

Fraenkel—*Forgotten Fragments of the History of an Old Jewish Family,* by Louis and Henry Fraenkel (Copenhagen, 1975). 162 pp. (CAJ)

Fraenkel—*Der goldene Tiegel der Familie Fraenkel,* by M. Fraenkel (1928). In German and Hebrew.

Frankel—See Mirels.

Frankel-Spira—*Neue Beiträge zur Geschichte der Familie Frankel-Spira,* by Ludwig Lazarus. (YIVO)

Franklin—*Records of the Franklin Family and Collaterals,* by Arthur Ellis Franklin (London, 1915). (CAJ)

Franks—*An Old New York Family,* by Albert Gardner (New York, 1963). Franks and Gardner families. (AJHS and CAJ)

Friedlander—*Chronik der Familie Friedlander-Lowenherz, 1760–1912,* by Molly Philippsohn. 51 pp. (CAJ)

Friedlander—*Das Handlungshaus Joachim Moses Friedlander & Söhne zu Königsberg,* ed by Ernst Friedlander (Hamburg: Lucas Grafe, 1913). 58 pp. plus family tree. (LBI)

Friedman—*An Old New York Family,* by Albert Gardner (1963).

Frydman—see Twerski.

Gans—*Zur Geschichte der Familie Eger-Gans-Gansmann,* by Walther Meyer. (LBI Pinkus Collection)

Gardner—see Friedman.

Geldern—*Stammbaum der Familie Geldern,* by Leopold Loewenstein (Breslau, 1907).

Gerstle—*Lewis and Hannah Gerstle,* by Gerstle Mack (New York, 1953). 131 pp. (HUC)

Gitelson—*The Chronicle,* published by the Gitelson-Komaiko Family Association (New York, 1961, *et seq.*). (YIVO)

Godchaux—*The Godchaux Family of New Orleans,* by Paul Godchaux (New Orleans, 1971). (AJA)

Godschalk—*Godschalk, 1777–1778,* by H. M. Corwin (Averbuch, 1901). In German. (CAJ) Also see Gottschalk.

Goldberg—"The Goldberg Brothers: Arizona Pioneers," by F. S. Fierman, in *American Jewish Archives,* Vol. 18 (April 1966).

Goldschmidt—"Die Familie Goldschmidt, Oldenburg: Geschichte im 18 und 19 Jahrhunderts," by Gerhard Ballin, in *Oldenburgische Familienkunde,* Vol. 17, No. 1 (January 1975). (CAJ)

Goldschmidt—*Verzeichnis der von S. B. Goldschmidt aus Frankfurt-am-Main,* by Richard Meyer (Frankfurt, 1879). 55 pp. (HUC)

Goldsmit—*Pedigree of the Family Goldsmit-Cassel of Amsterdam (1650–1750),* by Josef Prys, trans. from the Dutch by O. Schmerler (Basel, 1937). (HUC)

Goldsmith—see Price.

Golodetz—*History of the Family Golodetz,* by Lazar Golodetz (New York, 1954). 44 pp. (YIVO)

Gomperz—*Die Familie Gomperz,* by David Kaufmann and Max Freudenthal (Frankfurt, 1907). 437 pp. (YIVO)

Gordon—see Lee.

Gotfred—"Abraham Gotfred de Meza og hans familie," by Julius Margolinsky, reprinted from *Jodisk Samfund* (January 1955). In Danish. (YIVO)

Gotthelft—*The Gotthelft Family Tree,* by Frieda Sichel and Karl Hermann (Johannesburg, 1966). Covers 1670 to 1966. (AJHS)

Gottschalk—"Note on the Jewish Ancestry of Louis Gottschalk, American Pianist and Composer," by B. W. Korn, in *American Jewish Archives* (November 1963), p. 117. Also see Godschalk.

Grafenberg—*Stammbaumblätter der Familie Grafenberg,* by Selly Grafenberg (Frankfurt, 1916). 20 pp. (YIVO)

Guggenheim—*Samuel Guggenheim gest. 27 Dec. 1930* (Worms). (CAJ)

Guggenheim—*The Guggenheims: The Making of an American Dynasty,* by Harvey O'Connor (New York, 1937). 496 pp.

Guggenheim—*Die Nachkommen des Simon Guggenheim (1730–1799) von Endingen,* by Ludwig David Kahn (1969). (CAJ)

Guggenheim—*Stammbaum der Familie Guggenheim aus Worms,* by Siegfried Guggenheim (Offenbach, 1926). (HUC)

Gumpel—*Die Hamburger Familie Gumpel und der Dichter Heinrich Heine,* in *Zeitschrift für die Geschichte der Juden,* No. 1 (1969), by J. Raphael. (CAJ)

Gunzburg—*Zur Genealogie der Familie Gunzburg,* by Bernhard Friedberg (Frankfurt, 1903). 8 pp. (HUC)

Gunzburg—*Toledot Mishpahat Gunzburg,* by David Maggid (St. Petersburg: Verlag des Autors, 1899). 306 pp. (LBI)

Hahlo—see Hallo.

Halberstam—*Siah Yizhaki*, by Solomon Halberstam (Lemberg, 1882). The author (1832–1900) traces eminent rabbis on both sides of his family.

Hallo—*Geschichte der Familie Hallo*, by Rudolf Hallo (Kassel, 1930). 170 pp. (YIVO)

Hameln—*Die Kinder des Hildesheimer Rabbiners: Samuel Hameln*, by Abraham Lewinsky (Hildesheim, 1901). 26 pp. (HUC)

Harkavy—*Stammbuch der Familie Harkavy*, by Elhanan Harkavy (New York, 1903). (HUC)

Harris—see Moss.

Harris—*The Family of Isaac and Rebecca Harris*, by Rowena Lipman (Berkeley, Calif.: Western Jewish History Center, 1970). 8 pp. (AJHS)

Hartvig—*Levin Marcus Hartvigs efterkommende*, by Michael Hartvig (Copenhagen, 1928). In Danish. (CAJ)

Harzell—see Herzog.

Hays—see Myers.

Heine—*Aus Heinrich Heines Ahnensaal*, by David Kaufmann (Breslau: S. Schottlander, 1896). 312 pp. (LBI)

Heine—*Heinrich Heines Berliner Verwandte und deren Vorfahren*, by Bernhard Brilling (Berlin: Arani-Verlag, 1955). (LBI)

Heine—*Heinrich Heines Stammbaum väterlicherseits*, by Gustav Karpeles (Breslau: Schottlander, 1901). (LBI)

Heller—see Mirels; Straus.

Heller—*Heller Family Tree*, by Morris Heller and Robert Beer (New York, 1942). (AJA)

Henriques—*Stamtavlen Henriques, 1725–1948*, by Bendix Moses Henriques (Copenhagen, 1949). In Danish. (CAJ)

Herz—*The Descendants of Anschel Herz of Bonn*, by Siegfried Auerbach (London, 1964). 57 pp. (CAJ)

Herz—*Fünfhundert Jahre Familiengeschichte, 1430–1930*, by Ludwig Herz (1934). Includes Steinthal family. (LBI)

Herz—*Zur Geschichte der Familie Herz in Weilburg*, by Heinrich Herz (Aachen, 1906). 67 pp. (YIVO)

Herzl—*Theodor Herzls väterliche und mütterliche Vorfahren*, by Paul J. Diamant (Jerusalem: Bamberger and Wahrmann, 1934). 19 pp. (LBI)

Herzog—*Herzog and Lambert Genealogy*, by Ruth Goldstein (Santa Barbara, Calif., 1971). The Herzog family later became Hartzell. (AJHS)

Heydenreich—*Handbuch der Genealogie*, by Eduard Heydenreich (Leipzig, 1913). (CAJ)

Hirsch—*Die Familie von Hirsch auf Gereuth*, by Josef Prys (Munich: Selbstverlag, 1931). 112 pp. (HUC)

Hirschland—*Die Familie Hirschland*, by Albert Phiebig (Berlin, 1937). 80 pp. (YIVO)

Hofheimer—*The Descendants of Moses Son of Naphtali of Hofheim, or Moses Hofheimer, 1781–1962*, by Malcolm H. Stern (Norfolk, Va.: 1964). (AJHS)

Horowitz-Margareten—*Directory and Genealogy of the Horowitz-Margareten Family*, by Joel Margareten, et al. (Brooklyn, 1955). 212 pp. (NYPLJ and YIVO)

Hurwitz (Horowitz)—*Toledot Mishpahat Hurwitz*, by Bernhard Friedberg (Frankfurt, 1911). 24 pp. In Hebrew. (NYPLJ and HUC)

Hutzler—*Hutzler,* by Charles S. Hutzler (Richmond, Va.: 1957). In English.

Ibn Menasheh—"Los Hermanos Abenmenasse al servicio de Pedro el Grande de Aragon," by David Romano, in *Jose Millas-Vallicrosa commemorative book,* Vol. 2 (1956), p. 241.

Ibn Yahya—*Sefer Dibre ha-Yamim,* by Eliakim Carmoly (Frankfurt, 1850). 43 pp. In Hebrew. (HUC)

Jacob—see Unna.

Jacobi—*Stammbaum der Familie J. L. Jacobi,* by Georg Zielenziger (Bromberg, 1905). Families of Levin Jacobi and Mortje Witkowski from about 1750. (LBI)

Jaffe—*Der Schweriner Oberrabiner Mordechai Jaffe, seine Ahnen und Nachkommen,* by Moritz Stern (Berlin, 1933). 15 pp. (CAJ)

Jomtob—see Bondi.

Johnson—see Morris.

Josephthal—*Stammbaum der Familie Josephthal,* by Hans Josephthal (Berlin, 1933). (CAJ and HUC)

Kahn—*Die Familie Kahn von Sulzburg/Baden,* by Ludwig Kahn (Basel, 1963). 206 pp. (AJHS)

Kapp—see Koppel.

Karger—*Familienblätter zur Erinnerung an unseren verewigten Vater Raphael J. Karger,* by S. Gronemann (Frankfurt, 1898). (YIVO)

Katzenellenbogen—*Eileh Toledot: These Are the Generations,* by N. Rosenstein (Cape Town, 1969). The author, born in 1944, traces his line without a break back to the 14th century. Details and charts of the Katzenellenbogen family and its descendants; includes the families of Hillel, Rashi, Luria, Treves, etc. In English. (AJHS)

Katzenellenbogen—see Ellenbogen.

Katzenellenbogen—see Samuel.

Katzenellenbogen—*Genealogische Übersicht über einige Zweige der Nachkommenschaft des Rabbi Meir Katzenellenbogen von Padua,* ed. by Max Wollsteiner (Berlin, 1898). 16 pp. (LBI)

Kimhi—see Elmaleh.

Komaiko—see Gitelson.

Konigswarter—*Toledot Bet Konigswarter,* by Isaac Gastfreund (Vienna, 1877). 8 pp. Editions in German and Hebrew. (HUC)

Koppel—*Stammtafel Koppel,* by Albert Heckscher (Copenhagen, 1883). 24 pp. (HUC)

Kuhn—see Morris.

Kulp—*The Kulp Family: A Genealogy,* by Jacques Sichel (Union City, N.J., 1965). Detailed history of a family originally from Frankfurt-am-Main. 225 pp. (AJHS)

Kurtzig—*Ostdeutsches Judentum: Tradition einer Familie (Kurtzig),* by Heinrich Kurtzig (Stolp: Eulitz Verlag, 1927). 164 pp. (LBI)

Lack—*You Can't Live All Your Life: A Story about Fannie Lack,* by Ruth Lack (Houston, 1967). 63 pp. (AJHS)

Ladenburg—*Ladenburg: Familie und das Mannheimer Bankhaus Wilhelm H. Ladenburg & Söhne,* by Florian Waldeck. (LBI)

Lambert—see Herzog.

Landau—*B'nai Landau Lemishpahatim,* by Bernhard Friedberg (Frankfurt, 1905). 24 pp. In Hebrew. (HUC) See also Margolioth (Margulies).

Landauer—*Family Tree of Elias and Karoline Landauer (Hurben-Krumbach-Munich),* ed. by Elias Karl Frenkel (1968). (CAJ)

Landsberg—*B'nai Shlomo,* by Solomon Landsberg (Krotoschin, 1870). Autobiography and family history. 77 pp. In Hebrew. (HUC)

Landshut—*Neumark, Westpreussen und die Familie Landshut,* by Siegfried Landshut (Kiriat Tivon, Israel, 1962). 44 pp. (LBI)

Lauterbach—*Chronicle of the Lauterbach Family,* by Leo Lauterbach (Jerusalem, 1961 and 1962). (AJA)

Lee—*Book of the Descendants of Dr. Benjamin Lee and Dorothy Gordon,* by Gordon Baker and others (Ventnor, N.J., 1972). (AJHS)

Lehmann—*Der polnische Resident Berend Lehmann, der Stammvater der israelitischen Religionsgemeinde zu Dresden* (Dresden: Pierson, 1885). 74 pp. (LBI)

Lemann—*The Lemann Family of Louisiana,* by Bernard Lemann (Donaldsonville, La., 1965). (AJHS)

Levi—*Autobiografia di un padre di famiglia,* by Giuseppe Levi (Florence, 1868). 113 pp. (YIVO)

Levi—*Stammtafel und Register der Nachkommenschaft der Samuel Alexander Levi aus Frankfurt-am-Main,* by Wilhelm Dann (Frankfurt, 1870). (CAJ)

Levinson—*Isaac Levinson's Genealogy,* ed. by Nathan Drazin (Baltimore, 1948). Traces the subject's ancestry back to Hillel and King David. (AJA)

Levison—*Die Siegburger Familie Levison und verwandte Familien,* by Wilhelm Levison (1876–1947) (Bonn: L. Rohrscheid, 1952). 187 pp. (YIVO)

Lichtenstein—*The Virginia Lichtensteins,* by Gaston Lichtenstein (Richmond, Va.: 1912). (AJHS and AJA)

Lieben—*Fünfzig Jahre eines Wiener Hauses,* by J. Winter (Vienna, 1927). Lieben and Auspitz families. 104 pp. (HUC)

Liebmann—*Stammtafeln der von Liebmann-Schwarzschild (1555–1594) abstammenden Familien,* by L. Neustadt (Frankfurt, 1886).

Lilienthal—*The Lilienthal Family Record,* by Sophie Lilienthal (San Francisco, 1930). (AJHS and HUC)

Loevinger—*The Loevinger Family of Laupheim: Pioneers in South Dakota,* by Ludwig Kahn (Basel, 1967). 83 pp. (AJHS)

Loewengart—*Der Familie Loewengart (im Württemberg),* by Stephan Loewengart (Stuttgart, 1971). (CAJ)

London—*Shades of My Forefathers,* by Hannah London (Springfield, Mass.: Pond-Ekberg Co., 1941). 199 pp.; 500 copies printed. (PGS)

Lowenstein-Porta—*Chronik der Familie Löwenstein-Porta,* by Siegfried Porta (Bielefeld, 1922). 103 pp. (LBI)

Lowenthal—*The Descendants of Moritz Lowenthal of Ladenburg,* by Siegfried Auerbach (London: Perry Press, 1959). (CAJ)

Luria—*Die Familie Lourie (Luria),* by Anton Lourie (Vienna, 1923). 50 pp., with one tree tracing family in an unbroken line back to the 14th century. (NYPLJ)

Luria—*Mishpahat Luria,* by Abraham Epstein (Vienna, 1901). 63 pp. In Hebrew. (NYPLJ)

Luria—see Katzenellenbogen.

Luzzatto—*Autobiografia di S.D. Luzzatto: Alcune notizie storico-letterarie sulla famiglia Luzzatto* (Padua, 1882). (CAJ)

Luzzatto—*Die Familie Luzzatto,* by Markus Brann. 48 pp. (YIVO)

Maram—"Der Name Maram (Marum)," by Bernhard Brilling, in *Forschung aus Judentum,* Festschrift for 60th birthday of Rabbi Lothar Rothschild (Bern: Herbert Lang, 1970). (CAJ)

Margolioth (Margulies)—*Ma'alot ha-Yuhasin,* by Ephraim Zalman Margolioth (1762–1828), published by his grandson, A.B. Krochmal (Lemberg, 1900). Margolioth and Landau families. In Hebrew. (HUC and Dropsie University, Philadelphia)

Mayer—*Aunt Sister's Book,* by Sam Ullman (New York, 1929). (AJA)

Mayer—*Aus der Geschichte der Familie Ascher Mayer,* by Gustav Mayer (Berlin, 1924). 11 pp. (LBI)

Mayer—*Memoir and Genealogy of the Ferdinand and Jette Steiner Mayer Family, 1832–1971,* by Mrs. Richard Mayer (San Angelo, Texas: 1972 (AJA)

Melchior—*Moses & William G. Melchior, 1761–1961* (Copenhagen, 1961). (CAJ)

Melchior—*Stamtavlen Melchior,* by Josef Fischer (Copenhagen, 1920). In Danish. (CAJ)

Mendelssohn—"New Light on the Family of Felix Mendelssohn," in *Hebrew Union College Annual,* Vol. 26 (1955), p. 543.

Mendelssohn—"Die Familie Mendelssohn," by Robert Geis, in *Abraham unser Vater,* Festschrift for Otto Michel, ed. by Otto Betz (1963), pp. 216–21.

Merlin—*Une famille lorraine: Les Merlin de Thionville,* by Albert Paul (Metz, 1949). (YIVO)

Metzon—*Mine Forfaeder,* by Hans Metzon. (CAJ)

Meyer—*The Ancestors of Emil Louis Meyer and Helen Levy Meyer of Hannover, Germany,* by John H. Richter (Ann Arbor, Mich., 1963). 11 pp. (LBI)

Meyer—see Myers.

Michael—*Familie Michael (Hamburg), 1620–1924,* by Edward Ducksz (Altona, 1925). 49 pp. plus tables. (CAJ)

Mieses—*Toledot Fabius Mieses,* by E. Ginzig (Cracow, 1890).

Mirels—*Stammbaum der Familie Mirels-Heller-Frankel,* by Leopold Lowenstein (Mainz, 1903). (LBI)

Moise—*Moise Family of South Carolina,* by Harold Moise (Charleston, S.C.: R.L. Bryan, 1961). 304 pp. (HUC)

Moos—*History of the Family Moos,* by S. Moore (1964). (AJA and LBI)

Mordecai—"Some Notes on the Mordecai Family," by R. Nuermberger, in *Virginia Magazine of History* (1941). (HUC) See also Myers.

Morpurgo—*La famiglia Morpurgo di Gradisca, 1585–1885,* by Edgardo Morpurgo (1909). 110 pp.

Morris—*The Ancestry of Rosalie Morris Johnson, Daughter of George Calvert Morris and Elizabeth Kuhn,* by Robert Johnson (Philadelphia, 1905).

Moss—*Moss-Harris Pedigree,* by Sanford Moss (Somerville, Mass:, 1934, 1937, 1940, 1943). (AJHS)

Muhr—*Abraham Muhr: Ein Lebensbild,* by Markus Brann (1891). 65 pp. (LBI)

Muhsam—*Geschichte des Namens Muhsam*, by Siegfried Muhsam (Lübeck, 1912). 46 pp.

Myers—*Records of the Myers, Hays and Mordecai Families, from 1707 to 1913*, by Caroline Cohen (Washington, 1913). (AJHS)

Nachamson—*"Always Be Good to Each Other": The Story of the Nachamsons*, by Eli Evans (1968). (AJHS)

Munk—see Te'omim.

Nasi—*The House of Nasi*, by Cecil Roth (Philadelphia: Jewish Publication Society, 1948). 208 pp. (YIVO and HUC)

Nathan—*Marcus M. Nathan, København, 1859–1959* (Copenhagen, 1959). In Danish. (CAJ)

Pechenik—*The Pechenik Family*, by Ralph Selitzer (Passaic, N.J., 1969). 62 pp. (YIVO)

Penso—see Belmont.

Peres—*The Peres Family*, by Sam Shankman (Kingsport, Tenn.: Southern Publishers, 1938). 241 pp. (YIVO)

Perlmutter—*La famille Perlmutter*, by Istrati Panait (Paris, 1927). 253 pp. (YIVO)

Perls—*Megilath Yuhasin*, by Maier Perls (1718) (Warsaw, 1864 and 1889). A biography of the Maharal of Prague (1525–1609), with his connections to the Perls family. In Hebrew.

Philipp—see Unna.

Philipsen—*Familien Philipsen i Pilestraede*, by Josef Fischer and T. Hauch-Fausboll (Copenhagen, 1920). 145 pp. In Danish. (HUC)

Philipson—*The Philipsons: The First Jewish Settlers in St. Louis, 1807–1858*, by Donald Makovsky (St. Louis, Mo., 1958). (HUC)

Pinelo—*Los Leon Pinelo*, by Boleslao Lewin (Buenos Aires, 1942). 51 pp. (YIVO)

Pisa—*La famiglia da Pisa*, by Umberto Cassuto (Florence, 1910). 82 pp. (HUC)

Pochapovsky—*Descendants of Velvel Pochapovsky*, by Howard Picker (Albany, N.Y., 1971). (AJA)

Porges—*Stammbaum der Familien Porges* (Kassel, 1906). Porges family of Portheim. 63 pp. (HUC)

Posner—*The Posner Family Tree*, by Stanley Posner, Helen Posner Freed and Milton Posner (New York, 1953). 60 pp. (HUC)

Price—*Price, Goldsmith, Lowenstein and Related Families, 1700–1967*, ed. by Harriet Stryker-Rodda (New York, 1967).

Rabinowitz—*Nine Generations: 200 Years Memoirs of Our Family*, by Chaim Rabinowitz (Tel Aviv, 1970). (YIVO)

Rashi—*Rashi*, by M. Liber (1905), and *Eileh Toledot: These Are the Generations*, by N. Rosenstein (1969). Both in English.

Reznikoff—*Family Chronicle*, by S. Reznikoff (New York, 1963). (AJHS)

Ris—*Die Nachkommen des Rabbiner Raphael Ris* (Israelitischer Wochenblatt). (CAJ)

Rivlin—*Sefer ha-Hem Lemishpahat Rivlin*, by Eliezer Rivlin (Jerusalem, 1935–1940). (HUC)

Rivlin—*Yosef Rivlin Memorial Volume*, ed. by Hayyim Hirschberg (1964), pp. 47–77.

Rosanes—*La Genealogie de la famille Rosanes*, by S. Rosanis (Roustchouk: D.M. Drobnyak, 1885). (HUC)

Rosenbaum—*Familientafel der Nachkommen,* by Mendel Rosenbaum-Zell (Tel Aviv: Ha-Aretz Press, 1958). (CAJ)

Rosenbaum—*The Rosenbaums of Zell,* by Berthold Strauss (London, 1962). (CAJ)

Rosenfeld—*Descendants of Joshua, 1741–1971,* by Abraham Rosenfeld (1971). (AJA)

Rosenthal—*Toledot Mishpahat Rosenthal,* by Leopold Greenwald (Budapest, 1920). 103 pp. (HUC)

Rosenthal—*Zur Geschichte der Juden im Gebiet,* by Ludwig Rosenthal (1963).

Rothmann—*Stammbaum der Familie Rothmann,* by Samuel Rothmann (Berlin, 1913). 12 pp.

Rothschild—*Die Familie Rothschild,* by Walther Brewitz (Stuttgart: Kohlhammer, 1941). 193 pp. (LBI)

Rothschild—*Das Haus Rothschild in der Zeit seiner Blüte, 1830–1871,* by Egon Corti (Leipzig: Insel-Verlag, 1928). 511 pages. (LBI)

Rothschild—*The Rothschilds: A Family of Fortune,* by Virginia Cowles (New York: Knopf, 1973).

Rothschild—*The Rothschilds: A Family Portrait,* by Frederic Morton (New York: Athenaeum, 1962). 305 pp.

Rothschild—*Les Rothschilds: Une famille de financiers juifs au 19ème siècle,* by Edouard Demachy (Paris, 1896). 194 pp. (LBI)

Rottenberg—*A Link with the Future,* by Dan Rottenberg (Chicago, 1969). Includes Rottenberg, Rubin, Goldstein, Gralnick, Cohen, Margulies, Tamarin, Schwartz, Klein, Gudelsky, Mariansky, Vinshnupsky, Grapf, Sobel, Kirschbaum, etc., families. (AJHS)

Samson—*Die Genealogie einer jüdischen Familie in Deutschland: Die Geschlecht Samson aus Wolfenbüttel,* by Felix Theilhaber (1912). (LBI)

Samsonschen—*Stammbaum der Samsonschen Familie,* by Moritz Berliner (Hannover, 1912). 31 pp.

Samuel—*Records of the Samuel Family,* by J. Bunford Samuel (Philadelphia, 1912). A collection of various articles dealing with Samuel family ancestors like the Katzenellenbogens and Saul Wahl. (HUC)

Samuel—*The Samuel Family of Liverpool and London, from 1755 Onwards,* by Ronald J. Hart (London, 1958). 118 pp. (HUC)

Sassoon—*The Sassoon Dynasty,* by Cecil Roth (London, 1941). 280 pp. (HUC)

Sassoon—*The Sassoons,* by Stanley Jackson (New York: Dutton, 1968). 304 pp. (AJHS)

Schick—*Der Stammbaum der Familie Schick,* by Salamon Schick (Schueck) (Munkacs, 1903). 89 pp. In Hebrew.

Schneerson—see Slonim.

Schor—*Ateret Tiferet Israel,* by Wolf Kratuschinsky (Vienna, 1883). Contains an imperfect genealogy of Israel Schor (1823–1899).

Schor—*Toledot Mishpahat Schor,* by Bernhard Friedberg (Frankfurt, 1901). 24 pp. In Hebrew. (NYPLJ and HUC)

Schreiber—see Eger.

Schwarzschild—see Liebmann.

Seligman—*The Family Register of the Descendants of David Seligman,* by George Hellman (1913). (AJHS)

Seligman—*The Story of the Seligmans,* by George Hellman (New York, 1945). 329 manuscript pages. (NYPLG)

Selman—*The Selmans,* by V. R. Emanuel (New York, 1925). (YIVO)

Shimshelewitz—*Megilat Yuhasin,* by Zebi Shimshi (Jerusalem, 1957). 45 pp. In Hebrew. (HUC)

Shomer—see Zunser.

Simon—*Stiftungs-Urkunde betreffend die Moritz Simonsche Familien-Stiftung,* by Moritz Simon (Königsberg, 1890). 14 pp. (HUC)

Simons—*Stammbaum der Familie Michael Simons,* by Karl Simons (Düsseldorf, 1905). 49 pp. (HUC)

Simonsen—*Jacob Simonsen und Frau Rose, geb. Hahn, und ihre Vorfahren,* ed. by Josef Fischer (Copenhagen: H. Meyer, 1923). 87 pp. (LBI)

Skaller—*The Family History of Nicholas Paul Alexander,* by Ulrich Skaller (1972).

Slonim—*Toledot Mishpahat ha-rav mi-Ladi,* by Menachem Slonim (Tel Aviv, 1946). Slonim and Schneersohn families. 302 pp. In Hebrew. (HUC)

Solomon—*Records of My Family,* by Israel Solomon (New York, 1887). Also includes Levy family. (AJHS)

Spanjaard—*Die Familie Spanjaard,* by K. A. Citroen (Bern: Berith Shalom, 1964). 202 pages. (CAJ)

Speyer—*Stammtafeln der Familie Speyer,* ed. by Bethhold Baer (Frankfurt, 1896). 147 pp. (LBI)

Spielmann—*The Early History of the Spielmann Family,* by Percy Edwin Spielmann (Reading, England, 1951). 62 pp. (HUC)

Spira—see Frankel.

Spitzer—see Zweig.

Steg—*Denk ich an Deutschland in der Nacht: Die Geschichte des Hauses Steg,* by Emil Herz (Berlin: Ullstein, 1953). 329 pp. (LBI)

Steinberg—*Genealogie de la famille Steinberg,* by Bernhard Friedberg (Antwerp, 1934). Traces the family from the 14th century. 26 pp. (HUC)

Steinheim—*Salomon Ludwig Steinheim, Gedenheim,* by Hans-Joachim Schoeps (Leiden, 1966). In German. (CAJ)

Steinthal—see Herz.

Stern—*Stammtafel der Familie Abraham Stern,* by Arthur Stern. (LBI)

Stieglitz—*D. Stieglitz aus Arolsen, ihre Vorfahren und Nachkommen,* by Bodo von Maydell. (LBI)

Straus—*The Descendants of Emanuel Straus and Fanny Heller Straus,* by Edwin Levy, Jr. (Richmond, Va., 1970). (AJHS)

Straus—*Verzeichnis der von Hirsch Herz Straus aus Frankfurt-am-Main,* ed. by Elias Ullmann (Frankfurt: R. Morganstern, 1880). (LBI)

Szold—*The Szolds of Lombard Street,* by A. L. Levin (Philadelphia: Jewish Publication Society, 1960). 418 pp. (HUC and YIVO)

Teller—*Teller Family in America, 1842–1942,* by Chester Teller (Philadelphia, 1944). Descendants of Marx Teller (1778–1850) and his wife, Caroline Lorsch Teller (1788–1872). 221 pp. (HUC)

Te'omim—see Theomim.

Teutsch—*Geschichte der Juden der Gemeinde Venningen: Familie Teutsch von 1590–1936*, by Albert Teutsch (Karlsruhe, 1936). 112 pp. (LBI)

Theomim—*Die Identität der Familien Theomim und Munk*, by Markus Brann (1911).

Tietz—*Hermann Tietz: Geschichte einer Familie*, by Georg Tietz (Stuttgart, 1965). 212 pp. (HUC)

Touro—*The Touro Family in Newport*, by Morris Gutstein (Newport, 1935). (AJHS)

Treves—"The Treves Family in England: A Genealogical Sketch," by Lucien Wolf. Reprinted from the *Jewish Chronicle* (London, 1896). 20 pp. (CAJ and YIVO)

Twerski—*Sefer Ha-yahas mi-Tshernobil ve-Rosin*, by Aaron Twerski (Jerusalem, 1966). Twerski and Frydman families. (AJHS)

Unna—*Geschichte der Familie Unna (Hamburg-Kopenhagen)*. Includes Jacob and Philipp families.

Valentin—*Geschichte der Familien Valentin, Loewen und Manheimer-Behrend*, by Bruno Valentin (Rio de Janeiro, 1963). 82 pp. (LBI)

Wahl—see Samuel.

Wallich—*Die Familie Wallich*, by J. Schultze (Pressburg: Alkalay und Sohn, 1905). (CAJ)

Warburg—*Stamm- und Nachfahrentafeln der Familie Warburg, Hamburg-Altona* (Hamburg, 1937, 1953). (HUC)

Warburg—*The Warburgs: The Story of a Family*, by David Farrer (New York: Stein & Day, 1975). 255 pp.

Webster—see Baum.

Weil—*Weil–De Veil: A Genealogy, 1360–1956*, by Ernest B. Weill (Scarsdale, N.Y., 1957). Descendants of Juda Weil, including Weil, Weill, Weyl, De Veil, De Veille, De Weille. 44 pp. (HUC)

Weil—*Nathanael Weil, Oberlandrabbiner in Karlsruhe, und seine Familie*, by Leopold Lowenstein (Frankfurt: Kauffmann, 1898). 85 pp. (LBI)

Weil—*Strangers in the Land: The Story of Jacob Weil's Tribe*, by Moses Rountree (Philadelphia: Dorrance, 1969). 177 pages. (AJHS)

Weill—*Ahnentafel der Kinder des Nathan Weill in Kippenheim (1828–1894)*, by Alfred Sonder (Germany, 1935). Weill, Weil, De Veil, Weyl, etc. 50 pp. (HUC)

Weille—*Het Geslacht de Weille*, by G. J. and G. A. de Weille (Weesp, Netherlands, 1936). 160 pp. (HUC)

Wertheimer—see Wolf.

Wertheimer—*Samson Wertheimer, der Oberhoffactor und Landes-Rabbiner, 1658–1724*, by David Kaufmann (Vienna, 1888).

Wetzlar—*Das Testament der Baronin Eleonora Wetzlar von Plankenstern*, ed. by Bernhard Wachstein (Vienna, 1913). 8 pp. (LBI and HUC)

Wigoder—*Sefer Zikaron*, genealogy of Myer Joel Wigoder (Leeds, England, 1931). 13 pp. In Hebrew. (NYPLJ)

Windmuller—*Chronik der Familie Windmuller* (1938). 117 pp. (HUC)

Witkowski—see Jacobi.

Witkowski—*Forgotten Pioneer*, by Harry Golden. Biography of U.S. peddler Morris Witkowsky.

Witzenhausen—*Family Tree of Rabbi Moshe Witzenhausen, Ancestors and Descendants,* by Elias Karl Frenkel (Jerusalem, 1969). (CAJ)

Wolf—*Chronik der Familie Wolf,* by Victor Reis (Schluchtern, 1932). Five family trees. Includes Oppenheimer and Hamburger families.

Wolf—*Die Familie Wolf: Verzeichnis der Nachkommen des Leopold und der Rosa Wolf, 1800–1866,* by Ernst Wolf (Vienna, 1924). Six family trees; includes Wertheimer family. (CAJ)

Wolfes—*Geschichte der Familie Wolfes aus Mehle bei Hildesheim,* by Willi Schragenheim (Hildesheim, 1936). Descendants of Wolf Lazarus, born about 1690. 17 pp., twenty-one family trees.

Wolff—*Four Generations,* by Frances Nathan Wolff (New York: Colonial Press, 1939). Also includes the Nathan and Hendricks families. 192 pp. (AJHS)

Wolsky—*Yizkor,* by Boris Wolsky (New York, 1950). (AJHS)

Worms—*Genealogical History of the Family de Worms,* ed. by Elias Ullmann (Frankfurt, 1886). (LBI)

Wulff—*Aus der Heimat Mendelssohns: Moses Benjamin Wulff und seine Familie, die Nachkommen des Moses Isserles,* by Max Freudenthal (Berlin: Lederer, 1900). 304 pp. (LBI)

Yates—*The History and Genealogy of the Jewish Families of Yates and Samuel of Liverpool,* by Stuart Samuel (London, 1901). 69 pp. (AJHS)

Zumoff—*Our Family: A History of Five Generations, 1831–1956,* by Abraham Zumoff (New York, 1957). 127 pp. (YIVO)

Zunser—*Yesterday,* by Miriam Shomer Zunser (New York, 1939). Three generations of the author's family. 271 pp. (HUC)

Zunz—*Dr. Leopold Zunz und seine Frankfurter Ahnen,* by Markus Brann (1916). (LBI)

Zunz—*Die Familie Zunz,* by David Kaufmann and Markus Brann (Breslau, 1895).

Zweig—*Die Nachkommen von Moses (Josef) Zweig,* by Julius Roder (Olmutz, 1932). Includes Spitzer families and six family trees with more than eight generations and five hundred names. (CAJ and YIVO)

GENEALOGY AND GENERAL REFERENCE

American Newspapers, 1821–1936: A Union List Available in the United States and Canada, by Winifred Herould (New York, 1937).

American Origins, by Leslie G. Pine (New York: Doubleday, 1960). A guidebook for Americans who want to trace their ancestors in Europe. The 7-page section on Jewry is of limited usefulness, but the sections on individual European countries may be of some help to Jews. 357 pp.

Atlas of European History, by Edward Whiting Fox (New York: Oxford University Press, 1957). Provides a good idea of changes in European national boundaries. 64 pp. plus index, in paperback.

Bureau of the Census Catalog of Publications, 1790–1972 (Washington, D.C.: U.S. Government Printing Office, 1974). A complete bibliography of sources for Bureau of Census statistics from 1790 through 1972. 911 pp.

Families: A Memoir and Celebration, by Wyatt Cooper (New York: Harper & Row, 1975).

Genealogical Research: Methods and Sources, by Milton Rubincam and Jean Stephenson (Washington, D.C.: American Society of Genealogists, 1966). Extremely detailed guide to most sources of genealogical data.

The Genealogist's Encyclopedia, by Leslie G. Pine (New York: Weybright & Talley, 1969; also in paperback, Macmillan). Includes a brief chapter on Jewry plus summaries on most foreign countries.

Generations: Your Family in Modern American History, by Allen F. Davis and Jim Watts (New York: Knopf, 1974). Paperback.

A Guide to Foreign Genealogical Research, by Maralyn Wellauer (Milwaukee, 1973). This unpublished manuscript is available in the Genealogy Room of the Library of Congress and some other libraries. It contains basic information for research in most countries of the world. 78 pp.

Guide to Genealogical Records in the National Archives, by Meredith B. Colket Jr. and Frank E. Bridges (Washington: GPO, 1964). 145 pp.

A Handy Guide to the Genealogical Library and Church Historical Department, by Ronald Cunningham and Evan Evans (Logan, Utah: Everton Publishers, 1975). A guide to the Mormon Genealogical Society library in Salt Lake City and its branches.

How to Trace Your Family Tree, by the staff of the American Genealogical Research Institute (Garden City, N.Y.: Doubleday, Dolphin paperback, 1975). A clear, comprehensible guide for beginners. 191 pp.

Know Your Ancestors, by Ethel Williams.

Locating Your Immigrant Ancestor, by James C. and Lila Neagles (Logan, Utah: Everton Publishers, 1975). Contains much useful information regarding naturalization records, with anecdotes about the authors' dealings with specific court clerks.

Migration, Emigration and Immigration, by Olga K. Miller (Logan, Utah: Everton Publishers, 1974). Deals primarily with movements to and in the United States.

Morton Allan Directory of European Passenger Steamship Arrivals (New York, 1931). Lists ship-by-ship dates of arrivals in New York, 1890–1930, and in Baltimore, Philadelphia and Boston, 1904–1926.

New York Immigration Information Bureau, 1928 (reprinted San Francisco: R & E Research Associates, 1972). Directory relating to records of arrivals of passenger steamships. 136 pp.

New York Times Obituary Index, 1858–1966.

Newspapers on Microfilm, 4th ed. (1967).

Ritters Geographisch-Statistiches Lexikon, ed. by Johannes Penzler (Leipzig, 1905–1910). German gazetteer with alphabetical listing of towns throughout the world, down to the tiniest communities. Tells country, state, county, other details. Sometimes breaks down population by Protestants, Catholics and Jews. In German.

Stielers Hand Atlas. German atlas published in several editions between 1890 and 1920. Has detailed maps of Europe with an index of towns.

U.S. Board on Geographic Names has published gazetteers on standard place names for 128 different countries. These include the names of all places within a country's current boundaries (towns, counties, districts, lakes, hills, rivers, forests, islands, etc.). Gives the longitude and latitude and a reference to maps on which the place can be found.

Ways of Identifying Ancestors, by E.L. Reed (1947).

JEWISH REFERENCE BOOKS

Encyclopedias

Jewish Encyclopedia, 12 vols. (New York and London: Funk, 1901–1906). Still the best single source of Jewish genealogical information. Contains family trees and/or articles on some 575 Jewish families. Provides the sort of details that bring joy to a genealogist's heart (there is even an entry on "The Ant in Jewish Literature").

Universal Jewish Encyclopedia, 10 vols. (New York, 1939, 1943 and 1948). This set is much more tightly edited than the *Jewish Encyclopedia* and thus less likely to yield the sort of details that genealogists seek. It does, however, have a large quantity of biographical articles on Jews of East European origin born in the latter 19th century.

Encyclopaedia Judaica, 16 vols. (Jerusalem and New York: Keter, 1971 and 1975). Undoubtedly the best Jewish encyclopedia ever produced, although it does not approach the original *Jewish Encyclopedia* in its interest in genealogy. It is, however, much stronger in the quantity and quality of its articles on Jewish communities past and present, and on Jewish families and individuals in Africa, Asia and the Middle East.

Encyclopedia Judaica (A–L) (1928–1934). This German encyclopedia was never finished, due to the rise of Hitler; what it does cover, however, is extremely thorough. It is considered a more reliable source of genealogical information than the 1971 *Encyclopaedia Judaica* mentioned above.

Encyclopedia Judaica Castellana, 9 vols. (1948–1951).

Evreyskaya Enciklopedia, 16 vols. (Petrograd: Brockhaus-Efron, 1908–1913). This edition had 150 contributors but borrowed many articles from the *Jewish Encyclopedia.*

Jüdisches Lexikon, ed. by G. Herlitz and B. Kirschner, 5 vols. (1927–1930).

Standard Jewish Encyclopedia, ed. by Cecil Roth (New York: Doubleday, 1959). A valuable single-volume reference work, but superficial in terms of serious genealogical usefulness.

Valentine's Jewish Encyclopedia, ed. by Albert Hyamson and Dr. A. M. Silbermann (London: Shapiro, Valentine & Co., 1938). Contains numerous biographies.

Names

American Jewish Names, by Lee Friedman (New York: Historica Judaica, 1944). Deals with personal names.

Die Familiennamen der Juden, by Erwin Dreifuss (Frankfurt: J. Kauffmann, 1927). 143 pp.

"German-Jewish Names in America," by Rudolf Glanz, in *Jewish Social Studies* (July 1961), pp. 143–167.

"Jewish First Names Through the Ages," by Benzion Kaganoff, in *Commentary,* Vol. 20 (November 1955), pp. 447–452.

"Jewish Forenames," by Arthur E. Franklin, in *Genealogist's Magazine,* Vol. 7 (March 1936), pp. 244.

"Jewish Names," by Edgar Samuel, in *Genealogist's Magazine* (1961).

"Jewish Surnames Through the Ages," by Benzion Kaganoff, in *Commentary,* Vol. 22 (September 1956), pp. 249–259.

"Joodse Namen en Namen van Joden," by H. Beem, in *Studia Rosenthalia,* Vol. 3, No. 1 (1969), pp. 82–95.

The Name Dictionary: Modern English and Hebrew Names, by Alfred Kolatch (New York: J. David, 1967).

"Namen der Juden, 1837," by Leopold Zunz, in *Gesammelte Schriften,* Vol. II (1876), pp. 1–82.

"Notes on Transformation of Place Names by European Jews," by Max Markreich, in *Jewish Social Studies* (October 1961), pp. 243–267. Includes specific information about family names and their origins.

Russian Surnames, by B. O. Ungebaum (Oxford: Clarendon Press, 1972). Contains a name index as well as a 17-page section on names of Jewish origin.

These Are the Names, by Alfred Kolatch (New York: J. David, 1948). Deals with Jewish and English personal names.

What's in Our Names? by David Swiren (Wilmington, Del.: Star Publishing, 1920). Jewish names. 48 pp.

General Judaica

Bibliographia Genealogica Judaica, by Hermann M. Z. Meyer (Jerusalem, 1942). This bibliography contains about 1,000 references to Jewish genealogies, family histories and local Jewish histories. However, it is only 21 pages long, and only 22 mimeographed copies were produced. Major Jewish libraries should have it.

"Bibliographie der Stammbäume jüdischer Familien," by A. Freimann, in *Archiv für jüdische Familienforschung,* Vol. 2 (Vienna, 1916).

"Bibliographische Sammelwerke über Juden," in *Jüdisches Lexikon,* Vol. 1, cols. 1046–1049.

Guide to Jewish Libraries of the World, by Josef Fraenkel (London, 1959).

Index of Articles Relative to Jewish History and Literature Published in Periodicals from 1665 to 1900, by Moise Schwab (New York: Ktav, 1971).

The Jewish Communities of the World, by Roberta Cohen (New York: Crown, 1971). 167 pp.

Jewish History Atlas, by Martin Gilbert (New York: Macmillan, 1969). 112 maps dealing with Jewish history from Biblical times to the present. Many pinpoint specific towns and waves of migration.

Jewish Immigration to the U.S., 1881–1910, by Samuel Joseph (New York: Arno, 1969). 211 pp.

"Jewish Migrations," by Malcolm Stern, in *Genealogical Research* (Washington, D.C.: American Society of Genealogists, 1971). Deals mostly with Jewish migrations to the New World and sources for further research.

Jewish Newspapers and Periodicals on Microfilm Available at the American Jewish Periodical Center (Cincinnati, 1957). Lists periodicals available at the periodicals center in the Klau Library at Hebrew Union College, Cincinnati.

Jewish Travel Guide, ed. by Sidney Lightman, published annually by the *Jewish Chronicle,* London (Bridgeport, Conn.: Hartmore House). Lists synagogues, kosher restaurants, Jewish museums and centers, etc., in cities throughout the world.

Jüdische Familienforschung (Berlin, 1924–1938). Quarterly publication devoted to Jewish genealogy in pre–World War II Germany. Many articles on families outside Germany as well. Issues through 1930 are printed in Gothic script. Fifty issues published altogether; a cumulative index covers the first 37 (through 1934). Available at many major Jewish libraries.

Leo Baeck Institute Bibliothek und Archiv, Katalog, Band I (1970), Register s.v. Genealogie. (New York.) Lists holdings of the Leo Baeck Institute, New York. In German.

The National Jewish Blue Book, "an elite directory."

The St. Charles, American periodical published briefly pre–World War II by Dr. Walter Kraus, dealing with Jewish genealogy.

The Selective Guide for the Jewish Traveler, by Warren Freedman (New York: Macmillan, 1972).

Shiloah—Discovering Jewish Identity Through Oral/Folk History: A Source Book, by the Institute for Jewish Life (1976).

Sod Haibur, by D. Friedlaender (Budapest: M. Burian, 1880). Family registers. In German.

The Thirteenth Tribe, by Arthur Koestler (New York: Random House, 1976). The author explores the history of the Khazar Jewish Kingdom and argues that it is the source of most of modern Jewry.

To Dwell in Safety: The Story of Jewish Migration Since 1800, by Mark Wischnitzer (1949).

Who's Who in American Jewry (1926 and 1938–39).

Who's Who in the Old Testament, together with the Apocrypha, by Joan Comay.

Who's Who in World Jewry (1938, 1955, 1965).

World Jewish Notables (1972).

Zur Sippen- und Namenskunde der Priester- und Leviten-familien, by G. Samuel, in *Jüdische Familienforschung* (1937), p. 842.

INTERNATIONAL JUDAICA

Note: Books listed below represent only a geographical sampling. Not included are more than a thousand histories of Jewish communities.

Europe

European Library Directory, by Richard C. Lewanski (Florence, 1968). Has addresses of state libraries and others.

From East to West: The Westward Migration of Jews from Eastern Europe During the 17th and 18th Centuries, by Moses Shulvass.

The Landmarks of a People: A Guide to Jewish Sites in Europe, by Bernard Postal and Samuel Abramson (New York: Hill & Wang, 1971). In paperback.

Life Is with People, by Mark Zborowski and Elizabeth Herzog (New York: Schocken Books, 1952). Good description of customs and life in 19th-century Polish-Russian *shtetls.*

Sefer Hapremumerantin, by Berl Kagan (New York: Ktav, 1975). Enumerates existing Hebrew subscription lists for 8,767 communities in Europe and North Africa, 18th–20th centuries, with a total of 350,000 names. In Hebrew, but contains an introduction and an index to towns in English.

The Traveler's Guide to Jewish Landmarks of Europe, by Bernard Postal and Samuel H. Abramson (New York: Hill & Wang, 1971). In paperback.

Austria

Jüdisches Archiv (Vienna, 1927–1929). Monthly publication dealing with Jewish genealogy.

Archiv für jüdische Familienforschung (Vienna, 1912–18). Publication dealing with Jewish genealogy.

Vienna, by May Grunwald (Jewish Community Series, 1936).

Britain

Anglia Judaica, by Tovey (1738).

"Anglo-Jewish Coats of Arms," by Lucien Wolf, in *Transactions of the Jewish Historical Society of England,* 1894–95, pp. 153–169.

Anglo-Jewish Notabilities: Their Arms and Testamentary Dispositions (London: Jewish Historical Society of England, 1949). 233 pp.

Anglo-Jewish Portraits, by Alfred Rubens (London, 1935).

Archives of the United Synagogue, by Cecil Roth (London: 1930). 71 pp. Records of the congregation of London's Ashkenazic Jews.

Bevis Marks Records, ed. by L. D. Barnett, 2 vols. (London, 1949). Contains marriage registers of Bevis Marks Synagogue (Sephardic), 1687–1837, with an index.

Bibliotheca Anglo-Judaica: A Bibliographical Guide to Anglo-Jewish History, by Joseph Jacobs and Lucien Wolf (1st ed. 1888; revised and enlarged by Cecil Roth, 1937). 464 pp. Contains long lists of printed works, 1657–1886, a section on biographies and a valuable introduction dealing with manuscript sources of Jewish history.

Calendar of the Plea Rolls of the Exchequer of the Jews, by J. M. Rigg (London: Jewish Historical Society of England, 1905).

Hebrew Deeds of English Jews Before 1290, by Myer David Davis (Farnborough, 1969). 341 pp.

A History of the Jews in England, by Cecil Roth (1941).

History of the Jews in Great Britain, by Moses Margoliouth (1851).

Jewish Historical Society of England, Miscellanies of, 1925 onwards.

_____*Transactions of,* 1893 onwards.

Both contain vital records and other genealogical data. Volumes from 1893 to 1945 have been cumulatively indexed.

"Jewish Obituaries in the *Gentleman's Magazine*," (1731–1868), by Albert M. Hyamson, in *Miscellanies of the Jewish Historical Society of England*, part IV (1942).

Jewish Year Book, published annually since 1896 by the *Jewish Chronicle*. Has directory and list of Jewish burial grounds, names of old Jewish charities.

The Jews and Immigrants in England (1870–1914), by L. P. Gartner (Detroit: Wayne State University, 1960). 320 pp.

The Jews of Angevin England, by Joseph Jacobs (New York: Putnam, 1893). 425 pages.

The Jews of Medieval England, by Michael Adler (1937).

A List of Jews and Their Households in London, Extracted from the Census List of 1695, by Arthur P. Arnold.

"Old Anglo-Jewish Families," by Lucien Wolf, in *Essays in Jewish History* (London: Jewish Historical Society of England, 1934).

Pamphlets Relating to Jews in England, 17th–18th Centuries, WPA Project (Sacramento: California State Library, 1939).

The Rabbinate of the Great Synagogue of London, 1756–1842, by Charles Duschinsky (1921).

The Sephardim of England: A History of the Spanish and Portuguese Community, 1492–1951, by Albert M. Hyamson (1951).

700 Jewish Marshalls, Generals and Admirals, by Eli Rubin (London: De Vero, 1952). 300 pp.

Sources for Roman Catholic and Jewish Genealogy and Family History, by D. J. Steel and Edgar R. Samuel (London: Phillimore, 1974). Contains 19 pages on Jewry, with many specific sources in Britain.

"Sources of Anglo-Jewish Genealogy," by Wilfred Samuel, in *Genealogist's Magazine* (December 1932), p. 146. Updated in "Jewish Ancestors and Where to Find Them," by Edgar Samuel, *ibid.* (December 1953), p. 412.

Three Centuries of Anglo-Jewish History, by V. D. Lipman (1961).

The Western Synagogue Through Two Centuries, by Arthur Barnett (1961). Has details on Ashkenazic settlements in London.

Bulgaria

Jews in Bulgaria (1963). (YIVO)

Spravochnik na Bibliotekite v Bolgariya, by Snezhina Tosheva (Sofia, 1963).

Czechoslovakia

Information on Securing Family History from Czechoslovakia, brochure published by the Czech government.

The Jews of Czechoslovakia, by the Society for the History of Czechoslovak Jews, 2 vols. (Philadelphia: Jewish Publication Society, 1968 and 1972). Covers mid-19th century to the eve of World War II.

In Search of Freedom: A History of American Jews from Czechoslovakia, by Guido Kisch (London: Goldston & Son, 1949). 373 pages.

"A 17th Century Autobiography: Picture of Jewish Life in Bohemia and Moravia," in *Jewish Quarterly Review*, Vol. 8, pp. 269–304.

"1,000 Years in Czechoslovakia," in *National Jewish Monthly* (July-August 1968).

Denmark

Genealogical Guidebook and Atlas of Denmark, by Frank Smith and Finn A. Thomson (Salt Lake City, 1969).

History of the Danish Jews, by Benjamin Balsler (Copenhagen, 1932).

France

Analytical Franco-Jewish Gazetteer, 1939–45, by Zosa Szajkowski, with an introduction to some problems in writing the history of Jews in France in World War II (New York, 1966).

Franco-Judaica: A Bibliography, 1500–1788 (American Academy for Jewish Research, 1962). 160 pp.

"Jews in Agriculture in Southern France," in *Jewish Quarterly Review,* Vol. 10, pp. 317.

Medieval Jewry in Northern France, by Robert Charan (Hebrew University Press, 1973).

Les noms des israelites en France: Histoire et dictionnaire, by P. Levy (1960).

Germany

Archive im deutschsprachigen Raum, Minerva Handbücher, 2 vols. (Berlin and Elmsford, N.Y.: Walter de Gruyter, 1974). Guide to all archives in all German-language countries.

The Atlantic Bridge to Germany, by Charles M. Hall, 2 vols. (Logan, Utah: Everton Publishers). First volume covers Hessen, second Rheinland-Pfalz. Information for ancestor hunters.

Encyclopedia of German-American Genealogical Research, by Clifford and Anna Smith (New York: R.R. Bowker, 1976). 273 pp. Lists villages in which Jews were allowed to live in 18th and 19th centuries; also all known ships' passenger lists, etc.

Die Familiennamen der Juden in Deutschland, by G. Kessler (1935). (CAJ)

Grosse jüdische National-Biographie, ed. by S. Wininger (1925–1936). Seven vols.

"Jews in Germany in the 18th century and During the Seven Years' War," in *Jewish Quarterly Review,* Vol. 9, p. 110.

Jews of Germany: A Story of 16 Centuries, by Marvin Lowenthal (1936). 427 pp.

Mein Stammbaum: Eine genealogische Anleitung für deutsche Juden, by Arthur Czellitzer (1934). Methods of tracing Jewish ancestors in Germany.

Hungary

The Destruction of Hungarian Jewry, by Randolph Braham (New York: Pro Arte, 1963).

Hungarian Jewish Studies, ed. by Randolph Braham, 3 vols. (New York: World Federation of Hungarian Jews, 1966, 1969 and 1973). Vol. I has articles on migrations and communities.

Jahrbuch für die israelitischen Kultusgemeinden in Ungarn.

Magyar Zsido Lexikon, by Peter Ujvari (Budapest, 1929). 1028 pp. Hungarian Jewish encyclopedia. In Hungarian.

Ireland

The Jews of Ireland: From Earliest Times to Year 1910, by L. Hyman (Shannon: Irish University Press, 1972). 403 pp.

Italy

"Die Familiennamen der Juden in Italien," by S. Scharf, in *Jüdische Familienforschung*, Vol. 14 (1938), p. 906. (LBI)

"Stemmi di famiglie ebraice italiane" [Family Trees of Italian Jews], by Cecil Roth, in *Scritti in memoria di Leone Carpi* (Jerusalem, 1967), pp. 165–184.

History of the Jews in Venice, by Cecil Roth (1930).

The Pope's Jews, by Sam Waagewaar (Open Court, 1974). 487 pp.

Lithuania

Ir Wilna, by Hillel Maggid (1900). Contains biographies of more than 300 prominent Vilna Jews. In Lithuanian.

Vilna, by Israel Cohen (Jewish Communities Series, 1943).

The Netherlands (Holland)

Searching for Your Ancestors in the Netherlands, by Wijnaendts van Resandt. Booklet in English available for $2 from the Central Bureau voor Genealogie, Nassaulaan 18, The Hague. 16 pp.

Poland and the Soviet Union

Archives and Manuscript Repositories in the USSR, by Patricia Kennedy Grimsted.

History of the Jews in Russia and Poland, by S. M. Dubnow, 3 vols. (Philadelphia: Jewish Publication Society, 1916–1920).

"Identifying Jewish Names in Russia," by Benzion Munitz, in *Soviet Jewish Affairs*, No. 3 (May 1972), pp. 66–76.

The Jewish Community in Russia, 1792–1844, by Isaac Levitats (New York, 1943).

"Jews in Red Russia in 14th–18th Century," in *Jewish Quarterly Review*, Vol. 12, p. 8.

Jews in the Province of Posen, 18th–19th Century, by M. M. Zarchin (Philadelphia: Dropsie University Press, 1939). 115 pp.

The Jews of Poland, 1100 to 1800, by Bernard Weinryb (Philadelphia: Jewish Publication Society, 1972). 424 pp.

The Russian Jew Under Tsars and Soviets, by Salo Baron (New York: Macmillan, 1964). 427 pp.

World of Our Fathers, by Irving Howe (New York: Harcourt Brace Jovanovich, 1975).

Spain and Portugal

Encyclopedia Sefardica Neerlandica, 2 vols. (Amsterdam, 1949). Portuguese Jewish families.

Geschichte der Juden in Spanien und Portugal, by M. Kayserling (Berlin, 1861).

A History of the Jews in Christian Spain, by Yitzhak Baer, 2 vols. (Philadelphia: Jewish Publication Society, 1961).

History of the Jews of Spain and Portugal, by Lindo.

A History of the Marranos, by Cecil Roth.

The Jews of Moslem Spain, by Eliyahu Ashtor (Philadelphia: Jewish Publication Society). Vol. I of planned 3-vol. work covers years 711 to 1085. 469 pp.

Noble Families Among the Sephardic Jews, by Isaac da Costa (London: Oxford University Press, 1936).

Sefer Ha-qabbalah, by Abraham Ibn Daud, trans. into English by Gerson Cohen (Philadelphia: Jewish Publication Society). Classic history of Spanish Jewry from the Days of Alexander the Great to 1147. 510 pp.

The Sephardi Heritage, ed. by Richard Barnett (New York: Ktav, 1971).

Sources of Spanish-Jewish History, by Joseph Jacobs. Refers to family trees of Jewish families prepared for trials in the Inquisition.

Turkey

Jewish Life in Turkey in the 16th Century, by Morris Goldblatt (New York: Jewish Theological Seminary, 1952). 240 pp.

"Usos y Costumbres de los Sefardies de Salonica," by M. Molho, in *Biblioteca Habraicoespanola,* Vol. 3 (Madrid-Barcelona, 1950), p. 70, describes origins of family names. (CAJ)

Yugoslavia

"Fifty Years of Yugoslav Jewry," in *World Jewry* (September-October 1969).

"The Jews of Serbia," by I. Alcavay, in *American Jewish Yearbook* (1918).

Western Hemisphere

Argentina

"Argentina and Its Jews," in *National Jewish Monthly* (November 1969).

Brazil

The Records of the Earliest Jewish Community in the New World, by A. Wiznitzer (New York: American Jewish Historical Society, 1954). 108 pp.

Canada

"Jewish Communities of Montreal and Toronto," by M. Melamet, in *Jewish Digest* (May 1967), pp. 51–54.

Tracing Your Ancestors in Canada (Ottawa, 1967). Guide booklet.

The Caribbean

A Guide to Jewish History in the West Indies, by Malcolm Stern and Bernard Postal.

History of the Jews in the Netherlands Antilles, by S. M. Emmanuel, 2 vols. (New York: KTAV).

History of the Jews of Jamaica, by J. A. T. Andrade. Provides countless names, tombstones, documents, etc. An index for this book, compiled by Saul White, is available at the American Jewish Archives in Cincinnati.

Jewish Memorial Inscriptions in Barbados, by E. M. Shilstone (American Jewish Historical Society and Jewish Historical Society of England, 1957). Makes some cross-references to public documents.

"Jews Among the Barbadians," in *Jewish Digest* (September 1969), pp. 27–30.

Precious Stones of the Jews of Curaçao: Curaçaon Jewry, 1656–1957, by I.S. Emmanuel (1957). Contains biographies, genealogies and tombstone inscriptions.

Mexico

The Jews in New Spain, by S. B. Liebman (Miami: University of Miami Press, 1970). 381 pp.

United States

"An Estimate and Analysis of the Jewish Population of the United States in 1790," by I. Rosenswaike, in *Publications of the American Jewish Historical Society,* Vol. 50, No. 1 (September 1960), p. 23. Lists Jews by name and place. A similar survey of Jews in the 1820 census is found in Vol. 53, No. 2, (December 1963), p. 131.

An Inventory of American Jewish History, by Moses Rischin (1954).

Biographical Encyclopedia of American Jews, by M. Jacobs and L. M. Glassman (New York, 1935).

A Biographical Dictionary of Early American Jews, through 1800, by Joseph Rosenbloom (Lexington: University of Kentucky Press, 1960). 175 pp.

Early American Jewry: The Jews of New York, New England and Canada, 1649–1794 (Philadelphia: Jewish Publication Society, 1951).

Early American Jews, by Lee Friedman (Cambridge: Harvard University Press, 1934). 238 pp.

Jewish Adventures in America: 300 Years of Jewish Life in the U.S., by Elma Levinger (New York: Bloch, 1954). 243 pp.

Jewish Americana. Catalogue of books and articles by or about Jews printed in the United States from earliest days to 1850 and found at the library of Hebrew Union College, Cincinnati. A supplement to *An American Jewish Bibliography,* by A. S. W. Rosenbach (Cincinnati, 1954).

Jewish Notables in America, 1776–1865: Links of an Endless Chain, by Harry Simonhoff (New York: Greenberg, 1956). 402 pp.

Jewish Participants in the Civil War, by Harry Simonhoff (New York: Arno, 1963). 336 pp.

Jewish Pioneers and Patriots, by Lee M. Friedman (New York: Macmillan, 1943).

Jewish Pioneers in America, 1492–1848, by A. Lebeson.

Memoirs of American Jews, 1775–1865, by Jacob R. Marcus, 3 vols. (Philadelphia: Jewish Publication Society, 1955).

Monographs of the Jewish Archives (Cincinnati: Hebrew Union College, 1954). Listing of Jewish American writing.

Three Years in America, 1859–1862, by I. J. Benjamin (Philadelphia: Jewish Publication Society, 1956). Lists almost every important Jewish community.

"The Wills of Early New York Jews (1704–1799)," by Leo Hershkowitz, in *Studies in American Jewish History IV* (Waltham, Mass.: American Jewish Historical Society, 1967). A primary research and reference guide. Also deals with New England, South Carolina and the British West Indies.

Asia

Burma

"Once There Was a Burmese Jewry," in *Jewish Digest* (September 1969), pp. 11–14.

India

"Emigration of Baghdad and Basra Jews to India," in *Jewish Quarterly Review,* Vol. 17, p. 422.

"The Miracle," in *Hadassah Magazine* (December 1968), p. 14. Regarding the 400-year-old Jewish community of Cochin.

Iraq
"By the Waters of Babylon: The Romantic History of Iraqi Jewry," in *Jewish Digest* (August 1969), pp. 30–32.
A History of the Jews in Baghdad, by D. S. Sassoon (1949).

Africa

Between East and West, by André N. Chouraqui (Philadelphia: Jewish Publication Society). Study of the Jewish community of North Africa, from Carthaginian days to the present.

The Jews of North Africa, by Nahum Slouschz (Philadelphia: Jewish Publication Society, 1927). 488 pages.

Heibreurisms of West Africa: From Nile to Niger with the Jews, by J. J. Williams (1930). (PGS).

The Present State of the Jews in the Barbary States, by L. Addison (1675). An early discussion of the Jews of what we call Algeria.

Reflexions sur l'onomastique judeo-nord-afrique, by D. Corcos.

South African Jewry, ed. by Leon Felberg (Johannesburg: Fieldhill Publishing, 1967–1968). The major portion of this volume consists of "Who's Who in South African Jewry."

A World Passed By: Scenes and Memories of Jewish Civilization in Europe and North Africa, by Marvin Lowenthal (1933).

Australia

"On Tracing Australian Jewish Genealogy," by Anthony P. Joseph, in *Genealogist's Magazine,* Vol. XIV (December 1964), p. 425.

About the Author

DAN ROTTENBERG has been a newspaper editor in Portland, Indiana, a reporter for the *Wall Street Journal*, managing editor of *Chicago Journalism Review* and executive editor of *Philadelphia Magazine*, as well as the author of more than two hundred magazine articles covering a broad range of subjects. He writes a monthly column of film commentary and reviews for *Chicago Magazine* and is also the author of a book about football at the University of Pennsylvania, his alma mater. He was born and raised in New York and now lives in Philadelphia with his wife and two daughters.